MONEY AND CAPITAL MARKETS

MONEY AND CAPITAL MARKETS

TIM S. CAMPBELL
University of Southern California

Scott, Foresman / Little, Brown College Division
SCOTT, FORESMAN AND COMPANY
Glenview, Illinois / Boston / London

Acknowledgments

Acknowledgments for literary selections and charts and graphs appear in a section at the back of the book on page 601 which is an extension of the copyright page.

Library of Congress Cataloging-in-Publication Data

Campbell, Tim S.
    Money and capital markets / Tim S. Campbell
        p.   cm.
    Bibliography: p.
    Includes index.
    ISBN 0-673-18712-8
    1. Money market.   2. Capital market.   I. Title.
HG226.C36 1988
332′.0973—dc19

1 2 3 4 5 6-KPF-939291908988

PREFACE

If the individual decision-making skills emphasized in corporate finance are to be developed fully, students need to understand the operation and structure of financial markets thoroughly. Moreover, students also need a coherent description of the way financial markets and institutions have been restructured in the last few years. Finally, the analysis of markets and institutions should build upon and reflect the recent advances in academic literature.

This book is directed toward filling this gap. It brings modern economic and financial theory to bear on the organization and behavior of financial markets and institutions. Its purpose is institutional, but it draws heavily on theory. Every effort is made to present useful theory and to develop it concisely and directly. The only prerequisite for the student is an introductory-level treatment of economics, particularly microeconomics. A chapter (and appendix) on the basic theory of pricing risky assets and an appendix on present value allow the book to be used with students who have not had a corporate finance or investments class. However, most of the book presumes students are familiar with these basic tools of finance and helps them to understand applied price theory and to examine the financial world with the tools it affords.

The book is intended for a financial markets course that easily integrates with corporate finance, investments and capital market theory, or courses in financial institutions and/or money and banking that have a larger focus than simply monetary policy. The book also might be used in any sequence with these courses. The book may be best suited for a hybrid financial markets and institutions course that draws from the theory of finance, traditional money and banking, investments, and the economics of regulation.

ORGANIZATION OF THE TEXT

This book is divided into four parts. Parts 1 and 2 are concerned with asset pricing and interest rate determination. Parts 3 and 4 deal with the current operation of financial markets and institutions, principally in the United States but including some international examples. As a result, the first half of the book is more analytical in developing models to explain prices and interest rates. The second half of the book explains the forces that determine the evolution of market structure and describes the current operation of selected markets and institutions.

Part 1 (Chapters 2–5) develops the microeconomic foundations of financial markets and shows the determination of the value of real and financial assets in competitive markets. Chapter 2 uses both the basic Fisherian model and the flow of funds to concentrate on the real rate of interest. Chapter 3 and its two appendixes deal with the pricing of risky assets including a discussion of the merits of APT versus CAPM. Chapter 4 introduces contingent claims and options pricing emphasizing a conceptual foundation for later material. The chapter does not develop computation skills with Black-Scholes or other option pricing models. Chapter 5 is concerned with information, including both efficient markets and assymmetric information.

Part 2 (Chapters 6–11) deals with the determinants of market interest rates and the management of interest rate risk. Chapter 6 discusses interest rates and inflation as well as exchange rates between currencies. Chapter 7 focuses on the impact of default risk, taxes, and segmentation on interest rates. Chapter 8 details the term structure of interest rates. Chapter 9 explains interest rate risk management including hedging strategy using both futures and options as well as immunization of bonds. Chapter 9 uses the understanding built up in the chapters on interest rates and the material in Chapter 4 on contingent claims. Chapters 10 and 11 deal with monetary policy and interest rates. Monetary policy is approached as one of the forces influencing interest rates. Chapter 10 presents some basic mechanics about the way the Fed influences market interest rates. Chapter 11 describes and evaluates the ongoing debate about the way monetary policy should be conducted.

The government's role in regulating and controlling the banking industry is developed in Part 3. It focuses on the operation of financial markets, particularly on the way various markets are organized and regulated. Chapter 12 describes and gives examples of three basic forms of organizational structure—auction, over-the-counter, and intermediated markets. Chapter 13 concentrates on the theory or rationale for government regulation of financial markets and institutions. Chapters 14 and 15 focus on government regulation of securities markets and financial institutions, respectively. Chapter 16 is about innovation in financial markets.

Part 4 (Chapters 17–21) deals with the current operation of selected institutions and markets. Chapter 17 shows how recent deregulation has affected markets and institutions, particularly commercial banks. Chapter 18 analyzes the operation of the banking business while Chapter 19 concentrates on mortgage finance. Chapter 20 describes the current state of money markets including the new market for interest rate swaps. Finally, Chapter 21 describes how markets for financial futures and options operate.

SPECIAL FEATURES

My editor and I have tried to make this book both timely and relevant. We have also tried to make it rigorous without making it difficult. A tremendous amount of change has occurred in financial markets and institutions in the last few years. The long lead time involved in preparing a text makes it difficult to reflect recent changes. My analysis and description of the operation of financial markets and institutions in the mid-1980s is reflected in the topics in each chapter and the many boxed inserts about current events. For example, events as recent as Black Monday (October 19, 1987) are extensively discussed in the text. I also attempted to describe the evolution of market practices and regulation as well as theoretical concepts which provide insight into the way markets and institutions operate. Since this book does not require as much number crunching as most corporate finance or investment texts, no separate study guide or instructor's manual has been prepared. However, a set of answers to end-of-chapter questions is available to instructors and an IBM disk can provide drill in financial problem solving.

ACKNOWLEDGMENTS

Writing a book like this is a long and often painful experience. I want to thank all the people who helped me, especially those who made the process shorter and lessened the pain. I owe thanks to my co-author on other ventures, Bill Kracaw, and to Kim Dietrich for very helpful discussions and comments. A number of other individuals provided valuable comments:

Alan J. Daskin, Boston University
David R. Durst, University of Akron
Clifford Fry, University of Houston
Hoje Jo, University of New Mexico
Morgan J. Lynge, Jr., University of Illinois
George W. McKinney, Jr., University of Virginia
Donald J. Smith, Boston University
George Sofianos, New York University
Garry B. Stone, Northeastern University
J. Ernest Tanner, Tulane University

The editorial staff at Scott Foresman deserves special thanks. George Lobell provided excellent advice and encouragement, and it has been a real pleasure to work with Jane Steinmann, Kathy Richmond, and Jeanne Schwaba. I also want to thank the Graduate School of Business at the University of Southern California for its support and help throughout this project.

Tim S. Campbell

Contents

PART **3**   *FORCES SHAPING THE STRUCTURE OF FINANCIAL*
MARKETS   **301**

PART 4 CONTEMPORARY FINANCIAL MARKETS AND INSTITUTIONS 421

1

*I*NTRODUCTION

This book is about financial markets—how they work, how they might work better, and, in some instances, how they don't work at all. Of all the markets in the world, financial markets are among the most interesting and the most important. They are complicated, and it is a challenge to figure out how they work. To each of us, financial markets seem to hold out the possibility of making or losing a great fortune. In this sense, they have most of the attributes of Las Vegas.

Financial markets are intimately linked to every other market and every individual in the economy. They provide the mechanism by which every business firm raises funds to carry out its operations. As consumers we all use financial markets in order to improve our personal well-being. The returns we earn in other markets can be stored in the financial markets for future use. The importance of financial markets therefore lies in their linkage with all our spending decisions, both in our personal lives and in the business world.

As consumers and personal investors or as business people, we can take either an active or a passive role in financial markets. In fact, this flexibility is one of the beauties of competitive financial markets. If we are passive, we simply consult market prices or rates of return and borrow or invest at the most attractive rates. A well-functioning competitive financial market will assure us that this is an efficient investment. On the other hand, if we want to get more actively involved in the market, we can learn more about the prospective returns on various investments and, in the process, improve the odds a little. In a competitive market we should also expect a fair return on our investment of extra time and effort in learning about investments.

In this chapter our objective is simply to get oriented to the major topics we will address and the methodology employed throughout the book. The methodology used in the field of financial economics, of which this subject matter is a part, has exploded in complexity and sophistication in the decade of the 1980s. Relative to the tools and theories used today, those used more than a decade ago seem extremely crude. Technological growth has increased our understanding of financial markets; it has also made us acutely aware of what we still do not understand. In this chapter we will construct a secure enough foundation in the methodology of finance that you will be able to maximize the return on your investment in information as we proceed through the book.   ■

THE ROLE OF FINANCIAL ASSETS AND MARKETS

A **financial asset** is a claim on some future income. The asset might be as simple as a Treasury bill, which represents a promise by the U.S. Treasury to pay a certain amount, say $10,000, at a specified future date. It might be as complicated as a share of stock in a corporation. This is a promise to pay the holder a portion of the profits that the company earns and does not retain for its own investments. A **financial market** is the place or mechanism whereby financial assets are exchanged and prices of these assets are set.

> A **financial asset** is a claim on some future income.

> A **financial market** is the place or mechanism whereby financial assets are exchanged and prices of these assets are set.

Throughout this book we will deal with both financial assets and markets. We have some notion of what assets and markets can do for us as individuals. Probably the most obvious thing is that, if we are lucky, they can make us rich, and, if we are unlucky, they can make us poor. But our interest here is to understand what they can do for the economy. What useful economic functions do financial assets and financial markets serve?

TWO PRINCIPAL FUNCTIONS OF FINANCIAL ASSETS

Financial assets provide the economy with two services. First, they provide a means by which funds can be transferred from those who have a surplus to those who have profitable investments for those funds. Second, they provide the means to transfer risk from those who undertake investments to those who provide funds for those investments. Therefore, financial assets are the record or the claim that facilitates an exchange of funds and a shift of risk. These two functions are summarized in Figure 1–1.

The first function of financial assets is probably the most obvious. A competitive economy is composed of a number of businesses and individuals that have productive uses for more financial resources than they have on hand at any one time. The variety of these uses is enormous, ranging from high-technology investments by large corporations to investments in homes by individuals. In both examples, if there were no way to obtain funds from other sources, the investment would be impossible to undertake. Hence, the availability of outside resources is crucial to the level of investments and therefore to the level of employment and income in the economy.

These funds are supplied by those in the economy who have fewer profitable investments than resources. These entities can profitably lend to those with pro-

FIGURE 1–1
Principal functions of financial assets. Funds flow from those with a surplus to those who can make productive investments. Those who undertake risky investments transfer risk to those who supply funds.

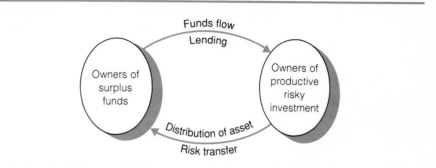

ductive investments if they can receive a reliable promise to share in the investment returns. The financial asset represents that promise. It is issued by the user or borrower of funds to the supplier of funds, and it represents a claim on the user or on the investment he or she is undertaking. The fact that such assets exist and are exchanged raises the level of income and wealth of the entire economy because more productive investment may be undertaken.

Unfortunately, the return on most productive investments cannot be predicted with certainty. As a result, such investments are risky. The incentive to undertake risky investments hinges on how the returns will be distributed or who bears the investment risk. If the party who undertakes the investment bears all the risk, then his or her incentive may be limited. But if that risk can be redistributed or shared with the suppliers of funds, then the incentive to go through with the investment will be enhanced. Financial assets provide the mechanism through which this risk sharing takes place.

TWO PRINCIPAL FUNCTIONS OF FINANCIAL MARKETS

Financial assets can be created and exchanged between a supplier and user of funds without ever utilizing an organized financial market. But in a developed economy, this is more the exception than the norm. Most assets are exchanged through some kind of financial market. These markets assume widely diverse forms, from public auction markets like the New York Stock Exchange to highly diffused markets like the market for savings deposits from financial intermediaries. Both of these examples are financial markets where financial assets are exchanged. The markets serve two useful functions above and beyond those served by the assets exchanged in those markets. The first function is that a market provides the holder of an asset with liquidity. The second is that the market reduces the cost of executing transactions.

A market provides **liquidity** by offering a place or mechansim through which financial assets can be resold or liquidated. Liquidity is an extremely valuable feature for an asset. If an asset is not liquid and cannot be resold, then the only way

Liquidity refers to the ability to sell an asset quickly with minimal cost of executing the sale.

FIGURE 1–2
Principal functions of a financial market:
liquidity and reduction of transactions costs.

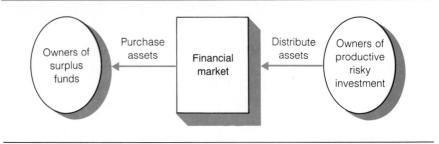

to receive the value of the asset is to wait to receive the future income promised by the asset. The future income is what makes the asset valuable. But there can often be contingencies when a particular owner of an asset would find it advantageous to pass title to that future income on to someone else in order to collect and use today's value of that future income. The existence of a market where assets can readily be bought and sold increases the options and flexibility of all market participants. They can either sell or wait, depending upon which promises the greater personal benefit.

In all such exchanges of assets there are costs. These are generally called costs of transacting and costs of contracting. One example of such costs is best understood if you consider the difficulties that would be involved in trying to hunt for the right exchange if there were no organized market. Suppose you owned shares of General Motors stock and you wanted to sell these and buy Exxon. Without an organized market, you would have to go hunting for someone who owned Exxon. Moreover, that person would have to be willing to take General Motors stock in exchange. You might resort to placing an ad in the barter column of the newspaper in order to find such a person. The financial market, however, performs this service for you. It reduces your transaction cost by eliminating the need for a costly search for someone who wants to trade what you want for what you have. The market can also reduce the cost of collecting information about the future returns on financial assets and about the activities of those who are undertaking productive investments to ensure that they are acting in your interests. It can help enforce the terms of contracts if it is discovered that breaches of contract have occurred.

The two principal functions of a financial market are summarized in Figure 1–2. The figure depicts the same sort of exchange process illustrated in Figure 1–1, but now the exchange passes through an organized market.

THE METHODOLOGY OF FINANCIAL ECONOMICS

Financial economics is or tries to be like any science in that its purpose is to understand the world. This understanding is then used as a basis to improve the world. That is, it leads to prescriptions about how things ought to be done. But unlike the physical sciences, financial economics, as well as other branches of economics, deals with the behavior of people in a market economy, introducing complexities and difficulties in methodology which other, traditional scientific disciplines have not had to deal with. Before we can examine various economic theories and the available evidence on them, we need to have a firm grasp on the methodology of financial economics.

POSITIVE AND NORMATIVE ECONOMIC THEORY

Any theory, particularly an economic theory, can be designed to serve one of two purposes. As a result, there have come to be virtually two types of economic theories: positive and normative. Because we will cover both positive and normative financial economics, it is important to understand what the difference is.

A **normative theory** is a procedure or set of rules for accomplishing a stated objective. It is an explanation of what ought to be. For example, one might propose a normative theory of how to play bridge, or bet on the horses, or invest in the stock market. Such a theory would essentially be a strategy for winning or investing successfully. In the case of stock market investing the objective might be to maximize your wealth. The theory would then be a set of rules that should lead you to the objective of maximizing wealth. It is a theory as long as it cannot be established that the set of rules in the theory will always lead to the desired objective with perfect certainty. There may, therefore, be competing theories about how to reach a given objective. In bridge, horse racing, and the stock market there are numerous theories of how to prosper. None can be verified with certainty, though some may be rejected more easily than others.

A **positive theory** is a statement of what is, rather than what ought to be. It is a description of how some part of the observable world works. For example, a positive theory pertaining to the stock market might offer a hypothesis as to how prices of assets in the market are actually determined. The positive theory in and of itself would not necessarily offer any guidelines for action. Of course, the ultimate usefulness of any positive theory lies in the improvements we can make in the world. That is, we construct positive theories to improve our understanding of how the world works, and we use that understanding to guide our actions and decisions.

It is fairly simple to imagine what a normative theory might look like. It is essentially a how-to book with a forecast of a desired result. However, it is not always obvious what a positive theory should look like. First of all, a positive theory should serve as a filing system or an outline. That is, a good theory should allow us to organize and classify the things we observe in the world. In this way it reduces the complexity of the world around us and helps us to divide the world into manageable parts. But a positive theory must do more. It must make some predictions about observable phenomena. And the prediction must be one that is at least potentially testable. For example, one theory we will explore in this book is known as Fisherian interest rate theory. In its simplest form the theory says that the interest rates we observe in the world can be broken into two components. The first is known as the real rate of interest and the second is a premium equal to the rate of inflation the market expects. This is a useful classification or filing system. It helps

A **normative theory** is a procedure or set of rules for accomplishing a stated objective.

A **positive theory** is a statement of what is, rather than what ought to be.

us decompose what we observe into understandable components, but it is not in itself a prediction of observable phenomena. However, we can add a proposition that makes it at least potentially testable: the real interest rate is constant through time. This implies that observed changes in interest rates can be accounted for by changes in the anticipated rate of inflation. If we could simply measure the anticipated rate of inflation, then we could test this hypothesis.

Another common feature of positive theories is that they are based on highly unrealistic assumptions. Students often find this troublesome, but it is important to understand that any theory is a simplification of reality, and any simplification must, by its very nature, be unrealistic. The lack of realism in a theory's foundations or assumptions should not be troublesome in itself. The relevant question is whether the theory makes useful predictions about behavior that is important and observable in the world. It is best to judge a theory by its predictions rather than by the realism of its assumptions. Good theories—that is, ones that make good predictions—are not often based on assumptions that ignore major ingredients of the real world. A theory with good predictions usually is based on assumptions that incorporate the key features of reality. But such theories still must be simplifications and will therefore appear unrealistic. The trick involved in constructing a good theory is to simplify reality in a way that does not ignore the important elements of the observable world. But the only test of what is important lies in the predictive power of the theory.

In this book we will utilize both positive and normative financial economics. We will lean more heavily on the normative side than many economics texts, but we will also lean more heavily on the positive side than many business texts. The reason is that our ultimate objective is normative, as is the purpose of any business training. But the immediate focus of this book is on how financial markets work, or the positive theories of financial markets.

EMPIRICAL METHODOLOGY

We have learned that any positive theory must have predictive power. It must include some testable hypothesis. Therefore, the tasks involved in financial economics can be divided into two main categories: constructing the theories and testing them. In this book we will not do any actual testing ourselves, but we will review empirical evidence produced by financial economists on a number of hypotheses about financial markets.

As in the physical sciences, the concern with testability has created a need for precision in formulating and stating positive theories. This demand for precision has led to a heavy reliance on mathematics, which allows us to be sure that a theory does not suffer from logical faults. All good theories should be statable in words, but it is often beneficial to state the more complicated ones in mathematics as well. The precision of the mathematical expression often makes it possible to understand relationships that are too complicated if expressed only in words.

Once a hypothesis is formulated and stated precisely, then it is necessary to test the hypothesis or verify its prediction. In constructing such tests, it is virtually impossible ever to prove a theory conclusively. All we can hope to do is confront the theory with more and more demanding tests and attempts to disprove it. If we discover that a theory survives a number of such tests, then we can begin to have confidence in it. We can never really establish the truth of a theory; the most we can hope for is failure to disprove it.

Most empirical testing in financial economics is based on classical statistics. The test is designed to discriminate between two competing hypotheses based on the assumptions about probability distributions. For example, returning to our theory about the determinants of observed interest rates, the Fisherian hypothesis says that we can use changes in anticipated inflation to explain changes in observed interest rates. If we could directly measure the anticipated rate of inflation, then we might test this hypothesis by writing an equation that says the interest rate is determined by the anticipated inflation rate. Such an equation would be written as follows:

$$\text{Interest rate} = a + b \ (\text{anticipated inflation rate}).$$

This equation says that we take the anticipated inflation rate, multiply it by the value of b, add this to the value of a, and we should have the interest rate. If we could conduct a controlled experiment, we would allow the inflation rate to increase and observe the resulting interest rate. From our observations we would be able to measure a and b. If we found that b was zero, we would reject the Fisherian hypothesis. But if it were equal to $+1$, we would conclude that the Fisherian hypothesis was correct, for the Fisherian hypothesis says that the interest rate is equal to the anticipated rate of inflation plus the real interest rate.

A problem common to almost all testing in financial economics is that we cannot conduct controlled experiments. We cannot cause the nation's inflation rate to increase just to see if interest rates will rise by the same amount. Rather, we have to use the evidence the world offers us and draw what conclusions we can from it. This limitation introduces a host of problems into our empirical testing. It does not make most empirical testing impossible, but it does mean we must use some ingenuity to be able to draw reliable conclusions from the evidence we can get. When we deal with empirical evidence in this book we will discuss some of the limitations on how it should be interpreted.

Many of the theories we will examine in this book are potentially testable. Some have been subjected to many tests, but the tests are not completely conclusive. No single theory has been left unscathed by all the tests. There are often competing explanations for observed behavior, particularly regarding how financial markets influence spending decisions in the rest of the economy and regarding the effects of regulation on financial markets. On both of these issues there are strong schools of thought or advocates of competing theories that often have little in common. When we discuss these topics, we will be particularly interested in isolating the key factors that account for the different theories and assessing the evidence that supports each side. In most cases, it will be impossible to say which school of thought is correct. Our purpose will be to understand both sides of these arguments.

TOPICS COVERED IN THIS BOOK

This book addresses four major topics. They can be stated most succinctly as simple questions:

1. How are financial assets priced?
2. How are interest rates determined in competitive international financial markets?
3. How are financial markets organized and regulated, and how do innovations in market organization develop?
4. What are the basic characteristics of the financial markets and institutions operating today, and how are they likely to evolve in the future?

The book is divided into four parts, corresponding to these four questions.

Part 1 is concerned with two principal concepts. The first concept is *uncertainty*. All of the returns to assets are uncertain. We need to understand how uncertainty influences value. The second is *information*. We need to understand how markets collect information and how the amount of information and the distribution of information influences asset prices.

In Part 2 we examine market interest rates or interest rates on different types of securities. Thus, we deal with more aggregate assets than in Part 1. The central issues are essentially the same as in Part 1. We examine the various determinants of market interest rates.

In Part 3 we examine the ways that financial markets can be organized, and we consider some examples of each form of organization. Then we explore the reasons for the emergence of financial intermediaries as a tremendously important part of our financial system. We also explore the regulatory system for financial markets, first concentrating on the economic rationale for regulating financial markets. Then we analyze the major features of our regulatory system. The regulatory system can be broken into three major parts pertaining to securities markets, commercial banks, and nonbank financial intermediaries. The late 1970s and the 1980s have been a time of considerable sentiment to deregulate the American economy. This had led to a resurgence of controversy over regulation of financial markets. In the case of financial markets, the current regulatory system has emerged gradually over a century, and it has been easy to lose track of the central reasons for it. In this part we carefully examine the evolution of and motives for regulation and assess the performance of the regulatory system.

Part 4 deals with the final question. We examine the operation of specific markets and classes of institutions. We begin with an analysis of the recent deregulation of financial markets in order to see how this process is influencing the operation of financial firms and financial markets. Then we focus on the banking business and on mortgage finance. Finally, we examine the operation of money markets and options and futures markets.

Summary

More than anything else, this book is intended to give the student of finance a sufficient background to be a sophisticated participant in the marketplace. This book is not a practical guide to investing, nor is it a route map through the complex decisions a practicing financial manager must make. This book is about the marketplace in which both the investor and the financial manager must operate. It is intended to provide the theory, evidence, and institutional detail that a market participant needs to be successful. Two other factors, skill and luck, you will not learn from this or any other book.

References

Friedman, Milton. ''On the Methodology of Positive Economics,'' *Essay in Positive Economics,* Chicago: University of Chicago Press, 1953.

*T*HE VALUE OF ASSETS

The first part of this book explains how individual assets are valued. The value of an asset is determined by the stream of income which accrues to that asset in the future. Two important characteristics of the income stream determine the value of that asset. The first is the time distribution of income—whether that income will be received in the near or the distant future. The second is the uncertainty surrounding that future income—or the risk pertaining to the magnitude of that income. These are the concepts which occupy Part 1. Chapter 2 concentrates on the determination of the real rate of interest, the interest rate which provides a compensation for postponing consumption. This rate is the foundation of all the interest rates we observe in the financial markets. Chapter 3 analyzes how risky assets are valued in competitive capital markets when investors hold diversified portfolios of assets. Chapter 4 deals with the value of contingent claims, or assets whose payoffs depend on the value of some other underlying assets. Contingent claims include options and futures contracts. Chapter 5 looks deeper into the way value is determined by exploring how information about future returns to an asset is generated. This chapter shows how a financial market produces and aggregates information about individual assets. It also introduces the concept of an efficient use of information. Throughout Part 1 the emphasis is on how *individual* assets are priced in the market. ■

2

DETERMINANTS OF REAL INTEREST RATE

Interest rate is the price of forgone consumption.

This chapter begins a discussion of the determination of market interest rates that will be continued throughout Parts 1 and 2 of this book. The focus here is on what is called the **real interest rate**.[1] The adjective *real* refers to the fact that the interest rate is expressed net of inflation or no change in the price of goods and services. At the outset it is simplest to think of the real rate as the rate that would exist without inflation and if financial market participants anticipated there would be no inflation in the future. The real interest rate discussed here is also one that applies to a single time period as opposed to more than one period. In addition, the real rate is free of risk and taxes. Therefore, the real interest rate pertains to a single-period, risk-free financial obligation where there is no inflation or deflation. But before we dive into the determination of the real interest rate, it is useful to start with a description of the various types of interest rates used in financial markets and how they are computed. ■

---

[1]This chapter relies heavily on the exceptional work by Joseph W. Conard, *Introduction to the Theory of Interest,* Berkeley: University of California Press, 1959.

INTRODUCTION TO THE RATE OF INTEREST

The interest rate can be thought of in the same way as any other price in the marketplace. There is nothing unique about the function of the interest rate as a price. The only distinction between this price and prices in other markets is that the product involved is a little more abstract. We must therefore attempt to define precisely the product that is priced by the interest rate. Here is one way to think of the interest rate: it is the price of postponing payment. This is still somewhat ambiguous because it is not the timeliness of the payment itself that is valuable; rather, it is what the payment can be used for, or the opportunity cost of not having the funds available. When an individual to whom a payment is due agrees to postpone that payment, he or she has forgone the opportunity to consume. The interest rate can therefore be viewed as the *price of forgone consumption,* for the opportunity cost of delayed access to the funds is the postponement of consumption. More often we think of the interest rate as the price of borrowing or the price of credit. In effect, this is simply the more typical way of saying that the interest rate is the price of postponing payment or of forgone consumption.

HISTORICAL PERSPECTIVE ON THE INTEREST RATE

Credit has been a valuable commodity, and therefore the interest rate an important price, for centuries. As far back as 1500 B.C. the Assyrians used credit instruments. Somewhat more recently interest rates became a focal point for special regulation by the central authority. In medieval and renaissance Europe that authority was the Catholic church. The church's position on charging a price for credit was not based on any kind of notion of what was a fair or conscionable price, but rather on the objectionable nature of the credit contract itself. The church objected to the temporal nature of the contract, the fact that it bridged time. From the church's standpoint, what transpired tomorrow was the domain of God, not man. Hence, for man to profit on God's domain was considered sinful, and interest of any amount was a sin against God. This created some difficulty in that a zero interest rate was a disequilibrium, albeit, a divinely inspired one. At a zero rate of interest, there was an excess demand for credit; more people wanted to borrow than wanted to lend.

The marketplace evolved a number of ways to resolve this disequilibrium. One way to circumvent the church's prohibition on interest was for a class of specialists to emerge as lenders. This role was filled by the Jews of medieval Europe, for whom the eternal penalties of the Catholic church were of little consequence. As long as the church relied upon divine punishment for the sin of charging interest, Jewish lenders felt immune. However, if the church opted to impose worldly penalties, as it periodically did, then the cost to the lender became substantially greater. In effect, the real return to lenders declined, and they were compelled to raise their prices to bring their real returns back to an equilibrium. But during this period, one did not necessarily have to go outside the ranks of those who professed church allegiance to find lenders who charged interest for credit. They simply had to be more discreet about their pricing than did the Jews. One method practiced by the Medicis of renaissance Italy was to include an implicit charge for interest in the pricing of currency exchanges between different cities, which at that time issued their own currencies. For example, the rate of exchange between the currencies of Barcelona and Florence for a merchant traveling between the cities depended upon the travel time involved and included a premium for the interest covering that time period. Raymond de Roover concluded from the terms of exchange for such a contract in 1438 that the annual interest rate was 10.2 percent.[2]

Ever since medieval times the interest rate has been singled out for special treatment by government authorities. It is impossible to say with certainty whether this is a holdover from the Catholic church restrictions against interest in the Middle Ages. These restrictions might have created a climate that allowed other interest rate restrictions to persist into modern times. One type of restriction is the law that prohibits a usurious rate of interest. Unlike the medieval church, **usury laws** do not prohibit interest per se; they prohibit interest rates that are perceived to be too high—that is, usurious. Many states have had usury laws until recently, particularly regarding mortgage interest rates. These laws stem from the belief that, if not restricted by the state, lenders have the ability to take unfair advantage of unwitting borrowers.[3]

Another form of interest rate restriction is placed on interest rates that financial institutions, specifically commercial banks and savings and loans, are allowed to pay savers. This restriction was imposed by the federal government and was motivated by quite different considerations from those that led to usury laws. These ceilings were imposed to limit the ability of financial institutions to compete against each other. Apparently government officials believed that if institutions were left unrestricted, such competition would drive large numbers of them into bankruptcy. We will look more closely at both types of interest rate restrictions in Part 4 of this book.

SOME DIFFICULTIES IN COMPUTING INTEREST RATES

The interest rate can be defined in a number of ways. At this juncture we will examine a few incarnations of the interest rate. Most of the distinctions between various interest rates provide foundations for more extensive treatments of particular financial contracts in later chapters. Throughout this discussion we will deal with single-period interest rates. We will consider six specific types of interest rates. Multiple-period rates will be analyzed in Chapter 8.

Usury laws prohibit interest rates which are perceived to be too high.

---

[2]See Raymond de Roover, *The Rise and Decline of the Medici Bank, 1397–1494*, New York: W. W. Norton, 1966. Also see Martin Mayer, *The Bankers*, New York: Ballantine, 1974, for an excellent discussion of banking in the Middle Ages and a synthesis of Roover's treatment of the Medici bank.

[3]For a recent study of one type of usury law, see George J. Benston, ''Rate Ceiling Implications of the Cost Structure of Consumer Finance Companies,'' *Journal of Finance*, 32 (September 1977), pp. 1169–94.

The Simple Interest Rate.   The simple interest rate is so named because it is the simplest to define. It is defined with reference to a bond or a loan contract. Suppose the amount of the loan or the initial value of the bond is represented by P_1 and the amount or the value of the bond due at the end of one period by P_2. Then the interest rate, represented by i and measured as a decimal is defined as

$$1 + i = \frac{P_2}{P_1}. \qquad (2-1)$$

The equation can be manipulated in either of two ways: If we know the initial value of the loan and the interest rate, then we can solve for the amount due. Or, if we know the amount due and the interest rate, then we can solve for the current value of the loan. If, for example, the interest rate is 9 percent and the amount due at the end of the period is \$1,200, then P_1 = \$1,200/1.09 = \$1,100.92.

Compound Interest.   When we deal with bonds or loans that are longer than one period, then we must be careful to distinguish between simple and compound interest. To see the distinction suppose we examine a bond with an initial value of P_1 as above, and a value of P_5 four periods later. What is the single-period interest rate earned by this bond, or the yield per period on this bond? One way to determine this rate is simply to divide the percentage price increase by the number of periods involved, in this case four periods. This is the average simple interest rate:

$$\frac{(P_5/P_1) - 1}{4} = i. \qquad (2-2)$$

For example, if P_1 and P_5 assume the values of 100 and 220, respectively, then the average simple interest rate is ((220/100) − 1)/4 = 30 percent.

This method does not provide an accurate measure of the interest actually earned by the asset in each period. The shortcoming of the procedure is that it ignores the fact that interest earned in early periods increases the base on which interest is paid in later periods. In effect, it ignores the fact that interest compounds. We therefore refer to the appropriate measure of the interest rate as the compound rather than the simple interest rate. To see how to define the compound interest rate we will trace through the growth of the value of the asset each period from 1 to 5. If we buy a bond that increases in value at an interest rate of i per period, then the relationship between its value in period 2 and its value in period 1 is defined as in Equation (2−1).

$$P_2 = P_1(1 + i) \qquad (2-3)$$

The relationship between the values in periods 3 and 2 can be defined in the same way:

$$P_3 = P_2(1 + i). \qquad (2-4)$$

But by substituting from Equation (2–3) for the value of P_2, this yields:

$$P_3 = P_1(1 + i)(1 + i) = P_1(1 + i)^2. \qquad (2–5)$$

This substitution process can be continued until we derive an expression for P_5:

$$P_5 = P_1(1 + i)^4. \qquad (2–6)$$

We can now easily use this expression to solve for the *compound* (as opposed to the simple) *interest rate*. We merely divide through both sides of Equation (2–6) by P_1 and take the fourth root:

$$i = \sqrt[4]{\frac{P_5}{P_1}} - 1. \qquad (2–7)$$

In the example used above where P_5 and P_1 are 220 and 100, respectively, the compound interest rate is 22 percent as compared to 30 percent for the average simple interest rate. *Whenever the interest rate is referred to henceforth in this book and other places, it should be understood that it is the compound rather than the simple interest.*

The Interest Rate on a Discount Loan.   The typical loan contract is usually stated with the following terms. For a single-period loan the initial amount of the loan is P_1 and the interest rate is equal to i. This means that at the end of the period the amount owed to the lender is $P_2 = P_1(1 + i)$. This is identical to the statement of simple interest above. However, the loan may instead be made on a discount basis. The amount of a *discount loan* is stated in terms of the amount to be repaid rather than the amount lent—that is, in terms of P_2 rather than P_1. In addition, the quoted interest payment is based on P_2 rather than P_1; that is, P_1 is determined as follows: $P_1 = (1 - i_d)P_2$, where i_d is the stated interest rate on a discount basis. This has the effect of understating the true interest rate that is paid, for one plus the true interest rate is still equal to $P_2/P_1 = 1/(1 - i_d)$. If, for example, the amount that is owed at the end of the period is $1,000, and the stated interest rate for the discount loan is 10 percent, then the amount that is actually lent is $900 and the actual interest rate on this loan is ($1,000/$900) − 1 = 11 percent.

The Coupon and the Market Interest Rates.   Many bonds have both a coupon and a market interest rate. In order to distinguish between these two interest rates it is necessary to explain the terms of a *coupon bond*. Most coupon bonds have maturities longer than one period. (We'll examine examples of these in later chapters.) At this point we will deal with a very simple coupon bond that has only one period to maturity. A coupon bond has what is termed a *face value*, and the face value along with the coupon rate determines the amount that will be paid to the lender at the bond's maturity. For example, a single-period bond with a $1,000 face value and 6 percent coupon interest rate will pay $1,060 at maturity. That is,

$$P_2 = (1 + i_c)F, \qquad\qquad (2-8)$$

where i_c is the coupon interest rate and F is the face value of the bond.

Now that we know how P_2 is determined we still can return to Equation (2–1) for the determinants of either the market value of the bond, P_1, or the market interest rate on the bond, i. If we know the market interest rate, then we can solve for the market value of the bond as follows:

$$P_1 = \frac{P_2}{1 + i}. \qquad\qquad (2-9)$$

Conversely, if we know the market value of the bond, we can solve for the market interest rate:

$$i = \frac{P_2}{P_1} - 1. \qquad\qquad (2-10)$$

For example, for the bond with a face value of $1,000 and a coupon interest rate of 6 percent, if the market interest rate is 10 percent, then the price of the bond must be $1,060/1.1 = $963. Only at this price will the bond have a yield which is the same as the one prevailing in the market. Therefore, the coupon rate merely defines the payment that will be made to the lender. It need not be the same as the interest rate which the market demands for lending funds.

Real and Nominal Interest Rates.   In our discussion of interest rates thus far we have not mentioned the possibility that the price level will change during the period covered by a bond or a loan. If the price level changes, then the real return received by the lender and the real cost paid by the borrower will change. This is because the values of financial contracts are denominated in terms of money, dollars, in the United States. This is clear from an examination of the value of the contract at its beginning and termination—that is, the value of P_1 and P_2. Both of these values are expressed in dollars. But if the general level of prices changes from time period 1 to time period 2, then the *ex post real interest rate, the actual interest rate net of observed inflation,* is altered. To make this statement more specific we will define the ex post real interest rate that is actually received by the lender, i_R, as

The **real interest rate** is the interest rate net of inflation.

$$i_R = \left(\frac{P_2}{P_1} - 1\right) - \text{observed inflation rate} \qquad\qquad (2-11)$$

$$= i_N - \text{observed inflation rate,}$$

where i_N is the nominal interest rate used in the equations above. For example, when the nominal interest rate is 10 percent, and the inflation rate is 6 percent, then the real rate is 4 percent.

When inflation rates are high and volatile, it is real rather than nominal interest rates that are of concern to investors. As as result, investors will adjust the nominal interest rates they demand so that the real returns they expect to receive are viewed as an appropriate compensation for lending funds. We will examine this process of adjusting the nominal rate in Chapter 7.

Before-tax and After-tax Interest Rates.   Most types of interest income are subject to income tax from both federal and state governments. Therefore it is important to distinguish between interest rates before taxes and after taxes. For any individual the distinction depends upon his or her **marginal tax rate,** the tax rate paid on the marginal amount of income that the interest payment represents. With this marginal tax rate represented by , the relationship between the before-tax and after-tax nominal interest rates for a particular individual can be expressed as

Marginal tax rate is the tax rate on the last dollar earned.

$$i_A = i_N(1 - \ell), \qquad (2-12)$$

where i_A is the after-tax nominal interest rate. Equation (2–12) indicates that the after-tax interest rate is equal to the before-tax interest rate reduced by the marginal tax rate of the individual in question. For example, if the nominal interest rate is 16 percent, then the after-tax nominal rate for a person in the 28 percent tax bracket is 11.5 percent.

We can combine the adjustments we have made for taxes and inflation rates to arrive at the after-tax real interest rate of an individual in the market. If we represent the *after-tax real interest rate* by i_{RA}, then its relationship to the nominal interest can be defined as follows:

$$i_{RA} = i_N(1 - \ell) - \text{inflation rate.} \qquad (2-13)$$

For example, for an individual with a 28 percent marginal tax rate who receives a nominal interest rate of 16 percent and experiences inflation of 10 percent, the real after-tax return will be $0.16 \times 0.72 - 0.10 = 1.5$ percent. The discrepancy between the real after-tax and the nominal interest rate is substantial. It highlights how misleading it can be to examine nominal interest rates without careful consideration of taxes and inflation. As the example shows, a 16 percent interest rate is not particularly high with 10 percent inflation and a 28 percent tax rate.

*F*ISHERIAN THEORY OF THE REAL RATE OF INTEREST

Our current understanding of the determinants of the real rate of interest dates back to the work of the famous economist Irving Fisher who published a book in 1930 titled *The Theory of Interest*. His principal contribution, if it is possible to summarize it succinctly, was to examine explicitly the trade-off between goods produced, purchased, and consumed in distinct time periods. Fisher's view of the interest rate has had tremendous staying power. It has been refined, expanded, and reinterpreted. But it remains, as its name suggests, Fisherian interest rate theory.

Fisherian interest rate theory is just basic microeconomics or price theory. The basic ingredients of the analysis include the individual's preference between goods consumed today and goods consumed tomorrow, as well as the production technology that permits investment in capital goods which are used to produce consumer goods for tomorrow.

The basic microeconomic problem is to determine the individual's optimal amount of investment in future goods as well as that person's amount of borrowing or lending with other participants in the market. An *equilibrium rate of interest* is then determined, where desired borrowing is equal to desired lending for all market participants. The purpose of the analysis is to discover and appreciate the factors that determine the real interest rate in any economy and the nature of the forces that tend to drive the market toward equilibrium.

TIME PREFERENCE

The first ingredient in determination of the real interest rate is each individual's attitude toward consumption today as opposed to consumption tomorrow. The choice can be thought of as the choice between two distinct commodities. For example, there is a trade-off between days spent skiing at Snowbird, Utah, this year and days spent there next year, just as there is a trade-off between days spent skiing in Utah this year and days spent skiing in Wisconsin this year. Each is a distinct commodity in that the typical skier is not indifferent about the way they are substituted.

The individual's attitude toward trade-offs between commodities, whether they are distinguished by time or other characteristics, is normally represented with indifference curves. These show the combinations of the commodities to which the individual would be indifferent. For example, a person might say that it didn't matter whether he or she had five days at Snowbird this year or seven days at Snowbird next year; either option would be equally satisfying. However, if the person had to give up one of the days this year, the only way the loss would be acceptable would be if he or she could have two days next year. This trade-off is illustrated with the curve labeled P_1 in Figure 2–1. This particular type of indifference curve, which is referred to as a *time-preference curve,* is drawn to reflect the assumption that as the individual is deprived of current consumption, ever larger amounts of future consumption are required to make him or her indifferent to the exchange. The curve is therefore drawn convex to the origin.

It is important to see that there will be an infinite number of indifference curves for each individual. The reason for this is that each curve represents the combinations of present and future consumption that leave the individual equally satisfied. But it is always possible to come up with combinations which create either more or less satisfaction. For example, ten days at Snowbird this year and ten next year is obviously better than five this year and seven next year. There will be a time-

FIGURE 2–1

Map of time-preference curves for an individual. Each curve shows the combinations of skiing this year and next to which an individual is indifferent.

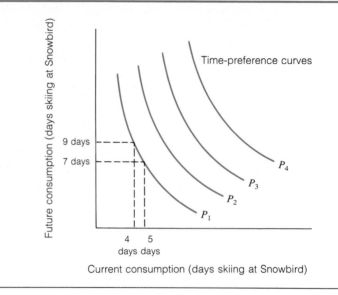

Current consumption (days skiing at Snowbird)

preference curve that goes through the point in Figure 2–1 representing 10 days this year and ten next which never intersects the curve drawn in the diagram that goes through the point representing five days this year and seven days next. The argument can be repeated indefinitely to construct as many time-preference curves as seems pleasing. Assuming that all individuals prefer more of almost any commodity to less (even skiing), the objective for any individual is to attain the highest time-preference curve possible. This means that any skier would seek the most skiing possible, maintaining the trade-off between present and future skiing. But the question arises as to what determines what is possible. What are the constraints on the individual that inhibit him or her from skiing the entire season?

INVESTMENT OPPORTUNITIES

There are two types of constraints that limit any individual's opportunities to consume goods today and tomorrow. Both relate to the opportunities for the individual to transform current into future wealth and vice versa. The first is the opportunity for the individual to forgo current consumption and invest in productive activities which increase wealth. The other is the opportunity to borrow wealth from or lend wealth to other individuals. It is useful to first consider the individual's choice between current and future consumption if there are no borrowing or lending opportunities and if there are only investment opportunities.

Thus far a few terms have been used a little loosely to introduce the constraints on each individual's choice. But more precise definitions of the terms saving, investment, borrowing, and lending are now in order. In common usage, saving

FIGURE 2–2
The investment-opportunity curve. The curve labeled II' represents the investment opportunities which are available to an individual or an economy. The slope of the tangent line at each point on the curve, such as the one at point A, represents the marginal rate of return on investment.

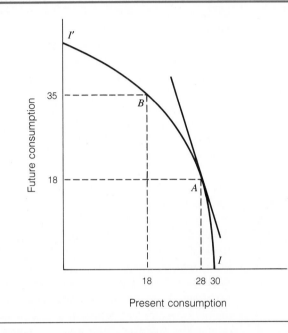

Saving is forgone consumption.

Investment is the creation of new wealth or capital goods.

Lending involves the exchange of funds today for a promise to repay the funds tomorrow.

Borrowing is the opposite of lending.

refers to both saving as it will be defined here and lending. **Saving** is really forgone consumption. It is that portion of current income that is not consumed. Saving makes no reference to the use to which this forgone consumption is put. Income that is saved can either be invested or lent. **Investment** is the creation of new wealth or capital goods. The classical example of investment is the planting of a forest. Current income is forgone in order to plant the seeds and maintain the forest. As the trees grow the capital stock of lumber, beauty, and recreational use increases. If the forest is cut, disinvestment takes place, and the capital stock is reduced by the consumption of the forest. By contrast, when the income that is saved is **lent,** a claim against future income is created, but no change in the capital stock takes place. Instead funds are exchanged today for a promise of repayment of funds tomorrow. Conversely, **borrowing** is simply the opposite side of this transaction. The individual who has acquired the funds today has issued a promise to pay tomorrow what was borrowed. Now that we have an understanding of how these words are used, we can return to the problem of how to represent an individual's choice between present and future consumption.

With the aid of Figure 2–2 it is possible to examine the individual's choice between present and future consumption, where there are no opportunities to borrow or lend but there are opportunities to invest. The horizontal axis in this figure measures the individual's current income and consumption, and the vertical axis measures his or her income and consumption tomorrow. We will assume that the individual in our example starts with $30 of current income, represented by the intersection of the II' curve with the horizontal axis. The constraint which this individual faces is defined by the set of investments available. The curved line labeled II' represents the possible combinations of current and future income the individual can reach by investing his or her initial income in real goods or services. For example, by moving to point A on the line II', the individual gives up $2 of current income to invest in the future. This investment generates a future income of $18, and this is the coordinate of point A on the vertical axis.

The rate of return or yield this individual receives on the investment can easily be calculated from curve II'. In this investment, which moved the individual from the initial point on the horizontal axis to point A, the return was $18 − $2 = $16. This is a rate of return of $16/$2, or 800 percent. This is an exceptionally attractive return, but we can tell from the shape of curve II' that as the individual continues to invest more current income, the rate of return will decline. For example, if the individual increased the investment from point A to point B, this would yield an additional $17 increase in future income. But this would require an additional $10 investment of current income. This would yield a rate of return of ($17 − $10)/$10 or 70 percent, which is a much smaller rate of return than the initial 800 percent. If we consider an infinitely small investment, the rate of return is measured by the slope of a line drawn tangent to the curve II' at that point of investment. This is illustrated by the tangent line at point A. We can see from the shape of the II' curve that as we move farther up the curve, lines drawn tangent to the curve will have flatter and flatter slopes. This means that the more the individual invests, the lower the rate of return will be. Another way of saying this is that the individual receives diminishing marginal returns on investment.

The problem facing the individual represented in Figure 2–2 is to choose the optimal amount of investment or saving (note that saving must equal investment for each individual when there is no borrowing or lending) given the investment opportunities available. From Figure 2–2 we can conclude that it will be optimal for the individual to position himself or herself on the II' curve *rather than inside it. The individual could always choose an investment opportunity which is represented by a point closer to the origin than the II'* curve, but the returns from such an investment would be less than a comparable investment which is on the II' curve. Since the II' curve represents the best the individual can obtain, it is impossible to be outside it. However, it is not possible to tell from Figure 2–2 what point on the curve is best. To do this we must incorporate time-preference curves, like those in Figure 2–1, into Figure 2–2. This is done in Figure 2–3. The optimal amount of investment in Figure 2–3 will be the point on the highest possible time-preference curve. This is represented by point A in Figure 2–3, where the II' curve is tangent to the time-preference curve P_1. This represents an optimal amount of investment and saving for the individual, because it is impossible to reach a higher time-preference curve, such as P_2, given the investment opportunities available.

The equilibrium illustrated in Figure 2–3 brings together two concepts of the real rate of interest. The first is represented by the slope of the investment oppor-

FIGURE 2–3

Optimal investment with no opportunities for borrowing and lending. This figure shows that an individual can reach the highest time-preference curve by investing until the investment-opportunity curve is tangent to a time-preference curve.

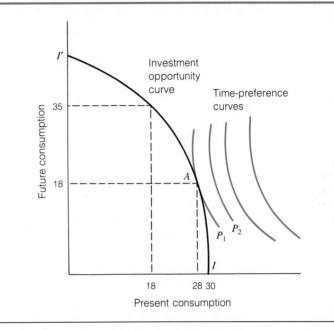

tunity curve II'. This slope represents the rate at which it is possible to transform current consumption opportunities into future consumption. The second is represented by the slope of the time-preference curve. This slope represents the rate of trade-off between present and future consumption that makes the individual satisfied with the exchange. It is called the **marginal rate of time preference.**

The important characteristic of equilibrium in the market revealed by Figure 2–3 is that these concepts of the interest rate must be the same. If this were not the case, the individual would search for a new level of investment where the trade-off between present and future consumption was more satisfactory. *Therefore, the initial insight into the real interest rate is that it is the rate where each individual equates his or her marginal rate of return on investment with his or her marginal rate of time preference.* In this sense, the real rate of interest represents an equilibrium.

EQUILIBRIUM WITH BORROWING AND LENDING

Now that we have seen how to describe an individual's optimal choice of consumption today and tomorrow when there are no opportunities to borrow and lend, we can expand this analysis to include borrowing and lending. To do this we have to

Marginal rate of time preference is the rate of trade-off between present and future consumption that makes an individual just satisfied with the exchange.

The initial insight into the real interest rate is that it is the rate where each individual equates his or her marginal rate of return on investment with his or her marginal rate of time preference.

add yet a little more to Figure 2–3. This is done in Figure 2–4. What we have to add is a straight line representing the opportunity to borrow and lend. The slope of this straight line represents the interest rate at which the individual in the figure can borrow or lend. The fact that the line is straight means that the interest rate does not change with increases or decreases in the amount of borrowing or lending. We could draw any number of these straight lines in Figure 2–4, showing opportunities to borrow and lend, just as we can fill the figure with time-preference curves of an individual. But we will draw in only one of these lines, *BL.* This line has a slope of −1.1. This means it is consistent with an interest rate of 10 percent. Line *BL* shows the borrowing and lending opportunities available to the individual whose choice we examined in Figure 2–3. The choices of two individuals are shown in this figure so that we can see how to represent the choices of someone who chooses to borrow and someone who chooses to lend. Table 2–1 provides a legend for Figure 2–4. Panel A shows the coordinates of each of the points in Figure 2–4.

To begin with, we will concentrate on individual 1 who chooses to borrow. When borrowing and lending opportunities were not available, as depicted in Figure

FIGURE 2–4
Equilibrium for two individuals who can borrow and lend. Individual 1 borrows and individual 2 lends.

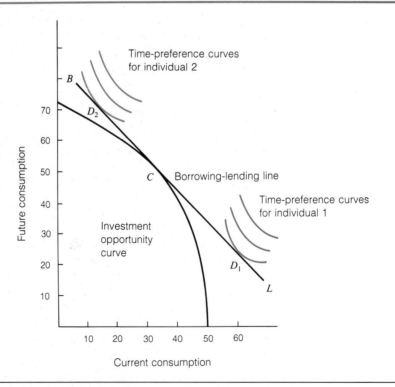

2–3, it was optimal for an individual to invest until the investment-opportunity curve was tangent with a time-preference curve at point A. But with opportunities to borrow and lend this is no longer optimal. It will now be optimal to invest until the investment-opportunity curve is tangent to the line representing borrowing and lending opportunities, as indicated by point C on line BL. Then individual 1 can borrow until he or she reaches point D_1, which is the point of tangency with his or her time-preference curve. To see that this is optimal, notice that the individual can move to any position on line BL by either borrowing or lending. A movement up and to the left sacrifices current income and is therefore a decision to lend, while a movement down and to the right sacrifices future income for current income and is therefore a decision to borrow. By either borrowing or lending and moving along this line, the individual is able to move to a position that is tangent to a higher time-preference curve (at point D_1) than the time-preference curve that is tangent to the investment-opportunity curve at point A. In this sense, the existence of opportunities to borrow and lend makes this individual better off.

Figure 2–4 also illustrates the decisions of a second individual. This second individual is assumed to start with the same initial amount of current income, \$50. The important distinction between the two is that the second individual chooses to lend rather than borrow. This results because his or her time-preference curve is tangent to the borrowing line above its tangency with the investment-opportunity curve at C. This individual finds it optimal to invest up to C and then lend at the prevailing interest rate of 10 percent. As a result, he or she will shift toward future rather than current consumption, whereas individual 1 uses borrowing to support current rather than future consumption.

Both of these individuals have an individual equilibrium in the following sense. They have chosen a level of investment and borrowing or lending that allows them to achieve their highest possible time-preference curve. In this equilibrium, they equate the marginal rate of time preference, the marginal return on investment, and the interest rate on borrowing and lending. This follows because the straight line representing borrowing and lending opportunities is tangent to both the II' curve and the time-preference curve. As a result, all three have the same slope. This means that the real interest rate is equal to all three of these alternative concepts of the rate of interest.

MARKET EQUILIBRIUM

We just characterized the equilibrium for a single individual. But this equilibrium will also apply to the market as a whole if total borrowing is equal to total lending in the market. In fact, for equilibrium in the whole market, the interest rate on borrowing and lending must adjust until desired lending is equal to desired borrowing. To see how this works we can use the two individuals in Figure 2–4 to represent a market of borrowers and lenders. For equilibrium to result, the desired borrowing of individual 1 must equal the desired lending of individual 2. We can

FIGURE 2–5
Illustration of how the market reaches an equilibrium real interest rate.

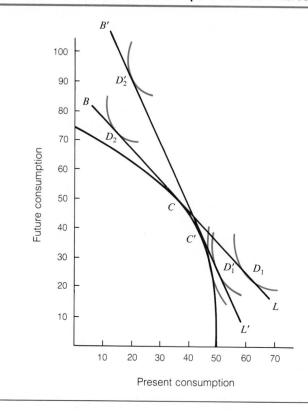

see that at the 10 percent interest rate used in Figure 2–4 this condition is met. When individual 1 borrows, he or she moves from point C with $38 of current income to point D_1 with $61 of current income. This means total borrowing of $23. Individual 2 moves from point C with $38 of current income to point D_2 with $15 of current income. This means lending of $23. As a result, with a 10 percent interest rate, desired lending is equal to desired borrowing.

Thus far, the discussion of borrowing and lending opportunities for individuals in the market started with a real interest rate that was an equilibrium rate. At the interest rate of 10 percent, represented by the BL line, individual 1 wanted to borrow the same amount that individual 2 wanted to lend. But the question arises as to how the market brings about this equilibrium. Is the market capable of adjusting toward an equilibrium if it begins in disequilibrium?

To consider this question suppose that the interest rate is initially at a higher rate, represented by the $B'L'$ line of Figure 2–5. This line represents a higher rate because it has a steeper slope. The introduction of the new borrowing and lending line is the only difference between Figures 2–4 and 2–5. Panel B of Table 2–1 shows the coordinates of the points added in Figure 2–5. At this higher interest rate both individuals will choose to invest a lower amount such that the marginal rate of return on investment is higher than before. Both individuals will choose to invest to point C' rather than point C. In addition, individual 1 will only choose to borrow $7 at this higher interest rate as represented by the tangency between $B'L'$ and the time preference curve at point D_1'. There will be a disequilibrium between desired borrowing and desired lending because individual 2 will choose to lend $26 as represented by the tangency at point D_2'. From Table 2–1, note that point C_1' includes consumption of $44, D_1' includes current consumption of $51, and point D_2' includes current consumption of $18. In order to induce individual 1 to borrow more and individual 2 to lend less, the interest rate will have to fall. It will fall until the real interest rate reaches 10 percent, as represented by line BL rather than $B'L'$. At this rate desired lending is equal to desired borrowing and the market is in equilibrium. The market has an incentive to make this adjustment, because at the high disequilibrium real interest rate there is excess lending. To attract additional borrowing it is necessary to reduce the real interest rate until the incentive to borrow and to lend are equal.

In equilibrium the real interest rate captures three important factors. It is, first and foremost, the rate at which borrowing and lending are in equilibrium. But, it is also equal to the marginal rate of return on productive investment for all participants in the market. Finally, it is equal to the marginal rate of time preference for market participants; the rate at which they desire to substitute between present and future consumption. The real interest rate, therefore, reflects an equilibrium among all of these important forces in the economy, which determine the economic trade-offs across time. The real interest rate is the fundamental component of all the interest rates observed in the marketplace.

Finally, with the introduction of borrowing and lending opportunities we have introduced a change in the way each individual conducts investment decisions. Without opportunities to borrow and lend, the criterion for optimal investment was to invest until the marginal rate of return on investment was equal to an individual's

TABLE 2–1
Legend for figures 2–4 and 2–5.

	Panel A	Panel B
	$C = 38, 48$	$C' = 44, 39$
	$D_1 = 61, 24$	$D_1' = 51, 28$
	$D_2 = 15, 73$	$D_2' = 18, 89$

Panel A shows the coordinates of points shown in Figures 2–4 and 2–5. Panel B shows the coordinates of new points added in Figure 2–5. Current income is listed first and future income second. For example, C is 38 current income and 48 future income.

FIGURE 2-6
The equilibrium real interest rate and the supply and demand for funds.

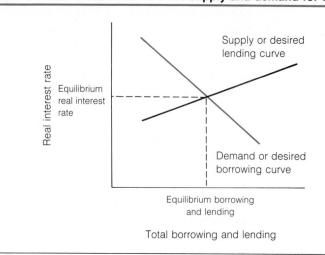

personal rate of trading future for present consumption. This is no longer true. With a market for borrowing and lending, investment is undertaken until the rate of return is equal to the market interest rate. Because the market interest rate is equal for all, the rate of return on investment is equalized across the economy. In addition, the investment decision is separated from the choice of how much to consume today versus tomorrow for each individual. In this way the investment decision is depersonalized.

A SIMPLE STATEMENT OF EQUILIBRIUM

It is useful to translate the Fisherian theory into a simple model of demand and supply for borrowing and lending. To do this we will assume that, as in the Fisherian model, everyone comes together to borrow and lend at once. As a result there is a single market for all borrowing and lending that clears at one time. In such a market there is no outstanding stock of past borrowing and lending. At the same time that people borrow and lend they also decide how intensely to use the existing stock of real productive capital goods.

We can use a diagram to illustrate how this simple market for borrowing and lending works. Figure 2-6 shows a downward-sloping demand curve and an upward-sloping supply curve. The vertical axis in the figure measures the interest rate, while the horizontal axis measures the total volume of borrowing and lending. The downward-sloping curve shows the desired amount of borrowing by everyone in the economy at different levels of the real interest rate. We can think of this curve as the demand for funds. This curve will have a negative slope, because, in the analysis of market equilibrium in Figure 2–5, we discovered that as the interest rate rises, desired borrowing falls. The upward-sloping curve in Figure 2–6 shows the desired amount of lending in the market as a function of the interest rate. We can think of this as a supply curve for funds. We also know from our examination of Fisherian theory that this will have a positive slope.

We can use Figure 2–6 to describe the equilibrium real interest rate. The real rate is the interest rate at which desired borrowing is equal to desired lending. This is illustrated in Figure 2–6 at the point of intersection between the two curves. Of course, we also know from Fisherian theory that the equilibrium rate must also be the rate of return on productive investment opportunities or on the economy's total stock of capital. This is not explicitly shown in this figure. As a result, the figure is only a partial description of the general equilibrium in the market. Nevertheless, it is useful to translate the Fisherian concept of equilibrium into the more familiar framework of a supply and demand diagram. From this diagram we can see that anything that causes the demand for funds to shift up to the right will put upward pressure on the real interest rate. Conversely, any factor that causes the supply curve for funds to shift back to the left will put downward pressure on the real rate.

*E*QUILIBRIUM IN PRIMARY AND SECONDARY MARKETS

The Fisherian theory of the real interest rate gives us a clear foundation for understanding the determinants of interest rates in the real world. It tells us that the real rate must equilibrate desired borrowing and lending, and it must equal the rate of return on productive investments and the marginal rate of time preference for everyone. It is difficult to understand the world around us without understanding these concepts. On the other hand, the imagined market of the Fisherian theory is not much like the markets we actually see in the real world. One of the most glaring discrepancies between the Fisherian model and real world markets is the fact that everyone in the world does not come together to borrow and lend all at once. Instead, people are borrowing and lending in distinct financial markets all the time. This means during any one period of time there is a large stock of outstanding financial contracts as a result of past borrowing and lending and there is new borrowing and lending taking place during the current period. Moreover, there are often distinct markets for existing financial contracts and new financial contracts.

A *primary market* is a market for new assets; a *secondary market* is a market for existing assets.

These are called *secondary* and *primary markets,* respectively. We will use our understanding of Fisherian theory to describe how the real interest rate is actually determined in primary and secondary financial markets.

When we introduce primary and secondary markets into our theory of the real rate of interest, we do not have to make any fundamental changes in the meaning or interpretation of the real rate. But we do have to recognize that the real interest rate must now be the equilibrium rate in both primary and secondary markets. To

FIGURE 2–7
Equilibrium in the secondary market. This figure shows that the real interest rate must be the equilibrium rate in the secondary market where the existing stock of assets is traded.

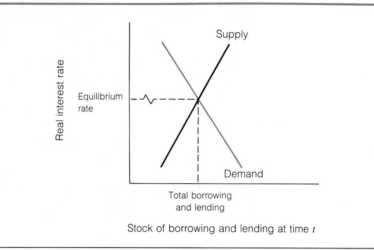

see what this means we need to analyze the equilibrium in both types of markets, just as we analyzed the equilibrium in Figure 2–6 where everyone borrowed and lent at the same time.

The *secondary market* comprises the market for outstanding financial assets. For example, the New York Stock Exchange is a secondary market for securities issued by major United States companies. The shares traded on the Exchange are shares that have previously been issued and are traded from one owner to another. In this sense they are used rather than new assets. When these assets are traded, they do not represent any new borrowing and lending. Rather, there is just a redistribution of existing borrowing and lending.

We can describe the equilibrium in this secondary market for assets with curves representing the total of all outstanding desired borrowing and desired lending, just as we did when we imagined a single instantaneous market. These curves now represent the total desired borrowing and lending at a point in time. In effect, they are the cumulative desired new borrowing and lending of all past periods in which financial contracts were written. This is represented in Figure 2–7. This figure shows the total desired borrowing and lending at a point in time labeled *t*. The real interest rate is the interest rate at which desired borrowing equals desired lending in this secondary market.

The real interest rate also has to be the equilibrium rate in the primary market. The primary market is the market for new borrowing and lending. It is the market where new securities are issued to obtain new funds. In many financial markets in the United States the primary and secondary markets, or the mechanisms through which new as opposed to old securities are traded, are quite distinct. However, the securities offered for sale on the primary and secondary markets are identical. A company that sells new securities to the market to raise new funds cannot expect its new securities to command a yield different from the yield on outstanding identical securities. This means that the prices and yields set in secondary and primary markets are tied together. In terms of our analysis of the real rate of interest, this means that the real rate of interest has to be the same equilibrium rate in both the primary and secondary markets.

The relationship between the primary and secondary markets is illustrated in Figure 2–8. Panel A of this figure shows the demand and supply curves for funds at two distinct points in time, t-1 and t. Panel B shows the demand and supply for funds in the primary market. The demand and supply in the secondary market is the

FIGURE 2–8
This figure shows how the demand and supply in the primary market is derived from the changes in demand and supply in the secondary market. The demand in panel B is equal to the quantity demanded on D'_1 less $\overline{B}$ and the supply is equal to S' less $\overline{B}$. $\overline{B}$ represents the total amount of borrowing and lending at time $t - 1$.

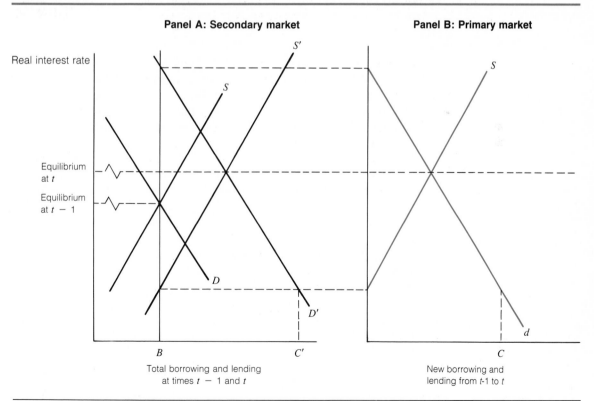

total of demand and supply at a point in time, while in the primary market it is the change in that demand and supply or desired new borrowing and lending between the two points of time that we see. This is what is illustrated in Figure 2–8. The demand and supply in the primary market can be derived from the changes in the secondary market at two different points in time. Panel A of the figure shows that both total demand and supply in the secondary market have shifted to the right between point *t*-1 and period *t*. The demand curve shifts from *D* to *D'* and the supply curve from *S* to *S'*. Panel B shows the new demand and supply for funds that develops between periods *t*-1 and period *t*.

In order to derive the demand-and-supply curves in the primary market, shown in panel B, from the changes in the demand-and-supply curves in the secondary market, we need to draw a vertical line in panel A representing the stock of assets at time *t*-1. This vertical line passes through the intersection of the *D* and *S* curves. The demand curve in the primary market is determined by the horizontal distance between this vertical line and the curve *D'* representing demand in the secondary market at time *t*. Specifically, the origin in panel B corresponds to the vertical line in panel A, and the distance between the origin and point *C* on curve *d* and the vertical line and point *C* on curve *D'* (or *C-B*) are the same. The demand curve in the primary market, *d*, therefore measures the new demand flowing into the market at each level of the real interest rate. The same procedure is used to construct the supply curve *s* in the primary market.

The important feature of equilibrium illustrated by Figure 2–8 is that the real interest rate is the rate which equilibrates the primary market between *t*-1 and *t*. Regardless of the magnitude of the shifts in the curves and therefore of the changes in the rate, the equilibrium real rate must be the same in both markets. Therefore, when examining flows of funds in the primary market, it is important to recognize that these are changes in the total stock of borrowing and lending. And the real interest rate determined in the primary market must be the same as the real interest rate determined in the secondary market.[4] As we learned from Fisherian theory, the equilibrium real interest rate is not only the rate that equilibrates borrowing and lending, it is also the rate of return on productive investment or the rate of return on the economy's capital stock. As a result, *when we examine the interest rate in the primary financial markets, in equilibrium that rate must be the same as the interest rate in the secondary market for financial assets and the same as the return on the economy's capital stock.* This is the principal link between the financial markets in the economy and the market for real goods and services.

When we examine the interest rate in the primary financial markets, in equilibrium that rate must be the same as the interest rate in the secondary market for financial assets and the same as the return on the economy's capital stock.

---

[4]It is important to recognize what Figure 2–8 and the accompanying discussion does not explain. It does not explain the path of the real interest rate through time nor the path of the flow of funds through time; it is as if we were using a still camera to record a continuous record of those movements. For example, we cannot tell whether the equilibrium interest rate shown in Figure 2–8 follows a straight line between the equilibrium levels at *t*-1 and *t* or follows a highly volatile path. We *do* know that new securities cannot sell at prices which differ widely from a much larger stock of identical outstanding securities as they flow in the market. But it is difficult, without considerably more analytical detail, to translate this statement into a precise statement about the path of the interest rate through time.

ANALYZING THE FLOW OF FUNDS

We have just learned that the real rate of interest is the equilibrium rate in both the primary and secondary markets for financial assets. We discovered that in the secondary market we were concerned with the outstanding stock of all borrowing and lending, while in the primary market we were concerned with the flow of new borrowing and lending. We will refer to this flow in the primary market as the **flow of funds.** Though we know the real rate is a function of what happens in both primary and secondary markets, it is often useful and interesting to focus attention on only the flow of funds in the markets. By examining the flow of funds within the economy we can tell where there are major changes in patterns of borrowing and lending. As a result we can acquire an indication of where there may be pressure on particular market interest rates. In order to make this kind of analysis possible, the Federal Reserve System measures the flow of funds or new borrowing and lending between various sectors in the United States economy. These data are called the flow of funds accounts.

> The **flow of funds** is the flow of new borrowing and lending in a given period of time.

We will analyze the flow of funds or the loanable funds market in the remainder of this chapter. To simplify our analysis we will begin by dividing the economy into four sectors. Within the Federal Reserve's flow of funds accounts there are actually a much larger number of sectors. But the four sectors we will start with are the major categories of borrowers and lenders in the economy. The four sectors are labeled households, nonfinancial businesses, financial institutions, and government (including federal, state, and local).

FINANCIAL STATEMENTS FOR ECONOMIC SECTORS

Each entity in each sector has a balance sheet and an income statement. An example of the fundamental items on such a balance sheet for the household sector is represented in Table 2–2. In this hypothetical example for the quarter period ending

TABLE 2–2

Hypothetical income statement for household sector for quarter ending December 31, 1987.

Current Income	$900
Current Expenditures	810
Saving	$ 90

Hypothetical Balance Sheet for Household Sector December 31, 1987

Assets	
Financial Assets	$1020
Real Assets	100
Total Assets	1120
Liabilities	940
Net Worth	180
Total Liabilities and Net Worth	$1120

TABLE 2–3
Hypothetical sources and uses of funds statement for household sector for quarter ending December 31, 1987.

Uses	
Other Financial Claims (Lending)	$ 37
Real Assets (Investment)	64
Total Assets	$101
Sources	
Liabilities (Borrowing)	$ 11
Net Worth (Saving)	90
Total Liabilities and Net Worth	$101

Financial assets refer to claims against future income.
Real assets refer to productive capital goods.

The income statement reports flows, while the balance sheet represents stocks.

December 31, 1987, the household sector has a total current income of $900 and current expenditures or consumption of $810, which implies the total saving by this sector is $90. The hypothetical balance sheet indicates that on December 31, 1987, households had total assets of $1,120. The assets are broken down into two broad categories, financial and real assets. The term **financial assets** refers to claims against future income, while **real assets** refers to productive capital goods. Liabilities or borrowing totals $940, and net worth equals $180.

An important distinction between the material contained in the income statement for a sector and the information contained in the balance sheet is that the income statement covers financial performance over a period of time, while the balance sheet represents the sector's financial position at a point in time. *The income statement reports flows, while the balance sheet represents stocks.* In order to analyze the flow of funds we must convert stocks into flows. To do so it is necessary to construct a sources and uses of funds statement for each sector of the economy corresponding to a period of time. The sources and uses of funds statement for a sector of an economy is just an aggregate of sources and uses of funds statements for individuals or firms. It merely shows the changes in each item that appear on the balance sheets between two points in time, and it classifies each change as to whether it is a source or use of funds. An example of a simple hypothetical sources and uses statement for the household sector is presented in Table 2–3 for the quarter ending December 31, 1987. In this statement changes in all the assets are treated as uses of funds while liabilities and net worth are treated as sources. The balance sheet identity requires that the sum of all uses equals the sum of all sources for each sector.

Each individual sector's sources and uses statement may be put together to form a flow of funds statement for the economy as a whole. An example of a hypothetical flow of funds statement for the four sectors defined above is presented in Table 2–4. This flow of funds statement illustrates that, within each sector, sources must balance uses. It follows, of course, that sources must balance uses for all the sectors combined.

The basic contribution of the flow of funds statement is that it allows us to analyze the pattern of borrowing, lending, saving, and investing for each sector and to make comparisons between sectors. In effect, it makes it possible to trace the flow of funds through the economy. In the example presented in Table 2–4 households save (90) more than they invest (64), and the excess savings is lent to other sectors. Households also acquire some financial liabilities, but lending still exceeds borrowing for this sector. Business firms, on the other hand, invest (85) more than they save (62). They acquire the necessary funds by issuing more liabilities than they acquire in financial assets. The financial institution sector saves very little and makes a negligible real investment. It largely exchanges financial assets for financial liabilities, that is, it is an intermediary. In this example governments dissave in that they run a deficit (−5). The deficit is financed by issuing more financial claims than are purchased.

The flow of funds table also illustrates one other important aspect of the economy. Actual investment must equal actual saving for the economy as a whole. This is definitely not true for any particular sector, as the household and business sectors make evident. However, total sources and uses must be equal for each sector and, therefore, for the entire economy. In addition, all financial claims are offsetting for the economy as a whole. Every dollar lent is offset by a dollar borrowed, so that total borrowing, which is equal to the change in liabilities, must equal total lending, which is equal to the total change in financial claims. As a result, the residuals, investment and saving, must be equal. This can be expressed in a simple algebraic form. For the whole economy:

$$\text{Investment} + \text{Lending} = \text{Saving} + \text{Borrowing}.$$

TABLE 2–4
Hypothetical flow of funds for four sectors for quarter ending December 31, 1987.

	Household Sector		Business Sector		Financial Institutions Sector		Government Sector		All Sectors	
	U	S	U	S	U	S	U	S	U	S
Net Worth (Saving)		90		62		2		−5		149
Real Assets (Investment)	64		85		0		0		149	
Financial Assets (Lending)	37		17		53		12		119	
Financial Liabilities (Borrowing)		11		40		51		17		119
	101	101	102	102	53	53	12	12	268	268

But because

$$\text{Borrowing} = \text{Lending},$$

it follows that

$$\text{Saving} = \text{Investment}.$$

This relationship between saving and investment and borrowing and lending is not something totally new. We can draw the same conclusion from the Fisherian theory of the real interest rate. In the Fisherian theory the real rate is the interest rate that results in an equilibrium between desired borrowing and lending. At the same time, because investment plus lending must equal savings plus borrowing for the entire economy, the Fisherian theory implies that aggregate savings must equal aggregate investment. As a result, we have another way to think about the equilibrium real interest rate. The equilibrium real interest rate is the rate at which desired saving is equal to desired investment.

Finally, we can use flow of funds data to analyze either net or gross flows of funds between sectors. For example, the household sector illustrated in Table 2–4 is really a net lender of $26—that is, an increase in financial assets of $37, less borrowing of $11. This net lending (or borrowing) is equal to the excess of savings over investment for any sector, by definition. Therefore, the analysis of net loanable funds is equivalent to the analysis of saving and investment. But the loanable funds actually traded in the market are gross not net loanable funds. In fact, if an analysis of net loanable funds is carried out, it virtually eliminates the financial institution sector as an important part of the market, because their net position is very small but their gross position is very large. In addition, the analysis of net loanable funds pretends that individuals and companies do not have motives for simultaneously borrowing and lending—or, even if they do, that this is unimportant. But corporations as well as individuals do find it optimal to both borrow and lend at the same. We all hold financial assets for their return and in case we need quick access to funds. At the same time, we generally have financial liabilities outstanding. This provides for a redistribution of risk throughout the market. As we will see in later chapters, financial intermediaries specialize in this kind of activity.

FLOW OF FUNDS FOR THE UNITED STATES, 1977–1986

Flow of funds data are estimated on a quarterly basis for the United States economy by the staff of the Board of Governors of the Federal Reserve. A flow of funds table that shows the actual amount of funds raised in financial markets by various sectors of the economy during the years 1977–1986 is presented in Table 2–5. Panel A of Table 2–5 shows the total net funds raised in credit and equity markets. The first section of this panel shows the total net borrowing by domestic nonfinancial sectors. For example, this portion of the table shows that U.S. government borrowing represented over 25 percent of total net borrowings by domestic nonfinancial sectors in recent years. It also shows that the largest single category of financial instrument issued was home mortgages. In addition, households and the corporate sector alternate from year to year as the largest borrower in the market. The historical perspective given in the table shows that some categories of borrowing fluctuate considerably as the condition of the economy changes. For example, consumer credit reached a low point in 1980 of $4.5 billion. This was a year or two prior to the time when interest rates hit their historical peaks and the economy was entering a recession. Both of these forces tended to depress consumer borrowing. By comparison, in the mid-1980s consumer borrowing rebounded very strongly.

Panel B of Table 2–5 shows the flow of funds statement for the household sector for the same period of time covered in panel A. This table breaks total or gross savings of the household sector down between net saving and capital consumption allowance or depreciation. For example, in 1984, capital consumption allowances represented roughly half of gross savings of $641.7 billion. Gross investment listed in this table includes both investment in real capital, such as residential construction and consumer durables, as well as net financial investment. Financial investment represented approximately one-third of gross investment throughout the 1977–1986 period.

Panel B provides some interesting information about the types of financial investments households make. For example, one of the most dramatic developments is the growth of money market funds. During the first few years of this period, consumer acquisition of money market funds was negligible. However, in 1981 consumers acquired $107.5 billion in money market fund shares. By 1982 money market funds had attracted in total investment of approximately $200 billion. Money market funds grew rapidly as market interest rates rose in the late 1970s. Regulations that restricted interest rates paid on deposit accounts at commercial banks and savings and loans made those accounts very unattractive. In 1983, there was a net outflow of consumer funds from money market funds. This occurred partly because of changes in federal regulations that allowed banks and savings and loans to offer deposit accounts which were competitive with money market funds. It was also a result of a consumer shift from money market investments into the equity markets. This shift is evident in line 31, which shows mutual fund shares acquired by consumers. This item grew from a level of $4.5 billion in 1980 to nearly $200 billion in 1986. This occurred at the same time that consumers were withdrawing from direct participation in the equity market in the form of direct holdings of equities. This withdrawal occurred throughout the ten-year period shown in this table. This is evident in line 32, which shows other corporate equities. Entries in this line are negative for every year shown, reflecting a net outflow of household funds in this category.

The flow of funds tables are useful for analyzing the general pattern of investment, saving, and financing for individual sectors in the economy. They are also useful for tracing the flows among sectors. These flows determine and are determined by the interest rates observed in various markets, all of which are based on the rate examined in this chapter. An understanding of the flow of funds provides a foundation for an analysis of the yields that will be developed in the following chapters.

TABLE 2-5
Flow of funds accounts of the United States.

Panel A: Summary of net funds raised in credit and equity markets, March 2, 1987, (unadjusted net flows in millions of dollars).

$ Billions

Net Credit Market Borrowing by Nonfinancial Sectors

	1977	1978	1979	1980	1981	1982	1983	1984	1985	1986
Total net borrowing by domestic										
1. nonfinancial sectors	316.9	371.9	385.7	344.9	375.8	387.4	548.8	756.3	869.3	827.7
2. U.S. government	56.8	53.7	37.4	79.2	87.4	161.3	186.6	198.8	223.6	214.3
3. Treasury issues	57.6	55.1	38.8	79.8	87.8	162.1	186.7	199.0	223.7	214.7
4. Agency issues & mortgages	-0.9	-1.4	-1.4	-0.6	-0.5	-0.9	-0.1	-0.2	-0.1	-0.3
Private domestic										
5. nonfinancial sectors	260.2	318.2	348.4	265.7	288.5	226.2	362.2	557.5	645.7	613.3
6. Debt capital instruments	171.3	200.7	212.5	189.1	155.5	148.3	252.8	314.0	461.7	447.0
7. Tax-exempt obligations	20.3	28.4	30.3	30.3	23.8	44.2	53.7	50.4	152.4	48.5
8. Corporate bonds	22.9	21.1	17.3	27.7	22.8	18.7	16.0	46.1	73.9	109.2
9. Mortgages	128.1	151.2	164.9	131.2	109.3	85.4	183.0	217.5	235.4	289.4
10. Home mortgages	93.3	110.2	116.6	94.2	72.2	50.5	117.1	129.9	150.3	200.6
11. Multifamily resid.	8.4	10.9	10.0	7.6	4.8	5.4	14.1	25.1	29.2	30.4
12. Commercial	18.2	21.9	24.4	19.2	22.2	25.2	49.0	63.3	62.4	64.4
13. Farm	8.2	8.2	14.0	10.2	10.0	4.2	2.8	-0.8	-6.4	-6.0
14. Other debt instruments	88.9	117.6	135.9	76.6	133.0	77.9	109.5	243.5	184.0	166.3
15. Consumer credit	38.1	46.7	42.7	4.5	22.6	17.7	56.8	95.0	96.6	67.9
16. Bank loans n.e.c.	26.5	40.5	50.5	37.8	57.0	52.9	25.8	80.1	41.3	80.2
17. Commercial paper	1.6	2.7	9.0	4.0	14.7	-6.1	-0.8	21.7	14.6	-9.3
18. Other	22.6	27.6	33.7	30.3	38.7	13.4	27.7	46.6	31.4	27.4
19. By borrowing sector:	260.2	318.2	348.4	265.7	288.5	226.2	362.2	557.5	645.7	613.3
20. State & local governments	10.5	16.5	17.6	17.2	6.8	21.5	34.0	27.4	107.8	60.0
21. Households	137.5	167.2	173.7	120.0	121.4	88.4	188.0	239.5	295.0	291.2
22. Nonfinancial business	112.2	134.5	157.1	128.5	160.3	116.2	140.2	290.6	242.9	262.2
23. Farm	13.4	15.6	23.5	15.2	16.6	6.8	4.3	0.1	-13.6	-11.7
24. Nonfarm noncorporate	29.5	33.8	37.9	31.8	38.5	40.2	76.6	97.1	92.8	100.7
25. Corporate	69.3	85.2	95.7	81.5	105.2	69.2	59.3	193.4	163.7	173.2
26. Fgn. net borrowing in U.S.	13.5	24.2	15.1	23.8	23.5	16.0	17.4	6.1	1.7	14.4
27. Bonds	5.1	4.2	3.9	0.8	5.4	6.7	3.1	1.3	4.0	5.2
28. Bank loans n.e.c.	3.1	18.3	3.1	11.8	3.0	-5.5	3.6	-6.6	-2.8	-2.1
29. Commercial paper	0.6	1.7	1.7	2.4	3.9	-1.9	6.5	6.2	6.2	11.5
30. U.S. govt. & other loans	4.8	0.7	6.5	8.8	11.1	13.0	4.1	5.3	-5.7	-0.2
31. Total domestic plus foreign	330.4	396.1	400.8	368.7	399.3	403.4	566.2	762.4	871.0	842.0

Net Credit Market Borrowing by Financial Sectors

	1977	1978	1979	1980	1981	1982	1983	1984	1985	1986
Total net borrowing										
1. by financial sectors	50.8	73.3	89.9	65.4	101.9	90.1	94.0	139.0	186.9	242.0
2. U.S. government-related	22.0	37.1	47.9	44.8	47.4	64.9	67.8	74.9	101.5	171.1
3. Sponsored credit ag. sec.	7.0	23.1	24.3	24.4	30.5	14.9	1.4	30.4	20.6	12.4
4. Mortgage pool securities	16.1	13.6	23.1	19.2	15.0	49.5	66.4	44.4	79.9	159.0
5. Loans from U.S. government	-1.1	0.4	0.6	1.2	1.9	0.4	—	—	1.1	-0.4
6. Private financial sectors	28.8	36.2	42.0	20.6	54.5	25.2	26.2	64.1	85.3	71.0
7. Corporate bonds	12.0	7.8	5.5	1.6	4.4	12.5	12.1	23.3	36.5	22.3
8. Mortgages	*	0.2	*	*	*	0.1	*	0.4	0.1	0.1
9. Bank loans n.e.c.	-0.2	1.8	0.5	-1.0	1.2	1.9	-0.1	0.7	2.6	3.6
10. Open-market paper	12.8	13.9	26.8	12.9	32.7	9.9	21.3	24.1	32.0	25.2
11. Fed. Home Loan Bank loans	4.3	12.5	9.2	7.1	16.2	0.8	-7.0	15.7	14.2	19.8
12. Total, by sector	50.8	73.3	89.9	65.4	101.9	90.1	94.0	139.0	186.9	242.0
13. Sponsored credit agencies	5.9	23.5	24.8	25.6	32.4	15.3	1.4	30.4	21.7	12.1
14. Mortgage pools	16.1	13.6	23.1	19.2	15.0	49.5	66.4	44.4	79.9	159.0
15. Private financial sectors	28.8	36.2	42.0	20.6	54.5	25.2	26.2	64.1	85.3	71.0
16. Commercial banks	3.7	-0.5	9.1	8.3	11.6	11.7	5.0	7.3	-4.9	-2.2
17. Domestic affiliates	3.8	7.5	4.1	6.7	6.8	6.8	12.1	15.6	14.5	4.5
18. Savings and loan assns.	6.9	13.5	12.6	7.4	15.5	2.5	-2.1	22.7	22.3	31.3
19. Finance companies	17.0	16.1	16.3	-1.3	18.5	4.3	11.4	17.8	52.8	36.9
20. REITs	-2.5	-0.4	-0.1	-0.5	-0.2	*	-0.2	0.8	0.5	0.5

Total Net Credit Market Borrowing, All Sectors, by Type

1. Total net borrowing	381.3	469.4	490.7	434.1	501.3	493.5	660.2	901.4	1057.8	1084.1
2. U.S. government securities	79.9	90.5	84.8	122.9	133.0	225.9	254.4	273.8	324.2	385.8
3. Tax-exempt obligations	20.3	28.4	30.3	30.3	23.4	44.2	53.7	50.4	152.4	48.5
4. Corporate & foreign bonds	39.9	33.1	26.6	30.1	32.6	37.8	31.2	70.7	114.4	136.6
5. Mortgages	128.0	151.2	164.8	131.1	109.2	85.4	183.0	217.8	235.4	289.4
6. Consumer credit	38.1	46.7	42.7	4.5	22.6	17.7	56.8	95.0	96.6	67.9
7. Bank loans n.e.c.	29.3	60.6	54.1	48.5	61.2	49.3	29.3	74.2	41.0	81.7
8. Open-market paper	15.0	17.7	37.5	19.3	51.3	5.7	26.9	52.0	52.8	27.4
9. Other loans	30.7	41.2	50.0	47.5	68.0	27.6	24.8	67.6	41.0	46.7
10. Memo: U.S. govt. cash balance	1.1	3.8	0.6	-3.8	*	7.3	-7.1	6.3	14.4	0.3
Totals net of changes in U.S.										
11. Net borrowing by dom. nonfin	315.8	368.1	385.1	348.7	375.8	380.2	555.9	750.0	854.9	827.4
12. By U.S. government	55.7	49.9	36.8	83.0	87.4	154.0	193.7	192.5	209.3	214.0

External Corporate Equity Funds Raised in U.S. Markets

1. Total net share issues	6.6	1.7	-3.9	21.2	-3.3	33.6	67.0	-31.1	37.5	115.3
2. Mutual funds	1.0	-0.1	0.4	4.5	6.0	16.8	32.1	-38.0	103.4	187.6
3. All other	5.6	1.8	-4.3	16.8	-9.3	16.8	34.9	-69.1	-65.9	-72.3
4. Nonfinancial corporations	2.7	-0.1	-7.8	12.9	-11.5	11.4	28.3	-77.0	-81.6	-80.8
5. Financial corporations	2.5	2.4	2.7	1.8	1.9	4.0	2.7	6.7	11.7	6.7
6. Foreign shares purchased in U.S.	0.4	-0.5	0.8	2.1	0.3	1.5	3.9	1.2	4.0	1.8

Billions of dollars. IV/86 based on incomplete information.

TABLE 2–5 (continued)

Panel B: Sector statements of saving and investment in households, March 2, 1987, (unadjusted net flows in millions of dollars).

		1977	1978	1979	1980	1981	1982	1983	1984	1985	1986	
							$ Billions					
						Households, Personal Trusts, and Nonprofit Organizations						
1.	Personal income	1607.5	1812.4	2034.0	2258.5	2520.9	2670.8	2838.6	3110.2	3314.5	3486.1	1
2.	− Personal taxes and nontaxes	228.1	261.1	304.7	340.5	393.3	409.3	410.5	439.6	486.5	514.1	2
3.	= Disposable personal income	1379.3	1551.2	1729.3	1918.0	2127.6	2261.4	2428.1	2670.6	2828.0	2972.0	3
4.	− Personal outlays	1288.6	1441.1	1611.3	1781.1	1968.1	2107.5	2297.5	2501.9	2684.7	2858.0	4
5.	= Personal saving, NIPA basis	90.7	110.2	118.1	136.9	159.4	154.0	130.6	168.7	143.3	114.0	5
6.	+ Credits from govt. insurance	22.5	27.9	24.4	35.3	39.7	43.9	53.5	63.9	66.5	68.6	6
7.	+ Capital gains dividends	0.6	0.7	0.9	1.8	2.4	2.4	4.4	6.0	4.9	11.6	7
8.	+ Net durables in consumption	53.3	58.8	54.0	31.9	37.4	37.2	62.7	92.7	102.9	113.6	8
9.	= Net saving	167.2	197.6	197.4	235.9	239.2	237.4	251.2	331.3	317.6	307.9	9
10.	+ Capital consumption	168.6	189.9	214.7	243.1	263.7	280.3	294.7	310.4	332.8	355.0	10
11.	= Gross saving	335.8	387.4	412.0	448.9	503.0	517.7	545.9	641.7	650.3	662.9	11
12.	Gross investment	351.3	401.2	434.2	491.5	565.0	610.7	606.1	732.0	712.8	722.9	12
13.	Capital expend. net of sales	284.2	327.7	356.1	342.7	362.0	355.0	427.8	500.2	535.3	581.4	13
14.	Residential construction	92.2	114.0	128.7	113.6	111.2	89.9	124.9	154.5	162.0	178.8	14
15.	Consumer durable goods	184.5	205.6	219.0	219.3	239.9	252.7	289.1	331.2	359.3	388.4	15
16.	Nonprofit plant and equip.	7.6	8.2	8.4	9.9	11.0	12.4	13.9	14.6	14.1	14.2	16
17.	Net financial investment	67.1	73.4	78.2	148.8	202.9	255.7	178.2	231.8	177.4	141.4	17
18.	Net acq. of financial assets	208.0	244.4	255.9	278.9	327.1	351.1	377.0	469.0	490.1	439.0	18
19.	Deposit & credit mkt. instruments (1)	159.0	183.4	208.2	205.4	265.3	257.0	284.3	433.2	367.8	258.2	19
20.	Deposits	125.1	128.4	134.1	168.2	203.6	170.6	193.9	290.7	182.8	235.4	20
21.	Checkable dep. & curr.	19.5	22.3	25.7	12.7	29.9	19.2	39.3	18.9	45.0	103.1	21
22.	Small time & svgs. dep.	95.1	67.3	61.2	82.7	47.3	134.2	210.0	153.2	142.9	117.6	22
23.	Large time deposits	10.2	31.9	12.8	43.6	19.0	−7.5	−11.3	71.4	−2.9	−6.2	23
24.	Money mkt. fund shares	0.2	6.9	34.4	29.2	107.5	24.7	−44.1	47.2	−2.2	20.8	24
25.	Credit mkt. instruments	33.9	55.0	74.1	37.2	61.7	86.4	90.4	142.4	185.0	22.8	25
26.	U.S. govt. securities	15.6	29.4	44.4	26.7	45.2	55.6	60.5	111.2	60.7	−1.2	26
27.	Tax-exempt obligations	−3.0*	4.1	10.4	7.0	11.0	24.7	37.8	28.7	59.4	4.4	27
28.	Corporate & fgn. bonds		−4.2	−4.5	−11.7	−4.0	2.0	−12.7	−3.4	13.2	11.5	28
29.	Mortgages	7.8	11.9	16.5	−17.5	18.0	13.3	0.4	6.4	4.0	5.7	29
30.	Open-market paper	13.5	13.8	7.3	−2.2	−8.6	−9.2	4.4	−0.5	47.8	2.4	30
31.	Mutual fund shares	1.0	−0.1	0.4	4.5	6.0	16.8	32.1	38.0	103.4	187.6	31
32.	Other corporate equities	−8.2	−6.2	−23.3	−10.8	−34.9	−14.7	−17.3	−74.3	−104.2	−118.3	32
33.	Life insurance reserves	9.5	11.2	10.7	9.7	9.2	7.2	8.0	5.2	10.7	10.2	33
34.	Pension fund reserves	68.5	77.3	95.4	108.8	106.8	120.1	142.2	129.1	139.7	137.8	34
35.	Net inv. in noncorp. bus.	−27.8	−30.2	−44.5	−49.6	−29.2	−45.7	−90.0	−68.5	−52.8	−57.0	35
36.	Security credit	−1.0	2.5	1.8	5.2	−2.1	3.7	2.4	−0.6	12.5	5.2	36
37.	Miscellaneous assets	6.9	6.6	7.2	5.6	6.1	6.8	15.3	7.0	13.1	15.2	37
38.	Net increase in liabilities	140.9	170.9	177.7	130.0	124.2	95.3	198.7	237.2	312.7	297.6	38
39.	Credit market instruments	137.5	167.2	173.7	120.0	121.4	88.4	188.0	239.5	295.0	291.2	39
40.	Home mortgages	89.7	108.6	117.6	96.4	75.0	49.5	110.4	129.3	149.4	196.8	40
41.	Installment cons. credit	35.0	41.0	35.6	1.1	16.9	14.9	48.9	77.0	82.4	60.0	41
42.	Other consumer credit	3.2	5.7	7.1	3.4	5.7	2.8	7.9	18.0	14.2	7.9	42
43.	Tax-exempt debt	3.4	2.6	2.9	3.1	4.4	8.5	11.4	10.2	30.2	−0.3	43
44.	Other mortgages	1.1	1.3	1.5	1.9	2.3	2.6	2.5	2.5	2.4	2.4	44
45.	Bank loans n.e.c.	2.8	4.1	2.6	5.3	6.0	2.6	3.6	−0.4	8.1	17.4	45
46.	Other loans	2.3	3.8	6.4	8.8	11.1	7.4	3.3	2.9	8.3	6.9	46
47.	Security credit	1.3	1.2	1.0	6.5	−1.7	3.8	8.4	−3.1	16.7	2.8	47
48.	Trade debt	1.2	1.5	1.7	2.3	2.7	2.4	1.8	1.8	2.2	2.5	48
49.	Miscellaneous	0.9	1.1	1.3	1.2	1.8	0.8	0.6	−1.0	−1.2	1.1	49
50.	Discrepancy	−15.6	−13.7	−22.2	−42.6	−62.0	−93.0	−60.2	−90.3	−62.5	−60.0	50

(1) Excludes corporate equities.

Memoranda:

Net physical investment:

	(A) Residential construction										
51.	Expenditures	92.2	114.0	128.7	113.6	111.2	89.9	124.9	154.5	162.0	178.8
52.	Mobile homes	3.9	4.4	4.9	4.3	4.7	4.6	6.1	6.2	6.1	5.3
53.	Other	88.2	109.5	123.8	109.2	106.5	85.3	118.8	148.2	155.9	173.6
54.	− Capital consumption	31.1	36.1	41.9	47.0	51.4	54.3	57.0	59.9	63.9	67.0
55.	− Home mortgages	89.7	108.6	117.6	96.4	75.0	49.5	110.4	129.3	149.4	196.8
56.	= Excess net investment	−28.7	−30.8	−30.9	−29.8	−15.3	−13.8	−42.6	−34.7	−51.3	−85.0
	(B) Consumer durables										
57.	Expenditures	184.5	205.6	219.0	219.3	239.9	252.7	289.1	331.2	359.3	388.4
58.	− Capital consumption	131.2	146.8	165.0	187.4	202.5	215.4	226.4	238.5	256.3	274.8
59.	= Net investment	53.3	58.8	54.0	31.9	37.4	37.2	62.7	92.7	102.9	113.6
60.	− Consumer credit	38.1	46.7	42.7	27.4	22.6	17.7	56.8	95.0	96.6	67.9
61.	= Excess net investment	15.2	12.0	11.3		14.8	19.5	5.9	−2.4	6.3	45.7
	(C) Nonprofit plant and equip.										
62.	Expenditures	7.6	8.2	8.4	9.9	11.0	12.4	13.9	14.6	14.1	14.2
63.	− Capital consumption	6.3	6.9	7.8	8.7	9.8	10.6	11.2	12.0	12.6	13.3
64.	= Net investment	1.3	1.2	0.7	1.1	1.2	1.8	2.6	2.6	1.6	0.9
	Percent ratios:										
65.	Effective tax rate	14.2	14.4	15.0	15.1	15.6	15.3	14.5	14.1	14.7	14.7
66.	Saving rate, NIPA basis	6.6	7.1	6.8	7.1	7.5	6.8	5.4	6.3	5.1	3.8
	Percent of disposable income adj.										
67.	Gross saving	23.9	24.5	23.5	23.0	23.2	22.4	22.0	23.4	22.4	21.7
68.	Capital expenditures	20.3	20.7	20.3	17.5	16.7	15.4	17.2	18.3	18.5	19.0
69.	Acquisition of finan. assets	14.8	15.5	14.6	14.3	15.1	15.2	15.2	17.1	16.9	14.4
70.	Net increase in liabilities	10.0	10.8	10.1	6.7	5.7	4.1	8.0	8.7	10.8	9.7
71.	Credit market borrowing	9.8	10.6	9.9	6.1	5.6	3.8	7.6	8.7	10.2	9.5
72.	(2) Disposable income adj. (NIPA) disposable income + govt.	1402.5	1579.8	1754.7	1955.0	2170.0	2307.7	2486.0	2740.5	2899.4	3052.2

Billions of dollars. IV/86 based on incomplete information.

Source: Federal Reserve Flow of Funds Accounts.

U.S. TREASURY YIELDS AND THE FLOW OF FUNDS

We have argued in this chapter that one of the most important uses of the flow of funds is to identify the patterns in borrowing and lending between sectors of the economy. We know from the Fisherian theory of the real interest rate that the equilibrium real rate will reflect the desired level of borrowing and lending in the financial markets. This is true in the aggregate economy, and it is true for specific types of financial instruments. As we begin to look at specific types of financial markets throughout this book, we need to remember that the real interest rate underlies the interest rates in all of these markets.

A good place to start our inspection of specific markets, and a good place to see how the flow of funds accounts can and cannot be used to understand changes in interest rates, is with the market for financing of the U.S. Treasury. The Treasury holds weekly auctions to sell new Treasury bills. Treasury bills are short-term obligations in that they have an original maturity of one year or less. Obligations of the Treasury with longer maturities are called notes and bonds. Unlike notes and bonds, Treasury bills are structured as pure discount instruments, which means there are no coupon payments. A bill is an obligation of the Treasury to pay a specific amount of cash on a specified date. We will have more to say about Treasury bills in later chapters, particularly Chapter 7.

The level of the interest rate on 90-day or three-month Treasury bills, as quoted in the secondary market, from 1929 until 1986 is shown in Figure 2–9. This figure also shows two other interest rates. One rate is the interest rate charged by the Federal Reserve Bank of New York on loans to commercial banks, referred to as the **discount rate**. The other is the **federal funds rate**, which refers to the prevailing interest rate on short-term loans between commercial banks and other financial institutions. You should notice that the interest rates on these three financial instruments move very closely together. This implies that the market views these securities as close substitutes.

You might attempt to relate the changes in interest rates plotted in this figure to the patterns of borrowing and lending in the Treasury security market or to the total amount of securities issued by the Treasury. Table 2–6 presents a ten-year history of Treasury financing drawn from the flow of funds data prepared by the Federal Reserve. The table indicates that total Treasury issues increased from $57.6 billion in 1977 to $214.7 billion in 1986, or increased nearly fourfold. The data in this table tell some interesting stories about who was buying these Treasury securities. For example, in 1986 households liquidated $68.3 billion of Treasury securities, excluding savings bonds. On the other hand, they purchased $53.5 Agency issues. These are obligations of agencies of the U.S. government, particularly agencies involved in mortgage finance (see Chapter 19). The largest categories of purchasers in 1986 were banks, foreigners, and mutual funds.

How can we use these flow of funds data to explain the gyrations of interest rates on Treasury bills shown in Figure 2–9? The answer is that we really cannot do this. The reason is that what we have learned in this chapter pertains to the real interest rate. As the Treasury attempts to borrow more, if this represents an aggregate increase in desired borrowing in the financial markets as a whole, then the real rate will have to rise to bring about a new equilibrium. This may in fact explain part of the general increase in interest rates we see in Figure 2–9. However, the interest rates in this figure are not real rates. They are nominal rates affected by the rate of inflation in the economy. We will learn in Chapter 7 that as the expected rate of inflation increases in the economy, then the nominal interest rate will be bid up. Therefore, we cannot be sure whether a change we see in actual nominal interest rates is due to shifts in desired borrowing, as say by the U.S. Treasury, or due to increases in expected inflation. Some financial analysts rely heavily on identifying the patterns of borrowing and lending, as de-

FIGURE 2-9
Short-term U.S. interest rates.

Discount rate, effective date of change; all others, quarterly averages

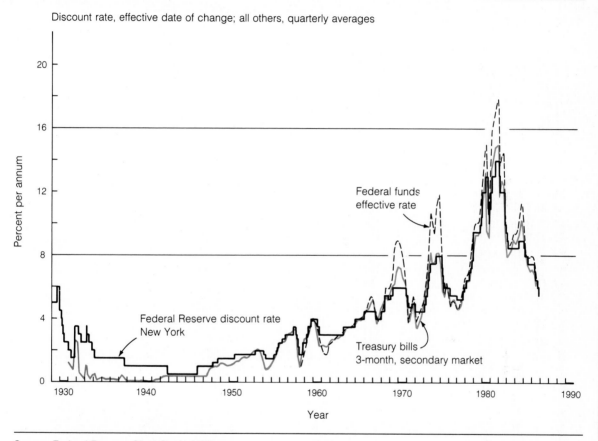

Source: Federal Reserve Chart Book, 1986.

picted in the flow of funds accounts, to explain and predict what will happen to interest rates. Others view this as of limited value due to the impact of inflation on interest rates. It is, of course, quite possible that real rates may be increasing with increases in desired bor- rowing while simultaneously nominal rates are falling due to declines in inflation rates. This might not be a bad explanation of the behavior of the nominal rates shown in Table 2–6 since 1982. We will have a lot more to say about this Chapter 7.

TABLE 2-6
Flow of funds for U.S. Treasury unadjusted net flows (in millions of dollars)

		1977	1978	1979	1980	1981	1982	1983	1984	1985	1986
							$ Billions				
	Total Net Issues by Sector and Type										
1.	Total U.S. government secur.	79.9	90.5	84.8	122.9	133.0	225.9	254.4	273.8	324.2	385.8
2.	U.S. government	56.9	53.8	37.5	79.3	87.5	161.4	186.6	198.9	223.7	214.4
3.	Spons. agencies & mtg. pools	23.1	36.7	47.3	43.6	45.5	64.5	67.8	74.9	100.5	171.4
	By instrument:										
4.	Treasury issues	57.6	55.1	38.8	79.8	87.8	162.1	186.7	199.0	223.7	214.7
5.	Household savings bonds	4.7	3.9	-0.8	-7.3	-4.3	0.2	3.1	3.0	5.3	13.6
6.	Treas. excl. savings bonds	52.9	51.2	39.6	87.1	92.2	162.0	183.5	195.9	218.5	201.1
7.	Other	22.3	35.3	46.0	43.1	45.2	63.7	67.8	74.8	100.4	171.1
8.	Budget agency issues	-0.5	-1.1	-1.1	-0.3	-0.3	-0.2	*	-0.1	*	-0.3
9.	Loan participations (1)	-0.2	-0.3	-0.2	-0.2	-0.1	-0.5				
10.	Spons. agency issues (2)	7.0	23.1	24.3	24.4	30.5	14.9	1.4	30.4	20.6	12.4
11.	Mortgage pool secur. (2)	16.1	13.6	23.1	19.2	15.0	49.5	66.4	44.4	79.9	159.0
	Total Net Purchases by Sector and Type										
1.	Total purchases, by sector	79.9	90.5	84.8	122.9	133.0	225.9	254.4	273.8	324.2	385.8
2.	U.S. govt. (agency secur.)	—	0.6	—	0.7	0.4	1.4	-1.3	0.6	1.3	0.9
3.	Sponsored credit agencies	-3.8	0.5	0.2	0.4	0.2	1.5	-0.8	0.4	1.2	1.5
4.	Treasury	-3.4	0.1	-0.2	0.2	0.2	-0.1	-0.4	0.2	0.1	-0.6
5.	Agency securities	-0.4	0.4	0.4	0.2	*					
6.	Monetary authority	7.2	7.3	7.6	4.4	9.8	8.5	12.0	8.8	21.6	30.2
7.	Treasury issues	5.8	7.7	6.9	3.9	9.6	8.4	12.6	8.9	20.5	30.0
8.	Agency issues	1.4	-0.4	0.7	0.6	0.1	0.1	-0.7	-0.1	1.1	0.2
9.	Foreign	31.5	23.5	-14.0	10.7	7.0	12.8	16.9	26.5	24.3	54.4
10.	Total private domestic	45.1	59.1	91.0	107.1	115.9	203.1	226.9	237.8	277.0	300.3
11.	Treasury issues	23.8	23.4	46.1	64.8	71.0	139.5	158.0	163.2	177.7	128.8
12.	Agency issues	21.3	35.7	44.9	42.3	44.9	63.6	68.9	74.7	99.2	171.5
13.	Private domestic nonfinan.	23.7	41.7	56.6	34.2	37.1	69.9	95.5	132.9	150.9	65.7
14.	Total Treasury issues	17.4	28.1	32.2	25.5	31.0	66.0	91.5	86.6	77.2	1.9
15.	Savings bonds (HH)	4.7	3.9	-0.8	-7.3	-4.3	0.2	3.1	3.0	5.3	13.6
16.	Other Treasury issues	12.7	24.2	33.1	32.8	35.4	65.8	88.3	83.5	71.9	-11.7
17.	Agency issues	6.3	13.6	24.4	8.7	6.1	4.0	4.0	46.3	73.7	63.8
18.	Households	15.6	29.4	44.4	26.7	45.2	55.6	60.5	111.2	60.7	-1.2
19.	Total Treasury issues	12.9	21.8	21.9	19.7	33.8	53.5	66.7	74.8	-5.1	-54.7
20.	Savings bonds	4.7	3.9	-0.8	-7.3	-4.3	0.2	3.1	3.0	5.3	13.6
21.	Other Treas. issues	8.2	17.8	22.7	27.0	38.1	53.3	63.6	71.8	-10.3	-68.3
22.	Agency issues	2.7	7.6	22.4	7.0	11.4	2.2	-6.2	36.4	65.8	53.5
23.	Nonfin. corp. business	-6.4	1.5	1.6	5.6	-1.0	5.3	8.0	7.2	-3.1	9.5
24.	Treasury issues	-6.0	0.8	2.8	5.1	-1.0	5.2	8.0	7.3	-3.0	9.6
25.	Agency issues	-0.4	0.7	-1.3	0.5	*	0.1	*	-0.1	-0.1	-0.1
26.	State and local govts.	14.6	10.9	10.7	1.9	-7.1	9.0	26.9	14.6	93.3	57.5
27.	Treasury issues	10.6	5.5	7.5	0.7	-1.8	7.3	16.7	4.5	85.3	47.0
28.	Agency issues	4.0	5.3	3.2	1.2	-5.4	1.7	10.2	10.1	8.1	10.5

#											
29.	Commercial banking	0.1	-0.8	9.6	25.8	11.6	26.6	48.6	0.6	9.7	46.5
30.	Treasury issues	-0.6	-7.8	2.0	16.1	1.8	19.4	47.8	1.9	12.1	7.0
31.	Agency issues	0.8	7.0	7.6	9.7	9.8	7.3	0.7	-1.3	-2.4	39.5
32.	U.S. commercial banks	-1.3	0.1	7.4	25.0	11.4	26.7	44.2	1.3	4.6	44.1
33.	Domestic affiliates	1.3	-1.3	1.7	0.2	-0.1	-1.2	1.6	-0.5	4.7	-1.2
34.	Foreign banking offices	-0.1	0.5	0.5	0.5	-0.6	0.8	1.7	-0.6	0.4	3.4
35.	Banks in U.S. possessions	0.2	-0.1	*	0.1	-0.3	0.3	1.1	-0.6	*	0.1
36.	Private nonbank finance	21.2	18.2	24.8	47.2	67.2	106.6	82.9	104.3	116.4	188.1
37.	Total pvt. nonbank finance	21.2	18.2	24.8	47.2	67.2	106.6	82.9	104.3	116.4	188.1
38.	Treasury issues	7.0	3.2	11.9	23.2	38.2	54.1	18.7	74.7	88.5	119.9
39.	Agency issues	14.2	15.0	13.0	23.9	29.0	52.4	64.1	29.6	27.9	68.2
40.	Savings and loan assns.	3.9	4.6	1.0	13.8	3.1	37.4	45.5	27.1	-8.9	50.9
41.	Treasury issues	-1.0	*	-2.9	5.7	-3.5	7.5	15.7	10.2	-10.1	10.5
42.	Agency issues	4.9	4.6	3.9	8.1	6.6	29.8	29.8	16.9	1.2	40.5
43.	Mutual savings banks	2.6	0.8	1.2	3.3	0.9	1.9	9.8	0.3	-1.2	6.8
44.	Treasury issues	0.1	-0.9	-0.2	0.8	-0.2	0.7	3.8	-0.2	-0.6	0.7
45.	Agency issues	2.6	1.7	1.3	2.5	1.2	1.2	6.0	0.5	-0.6	6.1
46.	Credit unions	0.5	-0.8	-1.1	1.0	0.3	1.2	3.1	0.4	3.6	3.4
47.	Treasury issues	0.4	-0.7	-0.1	0.3	0.1	0.3	1.4	0.8	2.5	1.7
48.	Agency issues	0.4	-0.1	-1.0	0.7	0.3	0.9	1.7	-0.4	1.1	1.7
49.	Life insurance companies	1.6	2.0	2.9	2.7	5.5	12.7	19.3	23.6	23.0	14.8
50.	Treasury issues	-0.1	-.5	0.1	1.0	2.3	8.4	12.1	12.6	10.5	8.1
51.	Agency issues	1.7	2.5	2.8	1.8	3.1	4.3	7.2	11.0	12.5	6.6
52.	Private pension funds	5.0	3.7	6.9	13.1	19.4	6.4	12.9	7.3	6.8	6.5
53.	Treasury issues	3.6	2.2	3.5	6.1	7.4	1.9	0.6	13.0	0.3	5.3
54.	Agency issues	1.4	1.4	3.4	7.0	11.9	4.5	12.3	-5.7	6.5	1.2
55.	St. & local govt. rtr. funds	5.5	7.1	6.6	9.9	11.8	19.4	17.0	23.1	17.5	19.6
56.	Treasury issues	2.7	2.7	5.3	6.2	6.6	9.3	12.0	19.0	18.6	11.8
57.	Agency issues	2.7	4.4	1.4	3.7	5.2	10.1	4.9	4.1	-1.1	7.8
58.	Other insurance cos.	3.0	1.2	1.3	1.8	2.2	2.2	5.5	9.1	18.8	13.7
59.	Treasury issues	2.5	0.7	0.2	1.6	1.4	0.6	3.3	5.9	10.6	9.4
60.	Agency issues	0.5	0.5	1.1	0.2	0.8	1.5	2.2	3.2	8.2	4.3
61.	Mutual funds (Treasury)	0.2	-0.2	*	0.3	0.9	2.3	0.6	6.4	52.9	70.1
62.	Money mkt. funds (Treas.)	-0.3	0.6	4.2	2.6	23.7	22.7	-18.4	6.2	0.3	0.5
63.	Securities brokers and dealers (Treasury)	-0.7	-0.8	1.9	-1.4	-0.6	0.4	-12.4	1.0	3.6	1.8

(1) For purchases, agency issues include loan participations.

(2) These issues are outside both the budget and the U.S. government sector in the flow of funds accounts. They are included in credit market debt of financial institutions. IV/86 based on incomplete information.

Source: Federal Reserve Flow of Funds Accounts.

SUMMARY

In this chapter we analyzed the most important underlying determinant of the multitude of interest rates we observe in the world. This factor, which all market interest rates have in common, is called the real rate of interest. The real interest rate refers to the rate of interest on a single-period risk-free loan when there is no inflation, deflation, or taxes.

The basic theory of the real rate of interest is referred to as Fisherian interest rate theory, after Irving Fisher, the economist who developed the analysis of the real interest rate. It shows that in equilibrium the real interest rate must be equal to three distinct concepts. The concepts are the marginal rate of return on real investment projects, or the rate of return on real capital; the marginal rate at which individuals choose to exchange present for future consumption, or the marginal rate of time preference; and the interest rate on borrowing and lending.

We divided the development of Fisherian theory into two parts. First, we examined what the equilibrium would be if there were no opportunities for borrowing and lending so that each person could choose only how much to invest in real productive investments. Each person would set the marginal rate of return on investment equal to his or her marginal rate of time preference. But there was nothing that would make these the same across individuals. Then we introduced the prospect that individuals could borrow and lend as well as undertake real investments. With this additional opportunity, market participants could generally move to a position that made them better off. Those who preferred current to future consumption could borrow and vice versa. With borrowing and lending opportunities a new equilibrium real interest rate would emerge. *The new requirement for equilibrium in the market was that the rate of interest on borrowing and lending equal the marginal rate of return on investment and the marginal rate of time preference for all individuals.* Moreover, an example showed that if the market started with an interest rate that was too high or low for equilibrium, market forces would drive the rate toward equilibrium. This concept of equilibrium underlies all the different interest rates in the marketplace.

The new requirement for equilibrium in the market was that the rate of interest on borrowing and lending equal the marginal rate of return on investment and the marginal rate of time preference for all individuals.

Next we examined the real rate from an alternative perspective. We briefly examined the aggregate supply and demand for funds in the market in the context of the traditional supply-demand diagram. We used the Fisherian theory to develop supply-and-demand curves that determined the real interest rate. Moveover, we found that in the real world there are two basic types of markets that simultaneously determine the real interest rate. These are referred to as *primary* and *secondary markets*. The secondary market represents the market for the outstanding stock of borrowing and lending at a point in time. The primary market is the market for new borrowing and lending that flows into the market during any period of time. Because new assets must trade at the same rate of return as old assets, the real interest rate must be in equilibrium in both markets. Therefore, though in practice we often concentrate on the flow of funds in the economy or the primary market, we must remember that this is a part of a larger, secondary market.

Finally, we examined the flow of funds in the U.S. economy. We constructed hypothetical financial statements for sectors of the economy and from these developed a statement of the sources and uses of funds in the economy as a whole. Within this framework, we explored the differences between borrowing, lending, saving, and investment in the aggregate economy, and we examined the basic equilibrium condition that for the economy as a whole, saving must equal investing. We used this hypothetical construction to examine the actual flow of funds in the U.S. economy.

QUESTIONS

1. What is the real rate of interest?
2. In equilibrium the real interest rate is equal to three distinct concepts. Explain what these are.
3. What is the time-preference curve? What does it show?
4. Calculate the rates of return an individual would earn at points A, B, and C on the following investment-opportunity curve. What do these rates of return indicate about increasing investments of current income?

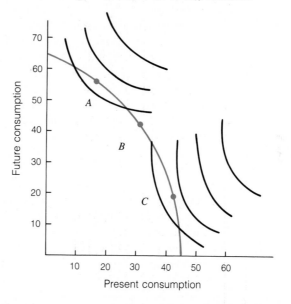

5. Now calculate the equilibrium interest rate using the time-perference curves for two hypothetical individuals shown in the figure in question 4.
6. Suppose you had two individuals with distinct investment-opportunity curves and with no opportunities to borrow and lend. Could there be a distinct equilibrium real interest rate for each of them? Would this be an equilibrium for each individual or a market equilibrium? Why?
7. Using the example presented in Figure 2–5 and Table 2–1, explain what would happen to desired borrowing and lending if the interest rate were 5 percent. Why is 5 percent a disequilibrium in this example?

8. What is a primary as opposed to a secondary market? Why does the primary market refer to the flow of funds while the secondary market refers to the stock of funds? What does this mean? What is wrong with concentrating on only one of these two markets in order to analyze the determinants of the real interest rate?

9. Explain the differences between lending, investing, and saving for an individual and for an economy.

10. What is the difference between net and gross flows of funds? Why does the financial institution sector of the economy have very large gross flows of funds but very small net flows of funds?

11. Describe the pattern of household borrowing and lending from the information given in Table 2–5. What significant pieces of information about the household sector of the economy can you discern from this information?

12. Which of the following statements are false?
    (a) For the economy as a whole: Saving = Investment.
    (b) For each economic sector: Borrowing = Lending.
    (c) For each economic sector: Borrowing + Lending = Saving + Investment.
    Explain your reasoning in answering these questions.

13. You are given the following hypothetical financial statements for the aggregate business sector of the U.S. economy. Construct a sources and uses statement from these financial statements and answer the following questions.

Balance sheet of business sector as of:

	12/31/85	12/31/86
Financial Assets	$ 460	$ 500
Real Assets	1200	1270
Liabilities	1350	1420
Net Worth	310	350

(a) How much did total investment exceed total saving for the business sector?
(b) How large was total borrowing?
(c) How much was real investment as a percent of total sources of funds for the business sector?
(d) What is the saving rate for the business sector for the year 1986?

REFERENCES

Conard, Joseph W. *Introduction to the Theory of Interest,* Berkeley: University of California Press, 1959.

Fisher, Irving. *The Theory of Interest,* New York: Macmillan, 1930.

Hirshleifer, Jack. *Investment, Interest and Capital,* Englewood Cliffs, N.J.: Prentice-Hall, Inc., 1970.

Van Horne, James C. *Financial Market Rates and Flows,* Englewood Cliffs, N.J.: Prentice-Hall, Inc., 1978.

3

PRICING RISK: A REVIEW OF BASIC CONCEPTS

Risky assets are assets with uncertain future returns. Risk is measured by variance or standard deviation of returns.

In the last chapter we laid the foundations for understanding how risky assets are priced in organized financial markets. That foundation entails developing a clear understanding of the real in-terest rate. The prices and therefore the expected rates of return on all risky assets are determined in part by the real rate of interest. We have learned that the real interest rate is a compensation for forgone consumption. This compensation must be included in the return on all risky assets. But now that we have become familiar with the real interest rate, we can turn our attention to the subject of risk. In this chapter we will concentrate on some of the most popular models of the pricing of risky assets. In the next chapter we will examine some special kinds of risky assets which are tremendously important in modern finance: options and futures.

The pricing of risky assets is often an integral part of any course in either corporate finance or investments. It is important to understand this material since virtually all the financial assets we will discuss involve some kind of risk. However, this book does not completely develop the theory of pricing risky assets. Instead, this chapter is a review or condensed version of material often found in texts dealing with corporate finance or investments. A reader who has never seen any of this material before may want to refer to Appendix B at the end of this book.[1]

In this chapter we will evaluate investments in risky assets and analyze the risk-return trade-off in an asset or a portfolio of assets. Next we will explore the difference between the systematic and the unsystematic risk of an asset and the importance of this to well-diversified investors. Finally, we will briefly review the two major approaches to the pricing of

---

[1]This chapter emphasizes the conceptual aspects of pricing risk. Appendix B emphasizes the computation of measures of expected return and risk and the beta of an asset (defined in this chapter).

risky assets that are currently popular in modern finance theory and some of the available empirical evidence that purports to test how risky assets are priced in organized securities markets. ∎

THE RISK-RETURN TRADE-OFF

In order to evaluate any risky investment it is necessary to begin by constructing some measure of the **expected return** and **risk** of that asset. Risk is usually measured by the *variance or standard deviation* of the asset's return. The data necessary to construct measures of expected return and variance must come either from subjective estimates of the future or from the historical record of return on an asset. For assets which are traded on well-organized markets, as opposed, say, to a new investment by a firm, historical data are usually used to construct measures of expected return and risk.

The basic premise upon which our analysis of investment decisions is based is that expected return is viewed as good—the more of it the better—and risk is viewed as bad—the less of it the better. The problem is to determine the amount of expected return a person or a market will demand in order to accept a certain amount of risk. That is, the problem is to determine the price for bearing risk. For this we must assess the individual's and the market's trade-offs between risk and return.

We will begin our analysis by considering the choice between mutually exclusive investments. We will explore how to choose between such investments as well as how risky assets are priced when they are not in portfolios. Next, we will see how to reduce risk by combining assets into portfolios, and we will examine how to choose the optimal combination of assets in a portfolio.

CHOICE BETWEEN MUTUALLY EXCLUSIVE INVESTMENTS

To begin our analysis let's suppose we have three mutually exclusive investments available with expected return and risk (measured in dollars), as shown in Table 3–1. The problem is how to select the best of the three investments.

Regardless of whether individuals consciously state trade-offs between risk and return, we can represent their choices between assets in terms of measures of

TABLE 3–1
Expected return, variance and standard deviation for three investments.

Investment	Expected Return	Variance	Standard Deviation
A	$7,000	850,000	922
B	7,000	4,800,000	2,191
C	9,000	4,800,000	2,191

FIGURE 3-1
Expected returns and standard deviations for the three investments in Table 3-1.

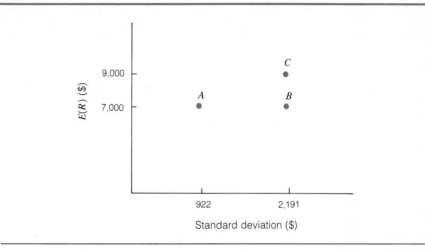

risk and expected return. To do so will utilize a diagram with expected return on the vertical axis and standard deviation of returns on the horizontal axis. Our purpose at the outset is merely to provide a graphical representation of the asset. The purpose of this particular graph is to facilitate comparison of the assets. Each of the three assets is plotted in Figure 3–1. Each assets corresponds to a unique point in the diagram. That point represents the expected return and standard deviation of the asset. For example, asset A plots at the point with coordinates of $7,000 and $922, corresponding to its expected return and standard deviation. We can utilize this diagram to examine the choice between the three risky investments.

To see how we can dissect the choice between these assets we will start by considering only the choice between assets A and B. Is one of these two assets or investments unambiguously superior to the other? That is, would you expect anyone who is risk averse to agree on which investment is superior? If all risk-averse individuals can agree, then we can conclude that personal preference is not relevant to the choice. The answer to the question is yes, A is unambiguously superior to B. A is superior because it has the same expected return as does B, but it has less risk. Therefore, anyone who prefers less risk to more would choose investment A over B.

Now consider the choice between assets A and C. We observe from Figure 3–1 that A and C have different amounts of both expected return and risk. Investment C has more of both than does A. This choice is not as clear-cut as the last one. The choice depends upon whether the additional return expected from investment C is sufficient compensation for the risk involved. This is strictly a matter of personal preference.

FIGURE 3–2

This figure divides Figure 3–1 into four quadrants centered on investment A. Investments which plot in quadrants II and IV will be unambiguously superior or inferior to A, respectively. Investments which plot in quadrants I and III will depend on the individual's attitude toward risk.

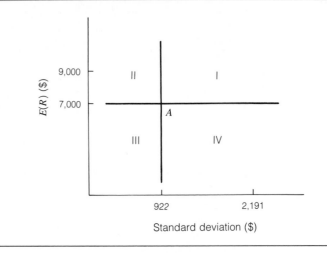

When examining investments in a diagram such as this, there is a simple way to determine whether the choice depends upon personal preference. What is necessary is to divide the diagram into quadrants centered on one of the available investments. This is illustrated in Figure 3–2, where the diagram is divided into four quadrants centered on asset A. Investments which fall in quadrant II, to the northwest of A, will always be unambiguously superior to A because they have less risk and more return. Investments which fall into quadrant IV will be unambiguously inferior to A because they have more risk and less expected return. The choice between A and any investment which falls in quadrants I and III will be a matter of personal preference because they will always have more or less, respectively, of both risk and expected return.

Now suppose that we have to make a choice between two investments like A and C, where personal preference matters. Is there some analytical procedure for determining which is best? The answer is no. You simply have to decide and choose! To represent the choice in this case, we can utilize the same type of diagram as that presented in Figure 3–1. To do this we will introduce a curve called an **indifference curve.** An indifference curve shows the alternative investments among which an individual is indifferent. To explain the idea behind an indifference curve, we will depart momentarily from our example of investments A, B, and C and consider five other investments. The first four of these each has more of both expected return and risk than the one before it. These investments are illustrated in Figure 3–3. An example of an indifference curve is also shown

Indifference curves show combinations of risk and return among which the investor is indifferent.

in Figure 3–3. This indifference curve slopes upward to the right and passes through the points labeled 1 through 4, which represents the first four investments. The fact that the indifference curve passes through them means that they are all equally appealing to the individual whose indifference curve this is. Each investment has just enough expected return to compensate for the additional risk, relative to the other investments. Because this compensation is just sufficient, the indifference curve passes through these four points. This indifference curve therefore represents this particular individual's trade-off between risk and return, or the premium or compensation demanded to bear risk. Suppose there is yet one more investment available to this individual, investment 5, which plots in the diagram to the northwest of the indifference curve. This person will then prefer investment 5 to any of the investments on this indifference curve. But we can go further, for there will also be an indifference curve passing through point 5, and it will never intersect the one passing through points 1 to 4. Any investment on this second indifference curve will be preferred to any investment on the initial indifference curve. We can represent this process indefinitely and fill the diagram with indifference curves, none of which will intersect.

A diagram with more than one indifference curve is shown in Figure 3–4. This diagram has the original three investments, A, B, and C, shown on it. A person who has the indifference curves shown in this diagram would prefer investment A to investment C because A falls on a higher indifference curve, that is, one further to the northwest. To this individual, the additional expected return in investment C is not worth the additional risk. Another individual might well

FIGURE 3–3
The upward-sloping line in this figure illustrates an indifference curve. The curve shows that an investor is indifferent between investments 1, 2, 3, 4 and finds investment 5 to be superior to each of the others.

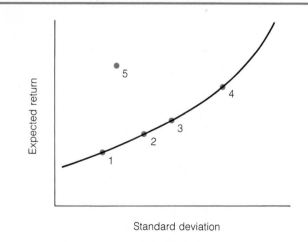

FIGURE 3–4
This figure illustrates the choice of a relatively risk-averse individual. His or her indifference curves are sufficiently steep that for this individual investment A is a better choice than investment B or C.

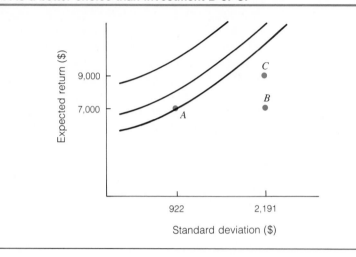

prefer C to A. The indifference curves of such a person are shown in Figure 3–5. This person would be less averse to risk because the additional risk would be more than compensated for by the extra expected return. This person would have flatter indifference curves than the person in Figure 3–4. The steepness of the indifference curve therefore reflects the degree of risk aversion. A person with very flat indifference curves would be less averse to risk than a person with very steep indifference curves. Another way to express this is that the indifference curve shows the trade-off between risk and return of a particular individual. All individuals are different and each will have a different trade-off.

Finally, we need to ask how to translate personal preference or attitude toward risk into a value that an individual will place on an asset. The value of an asset is determined by (1) the expected return on the asset, (2) the risk of the asset as measured by the variance or standard deviation of its future returns, and (3) the premium demanded to bear risk. Again, it is important to emphasize that there is no hard-and-fast or scientific way to quantify how these three factors are combined to determine value. There is no way to quantify the premium one should demand to bear risk. For example, in the case of investment A, the expected return is $7,000 and the standard deviation is $922. Each individual will value this asset differently, depending upon his or her attitude toward risk. Each person must ask what amount of money he or she would accept with certainty rather than have title to the risky investment A. One individual might say, for example, $5,500. Another might offer $6,000. This is the value of that asset to that particular individual.

FIGURE 3–5

This figure illustrates the choice of a modestly risk-averse person. His or her indifference curves are sufficiently flat that for this individual investment C is superior to investments B and A. To see the effect of differences in risk aversion it is helpful to compare this figure to Figure 3–4.

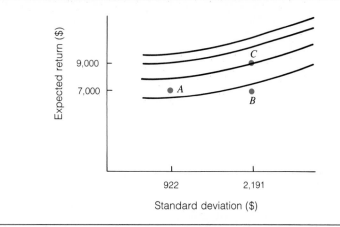

THE IMPACT OF DIVERSIFICATION ON RISK

Until now we have presumed that the investments available in the market were *mutually exclusive,* such that if you chose A, you couldn't also choose B. This is not always the case in the real world faced by investors. Investors can usually choose to purchase shares in different firms, spreading their investment across a number of assets. In this way investors construct *portfolios of assets.* As we shall soon discover, there are benefits for an investor if he or she chooses a portfolio of assets rather than just a single asset. The advantage of a portfolio is that the total amount of risk that each investor bears can be reduced through **diversification.** Our purpose is to understand what diversification is, how it works, and what benefits it can provide investors.

Diversification involves spreading investments across a number of assets to reduce risk.

The concept of diversification is illustrated in Figure 3–6. This figure plots the returns accruing to each of the three assets, A, B, and C, in each of five possible states of the world. Note that Figure 3–6 shows that the returns on assets A and B change in the same direction from one state of the world to the next. By contrast, the return to asset C changes in the opposite direction in that the return to asset C tends to be high when the returns to A and B are low. The idea behind diversification is that if any two assets that do not change in exactly the same way are combined in the same portfolio, then their returns would tend to offset each other so that the risk of the portfolio would be less than the risk of any asset held alone. The benefit of diversification is, therefore, that it reduces the total amount of risk to which an investor is exposed.

FIGURE 3–6
Alternative returns for three investments in each state of the world.

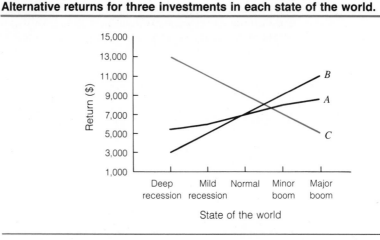

To see more specifically how this works we need to measure the risk and expected return of a portfolio of assets. We continue to measure risk using the variance, but now we need to measure the variance of a portfolio of assets. In order to measure the variance of a portfolio we need to know not only the variance and expected return of each of the individual assets that might go into that portfolio, but we also need to know the relationships between the returns on those assets, or the **correlation coefficients,** between them. When working with portfolios we also want to state returns in percentage rate of return rather than in dollar return as in Table 3–1. Table 3–2 shows the relevant information—expected rate of return, standard deviation, and correlation coefficient—for each of the three assets in our example.

In order to get to the form of the variance which allows us to capture the effect of diversification we have to go through considerable algebraic manipulation. Because these manipulations are not essential to understand the ultimate result, they are relegated to Appendix B. Suppose we form a portfolio out of assets

Correlation coefficient measures the correlation between rates of return on different assets.

TABLE 3–2
Covariance and correlation coefficients for rates of return of investments A, B, and C.*

Investments	Covariance	Correlation Coefficient
A · B	0.0008	0.99
A · C	−0.0008	−0.99
B · C	−0.0019	−1.00

*Assumes each asset has a price of $50,000 (see Appendix B).

A and B, where x represents the proportion of the portfolio in asset A and y represents the proportion of the portfolio in asset B. The expression for the variance of this portfolio that results from these manipulations is the following:

$$\sigma_{rp}^{2} = x^2\sigma_{rA}^{2} + y^2\sigma_{rB}^{2} = 2xy\rho_{AB}\sigma_{rA}\sigma_{rB}$$

We need to inspect this expression carefully. It says that the variance of the portfolio can be broken down into three terms. The first two terms are simply the individual variances of the two assets that go into the portfolio, each multiplied by the square of the proportion of wealth invested in that asset. Were it not for the last term, diversification would therefore have no impact on the variance of the portfolio. The important part of the last term is the correlation coefficient between the two assets, ρ_{AB}. We know that the correlation coefficient varies between $+1$ and -1. Therefore, the smaller the value of the correlation coefficient, the smaller the variance of the portfolio will be. We can imagine a situation where we have three different assets, all with the same variances but with different correlation coefficients. Then, regardless of how we created portfolios of those assets, the first two terms in the variance would be the same. But the third term would be lower for the assets that have the lower correlation coefficients. This is where diversification comes in. Assets with low correlation coefficients provide a greater diversification benefit and that benefit is a reduction in the variance of the portfolio of assets.

To see how this works in the case of our sample of three assets, we need to inspect Table 3–3 and Figure 3–7. The table shows the values of expected return

TABLE 3–3
Mean and standard deviation of portfolio rates of return.

Panel A: Investments A and C			
Percent in A	Percent in C	$E(r_p)$	σ_{r_p}
100	0	0.14	0.01844
75	25	0.15	0.00336
50	50	0.16	0.01285
25	75	0.17	0.02831
0	100	0.18	0.04382

Panel B: Investments B and C			
Percent in B	Percent in C	$E(r_p)$	σ_{r_p}
100	0	0.14	0.04382
75	25	0.15	0.02191
50	50	0.16	0.00000
25	75	0.17	0.02191
0	100	0.18	0.04382

FIGURE 3–7
This figure shows the combinations of expected rate of return and risk which can be obtained by constructing portfolios of investments A, B, and C.

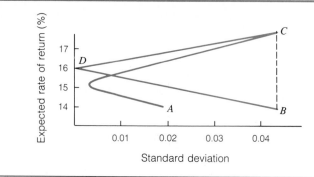

and standard deviation for alternative portfolios of assets. Panel A of the table shows various portfolios made from investments A and C, while panel B shows portfolios made from investments B and C. The portfolios are constructed by varying the percent of wealth invested in each asset. In both panels of the table we can see from the final column that by changing the proportion of wealth in each asset we alter the risk of the portfolio. In the second panel we can actually reduce the risk to zero if resources are split 50-50 between the two assets.

Figure 3–7 illustrates, in a diagram similar to the one first used in Figure 3–1, the combinations of risk and expected return defined in Table 3–3. The alternative combinations of risk and expected return that result from portfolios of assets B and C are represented by the solid lines between points C, B, and D. The line segment between points C and D shows the risk and expected return of portfolios with between 50 and 100 percent in C and zero and 50 percent in B. The lower line segment shows the other alternatives. With 50 percent in each, there is no risk at all. This occurs only when the correlation coefficient between two assets is −1. If it is even slightly larger than that, there will not be any combination of the two assets that eliminates risk entirely.

This is illustrated by the curve which goes from point A to point C. This curve shows that alternative combinations of risk and expected return resulting from portfolios made up the assets A and C. We know from Table 3–2 that the correlation coefficient between A and C is −0.99. As a result, there is no combination of A and C that yields zero risk.

Finally, the dashed vertical line shows the possible portfolios which would result from combinations of B and C if these assets had a correlation coefficient of +1 rather than −1. In this case, there would be no benefit from diversification with these assets. This is illustrated in the figure by the fact that as you move up or down the dashed line, regardless of how much is invested in B or C, there is no reduction in risk. There is simply a change in expected return.

CHOICE BETWEEN PORTFOLIOS OF ASSETS

Now let's consider the choice of the best portfolio comprised from assets A, B and C. To keep it simple let's assume we can combine any two of them rather than all three at once. In our previous example with mutually exclusive investments, we had to choose which one of the three assets we wanted. Now we have to choose which portfolio of assets we want. This means we have to first choose which assets to put into our portfolio and then what proportion to invest in each asset. As in the case of mutually exclusive assets, it may be possible to eliminate some alternative from consideration at the outset without being concerned with personal perferences. We have already excluded combinations of A and B. An inspection of Figure 3–7 leads to the conclusion that as long as you are averse to risk, you can always do better investing in combinations of B and C than you can by investing in A and C. This is because the line segment DC is always to the northwest of the curve between points A and C. The line DC represents the **efficient frontier** of the possible portfolios the investor can choose. This means there will always be a portfolio on this line that will be preferred by any risk-averse investor to any available inside this line.

However, the individual's attitude toward risk is the crucial determinant of the proportions to invest in assets B and C. Again, just as in the earlier case of mutually exclusive investments, there is no correct choice. You must decide how much risk you are willing to bear and select proportions to invest in each.

We can illustrate the choices of a highly risk-averse person and a less risk-averse person, however, just as we did earlier. To do so we have to utilize indifference curves as we did earlier. Figure 3–8 illustrates the choices of two individ-

> The **efficient frontier** is the set of portfolios which have the best available combinations of expected return and risk. They are best in that no other portfolio would be clearly preferred to any of these portfolios by all risk-averse investors.

FIGURE 3–8
This figure illustrates the choice of portfolios for a highly risk-averse person and a modestly risk-averse person. The upper panel shows the less risk-averse individual and the lower panel illustrates the choice of the highly risk-averse individual. Panel A shows that a modestly risk-averse person finds it optimal to bear some risk rather than eliminate all risk by choosing a portfolio of equal parts in assets B and C.

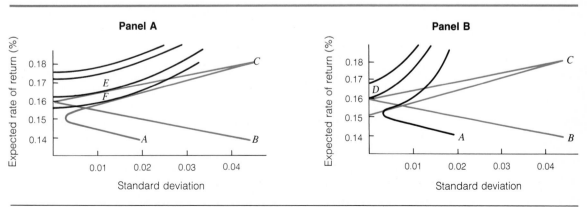

uals. The individual represented in panel A is only slightly risk averse. Panel B illustrates the choice of a person who is more risk averse. The more risk-averse person, in panel B, has steeper indifference curves than the person in panel A. These diagrams are simply the same as Figure 3–7, with indifference curves overlaid on the figure. The more risk-averse person chooses to split his or her investment equally between assets B and C and bear no risk at all. He or she knows that the return on this portfolio will be 0.16 regardless. The person in panel A finds that the additional return that can be gained from some additional risk is worth it. But she or he demands increasing amounts of expected return to take on additional risk, so that at point *E*, she or he finds that enough return has been added. This figure illustrates that no single portfolio is correct for everyone. The appropriate choice depends upon an individual's personal preference for risk as opposed to expected return.

Systematic and Unsystematic Risk

The total risk of an individual asset or portfolio of assets is measured by the variance or standard deviation of the asset's or portfolio's rate of return. Now we want to decompose the total risk of an individual asset into two components. One component is called *systematic risk,* and the other is called *unsystematic risk*. **Systematic risk** *is the part of an asset's total risk that cannot be eliminated by forming a diversified portfolio with all assets in the market*. **Unsystematic risk** *is the residual that can be eliminated through diversification*. Diversification does *not* change the total risk of an individual asset, even though it *does* change the total risk of a portfolio of assets. The total risk of an individual asset is still its variance or standard deviation, and this is unaffected regardless of what portfolio that asset may be a part of. Therefore, as we decompose the total risk of an asset into the systematic and unsystematic parts, we must remember that regardless of what we do with this asset, the sum of the two parts is always the same:

Total risk = Systematic risk + Unsystematic risk.

Systematic risk is the part of an asset's total risk that cannot be eliminated by forming a diversified portfolio with all assets in the market.

Unsystematic risk is the residual that can be eliminated through diversification.

INDIVIDUAL ASSETS AND THE MARKET PORTFOLIO

In the definition of systematic risk we said it is that portion of total risk that cannot be eliminated by forming a diversified portfolio with all other assets in the market. The idea of a portfolio of all the assets in the market is what is meant by a **market portfolio.** The market portfolio is the market as a whole. A portfolio made up of virtually every asset in the market offers the maximum amount of benefit from diversification. Therefore, the risk of the market portfolio is systematic risk, and the systematic risk of an individual asset is that part of its total risk that is tied to the market portfolio. This phrasing may seem a little ambiguous, for it is not clear exactly what it means to say that the risk is tied to the market portfolio. We need

Market portfolio represents the portfolio formed from all the assets available in the market.

to spell out the exact relationship between the return on the market portfolio and the return on a specific asset.

If we are going to take the definition of the market portfolio literally, then the market portfolio we use to determine systematic risk must actually be composed of every asset available in the market. If there were one million assets available in the market, then the portfolio would be composed of shares of each of these assets. Moreover, the proportion of each of these assets in the market portfolio would be equal to that asset's proportion of total value in the market. This means that if the total value of all shares of asset 1 available in the market is equal to one percent of the total value of all shares of all firms in the market, then this asset should represent one percent of the market portfolio. Again the idea here is that the market portfolio actually is the market.

In practice, it is impractical for an individual to construct a portfolio of all the assets in the market. Fortunately, this is not necessary in order to receive most of the benefits of diversification. As we increase the number of assets in a portfolio, the amount of unsystematic risk in the portfolio declines fairly rapidly. Therefore, we can choose a portfolio of, say, 30 or 40 assets, and that portfolio will be much like the true market portfolio. Like the true market portfolio, the risk of this portfolio will be almost entirely systematic risk, so that this portfolio gives almost as much benefit from diversification as the true market portfolio itself. This is illustrated in Figure 3–9, which shows what happens to systematic risk as the number of assets in a portfolio is increased. The line showing the total risk of the portfolio asymptotically or gradually approaches the line representing systematic risk. It has been shown from experiments involving portfolios with

FIGURE 3–9
Systematic and unsystematic risk in a portfolio. This figure illustrates how unsystematic risk declines as randomly chosen securities are added to a portfolio.

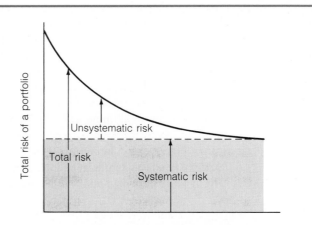

different numbers of securities that the risk of a portfolio actually declines in this manner.[2] This ensures that one does not have to include all the assets in the market in order to approximate the market portfolio with most of its diversification benefits.

There is one additional requirement, however, for this to work out: the securities in the modest-sized portfolio must be chosen randomly. It is certainly possible to construct a portfolio of, say, 30 securities that has a lot of unsystematic risk. For example, we could choose a portfolio of all energy stocks. But if the assets are chosen randomly, then this concentration will be avoided. As a result of this approximate relationship between modest-sized portfolios and the true market portfolio, well-diversified portfolios that are not really quite the total market have been used to represent the market portfolio. Two common examples that fill this role are the Standard & Poor's 500 and the New York Stock Exchange Index. These are indexes of returns on large, well-diversified portfolios of common stock.

Thus far we have learned that an individual asset always has both a systematic and an unsystematic component to its total return. Now we can begin to measure these components precisely by relating the return on an individual asset to the return on the market portfolio. To do so we want to specify how the rate of return on a particular asset, call it asset A, is related to the rate of return on the market. We will represent the rate of return on the market with r_M and the rate of return on an individual asset, A, as r_A. It is important to see what we are asking for in this relationship. At this point we are not asking for a theory of how an individual asset should be priced, given the return on the market. We simply want to quantify the observable relationship between the two rates of return, r_A and r_M.

We will quantify this relationship with the following linear equation:

$$r_A = \alpha_A + \beta_A R_M + \epsilon_A. \tag{3-1}$$

The **beta** of an asset measures the sensitivity of the rate of return on that asset to changes in the rate of return on the market portfolio.

The rates of return on asset A and the market portfolio are r_A and r_M. The term β_A represents the **beta** of asset A; that is, β_A is a measure of the systematic risk of asset A. The term α_A is a constant known with certainty. This means that α_A is not defined by a probability distribution. The term ϵ_A is an uncertain or random term referred to as a *residual*. The exact magnitude of ϵ_A is unknown, as it is determined by a probability distribution.

To see what Equation (3–1) means it is best to plug in some numbers and interpret its meaning in an example. Suppose that α_A and β_A have values of 0.02 and 2, respectively. (See Appendix B for a description of the procedure for estimating beta.) These are the two variables we know with certainty ahead of time. Now the equation can be read as follows: the return on asset A will be equal to two times the rate of return on the market, plus 0.02, plus an additional random

----

[2]The details of these experiments can be found in W. H. Wagner and S. C. Lau, "The Effect of Diversification on Risk," *Financial Analysts Journal,* 26 (November–December 1971), pp. 7–13.

factor, ϵ_A. For example, if the rate of return on the market were zero and the random factor were zero, then the rate of return on asset A would be

$$.02 = .02 + 2 \times 0 + 0.$$

If the rate of return on the market were 0.05 and the random factor ϵ_A were $-.03$, then the rate of return on asset A would be

$$.09 = .02 + 2 \times .05 - .03.$$

Equation (3–1) is simply a way of representing how the rate of return on a particular security is generated. It is a statistical approach in that it relates the return on the particular asset in question to the return on the market, where the intercept α_A and the slope coefficient β_A are the parameters in the relationship. It is not an approach that illuminates why the return on an asset is what it is. The return is actually determined by all sorts of factors pertaining to the firm involved and the products it produces. Equation (3–1) merely seeks to explain individual rates of return as having a component related to the market as a whole and a random residual component. As a result it is referred to as a **single-factor market model**, the single factor being r_M.

A **single-factor model** seeks to explain individual rates of return as having a component related to the market as a whole and a random residual component.

MEASURING SYSTEMATIC RISK

As it stands now, it may be difficult to see how to make use of Equation (3–1). But Equation (3–1) is useful because it provides a basis for measuring the systematic risk of an asset, that is, β. Because it is this part of total risk an investor actually bears when he or she holds a particular asset in a portfolio, it is valuable to be able to measure systematic risk. To measure the systematic risk of an individual asset we need to use Equation (3–1) to evaluate the variance of the rate of return on the asset. In Equation (3–1) we have defined the rate of return on asset A as a function of the two other random variables, r_M and ϵ_A. Therefore, the variance of r_A can be written as a function of the variance of these two random variables. The resulting equation for the variance of r_A is the following:

$$\sigma_{r_A}^2 = \beta_A^2 \sigma_{r_M}^2 + \sigma_{\epsilon_A}^2,$$

where $\sigma_{r_M}^2$ is equal to the variance of r_M and $\sigma_{\epsilon_A}^2$ is equal to the variance of ϵ_A.

To see how Equation (3–2) is derived we simply proceed to compute the variance of each of the three terms on the right-hand side of Equation (3–1). The first term, α_A, is a constant; thus its variance is zero. The second term is the constant β_A, multiplied by the random variable r_M. The variance of this product is β_A^2 times the variance of r_M. Next, it is important to note that ϵ_A and r_M are constructed so that they are uncorrelated with each other. This means they have a correlation coefficient of zero because the market portfolio has only systematic risk and therefore cannot be related to this residual term. As a result, the variance of the sum of r_M and ϵ_A is equal to the sum of their variances. That is, there is no covariance term that must be included. Note that there generally is a covariance term in the variance of a sum of two random variables, but when the correlation coefficient between the two variables is zero, the covariance term drops out. This is the case here. Therefore, the last term in Equation (3–2) is simply the variance of ϵ_A.

Now we can use Equation (3–2) to define the systematic and unsystematic components of the risk of asset A. The total risk of the asset is measured by the variance. The systematic component is that part of the total risk that is related to the market portfolio. Therefore, the first of the two terms in Equation (3–2) represents the systematic risk of asset A. The equation shows that the systematic component of the variance of any asset is the product of the variance of the rate of return on the market portfolio and the square of that asset's beta. The variance of the residual ϵ_A is the unsystematic component of variance of the individual asset.

$$\sigma^2_{r_A} \quad = \quad \beta^2_A \sigma^2_{r_M} \quad + \quad \sigma^2_{\epsilon_A}$$

$$\text{Total variance} = \frac{\text{Systematic}}{\text{component}} + \frac{\text{Unsystematic}}{\text{component}}.$$

The concepts of systematic and unsystematic risk are important for a very simple reason: investors who are well-diversified should not be concerned with unsystematic risk. Diversified investors should care only about systematic risks that cannot be diversified away in the market. As a result, in organized securities markets where most investors are well-diversified, the relevant risk, which should affect the price of an asset, is systematic rather than total risk or variance of the asset.

MODELS OF ASSET PRICING

In the remainder of this chapter we will discuss two theories of how assets are priced in organized securities markets. The first theory, known as the **Capital Asset Pricing Model (CAPM),** has been around for roughly 20 years. The second, known as the **Arbitrage Pricing Theory (APT),** is much newer. The purpose of a theory is to explain something which is observable in the world. It is debatable how well these theories accomplish this purpose. We will briefly summarize the empirical evidence on these theories, and you can judge for yourself.

OVERVIEW OF THE CAPM

The idea behind the CAPM is that if all investors make choices according to certain assumptions, then the CAPM provides a mathematical statement of the way the price is determined for each asset in the market. The mathematical expression is referred to as the *pricing equation*. The pricing equation is usually stated in terms of expected rate of return rather than price itself. But if the expected dollar returns are known, then for the expected rate of return to increase, the price must go down and vice versa; therefore the pricing equation is really an equation for the expected rate of return. Before we state the pricing equation itself, we need to discuss its basic ingredients. The first one we have already explored. It is the beta of an asset. The second one is called the *market price of risk*.

If we assume there is a risk-free rate of return, r_F, available in the market, then the premium investors will demand for bearing the risk of the market portfolio is reflected in the expected rate of return of that portfolio. That is, the expected rate of return on the market portfolio $E(r_M)$ will exceed the risk-free rate of return r_F by an amount that just compensates investors for holding the market portfolio. Given the expected absolute dollar returns for each asset in the market, the prices of those assets will adjust until investors are compensated for bearing the risk of the market portfolio. This difference between the expected rate of return on the market portfolio and the risk-free interest rate is called the **market price of risk:**

The **market price of risk** is the difference between the expected return on the market portfolio and the risk-free interest rate.

$$\text{Market price of risk} = E(r_M) - r_F.$$

Early in this chapter we emphasized that each individual must make up his or her own mind about the amount of risk he or she is willing to bear. In effect, each individual has his or her own price of risk. What the capital asset pricing model does is aggregate these prices into a market price of risk. This happens because, in the CAPM, each individual holds the market portfolio of assets. This occurs because all market participants are assumed to have identical expectations about the future.

When all investors hold the market portfolio, then the price of every asset in the market is determined by three factors: the market price of risk, the systematic risk of the asset, and the risk-free rate of interest. The pricing equation which defines the expected rate of return for an asset can be written, for asset A, as

$$E(r_A) = r_F + [E(r_M) - r_F]\beta_A. \tag{3--3}$$

The CAPM equation says that the expected rate of return on each asset in the market is equal to the risk-free interest rate plus the product of the market price of risk and the systematic risk of the asset. For example, if $r_F = 0.05$, $E(r_M) = 0.07$, and $\beta_A = 2$, then $E(r_A) = 0.09$. The risk-free interest rate represents the rate of return the asset would command in the market if it had no risk. The second term in the equation represents the compensation the market demands for risk. This compensation is equal to the measure of the systematic risk of the asset times the compensation demanded by the market to bear the same amount of systematic risk as the market portfolio. That is, if its beta were equal to one, then the price demanded to bear this risk would be the same as for the market portfolio.

FIGURE 3–10

The security market line. This figure illustrates Equation (3–3). Any security which has an expected rate of return above the line, such as I, has a return above that predicted by the CAPM. If it plots below the line, as does J, then the expected return is below that predicted by the CAPM.

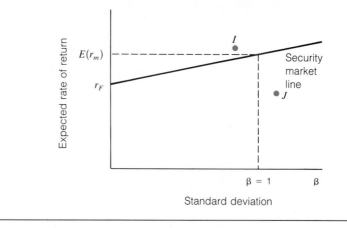

This relationship is illustrated by the upward sloping line in Figure 3–10. The vertical axis in this figure measures the expected rate of return and the horizontal axis measures the beta of an asset. The slope of the line is equal to the market price of risk, $E(r_M) - r_F$, and the intercept is equal to the risk-free interest rate. This line is called the **security market line** because it indicates the expected rate of return demanded by the market as a function of an asset's beta. The CAPM argues that the market should price assets so that they fall on the security market line. If they fall on this line, then their prices are determined according to Equation (3–3). If an asset plots above the line, as illustrated by point I in Figure 3–10, this means that the market is underpricing the asset, relative to the prediction of the CAPM. This is because the expected return in the market is above that predicted by Equation (3–3). On the other hand, if the asset plots below the line, as illustrated by point J in Figure 3–10, then the asset is overpriced relative to the prediction of the CAPM.

The security market line defines the expected rate of return demanded on an asset as a function of the asset's beta.

The greatest merit of the CAPM is its simplicity. You might not believe it if this is your first exposure to the CAPM, but almost nothing is simple at first. Compared to alternative theories that seek to examine how risky assets are priced in a market, the CAPM is really rather simple. The simplicity lies in the fact that Equation (3–3) has such a straightforward interpretation and is readily usable.

What the CAPM does is make use of the concept of beta in order to determine the price of an asset. What it offers is a standardized measure of the price of compensation for bearing risk. It depersonalizes the issue of how to state a proper compensation for risk. It does this by saying that the market portfolio provides the market's price of risk. The market's price of risk is the premium or difference

USING CAPM TO ESTIMATE DISCOUNT RATES

The normal procedure in estimating the value of a risky investment project is to construct estimates of the expected cash flows for that project and then calculate the present value of those cash flows. In doing such calculations it is critically important to choose an appropriate discount rate or hurdle rate. Specific models of how risky securities are priced can be used to estimate the discount rate in calculating the present value of a risky investment. We can express the present value equation as (see Appendix A for a development of present value):

$$\text{Present value} = \sum_{t=1}^{N} \frac{C_t}{(1 + i)^t}.$$

The symbol C_t represents the expected cash flow accruing to the project at time t in the future. We get these cash flows by analyzing the possible payoffs from the investment and constructing estimates of the best guess of what the cash flows will be. We also need to specify a value of i, the discount rate, in order to determine the present value. The advantage of the CAPM is that it suggests a procedure for accomplishing this.

In order to use the CAPM to construct a discount rate, it is necessary to have an estimate of the risk of the project under consideration. Furthermore, if the firm undertaking the investment has diversified shareholders, then we should only be concerned about the systematic risk of that investment. We have learned that the systematic risk can be measured by beta. Therefore, the first thing we need to know is the beta of the investment in question. For some types of investments this can be hard to obtain, but for many investments there are already companies in the business being considered. Their betas can be used as an indication of the risk in this business.

Once we know the beta, we need to know two other things in order to calculate a discount rate. We need to know the risk-free interest rate and the market price of risk. Then we can use Equation 3–3 to estimate the discount rate. We need to have a current measure of the risk-free rate, so we would consult the current level of Treasury bill rates, say the 1-year Treasury bill rate. To estimate the market price of risk we want a measure of what the market demands as a premium over the risk-free rate to hold a broadly diversified portfolio of assets. Ibbotson and Sinquefield have used a long history of returns on common stocks in the United States in order to estimate the historical difference between the return on a diversified portfolio of common stocks relative and the historical risk-free rate. They have estimated that this measure of the market price of risk has been 8.3 percent.[1]

Suppose you are considering an investment with expected cash flows of $5 million per year for 10 years. You estimate that the beta of this investment is 1.3, and the risk-free rate is 6 percent. How would you calculate the present value of this investment?

First you would calculate the appropriate discount rate as follows:

$$i = \frac{\text{Risk-free}}{\text{rate}} + \frac{\text{Market price}}{\text{of risk}} \times \text{Beta}$$
$$16.8\% = \quad 6\% \quad + \quad (8.3\% \quad \times 1.3).$$

Now we can use this 16.8% discount rate to calculate the present value of the expected cash flows. The present value is

$$\$4.693 \text{ million} = \sum_{t=1}^{10} \frac{10,000,000}{(1.168)^t}.$$

The moral of this story is that the beta and the CAPM provide a useful tool for making any adjustment for the risk of an investment when determining its current value.

[1]See R. G. Ibbotson and R. A. Sinquefield, *Stocks, Bonds, Bills and Inflation: The Past and the Future*, Charlottesville, Va.: Financial Analysts Research Foundation, 1982.

between the expected return on the market portfolio of assets and the rate of return on the risk-free asset. Since the measure of the risk of any asset, beta, is a measure of the risk of an asset relative to the market, the compensation demanded for the risk of an individual asset should be the product of the market price of risk and the beta of an asset. The pricing equation of the CAPM quantifies this:

$$E(r_A) = r_F + \underset{\substack{\text{Market price} \\ \text{of risk}}}{[E(r_M - r_F)]} \cdot \underset{\substack{\text{Risk of asset} \\ \text{A relative to} \\ \text{the market}}}{\beta_A}$$

SHORTCOMINGS OF THE CAPM

While the CAPM has been the preeminent analytical model of the pricing of risky assets in organized financial markets, it has its drawbacks. These drawbacks are sufficiently serious that an intense search for a superior theory of asset prices has been under way for some time. The issues involved in the rivalry between alternative models are exceedingly complicated and it is impossible to cover them in any depth here. It is possible, however, to give some indication of what the shortcomings of the CAPM are and why the search for an alternative theory is proceeding. To do this we need to examine the assumptions of the theory. All of the assumptions are unrealistic, but some are more troublesome than others.

One assumption is that there is a risk-free asset that every market participant can incorporate into his or her portfolio. But in reality, there is no such risk-free asset. The usual real-world counterpart for the risk-free asset is a Treasury bill. But with inflation the real return on Treasury bills, that is, the return after inflation, is not certain. As it turns out, it is not really necessary to have a risk-free asset to establish the CAPM. Instead, something called a zero-beta portfolio will work just as well.[3] To construct a zero-beta portfolio one has to be able to construct a portfolio of assets that is uncorrelated—that is, it has a correlation coefficient of zero—with the market portfolio. (While we will not show how to construct it here, in principle this is not very difficult to do.) And as long as this can be done, beta and the market price of risk retain their usefulness and can be interpreted as discussed above.

A more difficult problem centers on the assumption that all market participants agree on estimates of future returns on assets available in the market. This assumption leads everyone to hold a common market portfolio. One can still come up with an equation like Equation (3–3), but averages of every individual's estimates of expected returns and correlation coefficients now appear in the equation.[4]

---

[3]See Fischer Black, "Capital Market Equilibrium with Restricted Borrowing," *Journal of Business,* (July 1972), pp. 444–55, for the original development of the zero-beta portfolio and its application to the CAPM.

[4]See John Lintner, "The Aggregation of Investor's Diverse Judgments and Preferences in Purely Competitive Security Markets," *Journal of Financial and Quantitative Analysis,* (December 1969), pp. 347–400.

As a consequence, the resulting explanation of the prices of risky assets is not as simple and useful as the CAPM. They key to the usefulness of the CAPM is the concept of a market portfolio that lies on the frontier of all possible portfolios, as illustrated in Figure 3–8. If this portfolio does not exist in theory, or if there is no practical real-world measure of it, then the value of the CAPM is seriously compromised.

Another assumption of the theory is that investors deal in a world with only a single future period, which means there are no returns that continue into the future. This assumption is unrealistic because a central problem of financial economics is understanding how to value risky assets with returns occurring in many future periods. There is a version of CAPM that takes care of this problem,[5] but this version has its own restrictive assumptions. In particular, it assumes that the investment opportunities themselves do not change in the future. That is, it assumes there is no uncertainty about what future investments will be available, and this seems no more acceptable than the original assumptions of the CAPM itself.

These last two assumptions only hint at problems with the CAPM that limit its testability. The true test of any theory lies in its predictive power or how well it can explain the real world. Some prominent scholars have argued that for all practical purposes, the CAPM is not testable.[6] If this criticism is vindicated and no alternative is available, it would leave a gaping hole in financial economics. This criticism has been a strong part of the impetus to develop a viable alternative.

Simply stated, the criticism is as follows: the crux of the problem is that we don't know what the market portfolio actually is. It is always possible to pick some proxy for the true market portfolio with betas computed from that proxy that will satisfy Equation (3–3). For this to work the proxy for the market portfolio must end up on the frontier of possible portfolios as illustrated in Figure 3–8, for ex post returns. That is, if we construct a frontier from actual observed returns and our proxy for the market portfolio ends up on that frontier, then Equation (3–3) will be satisfied. If our proxy is not on the frontier, then the equation will not be satisfied. In either case, it is a matter of luck. The only way we can avoid this uncertainty is to know the true market portfolio, which we do not know. Moreover, if people have different estimates of future returns, there is really no common market portfolio. This criticism of testability is the most pessimistic and critical appraisal of the CAPM, and it is a powerful one. The best defense of the CAPM is that, while other theories seem to avoid some of the logical pitfalls of the CAPM, so far they do not have the simplicity of the CAPM and do not

---

[5]See Robert Merton, "An Intertemporal Capital Asset Pricing Model," *Econometrica,* (September 1973), pp. 867–88.

[6]See Richard Roll, "A Critique of the Asset Pricing Theory's Tests," *Journal of Financial Economics,* 5 (March 1977), pp. 129–79, for the original indictment of the CAPM. Also see Richard Roll, "Performance Evaluation and Benchmark Errors," *Journal of Portfolio Management,* (Summer 1980), pp. 5–12, for a less mathematical and formal discussion of the same topic.

provide superior predictions. With the intense research going on in this area, this assessment may change radically in the near future.

The principal alternative to the CAPM that has become popular in finance in recent years is called **Arbitrage Pricing Theory (APT).**[7] The APT avoids some of the criticisms of the CAPM: it is not based on many unrealistic assumptions about how individuals make investment decisions, and it does not require a well-defined and observable market portfolio. The essence of the APT is simply a statement that there may be multiple sources of systematic risk in the economy. These risks are systematic because they cannot be eliminated by constructing any kind of portfolio. The sources of risk are referred to as *factors*. Since the factors are sources of systematic risk, the expected return on any security should be related to these factors. If we assume that the relationship is linear, then this can be expressed as follows:

The **Arbitrage Pricing Theory** is a theory which explains expected returns on individual assets as a function of a set of systematic risks in the economy. These systematic risks are referred to as **factors**.

$$\text{Expected return on a stock} = \beta_1 \text{ Factor}_1 + \beta_2 \text{ Factor}_2 + \ldots + \beta_K \text{ Factor}_K.$$

Since there are K factors in this relationship, this is referred to as a *K-factor model*.

The APT says whatever systematic factors exist in the economy will turn out to be important in pricing assets. That is, if there is a source of systematic risk attributable to any observable factor, then this factor should influence the prices of securities. Moreover, the theory invokes what is called the **law of one price—** that is, a factor that is a source of systematic risk should not be priced differently for different securities at the same time. There should be one and only one price for this source of risk. The APT does not say what the factors that generate systematic risks may be, and it doesn't say how many there may be. This is essentially an empirical question; it is a matter of how many can be discovered to be important in the real world. Some recent research has argued that there are four sources of systematic risk in the economy.[8] The suggested candidates are unanticipated changes in

The **law of one price** says that assets with the same systematic risk should not be priced differently.

1. inflation
2. industrial production
3. risk premiums for default in interest rates
4. the term structure of interest rates. (See Chapter 8 for a discussion of the term structure.)

It is not clear that this is the correct set of factors, nor is it clear that this approach to pricing assets will be more useful than the CAPM. We will simply have to wait for more research in this area.

---

[7]The principal alternative is known as the Arbitrage Pricing Theory (APT). One of the first developments of this theory was in Steven Ross, ''The Arbitrage Theory of Capital Asset Pricing,'' *Journal of Economic Theory,* 13 (December 1976), pp. 341–60.

[8]See Chen, Nai-Fu, Richard Roll and Steven Ross, ''Economic Forces and the Stock Market,'' *Journal of Business,* 1987.

SUMMARY

In this chapter we learned how to analyze decisions when an individual faces uncertainty about future returns on investments. This subject is important not only because we want to make better decisions about uncertainty, but also because we want to know how uncertainty and people's reactions to it infuence the value of assets. We also analyzed the pricing of risky assets. We developed a measure of the risk of an individual asset when that asset is held in a portfolio, and we developed an explicit statement of the way the market prices assets when they are held in portfolios.

There is a natural limit to the extent to which we can make choice under uncertainty a scientific procedure. We can measure the expected return and standard deviation, but we can define no objective way to choose between risk and expected return. The right amount of risk to trade off for expected return is strictly a matter of personal preference.

In order to understand how assets are priced we decomposed the risk of an asset and of a portfolio into two components, systematic and unsystematic risk. The systematic risk is that part of total risk that cannot be eliminated through diversification. Unsystematic risk can be so eliminated. In order to measure systematic risk, we relied on the market portfolio, which is a portfolio of all assets available in the market. While it is difficult to measure the true market portfolio, indexes of returns on large numbers of securities can approximate the true market portfolio. Once we have a measure of the rate of return on the market portfolio, we can measure systematic risk. Systematic risk is measured by beta (β). The beta of an asset measures the effect of a change in the rate of return of the market portfolio on the rate of return of an individual asset.

We were able to develop the concept of systematic risk and measure it with beta without ever introducing an explicit theory of how assets are priced in the market when they are held in diversified portfolios. Therefore, neither the concept nor measure of systematic risk depends upon a particular theory. However, we need an explicit theory to explain the link between our measure of systematic risk and the prices of assets in the market. The preeminent theory is the Capital Asset Pricing Model (CAPM). Its pricing equation mathematically states the relationship between the price of a risky asset, its systematic risk, and the return on the market portfolio. The equation says that the expected return on the asset equals the return on the risk-free asset in the market plus the product of the asset's beta and the market price of risk. The market price of risk is the premium the market demands to hold the market portfolio and is equal to the difference between the expected rate of return on the market portfolio and risk-free interest rate.

The advantage of the CAPM is the simple composition and form of this pricing equation. It says that the price of an asset is determined by only three things, and the relationship among them is simple to write. However, there are potentially serious flaws with this theory of the pricing of risky assets. The most serious flaw lies in the logical difficulties involved in constructing a satisfactory method for testing the theory. Until a viable alternative appears, the CAPM remains the preeminent theory in this field. Moreover, the real benefit of the theory lies in the increased understanding of the market derived from understanding how the theory is developed. Even if this theory is supplanted, the insight it provides into the pricing of the systematic component of risk is still important.

QUESTIONS

1. Explain risk. Why do we use variance to measure risk? Suppose someone told you that risk should be measured by the probability of the lowest returns. That is, suppose there were two assets, one with a 5 percent chance of a rate of return less than zero and the other with a 10 percent chance of a rate of return less than zero. This person then said that the project with the greater percentage chance of a return less than zero was the more risky. What do you think of this as a measure of risk?
2. Do you think a risk-averse person is likely to buy insurance? Does a person have no aversion to risk if he or she gambles in Las Vegas? How would you explain a person who both buys insurance and gambles in Las Vegas?
3. The total risk of any asset can be decomposed into two parts. Explain what these two parts are. Can diversification reduce either part of the risk of an individual asset? The same decomposition can be applied to a portfolio of assets. Can diversification reduce either part of the risk of a portfolio? If so, then describe how this takes place.
4. How can we relate the rate of return on an individual asset to the rate of return on some index of the market? The slope coefficient in this relationship is referred to as beta. How does beta measure the systematic risk of the asset?
5. What is the market price of risk and how is it measured? How is it that the CAPM can depersonalize the trade-off between risk and return with a single market price of risk?
6. How is beta used in the CAPM? Explain its role in the pricing equation.
7. What is the security market line? Why is it said that "assets should price on the line"?
8. The CAPM has both serious strengths and weaknesses. What is its principle strength supposed to be? Do you agree? Why or why not?
9. Summarize the criticisms of the CAPM. What do you think of these criticisms?
10. Suppose you observed an asset that had a negative beta. What would this mean? How could you represent this with the security market line? Can you think of a real-world example of an asset that might have a negative beta?
11. Suppose you tried to find out if real-world securities plotted on the security market line. In your investigation you discover that the securities of small companies tended to plot above the line while those of large companies tended to plot below the line. Can you think of a rationale for this discovery?
12. Suppose you have three assets to choose from. To keep the problem simple, you can put all your wealth into any one asset or split your wealth equally

between any two assets. There are four possible rates of return for each asset corresponding to four possible states of the world. Also suppose each set of outcomes is equally probable (probability of 25%). The table showing possible returns is as follows:

State of the World	Rates of Return on Investment (%)		
	A	B	C
1	5	10	90
2	25	30	70
3	85	70	30
4	105	90	10

What portfolio would you prefer? You might want to consult Appendix B in answering this question.

13. Suppose you are considering two mutually exclusive investments. The two investments have risky cash flows which are distributed over ten years. Project A has expected cash flows of $10 million per year for ten years. Project B has expected cash flows which are expected to be $5 million per year for the first five years and $8 million per year for the next five years. You are told that the risk-free interest rate in the economy is 6 percent and that the beta of the first project is 0.8 while the beta of the second project is 1.4. Which of the two projects has the higher risk-adjusted present value?

14. Suppose you were constructing a portfolio made up of any combination of three assets. The assets have the following combinations of expected rate of return and risk as measured by beta:

Asset	Expected Rate of Return	Beta
1	0.15	1.0
2	0.225	1.5
3	0.17	1.25

What would you advise about the appropriate construction of a portfolio made up of these assets?

15. Given the following information on three assets, calculate the expected return, the variance, and the standard deviation for each one.

State of the World	Probability	Returns %		
		A	B	C
1	0.1	80	75	5
2	0.2	60	40	10
3	0.4	30	30	20
4	0.2	8	10	40
5	0.1	−10	−5	70

16. Given the above information, calculate the covariance and correlation coefficients for the possible combinations of pairs of assets.
17. What would be the expected returns and standard deviations of portfolios containing two assets in equal proportion? Plot the portfolios in a diagram with axes of risk and return. Which portfolio would you choose and why?

REFERENCES

Black, Fischer. "Capital Market Equilibrium with Restricted Borrowing," *Journal of Business,* (July 1972), pp. 444–55.

Chen, Nai-fu, Richard Roll and Steven Ross. "Economic Forces and the Stock Market," *Journal of Business,* 1987.

Copeland, Thomas E. and J. Fred Weston. *Financial Theory and Corporate Policy,* Reading, Mass.: Addison-Wesley Publishing Company, 1983.

Fama, Eugene F. and Merton H. Miller. *The Theory of Finance,* New York: Holt, Rinehart and Winston, 1972.

Lintner, John. "The Aggregation of Investor's Diverse Judgments and Preferences in Purely Competitive Security Markets," *Journal of Financial and Quantitative Analysis,* (December 1969), pp. 347–400.

Mossin, Jan. *The Theory of Financial Markets,* Englewood Cliffs, N.J.: Prentice-Hall, Inc., 1973.

Merton, Roberts. "An Intertemporal Capital Asset Pricing Model," *Econometrica,* (September 1973), pp. 867–88.

Roll, Richard. "Ambiguity When Performance Is Measured by the Security Market Line," *Journal of Finance,* 33 (September 1978), pp. 1051–69.

———. "A Critique of the Asset Pricing Theory's Test," *Journal of Financial Economics,* 5 (March 1977), pp. 129–76.

———. W. H. Wagner and S. C. Lau, "The Effect of Diversification on Risk," *Financial Analysts Journal,* 26 (November-December 1971), pp. 7–13.

Sharpe, William F. "Capital Asset Prices: A Theory of Market Equilibrium Under Conditions of Risk," *Journal of Finance,* (September 1964), pp. 425–52.

4 PRICING CONTINGENT CLAIMS

In this chapter we continue our analysis of the pricing of risky assets which we began in Chapter 3. However, here we will focus on an interesting set of financial assets, options and futures.

In the 1970s and early 1980s the markets for options and futures—or contingent claims on financial instruments—came of age. Prior to 1972 there were no organization markets on which options or futures on financial instruments were traded. Today there is a wide variety of options and futures on stocks, bonds, currencies and even on stock indexes. In fact, daily trading volume for stock options on the Chicago Board Options Exchange often exceeds trading volume on all stock exchanges in the country except the New York Stock Exchange.

It is no accident that the growth in options and futures occurred during this particular period. One of the forces behind the growth in these financial instruments appears to be the increased riskiness of the underlying financial instruments to which these options and futures apply. In the 1970s inflation increased the level and volatility of market interest rates on most fixed income obligations. The demise of fixed exchange rates between the dollar and other currencies led to increased exchange rate risk for many participants in the financial markets. Furthermore, the decline in the stock market in the mid-1970s also apparently led to increased desire for mechanisms to hedge the risk of investments in stocks. In addition, increased volatility in many financial markets led to a demand on the part of many market participants for new vehicles by which they could leverage their investments in financial instruments. Both in principle and in practice, futures and options satisfy all of these demands.

Because futures and options have become such an important part of the financial markets in the United States, a basic understanding of how these instruments work has become essential for anyone who intends to participate in the market. It is important to understand these markets not simply because it may be profitable to make use of them, but also because these markets are a critical part of a major transformation of the financial marketplace in the United States. During much of the post-war era in the United States many of the risks involved in financial transactions were shifted to various types of financial intermediaries, particularly the risk of fluctuations in market interest rates. However, as the volatility of interest rates has increased and as the financial institutions have changed, their risk-bearing role has been altered. Options and futures markets represent new vehicles for redistributing risks so that they can be borne more efficiently.

This chapter presents an introduction to how options and futures markets work and how risks are priced in these markets. However, the material presented here is only a very modest introduction to this fascinating but complicated topic. Options and futures are a growth industry in finance. They will be more rather than less important in the future.   ■

How options and futures work

DEFINITION OF TERMS

A **contingent claim** is a financial claim whose price depends or is contingent upon the price of another underlying security.

A **futures contract** is a commitment to provide or deliver a specific asset at a prespecified price and time.

A **call option** is a right to buy, and a **put option** is a right to sell an asset at a prespecified price.

The **strike price** of an option is the price at which the option can be exercised.

A **European option** can be exercised only at maturity. An **American option** can be exercised any time prior to maturity.

First of all it is helpful to define the terms we will be using. A **contingent claim** is a financial claim whose price depends or is contingent upon the price of another underlying asset. One example of a contingent claim is a futures contract. A **futures contract** constitutes a commitment to provide or deliver a specific asset at a prespecified price and time. In principle, in order to honor this commitment the asset involved would have to be purchased (or sold) at the market price prevailing when the commitment expires. Hence, a futures contract is a bet about the prevailing market price of the asset in question. The current value of the futures contract should depend on the available information about the future price of the underlying asset. A futures contract involves an obligation rather than an option. The obligation in the contract must be honored at its maturity or bought out for an appropriate price prior to maturity.

By contrast, an **option** on a financial instrument provides a choice to the holder of the option. The choice depends upon whether you have purchased the right to buy the underlying asset, referred to as a **call option,** or the right to sell it, referred to as a **put option.** The price at which the option may be exercised is called the **exercise** or **strike price.** Options are limited to a specific time period or maturity. Some options may be exercised only at maturity. These are known as **European options.** Other options may be exercised any time prior to maturity. These are known as **American options.**

The value of a call option, for example, derives from the fact that the holder may be able to exercise the option at a time when the value of the underlying security is greater than the strike or exercise price. For example, suppose you hold a European call option on an equity security with an exercise price of $50. If at maturity, the value of the underlying asset is greater than $50, then the proceeds you will receive from the exercise of the option will be equal to the difference between the value of the underlying asset and $50:

$$\text{Proceeds from exercise} = \text{Value of the asset} - \$50.$$

If the value of the asset is $75, then you have earned $25. On the other hand, if the value of the underlying asset is less than $50 at maturity, then the option will be worthless. As a result, the value of the call option at maturity will be equal to the difference between the value of the underlying security and the exercise price or zero, whichever is greater. This is illustrated in panel A of Figure 4–1. The vertical axis of this figure illustrates the value of the call option at maturity, while the horizontal axis shows the value of the underlying security at maturity.

Once you understand how a call option works it is relatively simple to understand a put option. The put represents an option to sell rather than buy the asset. If the value of the underlying asset is less than the exercise price at maturity, then the put option is equal to the difference between the exercise price and the value of the underlying security. Conversely, if the value of the underlying security exceeds the exercise price, then the put option is worthless. For example, if the exercise price of a put option is $50 and the price of the underlying security at maturity is $30, then the put is worth $20 at maturity. The relationship between the value of the put at maturity and the value of the underlying security is illustrated in panel B of Figure 4–1.

Figure 4–1 illustrates that the proceeds from an option always assume the form of the maximum of either zero or, in the case of a put, the difference between the exercise price and the price of the underlying asset. Hence, the proceeds from an option are never negative. This is inherent in the definition of an option, for the holder of the option can always choose not to exercise if the proceeds would be negative from so doing.

By contrast, the proceeds from a futures contract may well be negative. In effect, in a futures contract there is no option to refrain from exercising at maturity. The futures contract represents a commitment to deliver a financial instrument at a prearranged price and time. For example, suppose the futures contract requires that the holder of the contract must purchase the underlying asset at a price of $50 at maturity. This is referred to as a **long position** in the futures market. Then if the market price of the asset is greater than $50, the proceeds are equal to the difference between the market price and $50. However, if the price of the asset is less than $50, the proceeds are still determined in the same way. They are still the difference between the market price and $50. This is illustrated in panel C of Figure 4–1. The diagonal line in this panel shows that the proceeds are zero if the market price is equal to the contract price and increases and decreases proportionately with the market value of the asset.

Finally, consider the case of a **short position** in the futures market, or a commitment to sell the underlying asset at a prespecified price. As in the previous case, the payoffs will be symmetrical around the contract price of $50. However, now the holder of the futures contract will gain if the market price is below the contract price and will lose if it is above the contract price. This is illustrated in panel D of Figure 4–1.

A **long position** in a future involves the commitment or option to buy the underlying asset.

A **short position** in a future involves the commitment to sell the underlying asset.

FIGURE 4–1
Gross payoffs on options and futures.

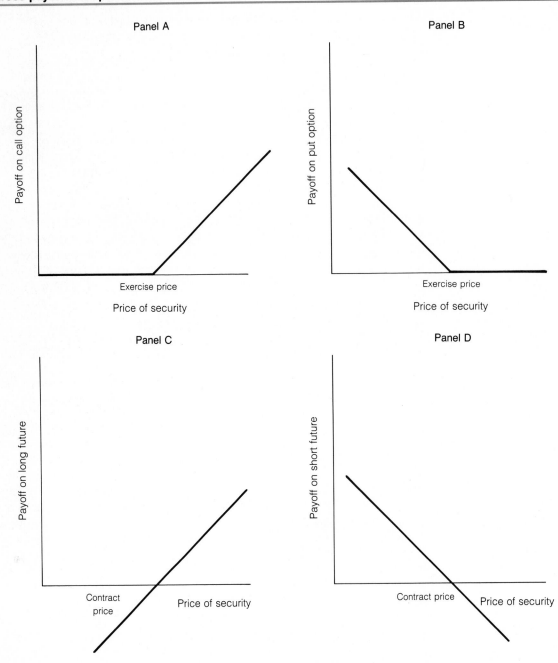

UNDERSTANDING FUTURES AND OPTIONS PRICE QUOTES

Before getting involved in the technicalities of how options and futures are used and how they are valued, it is important to see how the prices on these contingent claims are reported in the financial press. Figure 4–2 presents some selected options and futures quotations from the *Wall Street Journal*. The futures prices pertain to Treasury bonds, notes, and bills as well as foreign currencies. The options pertain to a selection of traded equity securities on the Chicago Board Options Exchange (CBOE). We will discuss exchanges as well as the procedures for trading both options and futures in Chapter 21.

Consider the futures quotations first. Price quotes for various futures contracts traded on June 2, 1986, are shown in panel A of Figure 4–2. Futures contracts in Treasury bills are listed for four months of the year: March, June, September, and December. These dates refer to the delivery or maturity dates of the contracts. To see how prices are quoted consider the June Treasury bill future listed in the first line of the relevant section of panel A of Figure 4–2. Reading across the page the first price quoted is the opening price for that day of trading. Next the high and low prices for the day are shown. Finally, the **settlement price** is listed. This is the closing price for that trading day. Next the change in price from opening to closing is shown as well as the discount interest rate and the change in this rate. (See Chapter 2 for a discussion of the discount rate.) The last column reports the **open interest,** which is the total number of March futures contracts outstanding at the end of the day. Note that each contract is for $1 million.

Panel B of Figure 4–2 shows prices prevailing on June 2, 1986, for options on selected equity securities. The first column in the table shows the closing price of the underlying security on the New York Stock Exchange. The second column shows the various strike or exercise prices for which option contracts are trading in that stock. The next three columns show the prices of call options maturing in June, July, and October corresponding to each exercise or strike price. The final three columns show the prices of put options maturing in June, July, and October corresponding to each exercise or strike price.

The price of the call options shown in this table are prices of the right to buy the underlying security at the specified exercise price. There is no directly comparable price for futures contracts. Futures contracts trade at only one contract price while options trade at a variety of distinct exercise prices, as illustrated in the options quotations shown in Figure 4–2. Therefore, the contract price quoted in the market for a futures contract has a special significance compared to the exercise price on an options contract. The significance is that the contract price is the market's best forecast of the future price of Treasury bills; that is, it is the contract price where there is no incentive for the market as a whole to switch from a short to a long position or vice versa. If there were put and call options on the same Treasury bill where there is a futures contract, the contract price on the Treasury bill future would be the exercise price on the options where the price of the put would be exactly the same as the price of the call. To see why this is true let's explore the relationship between options and futures in more detail.

The **settlement price** is the closing price at the end of the trading day.

Open interest is the total number of futures contracts outstanding.

FIGURE 4–2
Futures and options prices.

Panel A

– FINANCIAL –

BRITISH POUND (IMM) – 25,000 pounds; $ per pound

	Open	High	Low	Settle	Chg	High	Low	Open Interest
June	1.4680	1.4815	1.4670	1.4745	+ .0025	1.5525	1.15 ?	25,30?
Sept	1.4595	1.4715	1.4575	1.4650	+ .0025	1.5430	1.3240	4,818
Dec	1.4575	1.4650	1.4505	1.4565	+ .0025	1.5360	1.3250	460

Est vol 6,624; vol Fri 11,371; open int 30,584, –1,645.

CANADIAN DOLLAR (IMM) – 100,000 dlrs.; $ per Can $

	Open	High	Low	Settle	Chg	High	Low	Open Interest
June	.7198	.7217	.7164	.7171	–.0059	.7360	.6845	9,085
Sept	.7168	.7186	.7125	.7137	–.0066	.7305	.6809	4,713
Dec	.7150	.7155	.7095	.7102	–.0073	.7285	.6790	875
Mar87	.7131	.7131	.7072	.7032	–.0111	.7256	.6770	277

Est vol 5,030; vol Fri 3,724; open int 14,977, –458.

JAPANESE YEN (IMM) 12.5 million yen; $ per yen (.00)

	Open	High	Low	Settle	Chg	High	Low	Open Interest
June	.5701	.5748	.5690	.5729	–.0008	.6245	.4220	31,901
Sept	.5732	.5781	.5722	.5762	–.0006	.6280	.4690	5,610
Dec	.5760	.5810	.5760	.5800	–.0003	.6320	.4720	849

Est vol 19,497; vol Fri 22,712; open int 38,363, –1,336.

SWISS FRANC (IMM) – 125,000 francs-$ per franc

	Open	High	Low	Settle	Chg	High	Low	Open Interest
June	.5178	.5224	.5164	.5209	+.0035	.5580	.4190	24,204
Sept	.5205	.5253	.5194	.5239	+.0036	.5625	.4790	5,957
Dec	.5280	.5290	.5238	.5275	+.0035	.5660	.4878	598

Est vol 23,984; vol Fri 24,986; open int 30,766, –124.

W. GERMAN MARK (IMM) – 125,000 marks; $ per mark

	Open	High	Low	Settle	Chg	High	Low	Open Interest
June	.4294	.4325	.4286	.4314	+.0005	.4648	.3335	50,019
Sept	.4319	.4353	.4312	.4340	+.0006	.4675	.3762	8,110
Dec	.4338	.4375	.4338	.4366	+.0005	.4703	.4090	340

Est vol 27,927; vol Fri 27,016; open int 58,486, +2,450.

EURODOLLAR (LIFFE) – $1 million; pts of 100%

	Open	High	Low	Settle	Chg	High	Low	Open Interest
June	92.93	92.96	92.91	92.92	....	93.72	87.64	6,113
Sept	92.84	92.88	92.79	92.79	– .06	93.78	89.06	8,605
Dec	92.71	92.72	92.65	92.64	– .08	93.67	90.20	4,074
Mar87	92.48	92.48	92.43	92.39	– .10	93.46	90.80	1,980
June			92.08	– .10		93.15	90.85	580
Sept			91.80	– .10		92.95	91.99	210
Dec			91.54	– .11				108

Est vol 2,611; vol Fri 3,957; open int 21,769, +96.

STERLING (LIFFE) – £500,000; pts of 100%

	Open	High	Low	Settle	Chg	High	Low	Open Interest
June	90.20	90.30	90.20	90.26	+ .02	90.88	86.94	4,053
Sept	90.70	90.85	90.70	90.81	+ .06	91.49	87.53	5,590
Dec	90.94	91.03	90.94	90.98	+ .02	91.63	87.88	3,313
Mar87	90.95	91.04	90.95	90.98	....	91.63	88.00	2,186
June			90.91	– .02		91.45	90.08	1,202
Sept			90.70	– .02		91.30	90.48	883

Est vol 1,356; vol Fri 2,173; open int 17,289, –402.

LONG GILT (LIFFE) – £50,000; 32nds of 100%

	Open	High	Low	Settle	Chg	High	Low	Open Interest
June	123-07	123-13	123-00	123-04	– 0-14	130-03	108-00	3,078
Sept	123-11	123-24	123-03	123-06	– 0-15	130-10	123-03	10,975

Est vol 4,363; vol Fri 7,489; open int 14,253, –57.

EURODOLLAR (IMM) – $1 million; pts of 100%

	Open	High	Low	Settle	Chg	Yield Settle	Chg	Open Interest
June	92.96	92.96	92.85	92.86	–.07	7.14	+ .07	47,298
Sept	92.85	92.88	92.66	92.67	–.17	7.33	+ .17	63,812
Dec	92.69	92.71	92.47	92.47	–.17	7.53	+ .20	24,463
Mr87	92.45	92.45	92.20	92.20	–.21	7.80	+ .21	14,183
June	92.13	92.13	91.86	91.87	–.23	8.13	+ .23	8,953
Sept	91.82	91.84	91.52	91.55	–.26	8.45	+ .26	6,443
Dec	91.54	91.57	91.27	91.27	–.27	8.73	+ .27	4,259
Mr88	91.31	91.31	91.01	91.01	–.28	8.99	+ .28	4,477

Est vol 50,658; vol Fri 45,098; open int 173,888, +1,048.

U.S. DOLLAR INDEX (CTN) 500 times USDX

	Open	High	Low	Settle	Chg	High	Low	Open Interest
June	118.15	118.35	117.20	117.65	....	128.93	110.61	1,619
Sept	118.20	118.44	117.32	117.85	+ .10	129.00	110.71	1,510
Dec				117.85	+ .10	129.05	110.72	183

Est vol 750; vol Fri 796; open int 3,341, –55.
The index: High 118.03; Low 117.15; Close 117.49 –.02

TREASURY BONDS (CBT) – $100,000; pts. 32nds of 100%

	Open	High	Low	Settle	Chg	Yield Settle	Chg	Open Interest
June	93-29	94-17	91-26	91-30	– 62	8.868	+ .219	61,205
Sept	93-06	93-24	90-30	91-04	– 63	8.962	+ .225	124,232
Dec	92-15	92-31	90-07	90-12	– 63	9.050	+ .228	11,106
Mr87	91-22	92-04	89-14	89-20	– 62	9.139	+ .228	4,048
June	91-09	91-09	88-24	88-28	– 62	9.229	+ .231	3,356
Sept	90-19	90-19	88-06	88-06	– 62	9.313	+ .234	2,289
Dec	89-31	89-31	87-18	87-18	– 62	9.399	+ .236	1,175
Mr88	89-13	89-13	87-00	87-00	– 62	9.460	+ .239	1,148
June			86-16	– 62		9.522	+ .240	648
Sept	87-23	87-23	86-02	86-02	– 62	9.578	+ .242	206
Dec	87-00	87-00	85-22	85-22	– 62	9.626	+ .244	290

Est vol 300,000; vol Fri 293,299; open int 209,703, –818.

TREASURY NOTES (CBT) – $100,000; pts. 32nds of 100%

	Open	High	Low	Settle	Chg	Yield Settle	Chg	Open Interest
June	97-28	98-04	96-04	96-06	– 49	8.575	+ .234	20,300
Sept	96-30	97-07	95-02	95-06	– 51	8.731	+ .247	53,177
Dec	95-20	95-21	94-10	94-11	– 54	8.865	+ .265	799
Mr87			93-17	– 60		8.994	+ .282	270

Est vol 36,000; vol Fri 36,338; open int 74,546, +2,189.

TREASURY BILLS (IMM) – $1 mil.; pts. of 100%

	Open	High	Low	Settle	Chg	Discount Settle	Chg	Open Interest
June	93.72	93.74	93.60	93.61	–.10	6.39	+ .10	11,959
Sept	93.76	93.79	93.56	93.57	–.20	6.43	+ .20	20,791
Dec	93.70	93.72	93.47	93.48	–.21	6.52	+ .21	5,066
Mr87	93.41	93.50	93.26	93.27	–.21	6.73	+ .21	916
June	93.23	93.23	92.99	93.00	–.22	7.00	+ .22	684
Sept	92.97	92.97	92.72	92.72	–.24	7.28	+ .24	326
Dec	92.71	92.72	92.46	92.46	–.25	7.54	+ .25	120

Est vol 12,117; vol Fri 10,006; open int 39,882, +486.

LONG VERSUS SHORT POSITIONS IN OPTIONS

The simplest relationship between various options and futures contracts is the relationship between the person who buys or takes a long position in either a put or a call and the person who "writes" or takes a short position in the option. The payoffs received by the purchaser and the writer of an option always net out to zero. That is, the owner's gain is the writer's loss and vice versa. To see this suppose we return to the call option with an exercise price of $50. If the value of the underlying security at maturity is $75, then the option will be exercised by its owner for a gain of $25. This gain occurs at the expense of the writer of the option whose loss is equal to $25. The payoffs to the writer of the call option are illustrated in panel A of Figure 4–3. The figure shows that as long as the price of the underlying asset is equal to or less than the exercise price of the option, then the writer of the call receives a payoff of zero. If the price of the underlying asset at the maturity of the option is greater than the exercise price, then the loss in-

Panel B

CHICAGO BOARD

Option & NY Close	Strike Price	Calls–Last Jun	Calls–Last Jul	Calls–Last Oct	Puts–Last Jun	Puts–Last Jul	Puts–Last Oct
Amrtch	115	r	11 3/4	r	r	r	r
125 3/4	120	7	7 1/4	r	r	7/8	r
125 3/4	125	2 3/4	r	r	r	r	r
125 3/4	130	r	1 1/4	3 1/4	r	r	r
Atl R	45	s	r	r	s	1/16	r
55 1/2	50	r	6	r	1/16	r	1
55 1/2	55	1 3/8	2 3/8	3 5/8	1 1/4	1 1/4	3
55 1/2	60	r	3/8	1 3/8	r	r	r
BankAm	12 1/2	s	4 1/4	4 1/2	s	r	r
16 7/8	15	r	2 1/8	2 3/4	1/16	1/8	11/16
16 7/8	17 1/2	3/16	11/16	1 1/2	15/16	1	1 11/16
16 7/8	20	1/16	1/4	5/8	r	3 3/8	r
BellAtl	60	r	7 1/2	r	r	r	5/8
67 3/4	62 1/2	s	5 1/2	6 1/2	s	r	r
67 3/4	65	2 3/4	2 3/4	4 3/4	3/8	1	r
67 3/4	70	1/2	7/8	2	r	r	r
Citicp	50	r	r	r	r	1/16	3/8
61 5/8	55	r	7	r	r	5/16	r
61 5/8	60	2 1/4	3 1/2	r	11/16	1 1/4	2 3/4
61 5/8	65	r	1	2 1/2	3 3/8	r	r
Cullin	12 1/2	3 3/4	4	4 1/4	r	r	1/2
16 3/8	15	1 7/16	1 3/4	2 3/4	1/4	9/16	1 1/4
16 3/8	17 1/2	1/4	1/2	1 7/16	r	r	2 1/4
16 3/8	20	s	1/4	s	s	r	s
Delta	40	r	r	6	1/16	r	15/16
44 1/2	45	5/8	1 1/2	3	1 3/8	1 3/4	r
44 1/2	50	1/16	3/8	r	r	r	r
EKodak	45	s	r	15 3/4	s	r	r
59 5/8	50	s	10	r	s	1/8	5/8
59 5/8	55	4 1/2	5 5/8	6 7/8	1/8	1/2	1 11/16
59 5/8	60	1 3/16	2 3/8	4 1/8	1 7/16	2 1/4	3 5/8
59 5/8	65	1/4	3/4	2 1/8	5	5 1/2	r
Exxon	50	s	r	r	s	1/16	1/4
59 3/4	55	5 3/4	5 7/8	6 1/8	1/16	3/16	11/16
59 3/4	60	3/4	1 5/8	2 7/8	1	1 3/4	2 3/4
59 3/4	65	r	1/4	1	r	r	r
FedExp	50	s	12 1/2	s	s	r	s
61 1/2	55	7 3/8	8	r	1/16	1/2	r
61 1/2	60	2 3/4	3 5/8	6 1/4	1	1 5/8	3
61 1/2	65	5/16	1 1/2	3 3/4	r	4 1/4	5 1/2
61 1/2	70	1/16	1/2	r	r	r	r
61 1/2	75	s	1/8	r	s	r	r
Grumm	25	4 3/4	r	r	r	r	r
29 3/8	30	3/8	1	2 3/8	r	1 1/2	r
29 3/8	35	r	1/4	r	r	r	r
Halbtn	20	r	r	r	1/8	1/2	r
21 1/2	25	r	3/16	5/8	r	3 1/2	4
21 1/2	22 1/2	1/4	1/2	1 1/4	r	r	r
Homstk	17 1/2	r	5 1/4	r	r	r	1/4
22 5/8	20	2 1/2	3 1/8	3 1/2	1/16	5/16	7/8
22 5/8	22 1/2	r	1 1/8	2 1/8	9/16	7/8	r
22 5/8	25	1/16	3/8	7/8	r	2 1/2	2 15/16
22 5/8	30	s	1/16	r	s	r	r
I B M	130	s	23 1/2	s	s	1/16	s
152 1/2	135	s	19 5/8	s	s	3/16	s
152 1/2	140	12 5/8	13 3/4	17 1/4	1/8	1/2	1 15/16
152 1/2	145	8 1/2	10	13	5/16	1 3/8	3
152 1/2	150	4 3/8	6 1/2	10	1 5/16	2 11/16	5
152 1/2	155	1 13/16	3 7/8	7 1/4	3 3/4	5 1/8	7 1/4
152 1/2	160	1/2	1 15/16	5 3/8	7 1/4	8	10
152 1/2	165	1/8	1 1/16	3 3/4	12 3/4	12 1/4	12 3/4
In Pap	50	r	r	r	r	1/16	r
62 1/2	55	r	7 7/8	r	1/16	5/16	r
62 1/2	60	3 1/4	r	5 3/4	5/8	1 1/2	3
62 1/2	65	1/2	1 5/8	3 1/4	r	r	r
LAC	15	s	1 5/8	2	s	r	r
15 5/8	17 1/2	s	r	1 1/4	s	r	r
M M M	90	s	16 1/4	r	s	r	r
105 3/8	95	r	12	r	r	3/8	r
105 3/8	100	6 1/8	7 7/8	11 3/4	3/8	1 1/4	2 3/4
105 3/8	105	2	4 3/8	8	1 3/4	3	r
105 3/8	110	3/4	2 1/8	4 7/8	4	r	7 1/4
105 3/8	115	3/16	1 1/8	3 1/4	r	r	r
Pepsi	25	s	8 1/4	r	s	r	r
33 5/8	26 5/8	r	7	r	r	1/8	r
33 5/8	28 3/8	5	5	6 5/8	r	1/8	7/16
33 5/8	30	3 1/2	4	5 3/8	1/16	1/4	1
33 5/8	31 5/8	2 1/16	2 7/8	4	3/16	9/16	r
33 5/8	33 3/8	7/8	1 7/8	3 1/4	3/4	1 1/4	2 1/4
33 5/8	35	5/8	1 1/4	2 5/8	r	2 1/4	r
33 5/8	40	r	7/16	1 1/8	r	r	r
Polar	45	s	24	s	s	r	s
66 3/8	50	s	r	r	s	1/16	r
66 3/8	55	r	12	r	r	1/4	r
66 3/8	60	r	7	11 1/4	1/4	9/16	2 3/16
66 3/8	65	2 1/2	3 7/8	8	1 1/2	2 1/4	4
66 3/8	70	1/2	2 1/4	4 3/4	3	5	6 1/2
66 3/8	75	s	1 1/8	3	s	r	r
Sperry	50	r	24 7/8	r	r	1/16	r
74 3/4	55	19 7/8	20	20 1/4	r	r	r
74 3/4	60	15 1/8	r	r	1/16	1/16	r
74 3/4	65	r	10 1/4	r	1/16	1/8	r
74 3/4	70	5 1/8	5 1/8	5 3/4	1/16	5/16	3/4
74 3/4	75	5/16	3/4	2	1	1 3/8	1 7/8
74 3/4	80	r	r	1/16	r	r	r
Teldyn	280	s	r	s	s	3/16	s
339 7/8	320	r	r	r	r	1 7/8	5
339 7/8	330	15 1/4	r	r	1 1/2	3 1/2	r
339 7/8	340	6 1/4	11 1/4	r	4 1/2	8 1/4	r
339 7/8	350	2 1/2	7 1/2	r	9	11 3/4	r
339 7/8	360	5/8	4 3/4	r	r	r	r
339 7/8	370	7/16	3	10	r	r	r
339 7/8	380	s	1	r	s	r	r

Source: *Wall Street Journal,* June 3, 1986, pp. 48 and 54.

curred by the writer of the option is equal to the difference between the value of the underlying security and the exercise price.

The same relationship holds between the owner and the writer of a put option. The owner of a put chooses not to exercise if the price of the underlying asset exceeds the exercise price. In this case the payoff to both the owner and the writer of the put is zero. However, if the market price of the underlying asset is less than the exercise price, then the owner of the put will choose to exercise and his or her gain will be exactly equal to the loss of the writer of the put. The gross payoff to the writer of the put is illustrated in panel B of Figure 4–3.

It is apparent from Figure 4–3 that the writer of either a put or a call can never have a positive gross payoff as a result of the exercise of an option. Therefore, no rational investor will ever write an option without being paid to do so. The price for an option will be set so that all investors believe that the net payoff from writing an option represents a fair gamble. The net payoff received by the

FIGURE 4-3
Net payoffs on options.

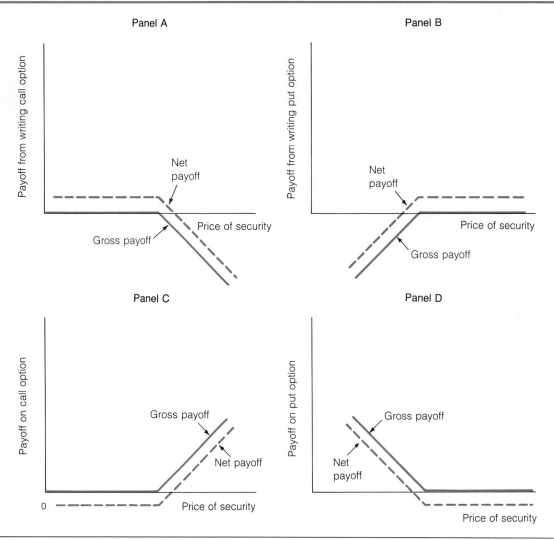

writer of an option is the sum of the price initially paid the writer for the option plus the payoff described above. The nature of the net payoffs to the writer of a call and put is illustrated by the dashed lines in all four panels in Figure 4–3. The dashed lines are derived by adding the price of the call or the put to the payoff illustrated by the solid line in each panel. Panels C and D in the figure show the gross and net payoff to the holder of a put and a call option. Thus far we have not learned how the price of an option is actually determined; we will examine this topic at the end of the chapter.

AN EXAMPLE OF PAYOFFS ON OPTIONS

In order to understand how options work it is very helpful to work through an example of the gains and losses that might result from changes in the value of the underlying security for each of the four basic possible positions in options contracts. The four positions include buying (long) or writing (short) in either a put or a call. We will enumerate these as follows:

Position 1—buy (long) a call
Position 2—write (short) a call
Position 3—buy (long) a put
Position 4—write (short) a put.

Suppose we are considering an option in the Volatile Circuits company which has puts and calls available with an exercise price of $25 per share. The price of the call is 75 cents per share and the price of the put is $1.75 per share. Since option contracts are written for 100 shares of the underlying security, if you buy a call, for example, you will have to pay the writer of the call $75 when the call is purchased. We want to see what your payoff will be if the price of the underlying security is greater or less than the exercise price for each of the four positions described. Therefore, we will consider three possible values for the underlying security at the maturity date of the option. The three values are $21, $25, and $27 per share. Table 4–1 defines the net payoffs—that is the gain or loss when the option is exercised—plus the value paid or received when the option was written, for each of the combinations of positions and prices of the underlying security at the maturity of the option. Let's start with the case where the price of the underlying security is $25.

Case A—Price = $25. In this case neither the put nor the call option can be exercised for a profit. As a result, the purchasers of both the put and the call will allow the option to expire at maturity. They will be out the initial cost of the option, $75 for the call and $175 for the put. The purchaser's loss is the writer's gain, so that the writer of the call experiences a net gain of $75 and the writer of the put experiences a net loss of $175.

Case B—Price = $21. In this case the call option cannot be exercised at a profit, so the owner of the call will allow it to expire. The net payoff for the purchaser and the writer of the call is identical to their payoffs in the case where the price at maturity was $25. However, the put option does have value since the exercise price exceeds the stock price by $4 per share; this means the put option can be exercised for a gain of $400. The net gain to the purchaser of the put is the difference between $400 and the price initially paid for the option of $175. Thus the net gain is $225. Once again, the gain for the purchaser of the put is the same as the loss for the writer of the put, so that the writer loses $225.

Case C—Price = $27. In this case the put option has no value at maturity, just like the call option in Case B. Therefore, the owner of the put will allow it to expire and will incur a net loss of $175. The writer of the put will have a net gain of $175. On the other hand, the call option has a value at maturity of $200. Therefore, the purchaser of the call will experience a net gain of $200 less the initial cost of the call of $75 or $125. Once again, the purchaser's gain on the call must be the same as the writer's loss, so the writer's net loss is also $125.

This example shows how investors in long and short positions in both calls and puts determine their net payoffs. The payoffs here are identical to those illustrated in Figure 4–2. Understanding the numbers and how to use the diagrams shown in Figures 4–1 and 4–2 is extremely important. If you master these ideas, options will become an important element in your knowledge of modern finance.

TABLE 4–1
Option payoffs at various stock prices.

Position	Price of Underlying Security at Maturity		
	$21	$25	$27
1. Buy call	−75	−75	125
2. Write call	75	75	−125
3. Buy put	225	−175	−175
4. Write put	−225	175	175

THE RELATIONSHIP BETWEEN OPTIONS AND FUTURES

Next let's consider the relationship between options and futures contracts. The most important distinction between an option and a future is that there is a symmetrical payoff with a futures contract whereas there is an asymmetrical payoff with an option. The nature of the symmetry refers to the pattern of payoffs around the exercise price for the option or the contract price for the future. This symmetry was apparent in Figure 4–1. There is no kink in the line describing the payoff for a futures contract. The owner of a (long) future gains if the market price at maturity is above the contract price and loses if it is below. With an option, the owner of either a put or a call never has a negative payoff. Hence, the payoff is not symmetrical around the exercise price.

This difference in symmetry between options and futures suggests that it might be possible to combine options in such a way that the payoff to a futures contract can be perfectly mimicked. In fact, this is quite easy to do. Suppose we consider a put, a call, and a futures contract on the same underlying asset all with the same exercise or contract price and maturity date. By inspecting Figures 4–1 and 4–3 we can see how to combine the put and the call to duplicate the payoff of the futures contract. If we buy the call, we will have duplicated the payoff to the futures contract if the market price of the underlying asset is above the exercise price at maturity. If we write the put, we will have duplicated the payoff to the futures contract if the market price of the underlying asset is below the exercise price at maturity. Therefore, by combining these two actions payoffs must be identical to those in the futures contract. This is called *put-call parity*. For example, Table 4–2 shows the payoffs to each of these contracts for alternative values of the market price of the underlying asset where the exercise price is $50. The table illustrates that the difference between the payoffs from the call and the put are equal to the payoffs from the futures contract. We can summarize this relationship as follows:

Value of a call − Value of a put = Value of a (long) future.

A similar relationship also holds for a short position in a futures contract—that is, a commitment to sell an asset at a prespecified price and time. A short position in a futures contract is the opposite of a long position in that the payoff in the long position is simply the negative of the payoff in the short position. Therefore, the payoff to the short futures contract can be duplicated by buying a put and writing a call or:

Value of a put − Value of a call = Value of a (short) future.

There is another important distinction between futures and options, in addition to the difference in symmetry of the payoffs. This distinction is a result of the way futures and options contracts are structured. The "price" quoted on a futures contract, as illustrated in Figure 4–2, is an index of the contract price at which

TABLE 4-2
Payoff on contingent claims with an exercise price of $50.

Price of Security	Call	Put	Future (long)
100	50	0	50
90	40	0	40
80	30	0	30
70	20	0	20
60	10	0	10
50	0	0	0
40	0	10	−10
30	0	20	−20
20	0	30	−30
10	0	40	−40
0	0	50	−50

the buyer or seller of the future is obligated to trade the underlying asset when the futures contract matures. (We will discuss the index in Chapter 21.) The market determines an equilibrium contract price for each futures contract at each point in time, and that is the only contract price available. By comparison, in the options market a variety of exercise prices is generally available for each security on which options are traded. Then, for each exercise price, the options market determines the equilibrium ''price'' or value of the option today. For example, Figure 4-2 shows there are three different exercise prices for call options on Bank of America and the prices of the calls decrease as the exercise price increases.

Given this difference in the way futures and options are structured, it might not appear to make sense to say the value of a call less the value of a put is equal to the value of a long future. The problem here is that the value of the futures traded in the market is implicitly always zero. To take a position in the futures market you do not have to pay a positive (or negative) price for the futures contract; in practice you do not have to put up cash to take a position in the futures market. Other than commissions or transactions costs, it doesn't cost anything. Your broker may require that you have access to cash or that you deposit funds in an account with the brokerage house to cover future losses if they occur. (We will discuss the margin requirement in Chapter 21.) But the cost of the future the day you buy it is still zero. The futures market is setting a contract price so that the fair value of the future today is zero. The next day the market will set a new contract price that may be higher or lower than the prevailing one. If you have a futures position and the price moves against you, you will have to settle your loss on a daily basis; this means that you must put up enough cash to cover your loss. However, once again, the cost of acquiring the futures position that day is still zero.

We can see from the relationship between futures and options that at the equilibrium contract price for the future, the value of the call must equal the value of the put, since their difference must equal zero. There will always be an exercise or contract price for which this is true. But options may be traded at any exercise price, not necessarily this particular one, while futures will be traded at only one contract price.

Finally we will consider the relationships between the payoffs on options and futures and the payoffs from owning the underlying asset directly. First, let's discuss the relationship between the futures contract and the underlying asset. The payoffs from a long position in the futures contract and from owning the underlying asset are illustrated in Figure 4–4. The lines that define these payoffs have the same slope, but they have different intercepts. We can duplicate the payoff in the futures contract simply by shifting the payoff line for the asset to the right, or by decreasing its intercept, by an amount equal to the contract or exercise price of the futures contract. This simply reflects the definition of the payoff on the futures contract, which is equal to

$$\begin{array}{ccc} \text{Payoff on the} \\ \text{future} \end{array} = \begin{array}{c} \text{Price of the} \\ \text{asset} \end{array} - \begin{array}{c} \text{Contract price} \\ \text{of the future.} \end{array}$$

FIGURE 4–4
Payoff on future and underlying security.

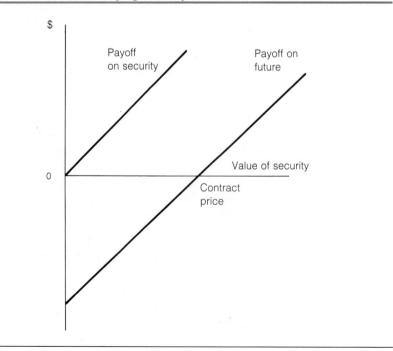

This implies that the relationship between the current values of these assets must be as follows:

Value of the future = Value of the asset
— Present value of the futures
contract price.

Since the payment of the contract price at maturity is risk free, the present value is calculated with the risk-free interest rate.

We can now make use of this relationship to examine the relationship between the value of options and the value of an investment in the underlying security. Specifically, we can substitute this expression for the value of a (long) futures contract into our previous expression for the relationship between options and futures:

Value of call = Value of (long) future = Value of asset
— Value of put   — Present value of
exercise price.

This expression may not be very intuitive at this juncture, so it is important to consider a simple example that illustrates the meaning of this relationship. Suppose you want to buy a particular share of stock but you don't have any cash. However, you do know that you will receive $50 in six months. One possibility is that you could borrow the present value of $50 and invest in the stock. What will your payoff be at the end of six months if you do this? It will be the value of the stock less $50. If we define $50 as the exercise price on an option, this payoff is identical to the payoff on the right-hand side of the above expression. How could we duplicate this payoff using options? We could buy a call and write a put both with the exercise price of $50. Our payoff is then the difference between the price of the underlying asset six months from now and $50.

VIEWING ASSETS THROUGH THE OPTIONS FRAMEWORK

Many financial instruments that at first glance might not appear to be options actually turn out to be so under close examination. This is one reason the topic is so interesting and useful. Once you recognize that a financial instrument is an option, it is often helpful to evaluate it with the methods of option pricing.

We will examine only one example of an asset that turns out to be an option, but this may be the most important example. The most obvious and widely used options are options on equity shares or stock of companies. However, the equity shares themselves are also options. They are options on the assets of the firm. More specifically, equity shares are call options on the assets of the firm. The exercise price of this call option is the amount borrowed from debtholders. If, at the maturity date for this debt, the value of the assets of the firm exceeds the obligation to debtholders, then the option will have a value equal to this difference. On the other hand, if the value of the firm's assets is less than the outstanding obligations to debtholders, then the option will expire worthless.

Using what we have already learned about options, we can also describe the position of debtholders. One way to view debt is that debtholders own the assets of the firm but have written a call on the firm to the stockholders. Therefore, the value of debt is equal to the value of the assets of the firm less the value of the call held by stockholders.

The debtholders' claim on the firm is illustrated in Figure 4–5, which uses the options diagram employed throughout this chapter to illustrate how debt can be described with options. The three panels in the figure illustrate the two alternative ways in which you can get to the same conclusion. The conclusion is shown in panel A. This panel describes the payoff from a debt instrument, a bond or a loan, in terms of the option diagram used in earlier figures in this chapter. In this case the underlying security shown on the horizontal axis is the value of the assets controlled by the firm. The exercise price is represented by the point labeled P on both axes. If the value of the assets is less than the payment promised to lenders, then the firm is bankrupt. In this event the lenders have the entire firm, so that the value of their claim moves up and down the 45-degree line in the figure. This is the value of debt at any value of the underlying assets less than P. If the value of the assets is greater than the promised payment to debtholders, then the debtholders still only get P. This is illustrated by the horizontal line emanating from point S in the figure. Therefore, the kinked line starting at the origin and going to point S, then becoming horizontal, defines the payoff to bondholders for all possible values of the assets of the firm.

FIGURE 4–5
Debt as an option on a firm's assets.

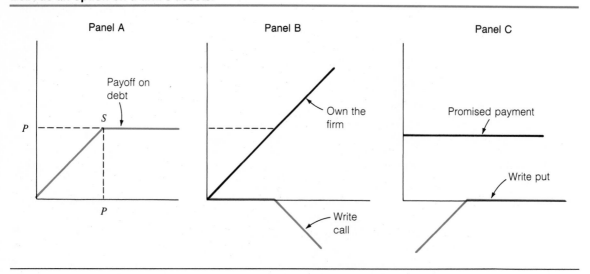

There are two ways to get to the conclusion shown in panel A of Figure 4–5 using options and the basic equilibrium relationship between puts and calls defined above. One way is to notice that the payoff described in panel A is equivalent to the payoff from owning the firm and writing a call with an exercise price equal to the promised payment to debtholders. These two claims are illustrated in panel B. One line shows the payoff to the writer of a call, just as in Figure 4–1. The other line shows the payoff to owning the underlying asset directly. When you add these two together you end up with panel A. Therefore, one way to view claims held by debtholders is that they own the assets of the firm but have written a call to stockholders with an exercise price equal to the promised payments from those stockholders.

There is another way to view the claims of debtholders using options. This alternative is shown in panel C. Debtholders also have a risk-free promised payment and have written a put option at an exercise price equal to the promised payment to debtholders. The risk-free payment is represented by the horizontal line in panel C. The other line in this panel is the payoff from writing a put. When these two are added together we also arrive at panel A.

We can justify the idea that these two characterizations of debt are equivalent by returning to the relationships between options and futures. We know from our discussion above that the following relationship always holds:

$$\text{Value of asset } = \text{ Value of call } - \text{ Value of put}$$
$$+ \text{ Present value of exercise price.}$$

We can use this relationship to derive the value of the debt:

$$\text{Value of debt } = \text{ Value of asset } - \text{ Value of call}$$
$$= \text{ Present value of exercise price}$$
$$- \text{ Value of put.}$$

Debtholders always receive the exercise price, which in this case is simply the contractual payment due bondholders. However, if the value of the assets of the firm is greater than the exercise price, then this is the total payoff to bondholders. On the other hand, if the value of the assets of the firm is less than the exercise price, then the put will be exercised and the bondholders will lose the difference between the exercise price and the value of the assets of the firm.

USES OF OPTIONS AND FUTURES

We have already noted that options and futures markets have experienced tremendous growth in the last decade. Apparently options and futures increase the alternative ways in which risk may be redistributed in society. But why are options and futures useful?

VIEWING LOCKHEED'S DEBT ISSUE AS AN OPTION

The securities of almost any company could be used to illustrate the idea that debt and equity can be viewed as options on the underlying assets of a company. Let's consider Lockheed as an example. On September 30, 1986, Lockheed had 49,095,000 shares of common stock outstanding. The closing price of Lockheed stock on that date was $44 ⅛, so the total value of Lockheed stock was $2.166 billion. This represents the value of a call option on Lockheed's assets. In order to know what the exercise price of this call option was we have to identify the book value of the outstanding Lockheed debt. We use book rather than market value because we want the actual obligation to debtholders. It is not always so easy to determine this for many companies that have a lot of different debt obligations outstanding with different provisions and maturity dates. In Lockheed's case we can simplify the matter by assuming that the total short-term assets of Lockheed just about offset its total short-term liabilities. Then we can count the book value of Lockheed's long-term debt as the exercise price of the option. The book value of long-term debt for Lockheed in September 1986 was approximately $500 million. Therefore, the exercise price for the call option represented by Lockheed's common stock is approximately $500 million.

Is the call on Lockheed's assets represented by its common stock very far in the money? One important clue is that the market value of Lockheed's outstanding long-term debt was virtually identical to its book value. This implies that the market rates Lockheed's probability of bankruptcy as very low. If we view the value of debt as the value of the promised payment less the value of the put option on Lockheed's assets, this suggests that the market is placing a very small value on this put option. Another way of saying this is that the call option represented by Lockheed's common stock is a deep-in-the-money option on Lockheed's assets. This is illustrated in Figure 4–6. This figure is just like panel A of Figure 4–5. It shows the payoffs to the debtholders depending on the values of Lockheed's assets, and the exercise price is $500 million. We have also drawn in a probability distribution for the value of Lockheed's assets. This is a subjective distribution because it merely guesses at what the market expects for Lockheed. It is drawn so that there is a very small chance that the value of the assets will be less than $500 million; this is what is meant when we say the call represented by the Lockheed common stock is deep-in-the-money.

FOR ACTING ON SPECIFIC INFORMATION

It appears that one of the greatest uses thus far of the new options contracts available in the United States is as a mechanism to speculate on the movements in prices of securities. Options provide a convenient way to make a leveraged investment in the underlying security. The fact that options can be used in this way follows directly from the relationship between the value of options and the value of the underlying security. By buying a call and writing a put, an investor takes the same position in a security as if he or she made a leveraged investment directly in the underlying asset. But by buying a call and writing a put, an investor also takes a position equivalent to purchasing a long futures contract in an asset. Hence, if the sole objective is to increase leverage in an asset, either futures or options are, in principle, equally attractive.

The unique attraction of options is that they provide more flexibility than futures. They allow an investor to take positions that are otherwise difficult or impossible to construct. The advantage arises from the asymmetrical nature of the

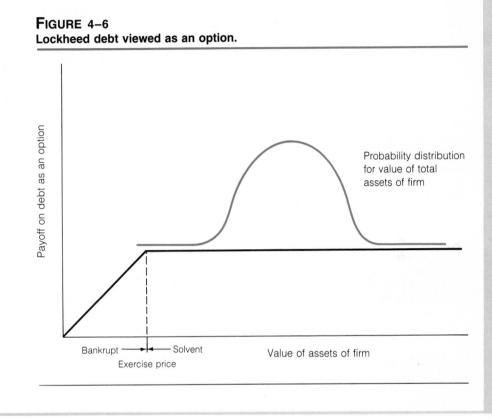

FIGURE 4–6
Lockheed debt viewed as an option.

Payoff on debt as an option

Probability distribution
for value of total
assets of firm

Bankrupt → ← Solvent

Exercise price

Value of assets of firm

option relative to the futures contract. This asymmetry is valuable if you have some specific information or belief about the direction of change of the price of an asset. An option provides a direct mechanism to place a bet on a specific direction of change in the asset price or even a specific range of the asset price. For example, if you think the price of a stock has a good chance of being greater than a specific value, say $100, you can purchase a call with an exercise price of $100. Without options markets there is no way you can make a specific bet on the price of an asset.

If you look closely at what types of investment positions you can take with options, you can construct ways to make almost any specific kind of bet you can imagine about the future performance of the value of an asset. For example, suppose you believed that the price of a specific asset would be exactly $30 six months from today. Using options you can construct an investment that pays you $1 if the price of the asset is exactly $30 and zero otherwise. The method for accomplishing this is called a *butterfly*. This particular butterfly would work as follows. Suppose that there are call options with one year to maturity that have exercise prices equal to every possible future stock price. Also, for simplicity, suppose the stock price can only assume integer values. Buy one call option with an exercise price of $29 and one call option with an exercise price of $31. Also write two call options with an exercise price of $30. Now let's see what happens at maturity. If the price at maturity is at or below $29, at maturity then all the options will be worthless, and the payoff will be zero. If the price is $31 or greater, the gain from the two long call options will exactly offset the loss on the two calls that were written at $30. If the price of the asset is precisely $30, both the $30 and the $31 option will be worthless, while the $29 option will have a payoff of $1. This example is only one of a wide range of possibilities.

A **complete market** is one in which every piece of information an investor might possess could be acted upon in the market with the available securities.

For a financial market options add to what economists call the market's **completeness.** To understand what a complete market is, imagine a market in which every possible investment outcome had an individual security associated with it. For example, there would be a security with a payoff of, say, $1 if the price of AT&T stock were precisely $112 one year from today and no payoff if the price assumed any other value. Such a security is called a *primitive security*. If a primitive security actually existed for every conceivable event or state of the world one could imagine, then the market would be complete. The attraction of a complete market is that every conceivable opinion or piece of information an investor might possess could be acted upon in the market with the available primitive securities. Real-world markets will never actually be complete. In fact, like any other product, new securities will develop when demand is sufficient for those securities. New securities are demanded when people want to make bets or act on information in ways that are not feasible with the available securities. Another way of putting it is that new securities arise because of a desire for a more complete market. Options accomplish precisely this purpose.

LIMITING RISK WITH OPTIONS

One of the most important uses of both futures and options is to hedge risks or to sell risks off to another party. Futures markets in commodities have been used for many years by various commodity producers to limit the risks of price fluctuations in the product they will have available for sale in the future. For example, a farmer who has planted a wheat crop may use futures markets to contract for a price when his wheat is ready for harvest. Without futures markets his profits would depend upon the uncertain price of wheat at harvest time. However, using futures markets he can shift that uncertainty to investors in the futures markets who are interested in speculating on the future price of wheat.

While futures markets have been used for many years to hedge the risk of commodity prices, only in the last decade have futures and options on financial instruments become widely used to hedge financial risks. Because Chapter 9 is devoted to hedging financial risks with futures and options, we will consider only two examples here of how options can be used to hedge financial risks.

Consider an investor who has a position in the stock of a company. Suppose this investor owns 1,000 shares currently valued at $50 per share. This investor is particularly averse to risk and does not want to accept the prospect that there might be large fluctuations in the price of the stock. Suppose the investor decides that she does not want to be exposed to more than a 20 percent fluctuation in the price of the stock. The way to accomplish this is to buy a put option with an exercise price of $40 and write a call option with an exercise price of $60. The results are illustrated in Figure 4–7. Panel A shows the payoff from holding the stock, while panels B and C show the payoffs from buying the put and writing the call. Panel D shows what happens when these distinct payoffs are combined. The solid line in panel D defines the payoff when the three positions are added together. The figure shows that if the price of the underlying asset is equal to or—

FIGURE 4–7
Hedging with options.

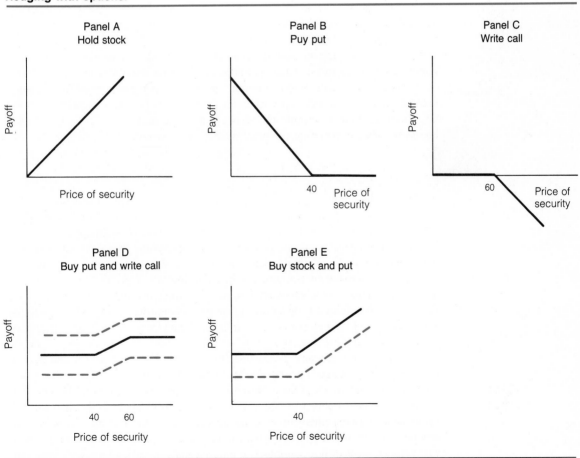

less than $40, then the payoff to the hedged position is $40. The payoff is exactly equal to the payoff from holding the stock if the stock price is between $40 and $60. If the price of the stock exceeds $60, then the payoff is only $60.

While the solid line in panel D is of substantial interest, it does not show the payoffs net of the prices of the options. In order to receive this payoff shown in the solid line, or what we might term the *gross payoff,* the investor must pay the going price for a put with an exercise price of $40. However, he or she will receive the going price for the call with an exercise price of $60. The dashed lines in panel D show hypothetical payoffs after these prices have been netted out. The two lines are drawn under two alternative assumptions. The dashed line above the solid line is drawn on the assumption that the price of the put is less than the price of the call, while the dashed line below the solid line is drawn on the assumption that the price of the put exceeds the price of the call.

The investor in this situation has purchased insurance against substantial declines in the price of the stock by buying the put. In effect, the price of the put can be thought of as an insurance premium. At the same time, using the call, she has sold off the prospect for substantial appreciation in the price of the stock. For this transaction she receives, rather than pays, a price. There is no reason why an investor has to engage in both of these transactions simultaneously. An investor might simply want to purchase insurance against substantial declines in the price of the stock. The payoff from this transaction, which includes holding the stock and buying a put, is illustrated in panel E of Figure 4–7. Once again, the solid line shows the payoff without taking account of the price of the put. The dashed line shows the net payoff if the price of the put is assumed to be $5.

HEDGING EXCHANGE RATE RISK

As another illustration of how futures and options can be used for hedging, consider a multinational firm which sells products denominated in a number of different currencies. Let's assume this company has its production facilities in Japan, the country in which it is domiciled. This company has two types of business. One type involves a relatively steady volume of sales of Japanese manufactured products in a number of countries. While the volume of production and sales is quite steady, there is a substantial production time involved. The second type involves sizable special orders from a variety of countries. Each order involves a substantial level of production, but it is uncertain how many orders might be received.

The Japanese company would find it optimal to use both futures and options to hedge the exchange rate risk between the yen and the currencies in which products are sold. It should use futures markets to hedge the risk in the first type of production and options to hedge the risk in the second. In both cases the risk being hedged is the prospect of price fluctuations in the currency in which the products will be sold during the time products are being made. However, with the first type of product the magnitude of the ultimate sales volume, and hence the amount of the currency that needs to be hedged, is known with certainty or is subject to little risk. A futures contract can be written in the amount of goods to be sold in the currency of each country where the firm has sales. If the price of currency in the country where the goods are sold declines, the firm will gain on its futures contract, but it will suffer from the changes in the exchange rate. Exactly the opposite happens if the price of the foreign currency increases. In this case the firm experiences a loss on its futures contract, but it is able to sell products for a higher price denominated in its home currency. As a result it has hedged its risk of fluctuations in foreign exchange rates from the first type of production in which it is engaged.

To see more precisely how this would work, suppose the Japanese company expects to sell 10,000 units of its product in the United States in one year for $10 each so that it will have $100,000 in revenue. If the exchange rate between yen and dollars were 20, then the revenue in yen would be 12,000,000 yen. To insure this level of revenue the Japanese company could sell short dollar futures in the amount of $100,000. Then if the value of the dollar denominated in yen declines or, equivalently, if the yen/dollar exchange rate declines, the company will earn a profit on its hedge. The payoffs from the hedged position are illustrated in Table 4–3. The table illustrates that if the exchange rate declines, then the firm will earn profits on the futures contracts, but the value in yen of the goods sold will decline. On the other hand, if the exchange rate increases, exactly the opposite will occur. The final column illustrates that the net proceeds from the hedged position will always be the same, regardless of the exchange rate. This is precisely the purpose of a hedge.

While it is preferable to use the futures markets to hedge the foreign exchange risk in the first type of production, it would not be so with the second type of production, because a futures contract makes a firm commitment to trade currency at a future price. The more attractive alternative is to have an option to do so. Let's compare what happens to this firm with an option versus a futures contract if no contract for production is signed. If the firm had originally hedged with futures—that is before it knew whether a contract would be signed—then it would face the symmetrical payoff characteristic of a futures contract. It would have

TABLE 4–3
Gain on short fuctures contract for $100,000 in yen with a contract yen/dollar exchange rate of 220.

Future Exchange Rate Yen/$	Gain on Futures in Yen	Value of Goods Sold in Yen	Net Proceeds from Sales and Futures
100	2,000,000	10,000,000	12,000,000
110	1,000,000	11,000,000	12,000,000
120	0	12,000,000	12,000,000
130	−1,000,000	13,000,000	12,000,000
140	−2,000,000	14,000,000	12,000,000

unlimited gains if the price of the foreign currency declined, but it would also have unlimited losses if the price of the foreign currency increased. Since there would be no sales of goods in that currency to offset these gains or losses, the firm would have assumed a speculative rather than a hedged position.

On the other hand, if it had utilized an options contract, it would have an asymmetrical rather than a symmetrical payoff pattern. The appropriate option would have been to purchase a put on the foreign currency. Then, if that currency fell below the exercise price, it could exercise the put option for a profit. If a production contract had been signed, that profit would have offset losses incurred due to the change in the exchange rate. However, if a production contract had not been signed, exercising the put option would yield a profit. Had the foreign currency increased in value, the put option would be worthless and remain unexercised, and the firm would not incur any direct loss on the option. In this situation had the firm used the futures contract, it would have been exposed to an unlimited loss. The moral of the story is that the options contract provides greater protection when there is uncertainty about the appropriate quantity of the hedge.

THE DETERMINATION OF OPTION PRICES

It is no simple task to figure out how an option should be valued. In fact, while options have been of interest for many years, it was only recently that somebody came up with a satisfactory analysis of how to value an option. In 1973 Fischer Black and Myron Scholes published a paper that presented a model for pricing options.[1] Their contribution was quickly recognized as a major breakthrough, and this model is now referred to as the **Black–Scholes model.** In the remainder of this chapter we are going to examine the principal determinants of options prices. First we will look at the problem intuitively in order to understand the basic relationships involved then briefly examine the actual Black-Scholes formula. Finally, we will review some empirical evidence on the determinants of option prices.

The **Black–Scholes Model** is an explicit pricing model for call and put options.

FACTORS THAT INFLUENCE OPTION PRICES

There are five principal variables which influence the price of an option. They are:

1. current price of the underlying security
2. exercise price of the option
3. variability of the price of the underlying security
4. time to maturity of the option
5. the risk-free interest rate.

---

[1]See F. Black and M. Scholes, "The Pricing of Options and Corporate Liabilities," *Journal of Political Economy,* 81 (May–June 1973), pp. 637–54.

TABLE 4–4
Determinants of option prices.

Cause of Price Change	Direction of Price Change
1. Current price of the underlying security	Positive
2. Exercise price of the option	Negative
3. Variability of the underlying security	Positive
4. Time to maturity of the option	Positive
5. The risk-free interest rate	Positive

We will explore why and how call option prices are influenced by each of these variables. Table 4–4 summarizes the qualitative relationship between the value of a call option and each of the five independent variables itemized above.

Current Price of Underlying Security.   Let's return to the call option on a share of stock with an exercise price of $50 that we considered early in the chapter. How will the value of an American call option be influenced by changes in the current price of the underlying stock? To answer this question suppose that the current price of the stock is above the exercise price. When this occurs, the option is said to be **in the money** because it could be exercised immediately for a profit. Therefore, the value of an American call option that is in the money must be at least equal to the difference between the current price of the stock and the exercise price. Furthermore, an option can never have a negative value since the payoff from an option will never be negative; this establishes a minimum value for the option for any value of the underlying security. This minimum value is illustrated in Figure 4–8 by the line identical to the one in Figure 4–1 which shows the payoff from a call option. We also know that the option can never be more valuable than the underlying security itself because the payoff from the stock will always exceed the payoff from the option. Therefore we can draw a 45-degree line emanating from the origin in Figure 4–8 to represent the maximum possible value of the option. The value of the option must lie between these two lines drawn in the figure.

An **in the money** option can be exercised immediately for a profit.

The relationship between the value of the underlying security and the value of a call option on that security hinges on the impact of changes in the price of the asset on the probability distribution of payoffs from the option. If the current price of the security increases, then there should be a higher chance of greater payoffs. This is apparent when the option is in the money, since the gain from an increase in the current share price could be realized by exercising the option immediately. But it is also true when the option is not in the money since an increase in the current price of the asset, in this case, must increase the chance the option will be in the money at some time prior to maturity. Therefore, regardless of whether the option is in the money, the higher the price of the security, the higher the value of the call option should be.

FIGURE 4–8
The value of a call option.

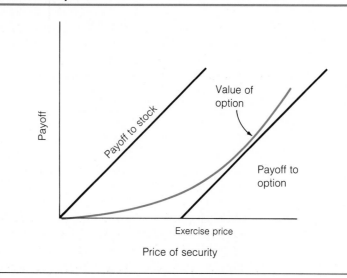

Price of security

If the price of the underlying asset is very high relative to the exercise price, the probability will also be very high that the option will be exercised. As a result, the value of the option must be very close to the value of the underlying asset less the exercise price of the option. This is illustrated in Figure 4–8: a solid curve shows the value of the option as a function of the price of the underlying security. This line is increasing throughout, which shows that an increase in the price of the underlying security leads to an increase in the price of a call option. The value of option line also approaches the line that shows the payoff to the option, or the value of the stock less the exercise price for an in-the-money option, as the stock price increases.

Exercise Price of the Options. A simple extension of the relationship discussed above will show how a change in the exercise price of an option influences its value. A decrease in the exercise price has the same effect as an increase in the current price of the underlying asset. For an in-the-money option it increases the payoff if it is exercised immediately. For an out-of-the-money option it increases the chance it will be in the money in the future. Therefore, a decrease in the exercise price must lead to an increase in the value of the option. This is illustrated in Figure 4–9 which presents curves representing the value of two options that differ only by their exercise price. One has an exercise price of $30 and the other has an exercise price of $50. The figure shows that the option with the lower exercise price has a higher value for any value of the underlying security. It is also evident in the options prices shown in Figure 4–2. For example, the prices of June call options on Federal Express decrease from $7\frac{3}{8}$ to $\frac{1}{16}$ as the exercise price increases from 55 to 70.

Variability of Price of Underlying Security.   The next variable that can influence the value of an option is the variability of the price of the underlying security. Imagine identical call options on two different stocks. Both stocks have a current value of $50. The first stock has a 50 percent chance that the price will either increase or decrease by $25, while the second stock has only a 25 percent chance of a comparable increase or decrease. The call option on either stock will be worthless if the stock goes down in value (assuming a $50 exercise price). However, the first stock has a greater chance of large positive payoffs than does the second. Therefore, the call option on this stock should be more valuable than the option on the second stock.

The probability of large changes in the price of a stock in any given period is determined by the variance of the stock price. Therefore, a call option on a stock with a high variance should have a higher value than a call option on a stock with a relatively low variance.

Time to Maturity.   The fourth variable that determines the price of an option, the time to maturity, also influences the probability that there will be large increases in the value of the stock. This is because the chance that there will be a large increase in price prior to maturity depends upon the variance applicable to the entire time until maturity. The variance of an asset is generally measured for a unit of time, such as a day. Therefore, the variance applicable to the period until maturity will increase as the length of the period to maturity increases.

The Risk-Free Interest Rate.   The final variable that determines the price of an option is the risk-free interest rate. To see why this is important, compare invest-

FIGURE 4–9
Values of options at two exercise prices.

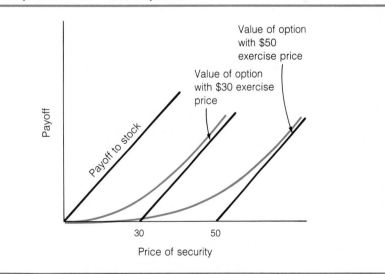

ing in a call option on a stock with investing directly in that stock. With either investment you are exposed to the same possible payoffs. If the risk-free interest rate increases, the cost of borrowing to finance the purchase of the stock will increase. This makes the call option more attractive, and its value must rise relative to the value of the stock. The implication is that increases in interest rates cause call options to increase in value. For this relationship to be correct, changes in interest rates must not directly cause changes in the value of the underlying asset. For options on equities this may be a reasonable assumption, but for options on bonds it is not.

THE BLACK–SCHOLES FORMULA

Black and Scholes developed their pricing formula for European options by doing a careful comparison of the alternatives of investing in a call option and making a leveraged investment directly in the underlying asset. Their actual analysis is quite formidable and is well beyond the scope of this book. However, it is helpful to be familiar with the form of the pricing equation they derived. It can be written as follows:

$$\text{Value of a call option } = PN(d_1) - Ee^{rt}N(d_2),$$

$$\text{where } d_1 = \frac{\log(P/E) + rt + \sigma^2 t/2}{\sigma \sqrt{t}}$$

$$d_2 = d_1 - \sigma \sqrt{t}$$

$N(d)$ = cumulative normal probability density function (the probability that a normally distributed random variable will be less than or equal to d)

E = exercise price of the option

t = time to maturity

P = current price of the underlying asset

σ^2 = instantaneous variance of the rate of return on the stock

r = risk-free interest rate (continuously compounded).

Fortunately, you do not have to understand this equation thoroughly to use it. Many participants in the options markets use the equation because it can be programmed into a hand-held calculator quite easily. If you intend to use this or any other model for pricing options, it is important to know when the equation is applicable and when it can be misused. A few references about the equation are listed at the end of the chapter.

EMPIRICAL EVIDENCE ON THE BLACK–SCHOLES MODEL

If the Black–Scholes model is to be used to price options, then it is extremely important to know how well the model explains observed prices of options. Black and Scholes were keenly interested in this when they developed their model. They conducted one of the first empirical studies of how their model performed. However, when they conducted their tests in the early 1970s, options were not traded on organized exchanges. The Chicago Board Options Exchange did not yet exist. Therefore, they collected data for options traded over the counter from 1966 to 1969. While we will avoid getting into the details of the procedure, we are interested in their conclusion. They concluded that the model tends to overestimate the value of options on securities with large variances, while it underestimates the value of options on securities with small variances.[2]

As data for options traded on the CBOE became available later in the 1970s additional studies of the Black–Scholes model were undertaken. Black found that the model systematically underpriced deep out-of-the money options and options which were close to maturity while it overpriced deep in-the-money options during the period from 1973 to 1975.[3] However, in a later study, MacBeth and Merville found that the bias reported by Black had reversed itself.[4]

This research pointed to a problem in attempting to apply the Black–Scholes European options formula to American options. There is really no significant difference between the prices of types of options if the stock to which the options apply does not pay dividends. However, most stocks used in the empirical studies cited do pay dividends. If a stock pays dividends, the value of a call option diminishes. The reason is simply that dividends reduce future share price; therefore, the payoffs to the option are reduced. Various proposals have been offered to correct the Black-Scholes formula to take account of dividend payments. One essentially ad hoc adjustment to the formula was proposed by Black. An alternative formula directly applicable to American options was proposed by Roll. Recent empirical evidence presented by Whaley, Sterk, and Geske and Roll indicate that most of the biases identified in the earlier empirical studies can be eliminated by using Roll's approach to pricing American options.[5]

Options and futures markets are large, growing, and they have become very important in only one decade. They will surely be more important in the future.

Summary

In this chapter we have examined contingent claims. *Contingent claims* are assets whose value depends on the value of some other asset. Most contingent claims can be classified as either options or futures. *Futures* represent a commitment to

---

[2]See F. Black and M. Scholes, "The Valuation of Option Contracts and a Test of Market Efficiency," *Journal of Finance,* (May 1972).

[3]See F. Black, "Fact and Fancy in the Use of Options," *Financial Analysts Journal,* 31 (July–August 1975), pp. 36–41, 61–72.

[4]See J. Macbeth and L. Merville, "An Empirical Examination of the Black–Scholes Call Option Pricing Model," *Journal of Finance,* 34 (December 1979), pp. 1173–86.

[5]See W. Sterk, "Tests of Two Models for Valuing Call Options on Stocks with Dividends," *Journal of Finance,* 37 (December 1982), pp. 1229–37; R. Whaley, "Valuation of American Call Options on Dividend-Paying Stocks: Empirical Tests," *Journal of Financial Economics,* 10 (March 1982), pp. 29–58; and R. Geske and R. Roll, "On Valuing American Call Options with the Black–Scholes European Formula," *Journal of Finance,* 39 (June 1984), pp. 443–55.

buy or sell an asset at a prespecified time and price. *Options* represent the right or option to buy or sell an asset at a prespecified time and price.

We examined how options and futures work and learned that the payoff from a futures contract is symmetrical around the contract price of the future. The buyer of a *long future* earns a profit equal to the difference between the price of the underlying asset and the contract price of the future. By contrast the holder of a *call option,* which is the option to buy a security, receives a payoff that cannot be less than zero. If the price of the underlying asset is greater than the exercise price of the option, then the holder of the call option will earn a profit equal to the difference between these two prices.

We also examined the relationship between options and futures and the underlying securities on which they are claims. The value of a call option less the value of a put option is equal to the value of a futures contract on that asset. The value of a call minus the value of a put is equal to the value of the asset less the present value of the exercise price of the option. We can use this relationship to see that an equity claim on a company is simply a call option on the assets of the firm. The value of the debt of the company can be characterized in terms of the value of options.

In exploring the actual and potential uses of options, we found that options allow market participants to act on specific information or to make specific bets that are otherwise unavailable in the marketplace. In this way options add to the completeness of the market, but options and futures also allow market participants to redistribute risk. Two examples demonstrated how futures and options may be used to hedge in the stock market and the risk of fluctuations in exchange rates between currencies.

Finally, we explored how prices of options are determined in organized markets. The price of a call option is determined by the exercise price, the current price of the underlying securities, the variance of the price of the underlying security, the time to maturity, and the risk-free interest rate. We also examined the formula for the Black–Scholes option pricing model, which relates the price of an option to these variables, and the recent empirical evidence on its effectiveness.

QUESTIONS

1. Distinguish between being long and short in both puts and calls. What are the payoffs in each position? How can they be illustrated graphically?
2. Explain the difference between a futures and an option contract. Why is there only one "contract price" for a futures contract but many exercise prices with options?
3. What is a complete market? How do options help to complete a market?
4. How can equity and debt securities issued by a firm be characterized as options? What is the underlying asset in these options?
5. What is a hedge? Give some real-world examples in which hedging might be desirable.

6. Suppose a firm is planning to borrow from a bank to finance some new inventory. The loan is going to be taken down in three months in the amount of $10,000,000. The bank is willing to commit to an interest rate for this future loan. However, the borrower is unsure whether she is getting a good price. How can the borrower use futures or options markets to accomplish the same guarantee as the banker provided? How can she check if the banker is providing a good price?

7. Why is it true that as the variance of an option increases the value of the option must increase? Does this conflict with the idea that variance measures risk and that value should go down as risk increases? Why or why not?

8. What is the nature of the bias discovered in early empirical studies of the Black–Scholes option pricing formula?

9. Suppose you had the job of approving the introduction of new options and futures contracts on the exchanges in the United States. How would you evaluate whether an option contract should be allowed to be traded on the exchange?

10. Consider a call and a put on the same stock with the same maturity date and an exercise price of $72. Suppose the current value of the stock is $75, so that the call is in the money. Suppose the current price of the call is $4.50 and the current price of the put is $1.50. Calculate the net payoffs to the purchaser and writer of both calls and puts if the value of the underlying security at the maturity of the option is $70, $72.50, $75, $77.50 and $80.

11. Suppose your Highly Variable Corporation has 400,000 shares of stock outstanding and the current price of the stock is $23.50. Also suppose it has total long-term debt with a book value of $10 million outstanding. This debt can currently be purchased for 95 cents on the dollar or for $9.5 million. Finally, suppose that it has short-term debt of $750,000 and short-term assets of $1,200,000. Describe how both the equity and the debt can be viewed as options. Quantify any option values and terms of the options, such as the exercise price, that you can using this data.

12. Suppose you owned 1,000 shares of Bank of America stock and that the current value of the stock and options available on that stock were as reported for Bank of America in Table 4–1. Suppose you wrote 10 July puts with an exercise price of 15. Define the net payoffs you would have from both your stock position and your options if the price of Bank of America stock varied from $5 to $25 at the maturity date of your options.

13. Return to the call and put options on Bank of America in Table 4–1. Now suppose you purchased both one July put and one July call of Bank of America. Define the payoffs that you would have for alternative values of the value of Bank of America stock at maturity. When would you be interested in taking this type of position using options?

14. Suppose you are comparing the values of two call options on different underlying assets. Both assets have the same exercise price, and the current prices of both assets are the same. However, the first asset has a higher variance than the second and its maturity date is shorter. Which of the two assets would you expect to have the higher value? Explain why.

REFERENCES

Black, F. and M. Scholes. "The Pricing of Options and Corporate Liabilities," *Journal of Political Economy,* 81 (May–June 1973), pp. 637–654.

———. "The Valuation of Option Contracts and a Test of Market Efficiency," *Journal of Finance,* (May 1972).

F. Black. "Fact and Fancy in the Use of Options," *Financial Analysts Journal,* 31 (July–August 1975), pp. 36–41, 61–72.

Bookstaber, R. and R. Clarke. *Option Strategies for Institutional Investment Management,* Reading, Mass.: Addison-Wesley, 1983.

Geske, R. and R. Roll. "On Valuing American Call Options with the Black–Scholes European Formula," *Journal of Finance,* 39 (June 1984), pp. 443–55.

Giddy, I. "The Foreign Exchange Option as a Hedging Tool," *Midland Corporate Finance Journal,* 1 (Fall 1983), pp. 32–42.

Goodman, L. "New Options Markets," *Federal Reserve Bank of New York Quarterly Review,* 8 (Autumn 1983), pp. 35–47.

Macbeth, J. and L. Merville. "An Empirical Examination of the Black–Scholes Call Option Pricing Model," *Journal of Finance,* 34 (December 1979), pp. 1173–86.

Sterk, W. "Tests of Two Models for Valuing Call Options on Stocks with Dividends," *Journal of Finance,* 37 (December 1982), pp. 1229–37.

Whaley, R. "Valuation of American Call Options on Dividend-Paying Stocks: Empirical Tests," *Journal of Financial Economics,* 10 (March 1982), pp. 29–58.

5

*I*NFORMATION AND FINANCIAL MARKETS

This chapter focuses on the role of information in financial markets. In the previous two chapters the value of an asset was determined by the expected return and risk of that asset. Yet an explanation of where the estimates of expected return and risk come from was conspicuously absent. This chapter fills in that gap, at least in part, by exploring the concept of information about future returns on an asset and the cost of acquiring that information. ▪

MARKET PRICES AND EFFICIENT USE OF INFORMATION

The **efficient markets hypothesis** contends that prices of assets reflect all available information about the future returns on those assets.

An exceptionally important issue about the performance of financial markets is whether they make efficient use of information about the future returns on assets. The hypothesis that markets use information efficiently has come to be known as the **efficient markets hypothesis.** The hypothesis merely states that markets do not waste information. Put another way, there will never be an *obvious* good buy the market *consistently* ignores. Because there is considerable misunderstanding about the efficient markets hypothesis, it is useful to focus attention on what the hypothesis really means. A little evidence will be discussed here concerning the degree to which markets actually are efficient, but more evidence will be sprinkled throughout the book.

The efficiency of financial markets is a very popular topic among practical people as well as academicians interested in financial markets. The efficient markets hypothesis in essence says that you can't beat the market or that investment advisors can't tell you anything useful. It is evident why practitioners would not believe in such a hypothesis. It is less evident why many academicians continue to insist that markets are efficient.

THE CONCEPT OF EFFICIENCY

Consider a little more carefully one of the arguments propounded by those who advocate the efficiency of markets. The argument is that security prices perform a *random walk*. This means that if you were going to estimate the price next period of a share of stock of XYZ company, your best estimate would be today's price; the past behavior of the stock price would be of absolutely no help in predicting its future course. This past behavior will already have been incorporated in the stock's current price. This form of the efficient markets hypothesis can be stated a little more formally by saying that the expected value of next period's price, given the entire history of the price of the stock, is equal to the current price. Therefore, there is no gain from studying past behavior. To understand this version of the efficient markets hypothesis, it is useful to examine Figure 5–1. This figure plots the performance of the price of our hypothetical XYZ company over a sample period. The random walk hypothesis says that the changes in this price through time are totally random. As a result, suppose you try to forecast what the price will be at time t_2 when the current price at time period t_1 is P_1. The random walk hypothesis says that the best guess of the price at t_2 is the current price, P_1 in this example. There is nothing to be gained from studying the past behavior of the price, that is, the line in the figure to the left of t_1, since it will give you no clue to its future behavior. Notice that the price at time t_2 eventually turns out to equal P_2, and this is much higher than the forecast of P_1. The efficient markets hypothesis does not say that your forecast of P_1 will prove accurate with hindsight. What it does say is that at time t_1, with what you know then about the past behavior of the price of the security, you cannot come up with a better forecast

FIGURE 5–1
The price of XYZ Company. This figure shows the behavior through time of the price of a hypothetical company named XYZ. If the market is efficient, then there should be no discernible pattern in the change in this price.

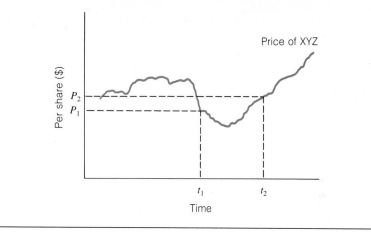

than to say that the future price will equal the current price. The very fact that there is uncertainty means that this forecast will not be perfectly accurate. It should, however, be the best available forecast.

Information about the past behavior of the price of XYZ company is easily available to anyone as long as XYZ is a publicly traded company. Moreover, the statistical techniques needed to find any information in the past prices of XYZ are readily available to anyone who chooses to study the subject. Therefore, it is not very costly to incorporate information about the past behavior of prices into the current price. But it is not as easy to conclude that the market has incorporated other information, such as an investment project XYZ is planning to undertake that is known only to the board of directors of the company. The market might not fully incorporate this kind of information into the price of XYZ company because it is very costly to obtain.

LEVELS OF MARKET EFFICIENCY

One of the reasons the efficient markets hypothesis is often misunderstood is that it is usually stated and applied with the assumption that information is not costly to acquire. The hypothesis usually makes use of the phrase, "the set of information available to the market at time t." The hypothesis then contends that the market efficiently uses all of the specified set of information. The basic strategy involved in testing such a hypothesis is to determine whether one could have expected to have made a profit on such information based on the market prices prevailing shortly after the information became available. It is logical, then, to relate the degree of market efficiency to the set of information the market is able to use efficiently and to the time required to incorporate the information.

The degree of market efficiency is divided into three forms according to the set of information which is used. These are:

Weak-form efficiency says the market sets the prices of assets efficiently with respect to the past history of the prices of those assets.

1. **Weak-form Efficiency.** In this form of the efficient market hypothesis the information set that the market is able to efficiently use comprises all of the history of the price of a security. This is the same as the previous example of XYZ company.
2. **Semistrong-form Efficiency.** In this form the information set comprises all publicly available information about a security (i.e., it is not restricted solely to price). For example, this might include the history of dividend payout rates or bond ratings in a recent *Wall Street Journal* article about a company.
3. **Strong-form Efficiency.** In this form the hypothesis includes what is called insider information. This includes information that is at least initially known only to the managers of the company.

Semistrong-form efficiency says the market is efficient with respect to all public information.

Strong-form efficiency says the market is efficient with respect to all inside information.

The weak-form efficient markets hypothesis has received the most attention both in the popular financial press and in academic journals. It is important to emphasize what this hypothesis does *not* say: it does not say that the best forecast of the next period's price of a security is this period's price. This statement is unconditional; it makes no reference to a set of information. The weak-form efficient markets hypothesis says that, *based solely on the past behavior of the price of the security,* the current price is the best forecast of the future price. Additional information might well improve the forecast, but such information is not included in the set of information relevant to the weak-form efficient markets hypothesis.

The categories of weak-, semistrong-, and strong-form market efficiency are useful for simplifying the problems created by the fact that information is costly to acquire and evaluate. The weak- and semistrong-form categories refer to information where the costs of acquisition are relatively low. This kind of information should readily be incorporated into market prices. A much stronger argument is that even information that is costly to acquire and that may be known only to insiders will work its way into the market and be incorporated into prices very quickly. The implicit argument here is that the incentives to use this information profitably are so strong that it will be disclosed rapidly to the market and incorporated into prices. This argument relies on the incentives for corporate insiders to disclose information rather than the incentives for outsiders to discover or collect information. Both kinds of forces are constantly at work to contribute to the efficiency of markets.

Monopolistic or excess returns are returns in excess of those necessary to induce an investor to hold an asset.

The real message which the efficient markets hypothesis seeks to communicate pertains to the state of competition in both the information and the financial markets. That message is that one cannot expect to earn **monopolistic or excess returns** from collecting information and trading on it. The hypothesis contends that financial markets and the market for information are competitive. This does not mean that, ex post, some participants in the market will not make exception-

INSIDE INFORMATION AND MARKET EFFICIENCY

One of the more important and interesting items regarding market efficiency pertains to the appropriate definition of inside information. From an intellectual standpoint the distinction between the semistrong-form and strong-form market efficiency hinges on this distinction. It also has tremendous practical importance since it is illegal to trade on inside information. The Securities Exchange Commission (SEC) has chosen to vigorously seek out and prosecute those who are believed to be engaged in such practices. In fact, in 1986 there were 30 enforcement actions against illegal trading and these actions generated $38 million in profits which were either given up or repaid.[1] A few cases have received tremendous notoriety. One in particular involves Ivan Boesky and Dennis Levine. Boesky attracted public attention as an arbitrageur who speculated on companies involved in potential takeovers. The SEC charged that Boesky profited from inside information supplied to him by Levine and others who worked for Wall Street firms directly involved in the takeover process. Both Boesky and Levine agreed to pay penalties and cooperate with the SEC in ongoing investigations. Levine agreed to pay $12 million and Boesky $100 million.

The SEC has historically relied on case-by-case litigation to determine the appropriate legal definition of insider trading. The case law has developed what is referred to as the theory of "misappropriation." This legal theory holds that it is illegal to trade on material, nonpublic information that has been misappropriated or obtained in a manner that constitutes a breach of fiduciary duty. As the case law has evolved, the perception of who has such fiduciary duty has been expanded. A narrow interpretation might suggest that only corporate officers and other clear insiders are covered under this definition. The courts have applied the definition to what might be termed temporary insiders such as lawyers, investment and commercial bankers, accountants, management consultants, and even financial printers. A recent case against R. Foster Winnans, a reporter for the *Wall Street Journal,* suggests that insiders can also include reporters, at least under some circumstances. At the time this is written, the case against Winnans is on appeal to the U.S. Supreme Court. As a result, the definition of insiders awaits further clarification. One of the complaints against the present system is that it is simply too difficult for anyone who is not a securities lawyer to know exactly what acts are illegal and what are not. Resolution of the Winnans case may clarify the situation or provoke a situation where clarification from the Congress is necessary.

There is considerable debate not only about how insider trading is defined under the law, but also about how it should be defined. One view, sometimes known as the equity or equal-information view, is that anyone trading based on superior information is, in effect, stealing from stockholders with whom this person trades. This goes beyond the misappropriation concept of how to define insider trading. Financial economists and others concerned with promoting the efficiency of financial markets generally have a low opinion of this equity view. They generally take the position that trading on superior information is necessary to improve the efficiency of the market. They also argue that it is impractical to make such insider trading illegal, since virtually all active investors constantly seek and sometimes find superior information as a basis for trading. If a broad legal definition of insider information were enforced, it would tend to stop much valuable investment in information and therefore tend to decrease the efficiency of financial markets.

[1]Bruce Ingersoll, "Demand Rises for Law Defining Insider Trading to Provide More than a Gut Feeling as a Guide," *Wall Street Journal,* March 26, 1987, p. 70.

ally large returns. Some will, just as there will be some who will earn very low returns. The hypothesis means that one cannot expect to earn such returns ex ante. Without barriers to competition, such excess returns will be eliminated in an efficient capital market.

EVIDENCE ON MARKET EFFICIENCY

Early tests of the efficient market hypothesis concentrated on the weak-form of the hypothesis, specifically that security prices perform a random walk. If the weak-form of the efficient markets hypothesis is correct, then the correlation coefficient between the prices of a security observed at two points in time, or autocorrelation coefficient, should be zero. This can be stated more formally as:

$$\rho_{P_t,P_{t-i}} = \frac{\text{Covariance } (P_t, P_{t-i})}{\sigma_{P_t}\, \sigma_{P_{t-i}}} = 0,$$

where P_t is the price of the asset at time t and σ_{P_t} is the standard deviation of P_t. Eugene Fama conducted some of the earliest tests of whether autocorrelation coefficients for publicly traded equity securities are zero. Table 5–1 shows some of the autocorrelation coefficients estimated in his 1965 study of the behavior of stock market prices. The table shows daily autocorrelation coefficients for lags (or differences between observed prices) of up to 10 days. The asterisks in the table indicate that the computed correlation coefficient is more than twice its estimated standard deviation. By normal standards, it is reasonable to accept the hypothesis that coefficients of this magnitude are different from zero. One would expect that simply by chance some reasonable number of these coefficients would be greater than twice their standard deviation. What is interesting about these results is how few asterisks there are in the table. The relatively small size of the autocorrelation coefficients is generally interpreted as evidence in favor of the weak-form of the efficient markets hypothesis.

Since Eugene Fama initially published these results in 1965, tests of the efficient markets hypothesis have become significantly more sophisticated, as well as more plentiful. The basic idea behind more recent studies of market efficiency is to determine whether there is some investment strategy that can consistently earn excess returns. A strategy might consist of a trading rule, such as buy a stock if it increases in value by a certain amount, or buy stocks with low dividend payout rates, or buy stocks in relatively small firms, or buy stocks in December and sell them in January. In fact some evidence has accumulated in the last few years that some of these strategies (as well as some others) work rather well—that is, they may earn excess returns.

One of the pitfalls with the efficient markets hypothesis is that it is not always obvious what may constitute excess returns. In order to measure excess returns it is necessary to have an acceptable measure of expected returns, and this, in turn, requires an acceptable measure of the risk of the security or some theory of how the asset in question is priced. Most empirical studies of the efficient markets hypothesis have used the Capital Asset Pricing Model as a basis for measuring expected returns on equity securities. This means that the expected return on an equity security will be defined as the beta of that security times the expected return on a well-diversified portfolio of securities which represents the market as a whole. Excess return in any single period is then defined as the difference between the actual return on a security in a given period less the expected return:

$$\text{Excess return} = \text{Actual return} - \left[\text{Beta} \times \frac{\text{Expected return}}{\text{on the market}}\right].$$

Some of the most interesting studies of market efficiency in recent years have focused on two types of investment strategies. The first strategy is to buy stocks

TABLE 5–1
Daily serial correlation coefficients for lags of 1, 2, . . . , 10 days.

	Lag									
Stock	1	2	3	4	5	6	7	8	9	10
Allied Chemical	.017	−.042	.007	−.001	.027	.004	−.017	−.026	−.017	−.007
Alcoa	.118*	.038	−.014	.022	−.022	.009	.017	.007	−.001	−.033
American Can	−.087*	−.024	.034	−.065*	−.017	−.006	.015	.025	−.047	−.040
A.T.&T.	−.039	−.097*	.000	.026	.005	−.005	.002	.027	−.014	.007
American Tobacco	.111*	−.109*	−.060*	−.065*	.007	−.010	.011	.046	.039	.041
Anaconda	.067*	−.061*	−.047	−.002	.000	−.038	.009	.016	−.014	−.056
Bethlehem Steel	.013	−.065*	.009	.021	−.053	−.098*	−.010	.004	−.002	−.021
Chrysler	.012	−.066*	−.016	−.007	−.015	.009	.037	.056*	−.044	.021
Du Pont	.013	−.033	.060*	.027	−.002	−.047	.020	.011	−.034	.001
Eastman Kodak	.025	.014	−.031	.005	−.022	.012	.007	.006	.008	.002
General Electric	.011	−.038	−.021	.031	−.001	.000	−.008	.014	−.002	.010
General Foods	.061*	−.003	.045	.002	−.015	−.052	−.006	−.014	−.024	−.017
General Motors	−.004	−.056*	−.037	−.008	−.038	−.006	.019	.006	−.016	.009
Goodyear	−.123*	.017	−.044	.043	−.002	−.003	.035	.014	−.015	.007
International Harvester	−.017	−.029	−.031	.037	−.052	−.021	−.001	.003	−.046	−.016
International Nickel	.096*	−.033	−.019	.020	.027	.059*	−.038	−.008	−.016	.034
International Paper	.046	−.011	−.058*	.053*	.049	−.003	−.025	−.019	−.003	−.021
Johns Manville	.006	−.038	−.027	−.023	−.029	−.080*	.040	.018	−.037	.029
Owens Illinois	−.021	−.084*	−.047	.068*	.086*	−.040	.011	−.040	.067*	−.043
Procter & Gamble	.099*	−.009	−.008	.009	−.015	.022	.012	−.012	−.022	−.021
Sears	.097*	.026	.028	.025	.005	−.054	−.006	−.010	−.008	−.009
Standard Oil (Calif.)	.025	−.030	−.051*	−.025	−.047	−.034	−.010	.072*	−.049*	−.035
Standard Oil (N.J.)	.008	−.116*	.016	.014	−.047	−.018	−.022	−.026	−.073*	.081*
Swift & Co.	−.004	−.015	−.010	.012	.057*	.012	−.043	.014	.012	.001
Texaco	.094*	−.049	−.024	−.018	−.017	−.009	.031	.032	−.013	.008
Union Carbide	.107*	−.012	.040	.046	−.036	−.034	.003	−.008	−.054	−.037
United Aircraft	.014	−.033	−.022	−.047	−.067*	−.053	.046	.037	.015	−.019
U.S. Steel	.040	−.074*	.014	.011	−.012	−.021	.041	.037	−.021	−.044
Westinghouse	−.027	−.022	−.036	−.003	.000	−.054*	−.020	.013	−.014	.008
Woolworth	.028	−.016	.015	.014	.007	−.039	−.013	.003	−.088*	−.008

*Coefficient is twice its computed standard error.
Source: Eugene Fama, "The Behavior of Stock-Market Prices," *Journal of Business,* (January 1965), p. 72.

The **small-firm effect** is the observed tendency of firms with low capitalization to earn apparently excess returns.

in low capitalization or small firms. The second strategy is to buy stocks at the right time of the week or year. The evidence indicates that there have been opportunities to make consistent excess returns from these strategies. These *anomalies,* as they are called, have become known as the *small-firm effect* and the *day of the week* and *January effects.*

One of the original and most important studies of the **small-firm effect** was carried out by Marc Reinganum.[1] Reinganum constructed a sample of NYSE and AMEX traded stocks during the 1970s which he divided into groups according to the size of the firm. Reinganum ranked the 535 firms that continued to be traded throughout his sample period by size and constructed 10 portfolios out of these securities. The daily returns of securities with market values in the lowest decile of this ranking were weighted equally to form a daily return portfolio he labeled *MV1.* Daily returns of securities in each of the other value deciles were also weighted equally to form the daily returns in the remaining portfolios, *MV2* through *MV10.*

Table 5–2 summarizes the results developed by Reinganum regarding the small-firm effect. The table shows mean excess daily returns for the one-year period after the expected return is computed. The table also shows the estimated portfolio beta, the average percentage of firms within the portfolio listed on the American Stock Exchange, the median value of the firms within the portfolio over the fourteen years of data, and the first three daily autocorrelations of the excess returns.

The table indicates that for the lowest market value portfolios, *MV1* through *MV4,* the estimated portfolio betas are virtually one. The two lowest market value portfolios are the only ones with positive excess returns. In addition, these estimates are statistically significant in that the numbers shown in parentheses, which are *t*-statistics (*t* statistics are computed by dividing the estimated coefficient by its estimated standard deviation), are relatively large (they are greater than 2.0 in absolute value). The first two portfolios stand out not only because of their positive excess returns, but also because they are heavily populated with firms that trade on the American Stock Exchange, 80 percent for *MV1* and 50 percent for *MV2.* Reinganum also carried out the same analysis for a two-year interval after the computation of expected returns and his results persisted. Portfolios of relatively small firms consistently earned positive excess returns.

If these results are taken at face value, they suggest one of two conclusions. Either the market is inefficient and cannot effectively distinguish the effect of size on value, or our methods of measuring expected returns are poorly developed. This problem is recurring in tests of the efficient markets hypothesis. Any test of the hypothesis is a joint test of two hypotheses. One hypothesis is that the market

---

[1]Also see Rolf W. Banz, ''The Relationship between Return and Market Value of Common Stocks,'' *Journal of Financial Economics,* (1981), pp. 3–18 for additional evidence on the small-firm effect.

is efficient. The other hypothesis is about how assets are priced. With tests of efficiency of pricing of equity securities, the Capital Asset Pricing Model is usually the basis for formulating measures of expected returns. If this model is flawed in ways that produce biased tests, then evidence might seem to point to market inefficiency when that is not the case. Without developing better theories of the pricing of assets, it is difficult (even impossible) to determine whether the model is wrong or the market is inefficient.

In addition to the size effect popularized by Reinganum there are also a number of potential calendar effects. These are systematic patterns in security prices that generate opportunities to earn excess return that are related to the calendar.

TABLE 5–2
Mean excess daily returns of 10 MV portfolios (based on equal-weighted NYSE-AMEX index).[a]

Portfolio	Mean Excess Returns	Beta	Average percent on AMEX	Average Median Value	Autocorrelations of Excess Returns		
					1	2	3
MV1	0.500	1.00	82.61%	8.3	0.06	0.03	0.06
	(6.42)	(101.7)					
MV2	0.193	1.02	48.35%	20.0	−0.05	0.01	−0.00
	(3.47)	(144.9)					
MV3	−0.033	1.00	23.81%	34.1	0.01	−0.00	0.02
	(−0.71)	(171.3)					
MV4	−0.050	1.00	11.29%	54.5	0.05	−0.02	0.00
	(−1.11)	(177.1)					
MV5	−0.115	0.94	8.59%	86.1	0.09	0.04	0.01
	(−2.60)	(170.3)					
MV6	−0.193	0.88	4.42%	138.3	0.20	0.07	0.11
	(−4.18)	(160.9)					
MV7	−0.189	0.90	4.35%	233.5	0.27	0.17	0.16
	(−3.99)	(156.8)					
MV8	−0.214	0.83	2.71%	413.0	0.37	0.22	0.17
	(−4.00)	(135.9)					
MV9	−0.292	0.83	2.46%	705.3	0.38	0.23	0.21
	(−5.14)	(126.3)					
MV10	−0.343	0.82	1.60%	1,759.0	0.37	0.25	0.21
	(−4.79)	(96.3)					

[a]Mean excess returns reported above are multiplied by 1000. *T*-values are in parentheses. An excess return is defined as the daily portfolio return less the equal-weighted NYSE-AMEX market return. Betas are market model estimates using this index. *MV1* is the lowest *MV* portfolio; *MV10* is the highest *MV* portfolio. The return statistics are based on 3505 daily observations from 1963 to 1977. Median values are stated in terms of millions of dollars. Only the average of the median values during the 14 years of the study is presented in the table. Similarly, the percentage of firms within each portfolio that are traded on the American Stock Exchange, averaged over 14 years, is presented.

FIGURE 5–2
Histograms of daily returns, in percent, from 1953 through 1977.

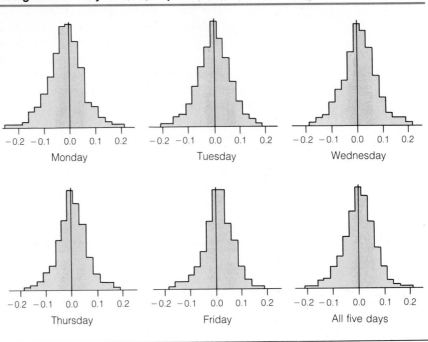

One such effect, which was identified by Kenneth French, is call the **weekend effect.**[2] The weekend effect can be summarized quite succinctly. Stock returns tend to be lower on Monday than on other days of the week. This pattern is shown in Figure 5–2, which is taken from French's study of the weekend effect. More detail is shown in Table 5–3, which shows average percentage returns by day of the week for each year from 1953 to 1977. One possible explanation for this behavior is that information released over the weekend tends to be unfavorable. While this does seem plausible, it is not a completely acceptable explanation of the stock market reaction to the timing of bad news. Investors should come to expect the release of unfavorable information on weekends and then discount stock prices appropriately throughout the week. Once again, it is necessary to conclude that either the market is inefficient or our models of asset pricing are not sufficiently well specified.

The **weekend effect** is the tendency of stock returns to be higher on Monday than on other days of the week.

---

[2]Similar results have been presented by Michael Gibbons and Patrick Hess in "Day of the Week Effects and Asset Returns," *Journal of Business*, (October 1981), pp. 579–96.

THE PROBLEM OF ASYMMETRICAL INFORMATION

The idea that markets are efficient means that prices of assets communicate all relevant information about the future returns on assets in the market. In the strong form this means that no one has any special information that is not accessible to everyone else. In other words, there are no asymmetries in access to the information, or the information possessed by market participants is symmetrical.

Asymmetrical information refers to situations where participants in market have different information about the value or quality of an asset traded in that market.

An alternative view, however, maintains that there are important asymmetries in information in the marketplace. This **asymmetrical information** argument is not really inconsistent with the available evidence on weak- and semistrong-form market efficiency. This evidence says that, on average, the prices of securities in the capital markets reflect publicly available information. The asymmetrical information argument is concerned with the following problem: suppose two firms have

TABLE 5–3
Average percent return from close of previous trading day to close of day indicated.[a]

Year	Monday	Tuesday	Wednesday	Thursday	Friday
1953	−0.2488	−0.0570	0.1181	0.0641	0.0110
1954	0.0362	0.0260	0.1746	0.1959	0.2524
1955	−0.2351	0.0857	0.2497	0.0020	0.3135
1956	−0.1445	−0.0393	−0.0649	0.0327	0.2069
1957	−0.5102	−0.0560	0.3083	−0.0237	−0.0949
1958	0.0301	0.0830	0.1166	0.1246	0.2043
1959	−0.1403	0.0865	0.0066	0.0485	0.1819
1960	−0.3487	0.0121	0.0286	0.0560	0.1604
1961	−0.0620	0.0440	0.2011	0.0631	0.1311
1962	−0.3263	0.0388	0.0404	0.0343	−0.1070
1963	−0.0836	0.1248	0.0525	0.0588	0.0969
1964	−0.0400	−0.0463	0.1023	0.0585	0.1692
1965	−0.1286	0.0505	0.0740	0.0354	0.1512
1966	−0.2645	−0.0414	0.1416	−0.1049	−0.0064
1967	−0.1755	0.1062	0.1343	0.2142	0.1026
1968	0.0007	0.0623	0.2410	−0.0664	0.0086
1969	−0.3503	−0.0691	0.0754	0.0404	0.0842
1970	−0.2790	−0.1230	0.2677	−0.0361	0.1370
1971	−0.0621	0.0872	0.0489	−0.0193	0.0899
1972	−0.1529	0.0206	0.1469	0.0501	0.1935
1973	−0.4738	0.0338	−0.0578	0.1293	−0.0877
1974	−0.3784	0.1677	−0.1015	−0.0956	−0.2676
1975	0.1918	−0.2279	0.1450	0.2250	0.2383
1976	0.1089	0.1496	0.1483	−0.0433	−0.0275
1977	−0.1274	−0.1126	−0.1091	0.0237	0.0403

[a]Returns for periods including a holiday are omitted. These returns are defined as $R_t = 1n (P_t/P_{t-1}) \cdot 100$.

THE CRASH OF 1987; AN EFFICIENT MARKET?

The efficient markets hypothesis argues that changes in the prices of securities on organized markets will be random and therefore unpredictable. Nothing in the hypothesis says that those changes cannot be large, even very large. On October 19, 1987, the Dow Jones Industrial Average (DJIA) of 30 blue-chip stocks recorded its largest one-day decline in history when it dove 508 points or 22.61 percent to a level of 1738.74. This first day of the most tumultuous week on Wall Street since the stock market crash of 1929 is known as Black Monday. Figure 5–3 shows the DJIA in 15-minute intervals over the week beginning October 19. Not only did stocks decline dramatically on October 19, but trading volume on the NYSE exceeded 600 million shares, well above the previous record trading day and more than triple the average trading volume on the exchange. In subsequent days trading volume remained at record levels, and by the end of the week, the NYSE closed early at 2:00 PM to attempt to keep track of the large volume. In addition, the decline in stock prices was not limited to U.S. exchanges or to DJIA blue-chip stocks. Exchanges throughout the world suffered significant declines and the U.S. over-the-counter stock market, the NASDAQ, experienced a decline that was roughly equivalent.

As Figure 5–3 shows, the October stock market crash entailed tremendous volatility of stock prices. While the decline was fairly consistent on Monday, on Tuesday the DJIA moved up by almost 200 points and then lost all of that gain before the trading day was half over. Before the close of trading Tuesday, the market had gained roughly 100 points. Prices then wandered without such significant changes over the next three days. But on Monday, October 26, the market had another near-record decline of 156.83 points on the DJIA or 8.04 percent.

The stock market decline needs to be put in historical perspective. In 1982, the stock market began

a major expansion that had no significant reversal until October, 1987. The dip to the mid-1700s on the DJIA set the market back to early 1986 levels. Some observers had argued that the market was overvalued and due for a correction. However, others observed that the market was simply a reflection of a positive future for U.S. business.

To some observers, the decline in the stock market, as characterized by such price volatility, was a sign of inefficiencies in the market. Since the efficient markets hypothesis argues that the market cannot be predicted, it has little patience with statements that the market is overvalued or due for a correction. The hypothesis argues that changes in the prices of securities are a result of new information entering the market which causes revised expectations or attitudes to risk. Critics of the hypothesis question what information between the close of the market on Friday, October 16, and Monday, October 19, could account for a revision of expectations worth 22.61 percent. There were no major news events over the weekend, although a number of events over the previous weeks pertaining to U.S. monetary and trade policies could have caused market participants to lower their expectations. Moreover, the critics also question what kind of new information could account for the volatility observed throughout the week, also illustrated in Figure 5–3. They contend that the market is in part driven by emotions, fears, or guesses about what other investors are guessing. Even if the market is dependent upon emotions, that does not question the idea that these emotions are unpredictable, which is the central message of efficient markets. However, one view of efficient market is that new information influencing security prices must be objective about the level or risk of future cash flows accruing to those securities. Critics of efficient markets find it difficult to reconcile this view with the events of October, 1987.

shares traded in the capital markets, and the market accurately prices those shares on average using all information available to it. Yet the managers of one firm know that their firm is really above the average, while the managers of the other firm know theirs is really below the average. They know this because they have

FIGURE 5-3
Performance of the *DJIA* during the week of October 19–23, 1987.

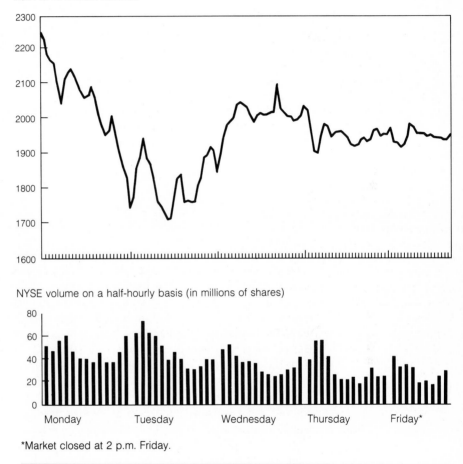

DJIA at 15-minute intervals

NYSE volume on a half-hourly basis (in millions of shares)

*Market closed at 2 p.m. Friday.

Source: *Wall Street Journal*, Oct. 26, 1987, p. 8.

inside information which the market does not. The market is still right, on average, and can therefore be efficient in the weak- and semistrong-form. But it is not efficient in the strong form because manager-insiders have special information. Managers who believe their firms are under- or overvalued might have incentives to take advantage of this situation or to try to correct it, and this can lead to various kinds of behavior that are difficult to explain if markets are thought to be efficient in the strong-form. In the extreme case, these asymmetries can lead to the breakdown of the market altogether.

THE LEMONS PROBLEM

Let's consider a particular market as an example of one of the problems that can be created by asymmetrical information. We will examine the market for used cars and explain why it is often thought of as a market for lemons.[3] Suppose there are only two kinds of cars produced. One kind is called *plums* because they perform beautifully, the other kind is called *lemons* because they perform terribly. When the cars are new it is impossible to tell a plum from a lemon; one can learn the distinction only by driving the car for a while. Therefore, everybody who owns a car knows whether it is a plum or a lemon, but potential buyers don't know the true quality of any individual car. Also, suppose that lemons are thought to be worth $2,000, while plums are worth $4,000, and the buyers know the number but not the identity of the existing lemons and plums. Finally, suppose that any car owner will sell his or her car if there is a profit to be made and will keep it if the sale involves a loss. There are no motives other than profit for selling or keeping used cars.

What will the market for used cars look like? Specifically, what will be the quality of cars sold in the used car market, and what will the going price for cars? If information were perfect—that is, if everyone knew whether each car was a lemon or a plum—then plums would sell for $4,000 and lemons for $2,000. But buyers don't know the quality of any car which someone has for sale. It is profitable for owners to claim their lemons are plums and try to sell them for $4,000. But no buyer will be willing to pay $4,000 because of the probability of being sold a lemon. If half the cars in the market were lemons and half were plums, then buyers might try offering $3,000 for cars, expecting that there was a fifty-fifty chance of getting a lemon or a plum. But at $3,000, owners of plums would not sell and buyers would, therefore, realize that they would be sure to get a lemon. In fact, at any price above $2,000 buyers would be certain to lose because no plums would be offered for sale. As a result, the market for used cars will be a market for lemons, and the price of used cars will approach $2,000. This is a result of the asymmetry in information between buyers and sellers of used cars.

The problem of asymmetrical information is potentially present in a number of markets. Essentially in this situation poor quality assets are driving out high quality assets until the market consists only of low quality products. However, if there are relatively low-cost mechanisms for correcting the information asymmetry, the efficiency of the market can be improved. In the used car market this may

---

[3]This analysis of the market for lemons is based on George A. Akerlof, "The Market for 'Lemons': Quality, Uncertainty and the Market Mechanism," *Quarterly Journal of Economics,* 89 (August 1970), pp. 488–500.

take the form of inspections or tests by unbiased mechanics or good record keeping for maintenance and repairs.

ADVERSE SELECTION IN AN INSURANCE MARKET

The lemons story illustrates how a market for relatively high quality products can be driven out of existence by asymmetrical information. In many types of financial contracts, information asymmetries such as in the used car example are an important feature of the market. In fact, many of the market's institutional features and the types of financial contracts used can be explained as a response to some kind of information asymmetry. In order to gain some insight into how contracts are influenced by asymmetrical information we can examine the problem of adverse selection in the context of an insurance market.

Adverse selection is simply another manifestation of asymmetrical information. Adverse selection occurs in insurance when purchasers know more about their own probability of incurring a loss than do the insurance underwriters. For example, it is common for health insurance purchasers to have a better idea of their risk of incurring regular but relatively minor medical expenses than does the insurance underwriter. When purchasers have better information about their own risks than do the underwriters, then the underwriters will be induced to develop complex contracts, sort out customers, or force them to reveal their information. For example, health insurers might offer contracts with different deductibles for minor expenses and different prices. Customers who believe they have a high probability of regularly incurring relatively minor expenses will be willing to pay a higher premium for the lower deductible. On the other hand, customers who perceive a low risk of incurring regular minor medical expenses will prefer a higher deductible and a lower premium.

In this kind of information asymmetry the insurance underwriter is subject to adverse selection. If an insurance underwriter made a single standard contract available to everyone, the market would be unstable. It would always be possible for another insurer to enter the market with a different contract specifically tailored for the lower-risk customer—for instance, for the health insurance customer with a lower probability of incurring regular but minor medical expenses. If these customers leave the original insurer and move to a new one, then the original insurer will not break even at prices that were fair when both kinds of customers were assumed to purchase the insurance. The first insurer is then said to have been adversely selected against and loses money because he or she attracts only the relatively high-risk customers. In order to remedy this situation all insurers must offer a set of contracts that compel customers to self-select according to their asymmetrical information. The insurer in our example will offer two contracts: one suited for high-risk individuals with a low deductible but higher price, and one suited for low risk individuals with a higher deductible but a lower price. When contracts are used in this way the market is said to have a **separating equilibrium** as opposed to a **pooling equilibrium.** A **pooling equilibrium** is an equilibrium with a single type of contract. This will work only when there is no information asymmetry and no potential for adverse selection.

Adverse selection refers to the incentive of market participants who have special knowledge of risks to select the types of contracts that are to their advantage and generally to the disadvantage of those who offer the contracts.

Separating equlibrium refers to the equilibrium in a market when distinct contracts are chosen by market participants who have different information.

Pooling equilibrium refers to the equilibrium in a market when a common contract is chosen by market participants who have different information.

The strong-form efficient market and the market with serious asymmetries in information may be viewed as extreme polar characterizations of the way real markets operate. In general, there are strong incentives that promote efficiency in any market. Later chapters will discuss the pressures and incentives that determine which characterization of a particular market is more accurate.

THE INFORMATION PRODUCTION INDUSTRY

Once we acknowledge the possibility that access to information in financial (or other) markets may be asymmetrical, then we also must ask how information asymmetries tend to be reduced or even eliminated. Much activity in financial markets is directed toward the production and communication of information. Our purpose now is to attempt to understand what mechanisms are employed to both communicate and produce information.

We will start by considering the various ways information is produced and packaged for distribution. An industry has developed to produce the information investors use to assess the value of alternative assets. Just as it is technically feasible for individuals in the United States and other developed countries to produce much of their own food, it is technically feasible for individuals to produce their own information about investment opportunities. But, as in the production of food, specialization is efficient. The economies and efficiencies in large-scale information production have led to the emergence of an industry that produces information and sells it to the consumer.

TYPES OF INFORMATION PRODUCERS

The information-production industry in the United States is diverse and complicated. At least four distinct types of information producers can be identified. They differ not so much by the nature of the production process used as in the way they market the product produced. Each type of producer is discussed below.

Information Production for Direct Sales.   The most obvious type of information producer is the company which seeks information relevant to economic conditions and, therefore, investment decisions, and publishes that information for direct distribution to investors. Probably the best-known organization of this kind in the United States is Dow Jones, Inc., publisher of *The Wall Street Journal* and other business-oriented publications. Other examples of the same type of publication are *Value Line,* Standard & Poor's *Stock Report,* and *Fortune.* Of course much of the material found in more general publications, such as *The New York Times,* is directly relevant to investment decision making. In addition, there are newsletters, consulting services, and a large number of graduate schools of business administration that are primarily in the business of directly distributing information as well as technically assessing information about investment decisions.

Sales of a Judgment about an Asset's Value. Some information producers do not directly distribute their information, but use it to produce an estimate of an asset's value and then sell the assessment of value. An obvious example of this is the rating services provided by Moody's and Standard & Poor's. These organizations continually collect information about the riskiness of the debt obligations of corporate and municipal borrowers and distribute the conclusions they draw from this information in the form of ratings to investors. The borrowers being evaluated find it profitable to pay for the service. Other examples of this type of information production are real estate appraisers and film, music, and drama critics.

Information Production Bundled with the Sale of an Asset. A number of firms produce information as a major part of their business, but only rarely sell it directly to any of their customers. An interesting example is the medical profession. Physicians are in the business of diagnosing illness and providing treatment, but they generally tie in the diagnosis with the treatment and do not sell the products separately. Only with an increased demand for second and third opinions is the diagnosis becoming known as a distinct product. The analogy with the securities brokerage industry is quite close. Securities brokers are in the business of producing information about securities to facilitate the sale of shares. However, information has not normally been sold as a distinct product. Instead, it is tied in with the service of executing a trade such that the broker's fee pays for both the transaction and the cost of the information. However, as with medical services, this tie-in arrangement has been changing somewhat in recent years.

Information Production and Intermediation. The final type of information producer is the financial intermediary, such as a commercial bank, savings and loan association, savings bank, insurance company, or mutual fund. These institutions are in the business of investing funds for their customers. They produce information about the investments they may make and return a share of the profits from the investments they undertake to those whose funds they manage. The profits they receive on their investments may be viewed as a return on their production of information.

PROBLEMS WITH QUALITY OF INFORMATION PRODUCED

Each of these four types of financial organizations is involved in collecting, processing, and, in some cases, evaluating information. They can be viewed as supplementing and/or supplanting the activity of information collection and evaluation by each investor. One problem is that there are great differences in the quality of information, and the information purchaser is usually not in a position to evaluate quality effectively. The very nature of information as a product presumes that the purchaser cannot assess quality at the time of purchase. Only as the information is used and evaluated, can its quality be ascertained. Thus, there is a strong incentive for information producers to try to misrepresent the quality of information to their customers. Information producers can easily claim that they have very valuable information and try to extract a high price for it. The problem for the market is to devise a way to separate good information from bad or to price information so that price reflects quality.

There are two factors market participants must consider when attempting to evaluate the quality of information. The first is the incentive of each producer to lie to the market. The second is the ability of the information producer to achieve a given level of quality. Hence, market participants must attempt to evaluate both *honesty and competence*.

The market can perceive there is no incentive to cheat if the information producer uses his or her own information. That is, if the information producer has a big enough stake in the outcome that any incentive to cheat is offset, then the market will accept the information at its face value. A similar mechanism depends upon the economic value of a firm's reputation. If a firm has a reputation for honesty, then this will influence the value of information it sells. The market can be reasonably sure that a firm will not misrepresent information if the gain from doing so is less than the value of a lost reputation. This will often depend upon the value of future repeat sales to the firm and suggests that the quality of information sold by an operation with little reputation will probably be low. In large reputable firms that have established a track record for honesty some lying might take place if it is difficult to detect. Moreover, there may occasionally be a big lie, as suggested by the maxim, "Be honest in all things small."[4]

The moral of this story is that when evaluating honesty it is necessary to be forward looking. The question is, will the product seller earn enough in the future from being honest to compensate him or her for refraining from cheating today? In contrast, when evaluating competence it is appropriate to be backward looking. The question then is, did this producer establish through past production that he or she has the ability to produce a high quality product? Hence, reputations generated through past behavior can be important for establishing competence. But to be important in establishing honesty, there must be a profit in remaining honest in the future.

ECONOMIES IN INFORMATION PRODUCTION AND THE ROLE OF SPECIALISTS[5]

A large number of institutions in the marketplace are essentially functioning as information producers. These institutions exist and function as they do because it is costly to acquire information. It is worth devoting some attention to exactly what is meant by the term *information costs*. In Chapter 3 the information that

---

[4]I believe that this maxim should be attributed to an anonymous but distinguished economist.
[5]The analysis presented here follows Armen Alchian's treatment of the subject very closely: "Information Costs, Pricing, and Resource Unemployment," *Western Economic Journal,* (June 1969).

was important about an asset was information about the probability distribution on returns: the expected value and variance of an asset's return as well as its covariance with other assets in the market. In order to understand information costs, it is necessary to ask how information about future returns might be acquired.

There are basically two approaches to this problem. The first can be labeled the statistical approach. The basic idea is to use past returns on the asset to estimate the expected value and risk on future returns on the asset. The implicit assumption is that the underlying probability distribution on return does not change with time. If the probability distribution from which future returns are drawn is different from the probability distribution that generated the historical returns, then the historical data will be of limited use. One view of information costs, then, is that they represent the costs of producing statistical estimates. But if this is the way market participants estimate returns, there seems little room for disagreement. Given that the correct statistical procedures are well defined and the actual historical returns on an asset are not subjective estimates, all market participants should agree on the estimated returns drawn from historical data.

The apparent shortcoming of this procedure is that probability distributions don't remain unchanged over time. For example, the market environment in which a firm operates changes as does its management, its cost of operation, and so forth. As a result, the second approach, and the one used by most market participants in conjunction with the first approach, is to assess all the information available about an asset and make a subjective estimate of the expected return and risk of an investment. In the case of a firm's stock, for example, this might involve assessing the market in which the firm operates and evaluating the strength of competitors or the skills of management. The cost of collecting and evaluating this information is what is referred to as information costs, and the institutions that produce or collect information are specialists.

OPTIMAL SEARCH

Another way of characterizing the idea of collecting information is as a process of search. It is possible to think of a search for a job, or a house, or an investment as the collection of information. In this context efficiency means that those who concentrate their efforts solely on searching for a new job will incur lower costs than those who do not specialize. The basic argument is that specialization is efficient; those who specialize can produce information at a lower cost than those who do not.

In order to explain the usefulness of specialists in producing information, we will concentrate on a particular search activity. The example concerns the sale of a house, and the search involved is the search for a buyer. The problem is presented in Figure 5–4. In Figure 5–4, time measured in days is represented on the horizontal axis, and dollars are represented on the vertical axis. Curve P_0P_t represents the maximum price the seller expects to attract, with a constant rate of search. That is, the point P_t on the curve measures the highest offer the seller would expect to receive if she searched at a constant rate for t days. To understand

FIGURE 5–4*
The value of assets and the cost of search. This figure shows two sets of curves. The lower set of curves shows the maximum expected price, maximum expected price net of search costs, and future values with the same present value for the owners of an asset who do not specialize in search. The higher set of three curves shows the same thing for a specialist who does not own the asset. The difference between Z^* and V^* represents the margin earned by the specialist.

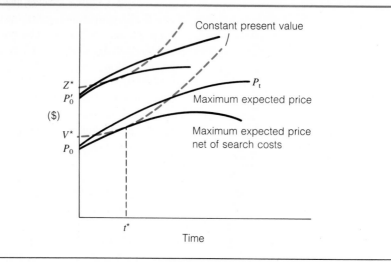

the meaning of this curve suppose that a house is for sale and the seller searches for buyers at a constant rate, 10 hours per week. With 1 week of search the maximum offer one might expect would be, say, $75,000. However, with additional days of search the chance increases that a higher offer will be received. The longer the seller searches for buyers, the higher the offers he can expect to receive. However, it seems reasonable to expect that the maximum expected offer would go up by smaller amounts with greater search. Therefore, the curve P_0P_t is drawn so that it increases at a decreasing rate. This, of course, assumes that buyers don't conclude that the house must be a lemon if it is on the market for a long time and hence reduce their offers.

Because search is a costly activity, it is necessary to incorporate the cost of search into the analysis. The cost of search represents the opportunity cost of the time spent and resources used in the search activity. For example, suppose a person values his or her time at $15 per hour and expends an additional $10 per hour on expenses. The marginal cost per hour of search is then $25. If the search is conducted at a constant rate or intensity, then this cost will be constant across time. Therefore, this constant cost of search per unit of time can be subtracted from the maximum expected price corresponding to the amount of time spent in search. The difference between the two can be plotted as a curve which is below

P_0P_t and represents the maximum expected price, net of search costs. The two curves diverge by an increasing amount because the marginal increase in the maximum expected price declines with increased search, but there is a constant marginal cost of search.

The first question that the seller must ask is how long to search or what offer to accept at each point in time. The answer depends upon the time rate of discount or interest rate she believes represents the opportunity cost. An additional curve can be drawn in the diagram representing, for a given interest rate, the quantities of dollars in any time period t that have the same present value in time period 0. This curve, represented by the dashed line through V^* in Figure 5–4, will increase at an increasing rate as long as there is a positive interest rate, due to compounding. To see this consider an example of the future value of $10 invested at 10 percent. After 2 years the $10 is worth $12.10. After 5 years it is worth $16.11, and after 10 years it is worth $25.94. It is evident the value of the $10 is increasing at an increasing rate with time. Returning to Figure 5–4, for a given interest rate there will be an infinite number of present value lines parallel to one another and intersecting each point along the vertical axis. Each corresponds to a different present value and is referred to as a constant (iso) present value line.

The objective for the seller is to obtain the highest attainable present value for her house. Therefore, the optimal waiting time or the optimal offer to accept at each point in time is the point that attains the line of highest constant present value, given the net gain available from search. The expected waiting time will be t^* periods. At this period the curve representing maximum expected price, net of search, is tangent to the curve representing constant present value. If the seller searched longer than this, she would be losing money because it would have been more profitable to accept an earlier offer and invest the funds at the interest rate that represents the opportunity cost. If the seller accepted an offer earlier than optimal, she would lose because she would have expected to gain more than the opportunity cost by waiting longer. This indicates that the value of the house for sale is equal to V^*, which is equal to the present value of the optimal offer.

THE ROLE OF THE SPECIALIST

Understanding search costs does not in itself give us a clear characterization of the role of specialists in the search for or production of information. To see how specialists fit in let's analyze how the example would be affected if an investor who specialized in real estate offered more than V^* today for the house. The question at issue is should the seller accept this offer? Yes, she should, because V^* is the value of the house to her today based on the cost of search. One might ask, however, how an investor could profitably offer more than V^*. After all, presumably the investor is not buying the house to live in and, therefore, only values it based on its resale value. In order to profitably offer more than V^*, the investor must do a better job of attracting offers than the seller. This means he must be more efficient at processing information or searching. In fact, the investor is more efficient at this kind of information processing because he specializes in this particular activity. As a result, it is possible to represent the curve the specialist sees showing the maximum expected price, net of search costs, as above that of the seller. It is shown in Figure 5–4 as the curve intersecting P_0', and the specialist's maximum expected price, net of search costs, is shown immediately below it. The highest line of constant present value the specialist can attain is the dashed line intersecting Z^*. Therefore, the specialist values the house at Z^* and can expect to earn a profit by buying it at V^*.

The analysis not only shows how specialized investors can profitably operate in a market, but it also illustrates an additional element in determining the prices of assets. Because there are costs for the search for and collection of information, assets may remain on the market for some time rather than sell immediately. Given the cost and intensity of a search, there will be an optimal waiting time for an optimal offer to accept. Moreover, it is not optimal to wait until the expected increase in the maximum price offer is equal to the marginal cost of searching for a new offer. Instead, the optimal waiting time is determined when the marginal gain from additional search, net the cost of search, is equal to the interest rate. These factors will be additional determinants of the observed prices of assets.

The basic reason information specialists exist is that they can compete with one another and earn a competitive return on producing information due to the economies which they enjoy over individuals who produce information. Information producers can therefore be viewed as contributing to the efficiency with which the market utilizes information in determining the market value of assets.

SIGNALING INFORMATION

Signaling is an important way information may be communicated from those who have it to those who do not. Many corporate finance analysts believe that many financial decisions, including dividend and capital structure decisions, involve a signal of inside information from managers to security holders. As a result, in order to understand many activities in financial markets it may be necessary to understand what constitutes a **signaling equilibrium.**

Signaling refers to the communication of assymmetrical information to the market through some action or decision.

The idea behind a signaling equilibrium is relatively simple. To understand the idea let's consider two competing firms which undertake new risky investments. The manager of firm A believes he has a project worth $10 million, while the manager of firm B believes she has a project worth only $5 million. The problem faced by the two managers is that the market does not know which of the two firms has the more valuable project. Suppose all the market knows is that one of the projects is worth $10 million and the other $5 million but not which is which. How could the manager of the firm A successfully communicate to the market that he has the more valuable project? In order to accomplish this he has to take some action that is costly for the manager of firm B to mimic. Hence, the ability of the manager of firm A to signal its value to the market depends on the cost of mimicking or the cost of signaling value to the market.

One type of signaling cost proposed in the finance literature is the penalty incurred by the manager if the firm goes bankrupt or experiences financial distress.

A manager is likely to be penalized in that he will lose his job and find it difficult to attain another equally satisfactory job if he is viewed as responsible for the firm's financial distress. The probability of bankruptcy depends both on the probability distribution of returns for a project and on the amount of leverage used to finance the firm. As a result, a firm with a more valuable investment project can afford to utilize more debt to finance that project than would another firm with a less valuable project and still run the same risk of incurring bankruptcy. This means that it will be more costly for the manager of firm B to attempt to leverage her firm to the degree of firm A. The cost involved is the ex ante or expected cost of the bankruptcy penalty that the manager could incur.

If both managers and investors in the market understand how leverage affects expected bankruptcy costs for the manager, then it is possible for leverage to signal value. The manager of firm A can increase leverage until the cost of the expected bankruptcy penalty is so large that it no longer pays for the manager of firm B to match the leverage of firm A. The expected cost of the bankruptcy penalty must be large enough, at some level of leverage chosen by the manager of firm A, that the manager of firm B is better off to reveal the identify of her firm to the market. If bankruptcy penalties are this large and managers use this fact to signal their value to the market, then it is reasonable to infer that higher leverage signals higher value investments. The empirical implication is that as we examine firms with different leverage we should conclude that the more leveraged firms are the more valuable ones. It is difficult to test this, however, since the point of the signaling story is that we cannot directly observe the value of investments. Therefore, it is difficult to attempt to examine the correlation between observed leverage and manager's perceived value.

Summary

This chapter has been about information and financial markets. The central idea is that information about the future returns on assets is costly to acquire. We explored five separate aspects of that idea: efficient financial markets, asymmetrical information, the information production industry, economies in information production, and the signaling of information.

The essence of the efficient markets hypothesis is that the market makes efficient use of information. In its simplest form this means that one cannot expect to make a profit by trying to predict future stock prices by studying their past behavior. This is called the weak-form of the hypothesis. The semistrong-form of the hypothesis contends that all publicly available information is efficiently incorporated into current prices. The strong-form says that even insider information is incorporated into market prices.

Next, we examined the implications of asymmetrical information between buyers and sellers of any product or asset. If the seller of an asset has better information than the buyer has, then the market could collapse. The reason is that the price will always be equal to the average value of all assets available for sale. As a result, the seller of the more valuable asset will withdraw from the market in order to avoid losses. This will continue until only the lowest quality assets remain. We also found that asymmetrical information can result in what is called adverse selection.

There is a large diversified industry in the United States that produces information about assets. The information is distributed in a number of different ways. Some is produced for direct sale, as in the case of many business publications. Sometimes it is tied in with an estimate of the impact of that information on particular firms, as in the case of rating agencies for bonds. Sometimes it is tied in with the sale of an asset, as in the brokerage industry, and sometimes it is tied in with the management of funds. Regardless of the way information is distributed, it is important that the information purchaser perceive it to be reliable. The market judges reliability by evaluating the incentive of each information producer to misrepresent the quality of its product and by the track record of competence.

We looked closely at why the market uses specialists to produce information by analyzing the cost and gain from search activity. The analysis showed how a specialist can operate profitably due to lower costs of search and demonstrated why it is often optimal to wait to sell an asset.

Frequently insiders who have access to special information can attempt to communicate it to others who do not have equivalent access. One such insider group is corporate managers; their decisions regarding the amount and form of financing investments may signal their information to the financial markets in general.

QUESTIONS

1. What does the phrase *information costs* mean? What costs are actually involved in collecting information? Can you give an example of a market besides financial markets where information is costly?

2. Explain what the size effect is. Why are tests of the size effect as much tests of the viability of a particular model for pricing securities as they are tests of the efficiency of financial markets?

3. Why are the small-firm effect and January effect called anomalies? What is really anomalous about them? Could these anomalies be due to problems in the underlying theory of asset pricing? Explain.

4. What is a signaling equilibrium? What is necessary for a signaling equilibrium to exist? How can the degree of leverage chosen by a manager of a firm signal the value of the firm's assets to the market? How can a firm's dividend policy signal value?

5. At least four distinct types of information producers can be identified. Can you identify them?

6. Why is reputation important in the information production industry? What has reputation got to do with the problem of asymmetrical information?

7. Why isn't information production a cottage industry? Can you explain how specialists in information can function profitably?

8. Distinguish between the weak, semistrong, and strong forms of the efficient markets hypothesis.

9. Explain your opinion of the following statement: If markets were really efficient, there would be no room for securities analysts.

10. Suppose you observed the price of a share of stock over a year-long period, and you plot that price as in Figure 5–1. How could you use this to forecast the future price of this stock? Could you use it to forecast the price of a different share of stock? Could you use it to forecast the price of Toyota Coronas?

11. What does it mean for a market to fail or break down? How can this happen if there is asymmetrical information?

12. What is adverse selection? Explain how adverse selection might be important in the market for mortgages. What types of procedures do you think might be developed by mortgage lenders and those who guaranty mortgage lenders to protect against adverse selection.

REFERENCES

Akerlof, George A. "The Market for 'Lemons'; Quality, Uncertainty and the Market Mechanism," *Quarterly Journal of Economics,* (August 1970), pp. 488–500.

Alchian, Armen. "Information Costs, Pricing, and Resource Unemployment," *Western Economic Journal,* (June 1969), pp. 109–27.

Banz, Rolf W. "The Relationship Between Return and Market Value of Common Stocks," *Journal of Financial Economics,* (1981).

Darby, Michael R. and Edi Karni. "Free Competition and the Optimal Amount of Fraud," *Journal of Law and Economics,* (April 1973), pp. 67–88.

Fama, Eugene. "The Behavior of Stock-Market Prices," *Journal of Business,* (January 1965), pp. 34–105.

————. "Efficient Capital Markets: A Review of Theory and Empirical Work," *Journal of Finance,* (May 1970), pp. 383–416.

———— and Arthur Laffer. "Information and Capital Markets," *Journal of Business,* (July 1971), pp. 289–98.

French, Kenneth R. "Stock Returns and the Weekend Effect," *Journal of Financial Economics,* (1980), pp. 55–69.

Gibbons, Michael and Patrick Hess. "Day of the Week Effects and Asset Returns," *Journal of Business,* (October 1981), pp. 579–96.

Gonedes, Nicholas J. "The Capital Market, the Market for Information, and External Accounting," *Journal of Finance,* (May 1976), pp. 611–28.

Grossman, Sanford and Joseph Stiglitz. "Information and Competitive Price Systems," *American Economic Review,* (May 1976), pp. 246–52.

————, Richard E. Kihlstrom, and Leonard J. Mirman. "A Bayesian Approach to the Production of Information and Learning by Doing," *Review of Economic Studies,* (October 1977), pp. 533–47.

Klein, Benjamin. "The Competitive Supply of Money," *Journal of Money, Credit and Banking,* (November 1974), pp. 423–51.

———, Robert Crawford, and Armen Alchian. "Vertical Integration, Appropriate Rents, and the Competitive Contracting Progress," *Journal of Law and Economics,* (October 1978), pp. 297–326.

Reinganum, Marc R. "Misspecification of Capital Asset Pricing: Empirical Anomolies Based on Earnings Yields and Market Values," *Journal of Financial Economics,* (1981), pp. 19–46.

Rothschild, Michael and Joseph Stiglitz. "Equilibrium in Competitive Insurance Markets: An Essay on Economics of Imperfect Information," *Quarterly Journal of Economics,* (November 1976), pp. 629–49.

Ross, Stephen A. "The Determination of Financial Structure: the Incentive Signalling Approach," *Bell Journal of Economics,* (Spring 1977), pp. 23–40.

2
PART

*D*ETERMINANTS OF MARKET INTEREST RATES

Part 2 leaves behind the question of how individual assets are valued and explores how aggregate market interest rates are determined. Throughout Part 2 and the rest of this book, observed market interest rates will be referred to as nominal as opposed to real interest rates. We learned in Chapter 2 that the real interest rate is the rate of interest which underlies all observable rates. In Part 2 we will see that nominal interest rates can best be understood as the sum of the real rate plus premiums for each of the important factors omitted from the real rate. The first chapter in this part, Chapter 6, explains how inflation affects nominal interest rates. It covers the link between inflation and interest rates in many countries, not simply the United States, so it also deals with exchange rates between currencies. Chapter 7 describes three other factors which affect nominal interest rates: default risk, taxes, and relative security supplies. Chapter 8 concentrates on the relationship between the nominal interest rate and the maturity of a debt instrument, the term structure of interest rates. Chapter 9, draws upon the material in Chapters 4, 6, 7, and 8, in order to analyze how the risk of changing interest rates and exchange rates can be hedged using options and futures contracts. Finally, Chapters 10 and 11 deal with the link between monetary policy and interest rates. Chapter 10 explains how the Federal Reserve influences the monetary aggregates and market interest rates, while Chapter 11 analyzes the ongoing debate about how monetary policy should be conducted. Taken together, Parts 1 and 2 provide a comprehensive picture of how individual prices and interest rates as well as aggregate market interest rates are determined in the United States and the global financial markets. ∎

6

*I*NFLATION, INTEREST RATES, AND EXCHANGE RATES

We began our analysis of market interest rates in Chapter 2 where we learned about the real interest rate. Unfortunately, it is very rare that we actually observe the real interest rate. The real rate is a bit like the nucleus of an atom: it is very difficult to actually see it, but it is the foundation of everything we do observe. Now we need to fill in the gaps between the foundation and the interest rates we actually observe in the world. We will refer to these observed rates as *nominal rates* to distinguish them from the underlying real interest rate. Five factors account for the difference between the real rate and observed nominal rates. They are inflation, default risk, taxes, relative security supplies, and maturity.

In this chapter we will deal with the link between inflation and interest rates, as well as the links between inflation and interest rates in different currencies. We will explore the basic relationship between exchange rates between currencies, inflation, and interest rates.

To see more specifically what is meant by observed nominal interest rates, it is helpful to examine a diagram that plots the levels of various yields in the United States over a specific historical period. Figure 6–1 shows the level of a collection of yields from 1981 to 1985. Panel A plots yields on short-term or money market debt instruments. Panel B plots yields on long-term instruments, including bonds issued by private corporations, the U.S. government, and state and local governments (municipal bonds). Municipal bonds generally had the lowest yield of all the debt securities indicated, and the next highest yields were on mortgages and federal funds at different times during the period. Finally, the yields on corporate bonds were consistently higher than the yields on Treasury bonds. ∎

FIGURE 6–1
U.S. interest rates.

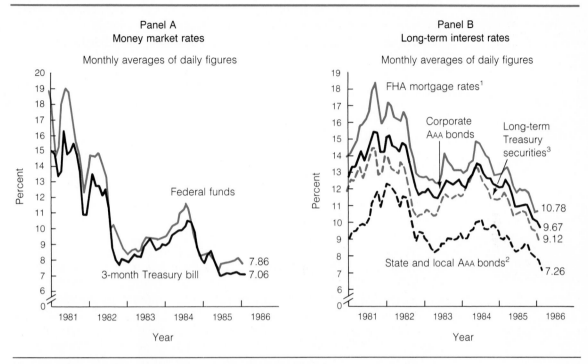

Panel A
Money market rates

Monthly averages of daily figures

Panel B
Long-term interest rates

Monthly averages of daily figures

[1]FHA 30-year mortgages; dashed lines indicate data not available.

[2]Monthly averages of Thursday figures.

[3]Average of yields on coupon issues due or callable in ten years of more excluding issues with federal estate tax privileges; computed by this bank.

Latest data plotted: February.

Prepared by Federal Reserve Bank of St. Louis.

DEFINITION OF TERMS

Before we consider the relationship between inflation and nominal interest rates we need to define some terms pertaining to interest rates. In addition, we must explore some concepts fundamental to the financial markets, like the distinction between yield-to-maturity and holding-period yield. We also want to be able to compute the market yield or yield-to-maturity on a Treasury bill and the holding period yield on a Treasury bill. In this chapter we need the latter number to compute the ex post real return on a Treasury bill. Moreover, we will distinguish between an ex post, or after-the-fact, return on Treasury bills and an ex ante return, in both real and nominal terms. These distinctions are synonymous with the distinction between holding-period yield and yield-to-maturity. Therefore, we should save a lot of confusion if we pin down these ideas now.

A **discount instrument** is a promise to pay a fixed amount at a future date or a bond without any coupon payments.

First, we will see how to compute the market yield or yield-to-maturity on a Treasury bill. A Treasury bill is a pure **discount instrument,** which means that it has no coupon payments. In the *Wall Street Journal* yields are quoted on Treasury bills in a specific format. For example, the *Wall Street Journal* of December 31, 1984, listed the following information on a specific Treasury bill in the section that shows current Treasury bill prices:

Maturity	Bid	Asked	Yield
3-28-85	7.80	7.60	7.85

The first column indicates the date this particular bill will mature. The second column indicates the discount interest rate that determines the price a dealer would pay for this bill. The third column indicates the discount interest rate that determines the price a dealer would sell this bill for. The final column indicates the yield you would earn if you bought this bill at the asked price and held it until maturity, or the **yield-to-maturity.** Before we go any further we want to decipher how to compute the yield-to-maturity of 7.85 for this bill.

The **yield-to-maturity** is the yield you would earn on a bond if it were held until maturity.

We start by counting the number of days until this bill matures. Since the bill was listed in the paper on 12/31/84, that means it was the price prevailing one day earlier (unless 12/31/84 was a Monday). Therefore, there were 88 days from the day the bill would have been acquired until it matured. By convention, the year is only 360 days long in the Treasury market. As a result, this bill will have a time to maturity expressed as a fraction of a 360-day year or 88/360. To compute the price the dealer is asking for this bill it is necessary to multiply this fraction by the asked discount interest rate of 7.60 and subtract this from 100:

$$\text{Asked price} = 100 - (88/360 \times 7.60) = 98.142.$$

This bill commands a price of $98.142 per $100 of maturity value of the bill. Now we can use this price to determine the yield-to-maturity. We simply need to ask what the yield is on an investment for which we pay $98.142 today and receive $100 in 88 days. The answer is

$$\text{Yield to maturity} = \left(\frac{100}{98.142} - 1\right)\frac{365}{88} = 7.85\%.$$

The **holding-period yield** on a bond is the yield you actually earn, taking into account the price you paid and the price you received when you sold the bond.

To compute the true yield-to-maturity we must correct for the fact that the discount asked interest rate was based on a 360 rather than a 365-day year, while the actual market yield to maturity is based on a 365-day year. The yield we have computed is a yield-to-maturity in that it is forward looking: it is the yield you would actually earn, after the fact, if you held this bill until maturity. This means the yield-to-maturity will also be your **holding-period yield** if you hold this bill to maturity. However, suppose you were to buy a bill with six months to maturity and then sell it when it had three months to maturity. The yield-to-maturity on that bill when you bought it would not be your holding-period yield, except by chance.

To see how to compute the holding-period yield in this situation we need to consider another example. Suppose that on June 30, 1985, you had purchased a Treasury bill maturing on December 26, 1985. The asked discount rate on that bill when you bought it would have been 7.21 percent, and the corresponding asking price would have been 96.415. If you had sold that bill on September 30, 1985, when it still had approximately three months until maturity, the bid price would have been 98.375. Therefore, the holding period would have been 91 days, and the holding-period yield can be computed:

$$\text{Holding-period yield} = \left(\frac{98.357}{96.415} - 1\right)\frac{365}{91} = 8.08\%.$$

The holding-period yield in this situation cannot be known with certainty when the Treasury bill is purchased because the price of three-month bills prevailing three months in the future cannot be known. Only if the bill is held to maturity will the holding-period yield and the yield-to-maturity be the same thing. The holding-period yield can be known with certainty only in this case. As we proceed through this chapter, we will distinguish between ex ante and ex post real interest rates. The yield-to-maturity is an ex ante yield, and the holding-period yield is an ex post yield. Now that we have defined these terms and we know how to compute these yields, we can move on to examine the relationship between inflation and interest rates.

THE LINK BETWEEN INFLATION AND NOMINAL INTEREST RATES

The real interest rate, as indicated in Chapter 2, is defined net of inflation. It is similar to real income or real gross national product in that the effect of inflation has been extracted. This does not mean that it is safe to ignore inflation because it has no impact on interest rates. Inflation, or more precisely, the *anticipated rate of inflation* is an important determinant of the interest rates observed in the world. When the interest rate is referred to inclusive of the effect of inflation, it is called the *nominal interest rate*.

REAL AND NOMINAL RATES DEFINED

The *real interest rate* is the equilibrium rate at which claims to future income are traded for current income. The real rate of interest is expressed without reference to prices. If the quantity of goods and services available for consumption in time periods 1 and 2 are represented by Q_1 and Q_2, respectively, then the real rate of interest is

$$\text{Real interest rate} = \frac{Q_2 - Q_1}{Q_1}. \tag{6-1}$$

This means that the real interest rate is the real rate of growth in available goods and services.

The **nominal interest rate** is the yield quoted in the market taking into account the future rate of inflation.

The **nominal interest rate,** on the other hand, takes into account the change in the price of goods and services. It values the quantity of goods and services in each time period at their going price. If the aggregate price level of all goods and services is represented by P_1 and P_2 in periods 1 and 2, respectively, then the nominal interest rate can be expressed as

$$\text{Nominal interest rate} = \frac{P_2 Q_2 - P_1 Q_1}{P_1 Q_1}. \tag{6-2}$$

In addition, the rate of inflation between periods 1 and 2 can be defined as

$$\text{Inflation rate} = \frac{P_2 - P_1}{P_1}. \tag{6-3}$$

A relationship between the real and nominal rates follows directly from these definitions. The nominal interest rate can be expressed as the sum of the real interest rate, the rate of inflation, and the product of the real interest rate and the rate of inflation:

$$\frac{P_2 Q_2 - P_1 Q_1}{P_1 Q_1} = \frac{Q_2 - Q_1}{Q_1} + \frac{P_2 - P_1}{P_1} + \frac{(Q_2 - Q_1)}{Q_1} \times \frac{(P_2 - P_1)}{P_1}. \tag{6-4}$$

Nominal rate = Real rate + Inflation rate + (Real rate × Inflation rate).

To see this, expand the right-hand side of Equation (6–4) and cancel terms until this expression for the nominal interest rate reduces to the one on the left-hand side of the equation.[1]

---

[1]We can rewrite Equation (6–4), after expanding the final term, as follows:

$$\frac{P_2 Q_2 - P_1 Q_1}{P_1 Q_1} = \frac{Q_2 - Q_1}{Q_1} + \frac{P_2 - P_1}{P_1} + \frac{P_2 Q_2 - P_2 Q_2 + P_1 Q_1}{P_1 Q_1}.$$

Next, we will multiply numerator and denominator of the first term by P_1 and the second term by Q_1. We then have:

$$= \frac{P_1 Q_2 - P_1 Q_1}{P_1 Q_1} + \frac{P_2 Q_1 - P_1 Q_1}{P_1 Q_1} + \frac{P_2 Q_2 - P_2 Q_1 - P_1 Q_2 + P_1 Q_1}{P_1 Q_1}.$$

Now we can cancel all the products of price and quantity that do not have the same time subscripts. What is left is the following:

$$= \frac{-P_1 Q_1}{P_1 Q_1} = \frac{P_1 Q_1}{P_1 Q_1} + \frac{P_2 Q_2}{P_1 Q_1} + \frac{P_1 Q_1}{P_1 Q_1}.$$

Finally, the first and last terms cancel and the expression for the nominal rate remains.

A convenient simplification for this equation results in a simple and usable relationship between the nominal rate and the rate of inflation. The simplification relies on the fact that the last term is the product of two small fractions. As a result, it is likely to be so small that it can be harmlessly dropped. For example, suppose that the real rate is 3 percent and the inflation rate is 10 percent; the product of the two will be 0.003. Generally, this is simply too small to make much difference. Therefore, the simple expression for the nominal interest rate is that the nominal rate is equal to the sum of the real interest rate and the rate of inflation:

$$i_N = i_R + \Delta P, \qquad (6-5)$$

where i_N is the nominal rate, i_R is the real rate, and ΔP is the inflation rate. For example, if the inflation rate is 10 percent and the real rate is 3 percent, then the nominal rate is 13 percent.

Thus far no economic hypothesis has been offered about the relationship between real and nominal interest rates. The expression just developed follows directly from the definitions of the real interest rate, the nominal interest rate, and the inflation rate. It therefore says nothing about how financial markets respond to inflation. To develop a hypothesis about financial markets and inflation, it is necessary to recognize that at any point in time the inflation rate is uncertain. The economic issue, then, is how anticipations of inflation affect the market.

EX ANTE AND EX POST INFLATION AND REAL INTEREST RATES

It is exceptionally important to distinguish between anticipated and unanticipated inflation, or, alternatively stated, between the ex ante expected rate of inflation and the ex post observed rate of inflation. Irving Fisher offered a hypothesis some years ago about the relationship between nominal interest rates and the market's **ex ante expected inflation rate;** that hypothesis is exceptionally relevant today. At first glance the hypothesis looks the same as Equation (6–5) above, but it is not. Equation (6–5) followed directly from the definitions specified above when uncertainty about the inflation rate was ignored. Fisher's hypothesis can be stated as follows:

The **ex ante expected rate of inflation** is the rate of inflation the market expects over a future period of time.

$$i_N = i_R + \Delta P^e. \qquad (6-6)$$

Nominal interest rate = The ex ante real interest rate +
The market's ex ante expected rate of inflation.

The equilibrium nominal interest rate is such that lenders receive a compensation equal to the real interest rate plus an amount that perfectly offsets the expected rate of inflation. If the nominal interest rate provided less compensation than this, then lenders would be expected to lose in real terms on financial transactions. Because, in equilibrium, lenders should not expect to lose on financial contracts, the nominal interest rate will have to rise to just cover the market's expectation of inflation plus the real interest rate.

Because the inflation rate is uncertain, the ex post or realized real return may be either more or less than the real interest rate demanded ex ante. To see this it is helpful to examine a modified version of Equation (6–6). Equation (6–7) says that the ex post real interest rate a lender actually receives, symbolized by i'_R, is equal to the nominal rate initially set for the financial transaction i_N, less the actual inflation rate in the period in question, symbolized by $\Delta P'$:

$$i'_R = i_N - \Delta P'. \tag{6–7}$$

The **ex post real interest rate** is the difference between the nominal interest rate and the actual inflation rate.

In any given time period the **ex post real interest rate** may be calculated from the actual nominal interest rate and the actual rate of inflation. But this ex post real interest rate is not the ex ante real interest rate in Fisher's theory. The ex post real interest rate will reflect the market's errors in guessing the inflation rate. For example, the ex post real interest rate earned by holding 90-day Treasury bills for 1977 and 1985 are shown in Table 6–1. These were computed according to Equation (6–7). For example, in January, 1977, $i_N = 4.6$ percent, $\Delta P' = 10.2$ percent, so that $i'_R - 4.6$ percent $- 10.2$ percent $= -5.6$ percent. These returns

TABLE 6–1
Historical ex post real interest rates.

Panel A: Ex Post Real Returns on Three-Month Treasury Bills for 1977,				Panel B: Ex Post Real Returns on Three-Month Treasury Bills for 1985,			
Three-month Treasury Bill Rate Issued in Month:		Subsequently Observed Inflation Rate[a] (%)	Ex Post Real Interest Rate (%)	Three-month Treasury Bill Rate Issued in Month:		Subsequently Observed Inflation Rate (%)	Ex post Real Interest Rate (%)
Month	Rate (%)			Month	Rate (%)		
January	4.6	10.2	−5.6	January	7.8	4.2	3.6
February	4.7	8.1	−3.4	February	8.2	5.1	3.1
March	4.6	8.3	−3.7	March	8.6	4.9	2.7
April	4.5	6.9	−2.4	April	8.0	4.4	3.6
May	4.9	6.1	−1.2	May	7.6	3.4	4.2
June	5.0	4.9	0.1	June	7.0	2.7	4.3
July	5.1	4.2	0.9	July	7.0	2.6	4.4
August	5.5	4.7	0.8	August	7.2	3.3	3.9
September	5.8	3.5	2.3	September	7.1	3.8	2.3
October	6.2	4.0	2.2	October	7.2	3.6	3.6
November	6.1	6.6	−0.5	November	7.2	3.6	3.6
December	6.1	8.2	−2.1	December	7.1	1.1	6.0

[a]This is computed from the 3-month change in the consumer price index, that is, for January this is the annualized change from January to April.

reflect the actual returns, after inflation, from holding Treasury bills during these years. They do not necessarily indicate the value of the ex ante real interest rate demanded by lenders. We simply do not see the ex ante real rate, in spite of its importance in lenders' decisions.

WEALTH REDISTRIBUTION DUE TO INFLATION

Monetary assets are assets with returns which are fixed in dollars or in nominal terms, such as Treasury bonds.

Real assets are assets with returns that are not fixed in nominal terms but which rise and fall with the inflation rate.

To better understand anticipated versus unanticipated inflation we will examine the impact on the balance sheets of lenders and borrowers of actual rates of inflation higher or lower than anticipated. To keep the discussion as simple as possible, we will assume that there are only two types of assets available in the economy. We normally think of these two types of assets as debt and equity securities, but we will refer to them as **monetary** and **real assets,** respectively. The two classification schemes are not completely interchangeable. Debt and equity securities have some characteristics that do not easily fit into the monetary-real classification. But to examine the effect of inflation, the distinction between monetary and real assets suits this purpose rather well. Debt is a claim on a future payment which is fixed in money terms, while equities, now called real assets, are not titles to fixed money payments. A money claim is a contractual agreement for one party—the debtor—to pay another party—the creditor—a prespecified dollar amount at some time in the future. Money claims include money itself; savings deposits; short-term debt instruments, such as Treasury bills; and long-term bonds, such as mortgages. On the other hand, real assets involve no claim to a prespecified dollar payment. Instead, they are generally residual claims to the income accruing to an asset after all monetary claimants have been paid.

We want to investigate what happens to money creditors and money debtors if there are unanticipated changes in the inflation rate. The difference between a money creditor and a debtor is simply a matter of whether an individual has borrowed more than was lent or has greater monetary liabilities than assets. If lending exceeds borrowing, the person is a money creditor; whereas if borrowing exceeds lending, he or she is a money debtor. Table 6–2 shows an example of a money creditor and a money debtor. The money debtor has borrowed $20,000 to add to initial equity of $10,000 and has invested $20,000 in real assets and $10,000 in money assets. By comparison, the money creditor has equity of $20,000 and has borrowed only $10,000 in order to invest $20,000 in money assets and $10,000 in real assets. The money creditor and debtor in this table are representative of all the money creditors and debtors in the economy: the money debts of one are exactly equal to the money assets of the other. This table shows the kind of redistribution of wealth that takes place as the inflation rate deviates from what is anticipated.

In Table 6–2, both market participants expect that the rate of inflation will be 100 percent. Furthermore, to keep the algebra simple, it is assumed that the real interest rate is zero. The table then shows the changes in the balance sheet of both individuals if the actual inflation rate turns out to be 50, 100, and 150 percent. The nominal value of money debts and money assets will be unaffected by the actual inflation rate. For example, the net money debtor contracts for $20,000 worth of debt at the beginning of the period and, with 100 percent expected inflation, agrees to repay $40,000 regardless of the actual inflation rate. The real return on such contracts fluctuates with the actual inflation rate in that the $40,000 payment will be less costly if the inflation rate has been 150 percent rather than 50 percent. On the other hand, the value of real assets rises perfectly with the inflation rate, and hence, their real value is fixed.

The fundamental point this table illustrates is that money debtors do well when the market underestimates the rate of inflation, while money creditors do well when the market overestimates the rate of inflation. Moreover, the gain of

TABLE 6–2
Balance sheets of money debtors and creditors (100% anticipated inflation).

	Before Inflation	After 50% Inflation	After Anticipated 100% Inflation	After 150% Inflation
Net Money Debtor				
Money assets	10,000	20,000	20,000	20,000
Real assets	20,000	30,000	40,000	50,000
Total assets	30,000	50,000	60,000	70,000
Money debts	20,000	40,000	40,000	40,000
Equity	10,000	10,000	20,000	30,000
Total	30,000	50,000	60,000	70,000
% Increase in equity		0%	100%	200%
% Change in real value of equity		−33%[a]	0.0%	20%
Net Money Creditor				
Money assets	20,000	40,000	40,000	40,000
Real assets	10,000	15,000	20,000	25,000
Total assets	30,000	55,000	60,000	65,000
Money debts	10,000	20,000	20,000	20,000
Equity	20,000	35,000	40,000	45,000
Total	30,000	55,000	60,000	65,000
% Increase in equity		75%	100%	125%
% Change in real value of equity		17%	0	−10%

[a]This is computed as follows:

$$1 - \frac{\text{Nominal value of equity in period 2}}{(1 + \text{inflation rate}) \times \text{Nominal value of equity in period 1}}$$

$$= 1 - \frac{10,000}{15,000}.$$

the money debtor is the loss of the money creditors. That is, unanticipated inflation, whether higher or lower than anticipated, redistributes wealth. It does not lead to a net change in wealth of all participants in the market.

To see that this is true, first examine what happens to the money debtor. If the inflation rate is exactly as anticipated, 100 percent, then there is no gain or loss on financial contracts in money terms. Therefore, the value of the money debtor's equity increases at the same rate as inflation. If the market overestimates the rate of inflation by 50 percent, then the money debtor loses $10,000 on net money debts, but also gains $10,000 on real assets; the nominal value of his or her equity remains unchanged, though the real value of this equity has declined by one-third. On the other hand, if the market underestimates the rate of inflation, he or she gains $30,000 on real assets and still only loses a nominal value of $10,000 on net money debts. Therefore the nominal value of his or her equity increases by 200 percent, which makes the real value of that equity 20 percent greater than it was before.

The pattern of gains and losses from unanticipated inflation is exactly the opposite for the money creditor. Again, he or she experiences no real gain or loss if the actual inflation rate is equal to the expected inflation rate, but if the market overestimates the rate of inflation, then there is a gain in real terms; that is, a net gain on money assets of $10,000 and a gain on real assets of $5,000. As a result, the nominal value of equity increases 75 percent, which means that the real value rises by 17 percent. If the market underestimates the rate of inflation, then the nominal gain on net money assets is still $10,000, but this now implies a smaller real gain. In fact, the real value of equity now declines by 10 percent.

The example illustrates that for the economy as a whole, where the net borrowing of all monetary debtors equals the net lending of all monetary creditors, the effect of unanticipated inflation is to transfer wealth. The money debtor paid the money creditor a net of $10,000 regardless of the rate of inflation. This was a good deal for the debtor if the inflation rate was above the expected rate, but it was a bad deal if the actual rate was lower than expected. Neither party would expect to profit from this, ex ante, given that they had the same information and expectations. Only if a market participant has superior information relative to the market can he or she expect to profit from inflation.

THE BEHAVIOR OF EX ANTE REAL RATE AND THE EFFICIENT MARKETS HYPOTHESIS: UNRESOLVED QUESTIONS

At least two interesting and important questions should be asked about the observed behavior of the nominal interest rate on debt instruments or on assets that have returns fixed in money terms. The first question is, how much of the changes in the nominal interest rate are due to changes in the real rate of interest as opposed to changes in the expected rate of inflation? The second question is, does the market efficiently use all available information in assessing the future inflation rate? The answers to these questions are not obvious. There is considerable disagreement not only about the correct answers, but also about how to determine the correct answers. Still, these questions are important and worth considering, at least briefly, even if no definite answers can be provided.

Irving Fisher is widely perceived to have argued that the real rate of interest is essentially constant. (Unfortunately, he is not around now to explain what he really meant.) According to Fisher, fluctuations in the nominal rate of interest basically represent changes in the expected rate of inflation. It should be understood that the real rate of interest is probably never exactly constant. The argument is that fluctuations in the real interest rate are relatively small. Therefore, when there are periods of fairly sizable changes in nominal interest rates, they should be attributed to changes in the expected rate of inflation. The alternative view is that there can be, and often are, rather large changes in the real interest rate. Therefore, changes in nominal rates cannot be attributed entirely to changes in inflation expectations.

The significance of the constant real rate hypothesis should not be underestimated. This view suggests that it is largely fruitless to worry about such things as analysis of the loanable funds market and the flow of funds. Changes in desired borrowing and lending basically all come out in the wash and equilibrate at the same real interest rate. The argument behind this is that the real interest rate also represents the marginal rate of return on the economy's capital stock. That capital stock is very large and changes only very slowly. Hence, changes in the real interest rate cannot be very large, at least in the short run.

The alternative view is that, for substantial periods of time, shifts in the supply or demand curves for loanable funds, which influence the real interest rate in financial markets, can take place. Only in a very long-run equilibrium do these changes have to induce similar changes in the real rate of return on the economy's capital stock. This argument implies that the real interest rate in the loanable funds market can move above or below the real return on capital for periods that may be as long as a year or two. For the purpose of understanding monthly, quarterly, or annual changes in interest rates on financial contracts, it is important to examine changes in the real rate of interest.

The second question, regarding market efficiency, is not quite so controversial. In this instance, the efficient markets hypothesis asserts that all available information is efficiently used by the market in assessing future inflation rates. This seems easy enough to accept, but it is very difficult to verify because it is impossible to observe the market's expected rate of inflation directly. This is true for the same reason that it is impossible to observe the market's ex ante real interest rate directly. It is possible to observe the ex post real interest and inflation rates, but these are not the direct subject of the efficient markets hypothesis.

Some conclusions can be drawn about market efficiency from the ex post real interest rate, however. One implication of the efficient markets hypothesis is that the market should not make systematic errors in guessing the inflation rate. For example, if there is some pattern in the way the actual inflation rate moves through time, then the market should figure out the pattern and it should not show up in the behavior of the market's ex post real return. If, for example, you looked at a graph of the ex post real interest rate, it should wander without any definable pattern.

This hypothesis has been tested statistically by Eugene Fama in a controversial but interesting study.[2] Fama shows that there is an identifiable pattern in the behavior of the inflation rate, and that when the real return on Treasury bills is computed, as in Table 6–1, the pattern does not show up in these returns. He concludes that the market efficiently uses the information contained in the consumer price index in assessing the future changes in that index. Other researchers have criticized some of Fama's methodology and have challenged his conclusions. This is a difficult topic, and more definitive conclusions about the market's efficiency in this instance may be hard to come by.

INFLATION AND THE RETURNS ON EQUITY SECURITIES

One way investors try to deal with inflation is to place their wealth in assets with rates of return that rise and fall with the actual inflation rate. In the simplified world presented in Table 6–2, these assets are all lumped under the heading of real assets. If an investor had no money debts and had all his or her wealth invested in real assets, then this would represent a perfect inflation hedge, for the real value of wealth would remain unchanged as the inflation rate fluctuates. In the late 1970s, when inflation rates were high and volatile, investors tried to do exactly this. They invested heavily in many commodities they believed would increase in value with inflation. Moreover, many of these assets did in fact increase.

One type of asset which was traditionally thought of as a good inflation hedge did not increase in value. That asset is common stock or equity claims on companies. Common stocks have generally been thought to be a good inflation hedge because they are the residual claims to all earnings after money debtors have been paid. Hence, if there is unanticipated inflation, it should work to the benefit of equityholders over debtholders. But in the 1970s it did not work that way. When inflation was high, the total returns on equities were quite low. Table 6–3 shows how low these returns were compared to returns on other investments, such as Treasury bills, real estate, and human capital. For example, during the 1971–1975 period the NYSE provided only a 1.6 percent nominal return while the inflation rate was 7.1 percent and Treasury bills earned approximately 6 percent.

There are at least three possible explanations for this behavior of common stock prices. One is the argument that corporate taxes increased with inflation so that inflation led to a decline in after-tax returns. The second is that investors were systematically undervaluing equity securities. The third is that inflation causes investors' expectations of future earnings to decline.

Consider the tax argument first. Its proponents contend that corporate taxes increase with inflation because of two peculiarities about the way taxable income is computed. First, income includes paper profits on inventories, that is, increases in the value of inventories due to inflation that will never actually be realized by

---

[2]See Eugene F. Fama, "Short-Term Interest Rates and Predictors of Inflation," *American Economic Review,* (June 1975), pp. 269–82.

TABLE 6–3
Average annualized nominal returns on assets (%) and inflation rates (% change in CPI).

Variable Inflation	1/53- 12/57 1.3	1/58- 12/62 1.3	1/63 12/67 2.2	1/68- 7/71 5.1	8/71- 12/75 7.1
Treasury bills					
1 month	1.9	2.2	3.7	5.5	5.7
2 month	2.1	2.7	4.0	5.9	6.0
3 month	2.3	3.0	4.1	6.1	6.4
Real estate r_1^a	1.0	0.6	1.7	5.9	6.2
Labor income h_1^b	2.2	3.4	5.2	4.7	6.1
Common stocks^c					
NYSE index	12.3	12.8	12.5	3.0	1.6

Source: Eugene F. Fama and William G. Schwert, "Asset Returns and Inflation," *Journal of Financial Economics,* 5(1977), p. 123.

^{a}Computed from the home purchase price component of the CPI.
^{b}Computed from changes in labor income.
^{c}Based on a value-weighted index of NYSE securities.

the company in question. Second, income includes depreciation, which is calculated on the basis of the original cost of the asset rather than the replacement cost. Both of these factors tend to overstate reported corporate profits for tax purposes. This leads to higher levels of taxes than would otherwise be the case, which in turn, reduce the real returns on the total capital of corporations. But a potentially offsetting effect tends to counter these tendencies for taxes to rise with inflation; that effect is the increased tax deduction for interest expense, which tends to reduce the total tax bill as a proportion of total profits. Some have argued that these two effects are largely offsetting. Therefore, total after-tax corporate profits adjusted for inventory, profits, and depreciation on a replacement cost basis, plus interest expense, were driven neither up nor down in the 1970s. If total corporate profits including interest have not significantly declined, then one might question whether the prices of equities were in some sense too low.

The second argument is that during the 1970s investors were making errors in valuing equities such that their assessment of value was too low based on any rational analysis. This argument is generally very distasteful to economists because it is based on the notion that the market is slow to learn or is relatively inefficient, but the argument has nonetheless been taken seriously by at least one economist with considerable reputation. One of the alleged errors the market may have been making is to capitalize profits by an inappropriate discount rate.[3]

[3]See Franco Modigiliani and Richard A. Cohn, "Inflation, Rational Valuation and the Market," *Financial Analysts Journal,* (March/April 1979), pp. 24–44.

To understand the nature of this error we need to examine a very simple model of the value of an asset. Suppose that the market expects the underlying stream of real earnings accruing to an asset to remain the same during each future period. This constant expected real rate per period is X. Also suppose the market expects the future nominal earnings of the asset to grow at an expected inflation rate, p. If this revenue stream were expected to go on indefinitely, then the value of the asset could be approximated as

$$V = \frac{X}{i_N - p} = \sum_{t=1}^{N} \frac{X(1 + p)^t}{(1 + i_N)^t}, \tag{6-8}$$

where i_N represents the nominal interest rate. Equation (6–8) illustrates that the appropriate discount rate for the nominal stream of earnings accruing to the asset is the nominal interest rate, but the appropriate discount rate for real earnings is the real rate.

The third argument is that the market was confused during the 1970s about the differences between real and nominal earnings in valuing corporate equities. The alleged mistake is that the market incorrectly capitalized reported accounting earnings at the nominal interest rate when they should be discounted at the real interest rate. This would lead to an undervaluation of equity securities, because inflation alters the meaning of reported accounting profits after taxes and interest. During inflation, these reported earnings no longer represent the true earnings of the equity owners of the firm, for inflation constantly shifts the value of the firm between debt- and equityholders. For example, if the nominal amount of debt financing in a company is left unchanged during a period of inflation, then the real amount must be declining. In such a situation the accounting returns to equity no longer represent the true nominal returns to equity. If the market does not understand this, then it may inaccurately value equity securities in general. The implication is that when the market discovers its error, it will revalue equities and the stock market will experience an appreciable increase. Precisely this type of appreciation in equity values has occurred in the 1980s. However, it is difficult to determine whether the appreciation in equity values in the last few years represents a correction of a mistaken undervaluation of assets or a change in the estimate of the future returns to assets.

It is virtually impossible to distinguish between this undervaluation argument and the alternative hypothesis that investors' expectations of future returns have changed. To see what this means we need to reconsider Equation (6–8). The undervaluation argument took expected future real returns, X, as given. Suppose that inflation affects the market's expectation of future real returns. This effect might be due to a belief that inflation will lead to wage and price controls, which will hurt corporate profitability, or to the belief that attempts to use monetary policy to halt inflation will cause a recession, which will hurt corporate profitability. Either reason suggests that inflation leads to corrective actions by the government that reduce future real profits. If inflation is perceived to be serious enough, it may cause a substantial decrease in X, and with it, the value of equity securities.

AN EXAMPLE OF MARKET RESPONSE TO INFLATION NEWS

During 1985 and much of 1986 the connection between anticipated inflation, nominal interest rates, and the stock market might have become a little hazy to many investors. Inflation rates were very low compared to the double-digit inflation rates of the late 1970s and very early 1980s. In addition, the stock market was booming and interest rates were relatively low (see Figure 6–1). However, in early 1987 the old worry of increasing inflation rates began to reappear. The basis for the concern was in part a result of the increase in oil and some other commodity prices and the decline in the value of the dollar relative to most currencies, particularly against the Japanese yen. Many analysts argued that as the value of the dollar declined, the cost of many foreign goods would be driven up. This, in turn, would decrease the pressure on domestic producers to keep prices low. Finally, there was concern that the Federal Reserve would allow inflation to accelerate with an accommodating monetary policy.

All of these concerns led to significant volatility in the stock market and in the markets for fixed income or debt obligations. For example, on Friday, May 15, 1987, the Dow Jones Industrial Average suffered its fourth worst loss for a single day in its history when it lost 52.97 points or 2.3 percent of total value. The Standard and Poor's 500 Index also fell 6.81 points which represented 2.31 percent of its value. The largest day's decline in the Dow Jones Index occurred on April 3, 1987.

An inspection of the headlines and news stories before and after the May 15 decline highlights the relationship between inflation, interest rates, and the stock market. For example, a *Wall Street Journal* story which appeared on May 15 focused on the producers' price index, an index of prices on a wide variety of various products sold on a wholesale basis. The performance of that index for April was announced on May 15. Prior to the announcement, various analysts developed forecasts of what the change in the index would be in April. The consensus forecast, as reported by the Dow Jones Capital Markets Report, was that the April increase would be 0.4 percent. In an efficient market, the anticipated level of the price index would already have been incorporated into interest rates and stock market prices by May 15. Therefore, on May 15 the financial markets should react to any new information contained in the announcement of the actual level of the producers' price index. As it turned out, the actual increase in the index was 0.7 percent rather than the anticipated 0.4 percent. The 0.7 percent increase for April translates into an 8.9 percent annual inflation rate in producers' prices if that rate of increase were maintained for an entire year. The price decline in the stock market that developed in response to this announcement was matched by an interest rate increase in the market for Treasury bonds. Bond prices fell and yields increased on 30-year Treasury bonds from 8.74 percent at the close of the market on Thursday, May 14, to 8.92 percent at the close of the market on Friday, May 15. This represented a 15-month high for yields to maturity on 30-year Treasury bonds.

This argument seems to be a powerful alternative to the proposition that the market has undervalued equities.

This final explanation for the poor performance of equity securities in the 1970s emphasizes the market's reaction to the long-run consequences of inflation. This hypothesis contends that inflation does not lead simply to a redistribution of wealth; rather it suggests that, if left unchecked, inflation itself will influence real income. It also implies that actions usually taken to try to control inflation also take their toll in real income. To understand why this may be true, we need to examine the link between monetary policy and interest rates, which we will take up in Chapters 10 and 11.

INFLATION AND NOMINAL INTEREST RATES IN DIFFERENT CURRENCIES

Thus far we have discussed the relationship between inflation and interest rates or rates of return on securities in the United States. The ideas here are not specific to any particular country, whether it be the United States, the United Kingdom, Japan, or Peru. The basic Fisherian theory that nominal rates are equal to a real rate plus the expected rate of inflation transcends national boundaries. In fact, if we go a little further and add to the Fisherian theory some basic ideas about the determinants of exchange rates between currencies, we can arrive at a very neat and concise set of relationships between exchange rates, inflation rates, and interest rates. Moreover, these neat relationships appear to fit in rather well with the real-world data. To develop these relationships, we need to start with some basic understanding of what spot and forward exchange rates are.

SPOT AND FORWARD EXCHANGE RATES

Whenever we purchase goods from another country we need to pay for those goods in the currency of that country. This means we need to be able to convert our currency, dollars in the United States, into the foreign currency. All such conversions of one currency into another involve going to the foreign exchange market. Actually, the foreign exchange market is not a formal auction market but rather a collection of dealers who hold inventories of currencies and trade those currencies. Most of us would go to a bank to exchange currencies. Banks are some of the largest dealers in foreign currency or foreign exchange.

The price we pay for buying a foreign currency with dollars, say in the case of yen, is the yen/dollar exchange rate. This tells us how many yen we can buy with one U.S. dollar. Figure 6–2 presents an example of the prices of foreign exchange quoted on a daily basis in the *Wall Street Journal*. Figure 6–2 shows that on March 6, 1987, the yen/dollar exchange rate was 153.55 per dollar. Conversely, one yen would be worth 0.006513 dollars. Notice this exchange rate is listed in Figure 6–2 as the first line pertaining to the Japanese yen. There are three additional lines under this one labeled 30-, 90-, and 120-day forward. The first line refers to the **spot exchange rate,** the rate prevailing that day for exchanges taking place that day. The 30-day **forward exchange rate** is the rate quoted that day for exchanges taking place 30 days in the future. Notice that the 30-day forward rate is lower than the spot rate. When this occurs the yen is said to be trading at a **forward premium.** When the forward rate is above the spot rate the currency in question is said to be trading at a **forward discount.** Most currencies have both forward and spot markets.

RELATIONSHIP OF INTEREST RATES, INFLATION, AND EXCHANGE RATES

Now that we have some understanding of what exchange rates are and how to read exchange rate quotes, we can begin to explore the relationship between interest rates, inflation, and exchange rates. We are going to develop four interre-

The **spot exchange rate** is the rate prevailing on a particular day for exchanges of currency occurring that day.

The **forward exchange rate** is the rate prevailing on a particular day for exchanges of currency occurring some time in the future.

A currency is selling at a **forward premium** when the forward rate is above the spot rate, and it is selling at a **forward discount** when the forward rate is below the spot rate.

FIGURE 6–2
Spot and forward exchange rates.

FOREIGN EXCHANGE

Friday, March 6, 1987

The New York foreign exchange selling rates below apply to trading among banks in amounts of $1 million and more, as quoted at 3 p.m. Eastern time by Bankers Trust Co. Retail transactions provide fewer units of foreign currency per dollar.

Country	U.S. $ equiv. Fri.	U.S. $ equiv. Thurs.	Currency per U.S. $ Fri.	Currency per U.S. $ Thurs.
Argentina (Austral) ...	.6502	.6954	1.538	1.4380
Australia (Dollar)	.6780	.6794	1.4749	1.4719
Austria (Schilling)	.07752	.07770	12.90	12.87
Belgium (Franc)				
Commercial rate	.02630	.02635	38.03	37.95
Financial rate	.02608	.02612	38.35	38.28
Brazil (Cruzado)	.05076	.05076	19.70	19.70
Britain (Pound)	1.5878	1.5862	.6298	.6304
30-Day Forward ...	1.5821	1.5806	.6321	.6327
90-Day Forward ...	1.5730	1.5715	.6357	.6363
180-Day Forward ...	1.5607	1.5587	.6407	6416
Canada (Dollar)	.7499	.7502	1.3335	1.3330
30-Day Forward ...	.7493	.7496	1.3345	1.3341
90-Day Forward ...	.7479	.7482	1.3370	1.3366
180-Day Forward ...	.7454	.7455	1.3416	1.3413
Chile (Official rate) ...	.004816	.004843	207.66	206.49
China (Yuan)	.2693	.2693	3.7128	3.7128
Colombia (Peso)	.004401	.004425	227.20	225.10
Denmark (Krone)	.1448	.1447	6.9050	6.9125
Ecuador (Sucre)				
Official rate	.006782	.006782	147.45	147.45
Floating rate	.006826	.006826	146.50	146.50
Finland (Markka)	.2216	.2209	4.5125	4.5275
France (Franc)	.1631	.1641	6.1295	6.0950
30-Day Forward ...	.1629	.1638	6.1373	6.1030
90-Day Forward ...	.1625	.1634	6.1555	6.1215
180-Day Forward ...	.1617	.1627	6.1840	6.1460
Greece (Drachma) ...	.007435	.007449	134.50	134.25
Hong Kong (Dollar) ..	.1281	.1282	7.8020	7.7995
India (Rupee)	.07698	.07692	12.99	13.00
Indonesia (Rupiah) ..	.0006072	.0006075	1647.00	1646.00
Ireland (Punt)	1.4535	1.4510	.6880	.6892
Israel (Shekel)	.6184	.6188	1.617	1.616
Italy (Lira)	.0007663	.0007686	1305.00	1301.00
Japan (Yen)	.006513	.006526	153.55	153.23
30-Day Forward ...	.006524	.006537	153.29	152.98
90-Day Forward ...	.006547	.006561	152.75	152.41
180-Day Forward ...	.006583	.006598	151.90	151.57
Jordan (Dinar)	2.9369	2.9499	.3405	.339
Kuwait (Dinar)	3.6088	3.5997	.2771	.2778
Lebanon (Pound)	.009434	.01	106.00	100.00
Malaysia (Ringgit)	.3964	.3964	2.5230	2.5225
Malta (Lira)	2.8531	2.8369	.3505	.3525
Mexico (Peso)				
Floating rate	.0009488	.0009470	1054.00	1056.00
Netherland(Guilder) ...	.4822	.4838	2.0740	2.0675
New Zealand (Dollar) .	.5590	.5580	1.7889	1.7921
Norway (Krone)	.1443	.1438	6.9300	6.9525
Pakistan (Rupee)	.05797	.05797	17.25	17.25
Peru (Inti)	.04955	.04873	20.18	20.52
Philippines (Peso)	.04859	.04873	20.58	20.52
Portugal (Escudo)	.007082	.007062	141.20	141.60
Saudi Arabia (Riyal) ..	.2666	.2666	3.751	3.751
Singapore (Dollar)	.4669	.4672	2.1420	2.1405
South Africa (Rand)				
Commercial rate	.4825	.4825	2.0725	2.0725
Financial rate	.2655	.2713	3.7664	3.6859
South Korea (Won) ...	.001169	.001168	855.00	855.80
Spain (Peseta)	.007773	.007776	128.65	128.60
Sweden (Krona)	.1556	.1552	6.4250	6.4450
Switzerland (Franc) ...	.6439	.6479	1.5530	1.5435
30-Day Forward ...	.6452	.6493	1.5499	1.5402
90-Day Forward ...	.6477	.6520	1.5438	1.5337
180-Day Forward ...	.6518	.6562	1.5342	1.5240
Taiwan (Dollar)	.02856	.02856	35.01	35.01
Thailand (Baht)	.03860	.03857	25.91	25.93
Turkey (Lira)	.001302	.001304	768.30	766.71
United Arab(Dirham) ..	.2723	.2723	3.6730	3.673
Uruguay (New Peso)				
Financial	.005291	.005291	189.00	189.00
Venezuela (Bolivar)				
Official rate	.1333	.1333	7.50	7.50
Floating rate	.04365	.04357	22.91	22.95
W. Germany (Mark) ..	.5424	.5459	1.8435	1.8320
30-Day Forward	.5436	.5470	1.8396	1.8282
90-Day Forward	.5458	.5491	1.8323	1.8213
180-Day Forward	.5489	.5520	1.8219	1.8115
		– – –		
SDR	1.26534	1.26211	0.790299	0.792325
ECU	1.13014	1.12541	....	....

Special Drawing Rights are based on exchange rates for the U.S., West German, British, French and Japanese currencies. Source: International Monetary Fund.

ECU is based on a basket of community currencies. Source: European Community Commission.

z-Not quoted.

Source: *Wall Street Journal*, March 9, 1987, p. 26.

lated propositions that create connections between interest rates, inflation rates, and exchange rates in different countries. Although each is important on its own, taken together they tell a complete story about nominal interest rates in different countries. Following a summary of these four relationships stated as four propositions, we will try to see what each one means.

Proposition I: Fisherian interest rate theory holds in every currency.
Proposition II: Relative interest rates in two currencies reflect the magnitude of premium or discount between the forward and spot exchange rates between the two currencies.

Proposition III: Forward exchange rates are equal to the market's best guess of the expected future spot exchange rate.

Proposition IV: Relative interest rates in two currencies are equal to the ratio of the market's expectation of the future spot exchange rate to the current spot exchange rate.

These four propositions may seem a little intimidating, but they are not as difficult as they appear at first glance. We will approach them one at a time, and then we will try to show how they are interrelated.

Proposition I: Inflation and Interest Rates.

Proposition I is the simplest to understand, given the background we have acquired earlier in this chapter. We have learned that the nominal interest rate is equal to the sum of the real rate of interest, or the price of forgone consumption, and the market's expectation of the future rate of inflation. When we developed this theory we approached it in the context of the U.S. economy. That is, we implied that the Treasury bill or bond rate in the U.S. was equal to the real rate of interest demanded in the U.S. plus the rate of inflation expected in the U.S. over the relevant period. This approach to the issue is far too provincial. Actually, Fisherian interest rate theory knows no national boundaries. The same proposition should be true in any currency. The one year risk-free interest rate in the United Kingdom or West Germany or Brazil should be equal to the real interest rate plus the rate of inflation expected in that country.

There is an important caveat about this proposition. In some countries financial markets are not as well developed as they are in the U.S. or say the U.K. They may have few competitive markets where interest rates are set, and governments may fix most interest rates. In such situations there is no reason to believe that the Fisherian interest rate theory holds. A government does not *have to* set interest rates the way Irving Fisher predicted they would be set in competitive financial markets. However, if a government does not do so, it will create problems in that country's economy. If the government sets the interest rate at 10 percent when most people expect 20 percent inflation, people will not be interested in investing their funds at the government-controlled rate. They will try to send their funds abroad to place them in competitive markets where Fisher's theory is working. Because of this most governments that attempt to control domestic interest rates find they must also impose exchange controls to restrict the outflow of capital. Within this country, for many years the U.S. government attempted to control the interest rates banks could pay depositors through what was known as Regulation Q of the Federal Reserve Board. When inflation expectations drove market interest rates above the ceilings imposed by the government in the late 1970s, depositors withdrew their funds from banks and savings and loans and placed them in other investments, which gave them a reasonable expected real interest rate. This is analagous to investors' sending their funds abroad when similar restrictions are imposed in smaller countries.

If Fisher's theory applies to interest rates in any country, then if we compare interest rates in two countries, we would expect that any differences would be attributed to one of two factors: differences in ex ante real interest rates across countries or differences in expected inflation rates in different countries. If there are no exchange controls or restrictions on the ability of investors to move their funds abroad and if there are no special risks in doing so, then we would not expect to see differences in ex ante real rates in different countries. It should then be the case that interest rates in different countries are purely a reflection of the differences in expected inflation rates in those countries. We can state this version of proposition 1 as follows:

$$\frac{1 + r_\$}{1 + r_y} = \frac{1 + E(P_\$)}{1 + E(P_y)},$$

where $r_\$$ and r_y refer to the risk-free interest rate in the U.S. and the risk-free interest rate in Japan, respectively, and $E(P_\$)$ and $E(P_y)$ refer to the expected inflation rates in the U.S. and Japan. Notice that we are using the U.S. and Japan as examples, and we will continue to do so throughout the rest of this chapter. But we could use any two countries.

Proposition II: Relative Interest Rates and Exchange Rates.   In order to see the relationship between interest rates in two countries and the exchange rates between the currencies of those countries, we need to consider the choice between investing in the risk-free rate available in two countries, say the U.S. and Japan. Under what circumstances would one investment be better than the other? Suppose you are a U.S. resident and you have dollars to invest. If you invest in the U.S., you simply receive the nominal interest rate in the U.S. If we assume that the nominal interest rate in the U.S. for a one year risk-free investment is 6 percent and if you have $100,000 to invest, then you would have $106,000 at the end of a year.

Now suppose you consider the investment in Japan; in order to make the investment you need to convert your $100,000 into yen. If the yen/dollar exchange rate is 155, then you could convert your $100,000 into 15,500,000 yen. Then you would invest your 15,500,000 yen at the one year risk-free rate in Japan. If this rate is 7 percent, then you would have 16,585,000 yen. Now you would want to convert the yen back to dollars at the end of the year. You could wait to see what the spot exchange rate between yen and dollars would be at the end of the year, but then you would be bearing the risk of fluctuations in the exchange rate. An attractive alternative is to contract today through the forward exchange rate for a certain rate of exchange in one year. What forward exchange rate must prevail for the same amount of dollars to result from the investment in Japan resulted from the risk-free investment in the United States? There will be $106,000 at the end of a year if we invest in the U.S. We also know that there will be 16,585,000 yen at the end of a year if we invest in Japan. Therefore, we need to determine the exchange rate that will allow us to convert our yen back into exactly $106,000. This is

$$\frac{16,585,000}{106,000} = 156.46.$$

Given the U.S. interest rate of 6 percent and the Japanese interest rate of 7 percent, and the current exchange rate of 155, any one year forward exchange rate other than 156.46 would give an advantage to either the Japanese or the U.S. investment. Hence, there will be an equilibrium or lack of arbitrage opportunities in the foreign exchange market only if there is a precise relationship between the interest rates and the spot and forward exchange rates in the two countries. The relationship can be stated as follows:

$$\frac{1 + r_y}{1 + r_\$} = \frac{f_{y/\$}}{S_{y/\$}},$$

where $f_{y/\$}$ and $S_{y/\$}$ represent the forward and spot exchange rates between yen and dollars respectively. This works in our example by plugging in the numbers:

$$\frac{1.07}{1.06} = \frac{156.46}{155.00} = 1.0094.$$

We can also state the same relationship using the dollar/yen exchange rate:

$$\frac{1 + r_\$}{1 + r_y} = \frac{f_{\$/y}}{S_{\$/y}}.$$

This form of writing the expression will prove to be useful when we put these propositions together.

This expression states a basic equilibrium relationship between interest rates and the spot and future exchange rates. The relationship is known as **interest rate parity:** the interest rate differential, or the ratio of one plus the interest rates, must equal the differential between forward and spot exchange rates. This is one of the most important relationships governing the operation of markets in foreign exchange and financial markets in countries around the world.

Interest rate parity indicates that the ratio of one plus the interest rates in two countries must equal the differential between forward and spot exchange rates in those two countries.

Proposition III: The Relationship Between Forward and Future Spot Exchange Rates. It is fairly hard to refute or deny proposition II. It has been confirmed by a large amount of empirical evidence, and it makes obvious sense once you see what is saying. However, proposition III is more debatable. It defines a specific relationship between forward and future spot exchange rates. The relationship says that forward rates are equal to the market's best guess of what the future spot exchange rate will be. For instance, if the one year forward rate on yen is 160, then the market expects the spot rate one year from now to be 160. The implicit argument in this theory is that the market demands no premium to take on the risk of fluctuations in exchange rates. In this sense it is much like the basic Fisherian theory of interest rates, which implicitly assumes that people demand no premium to take on the fluctuations in the inflation rate. This *expectations theory of the exchange rate,* as it is called, implies that the ratio of the current forward rate to the current spot rate is equal to the ratio of the expected future spot rate and the current spot rate. We can write this, as we have written the implications of the first two propositions, as follows:

$$\frac{f_{\$/y}}{S_{\$/y}} = \frac{E(S_{\$/y})}{S_{\$/y}}.$$

An alternative to the expectations theory of exchange rates is that participants in the foreign exchange market demand premiums to take on foreign exchange risk. For example, suppose you are going to sell goods in Japan and will receive yen in 30 days. You are hurt if the value of your yen in dollars declines or if the number of dollars you can buy with your yen declines. On the other hand, someone from Japan might sell goods in the U.S. and might receive dollars in 30 days that need to be converted to yen. He is hurt if the number of yen he can buy with dollars declines. If both of these people are exposed to exactly the opposite magnitude of risk, then they should be able to execute a forward contract in the exchange rate between yen and dollars without paying or receiving any premium for risk. This is because their needs are exactly offsetting. However, if there were twice as much demand to convert yen to dollars as dollars to yen in 30 days, then someone must be paid to take a position beyond the one that is generated from their own business. Such a person could well demand a premium to accept the risk that the value of the yen in dollars would decline. If this were the case, then the expectations theory of exchange rates would not hold.

Proposition IV: The Relationship Between Relative Interest Rates and Expected Changes in Exchange Rates. The final proposition is based on what is called the *law of one price,* which says that two commodities or two assets that are identical should sell for the same price. Of course, we know that if there are transactions costs or other costs involved in shopping for or acquiring a product then the law of one price cannot hold exactly. But the idea is that competition tends to drive prices on identical commodities toward equality. Just as Fisherian interest rate theory knows no national boundaries, neither does the law of one price. In its most extreme form, the law of one price says that two identical commodities for sale in Britain and the U.S. should have the same cost, when the exchange rate between the currencies is taken into account. This is also known as **purchasing power parity.** This means that:

Purchasing power parity says that two identical commodities for sale in two countries should have the same cost when the exchange rate between the currencies is taken into account.

$$\text{Price of good in dollars} = \text{Price of good in pounds} \times \text{Price of pounds}.$$

This cannot apply at all times to all goods in all countries. For example, the price of beer in Spain is not the same as the price of beer in New York adjusted for the exchange rate. However, competition tends to drive prices for similar goods together, within the limits set by transactions costs.

If the law of one price holds in general, then any change in relative prices in two countries must be matched by changes in the exchange rate between the currencies of those countries. This means that expectations of the relative inflation rates in two countries must be equal to the expectations of the rate of change in exchange rates between the currencies of those countries:

$$\frac{E(1 + P_\$)}{E(1 + P_y)} = \frac{E(S_{\$/y})}{S_{\$/y}}.$$

For example, if inflation were expected to be 10 percent in West Germany and 5 percent in the U.S., then the price of deutsche marks must fall by 5 percent in order to maintain purchasing power parity.

THE RELATIONSHIP BETWEEN THE FOUR PROPOSITIONS

Now that we have worked our way through the four propositions relating interest rates, exchange rates, and inflation rates, we need to see how these four propositions fit together. The relationship between them is illustrated in Figure 6–3. Proposition I defines the relationship between inflation and interest rates in any two countries. It is simply a restatement of the basic Fisherian theory of interest rates

FIGURE 6–3
Basic relationships in foreign exchange.

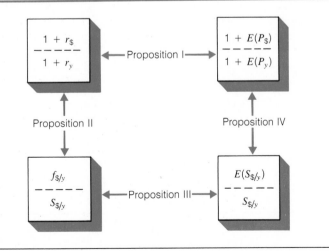

PURCHASING POWER PARITY IN THE 1980s

In the mid-1980s the spotlight has been on the relationships described in propositions I through IV. The value of the dollar declined dramatically since 1985 against most currencies, particularly against the Japanese yen. In addition, interest rates in the U.S. had fallen relative to their level in the early 1980s as both actual and anticipated inflation declined. But by early 1987, when the dollar reached an all-time low against the Japanese yen, inflation worries increased, and interest rates in the U.S. were beginning to be affected.

Many market participants asked how low the value of the dollar could fall and what the equilibrium value of the dollar might be. The appropriate reaction to this kind of inquiry is that the value of the dollar is whatever it will fetch in foreign exchange markets. If these markets are efficient, then any information

about what the value of the dollar may do in the future will be incorporated in forward exchange rates. But we also know that proposition IV or purchasing power parity tells us that the currencies should be priced so that, taking into the cost of acquiring different currencies, there is a rough parity across national boundaries in the costs of commodities.

A private research organization put together some information on the costs of various basic goods and services in a variety of different countries, taking into account the exchange rates between the dollar and the currencies in these countries. The results of their application of purchasing power parity are shown in Figure 6–4.

The upper left-hand corner of the table shows the value of the dollar from 1985 until early 1987 relative

FIGURE 6–4
Purchasing power parity in the 1980s.

Perspective on the Dollar

Its Decline

U.S. Dollar exchange rate vs. basket of 15 foreign currencies Plotted monthly, end of month, 1980-82 average = 100

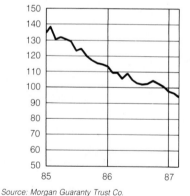

Source: Morgan Guaranty Trust Co.

Gauging It Two Ways

	Purchasing Power Parity Rate	Currency Market Exchange Rate	
U.S.	1.00	1.00	
Canada	1.24	1.39	Canadian dollars
Japan	223.00	169.00	Yen
Austria	17.15	15.27	Schillings
Finland	6.13	5.07	Markkaa
Norway	8.09	7.39	Kroner
Sweden	8.50	7.12	Kronor
Belgium	45.00	44.70	Francs
Denmark	9.83	8.09	Kroner
France	7.48	6.93	Francs
Germany	2.48	2.17	Marks
Greece	90.00	139.00	Drachmas
Ireland	0.71	0.75	Pounds
Italy	1329.00	1491.00	Lira
Luxembourg	43.30	44.70	Francs
Netherlands	2.47	2.45	Guilders
Portugal	76.00	148.00	Escudos
Spain	102.00	140.00	Pesetas
Britain	0.57	0.68	Pounds

(1986 exchange rates, 1985 pricing, currency units per dollar)

Source: Organization for Economic Cooperation and Development; Eurostat

154

to a market basket of 15 other currencies. The upper right-hand corner shows the exchange rate between the dollar and selected currencies which would satisfy purchasing power parity using this simple selection of goods and services. This purchasing power parity exchange rate was then compared to the actual exchange rate prevailing in 1986. Finally, the bottom panel of the table shows the cost of a selection of goods and services in various foreign cities measured in dollars.

The data in this figure indicate, that based on the purchasing power parity concept for these basic consumer goods, the dollar was undervalued at this point. Since the dollar's value declined further in 1986 and early 1987, the dollar was even further undervalued, relative to this concept of purchasing power

parity, by mid-1987. However, it is important to interpret these words carefully. Purchasing power parity does *not* mean that all goods must cost the same in all countries at every point in time. It does argue that over the long run, there is a tendency for prices of goods and services to equilibrate across countries. If this does not occur, then there is an incentive for entrepreneurs to take advantage of this by buying goods and shipping them abroad or ultimately by relocating. These kinds of forces may take a long time. In the meantime, the value of a currency is what it can command in the foreign exchange markets. In this sense a currency can be neither under- nor overvalued.

Its Purchasing Power Worldwide

Five common items in a typical major U.S. city vs. six cities abroad. Prices abroad in foreign currencies converted into dollars at recent currency exchange rates.

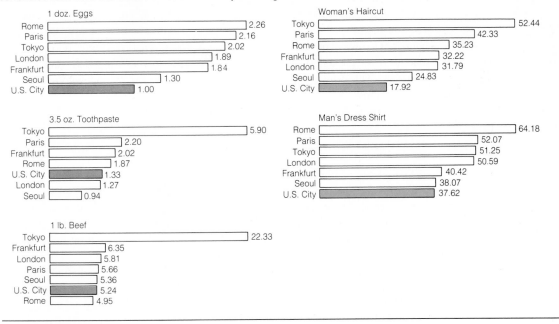

1 doz. Eggs	
Rome	2.26
Paris	2.16
Tokyo	2.02
London	1.89
Frankfurt	1.84
Seoul	1.30
U.S. City	1.00

Woman's Haircut	
Tokyo	52.44
Paris	42.33
Rome	35.23
Frankfurt	32.22
London	31.79
Seoul	24.83
U.S. City	17.92

3.5 oz. Toothpaste	
Tokyo	5.90
Paris	2.20
Frankfurt	2.02
Rome	1.87
U.S. City	1.33
London	1.27
Seoul	0.94

Man's Dress Shirt	
Rome	64.18
Paris	52.07
Tokyo	51.25
London	50.59
Frankfurt	40.42
Seoul	38.07
U.S. City	37.62

1 lb. Beef	
Tokyo	22.33
Frankfurt	6.35
London	5.81
Paris	5.66
Seoul	5.36
U.S. City	5.24
Rome	4.95

Source: Organization Resources Counselors Inc.; *Wall Street Journal*, April 15, 1987, p. 6.

in an international context. Proposition II, interest rate parity, defines the connection between interest rates in two countries and the spot and forward exchange rates between the currencies of those countries. A statement about international capital market equilibrium, it says that if there are no barriers preventing capital from flowing between two countries, then the interest rate differential must equal the differential between forward and spot exchange rates. This proposition is an implication of the internationalization of capital markets. Proposition III links forward exchange rates with expected future exchange rates. It postulates that in the aggregate there is no risk premium demanded in the exchange markets so that the forward exchange rate between two currencies is equal to the expected future spot exchange rate. Finally, Proposition IV closes the circle by linking the expected rate of change in exchange rates with the relative levels of expected inflation in the two currencies.

Taken together, these propositions provide an integrated picture of the determinants of interest rates in various countries. These propositions illustrate that interest rates in one country are tied to interest rates in other countries through the markets for foreign exchange. As the expected rate of inflation goes up in one country, so will the interest rate in that country. This, in turn, influences forward exchange rates in that country and the market's expectation of future spot exchange rates. These relationships highlight the interaction between financial markets in various countries around the world. This interaction has become increasingly important as the barriers between financial transactions across countries have diminished, internationalizing financial markets.

Throughout the chapters in Part 2 that deal with interest rates, we need to keep in mind that the factors that influence interest rates do not know international boundaries. Our capital markets are increasingly international, with borrowers and lenders from throughout the world playing active parts in the U.S. and in other countries. The principle of the determination of interest rates developed in these chapters apply throughout the financial markets of the world.

Summary

In this chapter we moved from the theoretical concept of the real interest rate to deal with the interest rates we see in the world, which we refer to as nominal rates. Five factors account for the differences between nominal rates and the real interest rate: inflation, risk, taxes, relative security supplies, and maturity. This chapter focused on inflation and interest rates and examined how inflation and interest rates in different countries are linked together.

Probably the most important difference between nominal rates and the real rate for the 1970s and 1980s is the premium the market demands for inflation. Excluding risk, taxes, and relative security supplies, the nominal rate is equal to the sum of the real rate and the market's expectation of inflation. Therefore, in a time of high inflation there will be a large difference between observed nominal rates and the underlying real rate. We focused on the distinction between the ex ante and ex post real interest rate. While we can compute the ex post real interest rate, this is not generally a perfect measure of the ex ante real interest rate, which we believe determines nominal interest rates. Instead, the ex post real interest rate is determined both by the ex ante real interest rate and by the market's errors in guessing the actual inflation rate. We also evaluated some of the available evidence on the degree to which the market efficiently incorporates publicly available information regarding future inflation rates into nominal interest rates.

We also examined some of the evidence on the link between inflation and the returns on various types of assets, including stocks. During the 1970s, when inflation was increasing in the United States, the stock market was performing relatively poorly. We evaluated various arguments about the connection between inflation and returns on publicly traded stocks. If the market believed that inflation would eventually make it difficult for corporations to earn significant profits, this could explain the poor performance of the stock market. However, it is difficult or impossible to confirm or reject any of the specific theories of the link between inflation and the stock market.

Next we turned our attention to the international financial markets, identifying four propositions about the relationship between interest rates, inflation, and exchange rates in different countries. Proposition I defines the relationship between inflation and interest rates in any two countries. It is simply a restatement of the basic Fisherian theory of interest rates, which we developed in the beginning of the chapter, but applied in an international context. Proposition II is known as interest rate parity; it defines the connection between interest rates in two countries and the spot and forward exchange rates between the currencies of those countries. A statement about international capital market equilibrium, it says that if there are no barriers preventing capital from flowing between two countries, then the interest rate differential must equal the differential between forward and spot exchange rates. This proposition implies the internationalization of capital markets. Proposition III links forward exchange rates with expected future exchange rates. It postulates that in the aggregate there is no risk premium demanded in the exchange markets so that the forward exchange rate between two currencies is equal to the expected future spot exchange rate. Finally, Proposition IV links the expected rate of change in exchange rates with the relative levels of expected inflation in the two currencies.

QUESTIONS

1. Explain the difference between holding period yield and yield to maturity.
2. What is the difference between the ex ante and the ex post real interest rate? Why can we observe one and not the other? Why do many economists argue that the real interest rate is essentially constant? Do you think the real interest rate is just as likely to be constant in the very short run (a week, a month, a quarter) as in the long run? Why?
3. What does it mean to say that the market efficiently uses available information about the future inflation rate in setting nominal interest rates? Why is it difficult to test whether this is true?

4. Summarize the competing theories offered to explain the poor performance of the stock market in the 1970s. Can you find holes in each of them?

5. Explain why the ex post real interest rates should wander around randomly. Should nominal interest rates wander randomly? Why or why not?

6. Explain the theory of interest rate parity. Why should this theory hold if there are no transactions costs or barriers to financial flows between two countries?

7. Suppose the expectations theory of exchange rates holds. Can you expect to make money by speculating on the future direction of exchange rates by investing in the forward market? Why or why not?

8. What is the law of one price? Give some examples of commodities where you would expect it would and would not hold. How could you construct a test of the law of one price?

9. Suppose the one year U.S. Treasury bill rate is 10 percent and the comparable rate in the U.K. is 12 percent. What combinations of forward and spot exchange rates between the dollar and the pound would be consistent with these interest rates?

10. What does it mean to say that a currency is selling at a forward discount or premium? How would you compute the discount or premium? Suppose the pound were selling at a forward premium relative to the dollar. What could you infer about expected inflation rates in the United Kingdom versus the United States?

REFERENCES

Black, Fischer. "International Capital Market Equilibrium with Investment Barriers," *Journal of Financial Economics,* (December 1974), pp. 337–52.

Cornell, Bradford. "Spot Rates, Forward Rates and Exchange Market Efficiency", *Journal of Financial Economics,* (1977), pp. 55–65.

Fama, Eugene F. "Short-Term Interest Rates and Predictors of Inflation," *American Economic Review,* (June 1975), pp. 269–82.

Modigiliani, Franco and Richard A. Cohn. "Inflation, Rational Valuation and the Market," *Financial Analysts Journal,* (March/April 1979), pp. 24–44.

Roll, Richard. "Violations of Purchasing Power Parity and Their Implications for Efficient International Commodity Markets," in M. Sarnat and G. P. Szego (eds.), *International Finance and Trade,* vol. I, Cambridge, Mass.: Ballinger Publishing Co., 1979.

Stulz, Rene M. "A Model of International Asset Pricing," *Journal of Financial Economics,* (December 1981), pp. 383–406.

Van Horne, James C. *Financial Market Rates and Flows,* Englewood Cliffs, N.J.: Prentice-Hall, Inc., 1978.

7

*F*ACTORS AFFECTING NOMINAL INTEREST RATES

In this chapter we continue our analysis of the determinants of nominal interest rates focusing on three factors that influence nominal interest rates: default risk, taxes, and relative security supplies.

In the last chapter we analyzed the impact of inflation on nominal interest rates. Many observers of financial markets would argue that most of the observed changes in nominal interest rates are probably due either to changes in the market's expectations of inflation or to changes in the real rate, possibly resulting from intervention in financial markets by the Federal Reserve. But this does not mean that the factors we will take up in this chapter are unimportant. If we are trying to explain changes in aggregate market interest rates like Treasury bill rates, then we need to look to changes in inflation or in real rates. But when we turn our attention to other types of debt instruments, ones that may have default risk and ones where there may be some tax effects, then the story may not be entirely one of inflation and real rates. ∎

PREMIUMS FOR RISK AND DEFAULT

Default risk refers to the risk that a debt instrument—a loan or a bond—will go into default.

Chapter 3 developed the basic theory of the value of risky assets. In this section we will extend that theory in order to explain how yields on debt securities are influenced by **default risk.** We will start by considering how default risk of a particular debt instrument influences the yield on that instrument. Then we will look at the historical evidence on risk premiums in corporate bonds. Finally, we will take up the interesting subject of junk bonds, analyzing the recent development of the market for junk bonds and assessing the risk involved.

DETERMINATION OF PREMIUMS FOR DEFAULT RISK

To see how nominal interest rates on debt securities are influenced by default risk, suppose a bank is lending to 100 companies. From experience the bank can expect 2 out of 100 companies to go into bankruptcy while the other 98 companies will pay off in full. Suppose, just to keep the example simple, that the two companies that go bankrupt never pay off anything on their loans. The bank decides that in order to take on the risk of lending to these customers, it will demand an expected return on lending of 12 percent, which we will assume represents a 200 basis point spread above the current Treasury bill rate of 10 percent. Would it make sense for the bank to charge a contract interest rate of 12 percent on on these loans? The answer is no! At a 12 percent contract interest rate the expected rate of return to the bank would be:

$$\text{Expected default rate} \times \text{Return on each default}$$
$$+ \text{ Expected payoff rate} \times \text{Return on each loan paid off.}$$
$$(2/100)(-100\%) + (98/100)(12\%) = 9.76\%.$$

This is obviously less than 12 percent expected return. The problem is that the contract interest rate on a debt instrument is the maximum possible rate that can be earned on each debt security. Therefore, if there is any chance of default, the expected return must be less than the contract rate.

If a lender demands an expected return of 12 percent to lend to the companies described above, it must determine what contract interest rate to charge so that its expected return is 12 percent. If we let i_c represent the contract interest rate, then it needs to solve for i_c in the following equation:

$$(2/100)(-100\%) + (98/100)(i_c) = 12.0\%.$$

In this example i_c is equal to 14.28 percent.

If we calculate the spread between the observed nominal contract interest rate and the risk-free Treasury rate, we will find a difference of $14.28\% - 10\%$ or 428 basis points. It would be incorrect to interpret this as a *risk premium* in the same sense as we might say the difference between an expected return and the risk-free rate (as used in Chapter 3) is a risk premium. Instead, the spread between

12 percent and 10 percent is the risk premium as used in Chapter 3: this is the amount of compensation, measured in terms of expected return, demanded by the lender to take on the risk of the loans described above. The 428 basis point spread between the contract interest rate and the risk-free rate is then the sum of the 200 basis point risk premium and an additional 228 basis point premium necessary to insure that the expected rate of return on the loans is 12 percent. We will refer to this additional premium as a *default margin.*

Another way to look at this is to divide up the probability distribution on returns to the firm that is borrowing money between that portion claimed by the lender and that which is left for the borrower. Examples of this are shown in panels A and B of Figure 7–1. Panel A shows a hypothetical probability distribution for returns measured in dollars on a particular asset. Three distinct amounts of dollar returns are marked on the horizontal axis, labeled x_1, x_2, and x_3. If we presume a specific face value of the debt claim on this income stream, say $100,000, then x_1 represents the amount of earnings that the firm would have to generate in order to pay the debtholders the risk-free rate of interest on their debt. If the risk-free rate were 10 percent, then x_1 would equal $110,000. But the bondholders do face risk. The probability distribution shows that their returns could be much lower than this $100,000. As a result, they will demand a contract interest rate that gives them an expected return higher than the risk-free rate of interest. Based on their estimate of the risk involved, they will demand an expected dollar return of, say, x_2. If the risk were such that the expected rate of return they demand were, say, 12 percent, as in the previous example, then x_2 would be

FIGURE 7–1

Uncertain returns on bonds and the assets on which they are claims. Panels A and B show probability distributions on two different assets. The debt claim in panel A is more risky than the one in B. x_1 shows the risk-free return on debt claims on these assets. X_2 and x'_2 show the expected return demanded. x_3 and x'_3 show the promised interest-rates demanded.

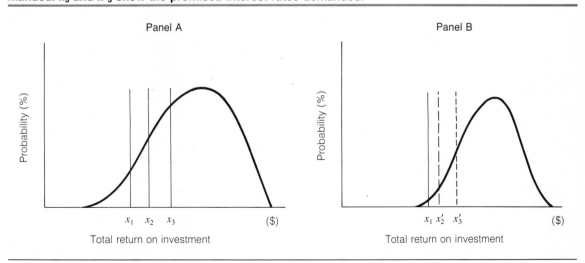

$112,000. The difference between x_2 and x_1 represents the same sort of premium for risk as was developed in Chapter 3. That is, it is the compensation demanded to bear the risk of the bond.

With the probability distribution given, the factor that actually determines the debtholders' expected return is the contract or promised interest rate. Investors will demand a contract interest rate that gives them an expected dollar return of x_2. In order to have an expected return of x_2, they must set the contract interest rate higher than x_2. If they set the contract return at x_2 and there were any probability of default—that is, a payment less than x_2—then the expected return could not be as large as x_2. There will always be a contract return, symbolized by x_3, that will lead to an expected return of x_2. For the probability distribution in panel A, the probability that return on the bond will equal or exceed x_3 is represented by the area under the curve to the right of the vertical line originating at x_3. The probability distribution to the left of this line shows the probabilities of return less than x_3. Finally, the distance between x_2 and x_3 represents the default margin.

As a result, the observed yield spread or risk premium, represented by the difference between x_3 and x_1, can be divided into two parts. First, there is the compensation for bearing risk, which is equal to $x_2 - x_1$. Second, there is the default margin, which is equal to $x_3 - x_2$:

$$\text{Risk premium of a bond} = \text{Compensation for bearing risk} + \text{Default margin.}$$

The same thing is shown in panel B of Figure 7–1, but in that case the probability distribution on returns is more concentrated around its expected value. As a result, the observed risk premium, measured as $x_3' - x_1$, is smaller than in the example shown in panel A.

EVIDENCE ON RISK PREMIUMS IN DEBT SECURITIES

It is one thing to understand what is captured in the observed risk premium on a bond. It is quite another to be able to assess the uncertain returns and determine the appropriate size of the risk premium for a particular bond. Because of the difficulties involved and the economies generated by specializing in this sort of activity, two firms, Moody's and Standard & Poor's, prepare and publish ratings on most publicly traded bonds. The expense of preparing the rating is paid by the companies being rated rather than by the users of the service. The ratings provide a qualitative judgment of the risk of each bond. The various rating categories employed by the agencies are shown in Table 7–1. The highest rating is a triple A. The two rating agencies usually agree on ratings, and the market generally is thought to have high regard for the rating agencies' judgments.

Not only do rating agencies provide ratings for newly issued bonds, they also update ratings on bonds already issued as they perceive that the riskiness of these bonds is changing. A number of studies have recently been conducted to determine whether updated ratings by the rating agencies provide new information to

TABLE 7–1
Bond ratings produced by Moody's and Standard & Poor.

Moody's	Explanation
Aaa	Best quality
Aa	High quality
A	Higher medium grade
Baa	Medium grade
Ba	Possess speculative elements
B	Generally lack characteristics of desirable investment
Caa	Poor standing; may be in default
Ca	Speculative in a high degree; often in default
C	Lowest grade

Standard & Poor's	Explanation
AAA	Highest grade
AA	High grade
A	Upper medium grade
BBB	Medium grade
BB	Lower medium grade
B	Speculative
CCC-CC	Outright speculation
C	Reserved for income bonds
D	In default

the market or whether the market has already adjusted the prices of bonds to reflect a change in perceived risk by the time the rating agencies announce rate changes. The most complete study of this issue, conducted by Mark Weinstein,[1] provides empirical evidence implying that rating changes convey no new information to the market. In effect, the market has already incorporated the information utilized by the rating agencies into bond prices by the time the rating agencies announce their new ratings. It is easy to interpret Weinstein's results to mean that rating agencies provide no useful information, but this would not be a valid inference from this evidence. Rating agencies act as an independent third party in evaluating the risk of new bonds coming to the market. It is these new ratings that firms pay for and that seem to be of value in the market. The fact that rating updates are anticipated by the market does not suggest that rating agencies are unimportant when new bonds are issued.

Over the years academicians have conducted empirical studies to see whether they can pin down the basic determinants of the risk premiums on different types of bonds. Some of the earlier studies tried to explain the differences in risk premiums across a number of different individual bonds at given points in time. More

---

[1] See Mark Weinstein, "The Effect of a Rating Change Announcement on Bond Price," *Journal of Financial Economics,* 5 (1977), pp. 239–350.

recent studies have attempted to identify the reasons the risk premiums on bonds with different ratings vary through time. The best-known study of the differences in risk premiums across firms was conducted by Lawrence Fischer in the 1950s.[2] In his classic study Fischer attempted to explain the differences in risk premiums as a function of three factors: the historical variability of the company's earnings, the company's ratio of debt to equity securities, and the length of time since any suspension of payments to creditors. Using these variables and a measure of the marketability of the firm's bonds, Fischer was able to explain approximately three-quarters of the variation in observed risk premiums for samples drawn in five different years. Fischer's was the first major study on the principal determinants of risk premiums. Moreover, it remains the definitive evidence on the subject.

More recent studies have concentrated on trying to account for the changes in risk premiums through time. Either of two basic factors can lead to such changes: the perceived probability of default can change or the degree of risk aversion of the market can change. Increases in either of these items will lead to increases in observed risk premiums. In recent years a number of researchers have attempted to measure these changes. One method has used a survey-based measure of consumer sentiment called "MOOD" to quantify investors' risk aversion. Not surprisingly, these studies have found that as consumers become more optimistic, risk premiums tend to decline. In addition, measures of the level of economic activity also tend to have a positive impact on observed risk premiums, suggesting that the perceived probability of default varies with the level of economic activity.[3]

DEVELOPMENT OF THE JUNK BOND MARKET

A junk bond is a publicly traded bond with a low rating or no rating from the major debt rating agencies.

A very interesting development in the bond markets during the 1980s is the so-called junk bond market. **Junk bonds,** as they are sometimes called, are publicly distributed bonds rated below investment grade by Moody's or Standard and Poor's. Investment grade usually means Baa or higher, according to Moody's rating category. For many years there were relatively few publicly distributed bonds that did not receive an investment-grade rating or that received no rating at all. Potential issuers of low rated bonds simply did not distribute their bonds in the public markets. Instead, they went to an insurance company for a private placement of debt or to a bank for a private loan. But in the 1980s the new phenomenon of the public distribution of low rated bonds or high-yield bonds developed.

---

[2]See Lawrence Fischer, "Determinants of Risk Premium on Corporate Bonds," *Journal of Political Economy,* 67 (June 1959), pp. 217–37.

[3]See Dwight M. Jaffee, "Cyclical Variations in the Risk Structure of Interest Rates," *Journal of Monetary Economics,* 1 (1975), pp. 209–325; also Timothy Q. Cook and Patrick H. Hendershott, "The Impact of Taxes, Risk and Relative Security Supplies on Interest Rate Differentials," *Journal of Finance,* 33 (September 1978), pp. 1173–86.

To a large degree the junk bond market is the invention of the investment banking firm of Drexel Burnham Lambert. Drexel Burnham Lambert developed a group of investors who were willing to invest in junk bonds if they carried a high enough yield to maturity, or spread over the yield to maturity on bonds with substantially higher rating. The question is whether the higher promised yield on these low rated bonds is worth the risk. This issue has attracted considerable attention in the last few years, in part because junk bonds have been so controversial. Part of the controversy arises from the fact that junk bonds have been used to finance many of the actual and threatened takeovers of corporations common in the 1980s. Many people who believe takeovers should be regulated or that significant abuses have occurred in the takeover process have also argued that junk bonds are excessively risky. Those who defend the use of junk bonds, particularly the issuers and the investment banks who have developed the market, argue that the relatively high promised yield to maturity on junk bonds make them very attractive investments. They contend that the high yield is at least a fair compensation for the risk involved.

The difficulty in evaluating the risk of these high-yield or junk bonds is that defaults on these instruments probably have a large systematic element. That is, defaults will probably occur for a number of these bonds at roughly the same time, if and when there is a significant downturn in the economy. The critics of junk bonds contend that companies that have issued these instruments are very heavily leveraged and that it is this high leverage that makes them risky. Defenders of junk bonds say they are simply the same types of loans banks and insurance companies once made, but that are now distributed to investors by investment bankers. It is necessary to separate the question of who buys them and who distributes them from the question of how much risk they pose for investors. It is possible that the new system for underwriting and distributing these issues has eliminated some of the safeguards that often were imposed by banks and insurance companies when they made loans to companies now issuing junk bonds. However, this is extraordinarily difficult to evaluate.

The other basic question at issue with junk bonds is whether their yields are a reasonable compensation for the risk involved. This is also difficult to answer with great confidence, but some interesting evidence has been collected on the subject. Before examining that evidence, it is important to clarify precisely how risk is measured in publicly traded bonds compared with loans made by banks or insurance companies. A loss is incurred by a bank or insurance company when a loan actually goes into default. If it does not go into default when the interest payments are made by the borrower, then there is no loss on the loan. With a loan there cannot be capital gains or losses on the value of the loan since there is no market for the loan where price is set. That is, the loan is not "marked to market," as a publicly traded security would be. With a publicly traded security the rate of return in any period would be both the dividend income, or coupon payment in the case of a bond, plus the capital gain or loss on the value of the security. With a bank or insurance company loan the return in each period is simply the coupon or loan payment.

With publicly traded bonds, it is quite possible to experience losses even if there is no default on a bond. The losses arise just as they would with equity securities—they result from declines in the value of the bond in the marketplace. Therefore, when we attempt to determine whether the yield on a bond is sufficiently high to cover the risk involved, we are talking not simply about the risk of actual default, but also the risk of capital losses due to declines in market value. Of course, one of the most important determinants of the value of the bond is the market's assessment of the probability of default. If the market perceives that the risk of default increases, then the value of the bond will decline. Therefore, an investor in public bonds can experience low returns even if the bond never defaults. The irony here is that had the same bond been financed as a bank loan, the bank would continue to report the interest payments on the bond as income and would never realize any paper losses from a decline in the price at which that loan could be sold.

A few recent studies on the returns on holding junk bonds have attempted to estimate the systematic risk of holding a portfolio of low-grade or high-yield bonds. (See Chapter 3 for a discussion of systematic and unsystematic risk.) One study, carried out by Marshall Blume and Donald Keim at the Wharton School of the University of Pennsylvania,[4] utilized data provided by the investment banking firms that had developed the junk bond market to analyze the realized or holding period returns on junk bonds from January 1980 to June 1984. Unfortunately, this is a rather short period from which to draw any reliable conclusion about the actual risk of low-grade bonds. Moreover, this period does not incorporate any significant downturn in economic activity, so it gives no indication of how junk bonds might perform during an economic downturn. Blume and Keim found that the realized return on a portfolio of low-grade corporate bonds was 1.14 percent per month, while the return on AAA corporate bonds was 0.69 percent per month. The difference of 45 basis points per month appears to be rather substantial. However, if one tests the hypothesis that the true expected returns on these two portfolios (of which the actual returns are only a sample) are actually different, that hypothesis would have to be rejected.

In another recent study, by Mark Weinstein,[5] of returns on low-grade bonds, rather than focusing on the limited amount of data on the large volume of low-grade bonds issued in the 1980s, Weinstein looked at yields on a sample of older low-grade public bonds for which he was able to obtain data. He utilized holding period returns on this bond portfolio from June, 1962 until July 1974. Weinstein utilized two definitions of high-grade bonds. First, he defined high-grade bonds as having ratings Aaa through Baa and low-grade bonds as having ratings of B and below. The second definition removes Baa rated bonds from the high-grade cate-

---

[4]See Marshall Blume and Donald Keim, "Risk and Return Characteristics of Lower Grade Bonds," University of Pennsylvania, mimeo., (December 1984).

[5]See Mark Weinstein, "A Curmudgeon's View of Junk Bonds," *Journal of Portfolio Management,* (1987).

gory and Ba rated bonds from the low-grade category. The basic results of Weinstein's analysis are presented in Table 7–2. The table presents the mean holding period returns, the standard deviations of those returns and t-statistic (ratio of estimated return to its standard deviation). Items (1) to (3) in the table are returns for the first definition of portfolios and (4) to (6) for the second definition. Within each group the first return is for the high grade, the second for the low grade, and the third for the difference between the grades. The table indicates that the low-grade portfolio does in fact have higher actual holding period returns, according to both definitions. In addition, the t-statistics for the differences [items (3) and (6)] are greater than 2, which indicates the hypothesis that the true expected return on the low-grade portfolio is greater than on the high-grade portfolio should be accepted.

Next Weinstein asked whether the differences in expected returns reflected differences in systematic risk. Therefore he estimated regressions for each portfolio where the actual rate of return was regressed on a market index. The results of these regressions are presented in Table 7–3. The first column in the table is the intercept, and the second column is the slope coefficient for the market index. The final column is the R^2 in the regression. The t-statistics for each coefficient are shown in parentheses under the estimated value of the coefficient. Equations (3) and (6) indicate that the estimated beta is significantly higher for the low-grade portfolio than for the high-grade portfolio regardless of which definition is used.

TABLE 7–2
Realized monthly returns on portfolios of high and low-grade industrial bonds.

Portfolio	Average Number of Bonds in Portfolio	Raw Returns		
		Mean Return	Standard Deviation	t-Statistic
1. RETH* [Aaa–Baa]	85	0.013%	0.060%	2.50
2. RETL [Ba and Below]	31	0.078	0.248	3.30
3. RDIF [(2)–(1)]		0.065	0.267	2.94
4. RETH1 [Aaa–A]	63	0.012	0.062	2.36
5. RETL1 [B and Below]	17	0.107	0.479	2.69
6. RDIF1 [(5)–(4)]		0.095	0.465	2.46
June, 1962–July, 1974 145 months				

*RETH = Return on high-grade bonds.
RETL = Return on low-grade bonds.

TABLE 7–3
Market model regressions on portfolios of high and low-grade industrial bonds.

Portfolio	Raw Returns		
	α	β	R^2
1. RETH	0.009	0.007	0.17
[Aaa–Baa]	(1.849)	(5.468)	
2. RETL	0.054	0.029	0.16
[Ba and Below]	(2.491)	(5.172)	
3. RDIF	0.045	0.023	0.11
[(2)–(1)]	(2.176)	(4.156)	
4. RETH1	0.008	0.006	0.16
[Aaa–A]	(1.716)	(5.152)	
5. RETL1	0.069	0.044	0.13
[B and Below]	(1.869)	(4.545)	
6. RDIF1	0.060	0.037	0.09
[(5)–(4)]	(1.673)	(3.438)	

June, 1962–July, 1974
145 months

t-statistics in parentheses.

Therefore, the data indicate that low-grade bonds do have more systematic risk than high-grade bonds. There were no defaults in Weinstein's bond data; all of the low returns on these bonds came from declines in market value rather than actual defaults.

The evidence seems to say that low-grade bonds are more risky than high-grade bonds, even when they do not actually go into default. But low-grade bonds also have a higher actual rate of return, at least as far as we have yet been able to observe. Of course, the real test will occur when we experience a significant economic downturn. Until then we cannot know how good a deal low-grade or high-yield bonds will be.

TAXES AND THE YIELDS ON SECURITIES

The next factor that has an influence on observed interest rates is taxes. The effects of taxes on the prices and yields of securities and on the investment decisions made in the market are as varied and complicated as the tax laws themselves. Basically, investors treat taxes like other costs—they try to minimize them. As a result, when judging investments, investors are interested in after-tax returns, which means the price and yield on an asset are determined by its after-tax returns rather than by the returns it pays before taxes are accounted for. Moreover, if investors are taxed at different rates, an asset with a particular before-tax return will often yield a different amount after taxes to two investors. Therefore, it is important to take into account not only the fact that different securities are treated differently in the tax law, but also the extent to which individuals and institutions are taxed at different rates. The effect of taxes on yields are particularly important because the Congress made historic changes in the United States tax code in 1986. The most important of these changes, for the purposes of the present discussion, is the movement toward a flat tax and the change in tax rates on regular income versus capital gains.

In this section we will concentrate on two effects of the tax laws on the yields on different securities. These are not the only effects of taxes in financial markets, but they are instances where the effects of taxes can be directly observed in the yield on debt securities. They are also of particular interest in light of the new U.S. tax laws. The first tax effect we will examine is the exemption of interest income on municipal securities from federal income taxes. Second, we will examine the effect of differential taxation of interest income and capital gains on the yields on debt securities.

SOME BASIC FEATURES OF THE TAX LAWS

Before we take up these issues, it is worth noting a few important aspects of the U.S. tax laws, including some changes incorporated in the 1986 tax law, which have a signficant impact on financial markets. One very important feature of the tax laws in the United States is that taxes on earnings on financial assets are based on nominal rather than real earnings. Suppose you were to invest in a one year Treasury bill with a nominal yield of 8 percent. The inflation rate at the end of the year turned out to be 4 percent, and you were in the maximum tax bracket in effect prior to the 1986 tax law, 50 per cent. Your after-tax real return would be:

$$\text{Nominal interest rate } (1\text{-Tax rate}) - \text{Inflation rate} =$$
$$8\% \ (1-.5) - 4\% = 0\%.$$

If the tax system allowed deductions for inflation expense, then the tax would be applied to real rather than nominal earnings. That is, you would pay a tax of 50 percent of 4 percent rather than 50 percent of 8 percent. But the tax system in the United States does not allow this kind of deduction. However, as the maximum marginal tax rate is reduced, the impact of this aspect of the tax law is reduced. The new 1986 tax law has stipulated that the maximum marginal tax rate will eventually be 28 percent. However, during 1987 and 1988 the maximum marginal tax rate will temporarily be at 38 percent. Notice that taxpayers benefit not simply from the impact of the lower rate on real earnings, but they also benefit from a reduction in the taxation of gains arising solely from inflation. But as long as we tax nominal rather than real income, we are, in part, taxing the return we demand simply to stay even with inflation.

Another important feature of the U.S. tax system is that interest expense is tax deductible on both individual and corporate tax returns. However, the 1986 tax law made an important change in the deductability of interest expense on

WHEN IS A DEFAULT A DEFAULT?

Throughout this chapter we discussed default risk as if default was a well-defined event and as if the losses incurred were well-defined. There is at least one very important real-world case of default risk where this is not the case at all. This is the debt to less-developed countries, or LDC debt, held by U.S. and some foreign commercial banks. Beginning in the 1970s, U.S. banks made extensive loans to private companies and governments in the third world. The loans to Latin American borrowers were particularly large. For example, Panel A of Table 7–4 shows the dollar magnitude of loans outstanding which constituted more than one percent of total assets for Bank of America and from Manufacturers Hanover, two of the banks with heavy exposure.

There were a number of reasons why U.S. commercial banks became interested in making such loans. One reason was that after the 1974–75 recession, there was never a complete rebound in the demand for loans by U.S. corporate borrowers. These borrowers began to develop alternative ways to raise funds which circumvented the banks, so commercial banks were hungry for new markets. In addition, a large amount of funds came into banks from countries profiting from the rise of oil prices—so-called petrodollars. The inflation of that period made it appear there would be sufficient long-term prosperity that foreign borrowers would have little difficulty paying for these loans. Finally, there was a widespread perception in banking circles that foreign governments would not default on these loans, so there was very little risk. The perception of low risk was accentuated by the fact that the riskiness of this type of lending was reduced if many U.S. banks were involved in the loans together.

As it turned out, LDC lending was very risky, which became apparent when the price of oil collapsed in the early 1980s and the economies of major debtor nations, particularly Mexico, deteriorated significantly. The foreign debt issue turned into what has been called a "crisis" when, in August, 1982, Mexico announced that it could not continue to pay its debt. Other Latin American countries encountered severe difficulties managing their debt obligations, but most were not as severe as in Mexico. Nonetheless, by early 1987 other countries, including Brazil and Equador, began to renounce their debt obligations. As a result, the banks and the U.S. government have become involved in highly complicated negotiations to restructure this foreign debt.

An interesting feature of the debt "crisis" is that it is not at all clear exactly what constitutes a default. Banks can continue to extend new loans to LDC borrowers, and the proceeds from the new loans can be used to pay off the old loans. This process can be used to hold out for some fortuitous event which will improve the borrower's economic situation, but for all practical purposes, these loans go into default when the banks decide, or are forced to decide, to write them off. A major step in this direction was taken in the second quarter of 1987 when Citicorp announced on May 19, 1987, that it would add $3 billion to its loan-loss reseves to cover write-offs of LDC debt. Citicorp's increase in loan-loss reserves meant that its reserves were equal to 25 percent of the amount of Latin American loans on its books. While increasing reserves does not actually constitute writing off 25 percent of the loans, this was a major step to recognizing that the LDC would probably never be fully repaid. Citicorp's announcement led to similar actions by other banks. Panel B of Table 7–4 identifies the magnitudes of the increases in loan-loss reserves announced by mid-June, 1987 for the second quarter of that year by major U.S. banks.

---

personal income taxes. Starting in 1987, personal interest expense will be tax deductible only if it is for qualifying mortgage loans. To qualify, the mortgage loan cannot exceed the purchase price of the home plus the value of any improvements in the property. This means that interest on credit cards and other personal loans will not be deductible. Nonmortgage consumer debt in the United States grew at a very rapid pace through the 1970s and 1980s. The new tax law implies

TABLE 7–4
LDC debt at U.S. commercial banks.

Panel A	Panel B

Panel A

BankAmerica

Foreign debt holdings exceeding 1% of total assets, as of March 31, 1987, in millions of dollars.

Country	Amount	As a Percentage of Total Assets
Brazil	$2,716	2.7%
Mexico	2,407	2.4
Venezuela	1,226	1.2

Manufacturers Hanover

Outstanding loans and investments in heavily indebted developing countries as of Dec. 31, 1986.

Country	Loans and Investments ($ billions)	As a Percentage of Total Assets
Brazil	$2.32	3.11%
Mexico	1.90	2.56
Argentina	1.46	1.96
Venezuela	1.00	1.35
Chile	0.82	1.10

Panel B

Foreign-Debt Problem

($ millions)

Bank	Addition to Loan-loss Reserves	Net 2nd Quarter Loss[1]
Citicorp	$3,000	$2,500
Chase Manhattan	1,600	1,400
BankAmerica	1,100	1,100
Chemical New York	1,100	1,104
First Chicago	800	700
First Interstate	500	205
Security Pacific	500	175
Mellon	415	500
Bank of Boston	300	80
Norwest (Minneapolis)	200	160
Mercantile (St. Louis)	75	33
Shawmut (Boston)	69	30
Reinier (Seattle)	58	19
NBD Bankcorp	54	15[2]
Merchants National (Indianapolis)	30	13
Banco de Ponce (Puerto Rico)	10	4
TOTAL	**$9,811**	**$8,008**

[1]Estimated.

[2]Net income, reduced by $22 million from year-ago level

Source for Panel A: Information from MHC's 1986 annual report reported in the *Wall Street Journal,* June 9, 1987, p. 3.
Source for Panel B: *Wall Street Journal,* June 16, 1987, p. 2.

that the interest expense on much of that debt will now have to be fully borne by the borrower rather than by both the borrower and the taxpayers.

One implication of this change is that the real cost of borrowing to fund consumer durable and other purchases will increase. Some borrowers will attempt to finance their purchases in such a way that they are using loans collateralized by their homes to pay for other purchases. But only borrowers who have the capacity to take out new debt and not exceed the original purchase price of their home, plus the value of any improvements, will have this option available. It is not obvious how large a portion of the population this will be. Many financial institutions are offering home equity lending programs tailored for these borrowers. This shows how changes in the tax laws can affect the nature of the financial contracts used in the economy.

Municipal bonds are bonds issued by state or local governments.

The 1986 tax law also includes important changes in the taxation of bonds issued by state and local governments, or **municipal bonds.** In an effort to reduce the cost of borrowing for state and local governments across the country, the U.S. government has made the interest income on municipal bonds exempt from federal income taxes. In addition, each state has declared that the interest income on its own bonds will be exempt from its state income taxes. Finally, some states and localities have given tax-exempt status to bonds issued by other states on a reciprocal basis.

The tax-exempt feature of the interest income on municipal bonds has made them attractive to individuals and institutions with high tax rates. Individuals who have historically faced a progressive income tax schedule have found that the higher the tax bracket, the more advantageous is the tax-exempt feature of the municipals. Corporations with a constant marginal tax rate (as long as their taxable income is over $25,000) have not found that the attractiveness of municipal securities varies directly with their income level in the same way as have individuals. In addition, some institutions with sizable amounts of funds to invest, such as pension funds and tax-exempt foundations, do not pay taxes and therefore find the tax-exempt feature of municipals totally unattractive.

Prior to the enactment of the 1986 tax law, the tax treatment of municipal bonds was relatively straightforward. However, the new tax law has made the situation much more complicated. The general thrust of the new tax law is to limit the ability of municipal governments to sell tax-exempt bonds. This limitation is motivated by the perception that municipal governments were abusing the privilege granted to them through the tax-exemption feature.

There were two principal types of perceived abuses. One pertains to the growth of industrial revenue bonds used to finance a wide variety of projects that were not deemed essential services of state and local governments. It was relatively common practice for state and local governments to issue bonds to fund private ventures. This was used extensively in campaigns to provide incentives for corporations to locate facilities in a particular town or region. The local government would fund the development of the new facility and related capital expenditures in order to provide an incentive for the firm to locate in that area. This reduced the cost incurred by the corporation since it was able to finance its project at the tax-exempt rate.

The second perceived abuse was that some state and local governments sold municipal bonds in order to reinvest the proceeds in higher yielding instruments. While explicitly prohibited by the IRS, it was very difficult to prove this was the purpose of a specific bond issue. As a result, Congress chose to limit the ability of state and local governments to engage in such transactions.

The 1986 tax law defines four classes of municipal debt:

Class 1 consists of public purpose bonds. These are issued by state and local governments or their agencies to meet essential government functions, such as highway construction and school financing. These bonds will continue to be tax exempt.

Class 2 includes bonds issued to finance what the tax law calls nongovernmental purposes, like housing and student loans. States will have a ceiling on the amount of class 2 bonds they can issue. Moreover, taxpayers who purchase such bonds will have to treat interest earned on them as a preference item on their tax returns; it will have to be added to taxable income if the taxpayer is liable for the new minimum tax included in the new law.

Class 3 includes taxable municipals, issued for purposes that Congress deemed nonessential, such as upgrading of pollution control facilities or building a sports stadium.

Class 4 consists of bonds issued prior to August 7, 1986, which will continue to provide tax-free income.

THE EFFECT OF TAXES ON MUNICIPAL BOND YIELDS

The attractiveness of tax-exempt municipal bonds hinges on the difference in yields between the municipal security and an otherwise comparable security which is fully taxable. For example, suppose that a municipal bond and corporate bond are identical in every respect except the tax-exempt status of the muncipal bond. The yield on the corporate bond is 10 percent, and the yield on the municipal is 6 percent. At what tax rate will it be profitable for an investor to hold the municipal rather than the corporate bond? The answer can be computed from the following formula:

$$1 - \frac{0.06}{0.10} = 0.40. \tag{7-1}$$

To see why this is true we must return to the statement that investors are interested in after-tax returns. The problem facing the investor is to determine the yield he or she will receive after taxes on a taxable bond paying 10 percent. The corporate and municipal bonds will yield identical after-tax returns if

$$i_c(1 - \ell) = i_m, \tag{7-2}$$

where ℓ is his or her tax rate, i_m is equal to the yield on the municipal bond, and i_c is equal to the yield on the otherwise equivalent taxable corporate bond. For a given yield on both the municipal and corporate bonds, we can solve for the minimum marginal tax rate where the municipal bond produces the higher after-tax yield:

$$\ell = 1 - \frac{i_m}{i_c}. \tag{7-3}$$

This is exactly the same equation as the example in Equation (7–1). It implies that anyone with a tax rate over 40 percent, in the example, will find the municipal bond to be a better investment than the corporate bond.

From the observed yields on municipals and roughly comparable securities that are taxable, it is possible to compute the implied marginal tax rate, as in this example. Figure 7–2 shows the recent yields on high-quality municipal bonds with a maturity of 20 years. It also shows the yield on long-term corporate bonds over the same period. Using the corporate bonds as the comparable security, it is possible to compute the marginal tax rate at which the municipal security becomes preferable, over the same historical period. The marginal tax rates are shown in panel B of the figure. There is considerable fluctuation in the computed marginal tax rate over the historical period. The figure also shows that the marginal tax rate has declined in recent years. In 1984 and 1985 the marginal tax rate was 24 percent, so that yields on municipals have tended to be roughly 76 percent of yield on other comparable bonds.

It is not obvious why this yield spread has been around 75 percent rather than some higher or lower amount, such as 85 percent or 55 percent. The size of the spread depends largely on who is attracted to hold municipals and who is not. Most municipal bonds are held by commercial banks, property and casualty insurance companies, and individuals who have been in high tax-brackets. Because commercial banks have the largest position in the municipal bond market, it has been argued that their decisions to buy or sell municipals are an important, if not the most important, determinant of the marginal tax rate. It is argued that as banks, which are subject to the corporate tax rate, move into or out of the market,

FIGURE 7–2

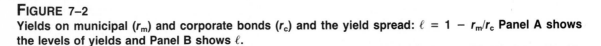

Yields on municipal (r_m) and corporate bonds (r_c) and the yield spread: $\ell = 1 - r_m/r_c$ Panel A shows the levels of yields and Panel B shows ℓ.

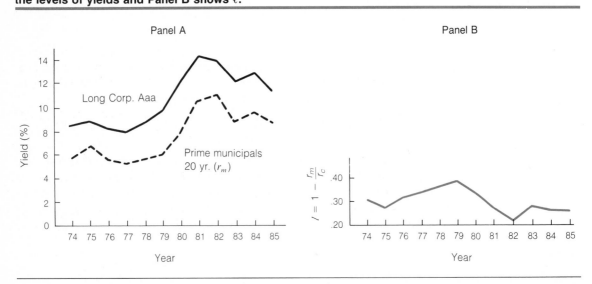

they increase or decrease the total demand for municipals. The slack has been taken up by individuals who have faced a progressive tax schedule. Therefore, when they must pick up additional slack, the marginal tax rate must fall to induce more individual investors to buy municipals. Demand for municipal bonds by commercial banks declined during the late 1970s and 1980s largely because banks had plentiful tax deductions from other sources, such as foreign tax credits and leasing operations. The rise in municipal bond rates relative to other taxable rates roughly coincided with this change in bank demand. However, it is difficult to determine whether this was the principal cause of the shift in yields or not.

Empirical studies that have attempted to explain the determinants of the spread between municipal and taxable yields have not generated conclusive results. Some studies have indicated that changes in demand for municipals by commercial banks have had a significant impact on these yield spreads. Others have attributed the changes in yield spread to changes in risk or to other differences between the securities.[6] One difficulty in this type of empirical work is that it is difficult to identify securities comparable to municipals in all respects except tax treatment. For example, the risk of default and the options open to security holders in the event of default are somewhat ambiguous with regard to municipal securities. The effective default of New York City in the late 1970s and the limited options open to investors due to the political nature of the problem highlighted the potential difficulties involved in municipal debt. Premiums for risk may therefore vary widely for even the most highly rated municipal securities, especially when the maturities are long. Another problem is that there are a number of peculiar pressures on commercial banks. For example, banks may find it necessary to liquidate municipal bonds to satisfy the commitments they have made to extend commercial loans. This prospect of untimely liquidation will alter the perceived return to banks from holding municipal bonds. These factors and others make it exceptionally difficult to measure true after-tax yield spreads between municipal and other securities as perceived by commercial banks.

THE SUBSIDY FOR INVESTORS IN MUNICIPAL TAX EXEMPTION

One interesting aspect of the tax treatment of municipals is that the combination of tax exemption of income on municipal bonds and progressive personal income tax creates a subsidy for investors in relatively high tax brackets. By comparison, a flat tax on personal income incorporates no such subsidy. Hence, the movement to a flat tax system which is part of the 1986 tax act will reduce the subsidy that has been a part of municipal financing for many years. To understand how this subsidy works we need to examine the incentive to purchase municipal bonds by investors who face a flat income tax as opposed to a progressive one. Let's consider the difference between a flat tax at 46 percent, which is what corporate investors have paid (assuming no other deductions reduced their tax liability), and a progressive tax. As long as corporate investors expect their investments will be

---

[6]See Cook and Hendershott, pp. 1173–86.

subject to full corporate taxes, then they will prefer municipal bonds over comparable corporate bonds if the yield on municipals is at least 54 percent of the corporate yield. This assumes no other tax shelters are available for this income so that the full 46 percent tax rate will be paid if the municipal bond is utilized. Because there is a constant tax rate, as long as the ratio of the municipal to the corporate bond yield is exactly equal to one minus that constant tax rate, then municipal bonds are as good as corporate bonds in terms of their after-tax yields. Moreover, there are no corporate investors with higher tax rates to be induced into the municipal market by offering higher yields. Therefore, if yields rise above the ratio of 54 percent, this would tend to increase the gain to corporate investors above what is sufficient to induce them to enter the market. Moreover, this gain comes at the expense of issuers of municipal bonds, for as the yield they have to pay increases relative to prevailing corporate yields, the subsidy they derive from tax exemption declines. As long as the ratio of the yields remains at 54 percent, municipal governments pay no more than is necessary to attract investors subject to the corporate income tax, and they maintain the maximum amount of their subsidy.

The situation is different, however, with a progressive as opposed to a constant tax schedule. To see why, consider the incentive to shelter income with municipal bonds for individuals in the 60 as opposed to the 40 percent tax bracket. The individuals in the 60 percent bracket will find it profitable to purchase municipal bonds as long as their yield exceeds 40 percent of the yield on a taxable bond. On the other hand, individuals in the 40 percent tax bracket require that the municipal yield rise to 60 percent of the corporate bond yield to induce them to purchase municipals.

Another way to see this is to compute the relative gain that an individual in a particular tax bracket would reap by investing in municipal rather than corporate bonds, depending upon the ratio of the yields. For example, if a person who is in the 60 percent tax bracket invested in corporate bonds, he or she would reap an

TABLE 7–5
Gain (or loss) from investing in municipal bonds.

	Tax Bracket		
r_m/r_c	40%	46%	60%
20%	$-0.4r_c$	$-0.34r_c$	$-0.2r_c$
40%	$-0.2r_c$	$-0.14r_c$	0
54%	$-0.06r_c$	0	$0.14r_c$
60%	0	$.06r_c$	$0.2r_c$
80%	$0.2r_c$	$0.26r_c$	$0.4r_c$

Gains on municipal bond investments relative to corporate bonds—gains are expressed as a multiple of the corporate bond rate. Each gain is computed as:

$$\left[\frac{r_m}{r_c} - (1 - l)\right]r_c$$

FIGURE 7–3

Bondholders' surplus. The downward-sloping line in this figure represents the demand for municipal bonds by individuals who face a progressive income tax. The marginal tax rate l implied by the ratio of municipal and corporate bond yields is on the vertical axis and the demand for municipal bonds is on the horizontal axis. The area under the demand curve above the horizontal line at 0.4 represents the bondholders' surplus if the marginal tax rate is 0.4 or the ratio of the yields is 0.6.

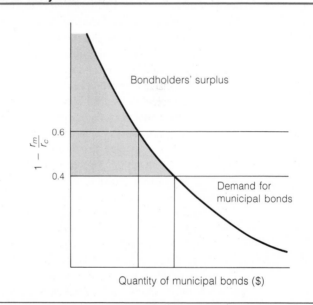

after-tax return equal to 40 percent of the corporate bond interest rate i_c. If the ratio of the yields is also 60 percent, $i_m/i_c = 0.60$, then the return from municipals is equal to 60 percent of the corporate bond rate. As a result, a person in the 60 percent bracket gains 20 percent of the corporate bond rate by investing in municipals. If the corporate bond rate is 10 percent, then this gain represents 200 basis points (or 2 percent interest). We can repeat these calculations for individuals in different tax brackets and for different yield spreads to see what the amounts of the gain and loss will be. The results of these computations are presented in Table 7–5. This table shows that as the ratio of the yields rises, individuals in lower tax brackets are induced to purchase municipal bonds, and the demand for municipal bonds rises.

We can represent this relationship with a demand curve for municipals by individuals as a function of their marginal tax rates. Such a demand curve is illustrated in Figure 7–3. It shows that individual demand rises as the ratio of yields rises, or as the marginal tax rate at which municipals becomes profitable falls. Now suppose that the ratio between the two yields is 60 percent, so that the critical tax rate at which it is profitable to invest in municipal bonds is 40 percent. All investors with marginal tax rates above 40 percent would be willing to buy municipals at yield spreads less than 60 percent. For example, the 60 percent bracket individual would be willing to purchase municipals if the municipal yield declined to 40 percent of the corporate yield. As shown in Table 7–4, at any yield spread greater than 40 percent this individual would reap some gain.

As a result, at any particular tax rate ℓ in Figure 7–3, the individual with exactly the tax rate breaks even on corporate or municipal bonds, and the higher tax bracket individuals receive a surplus. The surplus is the amount of interest income they would be willing to give up and still hold municipal bonds. In effect, this is a transfer of the federal subsidy from the state and local governments to the individuals in very high tax brackets. The total amount of this surplus, in the case where the ratio of the yields is 60 percent or ℓ equals 40 percent, is represented in Figure 7–3. The surplus is the shaded area under the demand curve above the horizontal line at the 40 percent marginal tax rate.

Bondholders' surplus refers to the extra return included in the yield on municipal bonds beyond what is needed to induce an investor in a particular tax bracket to hold those bonds.

Because of this, **bondholders' surplus** tax exemption, in conjunction with a graduated personal income tax, has been criticized as an inefficient subsidy. Rather than return all the subsidy to state and local governments, this system has diverted part of it to high tax bracket investors. Of course, if and when we eventually implement the 28 percent tax rate mandated in the 1986 tax law, then the bondholders' surplus will be significantly diminished.

TAXATION OF INTEREST AND CAPITAL GAINS: THE ADVANTAGE OF DISCOUNT BONDS

Historically, the tax laws have treated income derived from interest and income derived from capital gains differently. Capital gains income has been taxed at a lower rate than interest income. Until 1987, the capital gains rate was one-half of an individual's regular rate, but for high-income individuals the difference is smaller. Under the 1986 tax law capital gains taxes have been increased to eliminate the divergence between tax rates on regular income and on capital gains. However, other countries have chosen to go further than the U.S. had to encourage investment by taxing capital gains at a lower rate than regular income. For example, Japan has exempted certain types of capital gains from any income taxation. In spite of the equal treatment of capital gains and regular income in the new tax laws, it is important to understand how differential tax rates on capital gains can influence yields on securities. We will find this to be of particular importance in Chapter 16 when we examine zero-coupon bonds.

The implication of the differential taxation of interest and capital gains is that the price and yield of a bond can be influenced by shifting the income in a bond from coupon interest to capital gains. To see precisely what this means it is necessary to reconsider the price of a coupon bond (see Appendix A) and introduce taxes into the present value equation that determines its value. The value of an N period coupon bond with a value at maturity of $1,000 can be defined as

$$PV = \sum_{t=1,}^{N} \frac{A}{(1 + i)^t} + \frac{1,000}{(1 + i)^N}, \tag{7–4}$$

where i is the discount rate and A is the periodic coupon interest payment. Equation (7–4) implies that, given a discount rate or value for i, the price of the bond can be determined. Or, given a price for the bond, the equation implies a yield for the bond.

Once we try to take taxes into account, this equation still represents the relationship between the observed price and the observed before-tax yield, but it no longer tells us how the price is really determined because investors are concerned with after-tax yields and returns. Therefore, the value of the bond will be determined by investors discounting their after-tax returns at the after-tax discount rate they demand. We can imagine the market working in the following manner. Investors consider the returns on alternative investments on an after-tax basis. They bid for securities that look attractive after taxes. The prices of securities come to reflect investors' after-tax yields.

In order to specify how the price is determined, we have to state the relationship between price and the after-tax income stream accruing to the asset. To do this we will need some additional notation. We will represent the tax rate on regular income with the symbol ℓ, as we did above, and the tax rate on capital gains with the symbol g, and the after-tax interest rate demanded by investors as i_a. Now we need to state an equation for the present value of after-tax returns discounted at the after-tax rate i_a. This equation can be written as follows:

$$PV = \sum_{t=1}^{N} \frac{A(1 - \ell)}{(1 + i_a)^t} + \frac{1,000}{(1 + i_a)^N} - \frac{(1,000 - PV)g}{(1 + i_a)^N}. \qquad (7\text{–}5)$$

The first term is the present value of the coupon payments after taxes. The second term is the present value of the maturity value. The third term is the present value of the future capital gains tax. This equation determines the price that an investor will place on an asset based on its after-tax returns.

In order to illustrate how this equation is used to determine the price, we need to move the PV in the last term on the right-hand side of the equation to the left-hand side so that we can solve for PV. When we do this we have the following somewhat more complicated expression:

$$PV = \left[\sum_{t=1}^{N} \frac{A(1 - \ell)}{(1 + i_a)^t} + \frac{1,000(1 - g)}{(1 + i_a)^N} \right] \cdot \frac{(1 + i_a)^N}{(1 + i_a)^N - g}. \qquad (7\text{–}6)$$

However, while it is more complicated, we can plug a number into everything on the right-hand side. To illustrate, suppose that the tax rate on regular income is 50 percent, the tax rate on capital gains is 25 percent, and the after-tax discount rate is 5 percent. Also suppose this bond pays annual coupon payments of $50 and there are 10 years to maturity. Then we can solve for the price as follows:

$$PV = \left[\sum_{t=1}^{10} \frac{25}{(1.05)^t} + \frac{1,000(1 - .25)}{(1.05)^{10}} \right] \frac{1.63}{1.63 - .25} \qquad (7\text{–}7)$$
$$= [193 + 460][1.18]$$
$$= 771.$$

Equation (7–5) shows how the price of a coupon bond is determined with taxation of interest income and capital gains at different rates. In spite of the importance of after-tax yields to each investor, however, we observe only the before-tax yield of the bond quoted in the market. The before-tax yield is the one determined by Equation (7–4), and we can compute it by solving Equation (7–4) for the internal rate of return when the price is $771. The before-tax yield is still used by the market as just another way of stating the price of the security, but it no longer represents a yield demanded by security holders. The yield actually demanded is the after-tax yield i_a.

The effect of the differential tax rate on capital gains and interest income is to create a preference for bonds with low coupon rates.[7] These are called **discount bonds** because they sell at low or discount prices. The idea behind a discount bond is to shift income from coupon payment to capital gain in order to take advantage of the lower tax rates on capital gains. To see how this works we want to examine two bonds that have the same yield before taxes but have different proportions of capital gains as opposed to coupon interest income. The first bond has coupon payments virtually equal to the market interest rate. The second bond has much lower coupon payments. If these two bonds were traded in a world where there were no taxes, then the first bond would have no capital gain, because its current value would be exactly equal to its value at maturity. In order to maintain the same yield, the price of the second bond would have to fall until the capital gain was large enough to promise the same yield to investors as the first bond. Now suppose that interest income and capital gains are taxed, but with the capital gains rate lower than the rate on interest income, as was the case in the U.S. through 1986. The decrease in coupon payments on the second bond would then create a tax savings. We can see how this happens from Equation (7–5). As we decrease the coupon payments, the value of the bond declines and the capital gain in the third term increases to compensate. However, because of the tax savings, the value of the bond does not have to fall as much as it otherwise would to maintain the same after-tax yield. Because the price of the bond does not go down as far as it otherwise would, the before-tax yield, which is computed from Equation (7–4), should be lower for a discount bond than for a bond with a coupon rate close to the before-tax market interest rate.

This is, in fact, what has been observed in the market. For example, on November 23, 1979, the prices and yields on two Treasury bonds were as follows: one was a discount bond that matured in February, 1990 and had a coupon rate of 3.5 percent. The other offered little discount with a coupon rate of 8.25 percent and a maturity date of May, 1990. Because these bonds are nearly identical except for the discount coupon rates, they would have roughly the same market yield, were it not for the tax treatment of capital gains. The discount bond was priced at $75.20 with a before-tax yield of 6.69 percent. The bond with little discount was

Discount bonds are bonds which are issued with low coupon interest rates so that income is earned in capital gains.

---

[7]For a more detailed discussion, see James C. Van Horne, *Financial Market Rates and Flows,* Englewood Cliffs, N.J.: Prentice-Hall, chapter 8, 1978.

priced at $86.2 with a before-tax yield of 10.39 percent. The tax treatment of capital gains therefore drove down before-tax yield on the discount bond because the price did not have to fall as much as it would if not for the tax savings on capital gains.

THE IMPACT OF RELATIVE SECURITY SUPPLIES ON NOMINAL YIELDS

Segmentation refers to artificial divisions between financial markets not based on the cash flows paid on the securities.

The impact of relative supplies of securities on nominal yields hinges on the extent of **segmentation** in securities markets as opposed to the strength of substitution between different securities. The segmentation and substitution theories are polar extreme characterizations of the way financial markets operate. Basically, the segmentation theory argues that different securities or groups of securities have distinct markets with impenetrable barriers between them; the substitution view says that such barriers are nonexistent or minimal and that investors substitute back and forth between securities as they detect opportunities for excess returns. The implication of the segmentation view is that observed yield spreads are largely determined by changes in demand or supply for a given segment of the market. On the other hand, the substitution theory implies that factors that affect the real return to investors, such as risk and taxes, account for the observed differences in yields.

SEGMENTATION VERSUS SUBSTITUTION

The fundamental tenet of the segmentation theory is that specific securities have some characteristics that cause particular clienteles of investors to be interested in them and other investors to avoid them. The characteristics that lead to the formation of clienteles, or to market segmentation, are usually thought to be external to the innate risk and return characteristics of the security. The characteristics may be related to the tax treatment of some securities, or to some government restriction on the investments of financial institutions, or to some characteristics of the investors themselves that might make them choose securities on some basis other than the security's risk and return. Segmentation of the market into groups of investors who are willing to hold only particular types of securities is illustrated in Figure 7–4. The diagram shows the total population of investors divided into two groups according to some criterion unrelated to the actual returns on the securities. Each group holds only one type of security. As a result, there are effectively two markets with no links between them.

The empirical implication of the segmentation theory is that investors will be insensitive to changes in risk and return across the barrier that divides the markets. Therefore, factors that influence the distributions on returns for securities in different segments of the market will not explain the spreads between the yields on these securities. What will explain these yield spreads is the relative strength of supply and demand in the various market segments. The segmentation theory implies that the observable links between securities markets or between different

FIGURE 7–4
Segmented market. The figure shows that in a segmented market investors are divided into groups that hold distinct sets of securities.

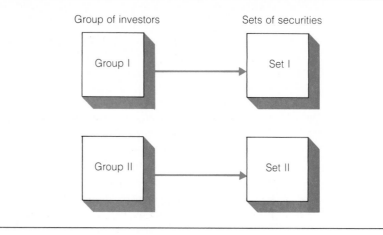

assets is weak. It implies that where segmentation exists, observed yields essentially follow their own independent paths and are not closely related.

The substitution theory argues that relative supplies and demands are not important determinants of security prices. Rather, all securities are priced to reflect the market's assessment of their risk and return. In this view, observed yield spreads are determined by all the factors affecting the return distributions on each security and any costs of substituting back and forth between securities. For example, if the income from different securities is treated differently for tax purposes, then this will affect the after-tax returns to investors, which will in turn influence the observed yields on these securities. The difference in yield will reflect the cost to investors of the differential tax treatment of the income of the securities. The substitution theory leaves no room for seemingly arbitrary or unexplained division of securities or investors into clientele groups that demand the yields on securities. It therefore argues that relative supply and demand will be unimportant in explaining differences in yields. The essence of this theory is that yield spreads must be due to perceived real differences in future returns.

Evidence on Segmentation and Substitution.   There are two types of evidence on the extent of segmentation in financial markets. One is indirect evidence, while the other is direct. Indirect evidence is drawn from attempts to account for observed differences in yield on different securities based on factors that directly affect the securities' future returns. This indirect evidence does not try to test the impact of relative security supplies directly. Instead it attempts to explain yield spread with the facts the substitution theory asserts are relevant. If this explanation proves adequate, then the segmentation theory is judged unimportant. Unfortunately, there is no unambiguous criterion as to what is an adequate explanation. It is impossible to account fully for observed yield differences in empirical studies. Therefore, what seems adequate to one person who reviews the evidence may seem inadequate to another. For example, Marshall E. Blume and Irwin Friend concluded after an extensive analysis of risk premiums on equity securities (using the capital asset pricing model) that the ability to explain observed differences in yields is sufficiently poor that "the evidence points to segmentation of markets as between stocks and bonds."[8] In general, a failure to explain observed yield spreads adequately with the identifiable factors affecting returns has led to the conclusion that there must be some segmentation.

Fortunately there is also some direct evidence on the impact of the relative supply and demand of securities. One of the more comprehensive studies of yield spreads on bonds that attempted to test the importance of relative supplies of securities directly was conducted by Timothy Cook and Patrick Hendershott.[9] They examined the yield spreads between long-term corporate and Treasury bonds. They made extensive adjustments for tax and technical factors influencing the yield data, and then attempted to isolate the influences of risk and relative security supplies on the observed yield spreads. However, their measures of relative supplies of corporate and Treasury bonds have no perceptible effect once risk and taxes are accounted for.

But, as Cook and Hendershott point out, the segmentation view requires that no large group of investors exists who are indifferent at the margin between the two securities in question. Even if this is not the case for high-grade corporate and Treasury bonds, it may be true for other securities. The discussion earlier in this chapter suggests that one more likely candidate might be the market for municipal securities. In that case, some have argued that the tax treatment of municipal bonds has created a segmented market dominated by commercial banks. In this case, the evidence is not as clear-cut. In one study of regional markets for municipal bonds, Hendershott and Kidwell found evidence of segmentation in the yield spreads between yields in the regional market and yields on nationally distributed bonds that could not be attributed to risk and other factors affecting returns.[10] But in another study of 20 years' worth of aggregate national yield data for municipal bonds and Treasury bonds, as well as between municipal bonds of different risk and maturity, no evidence was found of segmentation resulting from changes in banks' holdings of those securities.[11]

---

[8]See Marshall Blume and Irwin Friend: "A New Look at the Capital Asset Pricing Model," *Journal of Finance,* 28 (March 1973), pp. 19–33.

[9]See Cook and Hendershott, pp. 1173–86.

[10]See Patrick H. Hendershott and David S. Kidwell, "The Impact of Relative Security Supplies; A Test with Data from a Regional Tax-Exempt Bond Market," *Journal of Money, Credit and Banking,* 10 (August 1978), pp. 337–47.

[11]See Campbell, Tim S., "On the Extent of Segmentation in the Municipal Securities Market," *Journal of Money, Credit and Banking,* 12 (February 1980), pp. 71–82.

Finally, John S. Bildersee examined yield spreads between Treasury securities and other securities backed by the U.S. government but issued by other agencies within the federal government and called agency securities. Bildersee's study attempted to determine the extent of segmentation between the markets for these types of securities and identify the factors that accounted for changes in yield spreads over time. This particular issue has attracted some attention from market observers because the underlying securities are so similar, yet there are persistent yield spreads between the securities. Bildersee concluded that ''the yield spreads separating these markets are most consistently related to economic liquidity measures . . . and to market measures such as relative transaction rates and market size.'' Bildersee also draws an important conclusion about the general problem of segmentation and substitution in financial markets. He points out, ''it appears that the major questions that must be answered about the bond markets are not whether they are continuous and integrated or segmented. Instead, the questions must revolve around the issues of how continuous and integrated these markets are, how this continuity can be defined, and how it changes through varied economic conditions.''[12]

Markets become more segmented when there are barriers or costs to substituting between alternative types of investments. This includes the cost of evaluating the yield spread to determine whether it is justified by anticipated real returns and the transactions cost of selling one security and buying another. It seems exceptionally reasonable that such costs exist in substituting between various regional markets. It also seems reasonable that these costs may be large in the short run. This means that a short-run change in yield spreads may be slow to induce investors to alter their portfolios and make the adjustments necessary to force the yield spread back to what they believe is an equilibrium. This may be particularly true when a large change in investments may be necessary, which occasionally occurs in the municipal-bonds market.

These costs should dissipate over time. In effect, as the disequilibrium yield spread persists, more investors are able to make the substitutions which will return the yield spread to equilibrium. Segmentation therefore results when the costs of substituting between assets are large. As these costs diminish across time, or regional boundaries become less significant, segmentation diminishes.

Summary

In this chapter we concentrated on three factors that influence nominal interest rates: default risk, taxes, and relative security supplies. With debt securities there are both a premium for bearing risk, in the sense that we understand from Chapter

---

[12]See John S. Bildersee, ''U.S. Government and Agency Securities: An Analysis of Yield Spreads and Performance,'' *Journal of Business*, 51 (July 1978), p. 520. Copyright 1978 by the University of Chicago.

3, and a markup or margin for default. Both premiums represent differences between the contract or promised interest rate on a debt security and the expected rate of return on the investment that debt security is financing. Both factors in combination account for the difference between observed promised rates on debt securities and the risk-free real interest rate. Announcements of rating changes seems to provide no new information to the market about the risk of default.

Next we examined the growth of the market for junk bonds or low-grade, high-yield bonds. This was actually a market for publicly distributed debt that would have previously been privately financed by banks or insurance companies. This market has attracted a lot of controversy because junk bonds have been used to finance a number of actual and threatened takeovers of major U.S. companies. The controversy has focused attention on the riskiness of junk bonds. We examined some recent evidence on the returns on portfolios of low-grade bonds and found that the evidence indicates that low-grade bonds are more risky than higher grade bonds, and they have thus far earned higher actual returns. However, we have only experienced one major downturn (in October, 1987) in the financial markets since the widespread use of junk bonds, so it is difficult to say whether the extra promised yield is sufficient compensation for the risk involved.

Next we explored the effects of taxes on nominal yields. Taxes in the U.S. are based on nominal rather than real returns. We reviewed some of the principal features of the 1986 tax act. Two important examples of the effects of taxes on yields are the exemption from federal income taxes of interest income on municipal bonds and the taxation of capital gains at a lower rate than regular interest income. The tax treatment of municipal bonds tends to decrease municipal bond yields relative to yields on comparable securities with taxable income until the after-tax yields are the same. Furthermore, this tax treatment has tended to concentrate investments in municipals in the hands of those who have the least preferential tax treatment, particularly high tax-rate individuals, commercial banks, and property and casualty insurance companies. Regarding the tax treatment of capital gains, when capital gains are taxed at lower rates than regular income, it is possible to raise the after-tax yield of a bond by reducing coupon payments. We learned how to examine the after-tax yield of a discount bond and why after- rather than before-tax yield determines market prices.

Finally, we examined the impact of relative security supplies, or the segmentation argument. The segmentation argument asserts that there are clienteles of investors in the market who prefer specific types of securities at the exclusion of others. The formation of such clienteles is often thought to be due to something external to the factors that determine a particular security's future returns. The alternative theory, which was characterized as perfect substitution, asserts that no such external forces exist and each security's price and yield are determined by the return it is expected to offer and the risk surrounding that return. We found that evidence on segmentation often comes from two sources. Often times, when it is difficult to examine observed prices or yields empirically with available measures of the future returns, this disparity is attributed to the presence of segmentation. The other evidence is based on the contribution to yields of changes in the volume of supply of demand for securities. Most such direct evidence points to segmentation only in the short run or in markets with great regional dispersion.

QUESTIONS

1. In this chapter we differentiated between two components of the premium for risk in a bond. What are these two components, and what do they mean? Suppose market participants became more averse to risk. Which of these two components of the premium would this affect?

2. What are junk bonds? Why have they become so controversial?

3. Discuss the available evidence on the holding period returns on low-grade corporate bonds. How would you measure the risk of these bonds? Is the extra promised return sufficient compensation for the risk involved?

4. Suppose you noticed that the yields on Treasury bonds with 20 years to maturity and municipal bonds of the highest quality also with 20 years to maturity had yields of 12 percent and 9 percent respectively. What would be the marginal tax rate at which you would find it profitable to hold municipal rather than Treasury bonds?

5. What are the various classes of municipal bonds included in the 1986 tax law? How will these new provisions of the tax law affect municipal financing?

6. What is bondholder surplus? How is it affected by the new 1986 tax law?

7. What does it mean to say that a financial market is segmented? Many people who have studied segmentation of financial markets have concluded that segmentation is a transitory or short-run phenomenon. In the very long run there really is little or no segmentation. Does this make sense? Why?

8. How do announcements of rating changes affect the prices of bonds? What does this effect imply about the value of rating services to the debt markets?

9. Can you summarize the factors that lead to observable changes in nominal interest rates over time? What do you think has probably been the most important factor causing changes in nominal rates in the 1970s and early 1980s?

10. In 1986 the spread between municipal bond yields and comparable maturity Treasury bonds narrowed to an extremely low level. Can you explain the reduction in yield spreads?

11. How do you think the spreads between interest rates of comparable maturity but different default risk behave over the business cycle? Do you think these spreads increase or decrease? Why?

12. Calculate the contract interest rates on risky loans which would be charged in order to yield an expected return of 10 percent, given the following alternative assumptions: probability an individual loan will default—.05 percent and 2 percent, percentage loss on default—20 percent and 60 percent.

REFERENCES

Bildersee, John S. "U.S. Government and Agency Securities: An Analysis of Yield Spreads and Performance," *Journal of Business,* 51 (July 1978), pp. 499–520.

Blume, Marshall, and Irwin Friend. "A New Look at the Capital Asset Pricing Model," *Journal of Finance,* 28 (March 1973), pp. 19–33.

Blume, Marshall, and Donald Keim. "Risk and Return Characteristics of Lower Grade Bonds," University of Pennsylvania, mimeo., (December 1984).

Campbell, Tim S. "On the Extent of Segmentation in the Municipal Securities Market," *Journal of Money, Credit and Banking,* 12 (February 1980), pp. 71–82.

Cook, Timothy Q. "Some Factors Affecting Long-Term Yield Spreads in Recent Years," *Monthly Review of the Federal Reserve Bank of Richmond,* 59 (September 1973), pp. 2–14.

———, and Patrick H. Hendershott. "The Impact of Taxes, Risk and Relative Security Supplies on Interest Rate Differentials," *Journal of Finance,* 33 (September 1978), pp. 1173–86.

Fischer, Lawrence. "Determinants of Risk Premium on Corporate Bonds," *Journal of Political Economy,* 67 (June 1959), pp. 217–37.

Jaffee, Dwight M. "Cyclical Variations in the Risk Structure of Interest Rates," *Journal of Monetary Economics,* 1 (1975), pp. 309–25.

Hendershott, Patrick H., and David S. Kidwell. "The Impact of Relative Security Supplies; A Test with Data from Regional Tax-Exempt Bond Market," *Journal of Money, Credit and Banking,* 10 (August 1978), pp. 337–47.

Van Horne, James C. *Financial Market Rates and Flows,* Englewood Cliffs, N.J.: Prentice-Hall, Inc., 1978.

Weinstein, Mark. "The Effect of a Rating Change Announcement on Bond Price," *Journal of Financial Economics,* 5 (1977), pp. 239–350.

Weinstein, Mark. "A Curmudgeon's View of Junk Bonds," *Journal of Portfolio Management,* (1987).

8

THE TERM STRUCTURE OF INTEREST RATES

An important characteristic of debt securities not dealt with in the last two chapters is the maturity of the security. The impact of maturity on yield is an important enough topic that it warrants treat-ment separate from other factors influencing yield. In this chapter we examine the relationship between the yield on a debt security and its maturity, referred to as the *term structure of interest rates*. The term structure deals only with debt securities because only they have a stated maturity. In addition, the term structure refers to the relationship between maturity and yield for securities that are alike in all other respects—for example, in their risk and tax treatment. Therefore, the term structure is normally applied to Treasury securities because of their high degree of homogeneity across maturities.

The term structure of interest rates contributes to a general understanding of financial markets and is one of the most critical financial issues facing any corporation. If the financial manager of a company is assessing whether to obtain funds with short-term or long-term debt, his or her choice will be determined by the yields available at the alternative maturities. If the short-term interest rate is higher than the long-term rate, as it was in 1982 for 1- and 10-year maturities, for example, then he or she might conclude that long-term borrowing will be better. One of the theories of the term structure we will examine, the unbiased expectations theory, argues that the long-term rate is determined solely by the market's expectations of future short-term rates. If the unbiased expectations theory is correct, then the financial manager cannot expect to save by borrowing at the longer rate because it is lower. An understanding of the term structure is of tremendous practical importance. ∎

YIELD CURVES AND FORWARD RATES

This chapter is devoted to an examination of three alternative theories of the term structure of interest rates. But before we get into the theories themselves we need to develop some concepts important for all three theories. First, we need to understand what a yield curve is. Second, we need to understand both what forward interest rates are and the relationship between current rates and forward rates.

THE YIELD CURVE

The margin note: *The **yield curve** shows the yield prevailing at a given point in time for bonds that differ only by maturity.*

The term structure of interest rates is normally represented by what is called a **yield curve.** The yield curve shows the yield prevailing at a given point in time for bonds that differ only by maturity. As a result, a different yield curve or term structure exists at any such point. Examples of different yield curves that have existed in recent years are shown in Figure 8–1. The figure shows that the yield curve prevailing in September, 1974 had a largely downward slope. A largely upward-sloping yield curve prevailed in June, 1975 and November, 1981, which means that short-term interest rates were generally below long-term interest rates during those months, resulting in an upward-sloping yield curve.

Before we begin the more detailed analysis of the term structure, it is fruitful to examine briefly the behavior of the yield curve through time. For example, consider the changes that occurred in the yield curve during the 1974–75 recession. September, 1974 was near the peak of short-term interest rates during that recession. During that time short-term interest rates reached record high levels, though that record has since been shattered. For example, 90-day Treasury bill rates went as high as 9.33 percent. By comparison, long-term Treasury bond rates were not nearly as explosive, reaching a peak of approximately 8.5 percent. This is reflected in the shapes of yield curves observed at different points, as illustrated in Figure 8–1. At the peak of short-term interest rates in the 1974 recession, the yield curve was negatively sloped. Later in the recession, short-term interest rates fell relative to long-term interest rates and the yield curve became positively sloped, as illustrated for June, 1975.

This pattern of relatively volatile short-term interest rates and less volatile long-term interest rates has become a common feature of business cycles in the United States. The basic reason for this is that long-term rates reflect the market's expectations of what will transpire over a long period of time, probably including a number of business cycles. Hence, these rates reflect an average of those expected future events, but the short-term cost of credit is reflected directly in short-term rates. These rates rise and fall to reflect the equilibrium demand and supply for short-term funds. Long-term rates would have patterns that are as volatile as short-term rates only if the market expected the trend in short-term rates to continue. That is, if the market expected the short-term rate to increase and stay at the higher level, then long-term rates would make a similar adjustment. The volatility of short-term relative to long-term rates reflects the market's belief that changes in short-term rates will remain a short-run phenomenon.

It is particularly interesting to examine the shape of the yield curve in late 1980, as illustrated in Figure 8–1. Short-term interest rates again reached record high levels. Again the yield curve had a negative slope in that long-term rates were substantially below short-term rates. This was a time when the rate of infla-

FIGURE 8–1
Yield curves for Treasury securities.

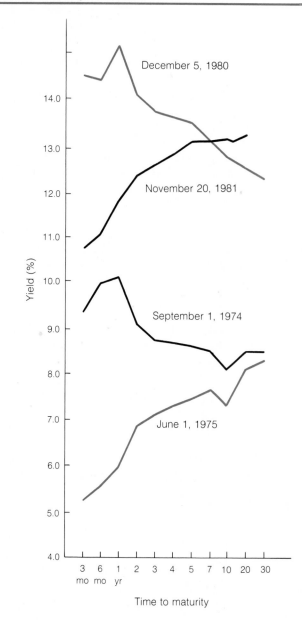

tion had accelerated sharply and was running in excess of 10 percent per year. It was widely perceived that short-term rates were rising in order to incorporate the expectations of inflation. But the fact that long-term rates were still substantially below short-term rates apparently reflected the market's belief that in the long run inflation rates would not remain at the levels experienced in recent years. The only alternative explanation of such low long-term rates would be that the market was willing to accept an expected long-run negative real return. In order to see more precisely the way the market incorporates its expectations into the term structure it is necessary to develop an understanding of forward rates.

THE MEANING AND COMPUTATION OF FORWARD RATES

The term structure of interest rates is the relationship between the current long-term and short-term interest rates. But underlying this there is really a relationship between the current long-term rate and the rates on current and future short-term loans. To see what this means suppose that there is a market for future short-term loans. In such a market you could arrange for a loan to begin, say, one year from now and receive a promise today of the interest rate you would have to pay one year from now. Such rates are called **forward rates.** And forward rates, or interest rates prevailing today for future loans, are an important part of the term structure relationship.

Forward rates are rates prevailing today pertaining to loans that begin at some point of time in the future.

In order to understand the role of forward rates in the term structure, consider the choice between two types of debt contracts. One type is a long-term bond at a single interest rate for N periods. The rate prevailing for such a contract today will be symbolized by $_tR_N$. The capital R means that it is a current rather than a forward rate. The subscript t means that it is the rate which prevails at time period t. The other contract involves N single-period loans contracted for in time period t. The rate of the first period will be $_tR_1$, which is the rate for single-period loans beginning today. The rate for loans in each future period which can be contracted for today is a forward rate. The forward rate will be symbolized as $_{t+1}r_1$, where the lower case r indicates it is a forward rate; the subscript $t+1$ indicates it is a rate on a loan beginning at $t + 1$ and the subscript $_1$ indicates it is a one-period loan. Figure 8–2 shows the time periods to which the forward rates and current rates apply in the case where $N = 5$. This figure illustrates that there are four forward rates which apply to the four year-long intervals between the maturity of the 1-year bond and the maturity of the 5-year bond. For example, the forward rate $_{t+1}r_1$ measures the interest rate prevailing today for a 1-year loan beginning 1 year from now.

If we relate this notation to the yield curve, we observe directly the R's on the yield curve, but we do not observe the r's. We can see this from Figure 8–1. For example, we can identify the rates prevailing in June, 1975 for Treasury securities of different maturities. A selection of these interpreted from the figure are listed below. (The right-hand subscript measures years to maturity and t means June, 1975).

$$_tR_1 = 6.04 \qquad _tR_{10} = 7.38$$
$$_tR_5 = 7.49 \qquad _tR_{20} = 8.17$$

FIGURE 8-2

Illustration of the time periods covered by forward interest rates (small *r*'s) and current interest rates (large *R*'s).

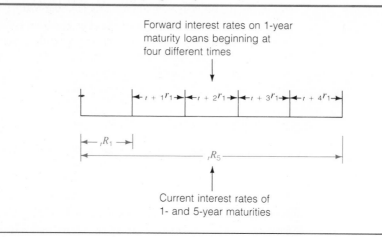

The yield curve directly measures the rates prevailing today for current loans with different maturities, the R's. On the other hand, the forward rates, the r's, are not directly shown in Figure 8–1.

Since we do not observe the forward rates on the yield curve, the natural question is where do they come from? We can compute forward rates from current rates of different maturities. To see how to do this we need to think about the choice between the two debt contracts just described, the long-term contract at a single interest rate and the alternative contract with a number of single-period future loans. We need to define the conditions under which the two contracts would have the same cost or the same future value. The two will have the same cost if the current and forward rates have the following relationship:

$$(1 + {}_tR_N)^N = (1 + {}_tR_1)(1 + {}_{t+1}r_1)(1 + {}_{t+2}r_1) \cdots (1 + {}_{t+N-1}r_1). \quad (8-1)$$

Equation (8–1) means that the value of the interest payments will be the same for either debt contract. Another way of looking at this is to say that the long-term rate implies a sequence of forward rates, and Equation (8–1) defines the relationship between them. For example, if the interest rate on a 5-year bond is 12.8 percent and the rate on a 1-year bond is 10 percent, then the following sequence of forward rates will satisfy Equation (8–1):

$$_{t+1}r_1 = 0.12, \; {}_{t+2}r_1 = 0.12, \; {}_{t+3}r_1 = 0.15, \; {}_{t+4}r_1 = 0.15.$$

We can make sure of this by substituting them in Equation (8–1). We find that both sides of the equation equal 1.82:

$$(1.128)^5 = (1.1)(1.12)(1.12)(1.15)(1.15) = 1.82.$$

When we observe the current interest rates on bonds with different maturities at a given point, we can use Equation (8–1) to solve for the forward rates these current rates imply. Suppose, for example, that we observe the current interest rate on 9-year bonds and 10-year bonds. We can use these to compute the forward rate for a 1-year loan beginning 9 years from now. The formula for the forward rate is as follows:

$$_{t+9}r_1 = \frac{(1 + _tR_{10})^{10}}{(1 + _tR_9)^9} - 1. \tag{8–2}$$

We can satisfy ourselves that this is correct by moving the one to the left-hand side of Equation (8–2) and substituting from Equation (8–1) for the values of $_tR_{10}$ and $_tR_9$:

$$1 + _{t+9}r_1 = \frac{(1 + _tR_1)(1 + _{t+1}r_1)(1 + _{t+2}r_1) \cdots (1 + _{t+8}r_1)(1 + _{+9}r_1)}{(1 + _tR_1)(1 + _{t+1}r_1)(1 + _{t+2}r_1) \cdots (1 + _{t+8}r_1)}.$$
$$\tag{8–3}$$

The equation is satisfied because the first nine terms in the numerator and denominator cancel out. To see how this can be used in an example, suppose that $_tR_{10} = 0.12$ and $_tR_9 = 0.11$. Then we can solve for $_{t+9}r_1$ as follows:

$$\begin{aligned} _{t+9}r_1 &= \frac{(1.12)^{10}}{(1.11)^9} - 1 \\ &= \frac{3.106}{2.558} \\ &= 0.21. \end{aligned}$$

So the rate for a 1-year loan beginning 9 years from now is 0.21.

Thus far we have dealt with forward rates which apply to future loans lasting only one period. In terms of our notation, the right-hand subscript on the forward rate has always been one. There is no reason to deal only with single-period loans. In principle, we could contract for a future loan to last any number of periods. We can solve for the forward rate on such a loan from the rates on current loans just as we did for single-period forward rates. From now on we will refer to the length of the future loan as K periods.

The formula for the forward rate on a K-period loan is similar to Equation (8–2), but with a complication introduced by the difference of K periods. If we observe current rates on an N-period bond and an $N + K$-period bond, then

$$_{t+N}r_K = \sqrt[K]{\frac{(1 + _tR_{N+K})^{N+K}}{(1 + _tR_N)^N}} - 1. \tag{8–4}$$

To see why this is equal to the forward rate on a K-period loan, we can examine the expression inside the radical ($\sqrt{}$). This can be rewritten as:

$$\frac{(1 + _tR_{N+K})^{N+K}}{(1 + _tR_N)^N} = \frac{(1 + _tR_1)(1 + _{t+1}r_1)(1 + _{t+2}r_1) \cdots (1 + _{t+N+K-1}r_1)}{(1 + _tR_1)(1 + _{t+1}r_1)(1 + _{t+2}r_1) \cdots (1 + _{T+N-1}r_1)}.$$

The difference between the numerator and the denominator is that the numerator includes the last K forward rates for single-period loans which are not included in the denominator. After canceling terms in both the numerator and denominator, we are left with

$$\frac{(1 + {_t}R_{N+K})^{N+K}}{(1 + {_t}R_N)^N} = (1 + {_{t+N}}r_1)(1 + {_{t+N+1}}r_1) \cdots (1 + {_{t+N+K-1}}r_1).$$

But using the reasoning in Equation (8–1), the product of these rates on the right-hand side of the equation will be the same as the forward rate on a K-period loan, raised to the Kth power. That is

$$(1 + {_{t+N}}r_K)^K = (1 + {_{t+N}}r_1)(1 + {_{t+N+1}}r_1) \cdots (1 + {_{t+N+K-1}}r_1). \qquad (8–6)$$

This means that the expression in the radical in Equation (8–4) is equal to

$$\frac{(1 + {_t}R_{N+K})^{N+K}}{(1 + {_t}R_N)^N} = (1 + {_{t+N}}r_K)^K. \qquad (8–7)$$

Equation (8–3) follows readily from Equation (8–7) in the special case where $K = 1$. The implication of this is that whenever we observe current rates with maturities which differ by K periods, we can compute the forward rate for a K-period loan which begins at the maturity of the shorter of the two bonds.

To illustrate these computations suppose we observe a sequence of current interest rates on bonds with maturities ranging from one to five years. An example of such rates is given in the left-hand column of Table 8–1. These current rates can be used to compute the equivalent forward rate on future loans over this 5-year period. For example, the current rates on 1- and 2-year bonds imply a forward rate for a 1-year loan beginning 1 year from now of

$$_{t+1}r_1 = \frac{(1.11)^2}{(1.12)} - 1 = 0.10.$$

Similarly the current rates on 3-year and 5-year bonds imply a forward rate for a 2-year loan beginning 3 years from now:

$$_{t+3}r_2 = \sqrt{\frac{(1.10)^5}{(1.105)^3}} - 1 = 0.09.$$

Other forward rates that can be computed from the first column of Table 8–1 are presented in column 2 of the table.

THE RELATIONSHIP BETWEEN FORWARD AND FUTURES RATES

Thus far we have made no attempt to relate the forward rates implicit in the term structure to the interest rates prevailing in the futures markets. However, these rates apply to the same type of investment. Selling Treasury bill futures, for ex-

TABLE 8–1
Example of current and corresponding forward interest rate.

Current Interest Rates for Selected Maturities	A Selection of Forward Rates which Can be Computed from Current Rates
$_1R_2 = 12.0\%$	$_{t+1}r_1 = 10.0\%$
$_1R_2 = 11.00\%$	$_{t+2}r_1 = 09.5\%$
$_1R_3 = 10.5\%$	$_{t+3}r_1 = 09.5\%$
$_1R_4 = 10.25\%$	$_{t+4}r_1 = 09.0\%$
$_1R_5 = 10.00\%$	$_{t+1}r_4 = 09.5\%$
	$_{t+2}r_3 = 09.3\%$
	$_{t+3}r_2 = 09.3\%$

ample, is essentially the same as betting on future Treasury bill rates by buying Treasury bills with different maturities. Therefore, futures and forward rates must be the same, if there are not any costless arbitrage opportunities to be found between these two markets.

To see that this is the case suppose we entered the futures market and promised to sell a 3-month Treasury bill with a maturity value of $10,000 six months from now at a price of $9,500. The $9,500 is referred to as the price of the contract. It is not a price we pay today, as is the price of a Treasury bill. Instead, it is the price at which we promise to deliver a Treasury bill in the future. We will break even on this bet if the actual price of Treasury bills six months from now is exactly equal to the price we promise, or $9,500. If the price is higher, we will lose, and if it is lower, we will make a profit. We can restate the nature of our position in terms of yield rather than price, as follows. At the price of $9,500, a 3-month Treasury bill would have to yield 21 percent. The yield is computed as the interest rate, r, which solves the following present value equation:

$$\$9,500 = \frac{\$10,000}{(1 + r/4)}.$$

Therefore, we are hoping that interest rates on 3-month bills will be greater than 21 percent 6 months from now, when we promise to supply a bill at a price of $9,500.

The same investment can be made by buying a 9-month Treasury bill and selling it in 6 months. We can infer the implicit price set for this transaction in the market by computing the forward rate for a 3-month bill 6 months from now. Since this is the same transaction as the one described above, the forward rate computed from the yield curve should be the same as the yield of 21 percent computed in the present value equation above. Both rates refer to the market's estimate of the interest rate prevailing on 3 month bills 6 months from now. If we know the spot or cash rates prevailing today on bills with 6 months and 9 months

CALCULATING FORWARD RATES FROM TREASURY BILL RATES

We can use our understanding of the forward rates implicit in the yield curve to calculate some actual forward rates from observed Treasury bill rates. Figure 8–3 shows the Treasury bill rates listed in the *Wall Street Journal* of Friday, June 26, 1987. These were the rates in the market on Thursday, June 25. To see how to calculate forward rates for these pure discount instruments, we will use the Treasury bill rates with maturities on 9–24–87 and 12–24–87. Beginning on 6–24–87 the first bill is a 91-day bill and the second one is a 182-day bill. We can determine this by counting the number of days between 6–24–87 and these two maturity dates. Now, we can solve for the forward interest rate on a 91-day bill beginning on 9–25–87. We will continue to use the same equation from our hypothetical examples, but now we must also account for the daily compounding. This means that we will count time in days and annual interest rates will be divided by 365. Our basic equilibrium equation, Equation 8–1, is:

$$[1 + (0.0599/365)]^{91} [1 + (_{91}r_{91}/365)]^{91} = (1 + (0.0634/365))^{182}.$$

We can use this to solve for the forward rate on a 91-day loan beginning 91 days from now or $_{91}r_{91}$ as follows:

$$[1 + (_{91}r_{91}/365)]^{91} = \frac{[1 + (0.0634/365)]^{182}}{[1 + (0.0599/365)]^{91}}.$$

Performing the calculations on the right-hand-side of this equation yields:

$$[1 + (_{91}r_{91}/365)]^{91} = \frac{1.0321}{1.0151} = 1.0168.$$

We can then solve for the forward rate as:

$$_{91}r_{91} = \sqrt[91]{(1.0168 - 1.0)365} = 6.69 \text{ percent.}$$

We could pick any two of the Treasury bill rates in Figure 8–3 and perform the same calculations to determine the forward rates that cover the periods of time between these two spot rates. Notice the forward rate we calculated is greater than either of the two spot rates because the rate on the 182-day loan is an average of the 91-day rate beginning 6–25–87 and the forward rate calculated here. As a result, since the 182-day rate is higher than the 91-day for bills beginning on 6-25-87, we would expect that the forward rate would be higher than either of the two spot or cash rates.

to maturity, we should be able to compute the forward rate according to Equation (8–4):

$$0.21/12 = {}_{t+6}r_3/12 = \sqrt[3]{\frac{(1 + {}_{t}R_9/12)^9}{(1 + {}_{t}R_6/12)^6}} - 1.$$

We can observe this forward rate directly from the futures market but we can only infer it from the yield curve in the cash or spot market.

Another way to see this relationship is the following. Suppose we consider two Treasury bills, one maturing in 6 months and one in 9 months, as well as a futures contract with a 6-month maturity. Suppose the price of the 6-month bill is P_6 and that of the 9-month bill is P_9. We are interested in determining what the contract price of the futures contract will be if there are no profitable opportunities to substitute between the bills themselves and the futures contract. We will represent this equilibrium price by the symbol P^*. Suppose that an investor buys the 9-month bill for the price of P_9 then sells a futures contract to obtain a certain price for the bill in 6 months of P^*. He or she now holds what is the equivalent

FIGURE 8–3
Treasury bill yields on June 25, 1987.

U.S. Treasury Bills

Maturity date 1987	Bid Asked Yield			Maturity date 1986	Bid Asked Yield		
	Discount				Discount		
				10-22	5.96	5.90	6.10
7- 2	5.41	5.33	5.41	10-29	6.04	6.00	6.21
7- 9	5.80	5.74	5.83	11- 5	6.01	5.97	6.19
7-16	5.78	5.70	5.79	11-12	6.03	6.01	6.24
7-23	5.54	5.50	5.60	11-19	6.04	6.00	6.23
7-30	5.45	5.41	5.51	11-27	6.03	5.99	6.23
8- 6	5.68	5.64	5.75	12- 3	6.05	6.01	6.26
8-13	5.68	5.62	5.74	12-10	6.08	6.06	6.32
8-20	5.66	5.62	5.74	12-17	6.07	6.05	6.32
8-27	5.66	5.62	5.75	12-24	6.09	6.07	6.34
9- 3	5.88	5.82	5.96	-1988-			
9-10	5.84	5.80	5.95	1-21	6.04	6.00	6.28
9-17	5.83	5.81	5.97	2-18	6.17	6.13	6.43
9-24	5.84	5.82	5.99	3-17	6.21	6.17	6.49
10- 1	5.93	5.91	6.09	4-14	6.26	6.24	6.58
10- 8	5.93	5.89	6.07	5-12	6.34	6.32	6.69
10-15	5.89	5.85	6.04	6- 9	6.32	6.30	6.69

Source: *Wall Street Journal*, June 26, 1987, p. 35.

of a 6-month bill. The only difference is that the certain payment to be received in 6 months is now P^* instead of the $10,000 face value of the bill. If the annualized yield demanded by the market is say, 16 percent, the value today of the 6-month bill is determined according to the present value equation as follows:

$$P_6 = \$10,000/(1 + 0.16/2).$$

But the value of the 9-month bill sold in the futures market must be such that it gives the same 6-month yield as the 6-month bill:

$$P_9 = P^*/ (1 + 0.16/2).$$

If the price in the futures market of the 3-month bill to be delivered 6 months hence is set, as in our example, at $9,500, then we can use this equation to determine the price of the 9-month bill today. It is:

$$\$8,796 = \$9,500/(1 + 0.16/2).$$

We can restate this in a way that emphasizes the relationship between the futures market and the market for Treasury bills of different maturities by combining the above expression for P_6 and P_9. Taken together, these two equations imply that

$$\frac{\$10,000}{P_6} = \frac{P*}{P_9}.$$

This means that the price of the 6-month bill must be in the same proportion to its maturity value as the price of the 9-month bill is to the price of the futures contract. If this were not true, there would be sure profits to be made by either buying or selling futures contracts and 9-month bills, depending upon the direction of the imbalance. The profit opportunities ensure that, in equilibrium, the market will price futures contracts according to the equation above.

This relationship will be only approximately true if there are costs involved in buying and selling Treasury bills and futures contracts. Most empirical studies indicate that the actual prices of futures contracts in Treasury bills conform reasonably closely to this relationship. For example, Rendleman and Carabini concluded there were some persistent but small opportunities for profitable trading between Treasury bills and futures.[1] They found that the opportunities were sufficiently small that if you included all of what they counted as the "indirect costs" for most market participants of conducting such trading, the opportunities would not be profitable. In other words, the equations developed above are a very close approximation of the actual relationship between Treasury bill prices and the prices of Treasury bill futures.

Thus far we only have the basic mechanics of the relationship between current interest rates on different maturities and the forward and future rates with which they are consistent. Now we need to examine the various theories about forward rates and current long-term rates.

THEORIES OF THE TERM STRUCTURE OF INTEREST RATES

Three basic theories have been designed to explain the term structure of interest rates. Two of the theories are extreme alternatives and the third is a hybrid of the first two. The theories are labeled:

Unbiased expectations theory
Segmentation theory
Preferred habitat theory.

We will examine each of these theories to see how they explain observed yield curves.

---

[1] See Rendleman, Richard J. Jr., and Christopher E. Carabini, "The Efficiency of the Treasury Bill Futures Market," *Journal of Finance,* (September 1979).

Throughout our investigation of each of these theories we will rely upon our understanding of yield curves and forward interest rates. Thus far we have looked at forward rates as interest rates contracted for today for loans that will actually take place at some time in the future. For example, $_{t+3}r_2$ is the rate available today on a two-period loan beginning three periods from now. However, we can also use the forward rate to represent the expected interest rate on future loans.

Suppose that we pretend there are no explicit contracts for future loans. Investors and borrowers cannot choose between a long-term bond today and a sequence of future single-period loans all contracted for today because the second option is no longer available. Investors and borrowers must choose between a long-term bond today and a sequence of future short-term loans, each contracted for when that loan begins. If a borrower chooses to borrow a year from today for one year, he or she must wait to pay the rate prevailing at that time rather than set that rate now.

To see more clearly what is meant, consider the problem facing an investor who wants to lend money for five years. If there are no futures markets in loans, the investor has the following three options. The simplest option is to buy a zero-coupon or pure discount bond with a 5-year maturity. Then the maturity of the bond held is exactly the same as the maturity desired. However, the investor could buy a short-term (1-year) bond each year for the next five years. As a result, he or she will earn the short-term interest rate that prevails in each future year. The investor's third alternative is to buy a bond with a maturity longer than 5 years, say 10 years, and sell after 5 years. The first option, that of buying a 5-year bond, is the simplest in that the only transaction is the initial purchase. But without knowing the interest rate today and in the future, and ignoring any costs involved in making transactions, it is not apparent which alternative will turn out to be the most profitable investment.

As we discuss the various theories of the term structure of interest rates, we will examine the question of how to choose between the kind of options described. The first theory of how to choose between these options and the prices of yields on bonds that result is called the **unbiased expectations theory.**

*The **unbiased expectations theory** states that the term structure is determined solely by the market's expectations of future interest rates.*

THE UNBIASED EXPECTATIONS THEORY

The best alternative open to the investor who wants to lend funds for five years depends upon his or her expectations of the rates that will prevail in the future on short- and long-term bonds. Suppose we use the forward interest rate to represent the investor's best guess of what the future short-term interest rate will be. For example, $_{t+1}r_1$ would represent the one-period interest rate that is expected to prevail one period from now. We can express this algebraically as

$$_{t+i}r_1 = E\,(_{t+i}R_1),\qquad\qquad (8\text{--}8)$$

where $_{t+i}R_1$ represents the interest rate on a one-period loan which will be observed in period $t+i$, or i periods from now, and E represents the market's best guess or expectation.

The unbiased expectations theory says that the investor in this example will find that he or she is indifferent between the option of buying five one-period bonds or one five-period bond if the following relationship holds between the long-term rate of $_rR_5$ and the forward rates:

$$(1 + {_rR_5})^5 = (1 + {_rR_1})(1 + {_{t+1}r_1}) \cdots (1 + {_{t+4}r_1}). \qquad (8–9)$$

This equation is merely an example of the more general equation in (8–1), but now the forward rates are equal to the expected future short-term rates. If Equations (8–8) and (8–9) hold, then the investor will not expect to gain by choosing either of these two options. More generally, if Equations (8–1) and (8–8) hold for any maturity or any value of N, not just 5, then each of the three options open to the investor will be expected to yield the same payoff. An investor cannot buy a bond with a maturity of 5 years and sell or cash it in at maturity and expect to earn more than he or she could by buying five one-year bonds at yearly intervals; this is what equations (8–1) and (8–8) say.

It is important to see the incentive the investor faces and the reaction of the market as a whole to his or her actions if Equation (8–1) does not hold but Equation (8–8) does, or when forward rates equal expected future rates. If, for example, a large number of investors believe the left-hand side of Equation (8–1) exceeds the right-hand side, these investors will shift investments from short-term bonds to long-term bonds because they can expect to earn a higher return by doing so. This substitution from short- to long-term bonds will increase the price and decrease the yield of long-term bonds. This process will continue until Equation (8–1) is satisfied. As a result, the incentive to substitute between bonds of different maturities forces yields into an equilibrium where long-term rates reflect the market's expectations of future short-term rates and Equation (8–1) holds. The process of substitution and the equilibrium to which it leads are represented by Equations (8–1) and (8–8). These equations constitute the unbiased expectations theory of the term structure.[2]

A useful way to interpret each of the three theories of the term structure of interest rates we will deal with pertains to the shape of the yield curve. Each theory offers a different explanation for upward-sloping, flat, and downward-sloping yield curves. The unbiased expectations theory says long-term interest rates are determined by the market's expectations of future short-term interest rates. Therefore, this theory implies that the market's expectations account for the slope of the yield curve. For example, the unbiased expectations theory suggests that the upward-sloping yield curve that existed in 1975, shown in Figure 8–1, implies the market expected future short-term interest rates to increase. By con-

---

[2]Irving Fisher first articulated the substance of the unbiased expectations theory in "Appreciation and Interest," *Publications of the American Economic Association*, 11 (August 1896), pp. 23–9 and 91–2. It was further refined by J. R. Hicks in *Value and Capital*, London: Oxford University Press, 1946.

trast, the downward-sloping yield curve observed in 1974 reflected expectations that short-term rates would decline.

The unbiased expectations theory can be an accurate description of the term structure only if there are no barriers or costs to substituting between bonds with different maturities. If it is costly to execute transactions (that is, to buy and sell bonds), then when Equations (8–1) and (8–8) hold, the returns from buying one new one-period bond each year will have to be lower than the returns from buying a single long-term bond. This is because Equation (8–1) ignores these costs of transacting, which include brokers' fees and the cost of time arranging the transaction. In most markets these costs are reasonably small. Therefore Equations (8–1) and (8–8) can still potentially be good approximations of the actual relationship between yields.

The unbiased expectations theory is an example of the perfect substitution view of the way financial markets work. Bonds of different maturities are viewed as perfect substitutes for one another. As a result, the difference in their prices should be determined totally by the differences in the market's expectations for the time periods they cover. Any other factors should be irrelevant because investors will substitute between bonds until an equilibrium that reflects only expectations is reached.

There are alternative explanations of the term structure of interest rates, where bonds of different maturities are not viewed as perfect substitutes. The polar extreme alternative is the segmentation view. We will examine this theory next.

THE SEGMENTATION THEORY

The **segmentation theory** states that the term structure is determined by the supply and demand for bonds at each maturity and that expectations of future interest rates are irrelevant.

Some people have argued that the markets for bonds of different maturities are segmented, just as the markets for securities that differ by tax treatment or risk are sometimes thought to be segmented.[3] As in these other cases, the fundamental implication of the **segmentation theory** of the term structure is that the yield at each maturity is determined by the relative strength of supply and demand for bonds at that maturity. If, for example, a large number of borrowers want to issue bonds with maturities of ten years, but few investors want to purchase such bonds, the promised yield will be driven up until there is an equilibrium between supply and demand at that maturity. As a result, in this theory the shape of the yield curve represents the relative strength of supply and demand for particular maturities. A downward-sloping yield curve means a shortage of demand in the shorter maturities. On the other hand, an upward-sloping yield curve means a shortage of demand for the longer maturities.

The segmentation theory of the term structure, like all examples of the segmentation theory, requires there be few investors who are willing or able to substitute between securities of different maturity. Without such arbitrageurs in the

---

[3]One of the original proponents of the theory was J. M. Culbertson, "The Term Structure of Interest Rates," *Quarterly Journal of Economics*, 71 (November 1957), pp. 489–504.

market, yield spreads could deviate widely from the market's expectations of future short-term rates. If investors are willing to substitute between maturities when they expect such substitution will be profitable, then yield spreads that are inconsistent with the market's expectations of future rates will not persist. Therefore, the segmentation theory in its strongest form hinges on the existence of barriers that prevent or discourage investors from any substitution across maturities.

One reason investors refrain from such substitution is to reduce or hedge some of the risks of their portfolios. This motive is most often attributed to financial institutions, though it may be applied to other corporations and individuals as well. Financial institutions generally have some of the best opportunities for arbitraging differences in yields; therefore, their motives are of particular interest. The type of risk that financial institutions are often thought to hedge is the risk of losses incurred because liabilities and assets do not have maturities that are matched. When an institution matches the maturities of both sides of its balance sheet, it is said to be in a **hedged position.**

An investor has a **hedged position** when the maturity of his or her assets are equal to the maturity of his or her liabilities.

To see more precisely what the risk is that the hedge eliminates we need to consider more carefully our example of how best to invest funds with a five-year maturity. What we have failed to consider as yet is the risk involved in the choice. One option is to purchase a bond with a maturity shorter than five years, say one year, and purchase another when that one matures. The risk involved here is that interest rates could fall below expectations at the end of a year and the investor would stand to lose income on the second bond. Another option is to purchase a bond with a maturity longer than five years and sell it prior to maturity. The price prior to maturity will fluctuate with market interest rates, and the price could be very low at the time when the bond must be sold. The strategy that eliminates all such risk is to buy a zero-coupon or pure discount bond with a maturity of exactly five years. The bond will be redeemed at maturity, and the maturity value is known with certainty. Therefore this type of risk can be eliminated by matching the maturities of assets and liabilities.

If most market participants perfectly hedge the maturity risks of their balance sheets, then there will be relatively little substitution between maturities. The segmentation theory argues that investors will choose to hedge regardless of how attractive the opportunities for substitution may become. Essentially the theory says that the incentive to avoid risk by hedging will be so strong that it will dominate any incentive to seek profits by substitution. A less extreme version of the theory asserts that if the incentive to substitute is large enough to compensate the investor for the risk borne, then substitution will take place. This represents a compromise between the pure segmentation and unbiased expectations theories and is known as the preferred habitat theory of the term structure.

The **preferred habitat theory** states that the term structure is determined both by expectations and by premiums for risk or liquidity.

THE PREFERRED HABITAT THEORY

The **preferred habitat theory** is a blend of the unbiased expectations theory and the segmentation theory in that it takes into account what each of those theories omits. The unbiased expectations theory ignores the risk that investors expose themselves to when they substitute across maturities. On the other hand, the segmentation theory ignores the expected profits of such substitution and concentrates exclusively on the incentive to avoid risk. We know that investors will bear risk if properly compensated to do so. Therefore, there is a third theory of the term structure, which incorporates the premiums that investors demand to bear risk.

The basic tenet of the preferred habitat theory is that each investor has a preferred maturity or habitat at which he or she would like to borrow or lend.[4] The maturity is determined by the nature of the investor's business. For example, if the investor wants to borrow money to build a factory with a long useful life, he or she will have a natural preference for a bond with a long maturity. Similarly, if a financial institution needs to obtain funds to lend to a customer for six months, it will generally seek to borrow for six months. The preferred habitat theory asserts that if the total amount of desired borrowing is equal to the total amount of desired lending at each maturity, then the term structure will be determined by the unbiased expectations theory. Because there is no imbalance between supply and demand at any maturity, investors at each maturity demand an interest rate that is fair based on the market's expectation of future interest rates. All investors avoid risk because they are all borrowing or lending at their desired maturity; hence, no premiums for risk are reflected in the term structure.

However, it is unlikely that total desired lending is very often exactly equal to desired borrowing at each maturity. More likely there are imbalances at most all maturities most of the time. To see what happens when such imbalances arise we can return to the example of an investor with a desire to invest for five years. Suppose there is an excess supply of such investable funds with this five-year maturity. This means that with a 5-year interest rate which is consistent with the unbiased expectations theory, there is a shortage of bonds with 5-year maturities. Therefore, the investor must lower the interest rate he or she is willing to accept for 5-year bonds until the supply of such bonds increases or else try to obtain bonds with either a shorter or longer maturity. The question at issue is, what happens to the prices and yields on bonds with different maturities when this kind of imbalance develops?

The answer is that interest rates will adjust until the investor in the example and the market as a whole are no longer willing to substitute between maturities. If investors are averse to risk, they will demand a premium to substitute between maturities. The interest rates on bonds of different maturities will adjust to a new equilibrium where investors will be compensated for bearing the risk of being out of their preferred maturity. In this example, the investor will pay a price for a 5-year bond which provides an inducement to some borrower to alter his or her desired maturity. Suppose, for example, that there is another participant in the market who wants to borrow $100,000, but with a maturity of 10 years. If this person borrows by issuing a 5-year bond now and another 5 years later, the risk

---

[4]See Franco Modigliani and Richard Sutch, "Innovations in Interest Rate Policy," *American Economic Review,* 56 (May 1966), pp. 178–97.

is that in 5 years interest rates will increase more than expected and the costs will go up for the second bond. The borrower will demand to be paid a premium by the investor to accept this risk of fluctuations in interest rates. This premium will take the form of a lower interest rate on the 5-year bond than on the 10-year bond.

This example provides an illustration of how markets work in the aggregate. If there is an excess supply or demand for bonds at any particular maturity, then an incentive has to be provided to induce investors to shift maturities and eliminate the excess supply or demand. The greater the excess supply or demand, the greater the premiums will have to be, because more investors will be exposed to more risk of fluctuation in interest rates or bond prices. The market will be in equilibrium when the premiums offered in the term structure are just sufficient to induce enough investors out of their preferred habitats to equilibrate desired borrowing and lending at each maturity.

This preferred habitat theory of the term structure can be represented by Equation (8–1) and a modified version of Equation (8–8). Equation (8–8) requires that the forward rates exactly equal the market's expectations of future short-term rates, but now we know that the forward rates can differ from expected future rates. In equilibrium, the difference will be a compensation for risk which equilibrates desired lending and borrowing at each maturity. We can represent this premium, referred to as a **liquidity premium** with the symbol $_{t+i}L_1$, which represents the liquidity premium for a one-period loan beginning at period $t+i$. More specifically, it is the premium demanded by the market to stretch its maturity one period, from $t+i-1$ periods to $t+i$ periods. Under the preferred habitat theory, each forward rate is equal to the sum of the market's expectation of what the future interest rate will be and the market's liquidity premium:

Liquidity premium is the premium for risk of changing interest rates.

$$_{t+i}r_1 = E(_{t+i}R_1) + {}_{t+i}L_1.$$ (8–10)

The implication of the preferred habitat theory is that the yield curve does not necessarily give a clear signal of the market's expectations of future interest rates. The preferred habitat theory implies that the yield curve is determined both by the market's expectations and by the imbalances in preferred habitats. If those imbalances are large, then premiums demanded to bring about an equilibrium will also be large. If those imbalances are small, then the premiums will be small and the observed yield curve will be determined largely by expectations.

For example, suppose there is a pattern in the liquidity premiums such that the longer the maturity, the larger the premium. The liquidity premiums would then satisfy the following inequalities:

$$0 < {}_{t+1}L_1 < {}_{t+2}L_1 < \cdots < {}_{t+N}L_1.$$ (8–11)

If liquidity premiums increased with maturity in this manner, the yield curve would tend to have a positive slope. Even if the market expected that short-term interest rates would remain constant, the yield curve would slope upward to reflect the increasing liquidity premiums. You can see this if you substitute Equation (8–10) into Equation (8–1) for bonds with longer maturities. The fact that the liquidity premiums are increasing will cause rates to increase with maturity even if expected future rates are all the same.

We can illustrate this with an example. To keep the example simple we will deal with only a 5-year time period. Suppose that the market expects future short-term rates to be constant at the current rate of 6 percent. But the market also requires the following liquidity premiums:

$$_{t+1}L_1 = 0.01 \qquad _{t+3}L_1 = 0.03$$
$$_{t+2}L_1 = 0.02 \qquad _{t+4}L_1 = 0.04$$

Using Equation (8–10) and these premiums, we can compute the forward rates beginning 1, 2, 3, and 4 years from now as follows:

$$_{t+1}r_1 = 0.06 + 0.01 = 0.07$$
$$_{t+2}r_1 = 0.06 + 0.02 = 0.08$$
$$_{t+3}r_1 = 0.06 + 0.03 = 0.09$$
$$_{t+4}r_1 = 0.06 + 0.04 = 0.10$$

Now we can use these data to compute the current rates on bonds with maturities of two to five years:

$$_tR_2 = [(1.06)(1.07)]^{1/2} - 1$$
$$= 0.065$$
$$_tR_3 = [(1.06)(1.07)(1.08)]^{1/3} - 1$$
$$= 0.07$$
$$_tR_4 = [(1.06)(1.07)(1.07)(1.09)]^{1/4} - 1$$
$$= 0.075$$
$$_tR_5 = [(1.06)(1.07)(1.08)(1.09)(1.10)]^{1/5} - 1$$
$$= 0.08$$

We can see from this example that the yield curve will increase if expected future rates are constant but liquidity premiums are increasing. We can also infer that if liquidity premiums are increasing and the yield curve is flat, the market must expect future short-term rates to fall.

Some people argue that liquidity premiums do in fact satisfy the inequalities in Equation (8–11).[5] They support this argument with their belief that lenders prefer to lend short rather than long. Therefore, larger premiums have to be offered to bear the additional risk of longer maturity loans. In fact, this is where the name *liquidity premium* arose. The liquidity premium is what must be paid to

---

[5]This was originally argued by Hicks, pp. 146–47. He referred to this as ''normal backwardation.''

lenders to induce them to forgo some liquidity. Another possible view is that there are enough investors with little or no risk aversion that liquidity premiums are really equal to or close to zero. This view contends that the unbiased expectations theory of the term structure is essentially accurate and that the yield curve represents the market's expectations of future short-term rates.

Most of the available evidence supports the view that there are liquidity premiums in the term structure of interest rates. Some of the original tests for these liquidity premiums conducted during the 1960s left considerable doubt as to which theory was essentially correct.[6] But, more recently, tests of the ability of long-term interest rates to forecast future short-term interest rates have made it almost impossible to escape the conclusion that liquidity premiums do exist. However, there remains little convincing evidence on the size and pattern of liquidity premiums over time.

INTEREST RATE FORECASTS AND THE TERM STRUCTURE

Unless the term structure of interest rates is completely explained by the segmentation theory, then the yield curve incorporates the market's expectations of future short-term interest rates. This means that long-term interest rates are determined, at least in part, by expectations. We know that the yield curve does not provide a perfect clue to the market's expectations as long as liquidity premiums are incorporated in the term structure. But, it is fruitful to ask what we can learn about expectations by studying yield curves. We will consider three aspects of this question. First, we will examine whether the market efficiently incorporates information about future interest rates into long-term interest rates. Second, we will examine various theories of the way expectations are formed. Third, we will explore how we can make practical use of yield curves as forecasts of future rates in financial decisions.

THE EFFICIENT MARKETS HYPOTHESIS AND THE TERM STRUCTURE OF INTEREST RATES

Any time the financial market incorporates a best guess of a future event into a price or interest rate we can ask whether, in so doing, the market efficiently uses available information. We first explored this concept of market efficiency in Chapter 5, where the basic idea behind the hypothesis was explained. In Chapter 6 we examined the hypothesis that nominal interest rates efficiently incorporate available information about future inflation rates. In this chapter we will examine briefly the hypothesis that long-term interest rates efficiently incorporate all available information about the values of future short-term interest rates.

---

[6]See James C. Van Horne, *Financial Market Rates and Flows,* Englewood Cliffs, N.J.: Prentice-Hall, 1978, for a review of the historical development of empirical evidence on this subject.

In order to see exactly what the efficient markets hypothesis is regarding the term structure, let us temporarily suppose that the unbiased expectations theory of the term structure holds. The forward rates implied by the yield curve observed at any point in time represent the market's expectation of the future short-term interest rate, or as stated in Equation (8–8),

$$_{t+i}r_1 = E(_{t+i}R_1).$$

The efficient markets hypothesis then implies that if we try to forecast future short-term interest rates with forward rates computed from yield curves, these forward rates ought to provide the best forecasts we can find. There should exist no other mechanism, based on publicly available data, that provides a better forecast of future short-term interest rates. For if the market is efficient, then any such forecasting mechanism should be incorporated into the forecast in the yield curve.

Eugene Fama has conducted a test of this hypothesis by comparing the forecasting ability of forward rates computed from the yield curve with alternative forecasts of short-term interest rates.[7] One very simple alternative is to assume that short-term interest rates are expected to remain constant for one period ahead or that the best forecast of tomorrow's short-term rate is today's short-term rate. Fama shows that the forward rates computed from yield curves provide forecasts inferior to the forecasts derived from this simple alternative forecast of the behavior of the short-term interest rate. At first glance, this might seem to be damning evidence against market efficiency. But remember the forward rate should equal the market's best forecast of the corresponding future short-term interest rate only if the market views securities of different maturities as perfect substitutes—that is, if there are no liquidity premiums. If there are liquidity premiums in the term structure, then forecasts of future short-term rates provided by the forward rates will be in error, on average, because of the existence of these liquidity premiums.

In order to develop more satisfactory tests of market efficiency, Fama attempted to measure the liquidity premiums present in the term structure of interest rates and extract those premiums from the forward rates to derive the market's true forecast of the future short-term interest rate. He compared this forecast to the simple alternative forecast of the future short-term rates based on the current short-term rate. Fama concluded from these types of comparisons that the forecasts of future short-term rates, which are embedded in the long-term rate, do as well as the simple alternative forecasting model. The performance of the term-structure model is not noticeably superior to the performance of the alternative model with which it is compared. This is evidence, albeit weak, in favor of market efficiency. The fundamental difficulty involved is in deriving accurate measures of the liquidity premiums demanded by the market. Thus far, no very satisfactory measures of these premiums have been devised. Without better measures

---

[7]See Eugene F. Fama, "Forward Rates as Predictors in Future Spot Rates," *Journal of Financial Economics,* 3 (1976), pp. 361–77.

of liquidity premiums, it may well prove difficult to devise better tests of this dimension of market efficiency.

An alternative way to evaluate whether long-term interest rates efficiently incorporate information about future short-term rates pertains to the behavior through time of yields on debt securities with different maturities. We should recall from our original discussion of the efficient markets hypothesis that the weak-form of the hypothesis implies that the past value of the price of a share of stock should be no clue to the future price level. That is, the best forecast of tomorrow's stock price is today's. The same argument applies to the yields on long-term bonds, such as 20-year U.S. Treasury bonds, but does not apply to short-term Treasury debt, such as 90-day Treasury bills.

To see why this is true we need to examine the difference between long-term bonds and short-term bonds. We can use 20-year and 90-day Treasury obligations as our example. Remember that what we observe in the market are the yields on both types of securities at discreet intervals. In terms of notation, we observe the yield on 20-year bonds at time t, then $t+1$, then $t+2$, and so forth. The interval between these dates is generally a week, month, or quarter, but it could be any interval you wanted to choose. In an efficient market, the yield on a 20-year bond at time t, $_tR_{t+20}$, will incorporate all information known to the market pertaining to the interval from t to $t+20$, that is, for the next 20 years. The interest rate on the 20-year bond will not necessarily provide an efficient forecast of a 20-year rate observed at time period $t+1$; because the periods of time these two rates cover do not overlap perfectly. This distinction between the time periods covered by two consecutive 20-year interest rates is illustrated in Figure 8–4. The figure shows that the periods covered by each rate differ by a single period at both the beginning and the end of the 20-year period.

The relevant question is whether this difference in periods of coverage influences the ability of the current interest rate to forecast the interest rate in the next

FIGURE 8–4

This figure shows the overlap in time included in the maturities of two 20-year bonds when the yields on these bonds are observed one period apart.

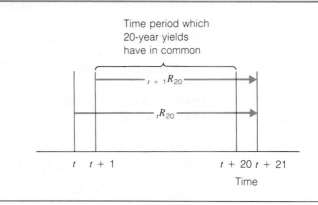

period. If we are actually dealing with interest rates on 20-year bonds that are observed 1 month apart, then the lack of overlap amounts to 2 months out of 240 months in the total 20-year interval. In this case, the lack of overlap is a minor problem. But suppose we are talking about 90-day Treasury bills. Out of the 3-month maturity on two bills observed a month apart, there are only 2 months in common or 60 out of 90 days. As a result, one would not expect the current 90-day bill rate to predict the future 90-day bill rate simply because, to a larger degree, each is covering a different time period.

The actual empirical evidence on the predictive ability of 20-year bonds and 90-day bills confirms these arguments. If we try to predict future rates on 20-year bonds, we find that we cannot significantly improve the predictive ability of the current rate by adding past rates to the prediction, as the efficient markets hypothesis implies. But the current rate on 90-day Treasury bills is not as good a predictor of the future 90-day Treasury bill rate. Here, past rates *do* add to the power of the current rate as a predictor, as the argument above suggests.[8] The available evidence therefore suggests that, like stock prices, long-term interest rates efficiently incorporate publicly available information. This is further evidence that financial markets efficiently use all publicly available information.

THEORIES OF THE FORMATION OF EXPECTATIONS

Except in the case of the pure segmentation theory, an important determinant of the term structure of interest rates is the market's expectations of future short-term interest rates. This has caused a number of scholars to try to explain how the market forms its expectations of future rates. Various theories have been proposed about the way the market uses past information to form its expectations, and these theories have been tested to see which best explains the available data on the term structure. Expectations of the future influence almost all economic decisions, and it is therefore exceptionally important to have some systematic understanding of how these expectations are formed.

There are two principal hypotheses about the formation of expectations which are referred to as extrapolative and regressive expectations. These two hypotheses are not mutually exclusive. In fact, many people argue that a combination of the two is the best available explanation of how interest rate expectations are formed. **Extrapolative expectations** simply mean that in the short run (i.e., for interest rates that will be realized just a few months in the future) the market extrapolates its current experience; that is, it expects currently observed patterns to continue. But in the long run (i.e., for rates well beyond a few months in the future), the market expects the rate to regress toward a normal rate of interest based on historical experiences. This normal interest rate is usually described as a weighted average of past observed interest rates where the weights decline with time. This implies that most recent experience has a larger impact on the market's concept of the normal rate than does less recent experience. When the regressive and

Extrapolative expectations means that the market expects current conditions to continue.

[8]For evidence consistent with this position, see Fama, *ibid.*

FIGURE 8–5
Weights in Equation (8–12) which are consistent with regressive and extra-polative expectations. The weights are small for short lags, then rise and fall again as the time lag increases.

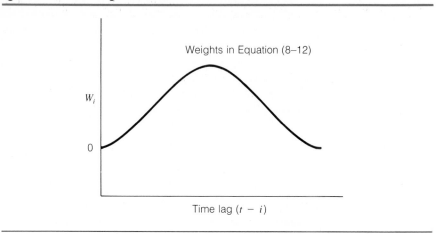

extrapolative hypotheses are combined, expectations are thought to be extrapolative in the short run and regressive in the long run.

In a sequence of studies published in the late 1960s and early 1970s, Franco Modigliani, Richard Sutch, and Robert Shiller argued that a term structure relationship could be constructed based on both the theories of regressive and extrapolative expectations.[9] The relationship can be expressed in the following algebraic form:

$$
{}^R_tL = \sum_{i=1,}^{N} W_i \, {}_{t-i}R_s,
\tag{8–12}
$$

where the subscripts L and S represent long and short maturities. Equation (8–12) says that the current long-term rate (e.g., the 20-year Treasury bond rate) can be expressed as a weighted average of past short-term interest rates (for example, the 90-day Treasury bill rate). In their formulation, the combination of regressive and extrapolative expectations resulted in a particular form of Equation (8–12) where the weight w_i follow a pattern that looks like an inverted U, as illustrated in Figure 8–5. The inverted U shape for the weights indicates that very recent short-term interest rates have little effect. This is because, for short maturities, the regressive and extrapolative expectations tend to cancel each other out. as the time lag in-

---

[9]See Modigliani and Sutch, *ibid.,* and Franco Modigliani and Robert T. Shiller, "Inflation, Rational Expectations and the Term Structure of Interest Rates," *Journal of Political Economy,* (February 1973), pp. 12–43.

volved increases, extrapolative expectations become unimportant and the weights reflect only only regressive expectations. **Regressive expectations** place less emphasis on events further removed in the past; hence the weights gradually decline, as illustrated in Figure 8–5.

Modigliani, Sutch, and Shiller have amassed a substantial amount of statistical evidence that purports to show that the actual relationship between the current long-term interest rates and past short-term interest rates is the one predicted by Equation (8–12), where the weights have the inverted U shape. They argue that this evidence shows that the market's expectations are a combination of regressive and extrapolative elements. However, there has been substantial criticism of the empirical evidence presented by Modigliani et al.[10] The essence of the criticism is that it is difficult if not impossible to produce statistically reliable estimates of the weights in Equation (8–12), hence difficult to confirm or reject the hypothesized inverted U shape. A development of the statistical problems involved is beyond the scope of this book, but the important point about this controversy is that if the criticism is correct, it will be difficult to develop reliable evidence as to whether the market combines regressive and extrapolative expectations. Despite the plausibility of the argument, for practical purposes this may well be an untestable hypothesis.

It should be recalled that however the market forms expectations, if the market is efficient, those expectations are incorporated in the current interest rate or price of the asset. Again, the implication is that long-term interest rates incorporate the market's best forecast of future rates, regardless of how these expectations are formed.

COUPON RISK AND PRICE RISK

Throughout this chapter we have ignored a very important practical element of the risk facing bondholders: the risk of income reinvestment received in the form of coupon payments on bonds. In fact, thus far, our entire discussion of the term structure of interest rates has simply ignored the presence of coupon payments. Before we leave this topic it is important to fill in the gap.

In our analysis of term structure we described the risk facing a particular investor with a specific planning horizon as follows. An investor with a 5-year horizon could buy a 10-year bond and sell the bond after 5 years. If he did so, he would be subject to the risk of the price of the bond after five years. Conversely, he could buy a sequence of 1-year bonds every year for 5 years. If he followed this strategy, he would be subject to the risk of changing future 1-year interest rates over the next 5 years. The first option involves a price risk and the second a reinvestment risk.

---

[10]See Llad Phillips and John Pippenger, "The Term Structure of Interest Rates in the MIT-PENN-SSRC Model: Reality or Illusion?" *Journal of Money, Credit and Banking,* 11 (May 1979), pp. 151–64.

THE USEFULNESS OF THE YIELD CURVE

The yield curve is often a rather maligned device because individuals ask too much of it. People often think that the yield curve is supposed to forecast future short-term interest rates—that individuals, business firms, or financial institutions can use the yield curve to construct estimates of future rates. We have learned that the yield curve has this practical use only if it is determined by the unbiased expectations theory. Only then will the forward rates implied by the yield curve represent the market's forecast of future short-term interest rates. But if, as the available evidence suggests, there are liquidity premiums in the term structure, then without good measures of these premiums, the market's forecast will be difficult to extract.

The nagging question this leaves is, of what use is the theory of the term structure? Term structure theory explains how prices and yields on assets that differ by maturity are determined in a competitive market. It can be used as a practical tool in the following manner: An investor with his or her own forecast of future rates in hand can compute forward rates from the observed yield curve and compare them to his or her independent estimate of future rates. If the difference is large enough to compensate the investor for the risk perceived in betting on future rates, then an investment outside a preferred habitat will look profitable.

For example, return to the Treasury bill rates in Figure 8–3. We used these rates to compute the forward rate on a 91-day loan beginning 91 days in the future. The forward rate in this example was 6.69 percent, while the current 91-day rate was 5.99 percent. Suppose your own forecast was that 91-day interest rates would increase by 30 basis points over the next 91 days. Your own forecast would be a rate of 6.29 percent. This means there is a 40 basis point liquidity or risk premium if your interest rate forecast is subtracted from the forward rate. You must decide whether the 40 basis point risk premium is enough to compensate for moving out of your preferred maturity. To see how this works suppose you want to invest for three months and are choosing between 91-day and 182-day bills. If you buy 91-day bills, you have no risk. If you buy 182-day bills, you are hurt if interest rates increase significantly because there will be less appreciation in the value of your bills as you approach the time you will sell them, 91 days in the future. The question is, will the 40 basis point risk premium you anticipate be enough to compensate you to take on the risk?

Price risk refers to the risk of capital losses on a bond.

A **zero-coupon bond** is a bond without coupon payments or a pure discount bond.

Reinvestment risk refers to the risk of reinvesting coupon payments at relatively low interest rates.

However, the actual risk in the first option is really limited to being a **price risk** only if the investor holds a pure discount or a **zero-coupon bond**—a bond with no coupon payments or for which the only cash flow is a single payment at maturity. If an investor buys a coupon bond, then he or she will be exposed to both a price risk and a **reinvestment risk.** The reinvestment risk arises because coupon payments must be reinvested at prevailing market interest rates. If the market interest rates decline, this will mean that the rate of return on reinvestment of coupon income will decline. Therefore, reinvestment income from coupon payments tend to be hurt by decreases and helped by increases in market interest rates. On the other hand, increases in rates cause bond prices to fall and vice versa. As a result, these risks respond in opposite directions to a change in interest rates.

One important implication of the presence of reinvestment risk for coupon payments: it can be very misleading to calculate yield curves and forward rates using bonds with different coupon rates. The bonds have distinct coupon payments so that the time pattern of cash flows from the two bonds would be quite different. It is not clear what the forward rates pertaining to a particular future time period that would be computed from these bonds might mean. However, it would not be the forward rate as defined earlier in this chapter.

The fact that reinvestment risk for coupon bonds exists and is important in no way compromises what we have learned in this chapter about the term structure of interest rates. However, we must be careful in applying what we know about the term structure to bonds with significantly different coupons. It also raises the question of how to deal with both the reinvestment and price risk of a coupon bond. This topic, as well as other aspects of interest rate risk management, is addressed in the next chapter.

SUMMARY

In this chapter we learned how debt securities, which differ only by their term of maturity, are priced. This relationship between debt securities of different maturity is *the term structure of interest rates*. The pricing of debt securities of different maturities entails another application of the theory of pricing of risky assets, from Chapter 3. In essence, the prices and yields of long-term securities are determined by the market's expectation of future short-term rates, the risk involved in betting on future short-term rates, and the amount of risk aversion of market participants.

We learned how to quantify the relationship between long- and short-term interest rates by relying on the use of forward interest rates. And we quantified the relationship between any long-term rate and the sequence of forward rates corresponding to the same time period. We also learned about the connection between the forward rates in the term structure and interest rates in futures markets.

Next we considered three theories of term structure which present a distinct explanation of the relationship between long- and short-term interest rates. The first, the *unbiased expectations theory,* says that the forward rates in the term structure relationship represent the market's expectation of future short-term rates. This theory hinges on the hypothesis that investors will substitute between maturities until the expected return from all maturities is the same. The second theory is the extreme alternative. The *segmentation theory* says that investors find substitution between maturities to be so risky and they are so averse to this risk that they avoid any substitution of their preferred maturity. Forward rates are unimportant because the yield at each maturity is determined by supply and demand at that maturity. The *preferred habitat* is a blend of the first two theories. It argues that individuals will substitute out of their preferred maturities, but only if they are paid a sufficiently large premium to compensate for the risk they bear.

All these theories are concerned with the ability of the market to forecast future short-term interest rates. It is natural then to ask how successfully the market does this and to inquire into how the market forms expectations. Evidence suggests that the market is efficient in the weak sense, but the difficulties involved in measuring liquidity premiums make it tough to evaluate the forecasting ability of the market.

QUESTIONS

1. What is the yield curve? What does it mean to say that the curve is upward or downward sloping? How does the yield curve usually change over the business cycle? What happened to the yield curve during 1980 and 1985? Why? (You won't find the answer to this last question in this book.)

2. Suppose you observed the following current rates from the yield curve: $_tR_{20} = 0.15$, $_tR_{15} = 0.14$, $_tR_{10} = 0.10$, and $_tR_5 = 0.05$. Compute all the forward rates you can from these current rates.

3. Explain what a forward rate is. Explain why you can use the procedure from question 2 to compute forward rates.

4. The unbiased expectations theory of the term structure is often referred to as the *perfect substitution theory*. Explain the connection between the ideas of perfect substitution and unbiased expectations. How does perfect substitution lead to unbiased expectations?

5. Explain the segmentation theory. Why is this referred to as the case of extreme risk aversion?

6. Compare the interpretations that would be placed on the slope of the yield curve if either the unbiased expectations theory or the segmentation theory were correct. How would these interpretations change if the preferred habitat theory were correct? Why do increasing liquidity premiums lead to a bias toward a positive slope in the yield curve? Explain what this means.

7. In what way is the preferred habitat theory a hybrid of the unbiased expectations and segmentation theories? What does the liquidity premium measure, and how does it affect forward rates?

8. The efficient markets hypothesis says that long-term interest rates should make efficient use of public information about future short-term interest rates. What does this mean? Why is it difficult to devise a very satisfactory direct test of this hypothesis?

9. What are extrapolative and regressive expectations? Suppose the market forms its expectations in a combination of an extrapolative and regressive manner. What would this say about the relationship between long- and short-term interest rates?

10. Suppose you wanted to attempt to forecast what the 90-day Treasury bill rate will be one year from now. One approach is to forecast that the best guess is simply today's 90-day bill rate. The other approach is to compute the forward rate from the current rates on 12-month and 15-month maturity Treasury obligations and use that forward rate as your forecast. Compare the merits of

these two approaches. What does the efficient markets hypothesis tell you about these two approaches?

11. Suppose you have $100,000 to invest for retirement and you expect to retire in 10 years. If you invest in a 10-year zero-coupon bond you will be able to lock in a return of 9 percent. A second alternative is to invest in a 5-year zero-coupon bond and then reinvest your funds at the end of the 5 years. Suppose the 5-year rate available today is 11 percent. Compute the total amount of money you will have under the second option if the 5-year rate 5 years from now ranges from 6 percent to 12 percent. How would you decide which is the best investment?

12. Now suppose that instead of deciding between the 10-year and the 5-year bonds in the previous question, you are comparing a 10-year and a 20-year bond. The current 10-year rate is still 9 percent and the current 20-year rate is 8 percent. Compute the total amount of money you will have at the end of the 10 years if you buy the 20-year bond and 10-year rates range between 6 percent and 12 percent. How would you decide which is the best investment in this situation?

REFERENCES

Culbertson, J. M. "The Term Structure of Interest Rates," *Quarterly Journal of Economics,* 71 (November 1957), pp. 489–504.

Elliott, J. W., and M. E. Echols. "Rational Expectations in a Disequilibrium Model of the Term Structure," *American Economic Review,* 66 (March 1976), pp. 28–44.

Fama, Eugene R. "Forward Rates as Predictors of Future Spot Rates," *Journal of Financial Economics,* 3 (1976), pp. 361–77.

_____. "Inflation, Uncertainty, and Expected Returns on Treasury Bills," *Journal of Political Economy,* 84 (June 1976), pp. 427–48.

Fisher, Irving. "Appreciation and Interest," *Publications of the American Economic Association,* 11 (August 1896), pp. 23–9 and 91–2.

Hicks, J. R. *Value and Capital,* London: Oxford University Press, 1946.

Meiselman, David. *The Term Structure of Interest Rates,* Englewood Cliffs, N.J.: Prentice-Hall, Inc., 1962.

Modigliani, Franco, and Richard Sutch. "Innovations in Interest Rate Policy," *American Economic Review,* 56 (May 1966), pp. 178–7.

_____. "Debt Management and the Term Structure of Interest Rates: An Empirical Analysis of Recent Experience," *Journal of Political Economy,* 75, Supplement (August 1967), pp. 569–89.

_____, and Robert J. Shiller. "Inflation, Rational Expectations and the Term Structure of Interest Rates," *Journal of Political Economy,* (February 1973), pp. 12–43.

Nelson, Charles R. *The Term Structure of Interest Rates*, New York: Basic Books, Inc., 1972.

Pesando, James E. "On the Random Walk Characteristics of Short- and Long-term Interest Rates in an Efficient Market," *Journal of Money, Credit and Banking*, 11 (November 1979), pp. 457–66.

Philips, Llad, and John Pippenger. "The Term Structure of Interest Rates in the MIT-PENN-SSRC Model: Reality or Illusion?" *Journal of Money, Credit and Banking*, 11 (May 1979), pp. 151–64.

Rendleman, Richard J. Jr., and Christopher E. Carabini. "The Efficiency of the Treasury Bill Futures Market," *Journal of Finance*, (September 1979).

Roll, Richard. *The Behavior of Interest Rates: An Application of the Efficient Market Model to U.S. Treasury Bills*, New York: Basic Books, Inc., 1970.

Van Horne, James C. *Financial Market Rates and Flows*, Englewood Cliffs, N.J.: Prentice-Hall, Inc., 1978.

9

Managing Interest Rate Risk

It wasn't very long ago that the topic of interest rate risk was of rather limited interest. Most individuals and even many financial institutions did not perceive that they were exposed to much interest rate risk. This was in the era, prior to the mid-1970s, when interest rates were relatively low and not particularly volatile, at least when measured by the experience of the early 1980s. Now interest rate risk has been elevated to the level of cocktail party conversation.

Before we get into this topic, we will explore some methods that essentially constitute a "zero-sum game:" that is, ways to shift interest rate risk from one party to another. We will not learn how to reduce the total interest rate risk in the marketplace, a much more formidable task.

We start with an examination of futures and options markets. Beginning with futures markets, we will see how they can be used to hedge interest rate risk. Then we shift to options on bonds to see how they can be used for the same purpose. Then we will learn how to "immunize" a bond portfolio or protect it against changes in interest rate risk. We will see how to immunize a portfolio with coupon bonds, that is, a portfolio which is subject to both price and reinvestment risk. ■

HEDGING INTEREST RATE RISK WITH FUTURES AND OPTIONS

HOW A HEDGE WORKS

A **hedge** refers to a position in one asset that will have a payoff opposite to the payoff on an asset that you already hold.

The idea behind a **hedge** is to take a position in one asset that will have a payoff opposite to the payoff generated by the asset or position you already hold. This will occur when you select a hedge or a hedge portfolio that is perfectly negatively correlated with the asset you want to hedge, or where the correlation coefficient between the changes in prices of the two assets is -1. When you use the futures market to hedge, then your position in the futures market should exactly offset your position in the cash market. If it is a perfect hedge, then any gain in the futures market will be offset by a loss in the cash market, and vice versa.

In any number of situations a market participant might want to hedge a position in the cash market. A depository financial institution that writes a loan intending to fund that loan with future short-term deposits might want to hedge the risk of future changes in the cost of those deposits. A mortgage broker who holds an inventory of mortgage-backed securities before they can be resold in the secondary mortgage markets might want to hedge the risks of changes in the value of that portfolio. A manufacturing firm may know that it needs to borrow from a bank in the future and may attempt to arrange a commitment from the bank. If the firm believes the bank is not offering attractive terms, it may attempt to lock in financing terms by hedging in the futures market.

To see how a hedge would work, let's examine the situation facing a manufacturing firm that wants to hedge the risk of changes in its cost of credit. The firm knows it will be purchasing materials for inventory in one month, and it will need a three-month loan to finance the inventory. It has approached its bank for a current commitment on the rate on the loan, but it suspects the bank rate is not in line with the market's estimates of future interest rates. We will assume that the future cost of borrowing from the bank is tied directly to the interest rate on 90-day Treasury bills. Therefore, the manufacturer decides to hedge its risk in the futures market for 90-day Treasury bills.

The appropriate position for the firm to take is to short futures on 90-day bills. Then, if interest rates increase, prices of 90-day bills will fall and the firm should make a profit off its futures position. At the same time the increase in interest rates will cause its cost of credit from the bank to increase. If the hedge works perfectly, these should be exactly offsetting. Table 9–1 illustrates how a perfect hedge would work in this example.

The table assumes that the firm attempts to lock in the rate on a discount loan beginning 30 days from now and that the forward rate on 90-day Treasury bills in the futures market is 12 percent. It also assumes that the amount of the loan is $10,000,000, which is the same as the amount of 10 Treasury bill futures contracts. Since the loan is a discount loan, the firm will not actually receive $10 million. (See Chapter 6 for a discussion of discount loans and treasury bill pricing.) Rather it will promise to pay $10 million after 3 months. It will receive the present value of that $10 million discounted at the 90-day rate applied to the loan.

For example, if the 90-day rate is 12 percent, the the firm will borrow $9,708,738 = $10,000,000/[1 + 0.12/(90/360)].

Table 9–1 shows the cost of borrowing and the gain or loss on the futures contract for five different levels of interest rates prevailing when the loan is to begin, that is, after one month. Since the forward rate for 90-day Treasury bills one month from now is 12 percent, the range of interest rates presented in the table is centered on 12 percent. The first column in the table shows the alternative interest rates. The second column shows the cost of borrowing through a discount loan for alternative interest rates. The third column shows the increase or decrease in the cost of credit over the cost at 12 percent. The fourth column shows the value of the futures contract on 90-day bills at maturity for different levels of the prevailing 90-day bill rate. Note that the contract price is the value of the futures contract if the prevailing interest rate is 12 percent. That is, the contract price for one contract is $970,873.8. The fifth column shows the gain or loss on the short futures position used in the hedge. If interest rates fall, then there is a loss on the short position. The gain is simply computed by taking the difference between the price of 10 contracts at the prevailing interest rate and the contract price of $9,708,738 for 10 contracts. The final column in the table shows the net cost of credit including the gain or loss on the futures contract. The table illustrates that this cost is always the same regardless of the level of interest rates. This is the result of a perfect hedge. The increase in the cost of borrowing, shown in column three, is always offset by the gain or the loss on the futures contract, shown in column five.

A **perfect hedge** is one that completely offsets the risk of changes in the payoffs in the asset you are trying to hedge.

This example is a case of a **perfect hedge.** It was possible to completely offset the risk of changes in the cost of borrowing by using Treasury bill futures. The loan contract was directly tied to Treasury bills so that the correlation coefficient between changes in Treasury bill rates and changes in the cost of the loan was one.

In practice, a perfect hedge is not generally attainable. There are two problems that can make a hedge less than perfect. Both of these problems generate

TABLE 9–1
Hedging the cost of bank credit.

90-Day Interest Rate (%)	Cost of $10 Mil Loan ($)	Increase in Borrowing Cost over 12% Forward Rate ($)	Value of Futures Contract at Maturity*	Gain on Futures Contract**	Net Cost of Credit
12.50	303,030	11,768	9,696,970	11,768	291,262
12.25	297,150	5,888	9,702,850	5,888	291,262
12.00	291,262	0	9,708,738	0	291,262
11.75	285,367	−5,895	9,714,633	−5,895	291,262
11.50	279,465	−11,797	9,720,535	−11,797	291,262

*If 90-day rate is 12.00 then price = 9,700,738 = $10,000,000/[1 + 0.1200(90/360)].
**Short position with contract price per contract of $970,873.8.

Basis risk occurs when the asset used to close out a hedge is not the same as the asset being hedged.

A **cross hedge** involves a hedge of one type of asset with a completely different asset. There are two key decisions in designing a hedging strategy. First, choose the appropriate futures contract to use, and second, choose the appropriate volume of futures contracts to acquire.

what is called **basis risk.** The first problem occurs when the maturity or desired length of the hedge does not coincide with the maturities or futures contracts available in the market. The second problem arises when no asset available in the marketplace is perfectly (negatively) correlated with the asset to be hedged. In this case it is necessary to construct what is called a **cross hedge.**

BASIS RISK

When the treasurer of the firm in our example attempts to hedge its risk, the first thing she might notice is that there are only four delivery dates for financial futures: March, June, September, and December of each year. (See Chapter 21 for some details on the structure of futures markets.) This is illustrated in the Treasury bill futures prices shown in Table 4–1 in Chapter 4. As a result, it probably would not be possible to execute the hedge described above exactly as shown in Table 9–1. Unless the date that the treasurer wanted to take out a loan corresponded with one of the four delivery dates, it would not be possible to write a futures contract that would mature on the precise date that the treasurer prefers. Therefore, she could not close out the hedge by delivering a 90-day Treasury bill; instead, it would be necessary to write a futures contract for one of the four delivery dates and close it out prior to maturity. This would be accomplished by buying back (since the hedge involved a short position in futures) the futures contract at the end of the hedge period but prior to the maturity of the futures contract.

This creates a problem: the prevailing price of the futures contract when it must be closed out may differ from the price that would yield a perfect hedge. In the context of the example in Table 9–1, the gain or loss on the futures contract may not exactly offset the change in the cost of borrowing as shown in the final column. The gain or loss on the futures contract will still be equal to the difference between the futures price when the hedge is initiated and the price of the contract used to close out the futures position. But in this case the latter price would be the price at the end of the hedge period of the same futures contract. In theory that price should be determined by the market's best guess of what interest rates will be when that futures contract matures. It will not be determined by the spot or cash 90-day Treasury bill rate prevailing when the contract is closed out.

For example, suppose that the futures contract used in the hedge above had two months to maturity when it was initiated. We will continue to assume that the maturity of the hedge is one month. Therefore, the futures contract must be closed out with one month to maturity in order to close out the hedge. When the futures contract is closed, it will be a one month future. The price or interest rate on the futures contract when it is closed should represent the market's best guess of cash or spot Treasury bill rates that will prevail in one month or at the maturity of the futures contract. If the forward rate prevailing for one month futures is 12.5 percent, then the price that must be paid to close out the ten contracts in the example in Table 9–1 is $9,696,970. The gain on the futures contract from the date of purchase would be $9,708,738 − $9,696,970 = $11,768, as shown in Table

TABLE 9–2
Hedging the cost of bank credit given that the futures contract is closed at an interest rate of 12.50%.

90-Day Interest Rate (%)	Cost of $10 Mil Loan ($)	Increase in Borrowing Cost over 12% Forward Rate ($)	Value of Futures Contract at Maturity*	Gain on Futures Contract**	Net Cost of Credit
12.50	303,030	11,768	9,696,970	11,768	291,262
12.25	297,150	5,888	9,696,970	11,768	285,382
12.00	291,262	0	9,696,970	11,768	279,494
11.75	285,367	−5,895	9,696,970	11,768	273,595
11.50	279,465	−11,797	9,696,970	11,768	267,693

*If 90-day rate is 12.00 then price = 9,708,738 = $1,000,000/[1 + 0.1200(90/360)].

**Short position with contract price per contract of $970,873.8.

9–1. However, this does not mean that the cash or spot 90-day Treasury bill rate will be 12.5 percent when the contract is closed. It could easily be any other value. Table 9–2 shows what would happen to the net cost of credit if the cash or spot Treasury bill rate varied from 12.50 percent to 11.50 percent while the forward rate in the futures market was fixed at 12.50 percent. For example, the table shows that if the cash or spot rate were 12 percent, the net cost of borrowing would be $279,494. This is the difference between $291,262, which is the cost of borrowing at 12.00%, and the gain on the futures contract of $11,768. As a result, the net cost of borrowing is no longer constant as in Table 9–1. Instead, it depends upon the difference between the price of the futures contract when it has to be closed, or the forward rate, and the value of 90-day Treasury bills at the same point in time. This, in turn, depends on what the market expects to happen to Treasury bill rates over the next month. The larger the difference between these two, the larger the variation will be in the net cost of credit.

The example presented in Table 9–1 is not constructed as a cross hedge because it was assumed that the cost of borrowing is directly tied to the Treasury bill rate. But suppose that the cost of borrowing were tied to the bank's prime rate and the prime rate was not specifically tied to any market interest rate. This is actually a more realistic description of bank borrowing terms. The problem facing the borrower in this case is that there is no futures contract on the prime rates of banks. There are futures contracts on commercial paper that might be used for such a hedge. But regardless of whether commercial paper or Treasury bill futures were used, there would still be basis risk because the prime rate could diverge from the interest rate in the future's contract.

HEDGING STRATEGY

The central strategic problem involved in hedging is to design a hedge so that you achieve a desirable combination of expected return and risk. There are two specific decisions which must be made in designing a hedging strategy.

A CROSS HEDGE IN THE MORTGAGE MARKET

To see how basis risk arises with a cross hedge, let's consider another example. Suppose an investor, such as a mortgage lender, has a portfolio of mortgages. These long-term assets are funded with short-term liabilities with a maturity of one year. To eliminate the mismatch in maturities, the lender decides to sell GNMA futures with a one-year maturity. An example of this transaction is shown in Table 9–3. Note that 8 percent GNMAs are used because that is the standard contract for GNMA futures. Panel A shows what happens in this example if the portfolio of mortgages owned by the mortgage lender were identical to the GNMAs in the futures contract. If this were the case, they could be delivered to close out the futures contract. Panel A shows that the investor locks in the price of the GNMAs at $62 through the futures market contract. Since the mortgages are valued at $64.2 at the beginning of the year, there is a loss of $2.2. In addition the investor receives a coupon payment of $8 during the year for a total return of $5.8. This results in a 9.0 percent rate of return on the initial value of the mortgages.

Now suppose that the investor does not have mortgages identical to the GNMAs. At the end of one year the investor will have to acquire GNMAs to close out the futures contract. If the value of his or her mortgages is exactly the same as the value of GNMAs, this will present no problem. No additional risk is created. However, if these two values can diverge, then basis risk is present. Panel B shows an example where the price of mortgages in the portfolio differs from the market value of the GNMAs at the end of one year. The value of the mortgages is $61, while the value of the GNMA is $63. This will lower the total return to the investor. Note that it is assumed that the mortgage portfolio pays 8 percent interest during the year just like the GNMAs. The rate of return received by the investor in this scenario will be less than that illustrated in Panel A because of the $2 disparity in the price of the mortgages and the GNMA price.

If the hedge is perfect, then the rate of return on the hedged position is fixed with certainty when the hedge is executed. The rate of return will be equal to the risk-free rate corresponding to the maturity of the hedge. Otherwise there would be risk-free arbitrage opportunities. For example, the rate of return in Panel A of 9.0 percent should be very close to the prevailing rate on one-year Treasury bills because the futures contract transforms the initial mortgage investment, assuming no basis risk, into a one year risk-free investment.

First, it is necessary to choose the appropriate futures contract to use for the hedge.

Second, it is necessary to choose the appropriate volume of futures contracts to acquire or the appropriate hedge ratio.

These decisions are simple when a futures contract that generates no basis risk is available. Such a contract is the one to use for the hedge. The choice of the amount of futures contracts to acquire is illustrated in panel A of Figure 9–1. This figure is similar to Figure 3–7 in Chapter 3, which shows expected return and risk in a portfolio of assets. Figure 9–1 shows the return to the investor's total portfolio that includes both a cash and a futures position. The vertical axis in the figure shows the investor's total expected return from the sum of the cash position and the futures position depending on how large a futures position is taken. The horizontal axis shows the variance of the investor's portfolio of cash and futures investments. Panel A of Figure 9–1 is constructed under the assumption that there is no basis risk. When this is the case, it will always be possible to reduce the variance of the investor's portfolio to zero by taking a futures position

TABLE 9–3
Results of hedging a mortgage loan portfolio.

Panel A		Panel B	
Initial position		*Initial position*	
GNMA cash position: Hold 8% coupon GNMA valued at	$64.2	GNMA cash position: Hold mortgages valued at	$64.2
GNMA futures position: Short 1-yr GNMA at	62.0	GNMA futures position: Short 1-yr GNMA at	62.0
Transaction at year end		*Transaction at year end*	
Deliver cash position to close future		Sell mortgages at market value of	61.0
		Buy back (close) GNMA future at	63.0
Rate of return		*Rate of return*	
Contract sale price in GNMA future	$62.0	Value of mortgages at year end	61.0
Less original value of cash position	64.2	Original value of mortgages	64.2
Capital gain	−$2.2	Gain on cash position	−3.2
Plus coupon income	8.0	Contract sale price in GNMA future	62.0
Total income	5.8	Cost of closing futures position	63.0
		Gain on future	−1.0
Original investment	$64.2	Plus coupon income	8.0
Rate of return	9.0%	Total income	3.8
		Original investment	$64.2
		Rate of return	6.0%

FIGURE 9–1
Optimal and minimum variance hedge ratios.

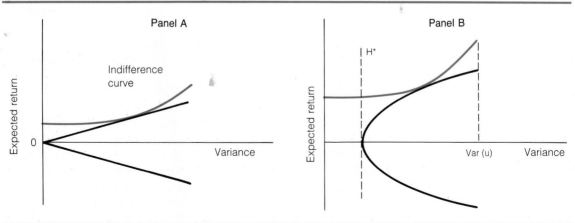

exactly equal in magnitude to the cash position. This is identical to the portfolio choice problem illustrated in Figure 3–7 in Chapter 3, where the correlation coefficient between the two assets in the portfolio is -1. The same idea is behind the perfect hedge illustrated in Table 9–1, where the correlation coefficient between the cash and futures position is also -1. The zero variance or perfect hedge position corresponds to the vertex of the triangle in Panel A of Figure 9–1. The diagonal lines which emanate from the origin to form this triangle define the feasible combinations of expected return and variance available to the investor, or the *opportunity set*.

Another way to describe the second choice facing the investor is to say that he or she must choose the appropriate hedge ratio. The **hedge ratio,** which we will symbolize by H, is defined as follows:

> The **hedge ratio** is (minus one times) the ratio of the quantity of the futures contracts held to the quantity of the cash position.

$$H = -\ \frac{\text{Quantity of futures held}}{\text{Quantity of cash position}}.$$

For example, if the investor is short the futures contract in an amount exactly equal to the size of his or her cash position, then the hedge ratio is 1. If the investor has a short futures position one half the size of his or her cash position, then the hedge ratio is ½. The hedge ratio is equal to 1 in Panel A of Figure 9–1 at the point where the variance of the portfolio is zero. Therefore, when there is no basis risk, a hedge ratio of one results in a perfect hedge, or a portfolio with zero variance.

Let's reconsider both of the decisions facing the investor if there is basis risk in all the futures contracts that might be used for a hedge. This means there is no futures contract available that will allow the investor to construct a perfect hedge. It is then necessary to choose the best instrument from available alternatives and to choose the best hedge ratio for that instrument. The best futures contract will be the one where the prices of the future are most highly correlated with the prices of the cash position or the asset to be hedged. The degree to which the futures contract is correlated with the asset to be hedged is called the **effectiveness of the hedge.**

> The **effectiveness of a hedge** is the degree to which the risk of the cash position can be eliminated with the hedge.
>
> The **minimum-variance hedge ratio** is the hedge ratio which will eliminate as much risk as possible in a particular hedge.

To see how to measure effectiveness we have to introduce what is called the minimum-variance hedge ratio. The **minimum-variance hedge ratio** for a particular futures contract is the hedge ratio that eliminates as much risk as possible using that futures contract for the hedge. This is illustrated in panel B of Figure 9–1, which shows the combinations of risk and expected return attainable in a hedge with basis risk. To understand what is represented in this figure it is useful to compare panels A and B: the line showing the opportunities open to the investor, or the efficient frontier, is now a smooth curve rather than a triangle. In addition, the minimum variance that can be achieved is no longer zero. While it is not evident from an inspection of the figure, the minimum variance, shown by the tangency of the dashed line labeled H^* with the opportunity curve, no longer occurs when $H = 1$. In fact, the value of H that minimizes variance, which is labeled H^*, could assume any value.

An effective hedge is one where it is possible to eliminate a large part, relative to other available alternatives, of the variance of the cash position. In terms of Figure 9–1, this would mean that the minimum variance would be close to the origin. One way to measure this is to measure the distance between the vertical axis and the dashed line representing H^* and divide that by the distance between the vertical axis and the dashed line through the point on the horizontal axis labeled Var(U). This point represents the variance of a completely unhedged cash position. This measure of the effectiveness of a hedge, which we will label e, can be defined as follows:

$$e = 1 - \frac{\text{Var}(R^*)}{\text{Var}(U)},$$

where Var(R^*) is the variance of the portfolio with a hedge ratio of H^*, or the minimum-variance portfolio. Though we will not get into detail here, it can be shown that[1]

$$e = \frac{\sigma^2_{CF}}{\sigma^2_C \sigma^2_F},$$

where σ_{CF} is the covariance of rates of return on the cash and the futures positions and σ^2_F is the variance of the rate of return on the futures position. This is simply the coefficient of determination or the square of the correlation coefficient between the returns on the cash and futures investments.

Now we can return to the question of how to choose the best futures contract for a hedge. It is necessary to evaluate the effectiveness using the measure e for each futures contract that might be used to hedge the risk of a specific asset. The futures contract with the highest measure of effectiveness will be the best instrument for the hedge in the sense that it will introduce the least basis risk.

Once it has been decided which of the available futures contracts is most effective, then it is necessary to choose the appropriate hedge ratio. One possible answer is to choose the minimum-variance hedge ratio. In order to compute this hedge ratio it is necessary is to conduct a regression analysis where the price of the asset to be hedged is regressed on the price of the futures contract used in the hedge. In effect, we are asking what is the expected change in the value of the asset to be hedged that is generated by a given change in the price of the futures contract. This is measured by the slope coefficient in a regression of the price of the cash position on the price of the future where H^* is the slope coefficient:

$$C_t = H^* F_t + u_t.$$

---

[1]See Louis H. Ederington, "The Hedging Performance of the New Futures Markets," *Journal of Finance*, (March 1979).

In the regression equation, C_t and F_t represent observed historical values of the price of the cash and futures positions, and u_t is the error term in the regression. The formula for the slope coefficient in a regression is as follows:

$$H* = \frac{\sigma_{CF}}{\sigma_F^2}.$$

Hence, the most effective hedge ratio in eliminating risk depends upon the relationship between the rates of return on the cash and futures investments. This makes sense since it is this relationship that determines the extent of the basis risk.

While we have focused our discussion on the minimum variance that can be achieved by a hedge, it is not obvious that an investor will find it optimal to minimize variance. As with all investment decisions, investors will generally want to balance risk against expected return. The investment opportunity curve shown in Panel B of Figure 9–1 shows the opportunities for trading risk against expected return provided by the futures market. The optimal portfolio, and therefore the optimal hedge ratio, will depend upon risk aversion of a specific investor. This can be represented by the indifference curves in Panel B. The tangency between the indifference curve and the opportunity curve for the hedge illustrates the optimal solution for the investor pictured here.

Evidence on Hedging Effectiveness. A number of researchers have computed measures of e and $H*$ for various types of hedges where the basis risk arises because of different maturities of the hedge and the futures contract used in the hedge.[2] By studying these measures we get a clear impression of how useful the futures markets actually are for hedging. Charles Frankle has estimated these values for 2-week and 4-week hedges in corn, wheat, 90-day Treasury bills, and GNMAs carried out during 1977.[3] For example, the 2-week hedge of Treasury bills involved the purchase of a 90-day bill and a short futures position that was closed out in 14 days. The 90-day bill would then be a 76-day bill, and it would be sold. Similarly, at maturity in a 4-week hedge, the original 90-day bill would then be a 62-day bill. Table 9–4 shows Frankle's estimates of $H*$ and e in each futures market. The estimates of $H*$ for both the 2- and the 4-week hedge are significantly different from one at the 0.05 percent level in each of the four cases for financial futures, but only one of four cases for commodity futures. The table indicates that the lowest measure of hedging effectiveness in all four markets is 0.65. Moreover, hedging effectiveness of financial futures appears roughly comparable to the effectiveness in commodity markets.

---

[2] See Louis H. Ederington, ibid.

[3] See Charles T. Franckle, "The Hedging Performance of the New Futures Market: Comment," *Journal of Finance*, (December 1980).

TABLE 9–4
Estimates of hedging effectiveness and minimum-variance hedge ratio.

The Futures Contract	Hedge Length	Estimated e	Estimated H^*
8% GNMAS	2-week	0.664	0.801*
	4-week	0.785	0.848
90-day Treasury bills	2-week	0.686	0.698*
	4-week	0.661	0.669*
Wheat	2-week	0.898	0.864*
	4-week	0.918	0.917
Corn	2-week	0.649	0.915
	4-week	0.725	1.021

*Significantly different from 1 at 5 percent level.

Commodity futures have been used to redistribute risk for many years. Hence, basis risk does not present an insurmountable obstacle to the practical use of financial futures. However, understanding basis risk is critical to understanding how useful financial futures will be in practice.

USING OPTIONS TO HEDGE INTEREST RATE RISK

Prior to 1982 it was difficult to engage in hedging activities using options as well as futures because there were no organized markets for options on fixed income obligations. However, in the last quarter of 1982 options trading began on a number of financial instruments, including bonds, foreign currencies, gold, and stock indexes such as the Standard and Poor's (S&P) Index. (See Chapter 21 for a discussion of the growth of options markets.) As a result it is now possible to construct hedges virtually identical, except for transactions costs and margin requirements, to the interest rate hedges constructed using futures markets.

CONSTRUCTING A HEDGE

To see how to utilize options markets to hedge interest rate risk we need to recall the relationship between futures contracts and put and call options. This relationship is examined in some detail in Chapter 4. A futures contract has a payoff symmetrical around the contract price. That is, the payoff is the difference between the price of the asset used to close out the futures contract and the contract price. By comparison, an option has an asymmetrical payoff. The payoff on the call option will be positive if the price of the underlying asset exceeds the exercise price of the option, and the payoff will never be negative since the option does not have to be exercised. Similarly, the payoff for a put option will be positive if the price of the underlying asset is less than the exercise price, and it will never be negative. These payoffs are illustrated in Figure 9–2. Panel A shows the payoff to a call option, while panel B shows the payoff to a put option with the same exercise price.

In order to see how to use options to hedge interest rate risk it is important to recognize that if you buy a call and write a put option with the same exercise price, the payoff will be the same as if you had a long futures contract in the same underlying asset with the same time to maturity and contract price. Therefore, the appropriate option position to take in order to hedge a cash position in an asset is simply to buy a put and write a call in that asset. This will be the equivalent of a short futures contract.

To see how this works let's reconsider the example of the mortgage lender who has a cash position in GNMAs. This lender was able to hedge that position by shorting a futures contract. The results are illustrated in Table 9–3. However, the same payoff can be received by buying a put and writing a call with the same maturity as the futures contract and with exercise prices equal to the contract price on the futures contract. This is illustrated in Table 9–5. This table shows the value of the cash position of the lender and the payoffs on the two options for alternative values of the price of the underlying security. It shows that the mortgage investor's losses on the call go up as the gains on the cash position increase. Similarly the investor's gains on the put increase as the value of the cash position declines. The final column of the table shows that the net gain on the cash position, includ-

FIGURE 9–2
Payoffs on call and put options.

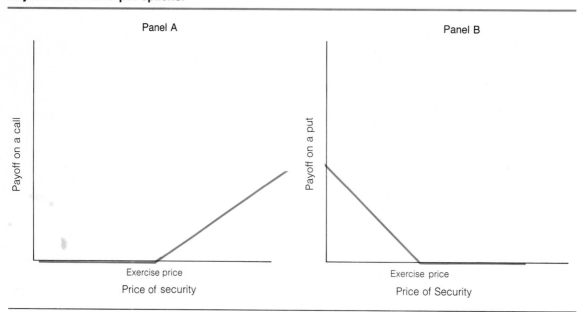

TABLE 9–5
Hedging a GNMA portfolio using options (assuming an exercise price of $67).

Price of GNMA at Maturity	Gain on Cash Position	Gain on Writing Call	Gain on Buying Put	Total Gain
70	5.8	−3.0	0.0	2.8
68	3.8	−1.0	0.0	2.8
66	1.8	0.0	1.0	2.8
64	−0.2	0.0	3.0	2.8
62	−2.2	0.0	5.0	2.8
60	−4.2	0.0	7.0	2.8

ing the put and the call, are always the same, regardless of the value of the GNMA. As a result, the investor is able to construct a perfect hedge using options just like the one illustrated in Panel A of Table 9–3 using futures.

ADVANTAGES OF OPTIONS IN MANAGING INTEREST RATE RISK

The principal advantage of options is that they are more flexible than many other types of securities. They allow an investor to take positions not otherwise available. This also applies to hedging. Options allow a market participant to construct hedges not feasible using futures contracts. We will examine two important examples of how options can be used to construct unique hedges.

One of the greatest potential uses of options on fixed income obligations is to offset risk from investments or other commitments that are themselves options. Consider the situation facing a bank or a construction lender that offers fixed rate lines of credit. These are commitments to lend in the future at fixed interest rates, and they are commonly used in commercial and construction lending. A lender who offers fixed rate lines of credit has, in effect, written a put option. If the cost of credit increases, or the price of fixed income obligation falls, borrowers are likely to increase their borrowing on fixed rate credit lines in order to take advantage of the relatively attractive interest rate. The lender will lose because, unless it has hedged its position, it will have to pay market interest rates to attract funds to support these loans. The lender receives a commitment fee for providing this credit line, and this is analogous to the price of the put option that has been indirectly written by the lender.

A lender who has written a put option in providing a line of credit can hedge its risk by acquiring an offsetting put option in the options market. A futures contract will not accomplish the same purpose because of its symmetrical payoff. With a futures contract the lender would gain or lose depending upon the price of the underlying security. On the other hand, by buying a put option the lender can simply offset the loss exposure created by the fixed rate line of credit.

The position taken by the lender if the fixed rate credit line is hedged with a put option as opposed to a futures contract is illustrated in Figure 9–3. The figure is constructed on the assumption that the lender receives a fee for providing a fixed rate line of credit. Panel A illustrates the magnitude of the losses incurred by the lender if interest rates increase and borrowers make use of their line of credit. The price of the underlying security shown on the horizontal axis is stated in terms of an interest rate representing the cost of credit in the marketplace rather than a dollar price. This will reverse the payoffs on put and call options. The interest rate might be represented by a 90-day Treasury bill rate. If rates do not fall below a critical level, represented by R_e, then the lender incurs no losses and, therefore, receives a gain equal to the fee paid for the credit line, or the commitment fee. R_e is the exercise price in the put option written by the lender stated in terms of interest rate rather than the price of the bill.

Panel B of the figure shows the payoff for the lender from a short position in Treasury bill futures with an exercise price, stated in terms of yield, of R_e. The line representing the payoff has a positive slope for a short position in the futures market for 90-day Treasury bills simply because the exercise price is stated in yield rather than in price of the Treasury bill. Panel C shows the net payoff to the lender if he or she attempts to hedge the risk of the credit line with the futures acquisition represented in panel B. It is apparent from panel C that by utilizing the futures market, the lender has not eliminated the risk inherent in the line of credit. The risk has simply shifted so that losses are incurred if interest rates fall rather than rise.

Panel D shows the net profit from purchasing a put option on Treasury bill futures. If interest rates are below R_e, then the put will not be exercised and the lender will lose the price of the put. If interest rates are above R_e, the put will be exercised at a gain. When the payoffs in panels A and D are combined, that is, when the line of credit is hedged with an option, the resulting payoff is constant. It is equal to the difference between the fee received by the lender for offering the line of credit and the price of the put option on 90-day Treasury bills. The spread between these two prices will be the risk-free return earned by the lender. This is illustrated in panel E.

The option markets can also create more flexible hedges against interest rates than the one illustrated in Figure 9–3. To illustrate one possibility, suppose the lender who offers a line of credit is willing to accept a limited amount of interest rate risk but prefers to be protected against large increases in interest rates. Protection of this type can be arranged using options by purchasing a put with an exercise price, stated in terms of yield, greater than R_e, as shown in Figure 9–3. The net payoff from hedging the line of credit with this option is represented by R_e^*. Since the exercise price, measured in yield, is higher than the one illustrated in panel D, it should command a lower price. Therefore, the spread between the fee earned on the line of credit and the price of the option should be larger than that shown in panel E. If interest rates are below R_e, then the lender will receive this spread. However, if interest rates are between R_e and R_e^*, borrowers will utilize their lines of credit and the lender will incur some losses. However, the lender will not exercise the put option purchased in the market. If interest rates

FIGURE 9–3
Hedging with options.

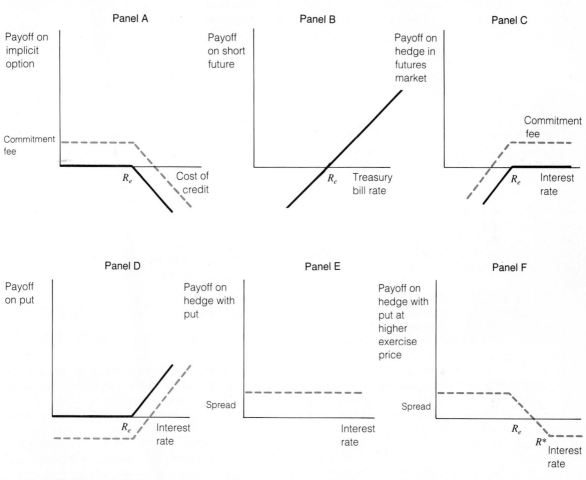

exceed R_e^*, the put option will be exercised and risk will be hedged, but the return will be lower than that earned in the risk-free hedge illustrated in panel E.

IMMUNIZING A BOND PORTFOLIO

Thus far we have approached interest rate risk by examining how to utilize the new markets for futures and options to sell interest rate risk to another party. It may also be possible for an investor to try to structure his or her balance sheet so that there is a natural hedge between the interest rate exposure of assets and liabilities. One way to do this is to select the maturity of assets to match the maturity of liabilities perfectly or to match the timing of cash flows. For example, suppose

WALL STREET'S HEDGING PROBLEM IN APRIL, 1987

It is not a simple task to construct a perfect hedge. Only under special circumstances is it possible since most hedges are exposed to some basis risk. While we have learned how to evaluate the magnitude of the basis risk involved in a hedge, it is important to understand that our measures of basis risk pertain to uncertain events. There can still be very large losses on a position that seems to have low basis risk if the value of the hedging instrument and the security being hedged move in widely different directions. A number of market participants, particularly in the mortgage markets, were reminded of this in April of 1987 when there was a significant increase in interest rates. It occurred largely because the Federal Reserve took steps to allow interest rates to increase in order to protect the value of the dollar, which had been falling against other major currencies. The interest rate increase caught many investors by surprise and was very painful to those who were not fully hedged.

The April, 1987, change in interest rates led to one of the largest trading losses ever reported—approximately $275 million incurred by Merrill Lynch & Co. Merrill Lynch blamed the loss on unauthorized trading in securities backed by mortgages. Shortly after announcing the loss, the firm fired one of its senior mortgage-backed securities traders, Howard A. Rubin, whom it blamed for much of the loss. Merrill Lynch claimed Rubin had accumulated a large unauthorized position in a new type of mortgage-backed security that was particularly risky. When interest rates went up in April, these securities experienced a significant decline in value. Figure 9–4 shows the level of mortgage interest rates and the value of mortgage-backed securities issued by the Federal Home Loan Mortgage Corporation for April, 1987. There was a significant decline in the value of these securities during a very short period. It has been estimated that Wall Street investment banking firms had approximately $5 billion of these types of securities in their inventory when the significant price decline occurred. Apparently, Merrill Lynch had the largest exposure of all the participants in this market.

To protect themselves against precisely this type of interest rate change, many market participants had implemented hedges using options or futures on 7- to 10-year Treasury bonds. These were chosen because the basis risk was believed to be rather low

FIGURE 9–4
Mortgage rate crosscurrents,

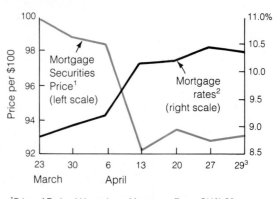

[1]Price of Federal Home Loan Mortgage Corp., 8½% 30-year mortgages sold in secondary market.
[2]Net yields required by Federal Home Loan Mortgage Corp. for 60-day delivery of 30-year mortgages.
[3]11 a.m. EDT.

Source: *Wall Street Journal*, April 30, 1987, p. 2.

with this hedging instrument. However, it appeared that a large number of market participants had failed to hedge their positions completely. In effect, many participants were speculating that interest rates would fall rather than rise and hence had chosen very small hedge ratios or no hedge at all. Beginning on April 10 when interest rates started to increase dramatically, people with unhedged positions attempted to dump their securities to protect themselves against further increases in rates. This drove down the prices of mortgage-backed securities and drove up their yields, relative to U.S. Treasury securities. This further increased the losses of unhedged investors in mortgage-backed securities. As a result, the basis between mortgage-backed securities and hedges using Treasury securities of investors who had been hedging increased. That is, their hedges became less effective than they thought they would be. This is an example of how the yield spread between two instruments can diverge in an unexpected way and seriously harm the effectiveness of a cross hedge. This particular episode represented a serious setback for many mortgage market participants.

you know that you will have a specific cash outflow of $100,000 five years from now. One simple way to hedge the risk involved in investing for that 5-year period is to buy a zero-coupon government bond with a 5-year maturity to immunize your position. This same problem started the last chapter when we developed the term structure of interest rates. However, the complication we are now going to introduce is coupon as opposed to zero-coupon bonds. We want to see how to immunize our investment if we invest in bonds with coupon payments, whereas we ignored coupon payments in the last chapter.

COUPON BONDS AND DURATION

The central problem we encounter when we examine coupon bonds is that the maturity of a bond is no longer a very satisfactory measure of the time pattern of cash flows from that bond. The cash flows are distributed over the life of the bond rather than concentrated in one payment at maturity. The maturity of the bond only measures when the last cash flow will be received.

Consider, for example, two bonds with coupon rates of 8 and 10 percent on a face value of $100,000. Suppose both bonds have 20 years to maturity and annual coupon payments. The cash flow for the first bond will be $8,000 per year and $108,000 at maturity, while for the second bond it will be $10,000 per year and $110,000 at maturity.

Is it possible to summarize the time pattern of these cashflows in a single measurement? One measure that seems to do a fairly good job is known as **duration.** Moreover, duration turns out to be quite useful in understanding how to immunize a portfolio.

Duration is a measure of the average time over which cash flows from a coupon paying bond are received.

There are a number of distinct measures of duration, but all of these are measures of time. The specific measure of duration we are principally interested in is called the *Macaulay duration.*[4] It is the weighted average of the points in time when the future cash flows accruing to a bond are to be received. The weight applied to each time is the present value of the cash flows received at that time as a proportion of the sum of the present values of all cash flows, where all present values are discounted at the yield to maturity for the bond. The Macaulay duration can be expressed as follows:

$$D = \frac{\sum\limits_{t=1,}^{n} \dfrac{C_t t}{(1 + r)^t}}{\sum\limits_{t=1,}^{n} \dfrac{C_t}{(1 + r)^t}},$$

where C_t = cash flow received at time t,

t = number of periods from present when cash flow is received,

r = yield to maturity,

n = number of periods to maturity.

[4]See Frederick R. Macaulay, *The Movement of Interest Rates, Bonds, Yields, and Stock Prices in the United States Since 1865,* New York: Columbia University Press, 1938.

The denominator of the expression for duration is the present value of the cash flows accruing to the holder of the bond. The numerator is the present value of the product of each cash flow and the number of periods in the future in which it is received. The durations of the 8 and 10 percent coupon bonds described can be computed as follows if it is assumed that the yield to maturity on both bonds is 10 percent. For the 8 percent coupon bond duration is computed as:

$$\frac{7273}{82973}\,1 + \frac{6612}{82973}\,2 + \frac{6011}{82973}\,3 + \ldots + \frac{1439}{82973}\,18 + \frac{1308}{82973}\,19 + \frac{16054}{82973}\,20 = 9.75,$$

where, for example, 7,273 is the present value, discounted at 10 percent, of the $8,000 received at the end of the first year of the life of the bond, and 16,054 is the present value of the $108,000 received after 20 years. These two values are multiplied by 1 and 20 years respectively and divided by the present value of the cash flows accruing to the bond, $82,973. The duration of the 10 percent coupon bond is computed as:

$$\frac{9091}{100000}\,1 + \frac{8264}{100000}\,2 + \frac{7513}{100000}\,3 + \ldots + \frac{1799}{100000}\,18 + \frac{1635}{100000}\,19 + \frac{16351}{100000}\,20 = 9.36,$$

where 9,091 is the present value, at 10 percent, of the $10,000 received at the end of one year, and $16,351, is the present value of the $110,000 received in 20 years. The value of the cash flows accruing to this bond when discounted at 10 percent is $100,000.

The duration is shorter for the higher coupon bond because more of the total cash flow is received earlier for that bond. This is not peculiar to this example. If other things are held constant, then an increase in the coupon rate will always cause the duration to decline. It is also true that if the discount rate is increased and everything else remains the same, then the duration will decrease. For example, suppose we use a discount rate of 12 percent rather than 10 percent in calculating the duration of the two bonds. The duration of the 8 percent bond will then be 8.94, and the duration of the 10 percent bond will be 8.60. For both bonds, the duration is lower at a 12 percent discount rate than it is at 10 percent. The duration of a bond is equal to its maturity if and only if it is a zero-coupon bond. For example, we would calculate the duration of a 20-year zero-coupon bond with a payment at maturity of $100,000, assuming a 10 percent yield to maturity, as follows:

$$\frac{100,000\,(20)/(1.10^{20})}{100,000/(1.10^{20})} = 20.$$

PROPERTIES OF DURATION

The specific measure of duration proposed above is only one of a number of possible ways to measure duration. The Macaulay duration has two attractive features: it is relatively simple, and it provides a measure of the relationship between a change in the yield to maturity and the change in the price of a bond. That is (for relatively low levels of interest rates), the percentage change in the price of a bond is inversely proportional to the change in the market yield to maturity.

$$\frac{\Delta P}{P} = -D \frac{\Delta r.}{1 + r},$$

where P represents the price of the bond, D represents duration, and r represents the yield to maturity. Thus, duration has the attractive interpretation that it measures the sensitivity of bond prices to changes in yield to maturity. The relationship implies that a bond with a short duration will be less sensitive to changes in yield than a bond with a longer duration. For example, based on the durations computed above for the 8 and 10 percent coupon bonds, a change in yield to maturity from 10 percent to 11 percent would result in a price change of 8.86 percent and 8.51 percent respectively, for the two bonds.

Ideally, we would like to have a simple measure of the time pattern of cash flows like the Macaulay duration but one that shows the relationship between bond prices and the entire term structure of market interest rates, rather than the yield to maturity. This is because changes in yield to maturity do not cause changes in bond prices. Instead, yield to maturity and price are two alternative ways of stating the same thing. The variables that logically determine the price and therefore the yield to maturity on a bond are the market interest rates that apply to different maturities—that is, the zero-coupon term structure of interest rates.

To see how the bond price is determined by the term structure of interest rates, recall that the market value of a bond is equal to the present value of the cash flows accruing to it where each cash flow is discounted by the market interest rate that applies to the maturity of that cash flow. For example, cash flows 10 years from now are discounted at the 10-year interest rate prevailing today. A simple way to express this is to say that the cash flows are discounted using the current zero-coupon term structure of interest rates.

Once the bond price has been determined by the cash flows to the bond and the term structure of interest rates, we can use the price and the cash flows to solve for the yield to maturity by solving for the single interest rate that satisfies the present value equation:

$$\text{Price} = \sum_{t = 1,}^{n} \frac{c_t}{(1 + r)^t}.$$

Fortunately, there are alternatives to the Macaulay duration that capture the relationship between the price of a bond and the term structure. Unfortunately, they are not simple, and we will not attempt to define them here. Moreover, these more complicated duration measures require knowledge of the way the term structure of interest rates fluctuates through time. Since this cannot be known with certainty, these more elaborate measures of duration must also be subject to uncertainty. Despite these shortcomings, the simple Macaulay measure of duration is a useful concept.

IMMUNIZATION

The basic strategy involved in immunization of a portfolio of coupon bonds is to try to transform the portfolio into the equivalent of a zero-coupon bond with a maturity equal to the decision maker's investment horizon. Interest rate risk can be eliminated entirely by investing in a zero-coupon bond with the same maturity as the investment horizon. The central problem involved in immunization is to try to transform a portfolio of coupon bonds into a portfolio that behaves as if it were made up of zero-coupon bonds with the preferred maturity.

A coupon bond involves two types of risks. First, it has the risk of price changes if it is liquidated prior to maturity. Second, it has the risk of changes in the interest rate at which coupon payments can be reinvested. As we have already learned, these risks respond in opposite directions to changes in market interest rates. The idea in immunizing a portfolio is to make these two risks fully offsetting so that the bond value plus the reinvested coupon payments will be the same at the end of the investment horizon, regardless of the level of interest rates.

The way immunization works is illustrated in Figure 9–5. The horizontal axis in this figure shows time; the vertical axis shows the value of the portfolio including reinvested coupon payments. The length of the investment horizon is represented by n. The solid line in the figure emanating from point V_0 on the vertical axis shows the value of the portfolio, including reinvested coupon payments, if there are no changes in interest rates. The value of the portfolio at the end of the investment horizon when it follows the solid line is labeled V_n. If interest rates

FIGURE 9–5
Value of an immunized portfolio.

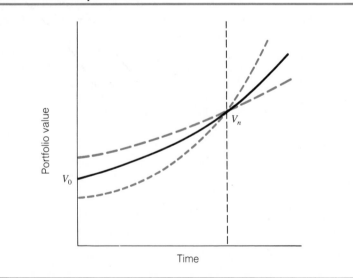

fall in time 0, that is, if the whole term structure shifts down, then the value of the portfolio will increase. At this new level of interest rates, the value of the portfolio, including reinvested coupon payments, will follow a new path over time defined by the dashed line above the solid one in the figure. This line starts from a higher initial portfolio value. The value of the portfolio appreciates at a slower rate due to the lower level of interest rates, which mean lower reinvestment income. Hence, the slope of this dashed line is lower at each point in time than is the slope of the solid line below it. Conversely, if interest rates increase at time 0, then the value of the bonds in the portfolio will decline initially. However, the higher interest rates will mean the reinvested coupons will appreciate at a higher rate. This is represented in the dashed line below the solid one. This line has a higher slope, at any point, than does the solid line.

All three of the curves in Figure 9–5 are drawn so that they intersect at one point, which represents the value of the portfolio at the end of the investor's investment horizon, V_n. The figure has not been constructed this way by accident. The fact that they intersect at this point means the portfolio will always have the same value at time n, regardless of how interest rates change at time 0. It turns out that the way to construct a portfolio so that it will behave like this is to choose the portfolio's duration so that it is equal to the length of the investment horizon, n. It can be shown that when the duration is equal to the length of the investment horizon, then changes in reinvestment income caused by changes in interest rates will offset changes in the price of the portfolio exactly.[5]

Unfortunately, it is not as simple as it sounds to set the duration of a portfolio equal to the investment horizon. There are at least two practical difficulties involved. First, as time passes both the investment horizon and the duration of the portfolio decrease, but they do not decrease at the same rate. Therefore, the portfolio must be altered as time passes to keep the duration equal to the remaining horizon. Adjustments must be made constantly in the portfolio if it is to be immunized perfectly.

Second, the duration that yields perfect immunization is the "true" duration of the portfolio, defined with respect to the entire term structure of interest rates. In general, this is not the Macaulay duration. The true measure of duration depends upon the way interest rates vary over time, or on the proper stochastic process for interest rates. Since this can't be known with certainty, it is not possible to immunize perfectly with certainty. This introduces a new risk into the problem of immunizing a portfolio: the portfolio may be immunized perfectly except that the measure of duration employed is not accurate. As a result, the value of the portfolio may differ from what was expected at the end of the investment horizon. Since this risk arises from the fact that the future behavior of interest rates cannot be known perfectly, it has been labeled **stochastic process risk.**

Stochastic process risk refers to the risk of changes in the way risky interest rates evolve over time.

---

[5]See G. O. Bierwag and George G. Kaufman, "Coping with the Risk of Interest Rate Fluctuations: A Note," *Journal of Business,* (July 1977), pp. 367–70.

Some researchers and market participants have attempted to develop procedures to minimize stochastic process risk.[6] Essentially, these procedures involve the construction of a portfolio with cash flows concentrated around the end of the investment horizon. Of course, the ultimate way to do this is to use zero-coupon rather than coupon bonds.

SUMMARY

The basic idea behind a hedge is to take a position in one asset which will have a payoff that is the opposite to the payoff generated by the asset or position you already hold. Hedging has a number of practical applications for both financial and nonfinancial firms. A bank may want to hedge the future cost of deposits; a manufacturing firm may want to hedge the future cost of borrowing; a firm operating in more than one country may want to hedge the future exchange rate between currencies.

Basis risk occurs whenever it is not possible to construct a perfect hedge—that is, whenever the asset being hedged does not coincide perfectly with the asset in the hedge. We considered two sources of basis risk: the first occurs when the maturity of the risk being hedged does not coincide with the maturity of the futures contract. This can occur quite easily since there are four dates each year when futures contracts mature. The second source of basis risk occurs when there is no futures contract available for the asset to be hedged. Some other futures contract must be used instead and this is called a *cross hedge*.

Whenever there is basis risk in a hedge, that is, whenever the hedge is not perfect, there is a strategic element involved in hedging. The strategy involves choice of the best futures contract for the hedge and choice of the appropriate hedge ratio. Selection of a hedging instrument can be made by comparing measures of the effectiveness of a hedge. Naturally, the most effective hedge is the best one to use. We also learned how to compute the minimum-variance hedge ratio, which yields the lowest attainable level of risk. However, an investor might not find the minimum-variance hedge ratio to be the best choice since it is a matter of personal preference or a choice of the appropriate trade-off of risk and return.

We also reviewed the available empirical evidence on the effectiveness of financial futures with respect to the mismatch of maturities of the asset being hedged and the futures contract. According to this evidence financial futures on

---

[6]See G. O. Bierwag, George G. Kaufman, and Alden Toevs, "Immunizing Strategies for Funding Multiple Liabilities," *Journal of Financial and Quantitative Analysis,* (March 1983), pp. 113–24 and Gifford H. Fong and Oldrich A. Vasicek, "Return Maximization for Immunized Portfolios," In Bierwag, Kaufman and Toevs, eds., *Innovations in Bond Portfolio Management,* Greenwhich, Conn.: JAI Press, 1983.

Treasury bills and GNMAs appear to be about as effective in limiting risk as commodity futures contracts such as corn and wheat.

Next we turned our attention to the use of options as hedging devices. We can always create the equivalent of a long futures contract by buying a call and writing a put with an exercise price equal to the contract price of the futures contract. Hence, if we are to find a special role for options as hedging devices, it must be because we can use them to split up a futures contract. Some types of risks in the marketplace might inherently be like options and might have asymmetrical payoffs. For example, a bank that has written a line of credit has implicitly written an option. For the bank to attempt to hedge the risk in that commitment with a future, it would simply trade one kind of risk exposure for another. However, it can hedge its risk by writing an option that offsets its risk exposure.

Coupon bonds entail both a reinvestment risk and a price risk that respond in opposite ways to changes in market interest rates. When interest rates rise, the value of payment at maturity is reduced. However, the reinvestment income earned on coupon payments rises. The idea behind portfolio immunization is to attempt to choose an investment in coupon bonds to offset these risks. To do this an investor attempts to choose the bond so that it has a duration exactly equal to the investor's desired holding period. One particular measure of duration is known as the *Macaulay duration*. The advantage of this measure is that it is simple to compute. The disadvantage is that, since it is not the true duration of the bond, it will not generally provide perfect immunization.

QUESTIONS

1. Describe the basic idea behind a hedge using futures markets.
2. What is basis risk? How does a cross hedge create basis risk? How does a mismatch in maturities between the asset being hedged and the futures contract in the hedge create basis risk?
3. Suppose you are managing a savings and loan which has a portfolio of mortgage-backed securities that earn 10 percent on a current market value of $800 million. You are funding half of this portfolio with long-term deposits matched with the maturity of your loan portfolio and half with 180-day deposits priced at the Treasury bill rate plus 50 basis points. You consider hedging the risk of changes in the cost of you 180-day deposits with Treasury bill futures. The Treasury bill rate implied by current futures markets contracts with six-month maturities on 180-day Treasury bills is 7 percent and the current 180-day bill rate is 6.5 percent. Compute what your profits (losses) on your portfolio would be over the next year if you hedge your risk in the futures markets as opposed to accepting the risk of fluctuations in futures interest rates on Treasury bills. Allow Treasury bill rates to vary from 5 percent to 9 percent in your computations.

4. Reconsider the problem in question 3. Recalculate your profits (losses) with hedge ratios of 0.5 and 1.5. Remember you are hedging half of the $800 million portfolio. How would you select the best hedge ratio?

5. Reconsider the problem in panel A of Table 9–3. Suppose that the current GNMA futures price is $67. How would this affect the rate of return in the hedge in this table? Suppose that at the same time you observed a GNMA futures price of $67 you observed that the one year Treasury bill rate was 10 percent. How could you take advantage of the trading opportunity? Explain how your actions willl affect the cash and/or futures prices of GNMAs.

6. How do you measure the effectiveness of a hedge? What is the relationship between the effectiveness of a hedge and the R^2 in a regression equation?

7. What does the evidence say about the effectiveness of financial futures as hedging devices compared with commodity futures?

8. Reconsider the problem posed in Table 9–1. Suppose that the loan was indexed to the bank's prime rate and there is no futures market in this prime rate. You examined the past behavior of the prime rate and found that the prime could be related to the Treasury bill rate by the following linear equation (where both the prime and the Treasury bill rate are measured in percent):

$$Prime = 2.00 + Treasury\ bill\ rate + u_t,$$

where u_t is a random number with an expected value of zero and a standard deviation of 0.75. Also assume that the standard deviation of the Treasury bill rate is 1. What would be the minimum-variance hedge ratio in the problem in Table 9–1, and what would be the effectiveness of the hedge?

9. Why would you ever use an option rather than a future in a hedge? Suppose you were a bank making a loan commitment. How would using a future contract simply exchange one type of risk exposure for another?

10. On April 30, 1987, the following Treasury Bonds had the yields and prices shown below.

Maturity Date	Coupon Rate	Market Yield (%)
Feb. 2007	7 5/8	8.38
Feb. 2002	14 1/4	8.53
May 1995	10 3/8	8.23
Feb. 1993	7 7/8	7.96

Compute the Macaulay duration for each of these bonds. How could the duration measures change with a 100-basis-point increase in market yield and with a 100-basis-point change in coupon rate?

11. Why mightn't you have perfect immunization if you chose the duration of a bond equal to your investment horizon if you used the Macaulay duration as the measure of duration?

REFERENCES

Bierwag, G. O., George G. Kaufman, and Alden Toevs. "Duration: Its Development and Use in Bond Portfolio Management," *Financial Analysts Journal,* (July-August) 1983, pp. 15–35.

Bierwag, G. O. and George G. Kaufman. "Coping with the Risk of Interest Rate Fluctuations: A note," *Journal of Business,* (July 1977), pp. 367–70.

Bierwag, G. O., George G. Kaufman, and Alden Toevs. "Immunizing Strategies for Funding Multiple Liabilities," *Journal of Financial and Quantitative Analysis,* (March 1983), pp. 113–24

Ederington, Louis H. "The Hedging Performance of the New Futures Markets," *Journal of Finance,* (March 1979), pp. 157–70.

Fong, Gifford H. and Oldrich A. Vasicek. "Return Maximization for Immunized Portfolios," in Bierwag, Kaufman and Toevs, eds., *Innovations in Bond Portfolio Management,* Greenwich, Conn.: JAI Press, 1983.

Franckle, Charles T. "The Hedging Performance of the New Futures Market: Comment," *Journal of Finance,* (December 1980), pp. 1272–79.

Jaffee, Dwight M. "Interest Rate Hedging Strategies for Savings and Loan Associations," *Managing Interest Rate Risk in the Thrift Industry,* Federal Home Land Bank of San Francisco, 1981.

Kaufman, George G. "Measuring and Managing Interest Rate Risk: A Primer," *Economic Perspectives,* Federal Reserve Bank of Chicago, 1982, pp. 16–29.

Khoury, Sarkis J. *Speculative Markets,* New York: Macmillan, 1984.

Macaulay, Frederick R. *The Movement of Interest Rates, Bonds, Yields, and Stock Prices in the United States Since 1865,* New York: Columbia University Press, 1938.

Poole, William, "Using T-Bill Futures to Gauge Interest-Rate Expectations," *Economic Review* of the Federal Reserve Bank of San Francisco, (Spring 1978), pp. 7–20.

Rendleman, Richard J. Jr. and Christopher E. Carabini. "The Efficiency of the Treasury Bill Futures Market," *Journal of Finance,* (September 1979), pp. 895–914.

10

*M*ONETARY POLICY AND INTEREST RATES

This is the first of two chapters that explore the link between monetary policy and interest rates as well as the contemporary debate about the conduct of monetary policy. In order to understand the link between monetary policy and interest rates it is useful to examine the structure and operation of the central bank in the United States, the Federal Reserve. In this chapter we see how the Fed (as it is called) influences the supply of money and market interest rates. Then, in the next chapter, we see how the Fed has conducted its policy in recent years, as well as the many criticisms of Fed policy and prescriptions for how it should operate in the future.

We start by examining the mechanics of the Federal Reserve operations and how it controls what is called the *monetary base.* Then we examine how control over the monetary base is translated into control of the total supply of money. Finally, we explore the link between the supply of money and the level of interest rates. ■

OPERATION OF THE FEDERAL RESERVE AND CONTROL OF THE MONETARY BASE

The United States did not always have a central bank. In fact it was not until 1913 that Congress created the Federal Reserve. The Congress passed the Federal Reserve Act in response to the Panic of 1907, which constituted a serious liquidity crisis in the U.S. commercial banking industry. The Federal Reserve was created to function as a "lender of last resort" or a source of liquidity to the industry. (We will learn more about the relationship between the Federal Reserve and the banking industry in Parts 3 and 4.) Since 1913, the functions of the Fed, as well as our understanding of its proper role in the economy, have developed considerably. Today, the Fed not only serves its traditional role of providing liquidity to the banking industry, but it also exerts control over the quantity of money in the economy and influences market interest rates. To understand how and why it has this power we need to know how the Fed is organized and how it conducts its business.

ORGANIZATION OF POWER WITHIN THE FEDERAL RESERVE

The Federal Reserve is an unusual government agency in many respects, but its most unusual characteristic is its apparent autonomy from both the executive and legislative branches of the government. Its autonomy comes both from the way it is organized and from its budgetary independence. The Federal Reserve is controlled by a seven-member Board of Governors. Each board member is appointed for a 14-year term, with one member's term expiring every 2 years. Appointments are made by the President with the consent of Congress and, because of retirements, are often made more frequently than the two-year interval. One of the seven members of the board serves as its chariman. The chairman is selected by the President for a four-year term. Unlike almost every other agency in the federal government, the Federal Reserve does not have to go to Congress for a budget. The Fed is self-supporting and, in fact, generally returns billions of dollars to the Treasury each year from the profits it earns on its portfolio of government securities.

The formal independence of the Federal Reserve may overstate the reality of the matter, for the Federal Reserve's independence persists only with the consent of Congress and the President. There is always the possibility that the Federal Reserve Act will be modified to alter the accountability of the Federal Reserve. Many have argued that this implicit threat has always been sufficient to compel the Federal Reserve to conduct monetary policy in a way that serves the interests of the President or of Congress.[1]

---

[1]See Raymond E. Lombra, "Reflections on Burns's Reflections," *Journal of Money, Credit and Banking* (February 1980), pp. 94–105, for a discussion of the political aspects of the conduct of monetary policy during Arthur Burns's term as chairman of the Federal Reserve Board.

The organizational structure and distribution of power within the Federal Reserve system is the result of a number of compromises made over the life of the system. When the system was created, the offices of the board were located in Washington, but the country was divided into 12 districts with a Federal Reserve bank in each. Considerable power was allocated to the district banks. Specifically, they had the power to grant loans and set the terms for those loans to individual commercial banks in each district and to buy and sell United States government securities on their own accounts. In the 1930s this power was consolidated in Washington under the direction of a committee that maintained representation from the district banks. This committee, known as the **Federal Open Market Committee** (FOMC), remains the single most important decision-making body within the Federal Reserve system. It is composed of the seven members of the Board of Governors, the President of the Federal Reserve Bank of New York, and, on a rotating basis, four of the other eleven district bank presidents. The FOMC has the real responsibility for determining monetary policy.

> The **Federal Open Market Committee** meets to decide on the monetary policy of the Federal Reserve.

The power of the FOMC results from its control of what are called *open market operations*. Open market operations involve the purchase or sale of U.S. Treasury securities by the Federal Reserve. This is the principal tool by which the Federal Reserve determines the money supply. The FOMC meets about once a month in Washington and on other, special occasions to decide on the future course of monetary policy. The meetings are held in secret, but as of 1980, edited minutes of the monthly meetings are published in the Federal Reserve Bulletin.

The chairman of the Board of Governors has historically been an immensely powerful figure within the system, though not always within the rest of the government. This is certainly not inherent in the system itself, as the chairman has little formal power. Within both the Board and the Open Market Committee the chairman has only one vote, just like other members. The chairman does not affect the tenure of the other board members, though he or she does have some control over their personal budgets and perquisites. The power that the chairman has historically commanded has been largely a result of the personality and political skills of the individuals who have occupied the job.

OPEN MARKET OPERATIONS AND CONTROL OF THE MONETARY BASE

Over the approximately 70 years it has been in business, the Federal Reserve has acquired a rather large portfolio of U.S. Treasury securities. As of December, 1985, the Fed owned $181 billion worth of Treasury securities, which represented approximately 9 percent of the total stock of such securities outstanding. This means that at that time the Fed owned 9 percent of the total national debt. The Fed doesn't buy such securities purely in order to make a profit. Instead, it is principally through the purchase of such securities that the Federal Reserve supplies reserves to the banking system. The Federal Open Market Committee sets the guidelines for the purchase and sale of such securities, and its operating arm, the **Open Market Desk** at the Federal Reserve Bank of New York, actually conducts the transactions. These transactions are referred to as *open market operations*.

> The **Open Market Desk** is the office in the Federal Reserve Bank of New York which buys and sells securities for the Federal Reserve.

THE SIGNIFICANCE OF THE CHAIRMAN OF THE BOARD OF GOVERNORS OF THE FEDERAL RESERVE

An interesting example of the importance of the individual to this job is provided by Arthur Burns, who served as chairman from 1970–77. Burns was appointed to the job by President Richard Nixon after he had already established one of the most successful careers in the economics profession. Burns' career spanned nearly the entire twentieth century. He was a professor of economics at Columbia University in his early twenties. (He was Milton Friedman's first economics professor.) He later became chairman of the Council of Economic Advisors for President Dwight Eisenhower. During these years he developed a close relationship with then Vice President Richard Nixon.[2] At the end of the Eisenhower administration, he became head of the National Bureau of Economic Research, the most widely known private economic research organization in the United States. Because of Burns' distinguished career prior to becoming chairman of the Board of Governors, and because of the political and economic skill he had acquired during this career, he became an extremely powerful if not dominating force within the Federal Reserve.

A similar characterization seems appropriate for Paul Volcker, who became Chairman of the Board of Governors in 1979. Prior to being appointed to this position by President Jimmy Carter, Volcker had been president of the Federal Reserve Bank of New York and served in the Department of the Treasury for a number of years. He was widely recognized as an authoritative and knowledgeable figure in monetary affairs, particularly with respect to international financial issues.

Though Volcker was appointed by a Democratic president, he won tremendous political support from participants in financial markets and Republican politicians. Volcker essentially led a fight against inflation in the United States in the late 1970s and early 1980s by controlling the growth rate of the money supply and allowing interest rates to increase to unprecedented levels in 1980 and 1981. Largely because of the broad support for his anti-inflation policies, Volcker was reappointed to a second term as chairman of the Federal Reserve Board by the Reagan administration in 1983. However, after his reappointment, a significant gap in policy objectives developed between Volcker and the Reagan administration. Volcker appeared to favor a less expansionary policy than did many in the Reagan camp. The expansionist view gained more support as the composition of the board changed with new appointments from the Reagan administration. The new board was much less willing to go along with Volcker and his policies. In 1986 and 1987 there were two occasions when Volcker's position lost a formal vote with the board. One issue pertained to the Fed's control of monetary policy and the other to bank regulation. As we will see in this chapter and the next, there are numerous competing views about how monetary policy should be conducted. These differences are directly visible in the composition of the board to a greater extent than may have been true in the past.

In mid-1987 Alan Greenspan replaced Paul Volcker as Federal Reserve Board Chairman. Greenspan was widely regarded as the best possible replacement as he had been chairman of the Council of Economic Advisors under President Ford and immediately prior to his appointment, he was president of Townsend-Greenspan Associates, a highly regarded economic consulting firm.

---

[2]See William Safier, *Before the Fall*, New York: Doubleday, 1975, for an interesting description of the relationship between Richard Nixon and Arthur Burns and for an account of Burns's role in the Nixon administration.

The basic mechanics of open market operations are relatively simple. When the Open Market Desk, under the direction of the FOMC, decides that Treasury securities should be purchased, it calls up any of a number of dealers in such securities. The Fed maintains a list of commercial firms, usually large brokerage houses or banks, that continually make a market in Treasury securities, and for any given transaction it chooses some dealer on this list. The Federal Reserve then agrees to buy a certain volume of securities at the going price, say $10 million worth of securities. The Federal Reserve Bank of New York issues a check to the securities dealer for $10 million, and the Federal Reserve receives title to the securities. If the securities dealer is not a commercial bank, then that dealer has the check from the Federal Reserve Bank of New York deposited in its bank. The deposit balances of the dealer are increased by $10,000,000, and the deposits the commercial bank holds with Federal Reserve Bank of New York are increased by $10 million. This represents a net increase in the reserves of the banking system, for there is no offsetting decline in the deposits of any other bank.

Fractional reserves are the reserves held by commercial banks as a fraction of outstanding deposit balances.

Before we go any further it is important to understand what reserves are. We operate in what is called a **fractional reserve banking system** in the United States. Regulations require that banks and other depository institutions such as savings and loans hold reserves behind deposit accounts that function like demand deposits. One way these reserves are held is in the form of deposits with the various Federal Reserve Banks. Therefore, when the Fed purchases securities and the deposits with the Fed of a commercial bank increase, this is equivalent to increasing the amount of reserves held by the banking industry as a whole.

The net impact of this increase in reserves is illustrated in the following hypothetical balance sheet. The demand deposits of the commercial bank in question, which are a liability on its accounts, are increased by $10 million. Offsetting this is a comparable increase in reserves in the form of deposits with the Fed. Hence, this bank and the banking system now have $10 million in new reserves that did not previously exist at all.

Balance sheet of commercial bank.

Assets	Liabilities and Net Worth
Reserves = +10,000,000	Demand deposits = +10,000,000

When open market operations take place, the public as a whole merely exchanges one type of asset for another—that is, when the Federal Reserve buys securities, the public exchanges Treasury securities for demand deposits. As a consequence of this exchange the banking system acquires new reserves because they are the deposits of commercial banks with the Federal Reserve. The unique and relevant characteristic of reserves is that they constrain the total supply of deposits the commercial banking system can make available to the public. If the required ratio of reserves to deposits is, say, 20 percent, and the total stock of reserves is, say, $20 billion, then the maximum amount of deposits that can be issued by the banking system is $100 billion (20 percent of $100 billion is $20 billion). Therefore, when new reserves are created the banking system can let deposits expand. On the other hand, if the Federal Reserve withdraws reserves through open market sales of securities, the banking system must limit deposits to a smaller volume than it did previously. To see the links between reserves and the total volume of deposits more clearly, we must examine what is called the *multiple expansion process*.

DETERMINANTS OF THE MONEY SUPPLY

DEFINING MONEY

In order to establish the link between open market operations and the aggregate supply of money we need to have a workable definition of what constitutes **money.** To see how to define money it is necessary to understand the function money serves in an economy. Money is an asset that serves as a unit of account and medium of exchange. Money serves as the unit of account because the prices of all goods and services are denominated in money (e.g., in dollars in the United States). In this sense money is simply a measuring device like inches, pounds, or liters. Moreover, the fact that we denominate the price of everything in money greatly simplifies the process of doing business. The alternative would be to state the price of every good in terms of every other good, that is, the price of lamb chops in terms of Toyota Coronas. It would be exceedingly difficult to carry out transactions, as this would essentially be a barter economy.

In our contemporary economy money also serves as a medium of exchange. People hold balances of money, which they exchange for goods and services they buy and sell. Hence, money is a commodity itself, not merely the unit of measurement in an accounting system. In our world it is difficult to imagine conducting business transactions without exchanging money. Regardless of what we purchase or sell, we are willing to accept money in exchange because we know it will be readily acceptable throughout the economy. As a result, we choose those items to use as money that minimize our costs of executing transactions. We would, for example, find it difficult to use cows as money. The difficulties might not be overwhelming if we wanted to purchase something that cost exactly one cow. We would merely have to worry about transporting, feeding, and cleaning up after the cow. Suppose we wanted to purchase something that cost half a cow. Then we would have to worry about butchering and preserving the meat. If we started using cows for money, we would eventually wind up exchanging frozen meat. In effect, hamburger would drive out cows as a medium of exchange. Similarly, if some other asset were viewed as presenting lower costs of transacting, it would come to replace hamburger as a medium of exchange. The implication is that an economy will naturally evolve to using those assets for a medium of exchange that involve the lowest cost of transacting. These assets are characterized as being the most liquid assets in the economy.

To see what serves as money today we can start with the assets that most clearly fit our concept of money. The first asset generally recognized as money is cash or currency. This includes the paper notes and metal coins issued by the Federal Reserve and the Treasury in denominations as small as a penny to as large as $1,000. The second asset generally understood to be money is **demand deposits** at commercial banks. These are the balances in checking accounts held by individuals and corporations throughout the country. They are thought of as money because they are universally accepted as a medium of exchange. It is certainly true that checks drawn on deposit balances are not always accepted without some guarantee of payment. But this does not mean that the demand deposits themselves do not function as money. What it does mean is that a check itself does not guarantee that the demand deposit exists. Hence additional proof or in-

Money is the asset in the economy that serves as a unit of account, in that prices are denominated in terms of this asset, and as a medium of exchange, in that this asset is exchanged for goods and services.

Demand deposits are balances in checking accounts payable on demand from commercial banks in the United States.

MONETARY POLICY IN 1987

Monetary policy and the behavior of the monetary aggregates was particularly interesting in 1986 and early 1987. In 1986 M_1 grew at a sizzling rate of 15.2 percent. The target rate set by the Fed for what it wanted to see in the growth of M_1 during 1986 was a range of 3 to 8 percent. The high rate of growth in M_1 caused many observers of financial markets to conclude that the Fed was pursuing a highly expansionary monetary policy. It also caused much concern that the Fed was allowing monetary policy to get out of control. However, the Fed believed that the usefulness of M_1 as a measure of the supply of money in the economy was becoming highly questionable. At the end of 1986 the Fed announced that it would no longer seek to control M_1 and would not announce targeted growth rates for M_1. However, the Fed continues to announce growth rates for M_2 and for more aggregate measures of the money stock (M_3). For 1987 the Fed announced that it would attempt to keep the growth rate of M_2 in a range of 5.5 to 8.5 percent.

Despite rapid growth in the money supply in 1986, the Fed was falling below its target range early in 1987. For example, during March of 1987, M_1 grew at a 3.3 percent rate while M_2 grew at a 1.7 percent rate. During the first quarter of 1987 M_2 grew at a 5.1 percent rate compared to its target range of 5.5 to 8.5 percent. When these money supply numbers were announced by the Fed in April, 1987, they created some surprise. The surprise was not simply that the growth rates had turned around so much, but that the Fed was then saying that the growth rates were important. For some months the Fed had been contending that the money supply numbers should no longer be given the significance they had been given early in the 1980s.

It is easy to be confused by all these money supply numbers and the various interpretations of them. One especially confusing part is an exceptional focus on short-term changes in these numbers. Week-to-week and even month-to-month changes in the money supply have little significance for the economy. Longer run changes in the supply of money can be important, and in this chapter and the next we want to find out why.

surance that the demand deposit exists and that the check will be paid upon demand is often required in order to purchase a commodity or service with a claim on a demand deposit. If the reliability of payment of deposits were seriously enough impaired, then they would cease to function as money. But in the United States today these are generally accepted as money or the medium of exchange. Figure 10–1 shows the magnitude of cash in the hands of the public and demand deposits at commercial banks in the United States from 1978 to 1985. Historically, the sum of these two assets was labeled M_1, representing the first possible definition of the quantity of money in the economy.

Recent Problems in Defining Money. In recent years a number of close substitutes for demand deposits at commercial banks have become available to the public. This is largely a result of relaxation of various federal regulations on depository institutions. These developments will be discussed in detail in Part IV. One of the recent substitutes for demand deposits has been money market mutual funds. A money market mutual fund functions like a demand deposit in that checks can be written on the account. The interest rate is determined by the earnings of the fund, and the balances of the fund are invested in a variety of short-term instruments. Other substitutes have also emerged to compete with demand deposits. These include **share drafts** offered by credit unions, which are essen-

Share drafts and **NOW accounts** refer to accounts offered by credit unions and savings and loans which operate very much like demand deposits.

tially demand deposits that pay interest, and similar types of accounts called **NOW** (Negotiated Order of Withdrawal) **accounts** offered by savings and loans.

The growth of these close substitutes for demand deposits caused the Federal Reserve to alter the definition of M_1. In February, 1980, the Federal Reserve started publishing data for an expanded definition of the supply of money that included transactions accounts at other depository institutions. These were called *other checkable deposits* and the new measure of M_1 was called M_{1b}. The traditional definition of the supply of money was then referred to as M_{1a}. However, after a few years, the Fed dropped the distinction and started calling the expanded measure of M_1 simply M_1. As a result, **M_1** now includes cash in the hands of the public, demand deposits at commercial banks, and other checkable deposits at nonbank depository institutions (as well as traveler's checks).

There has been a long-standing debate about whether the money supply should also include time and savings deposits at commercial banks. Some argue that people substitute back and forth between these assets so closely that it is unreasonable to exclude them from the definition of the money supply. When these are included in the money supply, along with cash and demand deposits, the money supply is referred to as M_2. In addition, the Fed reports M_3, which also includes money market funds. Figure 10–1 shows the recent behavior of currency, M_1 and M_3. Growth rates for M_1, M_2, and M_3 for mid-1985 are shown in Figure 11–4 in the next chapter.

M_1 includes cash in the hands of the public and bank reserves. M_2 includes M_1 plus time deposits at commercial banks.

FIGURE 10–1
Growth rates of monetary aggregates.

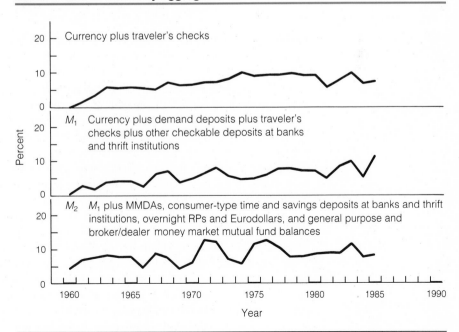

Source: *Federal Reserve Chart Book*, 1986.

The **monetary base or high-powered money** is the sum of bank reserves and cash in the hands of the public.

There is yet another possibility for defining the money supply which, in comparison to M_1 and M_2, involves less rather than more aggregation. This alternative definition of money is called **the monetary base or high-powered money.** The monetary base *(B)* consists of cash in the hands of the public and reserves held by institutions that offer transactions accounts. Reserves include deposits held with the Federal Reserve by institutions with transactions accounts and cash held in the vaults of commercial banks. The base is called *high-powered money* because more aggregate measures of the money supply, such as M_1 and M_2, are multiples of the base. Therefore, if the base expands, M_1 will expand by a multiple of the expansion in the base. The idea that the base represents money hinges on the argument that when transactions are made using demand deposits, the asset banks exchange is reserves. As a result, this high-powered money really underlies all other transactions. As long as there is a clearly definable, unique set of assets individuals and corporations use as a medium of exchange, the base is a less attractive definition of money. But in today's financial environment, with a multitude of special types of liquid assets that are close substitutes for demand deposits, the concept of a distinct money other than the base is becoming more nebulous.

While it is not obvious which definition of the supply of money is most appropriate, it is necessary to choose one in order to proceed. We will use M_1 in the remainder of this book. However, in the next chapter we will also discuss some of the difficulties created for monetary policy by the ambiguity surrounding the appropriate definition of money.

THE MULTIPLE EXPANSION PROCESS

In order to examine the links between reserves and M_1 we begin with a simple example of a banking system with no cash and only one type of deposit—demand deposits. We also assume that all institutions that offer these deposits are subject to reserve requirements. We call these institutions banks and assume that all banks always try to hold exactly the amount of reserves that are required. The required ratio of reserves to demand deposits is represented by *v,* and it is assumed to be equal to 20 percent. Since there is no cash in this simplified world, the monetary base is equal to reserves held by the banking system. Therefore, we can use reserves and the base interchangeably. We want to examine the impact on the total supply of demand deposits of an increase in reserves through an open market purchase of, say, $10,000.

Suppose that the initial purchase of Treasury securities by the Open Market Desk of the Federal Reserve Bank of New York is from a securities dealer named Jones & Henry. Jones & Henry has its demand deposit account with First Bank. When the transaction is made between Jones & Henry and the Federal Reserve Bank of New York, Jones & Henry has the payment made by the New York Fed credited to its demand deposit account at First Bank. Therefore, the demand deposit balances of First Bank increase by $10,000, and its reserves with Federal Reserve Bank of New York increase by an equal amount. The hypothetical balance sheet for First Bank before this transaction is:

Balance sheet of First Bank before open market purchase.

Assets		Liabilities	
Reserves	200,000	Deposits	1,000,000
Loans	800,000		

Before the Open Market purchase the actual reserves maintained by First Bank were exactly equal to the reserves required by the Fed—that is, 20 percent of its demand deposits. After the transaction the balance sheet looks as follows:

Balance sheet of First Bank after open market purchase.

Assets		Liabilities	
Reserves	210,000	Deposits	1,010,000
Loans	800,000		

Now First Bank has $8,000 in reserves above what the Fed requires, which can profitably be used to fund new loans.

Suppose that First Bank extends a new loan to someone who wants to purchase a car. The car purchaser receives a check for $8,000 from First Bank and presents it to the car dealer. The car dealer then deposits the check in his or her bank, say Second Bank. The accounts of First Bank will be altered so that loans are increased by $8,000 and reserves are decreased by the same amount:

Balance sheet of First Bank after extension of new loan.

Assets		Liabilities	
Reserves	202,000	Deposits	1,010,000
Loans	808,000		

Similarly, the books of Second Bank will show an increase in reserves of $8,000 and an increase in deposits of the same amount. Suppose Second Bank has exactly the required amount of reserves, 20 percent of deposits, before this transaction, as shown below:

Balance sheet of Second Bank before automobile purchase.

Assets		Liabilities	
Reserves	120,000	Deposits	600,000
Loans	480,000		

Once the car has been purchased, the $8,000 additions to reserves and deposits will be reflected as follows:

Balance sheet of Second Bank after the automobile purchase.

Assets		Liabilities	
Reserves	128,000	Deposits	608,000
Loans	480,000		

Second Bank is now in the same position First was when it received the initial $10,000 increase in reserves: it has excess reserves that it did not previously have. The magnitude of the excess reserves is smaller than for First; they now represent 80 percent of $8,000, or $6,400. Second Bank may now extend a new loan and generate new deposits of $6,400 for some other bank and still meet its reserve requirements exactly. Another bank will then receive $6,400 in new reserves and 80 percent of that will be in excess of that which is required. The process will continue almost indefinitely until all reserves held in the system become required.

As these reserves are distributed throughout the banking system and new loans are created, the total stock of deposits continually increases. Initially, when the Open Market Desk purchased Treasury securities from Jones & Henry, demand deposits increased by $10,000. With the loan made by First Bank, they increased another $8,000 and with the loan by Second, $6,400. As more loans are made, demand deposits will continue to increase by $5,120, then $4,096, and so on. This multiple expansion process will lead to a total increase in demand deposits that can be represented as follows:

$$\Delta D = \Delta B + (1-v)\Delta B + (1-v)^2\Delta B + (1-v)^3\Delta B + (1-v)^4\Delta B + \ldots , \quad (10\text{--}1)$$

where ΔD represents the total change in deposits and ΔB represents the initial change in the base or reserves. In this example, where the reserve requirement is 20 percent and the initial increase in reserves or the base is $10,000, this can be expressed:

$$\Delta D = 10,000 + 0.8 \times 10,000 + 0.8^2 \times 10,000 + 0.8^3 \times 10,000 + \ldots \quad (10\text{--}2)$$

Because Equation (10–1) is a convergent series (this means that the terms get smaller and smaller and converge, in this case, on zero), it is possible to rewrite it in a much simpler form so that it is relatively easy to calculate the total increase in deposits. The simpler expression is[3]

---

[3]Equation (10–3) can be derived as follows: Equation (10–1) indicates that:

$$D = B + (1-v) B + (1-v)^2 B + (1-v)^3 B + \ldots \quad (10\text{--}1)$$

Multiplying both sides of equation (10–1) by $(1-v)$ yields

$$(1-v) D = (1-v) B + (1-v)^2 B + (1-v)^3 B + \ldots \quad (10\text{--}1a)$$

Subtracting Equation (10–1a) from (10–1) yields:

$$D - (-v) D = B.$$

This can be simplified to read:

$$D v = B,$$

or

$$D = \frac{1}{v} B.$$

$$\Delta D = \frac{1}{v} \Delta B. \qquad (10\text{--}3)$$

In this example the total increase in deposits is five times the initial increase in reserves, or $50,000 = (1/0.2) \times 10,000$.

The multiple expansion
process refers to the
process by which new
bank reserves are
expanded into a multiple
increase in total deposits
outstanding.

The idea behind this **multiple expansion process** is that reserves place a constraint on the total volume of deposits banks can issue. As a result, as the volume of reserves goes up or down, the volume of deposits the system as a whole can support increases or decreases by a multiple of that amount. But the idea that the magnitude of the multiple expansion in deposits is equal to $1/v$ hinges on the assumption that all banks will increase deposits to the maximum extent and that there are no other leakages from the system. However, there definitely are leakages from this system in the real world.

LEAKAGES FROM THE MULTIPLE EXPANSION PROCESS

There are two principal types of leakages from this multiple expansion process which tend to reduce the magnitude of the ultimate expansion of deposits. These are leakages into cash and excess reserves. We will briefly analyze the effects of each type.

First, as described, the multiple expansion process assumes that people never choose to hold a portion of their new deposits in cash. Yet if people choose to convert part of each round of increase in deposits into cash, the expansion of the money supply will tend to be smaller than it otherwise would be. Each time people choose to hold cash rather than demand deposits, the reserves of the banking system decrease, and with this goes a decrease in the stock of deposits the reduced volume of reserves can support. Increases in the public's cash holdings entail decreases in reserves because the total stock of reserves is composed of cash held in bank vaults and deposits with the Fed. As a result, when the public exchanges demand deposits for cash, reserves decline and so must the total supply of money. We can summarize the effect of a leakage into cash with a modified form of Equation (10–3). To derive this equation we first need to decompose the change in the base (ΔB) into its component parts, a change in reserves (ΔR), and a change in cash held by the public (ΔC):

$$\Delta B = \Delta C + \Delta R. \qquad (10\text{--}4)$$

But we know that the actual change in reserves will be equal to the required reserve ratio v times the ultimate change in deposits, ΔD. In addition, if we postulate that the change in cash holdings will be some fraction c of the change in deposits, then by substituting these expressions in Equation (10–4), we have:

$$\Delta B = v\,\Delta D + c\,\Delta D. \qquad (10\text{--}5)$$

This can be further simplified to read:

$$\Delta B = (v + c)\,\Delta D. \qquad (10\text{--}6)$$

Next we can divide both sides by the sum of the required-reserve ratio and the cash-demand deposit ratio $(v + c)$, and we have an expression for the increase in deposits similar to Equation (10–3):

$$\Delta D = \frac{1}{(v + c)} \Delta B. \qquad (10–7)$$

The important difference is that the total expansion in deposits is now smaller than it was before c was introduced. If c is equal to 0.05, then in the example above deposits will expand by a multiple of 4 $[1/(0.20 + 0.05) = 1/(0.25)]$ rather than 5.

Another type of leakage takes place because banks choose to hold some excess reserves. In effect, some banks choose to hold more reserves than required as a cushion against a future deficiency. Banks will incur a penalty if they run short of reserves; hence, there is an incentive to avoid it. The nature and magnitude of this penalty depends upon the method the bank uses to cover its shortage of reserves. A bank that experiences a reserve deficiency has essentially three options. First, it can sell an interest-bearing asset. The cost in this case is the forgone yield on this asset. Second, it can borrow from the Federal Reserve. In this case, the cost includes the interest rate that must be paid to the Fed, known as the discount rate, plus the prospect that this increased borrowing may lead to closer supervision of the bank's activities. Repeated borrowing often leads to such increased attention, or at least there is a general belief that this is the case. Third, the bank can borrow from the federal funds market. In this instance, the cost is the yield that must be paid to obtain federal funds.

We represent the desired level of excess reserves as some proportion of total demand deposits. If we define e as the ratio of excess reserves to demand deposits, then the expansion process can be modified to incorporate excess reserves as follows:

$$\Delta D = \frac{1}{(v + e)} \Delta B. \qquad (10–8)$$

Again, as in Equation (10–7) where we examined the effect of a leakage into cash, the result of this leakage is that the multiple expansion process leads to a smaller volume of deposits than would be the case if banks held no excess reserves. If banks tend to hold, say, 1 percent of deposits in excess on average (and in the 1980s e was 1 percent or less), the magnitude of the multiple expansion in the example above would fall from 5 to $1/0.21 = 4.76$.

The **money supply function** is the relationship between the supply of money in the economy and the monetary base.

We can summarize this relationship between the base and the money supply with what we will call the **money supply function,** which simply says that the money supply represented by M_1 is determined by the product of the base and the money supply multiplier, where the money supply multiplier is, in turn, dependent upon the three ratios v, e, and c:

$$M_1 = B \, m(v, e, c). \qquad (10–8)$$

THE DEMAND FOR REAL MONEY BALANCES

The next step in our analysis of the link between monetary policy and interest rates is to develop an understanding of the demand for money. We will then be able to put money supply and money demand together and define the link between monetary policy and interest rates. We are actually interested in the demand for real money balances, rather than simply the demand for money. When we refer to money without qualification, we generally mean the nominal stock of money or money balances, without adjustment for inflation. By **real money balances** we mean the stock of money adjusted for the level of inflation. Using M_1 as our definition of money, the total nominal stock of money balances in the economy is simply M_1. But total real money balances are M_1/P, where P represents the aggregate price level. For example, the consumer price index in October, 1979, was 225.5, with a base of 100 in 1967. This means that during the interval from 1967 to October, 1979, consumer prices increased 125.5 percent. During October, 1979, M_1 was equal to 383.9. Real money balances were, therefore, 170.2 (383.9/2.255). This means that the money supply in October, 1979, was equal to 170.2 expressed in 1967 dollars. The absolute amount of the real money supply is not particularly meaningful. The usefulness is in the ability to compare real numbers for two time periods when they are expressed in prices defined at the same point in time.

Real versus nominal money balances distinguishes between the outstanding money stock adjusted for inflation and the money stock unadjusted for inflation, respectively.

To understand the demand for money is to understand why economic agents—that is, individuals and corporations—hold their wealth in money rather than other forms. The factors that determine this choice are not fundamentally different from those that determine the demand for any commodity one might consume. We think of the demand for any commodity as being determined by the level of income, the price of that commodity relative to the prices of other goods that may be complements or substitutes, and finally the tastes of individuals. Similar factors determine the demand for money.

SPECIFYING THE DEMAND FOR MONEY

The demand for money is the public's desired level of money balances as determined by interest rates, the level of income, and other relevant economic variables.

To specify the **demand for money** is to identify the variables that influence people's desire to hold money and define the nature of their impact on the demand for money. We will represent this relationship between money demand (M_d) and its determinants with a demand for money function. If we let X represent the set of variables that measure wealth and the relative rates of return on money and other forms of wealth, then we can express a demand function for nominal money balances as follows:

$$M_d = f(X). \tag{10-9}$$

The task at hand is to specify carefully the variables contained in X. We will identify three types of variables that influence the demand for real money balances. They are wealth or permanent income, the rates of return on alternatives to money, and the expected rate of inflation.

The first and possibly most important variable is the level of wealth, W. The basic decision involved in choosing a level of money is how to allocate wealth across various types of assets. As a result, the principal constraint on an individual's or the economy's decision about how much money to hold is the level of wealth. However, it is relatively impractical to try to measure the total stock of wealth for the society as a whole, as some components of wealth do not have readily defined market values. This is particularly true of human capital. But we can think of wealth as simply a capitalized income stream. Hence we can use income as a proxy for wealth, if we find it easier to actually measure income.

In order to make use of income as a proxy for wealth we cannot simply substitute the level of nominal income, measured at a particular point in time, for the level of wealth of the economy at that time. Wealth is the discounted value of expected future income, and measured income in any one period may well be above or below the expected level of long-run future income. Instead, we substitute what is called **permanent income.** Milton Friedman popularized the concept of permanent income as a basis for explaining aggregate consumption of all commodities, as well as the demand for money. Friedman's concept states that permanent income is the level of long-run income people expect they will average in the future. We will represent nominal permanent income with the symbol Y'.

Permanent income is the long-run expected or equilibrium level of income in the economy.

The next important determinant of the money demand function is the relative rate of return on alternatives to money as ways of holding wealth. By *relative rate of return* we mean the return on some other asset, such as equities, relative to the return on money. The difficulty inherent in specifying these relative rates of return is that we cannot directly observe the rate of return on money. In the United States the government has long fixed the explicit nominal rate of return on money at zero by paying no interest on cash and by prohibiting the payment of interest on demand deposits. While a large portion of demand deposits now earn a market interest rate, cash still earns a nominal rate of return of zero, but this by no means implies that the actual return on money is zero. In fact, if people received no benefit or return from holding money, they would not hold it. Instead, the return on money is by and large a service flow. That is, the maintenance of money balances eases the cost of buying and selling goods and services or executing transactions. If we had to convert some kind of bond or equity into the medium of exchange, money, every time a purchase of goods or services was to be made, we would incur substantial costs of transacting. These include the costs imposed by the market of actually selling the security as well as the cost of expending our time and effort on making the transaction. As technology has become more sophisticated, many of these costs have been reduced, but as long as such transaction costs exist, money will yield a service flow and we will hold positive balances of it. Unfortunately, practical problems of measuring this return on money still remain. To circumvent these problems it is generally assumed that the value of the services that money provides remains constant or, at least, is independent of changes in yields on other forms of wealth.

The other aspect of relative return is the expected rate of return on other forms of wealth. We might set out to specify and measure each of the rates of return on distinct assets for inclusion in the money demand function. Other important items are the expected rate of return on equities, r_e, and the expected rate of return on bonds, r_b. As either of these rates of return is perceived to increase, the opportunity cost of handling money increases and the demand for money declines.

The final element affecting the return on money is the rate of inflation. Inflation penalizes those who hold their wealth in money, for the value of money holdings declines directly with the rate of inflation. Moreover, people's expectations of the future rate of inflation influence the rate of return they anticipate from holding money. Therefore, it is the expected rate of inflation, P^e, that is normally included in the money demand function. As the expected rate of inflation increases, the demand for money decreases.

So we can summarize the money demand function as follows:

$$M_d = f[\overset{+}{Y'}, \overset{-}{P^e}, \overset{-}{r_e}, \overset{-}{r_b}]. \qquad (10\text{--}10)$$

The positive or negative sign over each variable influencing money demand indicates whether money demand increases $(+)$ or decreases $(-)$ as the variable in question increases.

REAL VERSUS NOMINAL MONEY DEMAND

Real versus nominal money demand refers to the demand for real versus nominal money balances.

Our purpose is to define the demand for real money balances. So far we have defined the demand for nominal money balances. To move from nominal to real demand we can start by trying to simplify Equation (10–10). The first ambiguity is whether the appropriate rates of return for equities and bonds are real or nominal returns. If the rates of return are nominal, then the explicit introduction of the expected rate of inflation is unnecessary, because the market's estimate of the expected inflation rate is contained in the nominal interest rate. If we include nominal interest rates in the demand function, this incorporates a measure of expected inflation, and it also handles the difficult problem of measuring the expected inflation rate. The best available measure is the one provided by the market and included in the nominal interest rate. Henceforth, the interest rates in the money demand function should be thought of as nominal rates.

Another simplification often used in dealing with money demand is to collapse the rates of return on bonds and equities into a single interest rate. The only substantial justification is that there may not be enough differences in the returns of these types of wealth to warrant dealing with them separately, and in long-run equilibrium this should be true. Therefore, if we represent the nominal interest rate as r, the simplified money demand function can be written:

$$M_d = f(Y', r). \qquad (10\text{--}11)$$

Now we can distinguish between the demand for money in real and in nominal terms. In Equations (10–10) and (10–11) money demand is measured in nominal rather than real dollars: it is not adjusted for inflation. The conversion from nominal money demand to real money demand should involve no change in the determinants of the demand function. The same functional relationship should hold with nominal changed to real money and income. This presumes that people do not alter their behavior in any significant way if the unit of measurement in which their transactions take place is altered. For example, suppose we double the number of dollars required to make every purchase and simultaneously double the level of total income in the economy. The effect should be to double the demand for money. An increase of a smaller or lesser amount would constitute a substantive change in behavior, yet the only change that has taken place is a change in the unit of measurement. When people's money demand can be expressed in this way, they are said to be free of **money illusion.**

Money illusion occurs when people are fooled into believing their real purchasing power changes when prices and income increase or decrease by the same relative amounts.

To see the impact of a change in the price level on money demand, we could divide the level of nominal permanent income Y' by the price level P. The resulting income variable is now real permanent income, or y'. Assuming that this increases money demand by the same proportional amount it reduces Y', then we should simultaneously multiply the money demand function by P in order to offset the effect of dividing Y' by P. Hence, we should be able to write the money demand function as follows, for any value of P:

$$M_d = P f(y', r). \tag{10-12}$$

Alternatively, we can move the P that multiplies the function to the left-hand side of the equation:

FIGURE 10–2
The demand for nominal money balances. The slope of the two money-demand curves shows that money demand is negatively related to the interest rate. The shift in the curve from $M_d(y_1, r)$ to $Md(y_2, r)$ illustrates that money demand is positively related to permanent income.

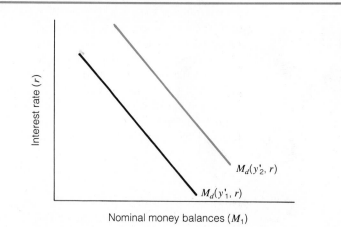

$$M_d/P = f(Y',r). \qquad (10\text{--}13)$$

This says the demand for real money balances depends on permanent income, in real terms, and the nominal interest rate, according to a function independent of changes in P.

We can illustrate this money demand function with a diagram as in Figure 10–2. The vertical axis in the figure measures the nominal interest rate r, while the horizontal axis measures the nominal quantity of money demanded. The relationship between these variables is illustrated by the slopes of lines labeled M_{d1} and M_{d2}. These lines are drawn for two distinct values of y': y'_1 and y'_2. Because increases in permanent income increase the demand for money, higher values of y' correspond to lines drawn further to the right. For example, line M_{d2} represents the quantity of money demanded at different levels of the nominal interest rate if permanent income is y'_2.

INTEREST RATE DETERMINATION

We need to consolidate our analyses of money supply and money demand in order to see how monetary policy influences interest rates. There are three separate effects of monetary policy on interest rates. They can be identified as follows:

1. **Liquidity effect.** The initial decrease in interest rates caused by an increase in the money supply.
2. **Income effect.** The tendency for the initial interest rate decrease to be moderated by the effect of increased income on money demand.
3. **Price anticipations effect.** The increase in nominal interest rates that results as money supply changes cause the market to expect higher rates of inflation.

The **liquidity effect** is the initial decrease in interest rates caused by an increase in the money supply.

The **income effect** is the tendency for the initial interest rate decrease to be moderated by the effect of increased income on money demand.

The **price anticipations effect** is the increase in nominal interest rates that results as money supply changes cause the market to expect higher rates of inflation.

LIQUIDITY AND INCOME EFFECTS

In order to see how these effects work we need to return to the money supply and money demand functions. The money supply function indicated that the quantity of money supplied is determined by the product of the monetary base (B) and the money supply multiplier (m):

$$M_s = Bm.$$

The simplest version of the money demand function indicates that the nominal quantity of money demanded is dependent on the level of permanent income and the nominal interest rate. We represented this equation as follows:

$$M_d = F(Y', r).$$

We can see directly from the money demand function that money demand is dependent upon the interest rate. Moreover, we know that the relationship is negative, so, as the interest rate increases, the quantity of money demanded decreases.

On the other hand, it is not obvious from the money supply equation how nominal interest rates affect the quantity of money supplied. To determine this relationship we must examine the effect of changes in nominal interest rates on the monetary base and the money supply multiplier. The base will increase with nominal interest rates because, with the discount rate charged by the Fed for loans to banks unchanged, higher nominal interest rates will encourage banks to borrow more from the Federal Reserve, leading to an increase in reserves and the base. Similarly, a higher nominal interest rate will encourage banks to lower their excess reserves, which will lead to an increase in the money supply multiplier and the money supply. We therefore conclude that the quantity of money supplied is positively affected by the level of the nominal interest rate.

We can represent the relationships between the nominal interest rate and the quantities of money supplied and demanded in Figure 10–3. The vertical axis in the figure measures the nominal interest rate, while the horizontal axis measures the quantity of money. The downward sloping curve represents the money demand function, while the upward sloping curve represents the money supply function. This diagram shows how the equilibrium interest rate is deterimined at the point of intersection between the supply-and-demand curves for money. The figure illustrates that, for a given level of permanent income, there is a unique interest rate that equates the quantity of money demanded with the quantity of money supplied.

Figure 10–4 can be used to illustrate the liquidity effect of changes in monetary policy on the interest rate, holding the level of income constant. If the Federal Reserve purchases securities in the market, it leads to an increase in reserves

FIGURE 10–3
Equilibrium between money supply and money demand. The figure shows that there is a unique interest rate at which money supply is equal to money demand.

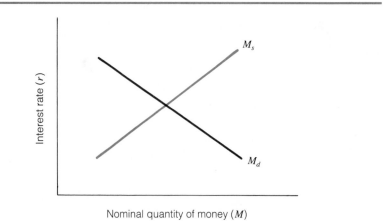

FIGURE 10-4
Effect of an increase in the base on interest rates. As the base increases, the
money supply curve shifts to the right causing interest rates to decline.

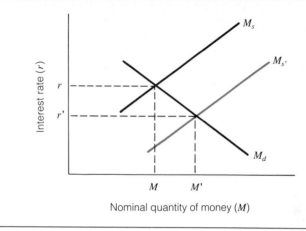

and the base, and this shifts the money supply function to the right, which increases M_s to M_s' in Figure 10–4. In order to achieve a new equilibrium so that the quantity of money demanded is equal to the new larger supply of money in the economy, something in the system has to change. If we hold income constant and the quantity of money demanded is negatively related to the level of the interest rate, then the interest rate will fall until a new equilibrium is achieved. The new and lower equilibrium level of the interest rate is represented as r' in Figure 10–4. Only at the lower interest rate is the quantity of money supplied equal to the quantity demanded.

You might get the impression that the sole function of the rate of interest is to influence the money supply-and-demand functions, but we know that the interest rate serves a much broader role in the economy. Chapter 2 explained that the real interest rate is the price that allocates resources across time, and, in equilibrium, it is the price that equilibrates both desired saving and investment and desired lending and borrowing. To relate the analysis of money supply and money demand to the analysis of the determinants of the real interest rate we need to examine the effect of changes in the supply of money on the market for borrowing and lending or the loanable funds market.

In the loanable funds market we treat the supply of money as a component of the supply of loanable funds or as a source of lending. This means that increases in the volume of money in the economy represent increases in borrowing and lending. As the quantity of money supplied is increased, this represents new lending in the economy as a whole. Hence, we can think of this as shifting the curve showing the total amount of lending at each level of the real interest rate to the right. This shift is illustrated in Figure 10–5. The supply curve for loanable funds

FIGURE 10–5
The effect of an increase in the money supply on the loanable funds market. An increase in the base causes the supply of loanable funds (lending) to increase, which leads to a reduction in interest rates.

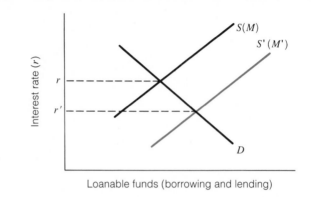

labeled s indicates the supply of funds in the market or the total desired amount of lending at each level of the real interest rate. A part of this desired lending is based on a given level of the money supply, M. If the Federal Reserve increases the money supply to a higher level, say, M', this causes the supply curve to shift to the right. This, in turn, will cause a decrease in the level of the real rate of interest. The new equilibrium is reached where the desired level of lending is equal to the desired level of borrowing, represented by the curve labeled D at r'.

The equilibrium rate of interest in the loanable funds market is the same as that which creates an equilibrium between money supply and money demand. The distinction between the analyses is that in the money supply-and-demand analysis we are implicitly assuming other factors that affect desired borrowing and lending remain unchanged, while when we examine loanable funds, we are simply not according money supply and money demand any special significance. But a crucial factor is held constant in each analysis: with both approaches the equilibrium interest rate is determined with the level of nominal income held constant. If we also take into account the affect of interest rates on income and then, in turn, the effect of income on money demand, we can understand the income effect of monetary policy on interest rates.

Under the income effect, the initial decrease in interest rates caused by the increase in the money supply makes income increase. The increase in income causes the money demand curve to shift back to the left, as illustrated in Figure 10–6. This in turn tends to moderate the initial decrease in interest rates caused by the increase in the money supply. Hence, the income effect tends to work in the opposite direction of the liquidity effect.

WHICH INTEREST RATES ARE WE TALKING ABOUT?

So far the discussion has been devoted to explaining the liquidity and income effects of monetary policy on interest rates. But even after we understand the logic involved, it is sometimes difficult to pin down exactly what interest rate or rates we are talking about in the real world. It is therefore important to relate this discussion to the actual conduct of monetary policy and to observed behavior of both short- and long-term interest rates.

There are vast numbers of short-term interest rates, each one applying to a particular type of security or debt contract. Generally, when we speak of the short-term interest rate we mean all of these rates, because we think of a common interest rate that underlies them all. The factors unique to each security account for all the differences between these rates.

Despite the generality of the concept of a short-term interest rate, the federal funds rate is of paramount practical importance both because it has long been the focus of monetary policy and it represents one of the shortest term rates generally available in the market. The **federal funds rate** is the rate paid for loans that generally have a maturity of one day and are made between financial institutions. When the Federal Reserve engages in open market operations, it directly affects this interest rate. Expansionary open market operations immediately increase the supply of federal funds and drive down the federal funds rate. Rates on financial contracts with longer maturities are closely linked to the federal funds rate. The

The **federal funds rate** is the rate paid for loans that generally have a maturity of one day and are made between financial institutions.

FIGURE 10–6

The liquidity and income effects of money on interest rates. The figure illustrates that the initial liquidity effect of an increase in the money supply is to reduce interest rates from r_1 to r_1'. The income effect moderates this decline and the interest rate settles at r_2.

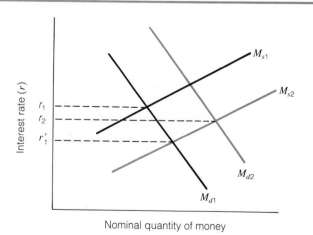

process of substitution between alternative financial contracts, if there is a profitable opportunity to do so, ensures this. If there are only limited barriers to substitution between financial instruments, then the federal funds rate cannot be driven down and held there without the rates on other financial instruments following a similar course. So, as the Federal Reserve puts pressure directly on the federal funds rate, this pressure soon affects other short-term rates as well, such as Treasury bill rates, commercial paper rates, and even prime interest rates. Only if the markets for these other securities are segmented, such that little substitution takes place between markets, would the interest rates move in diverse directions.

In order to link changes in monetary policy to changes in long-term interest rates we have to return to the three theories of the term structure of interest rates developed in Chapter 8. The *unbiased expectations theory* argues that long-term interest rates are equal to the geometric average of the market's expectation of future short-term rates. On the other hand, the *segmentation theory* argues that each maturity represents a separate market, and the interest rate prevailing for that maturity is the rate that equates desired borrowing with desired lending at that maturity. In the segmentation theory long-term rates are unrelated to the market's expectations of future short-term rates. The *preferred habitat theory* blends the two theories and implies that long-term rates represent the sum of the market's expectation of future short-term rates and a premium market participants demand as compensation for investing with a maturity longer or shorter than they prefer.

These theories have different implications for the Federal Reserve's ability to influence long-term rates. First, consider the segmentation theory. If each maturity represents a distinct market, then actions taken by the Federal Reserve that influence short-term interest rates will have no effect on long-term rates. Long-term rates will be determined solely by the demand and supply for long-term funds. Only if the Federal Reserve directly entered the long-term market would it have any effect on the long-term interest rate.

On the other hand, if the unbiased expectations theory is correct, then changes in expected future short-term interest rates would directly affect current long-term interest rates. As a result, Federal Reserve actions that affect today's short-term interest rate must be perceived as a long-term change. It must be perceived as permanent. If the market expects that a change in short-term rates will be reversed some months hence, then the effect on long-term rates will be slight. Because the long-term rate represents an average of a long period of expected short-term rates, a change in expectations for even a year or two will have only a limited effect. This does not mean that even relatively short-lived, high, short-term rates will have no effect on the economy, but the effect on long-term interest rates will be limited.

The **liquidity premium** refers to the compensation demanded by investors to invest in a security with a maturity other than that which is their desired holding period.

Essentially the same argument applies if the preferred habitat theory is correct, but the argument becomes less and less relevant as the **liquidity premiums** become larger. If liquidity premiums exist but are relatively small, then long-term rates are largely determined by expectations of future short-term rates. Changes in these expectations will be the principal determinants of changes in the long-term rates. As liquidity premiums become larger, however, they begin to dominate the effect of expectations. If expectations become totally irrelevant, then we return to the segmentation theory, where monetary policy can affect long-term rates only if the Federal Reserve directly buys and sells long-term securities. The bottom line is that if liquidity premiums are significant determinants of long-term rates and if they change through time, then the link between short-term and long-term rates is not very well defined.

The idea that long-term rates are, at least in part, reflections of the market's expectations of future short-term rates suggests that short-term rates ought to be more volatile than long-term rates. For, while short-term rates may go up or down, only if the market expects that these rates will go up (or down) and stay there, will the long-term rate change by a comparable amount. This prediction about the relative volatility of rates has been confirmed by experience. For example, Figure 8–1 shows the yield curves that existed near the interest rate peak of the 1974 recession and approximately 9 months later in 1975, when rates had fallen considerably. The figure illustrates that short-term rates changed by quite large amounts relative to long-term rates. This type of pattern has been common to all business cycles in contemporary U.S. history. Moreover, this pattern emphasizes that it is more difficult for the Federal Reserve to alter long-term rates than short-term rates, because long-term rates reflect the market's expectations about the Federal Reserve's actions over an extended period.

THE PRICE ANTICIPATIONS EFFECT

As we have examined the effect of changes in the supply of money on interest rates, we have made the implicit assumption that the inflation rate in the economy remains constant. That is, we have assumed there is no link between monetary policy and inflation. This is a terribly unrealistic assumption: there is a link between monetary policy and inflation, so now is the time to drop this assumption. Chapter 6 showed that nominal rates increase with increases in the expected rate of inflation. Therefore, if there is a positive link between monetary policy and inflation, such that increases in the supply of money lead to inflation, then it should also be true that increases in the supply of money will cause interest rates to increase as the market's expectations of inflation increase. This link between monetary policy and interest rates is the third effect described above, the price anticipations effect.

Monetary policy is argued to have a strong influence in determining prices and income. If the economy is near capacity or full employment, then high rates of change in the money supply generate expectations of inflation. These expectations of inflation increase nominal interest rates. Furthermore, if markets are efficient in incorporating information about future inflation rates, nominal interest rates rapidly and efficiently respond to high rates of growth in the money supply by incorporating the expected inflation rate that the money supply implies. This logic leads to the conclusion that increases in the money supply tend to increase, rather than decrease, observed interest rates.

The historical evidence on the link between growth in the money supply and inflation documents a fairly strong correlation between the two. The evidence is basically of two types. One is the history of parallel movements in the money supply and inflation in individual countries, including the United States. This is illustrated in Figure 10–7, which presents a long time series of data on the level of M_1 and the level of consumer prices in the United States. Over long periods of time these two data series move quite closely together. The second type of evidence is the tendency for inflation rates and growth rates in the money supply to be highly correlated across countries. When a country experiences a high rate of inflation, it almost always experiences a high rate of growth in its domestic money supply, too. This is illustrated in Figure 10–8, which shows how historical average inflation rates and growth rates in domestic money supply vary across countries. The observations in the figure generally plot upward to the right, indicating that inflation and high growth in the supply of money go hand in hand. An important caveat about this evidence should be taken into account. Evidence on a close correlation between inflation and money supply changes does not necessarily indicate that large changes in the supply of money cause inflation. There may be some other cause of inflation that also happens to be highly correlated with money supply changes. We need to be careful about inferring causation from high correlation. We will look a little more closely at the nature of the link between monetary policy and inflation in the next chapter.

You may have noticed a confusing point about the three effects of monetary policy on interest rates. The liquidity effect implies that increases in the money

FIGURE 10–7
Inflation and money growth.

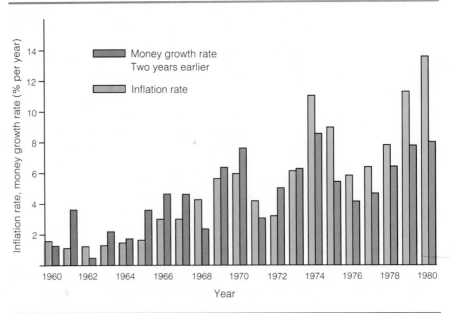

Source: *Economic Report of the President.*

FIGURE 10–8
Inflation and money growth rates in Latin America: 1974–1984.

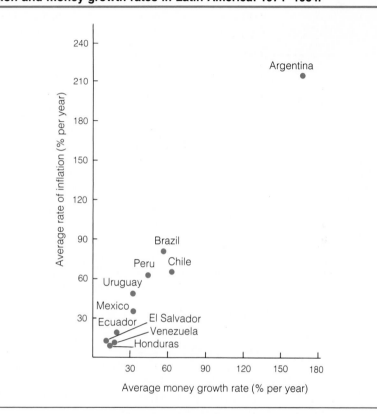

Source: *International Financial Statistics; Economic Report of the President.*

supply cause interest rates to decline. The other two effects indicate that increases in the money supply cause interest rates to increase. If you are rather perplexed about which of the three effects described above really explains how interest rates respond to monetary policy, you are not alone. The fact that these distinct effects lead to opposite predictions about the direction of the link between monetary policy and interest rates is one of the major causes of a long standing debate about how monetary policy should be conducted. Critics of U.S. monetary policy have often charged that the Federal Reserve cannot separate these three effects and therefore often gets confused about the impact of its policy decisions on the economy. Some critics argue that the Fed would be best served if it simply concentrated on trying to control the growth of money supply and did not worry about trying to influence interest rates or other prices of assets. This debate has gone on for some time and will probably continue in the future. We will take up this very important debate for understanding the operation of a modern economy in the next chapter.

SUMMARY

In this chapter we examined the links between monetary policy and interest rates, specifically focusing on how the Federal Reserve regulates the supply of money in the economy, how the demand for money is determined, and how the demand and supply for money interact to influence market interest rates. This chapter should be viewed in context with Chapter 11, which focuses on the debate about how monetary policy ought to be conducted.

We began with a brief overview of the structure of the Federal Reserve system and the structure of power within the Fed. The Federal Open Market Committee is the most important decision-making entity within the Federal Reserve System because it decides on the volume of open market operations. Open market operations refer to the purchases and sales of Treasury securities by the Fed. When the Fed purchases (sells) securities, it increases (decreases) the volume of reserves in the banking system. This constitutes an increase in the monetary base which is equal to the sum of reserves and currency in the economy.

Next we learned that the total volume of reserves places a constraint on the total volume of deposits in the system or on the supply of money. Because reserves must be held at a fixed percentage of deposits, any increase or decrease in the volume of reserves increases or decreases the volume of deposits financial intermediaries can support. As a result, whenever reserves increase, there is a multiple expansion in the volume of total deposits and therefore in the supply of money. The magnitude of this expansion is determined by the amount of the required reserve ratio, the ratio of cash to demand deposits, and the desired excess reserve ratio. These variables determine the money supply multiplier, and the money supply can be expressed as a product of the monetary base and the money supply multiplier. This relationship shows how actions taken by the Federal Reserve influence the total supply of money.

The idea behind the demand for money is that there is a stable and predictable relationship between the quantity of money people choose to hold and other important variables in the economy. The demand for money is principally dependent upon the level of permanent income and the nominal interest rate. We also found it was important to distinguish between nominal and real money balances. The demand for real money balances is dependent on real permanent income in the same way that the demand for nominal money balances is dependent upon nominal permanent income.

Finally, we were able to identify the ways monetary policy influences interest rates by combining our analyses of money supply and money demand. There are three effects of changes in the supply of money on market interest rates. The liquidity effect results from the fact that demand for money is negatively related to the level of interest rates. Therefore, as the supply of money is increased, interest rates must fall to maintain equilibrium between the demand and supply for money. The second effect, the income effect, refers to the fact that increases in income caused by increases in the money supply cause the demand for money to increase. This, in turn, causes interest rates to fall, mitigating the initial liquidity effect. Finally, the price anticipations effect pertains to the link between increases in the money supply and inflation. As increases in the money supply generate expectations of inflation, these expectations cause nominal interest rates to increase. Hence, increases in the supply of money can cause interest rates either to rise or fall, depending on the strength of the connection between money supply changes and inflation expectations.

QUESTIONS

1. What serves as money in the contemporary U.S. economy? Why was it necessary to change the definition of money in the late 1970s?
2. What is the Open Market Committee and what is its purpose? Why has it been described as the most important decision-making body within the Federal Reserve System?
3. Some argue that the Federal Reserve is virtually an arm of the executive branch of government; others argue it is independent. Evaluate the merits of each position.
4. Suppose there are no leakages in the multiple expansion process. Why is the multiplier then equal to $1/v$? How do leakages into cash and excess reserves influence the multiplier?
5. Suppose the Federal Reserve Bank of New York sells $100 million worth of Treasury securities. Trace trhe impact of this transaction through the banking system if reserve requirements are 15 percent.
6. What is the monetary base, and why is it called *high-powered money?* Suppose you thought that the money supply multiplier for M_1 would vary between 2.8 and 3.2 over the next year. You also expected you could control the rate of growth of the base within a margin of error of 10 percent. (That is, if you tried to make the base grow at a rate of 10 percent, the actual growth rate could vary between 9 and 11 percent.) Suppose you attempted to set the growth rate for the base at 6 percent, 10 percent and 14 percent. What ranges in the growth rates of M_1 would you expect would occur?
7. What is permanent income? Why is it important in determining the demand for money?
8. What is the difference between the demand for real as opposed to nominal money balances? How would the demand for money change if both nominal income and prices increase by 10 percent, assuming market participants suffer from money illusion? How might the presence of money illusion affect the conduct of monetary policy?
9. Distinguish between the income effect and the liquidity effect. Why do they cause interest rates to change in opposite directions?
10. Some people argue that an expansionary monetary policy means low interest rates, and others argue that an expansionary monetary policy means high interest rates. How can you reconcile these two views?
11. What kind of evidence is there that links money supply changes and inflation rates? Does this evidence imply that high rates of growth in the supply of money *cause* inflation?

REFERENCES

Friedman, Milton. *A Theory of the Consumption Function*, Princeton, N.J.: Princeton University Press, 1957.

———. "The Quantity Theory of Money: A Restatement," in Milton Friedman (ed.), *Studies in the Quantity Theory of Money*, Chicago: University of Chicago Press, 1956.

Lombra, Raymond E. "Reflections on Burns's Reflections," *Journal of Money, Credit and Banking*, (February 1980), pp. 94–105.

Poole, William. "Burnesian Monetary Policy: Eight Years of Progress?" *Journal of Finance* (May 1979), pp. 473–84.

Safire, William. *Before the Fall*, New York: Doubleday, 1975.

11

*T*HE MONETARY POLICY DEBATE

We have learned about the various ways in which changes in the money supply can influence interest rates. In this chapter we will focus on how the Fed actually conducts monetary policy as well as how people believe it should conduct monetary policy. Unfortunately, there is no commonly accepted program for conducting monetary policy. Instead, there is an ongoing debate about how monetary policy ought to be conducted. The number of theories or schemes for how to conduct monetary policy is almost unlimited.

First we will briefly describe the nature of the choices facing the Fed regarding the conduct of monetary policy, then we will review the conduct of monetary policy in recent years. Next we will explore the implications of efficient financial markets for the conduct of monetary policy and examine some recent evidence on the response of prices in various financial markets to money supply changes. Then we will turn our attention to the debate about how monetary policy should be conducted by examining one of the most vehement and long-standing criticisms of U.S. monetary policy in recent years—the monetarist critique. Finally, we will briefly look at how monetary policy is affected by the international monetary system, specifically by whether a country has fixed or floating exchange rates. ■

A *BRIEF HISTORY OF RECENT MONETARY POLICY*

INTEREST RATES VERSUS AGGREGATES AS TARGETS OF MONETARY POLICY

The contemporary debate about monetary policy focuses on what should be the proper target for monetary policy and, if that target is the rate of growth in the money supply, then how the supply should be controlled. One view of how to control the money supply is to use the analysis of the link between the monetary base (or some other measure of bank reserves) and the money supply developed in Chapter 10. From this view the Federal Reserve would conduct open market operations in a manner that leads to a desired change in the supply of money by altering the monetary base at a certain rate based on an estimate of what the money supply multiplier will be. The problem is that if the multiplier changes, it will alter the change in the base needed to achieve a desired rate of change in the supply of money. As long as the money supply multiplier remains constant, if the Fed wants the money supply to change by, say, 6 percent, it has to increase the base by 6 percent. Therefore, the Fed must try to estimate what the multiplier is likely to be and then try to change the base by an amount that leads to the desired increase in the money supply. The problem of forecasting the money supply multiplier is not a simple one. As a result of this volatility and other problems involved in directly controlling reserves, the Fed can never precisely control the supply of money. So the question is, can the Fed achieve control of the money supply within some reasonable margin of error?

Throughout its history the Federal Reserve has been reluctant to try to control the money supply in the manner described above. It has had two basic objections to the suggestion that it should try to control reserves directly.[1] The first, and probably less serious in the long run, is that it is difficult to forecast the multiplier and to know what reserves and the money supply really are from week to week. Hence, there are real, practical difficulties involved in trying to directly control reserves in the very short run. Critics have argued that many of these difficulties were created by the Fed for itself and they should not stand in the way of proper long-run control of the money supply.[2] The second objection is that by attempting to control reserves the Fed will sacrifice control over short-term interest rates and cause serious problems in financial markets. The critics respond that it is generally impossible to control both interest rates and reserves simultaneously; therefore, if the Fed really seeks to control interest rates, it loses control of the supply of money.

---

[1] For a detailed statement and defense of the Fed's long-held position on this issue, see Alan Holmes, "Operational Constraints on Stabilization of Money Supply Growth," in *Controlling the Monetary Aggregates,* Federal Reserve Bank of Boston, (June 1979), pp. 65–77.

[2] One of the road blocks which the Fed allegedly set in its own path is lagged-reserve accounting, where reserve requirements today are based on deposit balances maintained in a prior period. This policy was abandoned in the early 1980s.

To see what is involved in this argument about interest rates it is important to briefly examine how the Fed has operated in recent years. For some time the Federal Reserve has conducted its policy by trying to control the interest rate on federal funds.[3] It has done this by standing ready to conduct open market operations—that is, buying or selling Treasury securities that increase or decrease reserves—and thereby to affect the supply of federal funds directly and consequently the federal funds rate. If the Open Market Desk at the Federal Reserve Bank of New York observed that the federal funds rate started to rise above the target set by the Open Market Committee, then it would buy securities or supply reserves to the market in order to drive the funds rate back down. This is illustrated in Figure 11–1. The figure shows a band within which the federal funds rate is allowed to vary. If the funds rate approaches the upper range of this band, the Fed interevenes in the market to buy federal funds or Treasury bills and drive down the rate. If the funds rate approaches the lower band of the range, then the Fed sells federal funds to drive the rate up. In this way the Fed has tried to keep the funds rate very close to its stated target or within a target range. It has always been difficult to measure directly how successful this policy has been, because when it becomes difficult to maintain a given target rate, it is always possible to change the target. Because the Fed has chosen its federal funds target based on a long-run range for growth in the money supply, it was always possible to try to justify a change in the target. In any event, the target has never been explicitly stated ahead of time; rather, the target always had to be inferred from watching to see what interest rate the Fed tried to maintain.

FIGURE 11–1
Monetary policy target of band around federal funds rate.

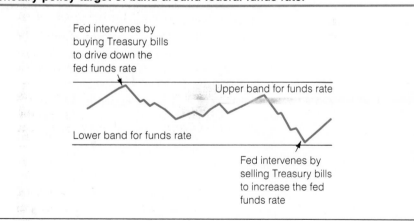

Fed intervenes by buying Treasury bills to drive down the fed funds rate

Upper band for funds rate

Lower band for funds rate

Fed intervenes by selling Treasury bills to increase the fed funds rate

---

[3]For a critical review of the Fed's conduct of monetary policy prior to October, 1979, see William Poole, "Burnesian Monetary Policy: Eight Years of Progress?" *Journal of Finance,* (May 1979), pp. 473–84.

But the result of this method of operation is that reserves will increase or decrease by whatever amount is necessary to achieve the desired control of the federal funds rate. Depending upon how the federal funds rate target is chosen, this may lead to large increases or decreases in the supply of money. Indeed, a major criticism of Federal Reserve policy in recent years is that it has allowed the money supply to grow at a high rate when the economy is in a boom and has permitted its growth rate to decline when the economy is in a recession. Critics contend that if the Federal Reserve would follow a policy of more direct control of reserves, rather than interest rates, the problem could be avoided.

In one form or another, this debate about monetary policy has been going on throughout the life of the Federal Reserve. To appreciate the significance of the issue it is useful to review the major episodes in the history of Federal Reserve policy.

FEDERAL RESERVE POLICY UNTIL THE EARLY 1950s

The principal powers given to the Federal Reserve upon its creation were the ability to extend loans to member commercial banks, the ability to buy and sell government securities, and the power to compel member banks to hold reserves. As it has turned out, probably the most important result of the Federal Reserve Act is that a central bank was created and empowered to control the money supply through its control of bank reserves. Yet at the outset, the Federal Reserve's perception of its purpose was not to control the supply of money. Instead, it was to provide what has been referred to as an "elastic currency." This means it was designed to prevent liquidity crises like those that plagued the U.S. banking system before the Fed was created. It was not wholly successful, however, as the largest such crisis in the history of the U.S. occurred in the 1930s, after the Fed had been in operation for some 16 years.

The **real bills doctrine** refers to the theory that money and credit should be made available by the Fed to provide for the needs of trade and commerce rather than to maintain stable prices or pursue some other social objective.

The idea of ensuring an elastic currency essentially meant that money and credit would be available to provide for the needs of trade and commerce rather than to maintain stable prices or pursue some other social purpose. This is known as the **real bills doctrine.**[4] The essence of the real bills doctrine incorporated two principles. The first was that as the economy expanded, the Federal Reserve's function was to ensure that enough money and credit were available so as not to hamper that expansion. The second was that the Fed was to discipline bankers so they did not engage in or finance what was judged excessive speculation. If the economy contracted, then money and credit should contract with it. The real bills doctrine meant that the Federal Reserve should assume a passive role as far as the money supply itself was concerned. In this view the money supply, or its rate of growth, was a by-product of economic events. This view implied that the Federal

---

[4]See Robert Craig West, *Banking Reform and the Federal Reserve, 1863–1923,* Ithaca, N.Y.: Cornell University Press, 1974, for an extensive discussion of the real bills doctrine and its role in the development of the Federal Reserve System.

Reserve should allow the money supply to pursue whatever course the economy dictated. As long as the Federal Reserve made loans and reserves available to banks to guarantee their liquidity, it was fulfilling its principal purpose.

The debate about the real bills doctrine dates back to the first few decades the Fed existed. Prior to the Great Depression of 1929, there was a struggle for power between the Board of Governors of the System, located in Washington, and the 12 regional Federal Reserve Banks spread throughout the country. This power struggle partly reflected a difference of opinion as to exactly what the purpose of the System was. Most of the district bank presidents believed that the Federal Reserve was to function as a banker's bank. They espoused the real bills doctrine. But throughout those years, they were often dominated by the forceful president of the New York Federal Reserve Bank, Benjamin Strong. The New York bank was originally, and remains, the most important bank in the system, in part because New York has long been the financial center of the country, but also because the New York bank dealt directly with foreign banks and governments. Strong argued that the Fed should not be entirely passive, but should use its powers to buy and sell government securities in order to influence reserves in a countercyclical manner. After Strong died in 1928, the view that the Fed should be a passive entity concerned with the stability of interest rates again became the dominant belief within the system as the country approached the Great Contraction of 1929.

Contemporary critics of the Federal Reserve, particularly Milton Friedman, have argued that this passive policy, if not responsible for the Depression itself, was a principal contributing factor to its depth and longevity. Between 1929 and 1933 the supply of money in the United States declined by approximately one-third. While clearly concerned with the Depression itself, the Federal Reserve evidenced little direct concern for behavior of the money supply or of other aggregate measures of credit in the economy. The Board members simply did not perceive it to be their responsibility to try to influence these variables.[5] Their view was summarized aptly by Governor Norris of the Philadelphia Federal Reserve Bank in September, 1930, when the system was considering a proposal to undertake actions to influence reserves in a countercyclical manner. The proposal was voted down by the Governors of the individual banks, and Governor Norris expressed their view:

We have always believed that the proper function of the System was well expressed in the phrase used in the Tenth Annual Report of the Federal Reserve Board (1923)-"The Federal Reserve supplies the needed additions to credit in times of business expansion and takes up the slack in times of business recession." We have therefore necessarily found ourselves out of harmony with the policy recently followed of sup-

[5]See Jane W. D'Arista, "Federal Reserve Structure and the Development of Monetary Policy: 1915–1935," Staff Report of the Subcommittee on Domestic Finance, Committee on Banking and Currency, House of Representatives, (December 1971) for an extensive account of the view of the board and the debate within the board at this time.

plying unneeded additions to credit in a time of business recession which is the exact antithesis of the rule above stated.[6]

In his memoirs Herbert Hoover wrote rather disparagingly of this dominant view within the Federal Reserve System, one also held by then Secretary of the Treasury Andrew Mellon:

> [These people] felt that government must keep its hands off and let the slump liquidate itself. Mr. Mellon had only one formula: "liquidate labor, liquidate stocks, liquidate the farmers, liquidate real estate." He insisted that, when the people get an inflation brainstorm, the only way to get it out of their blood is to let it collapse. He held that even a panic was not altogether a bad thing. He said, "It will purge the rottenness out of the system. High costs of living and high living will come down. People will work harder, live a more moral life. Values will be adjusted, and enterprising people will pick up the wrecks from less competent people."[7]

In the early 1940s the United States emerged from the Great Depression as it entered World War II. As the economy expanded to meet the production needs of the war, the problems of the Federal Reserve were also refocused on financing the war. The Fed agreed to help the Treasury finance it by pegging interest rates at the levels that had prevailed before it. This was ⅜ of 1 percent on Treasury bills and 2½ percent on long-term Treasury bonds. The Fed used these interest rates as their targets for monetary policy. If interest rates started to rise above these levels, the Fed would purchase Treasury bills or bonds and drive down the interest rates; the Fed would sell Treasury bills or bonds if rates fell below these levels. Since the Treasury was selling a large volume of new debt, the Fed had to buy this debt in order to keep interest rates low, which led to a significant increase in the money supply. However, since the wartime U. S. economy operated under wage and price controls, inflation expectations remained low, and the Fed was able to maintain control over interest rates and still inject a substantial amount of money into the economy.

The Fed continued to conduct monetary policy by pegging interest rates until 1951. Its decision to abandon its policy of pegging interest rates was prompted by the substantial increase in consumer prices that occurred during the Korean War. During this period the U.S. economy was expanding rapidly, but there were no wage and price controls to hold down inflation. As a result, the policy of pegging interest rates at pre-World War II levels became untenable. In March, 1951, the Fed and the Treasury agreed to abandon their previous policy, an agreement known since then as the **Accord.** The Fed did agree to prevent interest rates from increasing precipitously, and this continuing concern for control of interest rates has been an important feature of Fed policy ever since.

The Accord is the agreement between the Federal Reserve and the U. S. Treasury in 1951 for the Fed to discontinue its efforts to maintain stable interest rates.

---

[6]*Ibid.*, p. 128.

[7]*The Great Depression, 1929–41, The Memoirs of Herbert Hoover,* New York: Macmillan, 1952, p. 30. Reprinted by permission.

FEDERAL RESERVE POLICY FROM 1950 TO 1979

From 1951 until a few years ago the Federal Reserve aimed monetary policy at short-term interest rates. When it wanted monetary policy to be tight, it set out to raise short-term interest rates. On the other hand, when it wanted monetary policy to be loose, it set out to lower short-term interest rates. Moreover, it has always been concerned with preserving orderly conditions in financial markets—or that interest rates not be too volatile.

This approach to monetary policy was initially carried out by Chairman William McChesney Martin, who was chairman of the Board of Governors from 1952 until 1970. Martin's view was that the Fed should base its policies on the intuitive feel or judgment of the members of the board about conditions in financial markets. This included short-term interest rates as well as measures of reserves in the banking system. Specifically, the board focused on what were called **free reserves** during this period. Free reserves are defined as:

Total reserves - Required reserves - Borrowings from the Fed.

Free reserves were deemed to be important because they were interpreted as a good measure of the degree of slack in the banking system. The Fed was perceived to be tightening policy if it reduced the amount of slack and loosening policy if it allowed the amount of slack to increase.

In 1970 President Richard Nixon appointed Arthur Burns chairman of the Board of Governors. This appointment occurred at a time when interest rates and inflation rates were beginning to increase in the United States to levels not observed since the Korean War. Not surprisingly, this escalation of inflation and interest rates coincided with the Vietnam War, when the U. S. Treasury was attempting to fund relatively large federal deficits (by historical standards). Monetary policy was beginning to be the focus of increasing public attention and controversy as the concern for reducing inflation and interest rates increased.

Until the 1970s the Fed had been attempting to control interest rates and free reserves or the degree of slack in financial markets. This method of doing business began to face serious criticism in the mid-1960s. The principal objection was that by concentrating on interest rates, control of the money supply was sacrificed. Critics argued that the real test of whether monetary policy was tight or loose was whether the money supply was growing at a fast or a slow rate.

In the early 1970s, the Federal Reserve began to respond to this criticism by concerning itself more directly with rates of growth in the money supply. In 1975, for the first time in its history, the Federal Reserve agreed to report targets for the future rate of growth in the money supply to Congress on a quarterly basis and to be accountable for meeting those targets. This agreement is known as House Concurrent Resolution 133. Though by this time there was a general agreement that the Federal Reserve should seek to control the supply of money, there was no agreement that the Fed should totally abandon attempts to control short-term interest rates closely. The Fed continued to use the federal funds rate as its direct target for monetary policy. The policy therefore attempted to control the long-run

Free reserves refer to total reserves less required reserves and borrowing from the Fed. They measure the slack in the banking system.

growth of the money supply by controlling the federal funds rate in the short run. The Fed would publicly announce a target range for the growth of M_1 and M_2, for example, of 3 to 6 percent for M_1. At the same time the Federal Open Market Committee would direct the Federal Reserve Bank of New York to conduct its trading operations to maintain the federal funds rate in a narrow prescribed band, say 7 to 7.5 percent. Unfortunately, it would be pure luck if the target range for the federal funds rate turned out to be consistent with the intended range for the growth of M_1. Unless their luck held, and it generally did *not* during the 1970s, the Board of Governors and the Open Market Committee would continually be forced to choose between abandoning its publicly stated targets for M_1 or altering its private operating range for the federal funds rate. During much of the 1970s it appears that, more often then not, the Fed stuck with the range for the federal funds rate and allowed M_1 to grow out of its range.

The basic problem here is that if the economy is booming and interest rates are rising, it will prove difficult for the Fed to maintain both types of targets effectively. If it attempts to maintain the federal funds rate target, then this will lead to large increases in the supply of money. Increases in the money supply in a booming economy will lead the market to expect inflation, and this will tend to increase interest rates. This is the price anticipations effect operating. The increased pressure on interest rates will make it harder yet for the Fed to maintain its federal funds rate target. The opposite can happen if there is an unexpected decline in income and interest rates. Then, as the Fed tries to maintain its funds rate target, it will withdraw reserves from the banking system and the money supply will decline. This can lead to a decline in inflationary expectations and a further decrease in interest rates. This kind of policy will lead to a procyclical pattern of money growth—that is, the money supply will tend to rise and fall with the economy, rather than offsetting the fluctuations in the level of income. Critics of monetary policy in the 1970s argued that this was precisely what occurred.

On October 6, 1979, in the wake of growing pressure on financial markets, the new chairman of the Board of Governors of the Federal Reserve, Paul Volcker, formally abandoned the policy of trying to control the federal funds rate tightly. The Fed announced that it would try to control reserves directly, and through reserves, the supply of money. Within a fairly wide range, it would allow the market to set the federal funds rate on a week-by-week basis. While there has been considerable disagreement about how much of the change was really cosmetic as opposed to substantive, this was probably the most dramatic alteration in the stated purpose of monetary policy in the history of the Federal Reserve System.

MONETARY POLICY AND MARKET EFFICIENCY

Thus far, our treatment of monetary policy in this chapter and the last has proceeded without much attention to the concept of efficient financial markets. You will recall from Chapter 5 that the semistrong-form of the efficient markets hypothesis maintains that all publicly available information about the future values of financial assets will be incorporated in the current prices of those assets. Publicly available information about how the Fed conducts monetary policy, including information about changes in the monetary aggregates, fits this description quite well. As a result, it is important to see how monetary policy influences financial markets when financial markets are efficient, at least in the semistrong-form sense.

HOW MONETARY POLICY WORKS IN AN EFFICIENT MARKET

When the current money supply change is announced by the Federal Reserve, any information contained in that change is immediately used by the market to alter prices. Therefore, in an efficient market, past changes in the supply of money, or other policy actions by the Fed, cannot have a *current* effect on financial markets or interest rates. What *can* influence current prices in financial markets is any new information about the future course of monetary policy that is contained in the current change in the money supply. For example, if the market expects the Fed to restrain growth in the money supply, and yet a large rate of growth is announced for the current week, then the market may revise its expectations, and financial markets will respond accordingly.

Rational expectations is another name for the concept of efficient markets.

The efficient markets argument is often given another name when it is applied to the market's reaction to changes in the money supply or changes in other policies of the government. That name is **rational expectations.** There is no fundamental distinction between the hypothesis that expectations are rational and the hypothesis that markets are efficient. Regardless of the name applied, the hypothesis asserts that markets make efficient use of information. Another way of stating this, a way often associated with the rational expectations label, is that people do not make systematic mistakes—in the long run they behave as if they understand how the economy works. For if people efficiently use available information, and this in fact leads to *systematic* over- or underestimates of some important economic variable, then the systematic over- or underestimate will itself become relevant information that can be used to correct the market's estimates. Any alternative explanation of a market's long-run behavior relies on a belief in systematic mistakes.

The implication of the rational expectations argument can be summarized with the maxim: You can't fool all the people all the time. The market sets the prices of assets based on what it expects will be the returns to those assets in the future. As a part of this process the market forms an expectation of the future course of action of the Federal Reserve in determining the supply of money. In the short run the Federal Reserve can fool the market, and thereby change asset prices, but in the long run the market will gradually learn from the Federal Reserve's behavior.

This has a very important implication for understanding how the Fed influences the economy. The market forms expectations of future policy actions based on all available, current information about the way the Fed makes its policy decisions. If the Fed makes the anticipated decision—for example, if the Fed allows the money supply to grow at the rate anticipated by the market—then that policy

MONETARY POLICY SINCE 1979

The change in monetary policy announced by Paul Volcker in October, 1979, must be placed in context. The money supply had been growing at a rate slightly above 8 percent for several years, as illustrated in Figure 11–2, which shows quarterly average growth rates in M_1 from 1976 to 1986. In addition, U.S. interest rates and inflation rates had reached unprecedented levels (see Figure 7–1). In effect, Volcker's change in policy constituted an acknowledgment that if the Federal Reserve continued to walk the tightrope of controlling both interest rates and the supply of money, it would not control either effectively or have any impact on inflation. The change in policy appears to have been designed to break market expectations of inflation by persuading the market that the Fed would seriously attempt to control monetary aggregates.

There is at least one other way to interpret Volcker's historic decision: he wanted to raise interest rates sufficiently to bring about a recession that would in turn reduce inflation. However, it was politically impractical to announce a policy of allowing interest rates to rise to such a level. Therefore, he chose to disassociate the Federal Reserve publicly from control of interest rates. By seeming to control monetary aggregates he could really pursue a policy of allowing interest rates to rise. More specifically, he could abandon the policy of using the Federal Reserve to attempt to hold down interest rates.

Interest rates did increase significantly after October, 1979. Figure 11–3 shows that Treasury bill rates peaked in 1980 and short-term interest rates, particularly the federal funds rate, become substantially more volatile after October, 1979. This seems to have been a direct response to the change in operating procedure.[8] Once the Fed relaxed the ban in which it had attempted to maintain the federal funds rate, then the variance of the funds rate increased significantly.

By the fall of 1982 the Federal Reserve had begun to back away from its dramatic change in procedures for monetary policy. In part, this retrenchment seems to have been due to a disenchantment within the Fed with its ability to control the supply of money effectively. Also there was a perception that high interest rates that resulted from the new policy threatened to cause severe financial distress in the international economy because many loans from U.S. banks were denominated in dollars and pegged to U.S. interest rates. Interest rates in the United States had risen so high that many foreign borrowers were facing insolvency. The Fed backed away from its previous policy partly to avoid bankruptcy for many foreign borrowers.

In early 1987 the Fed moved even further from targeting monetary aggregates by refusing to pub-

FIGURE 11–2
Money supply (M_1) in the United States.

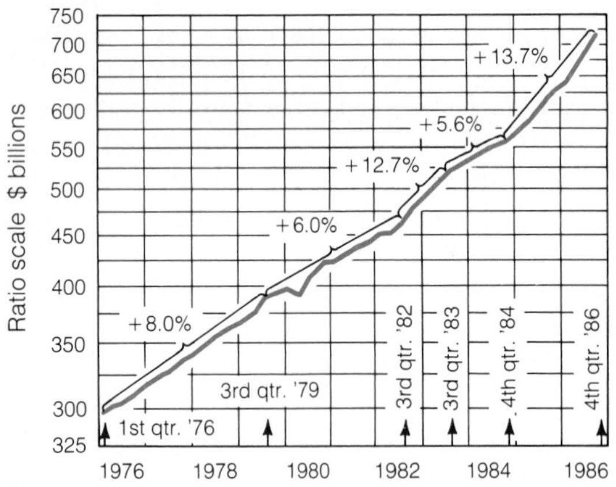

Percentages are annual rates of change for periods indicated.
Source: Prepared by Federal Reserve Bank of St. Louis.

---

[8]See Madelyn Antonvic, "High and Volatile Real Interest Rates: Where Does the Fed Fit In?" *Journal of Money, Credit and Banking*, 18, (February 1986) pp. 18–27, for some evidence on the link between the change in Fed policy and the change in volatility of interest rates.

FIGURE 11–3
Selected interest rates; averages of daily rates ended Friday.

licly release a target for M_1. The Fed does continue to publish targets for M_2 and M_3. Apparently this move was prompted by a belief that with all of the changes in regulation and use of the specific components of M_1 it had become unreliable as a target for monetary policy. However, it remains unclear how long this policy change will remain or to what extent the Fed may actually be using monetary aggregates.

With all the immensely important changes in monetary policy since Volcker's announcement in October, 1979, it has been difficult to say exactly what U.S. monetary policy has been in the 1979–1987 period. Many observers of the Fed say that the Fed followed a *Volcker standard* during this period, pursuing whatever course of action the board chairman thought appropriate. It will be interesting to see whether such a personal and eclectic policy will be continued under Alan Greenspan's tenure.

cannot have any effect on financial markets or the economy. The effect will already take place when the policy is anticipated. Therefore, if the Fed wants to change the level of inflation or some other important variable in the economy, it must attempt to fool the market. It must do something unanticipated. But over the long term, actions that fool the market in the short run will come to be anticipated. The point of the rational expectations argument is that the best thing the Fed can do is develop a stable and predictable policy that the market can understand. Individual decisions and specific actions taken by the Fed will not have an impact unless they are perceived to be a change in policy.

THE LINKS BETWEEN MONETARY POLICY AND INTEREST RATES IN AN EFFICIENT MARKET

Over the years, a specialized industry known as *Fed watching* has emerged. Fed watchers predict the future course of monetary policy. They form weekly estimates of the likely change in the money supply, and many institutions take positions in the financial markets based on these estimates. The process of forming weekly estimates of the change in the money supply results from the Fed's practice of making weekly announcements of the changes in the money stock (M_1) for the week ending 10 days earlier. These announcements are usually made on Thursday afternoons at 4:30 Eastern Standard Time.

The Fed's weekly announcements took on increased importance in the early 1980s as the market came to perceive that the Fed was basing its policy on the growth rates in the money supply. Especially since October, 1979, participants in financial markets have evaluated the success of monetary policy by how effectively the Fed is managing to keep the growth of monetary aggregates within its publicly stated range. The importance of the Fed's target ranges for the money supply are illustrated by the attention they receive in the financial press. For example, publications such as the *Wall Street Journal* regularly publish analyses of monetary policy that portray the Fed's target ranges, as in Figure 11–4. This example is taken from the July 11, 1986, edition of the *Wall Street Journal*. It shows both cones and tunnels for M_1, M_2 and M_3, which graphically illustrate the possible ranges of these aggregates over time, if their growth rates stay within their target ranges. The cone is the solid triangle shown in each panel of Figure 11–4. It defines the levels of the relevant monetary aggregate that would be consistent, at each point in time, with the announced target range of growth rates for that aggregate. The tunnel is the dashed line surrounding the cone in each panel of Figure 11–4. This shows the maximum or minimum level of the aggregate, at each point in time, that would keep the aggregate within its target range at the end of the horizon (November, 1986) if it grew at the middle range of growth rates for the rest of the period.

Since the weekly money supply announcements provide new information to the market about the current state of monetary policy, they have become an important way to assess the nature and extent of the effect of monetary policy on interest rates. By examining the link between the announcement and changes in the money supply and the immediate response of interest rates, we can acquire a better understanding of how efficient financial markets respond to Federal Reserve policy.

In order to form a complete picture of the link between monetary policy and financial markets, we must combine our understanding of how monetary policy is conducted with our theories of the impact of monetary policy on interest rates. We can formulate two combined hypotheses, that is, combinations of two of the effects of changes in the money supply on interest rates and two hypotheses about

FIGURE 11–4
Cones and tunnels for monetary aggregates.

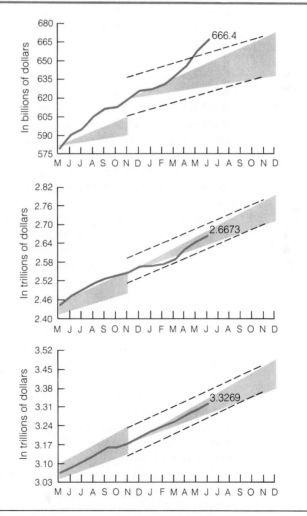

Source: *Wall Street Journal,* July 11, 1986, p. 34.

A **credible aggregates policy** is a policy of controlling monetary aggregates that is believed by participants in financial markets. A **noncredible policy** is a stated policy that is not believed.

how the market perceives the Fed is conducting monetary policy. The two effects of changes in the money supply on interest rates are the liquidity effect and the price anticipations effect. We will call the two hypotheses about the conduct of monetary policy by the Fed a **credible aggregates policy** and a **noncredible aggregates policy.** If the Fed has a credible aggregates policy, then the market believes the Fed is actually pursuing an aggregates policy. In this case the market should conclude that an increase in the money supply above the middle of the target range will cause the Fed to want to offset this change in the future. On the other hand, even when the Fed publicly announces target ranges for the money supply, the market may perceive that the Fed is not actually pursuing an aggregates policy. In this case we label the Fed's policy noncredible. The market will not conclude anything about the necessity to offset high (or low) changes in the money supply in the future under this view of Fed policy.

We can formulate two combined hypotheses about the way the market responds to money supply announcements.

Credible Aggregates Policy–Liquidity Effect.   This hypothesis says the market perceives that the Fed is following an aggregates target and the principal impact of money supply announcements on interest rates is the liquidity effect. Under this hypothesis, a large increase in the announced money supply will cause interest rates to rise. The market will expect the Fed to offset an increase in the money supply in the future, and it will expect this action to drive up nominal interest rates. In an efficient market this will cause investors to drive interest rates up now in anticipation of the future policy action.

Noncredible Aggregates Policy–Price Anticipations Effect.   This hypothesis says the market perceives that the Fed is not pursuing an aggregates policy despite its public announcement of aggregates targets. Under this hypothesis, if there is a large increase in the money supply and the market perceives that this will cause the inflation rate to increase in the future, then interest rates should increase.

There is an additional important feature of both of these combined hypotheses: it is only *unanticipated* changes in the money supply that should have any impact of returns on financial assets. Each week market participants formulate estimates of what they believe will be the announced change in the supply of money. As they form these estimates, market participants take positions in financial assets consistent with these expectations. If their expectations are correct—that is, if the actual change in the money supply is equal to the expected change—then the actual change should have no impact on interest rates, regardless of which of the two hypotheses is correct. Therefore, the hypotheses are actually making statements about the relationship between interest rates and the unexpected announcement of the change in the supply of money.

These hypotheses indicate that there are two alternative ways to explain a positive reaction of interest rates to announcements of increases in the money supply. One way is to assert that the market expects large increases in the money supply to be offset, so that the liquidity effect will drive up interest rates. The other is that the market does not expect large increases to be offset, so that the price anticipations effect drives up interest rates. Therefore, both hypotheses have the same prediction for the direction of the link between announcements and interest rates.

EVIDENCE ON MONETARY POLICY AND INTEREST RATES

There is a way to attempt to distinguish between these two hypotheses, despite the similarity of their prediction for announcements and interest rates: they have opposing predictions for the impact of monetary policy on exchange rates between the dollar and other currencies. The two hypotheses imply different responses of *real* as opposed to *nominal* interest rates to an unanticipated change in the money supply announcement. The first hypothesis asserts that the real rate of interest will increase in response to an increase in the money supply announcement because the liquidity effect operates on real rates as opposed to inflation expectations. The second hypothesis asserts that a large unanticipated money supply announcement will drive up the expected inflation rate but will leave the real interest rate unaffected. If the real interest rate increases, as under the first hypothesis, then the value of the dollar relative to other currencies should increase, since the real return on investments in dollar-denominated assets will now be higher. On the other hand, if nominal interest rates increase solely because of an increase in the expected rate of inflation, as in the second hypothesis, then the value of the dollar should fall relative to foreign currencies. As a result, by examining the impact of unanticipated money supply announcements on domestic interest rates as well as exchange rates, it is possible to compare these two hypotheses.

One of the principal empirical investigations of these hypotheses was carried out by Brad Cornell.[9] Cornell used historical data on Treasury bill rates and the exchange rate between the dollar and the deutsch mark for periods before and after October 6, 1979. He also used the average of analysts' predictions of the money supply announcement that are collected and published by Money Market Services as a measure of the anticipated money supply announcement. Then he was able to measure the unanticipated announcement by taking the difference between the actual announcement and this forecast.

Cornell found, and other studies have confirmed, that both Treasury bill rates and the dollar/mark exchange rate were not influenced by *anticipated* changes in the money supply announcement either before or after October, 1979. This is consistent with both of the hypotheses and with market efficiency. He also found that neither Treasury bills nor exchange rates responded much to unanticipated announcements *prior to October 1979*. However, after that date there is a large and statistically significant positive reaction of Treasury bill rates to the unanticipated money supply announcement. Cornell intereprets this as evidence against

[9]See Bradford Cornell, "The Money Supply Announcements Puzzle: Review and Interpretation," *The American Economic Review*, 73, (September 1983) pp. 644–56.

TABLE 11–1
Summary of results of Cornell's study of the impact of money supply announcements on Treasury bills and exchange rates.

	Treasury bill		R/Mark exchange rate	
	A	U	A	U
Pre-October, 1979	0	0	0	0
Post-October, 1979	0	+	0	−

The table shows the sign of the response of each price to anticipated (A) and unanticipated (U) money supply announcements. Source: Bradford Cornell, "The Money Supply Announcement Puzzle: Review and Interpretation," *American Economic Review*, (September, 1983).

the price anticipations effect and for hypothesis 1. It would seem that if price anticipations are significant in the link between money and interest rates, then the impact of unanticipated money supply announcements should be consistent before and after October, 1979. That is, there should be a positive reaction of interest rates to unanticipated announcements, regardless of whether the Fed has a credible aggregates target. The evidence indicates a strong effect only after the October 6, 1979, announcement. Presumably the market inferred that the Fed was going to follow an aggregates target at least for a while and responded to money supply announcements accordingly.

This interpretation is supported further by additional evidence reported by Cornell, which indicates that the dollar/mark exchange rate is negatively related to unanticipated money supply announcements after October 6, 1979, and independent of those announcements prior to this date. The decline in the exchange rate corresponds to an increase in the value of the dollar, which is consistent with the first hypothesis where the real rate responds to the unanticipated money supply announcement. The results of Cornell's study are summarized in Table 11–1, which shows the sign (+, −, 0) of the estimated relationship between both Treasury bill rates and the dollar/mark exchange rate and money supply anouncements before and after October 6, 1979.

THE CRITIQUE OF THE CONDUCT OF MONETARY POLICY

Now that we have some understanding of how the Fed can influence interest rates in principle and what the Fed has been up to in recent years, we can turn our attention to the debate about how the Fed *ought to* conduct its business. It seems to be good sport to attack the Federal Reserve, and the attacks come from a number of camps. Probably the oldest and most vocal critics are the monetarists. But there are also the rational expectations and open economy camps. We encountered the rational expectations camp earlier in this chapter. Therefore, the remainder of it summarizes the monetarist position, as well as presents a brief account of the way the structure of the international monetary system affects the conduct of monetary policy.

THE MONETARIST CRITIQUE

The **Monetarist view** is the opinion that the Fed should focus on controlling the supply of money, which has long been advocated by Milton Friedman.

The **monetarist view** of monetary policy is associated with a long tradition of economics taught at the University of Chicago during the latter part of the nineteenth and the entire twentieth centuries. The monetarists use the following simple equation as the vehicle for explaining their view of monetary policy:

$$MV \equiv Py, \qquad (11\text{--}1)$$

where y is real income, V is the velocity of money, M is the stock of money, and P is the price level. In fact, this equation is an identity, which means it is true by definition. We use the symbol $\equiv$ for an identity. The attractiveness of this identity lies in its simplicity and in the interpretation or usefulness of the concept of velocity. To understand the arguments of the monetarists we must understand their concept of velocity.

The monetarists argue that, within some limits, the Federal Reserve can make the money supply whatever it wants. Hence, we treat the money supply as determined independently of the rest of the economy. In addition, monetarists argue that the money demand function is a very stable and predictable relationship. They contend that equilibrium in the economy can be represented by an equilibrium between the quantity of money supplied and the quantity of money demanded. This equilibrium condition can be represented as follows:

$$M_s = M_d = f(Y',r). \qquad (11\text{--}2)$$

Suppose that the level of nominal permanent income and the interest rate are such that this equilibrium condition is satisfied. At the existing level of income and interest rates, people are willing to hold the quantity of money supplied by the Federal Reserve. Now suppose the Federal Reserve disturbs this equilibrium by increasing the supply of money so that

$$M_s > M_d. \qquad (11\text{--}3)$$

Monetarists argue that people do not accept these excess money balances passively unless something determining money demand changes to restore equilibrium. If the money demand function is stable, which is to say that people do not willingly accept new money balances without some substantive inducement to hold them, then either nominal income or interest rates must change to bring about a new equilibrium. Furthermore, monetarists generally argue that the variable that does, in fact, change to bring about the new equilibrium is the level of nominal permanent income. They argue that the effect of interest rate changes on money demand is generally so small as to be inconsequential.

This monetarist explanation of the effect of money on income is usually made using velocity and Equation (11–1). To see how the argument can be recast in this form, we need to alter Equation (11–1) slightly by dividing through by M, so that we have velocity on the left-hand side:

$$V = \frac{Py}{M}.$$

(11–4)

Now, we can define velocity in two ways, just as we can approach the quantity of money in two ways: the quantity supplied and the quantity demanded. First, we will examine **desired velocity,** V_d. Typically, when monetarists refer to velocity, they are referring to desired velocity, for they argue that velocity is simply an alternative way of stating the demand for money. Hence, desired velocity is simply the public's desired ratio of nominal income to nominal money balances:

Desired and actual velocity refer to the desired and actual ratios of nominal income to nominal money balances.

$$V_d = \frac{Py}{M_d} = \frac{Py}{f(y',r)}.$$

(11–5)

However, just as there can be a disequilibrium between the quantity of money supplied and the quantity of money demanded, there can be a difference between desired and actual velocity. Actual velocity, V_a, is the actual ratio of nominal income to nominal money balances:

$$V_a = \frac{Py}{M_s}.$$

(11–6)

But in equilibrium, when the public's demand for money is equal to the quantity of money supplied, actual velocity must equal desired velocity:

$$V_a = V_d.$$

(11–7)

We can summarize this equilibrium relationship by interpreting the M and V in the original Equation (11–1) as the quantity of money supplied and the equilibrium-desired level of velocity, respectively:

$$M_s V_d = Py.$$

(11–8)

The logic conveyed by this equation is as follows: suppose the money supply is increased. In order to maintain equilibrium, either velocity must decline or nominal income must increase. If it is nominal income that changes to bring about an increase in the demand for money, then the right-hand side of Equation (11–8) will adjust in the new equilibrium. But if people respond passively to changes in the money supply, such that income does not have to change for the demand for money to change, then a decrease in velocity may absorb the entire money supply increase.

Diagramatically we can represent the monetarist interpretation of a change in the money supply as inevitably leading to a change in nominal income:

$$\uparrow M_s V_d = \uparrow Py.$$

Conversely, a money supply change might simply be absorbed by a change in velocity:

$$\uparrow M_s \downarrow V_d = Py.$$

This could happen if either the money demand function itself changes as the supply of money changes, or if interest rates decline and that decline causes no change in income. The first probability is usually characterized as a situation where money demand, and hence velocity, is unstable.

To see more specifically what is involved in explaining velocity, it is useful to examine Figure 11–5, which shows the behavior of velocity from 1970 to 1985. Velocity tended to increase over this time period, but it also had a procyclical pattern; that is, it tended to rise and fall with the level of income. A procyclical pattern is evident in velocity's tendency to fall during or near the shaded time intervals in the figure, which represent periods of recession.

There appears to be a relatively simple explanation for the tendency for velocity to increase over recent years. The long-run increases in velocity can be attributed to increased efficiency in the process of carrying out transactions. This

FIGURE 11–5
Level and changes of velocity.

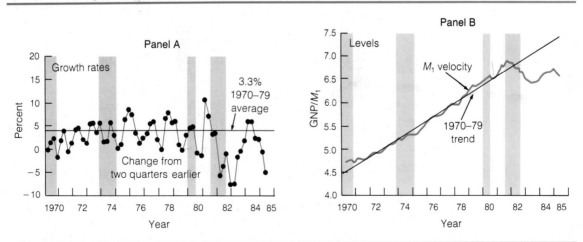

Shaded areas represent periods of recession, as defined by the National Bureau of Economic Research.
Sources: U.S. Department of Commerce and Board of Governors of the Federal Reserve System.

has led to a decreased demand for money relative to income. Since the late 1940s, a number of financial assets have developed that are viewed as substitutes for money—for example, credit union shares and money market mutual funds. Moreover, the speed and efficiency with which the payments mechanism works has increased. As a result, the cost of transacting has declined and with it, the need for money balances. This has been particularly noticeable in very recent years as the technology for efficient cash management has blossomed. It seems likely that this trend will continue and even accelerate.

The procyclical pattern in velocity can be explained in two ways. One explanation, advanced by Milton Friedman,[10] relies on the fluctuations of permanent income relative to nominal income in any given period. Because permanent income represents expected future long-run income, it changes less in any given period than does nominal income. Only if the change in nominal income were perceived to be permanent would permanent income change by the same amount. Most changes in nominal income are perceived to be transitory, so that only part of the change is reflected in permanent income. If part of this perceived change in permanent income is allocated to money balances, then the change in money must be less than the change in permanent income, which, in turn, must be less than the change in measured nominal income. This means that when nominal income changes, the numerator in Equation (11–5) will be altered by a greater amount than will the denominator; therefore, velocity will tend to rise and fall with income.

An alternative explanation for the procyclical behavior of velocity relies on the observation that interest rates move procyclically. Because the quantity of money demanded is negatively related to the level of interest rates, an increase in interest rates will lead to a decline in desired money balances. This will tend to diminish growth in the demand for money caused by an increase in income, and velocity will move procyclically.

While over long historical periods velocity has tended to behave as described above, velocity (at least M_1 velocity) has behaved very differently in the 1980s then it did in the 1970s. After increasing about 3.5 percent per year during the 1970s, M_1 velocity showed no growth from 1980 to 1985. This is illustrated in Panel B of Figure 11–5. In addition, the volatility of M_1 velocity also increased considerably, as is illustrated in Panel A of Figure 11–5. Velocity growth in the early 1980s (measured from the fourth quarter of one year to the fourth quarter of the next) ranged from -5.6 percent ot $+ 5.3$ percent. Over the entire decade of the 1970s, the range was from -0.1 percent to $+ 6.0$ percent. One possible reason for this change in velocity is the growth of substitutes for traditional demand deposits at commercial banks. Another possible reason is the sharp drop in

---

[10]See Milton Friedman, ''The Quantity Theory of Money: A Restatement,'' in Milton Friedman (ed.), *Studies in the Quantity Theory of Money,* Chicago: University of Chicago Press, 1956, and Henry A. Latane, ''Income Velocity and Interest Rates: A Pragmatic Approach,'' *Review of Economics and Statistics,* 42 (November 1960), pp. 445–49.

interest rates in the 1980s and the resulting change in the demand for money. However, these kinds of changes are themselves hard to predict, which has made velocity hard to predict. This, in turn, has made it difficult for the Fed to evaluate what the appropriate growth rate in the money supply should be.

THE MONEY SUPPLY RULE

Monetarists argue that the money supply should be controlled directly by the Federal Reserve. Moreover, they argue that interest rates should be left free of fluctuation to whatever extent the market dictates. They believe that any attempt by the Federal Reserve to achieve short-run control over interest rates inherently sacrifices long-run control over growth in the quantity of money.

A **money supply rule** is a rule for conducting monetary policy which stipulates that the Fed should force the supply of money to grow at a prespecified rate each year.

Monetarists also argue that monetary policy should be conducted according to what is called a **money supply rule.** To see what this means we need to return to the basic equation of the monetarists stated in Equation (11–1):

$$MV \equiv Py.$$

In order to use this equation to talk about the conduct of monetary policy, we need to restate this equation in terms of the rate of change in each variable. If we let Δ stand for the change in a variable so that, for example, $\Delta M/M$ means the rate of change in the money supply from one period to the next, then Equation (11–1) can be rewritten as follows:

$$\frac{\Delta M}{M} + \frac{\Delta V}{V} = \frac{\Delta P}{P} + \frac{\Delta y}{y}.$$

This means that the rate of change in the money supply plus the rate of change in velocity must equal the rate of inflation plus the rate of change in real income.

The question the monetarists ask of this equation is, what should be the appropriate rate of growth in the money supply? To answer this question we will alter the equation somewhat by moving velocity to the right-hand side:

$$\frac{\Delta M}{M} = \frac{\Delta P}{P} + \frac{\Delta y}{y} - \frac{\Delta V}{V}.$$

In order to determine the rate of growth in the money supply we have to specify the values of the variables on the right-hand side of the equation. The logic in choosing these variables is the following. From historical evidence we observe that velocity has a tendency to grow at a certain percent, say 1 percent. We observe from long-run historical evidence that real income tends to grow at a certain percent, say 3 percent. Therefore, if we expect that the long-run patterns of growth in velocity and real income will be the same in the future, then we can fill these in on the right-hand side of the equation. Given these future growth rates

THE POLITICS OF MONETARISM

For many years, the monetarist point of view was not taken particularly seriously by those who held power in Washington, D. C., especially from the post-World War II era until the late 1970s. The key economic fact which began to improve the political standing of monetarists was inflation. Monetarists argued inflation was linked to monetary policy and could be cured by controlling the supply of money. Since other methods for curing inflation did not appear effective, more attention began to be focused on the monetarists' arguments.

Monetarists argued that by using a money supply rule, the economy would eventually settle down to a stable growth rate with very little inflation. Furthermore, they believed that without such a rule, the Fed is forced to anticipate what will happen in the economy and take actions to offset undesirable future economic fluctuations. However, since we have rather imperfect knowledge of how and with what speed Fed actions influence the economy, its attempts to operate a countercyclical policy often backfire. In fact, one of the principal criticisms offered by monetarists such as Milton Friedman is that monetary policy has tended to be procyclical—that is, the money supply tends to grow at a fast rate in an economic expansion and at a slow rate in an economic contraction. A money supply rule would force the Fed to abandon its allegedly misguided attempts to anticipate and offset future economic fluctuations.

A second reason monetarists advocate a money supply rule relates to the circumstances that govern modern international monetary arrangements compared with those that existed earlier in history. Until the middle of this century, the United States was on a gold standard. In other words, the government's money was backed by gold and, as a consequence, the supply of money was determined by the supply of gold. The disadvantage of this system is that the economy may grow faster than the gold supply, and deflation will result. The advantage of such a system is that the government is unable to increase the money supply at a rate that produces high inflation unless the supply of gold permits. The government's natural temptation to resort to inflationary increases in the money supply to support deficit spending is limited by the available supply of gold.

The discipline enforced on the government by a gold standard is arbitrary; that is, changes in the supply of gold may be unrelated to a given country's rate of economic growth. Hence, essentially by chance there may be either inflation or deflation. For this reason the gold standard was eventually abandoned, yet monetarists seek a mechanism that replaces the discipline of the gold standard, one that eliminates the government temptation to inflate. Of course, politicians who seek power, even conservative ones, generally find such constraints unattractive. As a result of this, as well as the rather erratic performance of the velocity of money illustrated in Figure 11–5, Washington briefly embraced monetarism in the early 1980s. Monetarism and, with a few exceptions, monetarists lost favor in the government. The monetarist point of view will always be around and have articulate advocates. Whether it will ever be in favor again in Washington is difficult to predict.

---

for velocity and real income, if we want the future inflation rate to be zero, then the rate of growth in the supply of money must be 2 percent.

$$2\% = 0 + 3 - 1.$$

The assumption underlying this conclusion is that changes in the growth of velocity and real income are not influenced by monetary policy in the long run. Rather, the influence of monetary policy is largely on the rate of inflation. Hence, we can extract our estimates of the growth of velocity and income from the historical evidence, and then we can choose the rate of growth in the money supply that will generate the desired rate of inflation. Presumably, this desired rate of inflation is zero.

Despite the fact that this argument is relatively simple, there are difficulties involved in estimating the actual future growth rates in velocity and real income. Arguments over the proper values of these estimates have persisted for some time, and it will never be possible to know these values with certainty. But monetarists argue that even with imprecision about the exact rate of growth in the money supply that is best, a fixed rule is better than no rule at all.

THE OPEN ECONOMY CRITIQUE OF MONETARY POLICY

The **open economy critique** of monetary policy argues that the appropriate targets of monetary policy in the United States and other countries is linked with the form of exchange rate system in the world.

The **open economy critique** of the conduct of U.S. monetary policy is based on the fact that the U.S. economy is increasingly integrated with the economies of other countries. As a result, the exchange rate between the dollar and other currencies is of tremendous importance to the U.S. economy. In addition, the exchange rate is a barometer of the state of monetary policy in the United States. This is because the basic determinant of the exchange rate between two currencies is the relative level of prices of goods and services in those economies. We first encountered this relationship, known as *purchasing power parity*, in Chapter 6. We can summarize it in the following manner: let the price of goods in one country (say the U.S.) be P_c and the price level in any other country in the world be P_w. Let the exchange rate between the two currencies be represented by E. Therefore, if you can buy 2 units of the other country's currency with your currency, then $E = 2.0$. The exchange rate must be related to the prices of goods in the two countries as:

$$P_c E = P_w.$$

This is purchasing power parity. If it did not hold, it would be profitable to transport goods (with low transportation costs) from one country to the other for sale.

Now, if the U.S. follows a monetary policy that tends to drive up the prices of goods in the U.S. relative to other countries, so that P_c rises while P_w remains stable, then the exchange rate between the two currencies must decline. When the exchange rate declines, the value of the dollar goes down. As a result, if the monetary policy of one country is expansionary, compared with that of another, so that the first country experiences more inflation than the other, then the exchange rate between the two must adjust to satisfy purchasing power parity.

The fact that exchange rates are so closely linked to monetary policy means there is another possible target for the conduct of monetary policy. The Fed could use the exchange rate between the dollar and other major currencies, say, the yen or the deutsche mark, as its target of monetary policy. If the value of the dollar is rising, as it was in the early 1980s, then this would indicate that monetary policy is tight, regardless of what might be happening to the monetary aggregates. Conversely, if the value of the dollar is declining, as it was in 1986 and 1987, then this would indicate that monetary policy is loose.

MONETARY POLICY AND THE CRASH OF 1987

On Black Monday (October 19, 1987), the Dow Jones Industrial Average of 30 blue-chip stocks (DJIA) recorded its largest one-day decline in history when it plunged 508 points or 22.61 percent to a level of 1738.74. This unprecedented decline constituted a significant reversal or correction in the bull market which began in 1982. This flight from equities was not limited to U.S. markets nor was it a result of actions solely by U.S.-based investors since equity markets in London, Tokyo, and Hong Kong also experienced significant declines.

While it is difficult to explain why such an abrupt correction occurred in stock prices and why it occurred when it did, it is easier to identify some fundamental factors which caused investors to be concerned about the future of the U.S. economy. An often-cited source of concern among foreign investors had been persistent U.S. budget deficits throughout the Reagan administration. Investors argue that deficits require the U.S. to consistently borrow substantial amounts from foreign investors. In turn, dependence on foreign investors requires the Federal Reserve to keep interest rates high so that U.S. Treasury obligations are attractive to foreign investors. At the same time relatively high interest rates tend to discourage investment in the U.S. and to increase the likelihood of recession. Foreign investors also worry about record U.S. trade deficits with the rest of the world. These forces have led to a decline in the value of the dollar throughout the middle 1980s.

These problems are complicated by the U.S. Treasury's ability to finance its deficit which depends on the absolute level of U.S. interest rates, the level of U.S. rates relative to other interest rates, the relative values of various currencies, and their inflation rates. Major western nations reached an agreement, the Louvre accord, in early 1987 to stabilize the relative values of major currencies by coordinating their monetary policies. In September, 1987, West Germany seemed to be moving away from the Louvre accord by allowing German interest rates to increase. Policymakers in Washington believed that Germany should be less concerned with future inflation and reduce interest rates to stimulate the economy. In the week before the stock market crash, U.S. Treasury Secretary James Baker repeatedly criticized the German government for its actions. Baker was concerned that if the United States did not also raise interest rates, the dollar would decline significantly in value; however, if a significant increase in interest rates were allowed, the risk of a recession would increase.

As a result of this policy dispute, the major western governments allowed the dollar to trade more freely in foreign exchange markets. Whether this was because of a decision to reduce support or because of the difficulty in maintaining the level of the dollar is difficult to discern. In any case, as the stock market fell, the movement out of stocks into fixed-income instruments drove down United States interest rates. The dollar then declined in value against major foreign currencies, and by early November it reached a record low against the Japanese yen of 134.15. The

There is another important implication of the relationship between monetary policy and exchange rates. Unless the Fed has extraordinarily good luck, it cannot control both exchange rates and the supply of money. This is true for the same reason that, unless it is lucky, it cannot control both domestic interest rates and the monetary aggregates. Exchange rates, domestic interest rates, and monetary aggregates are all alternative measures of the impact of monetary policy. As a result, if a country attempts to operate with a system of fixed exchange rates, as did the U.S. and most of the world under the Bretton Woods Agreement from the end of World War II until 1971, it cannot pursue an independent course for the supply of money. This is readily apparent from the purchasing power parity equation. If the U.S. fixes E by having the Fed intervene in the foreign exchange

FIGURE 11-6
The value of the dollar after the stock market crash of 1987.

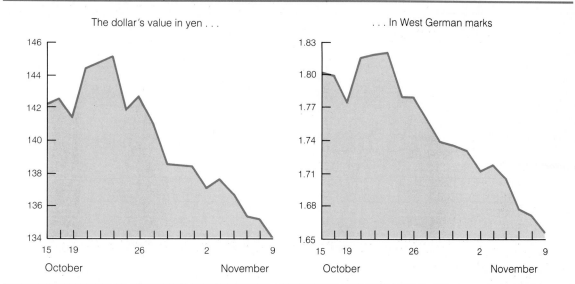

The dollar's value in yen . . .   . . . In West German marks

Source: *Wall Street Journal*, November 10, 1987, p. 3.

performance of the dollar against the Japanese yen and the German deutsche mark is shown in Figure 11–6.

Also after the crash, Federal Reserve Chairman Alan Greenspan had a dilemma to face: if the monetary policy were too tight, might we see a repeat of circumstances that led to the Great Depression? Or should monetary policy be loosened and risk a return to the years of high inflation? Steering a middle course was desirable but difficult. Fearing a post-1929 scenario more, Greenspan chose to pump money into the economy. Within a couple of weeks, interest rates declined. As of this writing, it is too early to tell if he chose the middle path or if inflation would worsen.

markets, then the relative level of prices between the U.S. and any other country must also be fixed. The intervention by the Fed in the foreign exchange market causes the U.S. money supply to change in a way that is sufficient to alter U.S. inflation relative to foreign inflation to the point that purchasing power parity holds. That is, domestic monetary policy becomes a by-product of the effort to maintain the fixed exchange rate.

Many contemporary critics of the Fed have argued that if we judge monetary policy by the value of the dollar relative to major foreign currencies, then monetary policy was highly contractionary during the first few years of the 1980s and then loosened. This is illustrated in Figure 11–7, which shows the exchange rate between the dollar and major foreign currencies in 1984 and 1985. Since the early

FIGURE 11–7

Spot exchange rate indexes; Dollar and weighted-average prices, Averages for week ending Wednesday (Dollar prices, solid line; Weighted-average prices, dashed line).

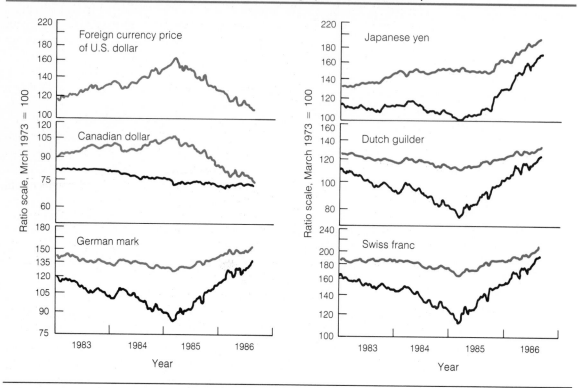

Source: *Federal Reserve Chart Book*, 1986.

1970s the U.S. and most other major Western countries have operated with flexible exchange rates. Hence, exchange rates served as indicators of what was happening to domestic monetary policies and therefore to relative inflation rates in these countries.

Often the open market critique goes hand in hand with the suggestion that the U.S. return to a gold standard. During the post-World War II or Bretton Woods era, most major countries in the world pegged their exchange rates with respect to the dollar and the U.S. pegged the price of gold in terms of dollars. This amounted to a system of fixed exchange rates with the value of the individual currencies tied to gold. As we have seen, the current attraction of this system is that it eliminates the discretion for conducting monetary policy currently enjoyed by the Federal Reserve and replaces it with a formula for the conduct of monetary policy. There is substantial difference of opinion among the experts as to whether the money supply rule advocated by the monetarists or the gold standard would be more effective as an alternative to the present system. However, it does not seem likely that either will receive widespread political support in the near future.

SUMMARY

In this chapter we examined the contemporary debate about the conduct of monetary policy. We began with a brief statement of the conflict between an aggregates and an interest rate target for monetary policy. Unless the Fed is very lucky, it will be unable to satisfy both types of targets. If if tries to maintain an interest rate target and the economy starts expanding, the attempt to hold down interest rates will require the Fed to increase the supply of money at a high rate. This, in turn, will cause the market to expect increased inflation, which will cause interest rates to increase. Hence, the Fed may be forced to choose between the two targets.

Next we discussed the evolution of monetary policy over the life of the Federal Reserve. During the early years of the Federal Reserve there was a debate within the Fed about its obligations and objectives. One view was that it should simply provide an elastic currency, allowing credit to expand and contract with the economy. This view, called the "real bills doctrine," appears to have dominated as the Depression began, because the Fed did not attempt to prevent the decline in the money supply which occurred. As World War II began, the Fed shifted to a policy of pegging interest rates motivated by a desire to accommodate the Treasury's need to finance the war without driving up interest rates. This policy continued until 1952.

From the early 1950s until the 1970s the Fed principally used interest rates and general economic conditions as its target for monetary policy. In the 1970s, as inflation increased in the U.S., there was increased pressure on the Fed to switch to monetary aggregates as targets for monetary policy. The Fed gradually paid more attention to the aggregate supply of money during this period. In October, 1979, Federal Reserve Chairman Paul Volcker announced that the Fed would abandon interest rates as targets of monetary policy and switch to monetary aggregates. This policy lasted until 1982, when conditions in financial markets convinced the Fed once again to adopt a more eclectic policy of focusing on both interest rates and monetary aggregates.

With an understanding of the recent history of monetary policy, we turned our attention to the link between announcements of changes in the supply of money and market interest rates. If financial markets are efficient, then market interest rates should reflect all available information about the future conduct of monetary policy. Moreover, as new information becomes available, this information should have an immediate impact on prices in financial markets. This feature of an efficient market implies that the Fed can have an impact on financial markets only if something occurs that the market has not already anticipated.

We reviewed the evidence on the link between financial markets and money supply announcements. The impact of these announcements depends on whether the market perceives that the Fed is pursuing an aggregates target. Before October 1979, unanticipated announcements of money supply changes had no significant impact on either domestic interest rates or foreign exchange rates. However, after October 1979 domestic interest rates increased, and the value of the dollar rose as the size of the unanticipated money supply announcements increased. This suggests that money supply announcements reflect the Liquidity Effect defined in Chapter 10 or cause changes in real interest rates.

Finally we considered the major criticisms of recent monetary policy. Our examination of the monetarist argument started with the demand for money. The idea behind the demand for money is that there is a stable and predictable relationship between the quantity of money people choose to hold and other important variables in the economy. We found that the demand for money is principally dependent upon the level of permanent income and the nominal interest rates. Velocity, according to the monetarists, is another way of expressing the demand for money; it is the desired ratio of nominal money balances to nominal income. Monetarists assert that within some limits the Federal Reserve can make the quantity of money whatever it chooses. If the Federal Reserve increases the supply of money, then it creates an imbalance between the quantity of money people want to hold and the quantity of money in the economy. Once this change has occurred, something must adjust to create a new equilibrium so that $MV = Py$. The monetarists argue that it is not velocity that adjusts, but the level of nominal income. The key to this argument is the demand for money, for if money demand is unstable or unpredictable, then changes in the money supply or money may well be offset by changes in velocity or money demand.

Monetarists argue that monetary policy should be determined by a money supply rule. The basic idea behind a money supply rule is that there is a rate of growth in the money supply which, if maintained in the long run, would lead to a zero rate of inflation. Monetarists contend that the Federal Reserve should be constrained to permit the money supply to grow at that rate to eliminate the temptation to finance federal government deficits by increasing the money supply at an excessive rate. In this way, a money supply rule provides the same external constraint that the gold standard provided in earlier times.

The other major critique of monetary policy comes from those who argue that monetary policy must account for the fact that the U.S. increasingly operates in an open international economy. In an open economy where the U.S. does not have fixed exchange rates with other currencies in the world, U.S. monetary policy also has an impact on the value of the dollar. An expansionary monetary policy will tend to drive up inflation which will reduce the value of the dollar relative to other currencies. Hence, in a world without fixed exchange rates, monetary policy can be evaluated in part by its impact on the value of the dollar. In a world with fixed exchange rates, a country cannot conduct an independent monetary policy. In effect, its monetary policy must be used to maintain the fixed exchange rate.

QUESTIONS

1. What is the real bills doctrine? Is it still influencing monetary policy today?
2. What is the Accord? Explain its significance.
3. How do money supply announcements influence the exchange rate between

the dollar and other currencies? Why will these announcements have an impact on exchange rates under the liquidity effect different from that under the price anticipations effect?

4. What happened on October 6, 1979, and what is its significance?

5. How did market interest rates tend to respond to money supply announcements both before and after October 6, 1979?

6. Why do monetarists say that velocity is simply the demand for money? Why is it important to their theory that velocity be a stable and predictable function? How do the monetarists account for the procyclical pattern in velocity?

7. What happens to monetary policy if a country has fixed exchange rates? How will monetary policy influence the value of the currency if a country has flexible exchange rates?

8. Why should there be a difference in the response of market interest rates to anticipated versus unanticipated announcements of changes in the supply of money?

9. Return to Table 11–1. What is the significance of breaking the data in Cornell's study into two periods, before and after October, 1979? Suppose the results had been the same in each period instead of that which appears in Table 11–1? How would you attempt to explain such a change? Imagine you had more recent data for a similar study and you divided the data again at a point somewhere between 1981 and 1987. What would be a good time for the division between the two periods, and what would you expect to find?

10. Based on your understanding of the liquidity, income, and price anticicipations effects of monetary policy on interest rates, analyze the viability of conducting monetary policy by creating a band around the federal funds rate, as shown in Table 11–1. Under what types of economic circumstances is such a band likely to be most (least) effective?

11. In 1986 and 1987 there was a significant decline in the value of the dollar relative to the yen, while earlier in the decade precisely the opposite occurred. What do these changes in exchange rates tell you about U.S. and Japanese monetary policies during these two periods?

12. How should the decrease in the value of the dollar relative to the yen in 1986–1987 affect U.S. interest rates? How can and should the Fed respond to these changes in exchange rates in its conduct of monetary policy?

*R*EFERENCES

Antonvic, Madelyn. "High and Volatile Real Interest Rates: Where Does the Fed Fit In?" *Journal of Money, Credit and Banking,* 18, (February 1986), pp. 18–27.

D'Arista, Jane. "Federal Reserve Structure and the Development of Monetary Policy: 1915–1935," Staff Report of the Subcommittee on Domestic Finance, Committee on Banking and Currency, House of Representatives, (December 1971).

Friedman, Milton. *A Theory of the Consumption Function,* Princeton, N.J.: Princeton University Press, 1957.

————. "The Quantity Theory of Money: A Restatement," in Milton Friedman (ed.), *Studies in the Quantity Theory of Money,* Chicago: University of Chicago Press, 1956.

————, and Anna Schwartz. "Money and Business Cycles," in Miltion Friedman (ed.), *The Optimum Quantity of Money and Other Essays,* Chicago: University of Chicago Press, 1969, pp. 230–31.

————, and ————. *A Monetary History of the United States 1867–1960,* Princeton, N.J.: Princeton University Press, 1963.

Holmes, Alan. "Operational Constraints on Stabilization of Money Supply Growth," in *Controlling the Monetary Aggregates,* Federal Reserve Bank of Boston, (June 1979), pp. 65–77.

Hoover, Herbert. *The Great Depression, 1929–41, The Memoirs of Herbert Hoover,* New York: Macmillan, 1952.

Latane, Henry A. "Income Velocity and Interest Rates: A Pragmatic Approach," *Review of Economics and Statistics,* 42 (November 1960), pp. 445–49.

Radecki, Lawrence J. and John Wenninger. "Recent Instability in M1's Velocity", *Quarterly Review,* Federal Reserve Bank of New York, (Autumn 1985), pp. 16–22.

Rozeff, Michael S. "Money and Stock Prices; Market Efficiency and the Lag of Effect of Monetary Policy," *Journal of Financial Economics,* 1 (September 1974), pp. 245–302.

Sheehan, Richard G. "Weekly Money Announcements: New Information and Its Effects", *Review,* Federal Reserve Bank of St. Louis, (August/September 1985), pp. 25–34.

3
PART

*F*ORCES SHAPING THE STRUCTURE OF FINANCIAL MARKETS

Part 3 moves away from the questions of how assets are valued and how market interest rates are determined and explores how the markets themselves operate. This part of the book has two basic purposes. The first is to create a taxonomy or organizational structure for financial markets so that it is possible to make sense out of the multitude of different markets in the U.S. economy. The second is to describe the major forces that shape the organizational structure of financial markets that currently exists. Part 3 is composed of five chapters. Chapter 12 describes the three basic types of markets which can be found in the United States—auction, over-the-counter and intermediated markets—and gives a few examples of each. Chapter 13 explains how government regulation shapes the organizational structure of markets and presents a theory for the regulation of financial markets that is the basis for the analysis in the next two chapters. Chapter 14 discusses the regulation of auction and over-the-counter markets, or securities markets. Chapter 15 deals with the regulation of financial intermediaries, particularly banks and savings and loans. Chapter 16 explains why so much innovation in financial markets has occurred in the late 1970s and 1980s and gives three examples of major innovations: securitization, the development of original issue discount bonds, and the growth of the NASDAQ market. ∎

12

*T*HE ORGANIZATION AND STRUCTURE OF FINANCIAL MARKETS

To the uninitiated, financial markets look like a maze. There are so many different types of assets, institutions through which these assets are bought and sold, and participants in the market, that just categorizing these diverse elements is a huge task. Therefore, the purpose of this chapter is to examine how financial markets are organized. We focus on what are called auction, over-the-counter, and intermediated markets. These labels characterize the way the markets operate.

An auction market involves some kind of centralized facility where buyers and sellers, or their commissioned agents, come together to execute trades. Over-the-counter markets have no centralized mechanism or facility for trading. Instead, they are composed of dealers who stand ready to buy and sell assets with anyone who chooses to trade. Auction and over-the-counter markets are, by their nature, public markets. Anyone who finds it economical to do so can buy or sell. Another type of market, the intermediated market, we think of as a private market where securities are issued only to a financial intermediary and the intermediary issues its own liabilities in order to supply the funds for these private borrowers. In an intermediated market financial intermediaries perform the function of a dealer, but they also change the nature of the asset traded. Financial intermediaries acquire one type of asset, create a claim on themselves—which is a new asset—and sell this new asset. Financial intermediaries are by no means restricted to dealing only in such private distributions. They also purchase from public auction or over-the-counter markets.

We will examine the basic characteristics of each of these three forms of markets and how and why markets may change or evolve from one form into another. This chapter should be considered a precursor to the material in the remaining chapters, since it provides a framework for analysis of a number of specific markets and institutions. ■

AUCTION AND OVER-THE-COUNTER MARKETS

There are a number of ways to decompose financial markets, and each such taxonomy sheds a little more light on the operation of the markets. It is important to recognize that no taxonomy is perfect. There are always exceptions or special cases that do not quite fit the taxonomy, but it is much easier to understand financial markets if they are organized into some kind of structure, even an imperfect one. The one we will settle on is not perfect. We will find exceptions which do not quite seem to fit. In spite of the imperfections, we will gain much more than we will lose by utilizing this taxonomy.

Probably the most obvious way to classify financial markets corresponds to the types of securities traded in those markets. Equities, mortgages, bonds, short-term debt instruments, deposits, and the like are often treated as having distinct markets, and we have done so throughout this book. Another extremely useful way to classify markets is according to who wants to borrow and who wants to lend. But both of these ways of organizing financial markets fail to emphasize the mode of operation of the market, and that is what we will explore here.

We can start examining the market itself, rather than the securities traded or the people trading them, by identifying the three basic functions a market serves. First, it provides the facility or the mechanism through which funds flow from those who want to lend to those who want to borrow. The market provides the means by which assets can be exchanged and also the recordkeeping function that goes with this flow of funds. Second, the market provides the vehicle by which prices are set both for new assets that accompany newly lent funds and for the existing stock of assets. In this sense, the market serves the function of valuing assets. Finally, the market acts as a collector of information. The market is the facility used to process and aggregate information about the values of assets and the flows of funds from lenders to borrowers. To a large extent, the costs of collecting and aggregating information determine the type of market organization that will emerge. Now that we have identified the functions of a market, we can look more carefully at the characteristics of auction and over-the-counter markets.

AUCTION MARKETS

In an **auction market** some kind of centralized and open competitive bidding process exists where all trades in an asset take place.

The essence of an **auction market** is that some kind of centralized and open competitive bidding process exists where all trades in an asset take place. This kind of exchange process cannot operate successfully in every financial market. Four basic requirements are necessary for such an auction market to be viable. They are

1. A central trading facility,
2. Homogeneous assets,
3. A minimum volume of buy and sell offers,
4. A profitable market maker.

We will examine each of these in turn.

At one time it might have been relatively simple to picture exactly what a central trading facility would look like: one large room where buyers and sellers of assets or their representatives could meet to make their bids and exchange assets. But in some cases technology has rendered this conception obsolete. A centralized trading facility need no longer always be a central physical location where people who want to trade, or their representatives, congregate, like, say, the New York Stock Exchange. Instead it can be a computerized trading facility where all trades are processed with no traders physically present. The essence of today's central trading facility is that all trades must be executed through a mechanism that preserves ready access. The central trading facility makes all trades and prices known to all market participants on an ongoing basis, and no trades are priced and executed away from the central facility. The central facility relieves the market participants of the burden of searching for individual prices. All the market's information about prices and exchanges is centralized in one location.

The second requirement for an auction market to operate successfully is that assets must be reasonably homogeneous. The centralized trading facility in an auction market collects information about bids and prices of assets. If each is a distinct asset that cannot be succinctly described, a central market cannot successfully collect the necessary information. But, if assets are homogeneous, the cost of collecting information can be spread over a number of homogeneous assets so that a central distribution of this information becomes economical. For example, consider the market for mortgages on residential real estate. Mortgages on residential property have traditionally not been distributed through an auction market. One of the principal reasons is that each asset is so distinct. A centralized auction market could not economically process all the information necessary to describe each mortgage offered for sale. The same could be said for equity shares in corporations were it not for the provision of limited liability. *Limited liability* means that the value of a share of equity stock is independent of its holder. If liability were not limited in this way, the value of the security would change if a rich person sold it to a poor person simply because the personal assets standing behind the security would be reduced. Limited liability has meant that all equity claims on a particular company are **homogeneous assets.**

Homogeneous assets are assets which have similar characteristics and therefore similar cash flows.

A closely related requirement to that of homogeneity is that the market not be too "thin" in an asset. There must be some minimum volume of transactions in the asset and a desire to exchange the asset. If there are too few shares of a homogeneous asset or if most of the shares are held by individuals who choose not to trade in the asset, then the centralized facility does not work efficiently. The costs of collecting and maintaining access to an asset in a centralized facility are largely fixed, in that they do not rise and fall with the volume of trading. Therefore, it is difficult to maintain a centralized market in an asset traded only infrequently.

The **market maker** serves the function of the auctioneer in an auction market.

Finally, there must be some **market maker,** someone or something that serves the function of an auctioneer. To function in the long run this market maker must earn a profit. At one time the market maker was literally an auctioneer who called out prices bid and asked, but now, to a large extent, the auctioneer's function can be mechanized. The function may be limited to that of bringing together all the buyers and sellers without the market maker's even holding an inventory of the assets traded. On the other hand, the market maker may also function as a dealer, purchasing securities for resale. The distinction between an auction market and an over-the-counter market is not as pure as it might be, if what we call dealers can operate in auction markets. The fact that a market maker may purchase securities for resale and therefore become a dealer does not in itself alter the auction nature of a market. What distinguishes an auction market from others is the presence of a centralized facility through which exchanges are made and the lack of private exchanges between individual parties or traders off the centralized exchange. When trading off the central exchange becomes significant, we have an over-the-counter market. We might say that the presence of dealers in an auction market only diminishes the purity of the market form.

> A **call market** operates with simultaneous offers to buy and sell an asset all placed at one time.

Auction markets can be further divided into two types of auctions, referred to as *call* and *continuous* markets. A **call market** operates with simultaneous offers to buy and sell all placed at one time. All the bids and offers are then collected, and exchanges take place at once. The market then ceases to function until there is sufficient demand for another round of exchanges, at which time the market operates again. The alternative type of auction market is a **continuous market,** in which offers to buy or sell can be placed at any time the market is in operation, and exchanges take place on a continuous basis. The continuous market increases the flexibility of the market participants so that they are not constrained to wait until the times when the market operates, as in a call market. However, in a continuous market the offers to buy or sell may be quite spread out in time. As a result, there will be opportunities for imbalances between offers to buy and sell, called **trading imbalances,** to develop. The market price can rise or fall as excesses of buy or sell offers develop. These imbalances create the opportunity for dealers to enter the market.

> In a **continuous market,** offers to buy or sell can be placed at any time the market is in operation and exchanges take place on a continuous basis.

> **Trading imbalances** refer to an excess of offers to either buy or sell an asset.

OVER-THE-COUNTER MARKETS AND THE ROLES OF BROKERS AND DEALERS

> An **over-the-counter** market has no central exchange facility.

There are two important features of an **over-the-counter** market. First there is no central exchange facility, as in an auction market. Second, the market operates through middlemen (or women) who stand ready to buy or sell a given security upon request. These middlemen are referred to as **dealers.** Dealers are distinguished from brokers on the one hand and financial intermediaries on the other. Brokers do not buy and sell assets on their own. Rather they act as salespersons and receive commissions. Dealers are principally engaged in selling the same securities they buy, whereas financial intermediaries create and sell new claims on themselves in order to fund their holdings of the securities they purchase. Dealers' holdings of securities are small relative to their turnover of those securities. In this sense they operate like the typical retailer: they buy assets not to hold them for long periods but to sell them quickly, so that the stock of assets they hold at any one time is an inventory maintained for resale.

> **Brokers** act as sales agents in arranging a sale of assets, while **dealers** hold inventories of assets and stand ready to buy or sell out of that inventory.

In many respects, an auction market and an over-the-counter market can be quite similar. Over-the-counter and auction markets function better the more homogeneous the assets and the larger the volume of trades. In addition, dealers may perform a useful function in either market. In a continuous auction market, dealers will be able to operate profitably if there are periodic imbalances between orders to buy and sell and if market participants are willing to pay to reduce the impact those imbalances have on prices. The reason an auction market arises in one instance and an over-the-counter market in another hinges on the benefits perceived by the participants in the market of a centralized exchange facility. Such a facility serves essentially as a collector of information and a means of economizing on the costs of searching for alternative prices from dealers. Therefore, if communication among dealers and participants in a market is good enough and competition is intense, a centralized facility may be an unnecessary luxury.

Immediacy in trading refers to the service a dealer provides when he or she supplies someone on the other side of a trade.

The important feature of an over-the-counter market involves the nature of the service provided by dealers, though this service may be rendered in auction markets as well. The service provided by dealers has been referred to as **immediacy**.[1] The dealer allows the buyer or seller of an asset to make the exchange when he or she desires, rather than waiting to locate a party who wants to do business. It is important to emphasize the distinction between the service provided by a dealer and a broker. A broker acts as an agent in executing a transaction and collects a commission. The broker goes hunting for the party on the other side of the transaction. His incentive to hunt efficiently is improved if his fee is tied to the outcome, so it is usually stated as a percentage of the sale price. On the other hand, the dealer holds an inventory of the assets in which he or she deals and, therefore, stands ready to execute the transaction when the buyer or seller desires.

Holding costs are the costs an investor bears for holding a portfolio of assets that is not properly diversified.

Whether in an auction market or an over-the-counter market, dealers must be able to operate profitably in providing the service of immediacy. The costs that the dealer faces can be broken down into three components: holding costs, order costs, and information costs.[2]

Order costs are the costs of transacting in a given security.

Holding costs are the costs an investor bears for holding a portfolio of assets that is not an optimal combination of risk and return. In order to make a market in a particular asset, a dealer must hold an inventory larger than he or she would hold if the dealer were investing in the asset on his or her own. Dealers demand a compensation for holding an excess amount of such assets. In contrast, **order costs** are costs of transacting. These are all the costs of handling securities and the fixed costs of office and staff, recordkeeping, and so forth, involved in executing transactions. Finally, **information costs** arise because some investors will trade with a dealer based on special information that is not available to the dealer.

Information costs are the costs of trading with someone who has special information which you do not have.

---

[1] The concept of immediacy was articulated by Harold Demsetz, "The Cost of Transacting," *Quarterly Journal of Economics,* 82 (February 1968), pp. 33–53.

[2] This breakdown is found in Hans R. Stoll, "The Supply of Dealer Services in Securities Markets," *Journal of Finance,* 33 (September 1978), pp. 1133–51.

The dealer knows that some portion of his or her transactions are with parties who have superior information, and the dealer expects to lose on such transactions.

The dealer earns returns from a spread between offers to buy and sell. This simply means that the dealer attempts to buy low and sell high, on average. The difference between the price paid for assets and the price received is the **bid-ask spread.** In markets where dealers are involved, the bid-ask spread is a function of the dealer's costs and the degree of competition in the market.

The **bid-ask spread** is the difference in the price a dealer will pay to buy versus the price he or she asks for an asset.

PRIMARY AND SECONDARY MARKETS

Primary markets are the markets where new securities are bought and sold. This does not mean that no other securities like the new ones being sold can exist. It simply means that the particular securities being distributed have not been owned before. For example, a primary market exists in the stock of a particular company when it issues new shares, despite the fact that it may already have shares outstanding. We think of the primary market as the market for the new shares as opposed to the often virtually identical old shares. A **secondary market** is a market where the old (used) securities are traded. In a secondary market securities are not being sold principally by the party upon which they are a claim and therefore involve no new lending or borrowing. For example, all IBM shares sold in the secondary market would not be offered for sale by IBM. They would be sold by the parties who own them.

A **primary market** is a market for newly issued securities.

A **secondary market** is a market for securities which have been issued at some earlier time.

Primary markets are essentially a distribution device and act as the conduit through which new capital or funds can be acquired. These markets operate in whatever method is best suited to the purpose of collecting information and facilitating this initial distribution. The secondary market provides the similar function of being a vehicle for exchange. The difference is that the exchange opportunities offered by a secondary market provide liquidity for those who hold the security as well as a mechanism for valuing the outstanding stock of assets. In other words, the outstanding stock of assets has some market value that is determined through the secondary market. The asset need not actually change hands in order for the asset to be valued, as long as there is a secondary market where similar assets are traded. Therefore, the market serves even those who do not directly use it.

There is no necessary reason why primary or secondary markets would operate as auction or over-the-counter markets. Either form of operation is potentially feasible. With either primary or secondary markets, the essence of the auction form of operation is the centralized exchange facility. Such a facility can exist as an efficient means of collecting and processing information in either type of market. This facility is efficient only when there is a large number of assets distributed in the market on a regular basis. Therefore, an auction market will not work in a primary market where the market needs to process a large amount of special information with the distribution of an asset. But a primary market can be an auction market if new homogeneous securities are issued regularly. A secondary market can operate as an auction market if a volume of securities are actively ex-

THE NEW YORK STOCK EXCHANGE: AN AUCTION MARKET WITH DEALERS

The secondary market for equity securities provides an excellent example of the differences between auction and over-the-counter markets. The reason is that auction and over-the-counter markets operate side by side for different equity securities. Moreover, the cost of collecting and processing information about equities and conducting exchanges in equities are changing so rapidly that the equities market is evolving quickly. It has been possible, as a result, to witness significant changes in these markets in relatively short intervals of time.

Most corporate equities are traded on one or more of the major stock exchanges in the United States. Of all the exchanges, the greatest publicity is given to the New York Stock Exchange (NYSE) because it dwarfs the other exchanges in volume of trades executed yearly and in the value of the securities listed on the exchange. But there are a number of other stock exchanges which operate in the United States. The second largest is the American Stock Exchange (AMEX). While it is not far behind the NYSE in the total number of securities listed, the total value of these securities is a fairly small portion of the total value of securities listed in the NYSE. The other regional exchanges are far behind the NYSE both in number of securities and total value. Figure 12–1 shows trading volume on the NYSE and the AMEX. The figure clearly indicates that trading volume has increased steadily throughout the late 1970s and 1980s on the NYSE, and it shows the relative size of the NYSE and AMEX.

The NYSE is essentially a hybrid of a continuous and call auction market for corporate equity and debt securities. It is continuous in that it operates during regular business hours five days a week. However, it is also a call auction in the sense that anyone wanting to trade during hours when the exchange is closed must wait until the exchange opens on the next trading day. While this may seem like only a small problem, it has become increasingly important as active trading in NYSE-listed stocks has increased around the world. In London or Tokyo, the fact that the NYSE is open only during business hours in New York creates a significant inconvenience. As a result there is increasing pressure to increase trading hours, and this may ultimately lead to 24-hour trading on the NYSE.

The NYSE actually consists of a corporate association of about 1,500 members who own seats on the

FIGURE 12–1
Trading volume on major exchanges.

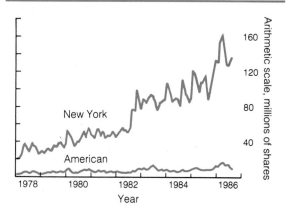

Source: *Federal Reserve Chart Book,* October 1986.

changed—that is, if the turnover of securities is sufficiently frequent. But it need not act as an auction market unless the centralized trading facility provides some efficiencies over a dealer system. All of these organizational forms are found in American financial markets.

Primary and secondary markets in the same security are not always different markets with distinct methods of operation, although they usually are. One case in which the two markets are virtually the same is the market for equity obliga-

exchange. A seat on the exchange entitles a member to trade on the floor of the exchange and, like a member of a country club, a new member of the exchange must be approved by existing members. The price of a seat on the exchange is determined by supply and demand for membership. As we shall see in Chapter 14, until the early 1970s, the NYSE was permitted to set minimum prices for brokerage services. Under this system, seats on the exchange became extremely valuable. Once minimum brokerage commissions were eliminated, prices of seats on the exchange declined significantly.

The NYSE functions as an auction market in the sense that all trading in a particular security is processed through a central market maker. The market maker on the NYSE is referred to as a *specialist*. Specialists are so named because they operate as dealers in particular stocks rather than in all the stocks listed on the exchange. The rules of the exchange are designed to limit the specialist's role as a dealer in order to minimize the costs of executing trades on the exchange. Specialists are required to give priority to the execution of orders between public investors rather than trades with themselves or for trades with other exchange members who are trading on their own account. This means when a specialist receives an order to buy or sell a stock, he or she must first seek to match it with an order from a nonspecialist. The specialist is permitted to execute his or her own order first only if its bid price is higher, or its offering price is lower than the prices of any public order on the exchange. As trading imbalances develop, the dealer is permitted to trade on his or her own account.

Individual specialists have formed partnerships or corporations with other specialists in order to control or diversify their risk exposure. These entities are usually called *specialist units*. Specialist units are important devices for limiting the specialist's risk exposure to traders who are trading on the basis of some special information. Specialists will generally expect to lose when trading against such informed traders and specialist units can spread some of this risk across the population of specialists.

In order to be listed on the NYSE a company must meet a set of minimum listing requirements pertaining to size and distribution of ownership of the firm's securities. In the mid-1980s there were more than 2,000 stocks listed on the NYSE. Of course, there are a large number of companies with publicly traded stock which do not satisfy the listing requirements of the NYSE and a smaller number who do satisfy those requirements but choose not to be listed. Many of these companies are traded on the over-the-counter market known as the NASDAQ (National Association of Securities Dealers Automatic Quotation System). The NASDAQ market differs from the NYSE in a number of important respects, but the principal difference is there is no centralized exchange or auction mechanism on the NASDAQ. Instead competing dealers make a market for stocks and trades are executed privately through those dealers. The NASDAQ market has been growing and changing dramatically in the 1980s. In fact, the NASDAQ market provides one of the more interesting cases pertaining to innovation in financial markets. In Chapter 16, after we have discussed the regulation of securities markets, we will approach the NASDAQ as a case study in innovation.

tions of a few very large corporations. In this case, some corporations are large enough that they can offer their new securities directly to the secondary market, as if they were someone who had used securities of a corporation to sell. In either case, a broker might be involved, but there would be no need for the particular type of dealer usually involved in the primary equity market, the investment banker. Such cases are not that frequent, however. In most instances the primary market operates in a somewhat different manner from the secondary market. The differences usually depend upon the number of securities to be sold relative to the volume and distribution of outstanding securities and the amount of information possessed by the market about the securities for sale.

INTERMEDIATED MARKETS

THE CONCEPT OF INTERMEDIATION

In order to understand the differences between the two types of markets discussed above and an intermediated market, it is useful to begin by comparing a financial intermediary with a dealer. A dealer buys and sells assets and lives off the spread and does not acquire assets for the long term. Rather, assets are held only for the purposes of providing an inventory, though dealers may also speculate for themselves and hold some assets for such purposes. As a result, the dealer's role as a middleman does not involve any changes in the assets traded or the creation of any new or distinctly different types of assets. Precisely the opposite is true with **financial intermediaries** such as commercial banks or insurance companies. Intermediaries purchase most assets as investments with a specific intended holding period. This means that intermediaries' holdings of assets do not serve essentially as inventories. Instead of reselling the assets they purchase, they create new assets and sell them to the market. The new assets constitute a financial claim on the intermediary rather than on the party who originally issued the asset purchased by the intermediary. Therefore, unlike the dealer, the intermediary does more than provide immediacy or absorb temporary trading imbalances; it creates and distributes new financial claims upon itself. This alteration of the nature of the financial claim distributed to the market is the concept behind the word *intermediation*.

> A **financial intermediary** is a firm that acquires an asset and funds that asset by issuing a claim on itself.

The distinction between a dealer and an intermediary is relatively clear-cut. The distinction between an intermediated market and either an auction market or an over-the-counter market is not quite as straightforward. An intermediary may participate in either an auction or an over-the-counter market. For example, commercial banks all buy and sell Treasury bills on a regular basis. Hence, depending upon whether they use the primary or secondary market, they are participating in an auction or an over-the-counter market. But commercial banks also participate in a private loan market. That is, they stand ready to make loans to business customers out of the funds they raise by offering various types of deposit accounts. This private loan market is certainly not an auction market, yet it does operate much like an over-the-counter market. The important difference between this market and an over-the-counter market is that the suppliers of loans are intermediaries rather than dealers. The same distinction applies to the liabilities offered by intermediaries. The market for the liabilities of an intermediary operates like an over-the-counter market, but the suppliers are intermediaries—that is, institutions that create new and distinct liabilities to fund their assets. Therefore, we will call these **intermediated markets.** The important concept here is that financial intermediaries are distinct entities because they create new financial claims, but

> An **intermediated market** is a market where assets are funded by financial intermediaries.

they may participate in all the types of markets we have identified. Hence, they create a distinct or new type of market, but they also bridge the gaps between markets.

It is not at all obvious why the services of a financial intermediary are needed. An intermediated market is more complicated than either an auction or over-the-counter market because an intermediary creates an entirely new set of assets. It therefore seems implausible that intermediaries provide a service that is essentially the same as the one provided by a dealer—that of immediacy. The question then becomes, what benefits do intermediaries offer to the economy that lead to some markets being dominated by intermediaries and others not? There is no single answer to this question. Intermediaries come in various forms and provide a number of distinct services to the market. These services can be grouped in two broad categories. First, intermediaries act as investment managers. They accept funds from those who wish to lend funds, issue these lenders liability claims, select the appropriate investments for those funds, and monitor those investments. In order to prosper as investment managers, intermediaries must be able to do something for their investors that they cannot do on their own. That is, there must be something inherent in the process of the intermediary managing funds for investors that generates some economies or efficiencies for the intermediary. Then, as long as there is competition among intermediaries, these efficiencies will be passed on to the suppliers of funds. The second category of services involves activities that can easily be tied in with the task of managing investments, such as managing payments. These services are not really a necessary part of the intermediation per se. In fact, some other type of firm could provide these services as well. But in performing the investment management function, the intermediary finds that these other services are naturally complementary with the investment management function.

SERVICES PROVIDED BY FINANCIAL INTERMEDIARIES

Financial intermediaries provide six services for the financial markets. They are:

Risk reduction through diversification,
Maturity intermediation,
Reduction in the cost of contracting,
Information production,
Management of the payments system, and
Insurance.

Almost all intermediaries provide some reduction of risk through diversification, but the other five services are more specialized. Some intermediaries provide two or more of these additional services, while others are more narrow.

RISK REDUCTION THROUGH DIVERSIFICATION

All financial market participants are interested in reducing risk through diversification. We learned in Chapter 3 that by choosing a portfolio of investments, rather than investing all one's resources in a single asset, an individual can reduce the total risk he or she is exposed to. The concept behind constructing a diversified portfolio is illustrated in Figure 12–2, which shows a hypothetical combination of expected return and risk measured by the variance of the portfolio. Various portfolios may be selected by allocating one's wealth in different proportions across the assets available in the market. Each such selection corresponds to a point in the shaded area to the right of line DD' in the figure. The curve labeled DD' represents the efficient frontier of the possible portfolios one might choose. Any combination of available assets that does not plot on that curve is inferior to some portfolio that does plot on the curve, because not enough risk has been diversified. The implication is that any risk-averse person will find it optimal to choose a portfolio of assets from the set of portfolios on this line. The optimal portfolio for any individual to choose is the one that provides what that individual perceives to be the best combination of expected return and risk from those combinations that plot on line DD'.

While this is a very useful representation of what constitutes any optimal portfolio and the impact of diversification, it is not necessarily a very practical guide for choosing investments. In order to use this as a practical guideline, one must estimate the risk and return on each asset one might choose and the relationships between these assets, or between individual assets and some representative market portfolio. As a result, portfolio theory recommends that individuals who have no special knowledge should choose a portfolio that closely approximates

FIGURE 12–2
Efficient frontier of portfolios of risky assets.

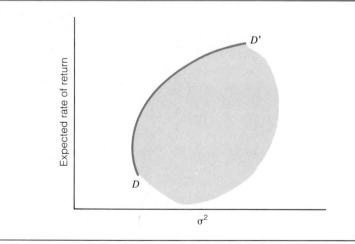

the market as a whole. As a practical matter, if one randomly chooses 20 or more equity securities from the market and spreads available funds across these securities, the resulting portfolio will be a close approximation of the return on the market as a whole. As one adds more randomly chosen securities to this portfolio, the benefits from diversification increase slightly. In the limit, one could choose to invest a small amount in virtually all securities in the market and thereby have a completely diversified portfolio.

There is one difficulty with following this advice directly: it does not account for the fact that it is costly to buy and sell securities in order to construct such a diversified portfolio. To illustrate the nature of the problem, suppose an individual had $10,000 to invest and wanted a highly diversified portfolio. In order to accomplish this, suppose that the person went to a broker with an order to purchase equal shares in each of the largest 100 corporations in the United States. Suppose the broker said that the brokerage fee would be $5 per share. The investor would then be able to purchase $95 worth of stock from each company, and the total cost for conducting the transaction would be $500. If the investor wanted to liquidate half of these holdings six months later yet still maintain the same degree of diversification, additional large transactions costs would be incurred.

Financial intermediaries can economize on such transactions costs by providing diversified portfolios for customers. The financial intermediary pools the funds of a number of investors and acquires a large diversified portfolio, then it sells claims on the entire portfolio of assets to individual investors. In this way, an individual who has $10,000 to invest and desires a diversified portfolio can purchase a portion of the larger portfolio of the intermediary. The intermediary does not have to buy small portions of each asset when individuals add to or withdraw their claims on the intermediary. Instead, the intermediary holds an inventory of assets that can be liquidated at low cost and uses these to provide funds to individuals when they withdraw. Similarly, it adds to this pool of low transactions cost assets when new funds are provided to it. As long as there is some balance between the inflow and outflow of funds, the intermediary can reduce the costs of transacting for all market participants who seek diversified portfolios.

MATURITY INTERMEDIATION

Many financial intermediaries currently provide the service of intermediating across maturities or borrowing short and lending long. This means that they accept funds from investors who desire to lend their funds with a short maturity, and they lend those funds out to borrowers who desire a long maturity. Borrowers and lenders who have different preferred maturities are thus not compelled to agree on a common maturity. But as we know from the theory of the term structure of interest rates (see Chapter 8), this cannot be accomplished without cost. By intermediating across maturities, financial intermediaries bear the risk of fluctuations in short-term rates. Lenders who supply funds to the intermediaries and receive short maturities are provided with liquidity that they would otherwise have to forgo or else purchase directly from borrowers without an intermediary in the transaction. When lenders deal with an intermediary, they still have to pay a price for this liquidity. Moreover, the risk involved is not a risk that can be reduced by diversification. Diversification is beneficial when assets can be combined that have probability distributions on returns that are less than perfectly correlated. The risk borne by an intermediary that borrows short and lends long is the risk that nominal short-term interest rates will rise, and it will have to match them in order to retain funds. If these rates rise above the rate of return on outstanding long-term loans, then the intermediary loses money. The risk of an increase in short-term rates is not a risk that can be diversified.

However, such risk can be transferred or sold off to another party and in this way reduced. Futures markets can be utilized to hedge the risk of these changes. But whether sold or held, a price will be charged as a compensation for bearing this risk. In spite of the fact that the intermediary cannot reduce the underlying risk involved in bridging the gap between preferred habitats, it can often perform this function more efficiently than other forms of market organizations. The intermediary must be able to generate some kind of economies by specializing in lending long and borrowing short for large numbers of borrowers and lenders. These economies come from two sources. First, individuals who supply funds in small amounts cannot easily estimate the risk involved in arranging long-term contracts. By specializing in this function, intermediaries are better able to assess these prospects. Second, they are able to package short-term liabilities and long-term loans in economical units. A borrower who is not large enough to sell debt claims effectively in an over-the-counter market, but who is large enough to require funds from a sizable number of lenders, will find it efficient to utilize an intermediary's services.

REDUCTION IN THE COST OF CONTRACTING

In almost all of the financial arrangements they engage in, financial intermediaries provide a reduction in the cost of contracting. There are two distinct types of costs included under the label of contracting costs. The first is simply the cost of writing and understanding the contract in the first place. The second is the cost of monitoring the contracting parties' activities to ensure that contract terms are observed (and enforcing them if they are not).

Financial intermediaries are able to reduce the costs of writing contracts in cases where lenders or borrowers find highly standardized contracts unsuitable. The intermediary is able to write a contract tailored to the needs of individual borrowers at a lower cost than would be possible in an auction or over-the-counter market. In these markets contracts are usually highly standardized without special provisions tailored to individual borrowers. To some extent, such special provisions make it difficult for the market as a whole to evaluate the financial instrument. Moreover, when specialized contracts are written with an intermediary, the borrower is also able to renegotiate the terms of the contract with relative ease, whereas this would be costly and difficult if financial claims were widely distributed to the public.

The financial intermediary can reduce the costs of monitoring and enforcement by centralizing these functions in one agent rather than distributing them across all bondholders. This centralization is efficient because each bondholder, acting on his or her own, has a limited incentive to expend effort in monitoring and enforcement activities. The same advantage in centralization leads to the use of trustees in public distributions of bonds who are given certain monitoring and enforcement tasks. Moreover, because the intermediary's own return is tied to the success of monitoring and enforcement activities, there is an incentive to perform those duties reliably. A trustee could also be compensated in a way that provides such an incentive, but the fact that the intermediary's return comes from the asset and is not sold off as a dealer would sell it accomplishes this as well.

Finally, the intermediary can provide a service for lenders if they are relatively unsophisticated compared to borrowers. The intermediary is interjected between a sophisticated party, usually the borrower, and an unsophisticated party, usually the lender. The intermediary is therefore in a position to write, monitor, and enforce contracts with greater skill than the individual lender. In effect, lenders find it profitable to pool their resources and hire a financial intermediary in the same way they would hire a lawyer.

INFORMATION PRODUCTION

An important service provided by financial intermediaries is the production of information about the value of assets. Intermediaries are certainly not the only type of information producer in the financial markets. The news media, brokerage houses, bond rating agencies, and other entities all produce information and so do intermediaries. Intermediaries expend considerable resources collecting, processing, analyzing, and interpreting facts and opinions about the future profits of the firms they finance. Investors could do this on their own, and to a certain extent, they do. It is as efficient to hire specialists in the production of information as it is to hire specialists to monitor the terms of contracts. The unique aspect of the financial intermediary as an information producer is that the intermediary generally does not redistribute information to the market as a whole. In other words, the intermediary does not collect information for direct resale to the market as *The Wall Street Journal* does. Instead, the intermediary collects information and uses it to guide investment decisions it makes for those who supply it with funds. Therefore, it can be thought of as tying the production of information in with the management of investments.

One of the major concerns about financial intermediaries as information producers is whether they perform this function reliably. The investor never directly sees the information and therefore needs some assurance that the intermediary is not in effect being bribed to invest in firms at too high prices. In this case, a bribe is some kind of extra payment paid to owners or managers of an intermediary to induce them to lend funds to a firm that might not qualify or to provide funds on terms that are not in the interest of the intermediary's suppliers of funds. The principal insurance the investor has that the intermediary will perform reliably is the stake the owners and/or managers of the intermediary have in the investments they choose for the intermediary's customers. The larger the amount of capital the intermediary's owners contribute to the intermediary, the more the owners have to lose if they place investments where they know they will not pay off. The market is therefore able to judge by the size of the intermediary's capital stock the extent of its reliability in gathering information and using it to guide investment decisions.

Intermediaries provide another service to the market that goes hand in hand with information production. They often receive information from corporate borrowers who seek to protect the confidentiality of their information. Confidential or inside information usually comes in two types—technological and strategic information. Technological information might include the knowledge of how to construct a Polaroid camera or a videocassette recorder. With a technological advance the product itself can be revealed to the market without revealing the method of production, and the market may be able to assess its value fairly. Moreover, the value of technological information is frequently protected by patent rights so that disclosure is possible. Much inside information is of a strategic rather than a technological nature. Strategic information refers to marketing and advertising strategies, collusive price agreements of an overt or a covert nature, organizational techniques, and research and development procedures. If the strategy of research and development procedures is completely disclosed, its value is diminished.

Firms that seek to protect such confidential information will find it advantageous to finance their activities from internal funds if and when they can. When they can't, they will find it advantageous to go to sources of financing where they can reveal the information in order to secure financing, but where its confidentiality will be protected. Financial intermediaries provide this option.

MANAGEMENT OF THE PAYMENTS SYSTEM

The services discussed thus far are provided by almost all intermediaries engaged in the management of investments. Now we will examine two important but more specialized services. The first, management of the payment mechanism, has long been provided by commercial banks. Banks provide the bookkeeping function of keeping track of receipts and disbursements for their customers as well as handling the exchange of funds. There is no reason why the management of payments has to be handled by a financial intermediary that also manages funds. For example, some European countries have payments systems, referred to as *giro,* that are not linked to commercial banks. Although these systems are not all alike, such systems allow individuals to authorize payments to a number of parties through the giro. Usually the giro system allows a user to specify a list of payments to be made and a bank account number from which the funds can be drawn. The bank is then notified of the total funds used. Automated giro systems are sometimes more closely related to the postal system in such countries than to commercial banks. The postal system handles the exchange of funds and provides the customer with a record of these exchanges, and the commercial bank merely maintains the balances of funds for the customer.

Management of the payments mechanism became tied in with the banking industry early in U.S. history. In the first half of the nineteenth century the banking industry issued bank notes that were like a bank's own currency. These notes did not always trade at the same value. That is, the notes issued by a very strong and reputable bank would exchange at a higher value than notes issued by a weak and risky bank. Each bank was willing to accept the notes of other banks at what they thought was a fair rate of exchange, and this constituted the payments mechanism. In the latter part of the century notes were replaced by demand deposits or checking accounts. Banks now began to keep records of transactions from demand deposit accounts, and they had to establish procedures for clearing checks back and forth. Banks set up clearinghouses to handle these exchanges, and large urban banks began to provide many of the collection and recordkeeping services for smaller banks. In the twentieth century, after the Federal Reserve System was created, it began to provide many check-clearing services for the banking industry.

More recently, innovations have dramatically changed the economics of the payments system. These changes are continuing at a rapid pace. First of all, credit cards are actively competing with checks as an efficient means of making payments. The credit card provides the customer with a direct link to a source of credit, but it also alters the method of recording and accounting for transactions. It increases reliance on automated recordkeeping and seeks to economize on the amount of paper that must change hands. Probably the most significant change in the payments mechanism is the prospect of an electronic funds transfer system. Such a system further minimizes the amount of paper that changes hands in the payments system while relying on electronic recordkeeping to the maximum extent possible. There are large potential economies in such a system, but it is difficult to estimate how rapidly we will progress toward a completely electronic system of funds transfer.

INSURANCE

Another service provided by some financial intermediaries is insurance. Insurance is a service which, like management of the payments mechanism, is easily tied in with the function of managing investments. In the process of insuring various contingencies, insurance companies receive premiums, which they invest, just as commercial banks invest the funds they receive in the course of managing payments for their depositors. While it might be possible to utilize a separate investment manager for funds collected by an insurance company, this is a less efficient means of insuring than combining the two services.

The basic idea behind insurance is essentially similar to the idea of diversifying risk in the stock market. Individuals and corporations are subject to risks that they would like to be able to avoid or shift to other parties. The risk may be the economic hardship imposed on a family by a death or the loss incurred by damage to property. People who are exposed to these risks are generally willing to pay a fee to have someone else bear at least part of that risk. This shifting of risk becomes economical when the risk can be diversified. For instance, consider the case of a company exposed to the risk of a fire. A company that is interested

TYPES OF FINANCIAL INTERMEDIARIES IN THE UNITED STATES

Now that we know why financial intermediaries exist, or at least the services they provide in financial markets, it is important to understand the different types of intermediaries which operate in the United States in the 1980s. In part the wide variety is a response to the market's demand for different financial services, but in part it is also due to government regulation which has fostered the growth of distinct or segmented financial institutions. There are seven basic types of financial institutions which are described briefly here. Table 12–1 shows the size of each classification by total assets at the end of 1986. We will look closely at some of these institutions and at their regulatory system in the chapters ahead.

Commercial Banks. These are probably the oldest, largest, and most diversified of financial intermediaries, and they have been the dominant source of business credit for centuries. In the United States commercial banking was a large and important enterprise before the New York Stock Exchange had even been founded. Commercial banks have provided mainly short-term debt financing to business borrowers. This traditional role limited the risk of intermediating across time. Risk is potentially significant for commercial banks, because most of their funds are obtained in highly liquid deposits. Banks offer demand deposits and saving deposits, which are interest-bearing accounts with a prespecified maturity. Historically, banks have been differentiated from other financial intermediaries by the fact that only banks were able to offer demand deposits. As a result, they alone were involved in managing the payments mechanism. However, recent changes in regulations have placed commercial banks and savings and loans on a more equal footing regarding both the asset and liability sides of their balance sheets.

Savings and Loans. These are depository institutions which specialize in making mortgage loans. They obtain funds through deposit accounts, both savings and time deposits, and they extend loans to finance residential property. They hold a small number of highly liquid securities, but these are held to maintain liquidity and not as profitable investments.

Historically, savings and loans invested principally in fixed rate, long-term mortgages, yet their deposits have very short maturities. As a result, they have provided the market with the service of intermediating across time. Until the passage of the Garn-St Germain Act of 1982, savings and loans were prevented from extending either commercial or consumer loans to any great extent and from accepting demand deposits. However, Garn-St Germain liberalized these restrictions on savings and loans so that their powers are now comparable in many respects with those of commercial banks. Some important differences in regulatory treatment of the two types of intermediaries remain, however. These include the treatment of holding companies, the funding of savings and loans through advances provided by the regulators, and the nature of supervision and capital requirements imposed on banks and savings and loans.

Mutual Savings Banks (MSBs). These institutions are a cross between commercial banks and savings and loans with some additional features. MSBs originated during the late nineteenth century in New England as an alternative to the commercial bank where working men and women could save funds and seek loans. Commercial banks did not commonly extend loans to consumers then as they do today, hence MSBs filled a distinct gap in the market. They were organized as cooperative or mutual organizations, so that the depositors are the owners of the organization. In MSBs depositors do not hold fixed interest claims with all residual income accruing to separate equity owners. Instead, the earnings of the MSB are paid to depositors. A large portion of the loans MSBs make are committed to home mortgages. They also provide other types of consumer loans to their members, and they invest a sizable portion of their funds in corporate bonds. Almost all MSBs today are in the New England states and New York. They have not spread to the rest of the country, probably because the growth of savings and loans and credit unions serve an essentially similar purpose.

Credit Unions. These are very much like mutual savings banks. They are organized as a mutual or

TABLE 12–1
Total assets of major classes of financial institutions, December 1986.
($ Millions)

Commercial banks	$2,799,700
Savings and loans	963,163
Savings banks	443,945
Credit unions	145,653
Finance companies	164,989
Investment companies	424,088
Life insurance companies	910,691
Total	$5,852,229

cooperative organization, and they provide an alternative to commercial banks where consumers can save money and obtain loans. Credit unions do not invest heavily in first mortgages because they are restricted from doing so, but they do finance most other types of consumer purchases. Credit unions got their start in the early twentieth century and existed in 38 states by 1934. Their largest growth occurred after World War II. Since then, they have had the highest growth rate of any financial intermediary in the country. The major distinction between a credit union and a mutual savings bank is that there is usually some common bond among the members of a credit union, for instance, their place of employment.

Finance Companies. This type of intermediary makes both business and consumer loans. Many finance companies are owned by commercial banks or nonfinancial corporations that produce or distribute consumer products. Many specialize in making consumer loans, often to more risky customers than banks deal with. These institutions evolved to circumvent many existing regulations on depository financial institutions. For example, many larger banks have operated finance companies that have offices outside of their permitted territories. Banks might do this to evade restrictions on branch banking and to be prepared in the event that commercial banks are allowed to have branches nationwide.

Investment Companies. These act as managers of investment portfolios for their customers. They provide all the services that go hand in hand with managing investments, such as reduction of risk through diversification, information production, and reduction in the cost of contracting. There are a variety of different types of investment companies, or mutual funds. Chapter 18 discusses the differences between two major types, closed- and open-end funds.

An increasingly important type of investment company is the pension fund. Pension funds accept funds from individuals during their working lifetimes, invest those funds, and pay them back to the individuals upon retirement. Like other intermediaries, they channel funds from lenders to borrowers. The contingency that triggers repayment of the funds lent is the lender's retirement. There are a number of different types of pension funds and pension contracts or terms for determining the funds lent and the repayment conditions. Investment companies are registered with and regulated by the SEC, while pension funds are regulated by the U.S. Department of Labor.

Insurance Companies. It is not always obvious that insurance companies perform a financial intermediary function similar to commercial banks or nonbank intermediaries, but they do. There are basically two types of insurance companies—life insurance and property and casualty insurance companies. These institutions differ according to the type of risk they insure and the investments they make, but not by the basic function they provide. Insurance companies accept premiums from those they insure and stand ready to pay off on the risks they insure. They also invest funds they receive, thus acting as a lender. As a consequence, they act much like commercial banks or other intermediaries.

in insuring against a fire faces a small probability that a fire will occur resulting in a large loss, and a large probability that no fire will occur resulting in no loss at all. A company which insures other companies against fire knows that some fires will always occur, but it knows that the probability that a large number of fires will occur at once is exceptionally small. As long as the insurance company has a large number of customers spread out geographically, it diversifies the risk of fire facing each customer. Therefore, the insurance company can offer customers a price for insurance that the consumer views as better than the prospect of no cost as long as no fire occurs, but large loss if it does.

From the standpoint of the economy, this kind of risk shifting is beneficial because it induces people to undertake productive activities they otherwise would perceive as too risky. The owners of a company might well be averse to constructing an expensive manufacturing plant if they alone had to bear the risk of its burning down. Therefore, risk shifting in general, and insurance in particular, serve a socially useful function.

Summary

We identified three distinct types of market organization: auction, over-the-counter, and intermediated markets. The important distinction between auction and over-the-counter markets is that all trades or exchanges take place in an auction market through some kind of centralized facility. At one time this meant that all buyers and sellers, or their brokers, had to meet in one location to trade in a competitive bidding process. But with modern computer technology, an auction market now requires only that there be a single facility through which all trading takes place or all transactions are recorded.

The alternative to the auction market is an over-the-counter market. The name is used to describe the operation method of any market that has no centralized trading or exchange facility, but, instead, has all trades handled by dealers. Dealers can also operate in an auction market. A dealer is a person who maintains an inventory of a particular security and buys and sells for that inventory with anyone who enters the market. The dealer provides immediacy to the market by offsetting imbalances between supply and demand. This service can be valuable in both auction and over-the-counter markets. In an auction market all trading with dealers takes place through a centralized facility, while trading is decentralized in an over-the-counter market.

We enumerated four requirements for a market to become centralized like an auction market. First, the market must have an economical, centralized facility for conducting exchanges. Second, the assets traded must be homogeneous so that a centralized trading facility is feasible. Third, there must be enough trading volume in the assets to make it efficient to operate the centralized facility. Finally, there must be some kind of market maker, a dealer, for example, who can operate profitably in the market. All of these requirements derive from the function of a market as an information collector and processor. If the assets traded in a market are homogeneous with a large trading volume, the process of collecting information and bringing it together can be centralized efficiently.

We also considered the distinction between primary and secondary markets. Primary markets are markets for new securities, and secondary markets are for used securities. There is no necessary connection between the primary-secondary classification and the auction versus over-the-counter classification for markets; both primary and secondary markets can operate as either auction or over-the-counter markets.

An intermediated market is one where financial intermediaries play a dominant role. A financial intermediary differs from a dealer in that an intermediary purchases assets and holds them as an investment rather than purchasing for resale and holding only an inventory. The intermediary acquires funds for these investments by selling claims on itself to the public. Therefore, unlike a dealer, the intermediary creates a new security and sells it to the market rather than reselling the securities it purchases.

We examined six services financial intermediaries provide to financial markets. The first few services are provided by almost all intermediaries, but the latter ones are more specialized.

Risk Reduction through Diversification. Financial intermediaries construct diversified portfolios of securities and sell claims on themselves to the market. In this way, they provide diversification to the investor. This is profitable because intermediaries find it less costly to construct a large diversified portfolio and sell small portions of it than individual investors would if they had to construct their own small diversified portfolios.

Maturity Intermediation. Many intermediaries acquire assets with long maturities and sell claims with very short maturities. This is referred to as intermediating across time or maturity intermediation. The intermediaries will demand a price that compensates them for the risk that they bear in bridging the gap between desired maturities.

Reduction in the Cost of Contracting. There are two principal costs involved in utilizing financial contracts. The first is the cost of constructing the contract, including the expertise required to know how best to structure the contract. The second is the cost of monitoring the parties' behavior to be sure the contract terms are observed. Investors who supply funds to financial intermediaries would find these costs to be quite large if they had to write, monitor, and enforce contracts with borrowers themselves. Financial intermediaries can lower these costs by specializing in financial contracting.

Information Production. Financial intermediaries produce information about the borrowers who are supplied with funds. They differ from other types of information producers because they do not directly distribute this information to the market. Hence, much of the information they receive is confidential.

Management of the Payments System.   A service historically provided by commercial banks is to keep records and provide for exchange of funds through demand deposits. Other types of intermediaries are competing with commercial banks in providing this service in the United States. This service is tied in with other services involved in managing investments for individuals and companies.

Insurance.   Many types of financial intermediaries provide insurance against particular contingencies, such as life insurance and fire and casualty insurance companies. These companies invest the funds received as premium income and repay these funds in the event of some event, such as fire, accident, or death. Though the management problems of insurance intermediaries are quite different from those of deposit intermediaries, they serve as a market for borrowing and lending just as other financial intermediaries do.

QUESTIONS

1. What are the important characteristics of an auction market? Why is the auction market held out as the economists' ideal of a market organization?
2. What is an over-the-counter market? Compare this to an auction market.
3. What service does a dealer provide? Explain the costs incurred by a dealer in providing this service.
4. Distinguish between a continuous and a call-auction market.
5. Distinguish between a primary and a secondary market. Can a primary and secondary market be either an over-the-counter or an auction market? Why?
6. Without the aid of an intermediary, investors can diversify portfolios and purchase securities with different maturities. Under what circumstances would they seek to use intermediaries to do this for them?
7. What does it mean to say that intermediaries can reduce the cost of contracting? What is included in the cost of contracting? What is the difference between an intermediary and the trustee of a bond?
8. What incentive does a financial intermediary have to produce reliable information? How does the market deal with the problem of unreliable information produced by financial intermediaries?
9. What is the payment system? How do commercial banks in the United States manage the payment system? Can you imagine an alternative, equally efficient system?
10. Insurance leads to a redistribution of risk. How can such a redistribution be socially beneficial?

REFERENCES

Arrow, Kenneth J. "Insurance, Risk and Resource Allocation," in Kenneth J. Arrow (ed.), *Essays in the Theory of Risk-Bearing,* New York: Markham Publishing Company, 1971, pp. 134–43.

Baltensperger, Ernest. "Alternative Approaches to the Theory of the Banking Firm," *Journal of Monetary Economics,* 6 (January 1980), pp. 1–38.

Benston, George, and Clifford Smith. "A Transactions Cost Approach to the Theory of Financial Intermediation," *Journal of Finance,* 31 (May 1976), pp. 215–231.

Black, Fischer. "Bank Funds Management in an Efficient Market," *Journal of Financial Economics,* (1975), pp. 323–39.

Campbell, Tim S. "Optimal Investment Financing Decisions and the Value of Confidentiality," *Journal of Financial and Quantitative Analysis,* 14 (December 1979), pp. 913–24.

———, and William A. Kracaw. "Information Asymmetries, Signalling and the Theory of Financial Intermediation," *Journal of Finance,* 35 (September 1980), pp. 863–82.

Demsetz, Harold. "The Cost of Transacting," *Quarterly Journal of Economics,* 82 (February 1968), pp. 33–53.

Diamond, D.W. "Financial Intermediation and Delegated Monitoring," *Review of Economic Studies,* 51 (1984), pp. 393–414.

Epps, Thomas W. "The Demand for Brokers' Services: The Relation between Security Trading Volume and Transaction Cost," *Bell Journal of Economics,* 7 (Spring 1976), pp. 163–94.

Fama, Eugene F. "Banking in the Theory of Finance," *Journal of Monetary Economics,* 1980, pp. 39–57.

Garbade, Kenneth D. and William L. Silber. "Structural Organization of Secondary Markets: Clearing Frequency, Dealer Activity and Liquidity Risk," *Journal of Finance,* 34 (June 1979), pp. 577–94.

Leland, Hayne E., and David H. Pyle. "Information Asymmetries, Financial Structure and Financial Intermediation," *Journal of Finance,* 32 (May 1977), pp. 371–87.

Mayer, Martin. *The Bankers,* New York: Weybright and Talley, Inc., 1974.

Miller, Merton, and Daniel Orr. "A Model of the Demand for Money by Firms," *Quarterly Journal of Economics,* 80 (August 1966), pp. 413–35.

Pyle, David H. "Descriptive Theories of Financial Institutions Under Uncertainty," *Journal of Financial and Quantitative Analysis,* 7 (December 1972), pp. 2009–29.

———. "On the Theory of Financial Intermediation," *Journal of Finance,* 26 (June 1971), pp. 737–47.

Stoll, Hans R. "The Supply of Dealer Services in Securities Markets," *Journal of Finance,* 33 (September 1978), pp. 1133–51.

Tinic, Seha M. "The Economics of Liquidity Services," *Quarterly Journal of Economics,* 86 (February 1972), pp. 79–93.

———, and Richard West. "Competition and the Pricing of Dealer Services in the Over-the-Counter Market," *Journal of Financial and Quantitative Analysis,* 7 (June 1972), pp. 1701–17.

13

*T*HE RATIONALE FOR
REGULATING FINANCIAL MARKETS

In general, financial markets are among the most heavily regulated of all U.S. markets. Yet both the extent and type of regulation varies tremendously across these markets. For example, the largest and most important type of financial intermediary, the commercial bank, is highly regulated; virtually every decision a commercial banker makes is subject to scrutiny by one or more government agencies. On the other hand, insurance companies are relatively free of regulation, at least at the federal level. For commercial banks and most other deposit intermediaries, regulation takes the form of government insurance for depositors against the prospect of losses and government supervision of loans and investments. In auction and over-the-counter markets, such as the market for corporate equities, regulation principally ensures the disclosure of relevant information to the public and maintains a competitive market.

The regulatory system that governs financial markets is complicated and often confusing. It is difficult to imagine that, if we could start over with a new regulatory system, we would create something exactly like what we have today. The system we have now evolved only gradually in response to crises. Regulations that dealt effectively with these crises were preserved, and the government institutions in charge of implementing those regulations grew. Oftentimes, however, institutions and regulations that failed were also preserved, so many features of today's system are rather difficult to justify.

Regulation is a timely topic for the 1980s. From the onset of the Great Depression in the 1930s until the late 1970s, the trend was toward increasing regulation in almost every U.S. industry. In the late 1970s the desirability of increased regulation came to be questioned seriously— not just by those who had obvious interests in reversing the trend, but by an increasingly broad cross section of Americans and their political representatives. This new sentiment has already had its impact on the regulation of financial markets, and it is likely that the regulatory system will continue to change in significant ways.

In order to understand how financial markets and institutions operate today, it is necessary to understand what constitutes the current regulatory system as well as how and why it is changing. The regulatory system is one of the major forces that has shaped the financial institutions and markets operating in the United States. In this chapter we concentrate on developing the rationale for the regulation of financial markets. ■

AN INITIAL PERSPECTIVE ON REGULATION

Before we get involved in the motives for and structure of financial market regulation, it is useful to acquire a broad perspective on the reasons for regulating *any* kind of market. Exploring the more general problem of regulation in any market is not to meander away from the principal issue at hand, but instead, it is to provide a meaningful context for the special problems of the financial markets.

REGULATION AND THE COMPETITIVE MARKETPLACE

A **perfectly competitive market** is one that has a large number of competitors that drive down prices to equal average cost, and there are no excess profits.

From the vantage point of society as a whole, the ideal kind of market is a **perfectly competitive** one. The opposite extreme from this ideal is a monopolistic one.

An industry is competitive if many firms sell their products at the lowest price and still find it profitable to remain in the industry. In this situation the firms are said to be earning no **excess or monopoly profits.** A more technical characterization of a competitive price is that it is equal to marginal cost. This means that the price charged by each firm is equal to the cost of producing the last unit of the firm's product. Where all firms price at marginal cost and where any firm that chooses can enter the industry and compete for customers, monopoly profits will not exist and the industry will be perfectly competitive.

Monopoly or excess profits are the excess of revenues over total cost where cost includes a normal return to the investors.

When an industry is controlled by a monopoly, the price charged by the monopolist will be greater than the price that would exist if that industry were perfectly competitive. In addition, the monopoly will reduce the quantity of goods produced in the industry relative to what would exist if the industry were perfectly competitive. By doing so the monopolist earns more profits than firms would earn if the industry were competitive. By keeping other firms out, the monopolist can raise price, lower quantity, and increase profits beyond the level that is just sufficient to keep the monopolist in the industry. For a monopoly to be successful, some mechanism must be devised to keep out the competition—that is, the monopolist must maintain a **barrier to entry.**

A **barrier to entry** is a device, such as a legal restriction, which prevents firms from entering an industry.

The rationale for regulation in a competitive economy is in some instances to encourage and in others to supplant the competitive marketplace. When used to encourage competition, regulation tries to prohibit practices by firms that interfere with the operation of a competitive market. When regulation is applied for this purpose, the presumption is that the market can operate competitively if the proper regulations are enforced. But regulation is also used to *supplant* the operation of a competitive market when a competitive marketplace is not feasible. In this instance the competitive market is said to have failed. Most regulation we observe in the United States can be traced to some kind of perceived or real market failure.

Market failure occurs when, for some reason, the private marketplace ceases to function at all or is unable to operate competitively, taking into account all the costs or benefits from production of a good. Market failure does not include the possibility that some firm or group of firms is able to establish a monopoly, unless there is something inherent in the market ensuring that competition cannot survive. There are three important ways in which market failure can occur: natural monopoly, externalities, and asymmetric information.

NATURAL MONOPOLY

A **natural monopoly** is a monopoly where the cost of producing the goods is decreasing with the scale or volume of production.

Most regulation in the United States has been developed to deal with industries subject to a particular kind of market failure called **natural monopoly.** It refers to a situation where an industry is inherently a monopoly. The principal natural monopolies are public utilities. For example, consider the prospect of competing electric companies providing service to the same community. Each company would have to build generators and construct electrical lines throughout the community. This is simply not feasible. It is much cheaper and more efficient to have a single set of electrical lines and generating facilities. The economist refers to an industry with a natural monopoly as a *decreasing-cost industry* or one subject to continuing economies of scale. The cost of production, per unit of output, decreases as the volume of output increases. When an industry has economies of scale, it is difficult to rely on competition to police prices. The electrical utility is by nature a monopoly, and this monopoly, if left to its own devices, would establish monopolistic prices. The solution to this problem has been to regulate the industry. Generally, public utility commissions have the responsibility for determining fair prices. What is fair is always debatable, yet this form of regulation has been applied to most electric power, gas, and communication utilities.

EXTERNALITIES

Externalities are costs not properly accounted for in the prices established in a competitive market.

A second type of market failure results from what are referred to as *externalities*. **Externalities** are costs not properly accounted for in the prices established in a competitive market. When externalities are present, there is said to be a divergence between social costs or benefits—that is, the total costs or benefits derived from the production of a product—and the private returns or costs derived by the purchaser or producer of the product.

Externalities can cut both ways. Social costs or benefits may be greater or less than private costs or benefits. The principal example of a situation where

A **public good** is a product people want to use or consume, but it is difficult or impossible to compel them to pay the price of their consumption.

social benefits exceed the private return from producing a product is referred to as the case of public goods. A **public good** is a product people want to use or consume, but it is difficult or impossible to compel them to pay the price of their consumption. The problem is best illustrated with an example. Suppose national defense were produced in a competitive market instead of by the government and paid for through taxes. While most individuals would prefer to consume some amount of national defense and would be willing to pay for it as they pay for other products, they know that if everyone else pays for national defense they can consume that defense without paying their share. In effect, they can ride free on the system; but when everyone recognizes the possibility of being a free rider, it is difficult for private producers of national defense to induce anyone to pay for their consumption. As a result, the production of national defense is less than most everyone would like. The root problem with a public good is that it is impossible to exclude someone who has not paid from the consumption of such a good. Hence, access to the good is public. Another way to view the problem is that the private return to the producer of defense is below the social return because of the free-rider problem. The externality involved in public goods leads to underproduction of those goods, and the role of regulation is to increase production to a level perceived to be socially optimal.

When an externality cuts the other way, the problem is that the private return from producing a product exceeds the social return from that product. This results when there is some social cost borne by society as a whole resulting from the production of a particular product, but the market does not compel the producer of the product to bear that cost. A contemporary example of this divergence between social and private cost is pollution. A wide variety of industrial products contribute to pollution of the environment, but in general, the market does not include the cost of that pollution in the private cost of producing those products. The problem is to devise a way to make the producers, and therefore ultimately the consumers, of the products that pollute bear the cost of that pollution.

There are two ways regulation can be used to accomplish this purpose. The first is to hold the producers liable for social costs or impel them to reduce the amount of pollution directly and hence the social costs of that pollution. The second is through taxes which transform the social costs into private ones. In this instance, unlike the case of the public good, the market produces too much rather than too little of a product because of the divergence between social and private cost. In both instances, government regulation is prompted to alter the level of production and the distribution of returns or costs.

ASYMMETRICAL INFORMATION

Asymmetrical information refers to information which is held by only one party to a transaction and which may be used by that party to her advantage.

The final type of market failure in competitive markets that has led to government regulation, asymmetrical information, was introduced earlier in this book (see Chapter 5). The earlier discussion of **asymmetrical information** was concerned with the problems of moral hazard, adverse selection, and ultimately market failure through what was called the "lemons" problem. You will recall the essence of the lemons problem: suppose there is a product for sale which is subject to a large variation in quality. Also, suppose that the quality of each such product is known to the seller but not to the buyer. The products might be automobiles, refrigerators, or medical services. If sellers sell only products when the price yields them a profit and buyers buy only when they believe they are getting a fair price, this market may be subject to a particular type of failure. Buyers know that every seller is likely to claim he has the highest quality product in the market. They also know that most of these sellers are lying, but they do not know who is lying and who is telling the truth. The price they are willing to pay will reflect the quality of the average product available in the market.

In this sense, the price is fair. The sellers who actually have high-quality products will be unwilling to sell at this price, as they must expect to take a loss by so doing. Hence, only the liars will be willing to trade at this average price. Recognizing that the sellers with high-quality products will drop out, the buyers will revise their idea of a fair price downward until all the higher quality products have been driven out of the market. In this kind of extreme situation, where nothing intervenes to alleviate the asymmetry of information, the market fails to deliver anything but low-quality products. Regulation may be useful in such instances to correct the information asymmetry and provide ways for buyers to discriminate among high-quality and low-quality products.

THE MOTIVES FOR REGULATING FINANCIAL MARKETS

Much of the regulatory structure that applies to markets other than financial markets has evolved to deal with the problems of natural monopoly and the types of externalities described above. But this is not true in financial markets. Although financial markets are heavily regulated, virtually no financial industries are natural monopolies. Moreover, while there certainly are externalities in financial markets, the externalities related to pollution, safety, and health that have led to such extensive regulation in other industries are not present.

We will identify four distinct rationales for regulation of financial markets. Three of these rationales pertain to difficulties arising from imperfections in information distribution, the most serious of which is market failure due to asymmetrical information. The other rationale is one that has led to regulation in other markets as well—the desire to limit monopoly power and promote competition.

1. Promote competition and prevent monopolistic paractices
2. Prevent or limit expropriation
3. Control the actions of agents
4. Prevent market failure.

These four basic rationales for regulation, the problems they create, and the types of regulation they have spawned are briefly summarized in Table 13–1. This table provides a useful frame of reference for the discussion of regulation throughout the rest of the book.

TABLE 13–1
Summary of the rationale for regulation of financial markets.

Motive for Regulation	Nature of Problem	Regulation to Deal with the Problem
1. Limit monopoly power and promote competition	1. Cartel behavior promotes monopolistic practices	1. Promulgate and enforce rules designed to prevent monopolistic practices
2. Limit opportunities for expropriation when there is a difference in information between contract parties	2. Unsophisticated parties—generally consumers—may be unable to protect themselves adequately against expropriations	2. Limit allowable contracts and require disclosure of information (truth-in-lending)
3. Limit opportunities for agents to act against the interests of their employers	3. Agents who have special information may be able to use that information for their own advantage at the expense of their employers	3. Mandate disclosure of information and limit opportunities for insiders to trade on information
4. Avoid market failure due to asymmetrical information	4. With unregulated financial intermediaries, depositors periodically withdraw from the market if they fear for the safety of their funds	4. Provide insurance on deposits and control the risk of financial intermediaries

REGULATION AND MONOPOLY POWER IN FINANCIAL MARKETS

We will begin by examining how monopoly power can develop in financial markets and then explore the ways that regulation can be used to limit monopoly power.

SOURCES OF MONOPOLY POWER

A significant amount of regulation applied to financial markets promotes competition or restricts practices perceived to be monopolistic. There are examples of this kind of regulation in auction and over-the-counter markets as well as in intermediated markets. The prospect that a monopoly might exist in U.S. financial markets has long been viewed as exceptionally pernicious, maybe more so than in most nonfinancial markets. The reason is probably that an important part of the structure of any democratic society is the concept that no citizen should be arbitrarily restricted from access to capital. A monopoly in the market for capital holds out the prospect that capital may be distributed in an arbitrary manner and, even if access is not restricted, prices will be set at monopolistic levels. As a result, it has been a strong part of the democratic tradition for the government to take actions assuring access to financial resources and explicitly forbidding practices that are clearly monopolistic.

In financial markets one of the principal devices that can be used to promote monopoly power is the trade association. A **trade association** is a club or organization formed by the firms in an industry to promote the good of the industry and to deal with common problems. It can serve many useful purposes—setting rules of behavior, promoting the industry, representing the industry in government proceedings, and performing research and educational tasks for firms—but a trade association can also be the front for a cartel. That is, it can serve as the means by which the industry establishes a monopoly and compels the firms to behave in a monopolistic manner. To serve this purpose it needs to set rules of behavior that jointly benefit all the firms acting in concert as a monopoly. The rules are needed because it is always to the benefit of any one firm in a cartel to cheat on the agreed behavior of the cartel. For example, the rules may stipulate a minimum price for a product. But if one firm cheats by lowering its price in secret, it would generate more profit than if it observed the minimum price. However, if all firms behave in this way, the cartel is doomed. Therefore, in order to be successful, a cartel needs to have enforceable rules of behavior.

Auction markets provide exceptionally good opportunities for the operation of cartels if these markets operate with brokers and dealers. In the purest of auction markets, without any brokers or dealers, the opportunities for cartel behavior are limited. Such a market is probably the closest in the real world to the economists' concept of perfect competition. But in auction markets where all sales are made by brokers or where dealers absorb temporary trading imbalances, there is a potential for a cartel to flourish. The markets essentially form a trade association in which one must be a member to act as a broker or dealer. If such a trade association is used to promote a cartel, then its principal objective will be to establish restrictions on permissible behavior that tend to generate monopoly profits for all brokers or dealers in the association. Rule enforcement comes through the ability to revoke membership in the association. The rules may directly govern pricing of the services member brokers and dealers are allowed to provide or the amount of information they can divulge to customers. All of these things will tend to establish monopoly power.

Another possibility for cartel behavior occurs in the distribution process of new securities—that is, in primary markets that do not function as auction markets. In the primary markets, securities are often distributed through investment bankers who come together to form syndicates in order to purchase and distribute securities. The syndicate distributes the risk of a particular security issue across separate investment bankers. The diversification motive is a very legitimate purpose of syndicates. However, there is at least the potential that the syndicate form of organization can be used to monopolize the primary markets. The success of

A **trade association** is a club or organization formed by the firms in an industry to promote the good of the industry and to deal with common problems.

EXAMPLE OF CARTEL BEHAVIOR

One of the most important historical examples of apparent cartel behavior in U.S. financial markets is the enforcement of minimum brokerage commissions on the New York Stock Exchange (NYSE) until the early 1970s. The NYSE regularly set minimum prices that could be charged by brokers for executing trades on the floor of the exchange. These fees had to be approved officially by the SEC as regulator of the NYSE. For many years the SEC regularly reviewed and approved minimum prices on the NYSE in spite of the apparent anticompetitive nature of this regulation. However, in the late 1960s the Antitrust Division of the U.S. Justice Department filed suit claiming that this practice violated antitrust laws. The NYSE fought and ultimately lost when Congress passed a law in 1975 prohibiting minimum brokerage commissions. The NYSE argued that the brokerage business was essentially a natural monopoly and therefore warranted this type of regulation. However, as we shall see in Chapter 14, the historical record presents strong evidence in contradiction of the NYSE's case.

A less dramatic but more current example of allegedly anticompetitive practices on an exchange is the use of broker groups on the floor of the Chicago Mercantile Exchange, particularly for trading futures contracts on the Standard & Poor's 500 Stock Index. The Merc uses an *open outcry* trading system where any offer to buy or sell a futures contract must be offered to anyone on the floor through an open outcry. However, brokers have formed groups to allow customers to trade in a number of pits, or locations where different futures contracts are traded, by contacting a single broker. Brokers in these groups trade largely with each other. Brokers who are not in a particular group argue that this practice violates the basic rules of the exchange regarding open outcry. They contend that customers are cheated because they often end up with prices that are inferior to what would be obtained if trading was done outside the group.

In early 1987 the Merc proposed that brokers be limited to 15 percent of their trading within a broker group. In addition, brokers who exceeded this limit would be subject to a $50,000 fine. In part, the pressures to change the practices on the Merc are a result of increased pressure from Wall Street securities traders who are more active in the futures markets as a result of new futures and options contracts on stock indexes. A conflict has emerged between two different segments of the finance industry: the commodities traders and the stockbrokers. The two largely separate businesses are now becoming increasingly interrelated, and each group is trying to protect its competitive position and limit the advantages of the other group. The securities industry argues that trading practices on the futures exchanges often benefit the entrenched position of commodities traders. The commodities traders are quick to defend their practices as being highly competitive and in the consumers' best interests. It is up to the regulatory authorities to decide what regulations are actually in the public's interest.

such a cartel depends upon the competitive forces at work in the industry, particularly how willing the issuers of securities are to circumvent the cartel. In this case, as with a trade association of brokers or dealers in an auction market, the cartel must have some mechanism for stipulating and enforcing rules.

In order for a cartel to be successful in the long run, it usually requires some kind of legal sanction. The legal sanction must not apply merely to the existence of the association that serves as the front for the cartel, but also to its rules and enforcement procedures. This is principally where regulation comes to bear in promoting competition in financial markets. Few financial markets are so dominated by a single firm that the firm can create a monopoly on its own without the support of a cartel. As a result, monopoly power in financial markets largely depends on cartel behavior, and regulation can be used to limit the ability of cartels to operate successfully. These regulations are directed at legitimate trade associations to insure that they do not directly fix prices, restrict the services members can offer, or restrict access to information that would lead to more competitive pricing.

REGULATION TO PROMOTE COMPETITION

It is useful to divide the regulatory actions taken to promote competition in financial markets into those which deal with auction and over-the-counter markets and those which deal with intermediated markets. While the issues are not totally separate, there are considerable distinctions.

Regulation in over-the-counter and auction markets is directed toward preventing cartel behavior. Responsibility for regulating these markets lies principally with the Securities and Exchange Commission (SEC) and with the Commodity Futures Trading Commission (CFTC) for specific futures and options markets. A good portion of the regulation conducted by the SEC is directed at the New York Stock Exchange, in part because it is the oldest and largest auction market in the country, and in part because it has been perceived as one of the ripest possibilities for cartel behavior. The SEC now explicitly prohibits minimum prices for brokers' services and closely supervises dealer activities on the exchange. In addition, it has major responsibility for determining what type of market organization will actually be used in the secondary market for corporate equities and bonds. These issues will be examined closely in the next chapter.

The task of promoting competition is less complicated in auction and over-the-counter markets than in markets where intermediaries play a large role. Problems pertaining to information distribution, which have led to the regulation of intermediaries, are not so severe in these markets. In auction markets, such as the New York Stock Exchange, the central problem is to be sure that the brokers and dealers who comprise that market offer competitive prices for their services. This is not significantly different from the issues regarding competitive versus monopolistic pricing that arise in other (nonfinancial) industries.

In intermediated markets, such as commercial banking, the fundamental difficulty is that many actions which tend to increase competition and lower prices also tend to interfere with the regulatory system that is designed to prevent market failure. A competitive market is one in which the weak and inefficient firms fail to survive. But in banking, such failure has often come all at once for a large number of institutions in response to a financial panic. Such failures threaten the stability of the whole industry and the economy. The regulatory system that has evolved to deal with the problem of market failure tends to ensure the survival of at least some banks that would not be profitable in a more competitive environment. Unfortunately, there seems to be no practical way to eliminate this conflict. As a result, the regulators of financial intermediaries often argue about how much competition to allow, and they often disagree with the Justice Department on these questions. These disputes are further complicated by the fact that it is possible to attempt to justify, as a necessary part of the regulatory system designed to prevent market failure, restrictions that do not really serve this purpose at all, but tend to reduce competition and increase the profits of existing financial institutions.

The important issues regarding competition in the intermediated markets relate primarily to the types of activities various intermediaries will be allowed to engage in and the amount of competition permitted in any region. Each type of intermediary is restricted as to what types of activities it may engage in. Many of these restrictions are designed to prevent conflicts of interest or to limit competition. The central issue is how much market fragmentation should be enforced by regulation versus how much competition should be encouraged. There appears to be no simple answer. With regard to regional competition, the underlying issue is essentially the same. As we will discover when we study bank regulation and the current conduct of the banking business, regulations on bank branching and bank holding companies tend to restrict the amount of competition in any given geographic area. Many such regulations are determined at the state rather than the federal level. Again, they tend to restrict competition apparently in order to reduce risk, though the motives here may be more to protect established regional monopoly positions than to protect the interests of depositors.

REGULATION AND THE PROBLEM OF EXPROPRIATION

As we have learned, an essential function of financial markets is to aggregate information about the future returns on assets and set the assets' prices. It is natural, then, that we should be concerned about how effectively an unregulated competitive marketplace can perform this job. We learned in Part I that if all participants in a market have equal information, the market can process information and set prices in a manner with which we can find little fault. But if participants in a financial market have significantly different information, then the market can have difficulties that may justify some regulation by the government or another third party. The most serious difficulty is that the market may fail, as described in the lemons paradigm. But even short of market failure, an imperfect distribution of information may lead to difficulties that give rise to regulation. Many people believe this has occurred in the U.S. economy in the twentieth century.

We will analyze three types of difficulties that can arise in a financial market when there is an unequal distribution of information. The most severe problem, market failure, has already been discussed. Our purpose here is to understand more thoroughly why and how regulation has been used to avoid market failure. The other two problems pertain to what we will call *expropriations* that can be carried out in financial markets and to the closely related problem of agency. In analyzing these topics we will try to understand how an unregulated, competitive market deals with them and then how regulation may be used as well. Our purpose

THE SEPARATION OF BANKING AND INSURANCE

The separation between the commercial banking and insurance industries represents an interesting example of the restrictions imposed on financial intermediaries that prevent competition. The laws that govern bank holding companies in the United States stipulate that they, or companies which own one or more commercial banks, cannot also be engaged in activities which are not deemed by the regulators to be "closely related" to banking. This has been used to enforce a separation between commercial banking and other forms of commerce. Bank regulators have held that insurance underwriting is not closely related to banking. As a result, commercial bank holding companies are prohibited from owning more than a 25 percent interest in an insurance underwriting firm. They are allowed to sell and underwrite insurance products directly tied with lending activities, such as credit life insurance, and they are allowed to act as an agency for separate insurance underwriters. However, they are not allowed to underwrite themselves.

While this restriction is enforced on commercial banks, in 1982 savings and loan holding companies were given the authority to own and operate insurance companies, including underwriting. At the same time, savings and loans were given expanded powers that left them with much the same authority for making loans and investments as commercial banks. Therefore, a system has developed where one type of depository institution has the authority to enter the insurance business, but the other does not.

There appears to be no good reason for enforcing a separation between banking and insurance other than to protect access to the deposit insurance system. There *is* concern that it is difficult or impossible to enforce a separation between bank and nonbank subsidiaries of a bank holding company, so that if a nonbank subsidiary developed financial difficulties, the bank's assets might be used to assist the nonbank subsidiary. The perception is that this might constitute an abuse of the support by the bank's deposit insurance system. However, aside from this concern, the major reason for maintaining a separation between banking and insurance appears to be a desire to limit direct competition between them to maintain their financial stability. This trade-off between concern with financial stability and maintaining competition underlies many of the policy issues involved in regulating financial intermediaries.

---

in this discussion is not to justify the extent of regulation we observe in the financial markets of the 1980s; instead, it is to understand why and how our present regulatory system evolved.

EXPROPRIATION IN PRIVATE CONTRACTS

Expropriation refers to an act which takes the property rights of an individual or corporation without appropriate compensation.

Virtually all financial assets involve some kind of legal contract. Legal contracts serve to both promote and protect the interests of all the parties involved. But whenever such contracts are agreed to, there are opportunities available for one party to take actions that tend to hurt or to **expropriate** the other party or parties. In fact, it is often because of these possibilities that such contracts are necessary. For example, consider the relationship between the owners of equity securities and the owners of debt securities in a particular firm. One way that equityholders might try to expropriate debtholders is to rob the firm of its assets by paying themselves excess dividends. This action increases the likelihood that the firm will be unable to meet its contractual obligation to debtholders and thereby expropriates their value. Another possible form of expropriation involves the relationship between securityholders and the managers of a firm. Managers may try to expropriate wealth from the firm's securityholders through the more explicitly illegal form of actually stealing funds from the firm, or it may involve excess consumption of perquisites such as hunting lodges, yachts, and other valued services provided by the company to management.

MARKET MECHANISMS TO DEAL WITH EXPROPRIATION

The unregulated market has essentially three methods for dealing with these expropriation activities, but each one has costs and hence may well not be used to eliminate such expropriation completely. The first method is called *ex ante pricing of expropriation*. Those who expect to be expropriated may charge a price when the contract is agreed upon that compensates them, ex ante, for the expropriation they expect will take place. For example, if stockholders are expected to pay themselves excess dividends, the bondholders will be unwilling to pay a price for the debt of this firm that is as high as they would pay for an otherwise identical firm where expropriation was not expected. That reduction in the price the debtholders will pay represents the charge demanded, ex ante, for the future expropriation. Once they have paid the price for this expropriation, the equityholders will be compelled to actually go through with the expropriation, so that this method of dealing with the problem does not curtail the expropriation itself. This method may work rather well when there is little ambiguity about the incentive of equityholders to actually expropriate—that is, when debtholders are able to anticipate the future expropriation perfectly—but if equityholders can estimate such expropriation opportunities better than debtholders, then ex ante pricing will work only imperfectly.

Covenants include restrictions on equityholders that limit their actions in ways which protect the interest of debtholders.

The second method the market uses to deal with expropriations is to include provisions in legal contracts that limit the ability of one party to expropriate the other. In the case of relations between equityholders and debtholders, such **covenants** would include restrictions on equityholders that limit the amount of dividends they can choose to pay themselves. Such restrictions are, in fact, often included in debt contracts. Unlike the method of ex ante pricing, these covenants are designed to prevent the expropriation from occurring rather than to seek compensation for it. The problem with covenants is that, as a rule, they involve costs that must be borne by the parties to the contract. The most obvious cost is in monitoring the party whose action is restricted to make sure that the convenant is observed. In many instances these convenants may be quite complicated, and therefore such monitoring can be quite expensive. A second cost is that the covenant may limit the flexibility of the restricted party in a way that is detrimental to that party's interests above and beyond the limits it places on his or her ability to expropriate. For example, covenants that restrict the amount of additional debt a firm may acquire may also restrict a firm's ability to engage in a new and profitable investment that becomes available when the stock market is at a low point and additional equity financing is exceedingly expensive. If the firm has to finance in a poor equity market, it might find the investment to be unprofitable and, with a restriction requiring it to use at least some new equity, its flexibility is reduced. Because of this kind of difficulty, debt agreements between corporations and private lenders such as banks and insurance companies are often renegotiated if the convenants begin to harm the borrower. But again, this renegotiation process is costly, so that the method of restricting expropriations with convenants cannot perfectly restrict all conceivable expropriations.

The final method utilized by the market for dealing with expropriations is referred to as **ex post settling up.** This might be thought of as the legal solution. It is really the opposite of ex ante pricing. If an expropriation takes place, then the courts will be used to extract damages from the party who does the expropriating. If ex post settling up can work perfectly, then the incentive to expropriate is eliminated; but if there are costs or difficulties involved, then at least some expropriation will take place regardless. Returning to the example of the relationship between debtholders and equityholders in a firm, consider the problem of deciding when an expropriation has taken place because of a payment of excess dividends. It is difficult to establish, in any objective manner, what is excessive and what is not. If the value of the securities owned by the debtholders goes down, they may claim it was because excess dividends were paid. But the equityholders may claim that it was because of some totally unrelated event. It is difficult, if not impossible, to establish who is correct in such cases, and it is costly to use the courts. Legal expenses mean that there will always be room for some expropriation where the gains from litigation are not worth the cost.

Ex post settling up refers to the arrangement of compensation, after the fact, for expropriations.

REGULATING THE TERMS OF CONTRACTS

The market's methods for dealing with expropriations are costly and complicated, even when parties to contracts are sophisticated and have a thorough understanding of how the market operates. But if some potential parties to financial contracts are unsophisticated or naive, then the opportunities for expropriation are enhanced. In contracts between corporate representatives, the general presumption is that parties are sophisticated or at least should be. But in consumer contracts this is not the case. Consumers engage in financial contracts on a relatively infrequent basis and therefore do not often have the opportunity to learn the ways they may be expropriated and the methods to protect themselves.

This possibility has provided a motivation for regulation that directly protects or helps the consumer to be self-protecting. The motivation for this kind of protection arises from the **doctrine of conscionability.** This legal doctrine holds that some contracts or actions by parties to contracts may be unjust, immoral, or unconscionable. From an economic viewpoint, this means that a relatively sophisticated party is attempting to take advantage of an unsophisticated party. The doctrine of conscionability leads to two general types of regulations. One involves restrictions on the allowable contracts that are legally binding. This means that some contract provisions may be completely prohibited because they are viewed as unconscionable. The second type of regulation is to impose requirements of disclosure on the relatively sophisticated party. Both of these are supplements to the methods utilized by the private market to deal with expropriation opportunities in contracts.

The **doctrine of conscionability** holds that some contracts or actions by parties to contracts may be unjust, immoral, or unconscionable.

A number of regulations imposed by the government are designed to prevent unconscionable contracts. Some of these regulations directly restrict the types of contracts in which market participants may engage. In other cases, the regulations are designed to improve the access to information of all contracting parties. There are a number of examples of each kind of regulation.

One example of a direct restriction on permissible contracts is provided by the limitations on the types of mortgage contracts that can be offered by savings and loans in the United States. These contracts are restricted by both state law and by federal regulators. Until the early 1980s, mortgage contracts other than the standard mortgage, with an interest rate fixed for the life of the mortgage, were prohibited for federally chartered savings and loans by regulation. While many regulators saw additional justifications for these restrictions, apparently an important motive was to protect consumers from mortgage contracts they might not understand. This kind of protection has often been criticized as paternalism but it is difficult to identify an objective criterion for what amount of regulation may be appropriate in this domain. Another example of this kind of restriction is usury ceilings, which seem to be an outgrowth of the religiously motivated restrictions on interest rates prevalent in Europe in the Middle Ages. The idea is that there are interest rates that are so high that people should be prevented from agreeing to them even if they understand the contract and choose to agree to its terms.

In recent years there has been a trend toward regulations that improve access to information rather than leave the uninformed in their unfortunate state and restrict the kinds of contracts to which they are allowed to agree. Principal among these regulations is truth-in-lending. Significant truth-in-lending legislation was first adopted by the U.S. Congress in the early 1970s. It requires that any firm that lends to consumers must comply with federal regulations regarding disclosure of the loan terms. In particular, the legislation requires that lenders present the true cost of the loan in a simple and understandable manner. This kind of legislation tends to limit the room for unconscionable contracts while keeping paternalism to a minimum. The drawback, however, is that such disclosure is costly. Many economists argue that, in most instances, the market will generate the optimal amount of disclosure if left to its own devices. But where relatively uninformed consumers are involved, this argument may well be weak. Yet the opposite extreme, one of extensive disclosure requirements, is also socially suboptimal, for truth-in-lending legislation raises the cost of providing credit, and all borrowers bear that additional cost.

REGULATION AND THE CONCEPT OF AGENCY

The **problem of agency** refers to the conflicts of interest between shareholders of a firm and the managers who operate that firm.

A special but important case of expropriation discussed above is the **problem of agency.** The idea of an agent applies to a wide variety of contractual relationships in our economy. Managers of firms are agents who make the decisions delegated to them by the stockholders. This applies to financial firms as well as nonfinancial firms. In an ideal world, agents act in the best interest of those who hire them, without having to be induced to do so. But the world is often not ideal, and the interests of agents often diverge from those of their employers. As a result, it is necessary for those who hire agents to devise mechanisms to induce them to behave as they would like. Actually, it is hopeless to try to induce an agent to act against his or her own interest in the long run. The trick is to make the agent's interests coincide with the interests of the employer to as great an extent as possible. The difficulties involved in accomplishing this trick are what constitute the agency problem.

SOURCES OF THE AGENCY PROBLEM

There are three sources of difference between the interests of agents and their employers. First, employers and agents have different attitudes toward the effort expended by managers. Employers view more effort on the part of their agents as unambiguously better because it leads to higher returns or lower costs for the investment that the agent controls. Agents, on the other hand, see the positive effect of effort that their employers see, but they also see more effort as less leisure. Agents, therefore, want to balance effort and leisure, while employers derive no benefit from agents' leisure.

The second source of difference, and probably the most important one for our purposes, pertains to information agents possess about the investments they control for their employers. Agents generally have better information about the value of the investments they manage than do owners, because they specialize in the acquisition of that information. If there were no barriers to disseminating that information to the market, this would provide them with no particular advantage. But it is often necessary for managers to limit access to a considerable amount of information, generally to keep it away from the firm's competitors. But, once much information remains private, managers must then choose the investments of the firm without the owners being able to review or observe those choices. The problem facing the employers is to provide an incentive for managers not to withhold information, unless it is in the interest of the employers to do so, and then to use that information to the employers' advantage. It is not obvious that the market has any effective way to resolve this problem.

The final source of difference between agents and their employers arises when managers have special information about the firm's actual earnings. If agents observe the actual returns on investments they manage and are responsible for reporting those returns to their employers, then they are provided with opportunities to use that information to their advantage. They can report lower earnings than actually accrued and keep the difference for themselves. One impediment that deters such behavior, or presumably does, is the threat of criminal prosecution for theft. The other method is for the employers of agents to hire accountants to audit agents' reported earnings and ensure that misuse of funds does not occur. There is, of course, the question of the auditors' reliability because they also may find misuse of funds to be profitable. If the gain is large enough, there will always be an incentive to cheat so that no such inspection system can be perfect. But, in general, the smaller the gap in information between agents and employers, the smaller the incentive for misuse of funds.

REGULATING AGENTS

Regulation which deals with the problem of agency is principally designed to decrease the disparity in information between agents and those people they represent. This type of regulation is referred to as **disclosure regulation.** Like truth in lending, it requires managers to disclose information to the capital markets about the value of their firms' investments.

Disclosure regulation refers to the regulations governing proper disclosure of information held by agents.

Existing disclosure regulations come under the domain of the Securities and Exchange Commission (SEC). They can be divided into two basic kinds. One kind of regulation requires disclosure to the market of information about a firm and its investments through periodic filing of financial statements as well as in the form of a prospectus when securities are issued to the market. These rules apply to all companies with 500 stockholders or $1 million in assets, so they apply to all but the smallest corporations in the United States. These disclosure restrictions provide a common basis of information for all current and potential owners of the firm's securities. The second kind of disclosure regulation is referred to as rule 10b–5 of the Securities and Exchange Commission. Rule 10b–5 requires that all corporate managers or other insiders—that is, people with access to the managers' information—must disclose all trading in the stock of the firm they manage. This rule is designed to prevent managers, and those in whom they confide, from using their inside information to buy or sell shares of their firm when they know something the market does not.

Since 1934 when the Securities and Exchange Commission was created and this type of regulation was first implemented, there has been considerable debate as to whether disclosure regulation of this kind is actually needed. As in the case of truth-in-lending legislation, many argue that the market will disclose, on its own, an appropriate amount of information. Because information generation and disclosure are costly, increased disclosure is not necessarily better. In the next chapter we will examine this debate about the need for the SEC's disclosure rules.

REGULATION TO LIMIT MARKET FAILURE

The prospect of a significant collapse of financial markets has been one of the prime reasons for market regulation in the United States for more than 150 years. During most of this period, such concerns centered around the banking industry because banks were involved in almost all financial transactions in one way or another. The country did not have the highly diverse types of markets and financial institutions that exist today. The problem that plagued commercial banks throughout the nineteenth century and into the early twentieth century was the periodic occurrence of financial panics. Financial markets periodically experienced varying degrees of market failure.

As we have seen, market failures have not been the result of natural monopoly or externalities such as pollution. Instead, they have principally been the result of the difference in information between those who owned and managed financial intermediaries and those who had deposits in them. Though the panics and failures were due to problems arising from differences in information, markets did not fail exactly as the lemons parable suggests; that is, firms with valuable assets did not withdraw from the financial markets. Instead, depositors who had little information about the value of an intermediary's assets and who feared that their deposits would be lost, withdrew their funds from financial intermediaries and hoarded them. Once the withdrawals began, the stability of the financial intermediaries was threatened and the incentive to withdraw funds increased. This kind of panic could, and in the early 1930s did, lead to the breakdown of the entire system, or to market failure. In Chapter 15 we look more closely at how and why these panics occurred.

The principal form of regulation that has evolved to deal with this problem involves a fundamental change in the nature of the financial contract that individuals agree to when they deal with a financial intermediary. The most important single feature of this regulatory system is insurance of deposits. Deposits with commercial banks and with savings and loans are now insured by the federal government up to a maximum of $100,000. Individual depositors at commercial banks need no longer fear that their funds will be misused when dealing with a financial institution that has vastly superior knowledge about financial markets and financial contracts. A depositer no longer needs to withdraw bank funds because he or she distrusts the banker's incentive to act in the depositor's interest. The government guarantees the banker's performance so that the underlying problem that leads to market failure is, at least in part, eliminated.

If deposit insurance alone were the only form of regulation used to eliminate the prospect of failure in financial markets where intermediaries play a large role, then it would not be successful. The reason is that the insured depositor no longer has any incentive to collect information and evaluate the banker's performance. In effect, the banker is no longer an agent of the depositor, but is now an agent of the government, which provides the insurance. The government must now perform all the functions that any sophisticated private party would perform who has contracted with the financial intermediary. The government has to devise schemes to protect against expropriation and monitor the banker's activities to see that his or her interests coincide with those of the government as much as possible. As we will discover in later chapters, most regulations imposed upon financial intermediaries are designed to accomplish these purposes.

In those financial markets not dominated by financial intermediaries, regulation designed to prevent market failure is much less extensive. This is true for two reasons. First, these markets tend to be ones where the social cost of market failure is less than it is in markets dominated by intermediaries. Specifically, market failure involving the commercial banking system has historically threatened almost all markets in the country. This results from the fact that banks provide the mechanisms of payment, through demand deposits and cash, used throughout the economy. When the banking system is threatened, the viability of the entire system for exchanging all goods and services is also threatened. Second, financial intermediaries exist and prosper in financial markets where there is a useful role to be served by some kind of specialist. The services intermediaries provide were discussed in Chapter 12. Most of these services involve some sort of information collection and processing for parties who want to borrow and lend. By its very nature, the intermediary comes to possess information not possessed by all the parties with which it deals. It is in precisely this kind of situation that there is the greatest potential for market failure. In markets where differences in information are relatively slight, there is neither the need for a financial intermediary nor as significant a prospect that there will be substantial market failure. Therefore, by and large, market failure is a problem that pertains to financial intermediaries, and the regulations that seek to prevent it are imposed upon financial intermediaries.

Summary

We have examined the rationale behind the regulation of financial markets and began by surveying the reasons for regulation of any type of market. One reason for regulation is to limit monopolistic practices in a market, and another is to supplant a competitive market when it would fail if unregulated. There are three basic types of market failure. The first is natural monopoly, which occurs when there are economies of scale in an industry so that the natural form of market organization is a monopoly. The second occurs when a market has significant externalities that create a divergence between private and social cost in the industry. The third occurs when asymmetrical information causes market participants to withdraw from the market. Much of the regulation developed in the 1960s and 1970s was directed toward the problem of natural monopoly and externalities, such as pollution, health, and safety, but these problems are relatively insignificant in financial markets.

Financial markets are regulated for two principal reasons. First, much regulation is designed to limit monopolistic practices and promote competition. Second, regulation is directed at problems that result from asymmetries in information, the most serious of which is the prospect of virtual collapse or failure.

Monopoly power in financial markets arises largely out of the potential for cartels to develop. One of the entities that can function as a cartel is a trade association. To function as a cartel a trade association must be able to enforce rules that prevent individual members from cheating on the cartel. To be successful in the long run such rules generally require legal sanctions. Trade associations are common in financial markets, both in intermediated markets and in auction and over-the-counter markets. One that has been the subject of considerable attention is the New York Stock Exchange, because it is one of the oldest and largest auction markets in the country and because it has had practices that have been viewed as supportive of a cartel. One of these practices was the maintenance of minimum prices for brokerage services; this practice is now restricted by the Securities and Exchange Commission. The SEC had the chief responsibility of regulation to prevent monopoly in auction and over-the-counter markets.

Problems in information distribution and the regulation to which they give rise can be broken down into three important categories. First is the general problem of expropriation between parties to a financial contract. The market has its own ways of dealing with expropriation, including ex ante pricing, restriction through protective covenants, and ex post settling up, but each of these approaches may be costly and imperfect. In cases where some parties to a transaction are unsophisticated or have inferior information, the market's methods for dealing with expropriation have been viewed as inadequate. This is often the case in financial contracts with consumers. Hence, the government has come to regulate the allowable terms of contracts and to require the disclosure of information to minimize the chances for expropriation.

The problem of agency has led to substantial regulation. An agent is someone employed to perform some action in the best interests of his or her employer. Mangers of nonfinancial firms and financial intermediaries are agents of the owners of those companies. The agency problem is the problem of inducing the agent to act in the owner's best interests or minimizing the differences between the agents' and owners' interests. These differences include different attitudes toward agents' effort and differences in information possessed by agents and owners. Regulation has attempted to reduce the differences in information and limit the conflicts those differences may create. The main approach to this issue has been to impose disclosure rules on agents and to define the legal responsibilities of agents to those whose interests they represent.

The last, and historically most serious, problem arises from asymmetries in information and is the prospect that financial markets may virtually collapse. In the United States this largely took the form of banking panics where depositors periodically withdrew their funds en masse. The principal form of regulation that deals with this problem involves a fundamental change in the nature of the financial contract to which individuals agree when they deal with a financial intermediary. This change took place in 1933, when deposits at commercial banks became insured by agencies of the federal government. The regulation later became extended to other financial intermediaries. The depositor now has a contract with the government rather than merely with a private financial institution. With the change in the contract came a system of government supervision and control of risk that is now the central feature of our regulatory system in intermediated financial markets.

QUESTIONS

1. Distinguish between perfect competition and monopoly. What is the purpose of a cartel? How does antitrust deal with monopolies and cartels? Compare this with the way regulation is intended to influence cartels.
2. Explain what an externality is. How can an externality cut both ways? How are they related to the concept of social cost?
3. In the simplest version of the lemons problem, sellers of all high-quality assets immediately withdraw from the market, and only the lowest quality assets are left. But this may well not happen directly and immediately in real-world markets. Explain why.

4. In any financial contract there may be methods for each party to try to do in or expropriate the other party. The unregulated marketplace has ways for dealing with this problem. What are they? Why are they not likely to stop such expropriation altogether?
5. How have financial markets been regulated to prevent market failure? Why is the regulation designed to prevent market failure oriented more toward intermediated financial markets than toward auction or over-the-counter markets?
6. Regulation can reduce the instances of unconscionable contracts in two ways. Explain and evaluate them.
7. What is an agent? How does the marketplace, if left to its own devices, try to control the actions of agents? How is regulation used to influence agents?
8. Why are those who are strong advocates of the efficient markets hypothesis, particularly the strong-form of the hypothesis, opposed to many regulations that are imposed upon financial markets?

REFERENCES

Akerlof, G. ''The Market for 'Lemons': Qualitative Uncertainty and the Market Mechanism,'' *Quarterly Journal of Economics,* 89 (August 1970), pp. 488–500.

Coase, Ronald H. ''The Problem of Social Cost,'' *Journal of Law and Economics,* 3 (October 1960), pp. 1–44.

Epstein, Richard A. ''Unconscionability: A Critical Appraisal,'' *Journal of Law and Economics,* 18 (October 1975), pp. 302–20.

Fama, Eugene F. ''The Effects of a Firm's Investment and Financing Decisions on the Welfare of its Security Holders,'' *American Economic Review,* 68 (June 1978), pp. 272–84.

———. ''Agency Problems and the Theory of the Firm,'' *Journal of Political Economy,* 88 (April 1980), pp. 288–307.

———. ''Banking in the Theory of Finance,'' *Journal of Monetary Economics,* 6 (June 1980), pp. 39–59.

Leland, Hayne. ''Quacks, Lemons, and Licensing: A Theory of Minimum Quality Standards,'' *Journal of Political Economy,* 87 (December 1979), pp. 1328–46.

Ross, Stephen. ''The Economic Theory of Agency: The Principal's Problem,'' *The American Economic Review,* 63 (May 1973), pp. 134–39.

———. ''Disclosure Regulation in Financial Markets: Implications of Modern Finance Theory,'' in F. P. Edwards (ed.), *Key Issues in Financial Regulations,* New York: Columbia University Center for Law and Economic Studies, Columbia University, 1978.

Smith, Clifford W., and Jerold B. Warner. ''On Financial Contracting: An Analysis of Bond Covenants,'' *Journal of Financial Economics,* 7 (1979), pp. 117–61.

14

REGULATION
OF THE SECURITIES MARKETS

In this chapter we examine the regulatory system that applies to auction and over-the-counter markets. A less technical name for these markets is *securities markets*. Specifically, we will examine how securities markets have been regulated to promote competition and limit monopolistic practices and to improve information distribution. While, as consumers, we do not all come in personal contact with securities markets, they are still extremely important to our economy. It is vital for all of us that they work efficiently and competitively and that the public perceive these markets as fair. The regulatory system is intended to accomplish all of these goals, but it has met considerable criticism in recent years. We will evaluate some of the criticism. This chapter and the next show how governmental regulatory policy can affect the organization and operation of financial markets and institutions. We will focus principally on the primary and secondary markets for corporate equities and bonds, because these markets have attracted the most attention from regulators and the more controversial issues pertain to these markets. ■

OVERVIEW OF THE REGULATORY SYSTEM FOR SECURITIES MARKETS

In this section we will outline the structure of the regulatory system that governs securities markets in the United States and explore how this system came to be. The securities laws governing auction and over-the-counter markets were written largely in 1933 and 1934. They have been amended since then but have remained essentially intact. Probably the most important amendments are contained in the Securities Acts Amendments of 1975.

Before we get involved in the historical development of the existing regulatory system for securities markets, we need to recall the basic rationale for regulation introduced in the last chapter. We learned that four central problems led to regulation. These were summarized in Table 13–1:

1. Promote competition and prevent monopolistic practices
2. Prevent or limit expropriations
3. Control the actions of agents
4. Prevent market failure

As we learned in the last chapter, the last three purposes for regulation arise from problems in the distribution of information, while the first one arises from various factors that present opportunities for monopolies to form in auction and over-the-counter markets. We will use these four purposes as a checklist in this chapter. As we analyze the specific types of regulations imposed on securities markets, we will refer back to these basic problems to clarify the central reason for each particular regulation. And when it is not clear that there is any good reason or when the reason is hotly disputed, we will try to note that as well. If you have read Chapter 13 carefully and understand the arguments behind each of these points, then the connection behind the rationale and each piece of regulation should be relatively easy to grasp. We will find that the big problems in securities markets, as opposed to intermediated markets, are items 1 and 3 on our checklist. In these markets, market failure and consumer protection from expropriations are much less important than they are in intermediated markets.

EVENTS LEADING UP TO THE SECURITIES ACTS OF 1933 AND 1934

From the end of World War I until late 1929, the United States experienced tremendous prosperity. This was an unprecedented time in U.S. history, and laissez-faire capitalism was at its pinnacle. Businesses and individuals were not only prosperous, they were also optimistic. That optimism was reflected in the performance of securities on organized securities markets. The 1920s witnessed an almost constant bull market. While the market experienced some short periods of retrenchment during the decade, it always rebounded very strongly. For example, the New York Stock Exchange experienced a decline during the first 3 months of

1928, but then, between April, 1928, and September, 1929, the Dow Jones Index increased by nearly 50 percent.[1] But October 24, 1929, known as Black Thursday, was the beginning of the end. On that day the market began its famous collapse.

The collapse of the securities market and the Great Depression that followed were a puzzle at the time. No one knew precisely why these events occurred. Time has increased our understanding, but it has by no means perfected it, for the underlying causes of the Great Depression and the appropriate measures to ensure it will never recur are still issues on which reasonable people differ. However, it became evident that the collapse was partly caused by abuse of the securities markets by those who had inside information or who sought to take advantage of less sophisticated parties. Whether the abuses that came to light after the crash were in fact one of its major causes can still be debated. But the crash did focus attention on these abuses, ultimately leading to an assortment of regulations governing almost every phase of the operation of securities markets.

Let us examine a few examples of the types of practices which took place on the exchanges during the 1920s. One of the most frequently cited abuses was a particular scheme to manipulate prices. A **pool** is essentially a device to push up the price of a stock by disseminating false information about it. The pool gets its name because, in order to be successful, such ventures usually require the efforts of more than one party. Hence, individuals come together to pool their resources in such an effort. When a pool is formed, the members try to acquire as many of the shares of some particular security as they can. The idea is to try to pay as low a price as possible for these shares, so the members keep the pool's intentions and identity secret. Such purchases are usually facilitated by the dissemination of negative information about this security, whether that information is accurate or not. Once a large enough position in the stock has been acquired, the whole process is reversed. Now the attempt is made to try to drive up the stock price so favorable information and hot tips are distributed about the security. In addition, the pool members can sell back and forth to each other in high prices to make it look as though the market value of the stock is actually increasing. When the price has been driven up, the members sell their holdings.

Anyone might try to operate such a pool, but the ability of the average investor to accomplish this sort of manipulation is quite limited. This may not be the case, however, if brokers or dealers form a pool. They can be in a position to distribute information to the market that will have an appreciable effect on the prices of securities, and they may also have the resources to support a successful pool. But because brokers are agents of the public, they also have a clear conflict of interest. When they engage in such activities, they are not acting in a way that tends to promote the efficient operation of the market, and they are not acting in the interests of the customers who employ them. This is an example of problem 3 on our checklist.

A **pool** is a device to push up the price of a stock by disseminating false information about that stock.

---

[1]See Robert Sobel, *The Big Board: A History of the New York Stock Market,* New York: The Free Press, 1965, p. 262.

A second abuse pertained to the distribution of information regarding new issues of securities. Insiders stood to make extraordinary profits and investors extraordinary losses if securities could be sold to the public based on false or inadequately disclosed information. There was no standard for what constituted false information, no requirement for disclosure of all pertinent information, and essentially no legal recourse on the part of the investor for misinformation or inadequate information. Federal Trade Commission investigations of security distributions from utility corporations disclosed several instances of these questionable practices.

A final example of the kinds of abuse that occurred at this time pertains to the provision of loans by banks and brokers to investors to fund the purchase of securities. Such loans are called **margin loans** or loans to purchase securities on margin. When the stock market crashed in 1929, a large volume of securities had been purchased on margin. This meant that when the prices of securities dropped, investors would face margin calls, and if they had no additional cash, they would be compelled to sell their securities. To see what this means, suppose securities have been purchased at a price of $1,000, which is financed with $200 from the investor and $800 borrowed from a broker. Should the market price fall below $800, then the broker will demand the difference through what is called a **margin call.** If the owner cannot pay the difference, then the broker will sell the security. If many investors purchase securities on very high margins, then relatively small declines in market prices can lead to widespread margin calls. If those investors cannot produce the cash to cover the margin calls, then the brokers are forced to sell, depressing market prices even further.

During the late 1920s many investors financed their securities holdings with large amounts of borrowed funds. There were no explicit restrictions at the time on the portion of stock purchases that could be funded on margin accounts or through loans from a broker. In many cases, the actual proportion was quite large. The role of margin accounts in the crash is illuminated by the precipitous decline in the total volume of such margin loans beginning in October, 1929. Loans from brokers to customers had risen to more than $8.5 billion in 1929, and this actually represented only a part of all the leveraged funds used to purchase securities. Within 10 days after Black Thursday, $3 billion in loans had been wiped out through margin calls or other means. Then the Depression set in, and by August, 1932, total loans from brokers had dropped to $242 million.[2]

Shortly after Franklin Roosevelt became President, a subcommittee of the Senate Committee on Banking and Currency hired Ferdinand Pecora as the committee's chief counsel to investigate abuses in the securities markets. The Pecora Committee was able to document 107 cases of pools on the New York Stock Exchange during 1929 alone, as well as a number of other abuses. The revelations of the Pecora Committee rival the revelations of the modern-day Watergate inves-

Margin loans are loans to purchase stock.

A stockbroker makes certain that an investor can cover losses incurred if a stock value declines by requiring that the investor make a **margin call.**

---

[2]See Irwin Friend and E. S. Herman, "The SEC Through a Glass Darkly," *The Journal of Business,* 27 (October 1964), p. 389.

PRINCIPAL FEATURES OF THE SECURITIES ACTS

Disclosure in Primary Distribution. The purpose of the 1933 act was to require disclosure of information in primary distributions of securities. The issuers of new securities must file a registration statement with the SEC and issue a prospectus to the public. What goes into the prospectus is stipulated by the SEC. Essentially, it acquaints the potential investor with all relevant information pertaining to the new issue. The issuer must wait 20 days after the prospectus is filed before securities may be sold. During this waiting period the investment banker for the new issue may engage in predistribution solicitations, but actual sales may not take place. If the SEC has not notified the issuer of flaws in the registration statement within the 20-day period, then the issue may be sold. During this interval, it must be written in red ink on the front of the prospectus that the SEC has yet to approve it. Such a prospectus is known as a *red herring.*

There are a number of exemptions from this registration procedure. A firm that issues less than $1.5 million per year in new securities is exempt. If the security is privately rather than publicly distributed, it need not be registered. If the security is issued in exchange for outstanding stock in a merger, it is exempt. Finally, if the security is a debt instrument with a maturity shorter than 270 days, it is exempt. These exemptions minimize the burden of preparing registrations and protect unsophisticated investors.

In addition, in 1982 the Securities Exchange Commission created what is known as **Rule 415,** which allows issuers of securities to preregister a security for future sale. This new process of shelf registration allows a firm to issue securities promptly without waiting for SEC approval of the distribution.

Disclosure for Publicly Traded Firms. The securities laws also require disclosure on a regular basis for firms that have publicly traded securities outstanding. Three types of financial statements must be filed with the SEC. The first is a **form 10k,** which constitutes detailed balance sheets, income statements, and supporting documents that must be filed on an annual basis. Second, **form 9k,** which includes less detailed statements, must be filed semiannually. Third, a short report **form 8k,** must be filed at the end of the month in which significant events have occurred; these include major changes in legal liability, in control of the corporation, or in the value of assets. In 1964 these disclosure requirements were applied to all corporations with at least 500 stockholders or $1 million in assets. This includes most publicly held corporations in the United States.

SEC Control of Secondary Markets. The securities laws give the SEC authority to regulate all organized exchanges for trading of securities, such as the NYSE. The SEC has the authority to set rules governing conduct of brokers and dealers on the exchange and to disapprove the rules of any association of brokers or dealers. It can take legal action against members of the exchange, and it has the authority to close down any exchange.

Margin Requirements. The securities laws gave the Federal Reserve authority to regulate margin loans extended by brokers, dealers, and commercial banks. The Federal Reserve was given this authority rather than the SEC because it was more closely tied to the Fed's general responsibility for regulating the supply of money and credit than to SEC responsibilities. The Federal Reserve sets margin requirements through its Regulations T and U. These requirements are altered from time to time, but they generally remain between 50 and 80 percent. For example, if the margin requirement is 75 percent, then the maximum amount of funds that can be borrowed to support securities purchases is 25 percent of the value of the securities.

Rule 415 of the SEC allows issuers of securities to preregister a security for sale.

Forms 8k, 9k, and 10k are financial statements which must be filed with the SEC quarterly, semiannually and annually by publicly held corporations.

Insider Activities. The securities laws take the position that people who have inside information about the value of publicly traded securities should not personally profit from it at the expense of the public and the owners of the corporation. To limit such opportunities, the SEC requires disclosure not of the inside information itself but of the investments of those who have access to such information. The SEC also prohibits short selling by insiders, and it can sue corporate officials who it believes have used inside information to acquire personal profits at the expense of the company's owners and the investing public. The SEC has utilized this authority and, through the courts, it has attempted to clarify what practices are permitted. During the 1980s, under Chairman John Shad, the SEC made enforcement of insider trading restriction a prime focus of the agency's activities. A large number of cases were filed and prosecuted.

Corporate Governance. A closely related realm of responsibility pertains to the SEC's authority to determine the system of **corporate governance**—that is, the methods by which boards of directors supervise corporate activities for shareholders and the accountability of those directors. The SEC has established rules to govern the solicitations of shareholder votes, or proxies, to be exercised during shareholders' meetings. These rules have made the process of governance of corporations as democratic as possible. In addition, the SEC encourages the use of outside members for boards of directors. This portion of the SEC's responsibility is evolving rapidly.

Antifraud Regulation. The securities laws stipulate that certain practices, which were believed to be common during the 1920s, are illegal. These include such things as dissemination of fraudulent information, as well as various schemes to manipulate prices, such as pools. Furthermore, the courts have interpreted these antifraud provisions so that it is not always necessary to prove fraudulent intent under the law. Instead, the courts have held that when securities are distributed, all persons responsible for that information, including accountants and underwriters, must exercise "due diligence" in determining that the information is factual. If they do not, they are liable.

Regulation of Investment Companies. The SEC has been given the authority to exercise almost complete control over investment companies and investment advisors. Investment companies are organized to manage investments for individuals. In this instance, a system of disclosure was not deemed adequate to protect against conflict of interest or fraud. The SEC has long supervised every aspect of this business. This power was not granted in the original securities acts but was conferred in two laws passed in 1940, the Investment Company Act and the Investment Advisor Act.

Separation of Commercial and Investment Banking. A final aspect of the regulatory system for securities markets, which was not a part of the Securities Acts of 1933 and 1934, is the requirement that commercial and investment banks must be separate. This requirement was a part of the Banking Act of 1933. Prior to this time, commercial banks and investment banks were often divisions of the same firms. This created a potential conflict because the investment banker could sell securities to his or her own bank—in effect, to depositors. Because the investment banker acted as both an agent for the firm distributing securities and for depositors who supplied funds, there was a potential for conflict of interest. As a remedy, the Banking Act of 1933 required all commercial banks to divest themselves of investment banking operations.

Corporate governance refers to the methods by which boards of directors supervise the activities of the corporation for shareholders and the accountability of those directors.

tigation for public attention and reform (even without television coverage). In this time of economic instability, political change, and public desire for reform, securities laws were drafted.

THE SECURITIES ACTS OF 1933 AND 1934

The demand for reform of the securities markets precipitated by the crash of 1929 and the Depression led to the enactment of two extremely important pieces of legislation, the Securities Act of 1933 and the Securities Exchange Act of 1934. (It also led to the Banking Act of 1933, which we will discuss later.) The first act was followed shortly thereafter by the second act because of apparent omissions and inadequacies in the initial legislation. These acts define the regulations governing securities markets that still apply today. The Securities Exchange Commission (SEC) was also created in this legislation and given power to administer most of the provisions of both acts. We will not be particularly concerned with identifying which law is responsible for what reform; instead we will discuss the two acts together. In addition, where appropriate, we will examine some recent changes or interpretations of the laws by the courts.

REFORM OF THE SECURITIES MARKETS IN THE 1970S

The securities laws, particularly the rules governing organized exchanges, stayed largely intact from the 1930s until the 1970s. But by the early 1970s, some major changes had taken place in the secondary market for corporate securities leading to major changes in the regulation of this market. The most important development was the withdrawal of individual investors from direct participation in the equity market and the growth of institutional participation in the market. Throughout the 1960s more and more individuals channeled their investments toward institutions, particularly pension funds, and diminished their direct participation in the market. This led to a significant increase in the portion of trading volume on the exchanges that involved institutions rather than individuals. For example, by the mid-1970s the proportion of total trading volume on the New York Stock Exchange that involved institutions reached 60 percent. This meant that an increasing portion of all trades was **block trades,** which involve large blocks of stock, usually in excess of 10,000 shares. Block trades represented less than 5 percent of total volume in the early 1960s, but approached 25 percent by the late 1970s.

> **Block trades** are trades involving large blocks of stock, usually exceeding 10,000 shares.

With the rise in importance of institutional investors in the market came increased pressure for competition in pricing brokers' services. Historically, the NYSE had been governed by a number of rules, sanctioned by the SEC, which tended to inhibit direct price competition by brokers. One such rule stipulated minimum commissions that could be charged by member brokers of the NYSE. In effect this allowed the NYSE to function as a cartel. This is an example of item number 1 on the checklist at the beginning of the chapter. Other rules tended to limit the entry of new brokers and to inhibit the ability of member brokers to conduct exchanges off the NYSE. For example, NYSE Rule 394 prohibited members from sending orders off the Exchange to be traded elsewhere. All of these rules were subject to some criticism prior to the growth of institutional participation in the market. But institutions that traded in blocks were in a better position than individuals to search for low-cost means of conducting exchanges. As a result, the increased growth of institutions put greater pressure on the rules governing brokers enforced by the NYSE.

Institutional investors sought a number of routes around the NYSE rules. For instance, brokers increasingly offered a variety of services to institutions to attract their business because they couldn't compete with prices. In addition, many of the institutions set up their own brokerage facility in one of the regional exchanges. In some cases, these brokers handled the transactions of the institution. In other cases, they handled business for a broker who was a NYSE member in exchange for handling trades of their parent institution on the NYSE. Another method was to move trades to the so-called **third market,** which was formed by a group of brokers who were not members of the NYSE in order to trade NYSE-listed securities off the exchange. They competed directly with the NYSE and without minimum commissions for conducting trades.

The **third market** refers to an informal market formed by brokers for trading NYSE-listed stocks off the exchange.

All of these actions to circumvent the rules of the NYSE led to fragmentation of the secondary market in corporate securities. Such fragmentation tended to change a highly centralized auction market into a collection of over-the-counter markets. It also tended to decrease public access to the prices at which assets were trading and generally to increase the cost of conducting transactions, that is, the cost that would have been incurred if the Exchange were not subject to rules limiting competition.

These developments led to reactions from the regulators and Congress that ultimately led to major changes in the rules under which the NYSE operates. Moreover, these changes have by no means completely run their course. One of the first events that seriously threatened the NYSE rules was a challenge to the practice of minimum commissions brought by the Justice Department. In 1968, when the NYSE made a relatively routine request for SEC approval of an increase in the level of minimum commissions, the Justice Department challenged this practice as illegal under antitrust laws. This and other events prompted the SEC to investigate intensively this practice and the broader problem of institutional investors in the secondary market for corporate securities. The SEC's study, known as the Institutional Investor Study, was one of the most important major investigations of the securities industry ever undertaken. It was submitted to Congress and published in 1971.[3] After some consideration the SEC ruled in 1975 that minimum commissions would no longer be permitted. This prohibition became effective on May 1, 1975, known as **May Day** on Wall Street.

May Day refers to May 1, 1975, when minimum brokerage commissions became illegal.

---

[3]See *Institutional Investor Study, Report on the Securities and Exchange Commission*, 92nd Congress, 1st Session, House Document No. 92–64, 1971.

Later in 1975 the Congress passed what is probably the most significant securities legislation since the original acts of 1933 and 1934. These regulations were intended to increase competition in the securities markets. The Securities Acts Amendments of 1975 made fixed minimum commissions illegal. It also mandated that the SEC develop a National Market System. The National Market System is intended to be an auction market for all outstanding securities that can feasibly be included. It is to be an automated system, with public access, linking all markets throughout the country. The exact design of such a system was not specified in the 1975 legislation. Rather, the legislation is a statement of intent and a mandate to the SEC to see that it is carried out. The SEC is currently studying such a National Market System.

The auction and over-the-counter markets for securities in the United States have undergone tremendous changes in recent years. In part this is due to advances in technology that have made new methods for conducting exchanges possible and to changes in the composition of those who trade securities as well as changes in the attitudes of regulators. It is unlikely that these changes will stop or even slow down appreciably. With some sense of the evolution of the regulatory process in hand, we can examine some of the more controversial issues regarding how effective the regulatory system is.

PROMOTING COMPETITION IN SECURITIES MARKETS

We will examine the two principal issues of the last decade that affect the extent of competition in the secondary market for corporate securities: the impact of the elimination of fixed minimum commissions on the NYSE and the possible form which a National Market System might take.

THE IMPACT OF ELIMINATING MINIMUM BROKERAGE COMMISSIONS

Those who advocated that minimum brokerage commissions should be abolished argued that the NYSE functioned as a cartel. The essential features of the cartel were that it limited entry to the Exchange, fixed prices for utilizing the Exchange, and compelled its members to trade only on the Exchange all listed securities. Because of this, a cartel is generally unstable unless a strong mechanism for rule enforcement can be devised. In the case of the NYSE, the ultimate method of enforcement was to deny a brokerage firm membership in the NYSE if it did not observe the Exchange's rules. Because the SEC had long agreed to these rules, the Exchange had the legal authority to enforce its restrictions. Hence, it had most of the prerequisites of an effective cartel, but a cartel must also prevent effective competition from outsiders. In this case, such competition came from regional exchanges and brokerage houses which were not members of the NYSE that traded in the third market. The difficulty facing the third market was that there were sufficient economies inherent in operating a single, large exchange; the

NYSE could operate at a lower cost than potential competitors that were considerably smaller. With large size come fewer trading imbalances and greater liquidity, and because many of the market costs are fixed, it is desirable to spread them over larger volume. Therefore, the opponents of fixed commissions argued that, in order to ensure a competitive securities market, it was important to eliminate the Exchange's ability to enforce fixed commissions.

In the debate that developed, the NYSE maintained that fixed commissions were a necessary part of a healthy stock exchange. To support their case they made essentially two arguments. The first was that without fixed commissions there would be a reduced incentive for Exchange membership, leading to its gradual disintegration. In effect, they argued that it was important to the economy to have a single central exchange. Moreover, an essential part of the nature of the Exchange was a brokerage industry with a number of prosperous firms with an incentive to behave reliably and honestly. If membership were not valued, the Exchange itself would disintegrate and so would the security and reliability of the market. The second argument was that competitive commission rates would lead to a large degree of consolidation in the brokerage industry, with a few large firms dominating the market. Here they argued that the economies in the industry were sufficiently substantial that if price competition were permitted, most brokerage firms would be driven out. Their argument was essentially that the brokerage industry was a natural monopoly and that, because of this, prices needed to be regulated, with a price floor enforced by the NYSE.

The NYSE lost the debate. But in addition, the historical record since 1975 seems to add additional evidence against the NYSE's case. First of all, it is important to see what the actual reduction in commissions amounted to after the May Day change. There is no doubt that elimination of fixed commissions led to a significant reduction in the cost of buying and selling securities, particularly for large institutional investors who can negotiate lower prices for higher volume. In its 1978 annual report the SEC assessed the impact on prices of the May Day change as of the end of September, 1978. It reported that:

> . . . individual investors' effective commission rates when measured as a percent of principal value declined 13.9 percent. Institutional customers, due to their larger average order size and greater bargaining power, have negotiated discounts averaging 48.8 percent from the exchange prescribed minimum rates.[4]

The evidence suggests that the NYSE's role as the principal marketplace for trading equities has been maintained. The demise of fixed commissions led to a decline neither in the amount of trading on the floor of the Exchange, nor in the proportion of all stocks traded this represents. Furthermore, there has been no noticeable decline in membership on the NYSE and only a slight decline in the total number of members engaged in brokerage business with the public, from 413 at the beginning of 1975 to 361 at the end of 1978.

------

[4]See Securities and Exchange Commission Annual Report, Washington, D.C., 1978, p. 7.

The evidence also shows no significant consolidation of the brokerage industry, with a few large firms emerging in a dominant position. This does not mean that brokerage firms were unaffected by the change, but the effect depended largely on the extent to which they served institutional rather than individual investors. Some firms that did a large portion of their business with institutions merged with more diversified firms. In addition, a group of **discount brokers** entered the industry. Discount brokers provide trading of securities at prices generally lower than those offered by full-line brokerage houses. However, discount brokers provide no investment advice or counseling in conjunction with their processing of trades. During the era of minimum commissions, brokers were compelled to compete with each other by providing services, such as investment advice. As a result, discount brokerage services could not operate in that market environment. In a review of how the elimination of fixed commissions affected the brokerage industry published at the end of 1979, Seha Tinic and Richard West concluded:

> To be sure, national full-line firms and institutional brokerage firms have increased their aggregate shares of commission business, gross revenue, and net pretax income during 1976–1978. But even more dramatic gains have been made by regional firms which primarily conduct an agency business. The securities commission revenues and pretax incomes of regional firms have increased at substantially higher rates than any other class of NYSE brokerage firms.[5]

Data released by the SEC in the few years after the minimum brokerage commissions were eliminated also show that discount brokers are becoming one of the most profitable and fastest growing segments of the brokerage industry. Within three years after the formal elimination of minimum brokerage commissions, or by the end of 1978, there were at least 55 discounters in business, 20 of which were started after the demise of fixed rates. Overall, their profit rates for 1978 were superior to those of NYSE member firms as a whole. Clearly the brokerage industry has not been one in which economies of scale have dictated that under competitive pricing, the largest four or five firms, or a particular group of firms, would grow inexorably at the expense of the rest. It now appears very probable that competitive commission rates will be a permanent aspect of the securities industry.

THE NATIONAL MARKET SYSTEM

Of even greater potential importance for the operation of securities markets is the prospect that a **National Market System** (NMS) for securities will emerge. The Securities Acts Amendments of 1975 mandated that the Securities and Exchange

Discount brokers provide trading without advisory services for a discount relative to the prices of full-service brokers.

The **National Market System** is the name given to a national trading system which Congress has mandated the SEC to develop.

---

[5]See Seha M. Tinic and Richard R. West, "The Securities Industry under Negotiated Brokerage Commissions: Changes in the Structure and Performance of New York Stock Exchange Member Firms," *Bell Journal of Economics,* 11 (Spring 1980), pp. 34–5.

Commission should move as directly as possible to develop and implement such a system. This was motivated by a desire to ensure the most competitive type of financial markets possible—that is, point 1 on our checklist. The idea behind a National Market System is to have a central computerized system for recording and executing all transactions in publicly available securities. It is not clear at this juncture exactly what features of the present system of trading securities would be retained and what would be replaced if and when a National Market System is instituted. But it is certain that such a system would significantly alter the structure and probably improve industry performance. Such a system involves, essentially, some kind of consolidation of all the regional and national stock exchanges as well as the over-the-counter market. All brokers would be given the right to access this market, which would encourage additional competition in the industry.

As envisaged by the SEC, the NMS would include five components, as well as some regulatory changes. The five components are:

1. A consolidated transaction reporting system
2. A consolidated quotation reporting system
3. A market linkage system (or systems)
4. A limit order protection facility
5. A national clearance and settlement system

A consolidated transactions system was first proposed by the SEC before the 1975 Securities Act was passed. The SEC developed what they called a Consolidated Transaction System for reporting all transactions in a given security. This system was implemented in 1976.

The second component of the NMS has also been completed and implemented: a system for consolidated price quotation, drawing on the national and regional exchanges as well as the over-the-counter market. This information has been printed in the daily press since 1976.

A system for linking existing exchanges could take one of two basic forms. One form involves separate display of prices and execution of transactions. It functions essentially as a communication link between separate exchanges. We will refer to this as the Intermarket Trading System (ITS). The other form involves a single integrated system for recording orders and executing transactions without regard for physical location. This plan leaves less room for a meaningful role for separate exchanges. A system of this kind began operation on the Cincinnati Stock Exchange as an experiment in early 1978. As a result, this system is often labeled CSE.

The NYSE and many of the other exchanges have come out in favor of an ITS, apparently because this system preserves the separate exchanges as meaningful trading centers. One component of the system is an automated display capability for bid and ask prices, which would display for anyone to observe all offers to buy and sell arriving in the system. A separate automated mechanism would handle actual orders. The initial version of this system operating on the NYSE in

1978 and 1979 allowed a broker on a particular exchange to check to see if a price available on his or her exchange was the best in the system. If it was not, he or she could use the system to trade on the exchange with the best available price.

One potential pitfall with this kind of system involves what are known as limit orders. **Limit orders** are orders from a customer to a broker to buy or sell a stock at a maximum or minimum price. For example, a customer might stipulate that a broker would sell a stock at a maximum or minimum price. For example, a customer might stipulate that a broker should sell a stock when the price rises to $50 per share. The difficulty here is that the SEC has proposed that the NMS incorporate nationwide protection of limit orders. For example, if a limit order to sell at $50 is given a broker on one exchange, the order should be executed when the stock rises to $50 per share on any exchange where it is traded, not merely the one where the broker is initially located. If brokers kept those limit orders themselves and watched the display terminal to see when anyone on any exchange was quoting a $50 price, this might work effectively. But traditionally limit orders have gone to dealers on the floor of the exchange who handle their execution, and the dealers' limit orders have not generally been public knowledge. Dealers pay attention only to their exchange and, hence, cannot execute limit orders on a nationwide priority. As a result, it is necessary to change that part of the dealer system and in some manner record all limit orders to be executed based on priority of price and time of arrival on the system.

The CSE system is inherently more capable of accomplishing this objective. In the experimental CSE system a central computerized system records all bid and ask prices and automatically arranges transactions based on the priorities given to the system. The priorities governing trades are that purchases are made at the lowest price offered and sales at the highest, and if prices are equal, then priority is given to time of entry. Anyone can purchase access to the system from anywhere in the country and never actually be present at the exchange. This kind of system can potentially carry all limit orders in the automated system and execute them in any priority. In addition, it provides a ready method of verifying transactions to ensure observance of SEC rules and regulations.

If a CSE system were implemented for all the exchanges, the role of dealers in such a market is left unclear. Traditionally dealers on the NYSE have derived a significant portion of their revenue from handling limit orders. If this function were automated, it is not clear if some other specialized function would arise to supplant this service. If it did not, the dealer's actual role in the market might be reduced to that of purely providing liquidity or absorbing temporary imbalances between supply and demand.

Probably even more fundamental is the future role of the separate exchanges themselves. Traditionally the central exchange offered the advantage of a single facility where brokers could meet for face-to-face auction of securities. If the face-to-face nature of the auction becomes obsolete, then so too may the concept of an exchange tied to any single location.

Limit orders are orders from a customer to a broker to buy or sell a stock at a maximum or minimum price.

REGULATING THE DISTRIBUTION OF INFORMATION

One of the important purposes of the securities laws is to limit the instances in which significant conflicts of interest can arise. Conflicts of interest are the essence of the problem of agency discussed in Chapter 13 (point 3 in our checklist). An agent is someone who is employed to work in the best interests of another party. A conflict of interest develops when either the interests of the agent and his or her employer diverge or when there are simultaneous agency relationships such that the interests of the parties who are employing an agent are in conflict. The securities laws have created different regulatory solutions for different cases of conflict of interest. In some instances the method employed has been to require disclosure so that the market can be fully informed about the actions of an agent who may face conflicts. In other cases the securities laws have simply eliminated simultaneous conflicting agency relationships altogether. Two of the more important and interesting regulatory issues surrounding potential conflicts of interest are restrictions on insider trading and disclosure regulation. We will examine the pros and cons of regulations designed to compel the manager-agents of corporations to disclose financial information. Then we will examine the debate about possible repeal of the Glass-Steagall Act, which creates a separation between investment and commercial banking.

INSIDER TRADING

A potential source of conflict of interest in the securities markets pertains to the use of either confidential or inside information. The facts that such inside information exists and that its confidentiality is often valuable to the corporation create potential conflicts. The conflicts center on the use of such information for personal gain by those who possess it.

Restrictions on insider trading have created substantial controversy, just as have rules pertaining to corporate disclosure. Some who have examined the subject argue that there should be no disclosure of insider trading. It is insider trading, they say, which causes prices to reflect fully all information (or which brings about strong-form market efficiency). Those who defend the requirement do not necessarily dispute this argument. Rather they argue that the method by which the information gets transmitted to the market is unfair to the party on the other side of the trade. This is usually about where the argument stops, with a comparison of the concept of fairness and the overall efficiency of the market. The conflict here is between the personal interests of the insiders and the interests of the public owners of the firm. Trading on the part of a firm's insiders tends to make the price a more accurate reflection of all information, but it also leads to a transfer of wealth from outside owners to insiders. The law's view has been that such conflicts should be held to a minimum.

Curiously, there is no mention of insider trading in the federal securities statutes. Instead, the legal stance on insider trading derives principally from the

SEC ENFORCEMENT OF INSIDER TRADING

Under the tenure of SEC Chairman John Shad, the 1980s have been a time of active prosecution of insider trading. From 1982 until the end of 1986, the SEC brought charges in more than 95 insider trading cases, as compared with only 77 in the previous two decades. Moreover, prosecution of insider trading has included charges filed and admissions made by some very prominent participants in the corporate takeover arena. The most notable example is the case against Ivan Boesky and David Levin. Boesky, who pleaded guilty to SEC charges, allegedly received tips from Dennis Levine, managing director of Drexel Burnham Lambert, regarding forthcoming takeover attempts. Boesky then took large positions in the stock of the takeover targets and reaped substantial profits from the subsequent run-up in the stock price. In return for his information, Levin was allegedly paid up to $12 million. The SEC also filed charges against one of the senior partners of Goldman Sachs for using inside information on takeovers to trade in stocks of the target companies.

The SEC's strategy in these cases appears to be to prosecute prominent violators of the law as harshly as possible to deter others from engaging in insider trading. This strategy appears based on the belief that most would-be violators are sophisticated enough to respond by avoiding insider trading. If the punishment is sufficiently severe, the strategy may work. An important part of this strategy is making sure that the punishment is, in fact, severe. The Insider Trading Sanctions Act of 1984 allows the SEC to sue a violator for three times the profits gained from the insider transactions. In addition, conviction carries a potential jail sentence. Prior to the 1984 act, a conviction simply meant that profits had to be disgorged.

An important element of the recent insider trading cases is the question it raises about the pervasiveness of such practices. A fundamental objective of security market regulation is to make those markets fair in the sense of minimizing abuses of agency or fiduciary responsibilities. If the public perceives that insider abuses are commonplace, this could undermine the markets' successful operation. The SEC, under John Shad, has been very concerned with seeing that this does not occur. In addition, the association of insider trading with corporate takeovers has threatened to impair the takeover mechanism. Those who believe that takeovers should be constrained do not view this aspect of the topic with alarm. But those who view takeovers as an important mechanism for dealing with agency problems in corporations are concerned that an abuse of insider trading may interfere with an important market process for disciplining corporation management.

Rule 10b–5 prohibits any device, scheme, or artifice to defraud.

SEC's enforcement of its **Rule 10b–5.** This ruling prohibits any device, scheme, or artifice to defraud. Prior to 1961 the SEC never brought any charges against anyone for insider trading. The case that initially clarified what constituted insider trading was the Texas Gulf Sulphur case which was decided by the Supreme Court in 1968. Texas Gulf Sulphur discovered some huge mineral deposits. Before the existence of these deposits was disclosed to the public, some officers of the company acquired large positions in the company's stock. The Court held that this constituted a violation of Rule 10b–5.

The Supreme Court has also held in other cases that a person who is not an officer of a company, or an outsider, also can violate the law when he trades on information provided by an insider. In addition, the insider who provides the information is also breaking the law. The Court took this position in the case against the former chairman of LTV Corporation, Paul Thayer, who was convicted of supplying inside information to a friend.

In recent years the SEC has been particularly concerned about the informational advantages that some specialists in corporate takeovers may possess. As a result, in 1980 it adopted **Rule 14e–3,** which makes it illegal for anyone with inside information about a takeover to trade the target company's stock. However, it is apparently still legal, at least in some circumstances, for an outsider to trade on material nonpublic information as long as the information was not acquired from an insider and it does not pertain to a tender offer. This situation results from the decision of the U.S. Supreme Court in a case involving Raymond Dirks, an analyst who uncovered a fraud involving Equity Funding in 1983. Dirks learned that Equity Funding had engaged in fradulent accounting and informed the clients of his brokerage firm before he informed the SEC. The SEC prosecuted Dirks, but the Supreme Court ruled that because he did not have a fiduciary responsibility to the investors in Equity Funding, he had not violated the law.

The SEC sought to prosecute Dirks under the **misappropriation theory.** This theory was originally articulated by the Supreme Court in a 1980 case against Vincent Chiarella, a proofreader who had acquired a stock after he correctly identified the firm from documents his firm was printing. The Supreme Court held that Chiarella had not violated any law, but it articulated the misappropriation theory. This theory views information as a commodity which can be stolen. The SEC used the misappropriation theory in the Dirks case, but the Court held that it was applied inappropriately since Dirks did not have a fiduciary responsibility. Hence, the misappropriation theory holds that there must be some breach of a fiduciary relationship in order to steal information.

Many discussions of insider trading do not explicitly consider the prospect that it may be in the best interests of the firm's shareholders to maintain the confidentiality of information. Some information is useful only if competitors do not know about it. For example, it may be best to keep competitors in the dark about the facts or even existence of a discovery of new mining deposits. If competitors find out, they will tend to take actions which decrease the value of the find. Such confidential information is, in fact, a commonplace thing in the world, and many financial arrangements are designed to protect the confidentiality of information. Commercial banks and investment banks receive such confidential information relatively frequently. Commercial banks receive it in the course of deciding on the loan terms to be extended to corporate borrowers. Investment banks receive it in the course of helping design and distribute new issues, such as private placements, or for other services, say, relating to mergers.

The existence for such confidential information has created a clear potential for conflict of interest. The recipient of the information, the commercial or investment bank, can utilize it for its own trading or to distribute to other customers. In the case of a commercial bank, these problems have attracted particular attention because banks operate trust departments required to be separate from the rest of the commercial banking operation. As a result, information acquired by a loan officer is not to be transmitted to someone in the trust department. These divisions of the bank are to be treated as if they were separate companies. They are to maintain what are referred to as **Chinese Walls** to separate these two sections of

---

Rule 14e–3 makes it illegal for anyone with inside information about a takeover to trade the target company's stock.

The misappropriation theory holds that information can be legally stolen when there is a fiduciary responsibility on the part of the person committing the theft.

Chinese walls refer to the alleged separation between divisions or between persons serving clients where there may be a conflict of interest in commercial and investment banks.

a bank. Investment bankers claim that the same Chinese walls exist between those personnel working for different customers. In the case of commercial banks the separation is created by regulation. In investment banks, the separation is maintained to protect the interests of clients without the inducement of regulation.

DISCLOSURE REGULATION

Another important form of regulation that the SEC imposes upon securities markets is the requirement that corporations disclose a wide variety of information to the public. Though these disclosure requirements date back to the Securities Exchange Act of 1934, during much of the 1960s and 1970s there was considerable sentiment for tightening these disclosure requirements. It is easy to get the impression that without government-mandated disclosure requirements there would be tremendous secrecy, but it is by no means obvious that this is true. Prior to the 1934 act, a considerable amount of information was disseminated to the market by managers of firms with publicly traded securities. Moreover, it is almost certain that if disclosure laws were repealed, there would still be much voluntary disclosure of information to the market. It is also evident that required disclosure is costly. Real resources are expended by all the firms that must comply with SEC regulations and by the SEC itself to enforce disclosure requirements. The question therefore arises as to whether required disclosure actually contributes significantly to the successful operation of the market. There are powerful arguments and considerable statistical evidence on both sides of this question.

Over the years a number of economists have attracted attention as critics of the SEC's disclosure regulations. But in recent years George Benston has made one of the most cogent cases against disclosure.[6] Because he has become one of the best-known critics of disclosure we will closely examine his criticisms and the rebuttals of some other well-known observers of the system. The essence of his position is that, since 1934, required disclosure has led to no measurable increase in the efficiency of financial markets. In effect he argues that competitive markets are efficient on their own, so required disclosure adds nothing. Because required disclosure is costly, it is best to eliminate or to reduce the requirements substantially. Benston has been criticized, particularly by Irwin Friend and Randolph Westerfield, both for the strength of his case concerning market efficiency and for the fact that he is unable to satisfactorily examine what they contend is probably the most important justification for the disclosure legislation.[7]

Benston's criticism of disclosure requirements hinges on the idea that the information disclosed must be perceived as valuable by the market as a whole. This means the disclosed information must be new and valuable to the market.

---

[6]See George J. Benston, "Required Disclosure and the Stock Market: An Evaluation of the Securities Exchange Act of 1934," *American Economic Review,* 63 (March 1973), pp. 132–55.

[7]See Irwin Friend and Randolph Westerfield, "Required Disclosure and the Stock Market: Comment," *American Economic Review,* 65 (June 1975), pp. 467–77.

The operational criteria for determining whether information is new and valuable is to determine whether the disclosure leads to observable and significant changes in the prices of the securities to which that information pertains. The bulk of Benston's case is devoted to the collection and assessment of evidence as to whether such a cause-and-effect relationship can be established between required disclosure and the observed prices of securities.

Benston uses three approaches to do this. The first approach is to select some time interval since the implementation of required disclosure and collect data on the prices of securities as well as the financial data disclosed according to SEC requirements over this time interval. In addition, he attempts to account for other factors that would affect these securities prices during the period, such as general market conditions and unanticipated changes in dividends. With these factors accounted for, the next step is to determine whether there is any significant statistical relationship between the disclosure and the prices of the securities in the sample. Benston conducts such a test for the year 1964 and reviews other researchers' tests of the same proposition. He concludes that there is no economically significant impact of disclosure.

Friend and Westerfield criticize Benston both for apparent shortcomings in his procedure and for the conclusion he draws from the evidence. Criticism of methodology aside, Friend and Westerfield argue:

> He in effect considers not too relevant for stock prices knowledge about changes in financial variables, in spite of the fact that he finds an increase of 100 percent in the annual rate of net sales is associated with an increase in price of 10.4 percent in the month of the announcement, and that changes in other variables are also associated with significant though proportionally smaller changes in price.[8]

Thus, the important disagreement hinges on what constitutes an economically significant effect of disclosure. While it seems inappropriate to dismiss totally the effect cited by Friend and Westerfield, it does not seem overwhelming. If this is the case upon which required disclosure regulation rests, it seems a weak case indeed.

Next Benston argues that his first test may understate the impact of disclosure for the following reason:

> It is often claimed that the detailed reports required by the SEC are more useful to trained analysts than to the ordinary stockholder. The analyst then passes on his information to his clients, or, in any event, trades on the information, thereby bringing its effect to the market. But does it get there by means of the financial reports required by the SEC?[9]

Benston reviews the studies of a number of researchers who have investigated analysts' ability to make use of special information. Again, he concludes that

[8]*Ibid.*, p. 468.
[9]Benston, p. 140.

information disclosed through the SEC is of no real value to them and therefore to the market.

Benston pursues an additional avenue to test the impact of required disclosure based on a potential flaw he saw in his first two tests:

> Even though the evidence reviewed does indicate that the financial reports required by the SEC, when made available, have almost no information content, this does not prove that the required disclosure is not valuable to investors. One might argue that the statements provide a confirmation of data previously released. Because investors know that a corporation's sales, operating expenses, extraordinary gains and losses, assets and liabilities will be reported, they may have some assurance that the preliminary reports, press releases, etc., are not prevarications. Thus when the financial statements are made public the data they contain are fully anticipated. But had it not been for the SEC's disclosure requirements, such a state of affairs might not exist.[10]

In order to account for this possibility, Benston examined the actual impact on the securities prices of the initial 1934 enactment of the legislation requiring disclosure. He collected data on the prices of a sample of securities for a period before and after the date the legislation went into effect and concludes, again, that required disclosure had no observable impact on the prices of securities traded in 1934.

The most telling criticism of these conclusions Friend and Westerfield have to offer pertains more to the issues Benston was not able to test than to any specific problems pertaining to the tests he did conduct. His tests did not pertain to what these authors refer to as the *fairness* of the market as between the public and insiders. Their concept of fairness is close, if not identical, to the concept of asymmetrical information. They argue that prior to the enactment of required disclosure, there were numerous opportunities for relatively well-informed insiders to take advantage of lesser informed investors. This allegedly led to numerous instances of actual expropriation or fraud and to a perception by investors that insiders had special information that provided them with an advantage in the market. Friend and Westerfield further argue that the instances of these kinds of abuse and, presumably, the potential for such abuse were reduced by required disclosure.

Benston's response to this criticism highlights one of the most pressing difficulties facing those concerned with the efficiency and fairness of our regulatory system. He said their criticism is based on impressions drawn from conversations with people in the industry and their reading of the historical record. He retorts:

> I have reviewed most of the cited materials and have found no more than anecdotes and assertions . . . Apparently we both have formed very different impressions based upon roughly the same 'evidence.'[11]

---

[10]*Ibid.*, p. 141.

[11]See George J. Benston, "Required Disclosure and the Stock Market: Rejoiner," *American Economic Review*, 65 (June 1975), p. 476.

The inherent difficulty is that, at this juncture, the issue which Friend and Westerfield raise is exceedingly difficult to test in the scientific manner in which Benston's tests were conducted. But decisions about the extent of regulation must be made, with or without such tests. The consensus judgment of those with responsibility for that regulation seems to support the position taken by Friend and Westerfield.

SEPARATION OF COMMERCIAL AND INVESTMENT BANKING

From a historical standpoint, one of the greatest alleged conflicts of interest has been between commercial and investment bankers. Commercial bankers provide loans to corporate customers and often receive special or inside information as a part of the loan relationship. The majority of funds for most commercial banks comes from various deposit accounts. As a result, the banker acts as the agent of the depositors who supply funds for business loans. On the other hand, investment bankers are dealers in the primary market for corporate securities. As such, they act as the distributors of new corporate debt and equity securities. Their principal responsibility is to the corporation whose securities they distribute. Moreover, they generally purchase these securities from the issuing company and bear the risk involved in distributing them to the market. Conflicts might arise when the same company operates both as a commercial bank and an investment bank. If an investment banker who experiences difficulty in distributing securities to the market is also a commercial banker, it is argued that there is a great temptation to eliminate the distribution difficulty by purchasing the securities for the commercial bank. In effect, the investment banker would have sold the securities to the depositors.

In order to eliminate the opportunities for such conflicts, Congress passed the Banking Act of 1933, which mandated that henceforth no company would be allowed to engage in both types of business.[12] This led to a major change in the commercial banking industry and primary securities markets as they then existed. Most banks chose to stay with their major line of business and close down or sell off their secondary line. For example, the First National Bank of Boston created a separate entity known as the First Boston Corporation, which is now a major investment bank. The bank founded by J. P. Morgan eventually broke into separate organizations known as Morgan Guaranty and the investment banking firm of Morgan Stanley. Since 1934 the SEC and bank regulators have devised an additional set of rules to enforce a separation between commercial banking and the sales distribution of marketable securities.

The allegations concerning conflict of interest were originally put forth during an era when there was little effective regulation of the securities markets. That is,

---

[12]This act is also popularly referred to as the Glass-Steagall Act. However, a less important piece of legislation, passed in February, 1932, is actually more accurately characterized with this name. While Senator Glass and Congressman Steagall had a major role in both pieces of legislation, we will refer to the 1933 act as the Banking Act of 1933.

DOES THE CRASH OF 1987 MEAN MORE REGULATION OF SECURITIES MARKETS?

In the aftermath of Black Monday (October 19, 1987) when the Dow Jones Industrial Average fell by 23 percent, there were numerous calls for more extensive regulation of the securities markets. A number of specific items came under the spotlight for regulatory scrutiny. For example, a *Wall Street Journal* article one week after the crash itemized the following issues which would receive new attention: "inadequate capital of some securities dealers, particularly New York Stock Exchange specialist firms; the lack of coordinated regulation among markets in the U.S. and abroad; the impact of highly leveraged options and futures contracts on equity trading; and the markets' vulnerability to brokers' and customers' computers . . ."[1] In fact, President Ronald Reagan appointed a panel led by investment banker Nicholas F. Brady, co-head of Dillon, Read & Co., to investigate that appropriate regulatory response to the market's decline.

Most of the problems highlighted by events of October, 1987, are not actually new ones. Instead, the crash appears to have focused public attention on issues surrounding the operation of securities, futures, and options markets that have received industry attention for some time. The public and political attention directed to these issues may well result in new regulatory actions, which would be no departure from the history of regulatory action in U.S. financial markets.

One issue attracting notice in October is the role of the specialist on the NYSE. Many specialists apparently lacked adequate capital to maintain orderly markets when demand plummeted. One solution is to draw more publicly owned firms with significant capital to the ranks of the specialists. The NYSE is attempting to entice large brokerage and investment banking firms as well as commercial banks into the specialist business. However, a more fundamental change would entail allowing competition among specialists as on the NASDAQ.

A second issue pertains to the ability of exchanges to handle high trading volume such as the more than 600 million shares per day traded during the week of October 19. With automated record keeping and back room operations, exchanges can handle processing records after trades occur. However, with the high trading volume of October, it was difficult for investors to get into or get access to the NYSE. High trading volume leads to a large accumulation of orders, some of which never get executed; as a result, the exchange runs far behind the order flow. Increased automation of the order process will be necessary to improve the exchange's ability to handle peak trading volume efficiently.

One of the most important and most controversial issues arising from the October crash pertains to the relationship between futures and options markets and the stock markets. The question is whether program trading and portfolio insurance were part of the cause of the crash. **Program trading** involves computerized arbitrage of any differences between prices of essentially equivalent claims on different markets. **Portfolio insurance** is a dynamic hedging strategy for protecting a portfolio of stocks against a market decline. The policy issue is whether some restrictions on futures and options trading would improve the overall efficiency and soundness of the markets. Some critics of the existing system go so far as to say that trading in stock index futures should be severely restricted or eliminated. Others contend that the problems have more to do with the lack of coordination between the futures and options and the stock markets than any inherent problem in the futures or options markets themselves. We will examine this issue in Chapter 21 which details the operation of futures and options markets.

---

[1] See Richard E. Rustin and Thomas E. Ricks, "Stocks' Plunge Brings Call for the Overhaul of Financial Markets," *Wall Street Journal*, October 26, 1987.

the abuses which led to the passage of the Glass-Steagall Act occurred before the enactment of the Securities Acts of 1933 and 1934 and after legislation was designed to limit the incentives of participants in the securities markets to engage in unethical and fraudulent behavior. As a result, while it may have seemed appropriate at the time to separate commercial and investment banking to limit conflicts of interest, it is more appropriate now to evaluate whether other forms of regulation may more effectively achieve the same end. The current system for bank regulation and supervision of bank investments did not exist when the Glass-Steagall Act was passed. The combination of disclosure and other regulations applied to investment banking and the close inspection by government regulators of bank loans provide substantially more protection for depositors than was available prior to the 1930s.

The separation between commercial and investment banking must also be evaluated in the context of the broader issue of the separation of commercial banking and other lines of commerce. This separation is an important feature of the regulation of bank holding companies in the United States. Bank holding companies (which are discussed in more detail in Chapter 15) are restricted by statute to a narrow list of allowable types of activities. The general purpose of these restrictions is to maintain a separation between banking and other lines of commerce in order to avoid conflicts of interest and concentration of economic power. The restrictions on bank holding companies have also maintained a separation between commercial banking and other types of financial services. For example, commercial bank holding companies are largely prohibited from underwriting insurance, except for lines of insurance directly linked to the extension of credit, such as credit life insurance. Taken together, the Glass-Steagall Act and the restrictions on bank holding companies have created a highly circumscribed set of financial services available to commercial banks.

The Banking Act of 1933—and the separation it created between commercial and investment banking—has probably become more controversial in the 1970s and 1980s than in any period since its inception. Neither commercial banking nor investment banking is quite the same industry it was then. Commercial banks now provide a wide variety of services both for corporations and consumers that did not exist in the 1930s. At one time commercial banks were unique in that they were the principal institutions that offered demand and savings deposits. These deposits were perceived by individuals and regulators as distinctly different from the more risky investments individuals might make in marketable securities. Hence, it was possible to create a real separation between these distinct types of investments and the institutions that offered them. As time has passed, these distinctions have blurred. In today's financial market, brokerage houses that deal in the secondary markets for securities also function as investment bankers and offer securities to consumers in the form of money market mutual funds and other accounts exceedingly close to demand deposits. At the same time, the large national commercial banks are continually seeking expanded authority to manage investments in securities traded on organized markets and to provide a wide variety of services to corporations that come very close to being those offered by an investment banker. Therefore, competition and innovation in the financial markets has made this separation more and more difficult both to rationalize and enforce.

The separation between banking and investment banking has also been diminished by actions taken by the regulators and courts to allow each type of business to be penetrated by the other. For example, at one time banks were not permitted to act as brokers in any corporate securities traded in over-the-counter markets or on organized exchanges. However, under certain circumstances, they were allowed to place orders for such securities with brokers but not act as brokers themselves. Recently the Federal Reserve has granted permission to some bank holding companies to acquire discount brokerage firms. The first and most highly publicized case was the acquisition of Charles Schwab and Company by Bank of America Corporation. This acquisition was not deemed to be a violation of the Glass-Steagall Act because Schwab functions as a discount brokerage house rather than a full-line broker. A discount broker does not provide investment advice but simply executes transactions. Moreover, it does not underwrite corporate securities.

One of the most important threats to the viability of investment and commercial banking separation comes from securitization. If markets once dominated by depository financial intermediaries gradually become securitized, the institutions operating in those markets must change the services they provide. Rather than making loans and offering deposits to fund those loans, they must function more like brokers and dealers. This tranformation will be difficult if regulation prohibits depository financial institutions from offering many of the services offered by dealers and distributors of securities. Therefore, if the markets themselves continue to change, there will be increased pressure on the regulators to accommodate that change in order to maintain the viability of existing institutions.

The issues we have addressed in the last portion of this chapter are as much about the regulation of commercial banks as they are about securities markets. In order to fully understand and appreciate these issues it is necessary to have a complete picture of how and why we regulate commercial banks. We will take that up in the next chapter.

SUMMARY

In this chapter we examined how securities markets—that is, auction and over-the counter markets—are regulated. We began by relating the discussion of securities markets regulation to the various rationales for regulation presented in Chapter 13. Most regulation of securities markets is designed either to promote competition and limit monopoly practices or to deal with the agency problem that comes out of imperfections in information distribution in the marketplace. Table 14–1 summarizes the major forms of regulation in securities markets and relates them to the appropriate underlying purpose for regulation.

A large part of our regulatory system emerged in response to the financial collapse of 1929 and the Great Depression. This collapse was viewed by many to be partly a result of abuses possible in the unregulated markets of the 1920s. As a result, the Securities Acts of 1933 and 1934 and the Banking Act of 1933 were passed which created a regulatory system that has remained largely intact to this day. These laws included new rules for ongoing information disclosure for publicly held firms and new securities distributed to the market, creation of the Securities and Exchange Commission to regulate the operation of secondary markets,

TABLE 14–1
Summary of principal regulations in securities markets.

Regulation to Promote Competition
1. SEC control of the rules of an exchange (e.g., NYSE) authorized in the Securities Acts of the 1930s.
2. Prohibition of minimum commissions on NYSE—1975.
3. Congressional mandate for a National Market System—1975.

Regulation to Control Agents
1. Disclosure requirement for new security issues and for publicly held firms.
2. Regulation of insider trading.
3. Laws restricting fraudulent activities.
4. Regulation of investment companies.
5. Separation of commercial and investment banking.

imposition of margin requirements for stock purchases, restrictions on insider trading, SEC regulation of the methods of corporate governance, definition of fraudulent activities, SEC regulation of investment companies, and the separation of commercial and investment banking. In the years since, there have been some relatively minor changes in the laws, but the most important changes came in the Securities Acts Amendments of 1975, which eliminated minimum commissions on the New York Stock Exchange and mandated a National Market System.

The issue of minimum brokerage commissions on the New York Stock Exchange took on significance because of changes in the Exchange during the 1960s and the early 1970s. During this period trading by individual investors declined in importance relative to trading by large institutions, which were often in a better position to demand competitive pricing of brokerage services than individuals with small trading volume. As a result, the long-standing rule of the Exchange that fixed minimum commissions began to cause the equities market to fragment. This focused attention on the role of the minimum-price rule as a device for supporting a cartel. After action by the U.S. Justice Department and by the Securities and Exchange Commission, Congress declared this minimum price rule illegal.

The 1975 Act also mandated that the markets move as fast as possible toward implementation of a National Market System, a central computerized system for recording and executing all transactions in publicly available securities. It is not clear exactly what features of the present system would be retained if and when a National Market System is implemented, but some recent experiments give a clue as to what the system might be like. One form preserves separate exchanges as they now exist, with automated display of prices and execution of transactions essentially as a communications link between exchanges. The other form involves a single integrated system for recording orders and executing transactions without regard for physical location.

Many of the provisions of the securities laws have been controversial since their inception. One feature is the set of disclosure requirements enforced by the

SEC. The criticism of required disclosure is that it has led to no measurable increase in the efficiency of financial markets. The argument is that competitive markets are efficient on their own, so that required disclosure adds nothing and is costly. There are two basic responses to this argument to reduce or eliminate disclosure. The first is to quarrel with the contention that there is no measurable increase in efficiency, which involves the collection and evaluation of statistical evidence as to whether disclosure leads to observable and significant changes in the securities prices to which the information pertains. The second counterargument is that required disclosure has reduced the opportunities for well-informed insiders to take advantage of less informed investors. Unfortunately, the evidence on this point is largely subjective and therefore can be interpreted quite differently by those on opposite sides of the issue. In any event, the debate on required disclosure promises to continue in the future.

An important opportunity for conflicts of interest was eliminated in the 1930s when commercial and investment banking were separated. However, during the 1970s and 1980s this separation began to receive a closer scrutiny as the operational distinctions between the two types of institutions have become less well defined. In today's financial market, brokerage houses which deal in the secondary markets for securities also function as investment bankers and offer securities to consumers in the form of money market mutual funds and other accounts quite close to demand deposits. At the same time, large commercial banks are seeking expanded authority to compete with large brokerage houses in their traditional lines of business. Whether it will be possible to maintain a meaningful separation in the future is hard to predict.

QUESTIONS

1. Explain how a pool works and why it is considered an abuse of the securities markets. What kind of conflict of interest does a broker or banker have who participates in a pool?
2. What are margin loans? How did margin loans contribute to the stock market crash of 1929?
3. Explain the position of the securities laws of 1933 and 1934 toward disclosure. What do you believe might be feasible alternatives to these disclosure rules?
4. Describe the circumstances or events that led up to the enactment of the Securities Acts Amendments in 1975. What were the fundamental features of these amendments?
5. Summarize the case made by the NYSE for preserving minimum commissions. What were the major arguments against this case? Compare and evaluate the two positions.
6. What is the National Market System? Describe the two basic ways such a system might operate. What are the most difficult issues involved in choosing between these alternatives?

7. Why have some people criticized disclosure regulation? What is the essence of their argument against this type of regulation?
8. Why does the concept of a fair capital market cause so much disagreement? Can you give a precise definition of what *fair* means in this context? How would you collect evidence to assess fairness? Suppose you couldn't collect any such evidence, yet you were responsible for choosing what regulations should be maintained or eliminated. Would you believe fairness was relevant?
9. Why have commercial and investment banking been separated? Why may this separation be more difficult to enforce in the future than it has been?

REFERENCES

Benston, George J. "Required Disclosure and the Stock Market: An Evaluation of the Securities Exchange Act of 1934," *American Economic Review,* 63 (March 1973), pp. 132–155.

Francis, Jack Clark. *Investments: Analysis and Management,* New York: McGraw Hill, 1972.

Friend, Irwin, and E. S. Herman. "The SEC Through a Glass Darkly," *Journal of Business,* 27 (October 1964), pp. 382–405.

———, and Randolph Westerfield. "Required Disclosure and the Stock Market: Comment," *American Economic Review,* 65 (June 1975), pp. 467–77.

Melton, William C. "Corporate Equities and the National Market System," *Quarterly Review,* Federal Reserve Bank of New York, 3 (Winter 1978–1979), pp. 13–25.

Offer, A. R., and A. Melnik. "Price Deregulation in the Brokerage Industry: An Empirical Analysis," *Bell Journal of Economics,* 9 (Autumn 1978), pp. 663–71.

Securities and Exchange Commission Annual Report, Washington, D.C., 1979.

Sobel, Robert. *The Big Board: A History of the New York Stock Market,* New York: The Free Press, 1965.

Stigler, George: "Public Regulation of the Securities Markets," *Journal of Business,* 37 (April 1965), pp. 117–42.

Tinic, Seha M., and Richard R. West. "The Securities Industry under Negotiated Brokerage Commissions: Changes in the Structure and Performance of New York Stock Exchange Member Firms," *Bell Journal of Economics,* 11 (Spring 1980), pp. 29–41.

Williams, Stephen L. "The Evolving National Market System" in *Market Making and the Changing Structure of the Securities Industry,* Yakov Amihud, Thomas S. Y. Ho and Robert A. Schwartz (eds.), Lexington, Mass.: Lexington Books, 1985.

15

THE REGULATION OF COMMERCIAL BANKS

The debate about the appropriate way to regulate commercial banks is probably the oldest public policy question pertaining to financial markets in the United States. It is also still one of the most important. In a sense, after the Great Depression the principal issues of bank regulation, which had raised such tremendous political controversies for over a century, were thought to be laid to rest. The system that was put in place in Franklin Roosevelt's first presidential term was perceived to be immensely successful. But in the 1970s and 1980s some of the perennial issues came to the fore again. The underlying reason for this is intimately linked to the problem of inflation and to the pace of technological progress in the financial services industry.

We will try to develop some understanding of the long-standing controversies concerning bank regulation. We will also get an overview of the basic structure of the current regulatory system for depository institutions. Much of this chapter describes the historical evolution of the current regulatory system for banks and savings and loans, a review that makes it possible to examine some of the contemporary problems of regulation with the advantage of some historical perspective. The historical material presented in this chapter is not intended to serve merely as a transition; it is really as important as current events. In the next decade we may experience changes in the regulatory system as dramatic as those in the 1930s. Only with a sense of historical perspective can these potential changes be understood. This chapter sets the stage for a more detailed analysis of recent changes in the regulatory system for depository institutions and for the contemporary operation of commercial banks and savings and loans presented in Part 4. ■

OVERVIEW OF THE BANK REGULATION SYSTEM

It is important to recall our list of reasons for regulation in financial markets developed in Chapter 13. Four underlying problems or motives for regulation make up our checklist:

1. Promote competition and prevent monopolistic practices
2. Prevent or limit expropriation
3. Control the actions of agents
4. Prevent market failure

In Chapter 14 we found that the big issues in regulating auction and over-the-counter markets were 1 and 3. In this chapter we will find that the big, even overwhelming, issue in regulating financial intermediaries is 4. Unfortunately, as we will discover, the regulations that have evolved to deal with market failure have made it more difficult to promote competition and prevent monopolistic practices. As a result, there is a trade-off between objectives number 1 and 4 on our checklist. We will explore the trade-off in this chapter.

The problems that have led to regulation of financial intermediaries are not strictly a matter of recent history. Instead, they have been with this country virtually since its birth. During most of the history of the United States there were periodic liquidity crises or panics where citizens sought to withdraw funds from financial institutions and hoard them. In effect, the banking industry was prone to market failure. Various methods were instituted by the government over the years in order to deal with these crises. With each additional approach to the problem, the regulatory system grew in complexity. It is imperative, in order to avoid getting lost in the maze of current agencies and regulations, that we examine the evolution of the regulatory system and only then assess its effectiveness.

To appreciate the complexity of the current system for regulating commercial banks and savings and loans, it is helpful to outline the major current regulations. Then we can turn to the historical evolution of these regulations and the rationale behind them. The regulations are listed roughly in the sequence in which they came into existence and in an order that facilitates a logical explanation of their purpose.

BANKING REGULATION THROUGH THE GREAT DEPRESSION

THE UNDERLYING ISSUE: CONVERTIBILITY AND STABILITY

The fundamental problem of instability facing depository institutions, virtually throughout history, results from the peculiar nature of deposits including the fact that they can be converted to cash, or historically to gold, upon demand. In the broadest sense, deposits are simply another type of debt claim, such as a bond or loan. As discussed in Chapter 13, one of the problems with any debt claim, in-

KEY FEATURES OF BANK REGULATION

Fractional Reserve Banking and National Currency. The National Banking Act of 1863 created a system of government-required reserves for nationally chartered banks, though no provision was made for expansion or contraction of those reserves. The legislation that followed shortly after led to the extinction of the multiple currencies issued by state banks that existed throughout the earlier nineteenth century.

Elastic Currency. In 1913 the Federal Reserve System came into existence and with it a provision for government control of the volume of currency and bank reserves. The Federal Reserve was designed to serve as a lender of last resort for commercial banks experiencing liquidity difficulties or to provide an **elastic currency.**

Restriction of Interest Payments on Deposits. Beginning with the Banking Acts of 1933 and 1935, the federal government imposed limits on the interest rates that could be paid on demand, savings, and time deposit accounts to limit competition. Interest payments on demand deposit accounts were entirely prohibited, and the Federal Reserve periodically adjusted interest-rate ceilings on saving and time deposits. These ceilings were eliminated in 1982.

Deposit Insurance. Since the Depression, deposits at commercial banks, as well as savings and loans, have been insured by agencies of the United States government. This insurance is provided for commercial banks by the Federal Deposit Insurance Corporation **(FDIC)** and for savings and loans by the Federal Savings and Loan Insurance Corporation **(FSLIC).**

Restrictions on Permissible Activities. Banks and savings and loans are restricted in the activities they can engage in and investments they can make. These restrictions were imposed in the 1930s and have been modified more recently as banks formed holding companies.

Capital Requirements. The government imposes minimum capital requirements on all depository institutions.

Entry Restrictions. Permission must be obtained from the banking or savings and loan regulators to create a new bank, savings and loan, or a new branch of an existing institution. Each state has the right to determine whether banks will be permitted to have branch offices and whether banks from another state can accept deposits in that state.

Inspection and Control of Riskiness. The government examines depository institutions to assess the riskiness of their deposit liabilities and can compel management to alter risky policies.

Segmentation of Banks and Savings and Loans. A separate regulator, the Federal Home Loan Bank Board **(FHLBB),** and a separate set of regulations were created for savings and loans in the 1930s. The Congress intended that savings and loans function mainly as suppliers of home mortgage funds. Therefore, they were subject to restrictions limiting their portfolios largely to home mortgages. These restrictions were significantly relaxed in 1982.

In a **fractional reserve banking** system, banks are required to hold reserves behind their deposits equal to some fraction of total deposits.

An **elastic currency** refers to the ability of the central bank to lend to commercial banks experiencing liquidity difficulties so the volume of money can expand and contract.

The **FDIC** stands for the Federal Deposit Insurance Corporation, the agency which provides insurance of deposits in commercial banks.

The **FSLIC** stands for the Federal Savings and Loan Insurance Corporation, the agency which provides insurance of deposits in savings and loans.

The **FHLBB** stands for the Federal Home Loan Bank Board, the federal regulatory agency for savings and loans.

cluding deposits, is the opportunity for the issuer of the debt claim, in this case the commercial bank, to engage in activities which tend to expropriate the claim holder. The most obvious kind of expropriation is for a borrower to take a lender's funds, issue a promise to repay, and simply disappear or spend the money and then claim bankruptcy. But there are a number of other, more devious methods to accomplish essentially the same thing, as will be evident from the banking arrangements in the United States in the nineteenth century. To prevent such problems, most formal debt contracts issued by corporations include covenants that constrain the borrower or require collateral the lender can claim if expropriation is attempted. The convenants restrict such things as future dividends and debt issues in order to limit the borrower's ability to divert funds from the corporation to equity owners, or to increase the company debt and therefore the risk to which existing debtholders are exposed.

But with depository institutions, it is exceedingly difficult to construct covenants that adequately protect against future increases in the debt issued by the institution because the business of a bank is to issue deposits. In order to function effectively banks must have the freedom to increase or decrease deposits as the need arises. It would be totally infeasible for the initial depositors to restrict the bank's ability to issue additional deposits. The volume of deposits fluctuates from day to day and must do so if the bank is to serve its customers profitably. Moreover, this same flexibility makes it impossible to assign collateral to specific deposits. Thus, an opportunity for expropriations is created.

The method that first evolved for dealing with this problem was for banks to back their deposits, or the antecedents of deposits called notes, with gold. Under such a system banks promised to redeem their notes or deposits in gold at a prespecified price. As a result, notes or deposits were titles to gold, and gold essentially fulfilled the role of collateral. But the promise to convert notes into gold on demand was a promise easily broken, so that the fundamental nature of the problem was not really changed. Banks invested only a small portion of their funds in gold as most funds were committed to loans and other investments. As a result, the commitment to convert deposits to gold could be honored only if a small portion of the total volume of deposits was presented for conversion at once. In essence, banks held gold as a reserve to satisfy the volume of conversions anticipated, plus some amount as a cushion. But because banks earned their profits from loans, the more gold they held in reserve, the less profitable they could expect to be.

This problem of balancing liquidity against profitability has always been the fundamental choice facing commercial banks. Throughout the history of the U.S. banking industry, panics developed when the public perceived either that banks were trying to expropriate them or that they had become too illiquid or were running too short on gold. If the panic became serious enough, it virtually guaranteed that the existing liquidity would be insufficient and the system would become unstable. We will explore some of the historical episodes of instability in the banking system as we examine how the regulatory system we now have evolved to deal with them.

EARLY REGULATION AND THE WILDCAT BANKING ERA

The **First and Second Banks of the United States,** which existed in the late eighteenth and early nineteenth centuries, were government-sponsored banks that functioned as the federal government's bank and regulated notes of independent state-chartered banks.

Shortly after the United States became independent, the government sought to establish a government-sponsored bank to serve as the government's bank and to regulate the note issues of independent, state-chartered banks. This bank, known as the **First Bank of the United States,** was chartered for a 20-year life in 1791. At that time each independent bank issued what amounted to its own currency, referred to as *bank notes*. These were paper notes that circulated largely in the geographic area each bank operated and that the banks promised to redeem in gold. The First Bank of the United States issued its own notes and offered deposits. But it also sought to regulate the issue of notes by state banks by regularly redeeming state banks' notes for gold rather than always recirculating them. The bank also was intended to serve the Treasury of the United States, and it did this by maintaining deposits for the Treasury and executing its payments.

Because of increased political opposition to the bank, the charter of the First Bank was not renewed in 1811. A large element of the population distrusted banks and believed the government should not sponsor a bank. For a while, at least, they won. Unfortunately, without the bank, the private banking system almost immediately experienced great instability as the volume of private bank notes expanded, leading to a general suspension of convertibility of notes into gold in 1814. Moreover, the Untied States entered the War of 1812 with Britain almost immediately after the charter of the First Bank expired, making it difficult for the Treasury to finance the war. After five years, in 1816, Congress reversed its earlier decision and chartered the Second Bank of the United States.

The **Second Bank of the United States** performed a function similar to that of the First Bank, but in the end its fate was the same. President Anderew Jackson was vehemently opposed to the bank and, in 1836, he permitted its charter to expire. Jackson represented largely agrarian southern and western groups, as opposed to the more industrial eastern section. By and large, the agrarian constituency believed that the Second Bank of the United States, particularly the able and powerful bank president, Nicholas Biddle, was not acting in its best interests. The bank consistently returned notes issued by southern and western banks for conversion to gold in an attempt to establish a national currency. Jackson's constituency objected strenuously to this policy and succeeded not only in reversing the policy but in eliminating the bank.

From the demise of the Second National Bank until the Civil War, the banking industry was virtually unregulated at the national level. Some states chose to impose relatively tight regulations, and Iowa went so far as to outlaw banking altogether.[1] In spite of the restrictions imposed in a few states, this period was one of almost totally unfettered competition. There were thousands of state banks

---

[1] See Robert Craig West, *Banking Reform and the Federal Reserve 1863–1923,* Ithaca, N.Y.: Cornell University Press, 1974, for a description of the attitudes of individual states toward banks during the wildcat banking era.

throughout the country that issued their own bank notes. The notes of each bank were exchanged at whatever price the market would bear. Bank notes often traded at their par value of a dollar note for a dollar note if the exchange took place in the immediate locale and if both banks were thought reputable. Notes often deteriorated in value with distance from the issuing bank because the perceived risk of convertability to gold increased. A small industry to collect information about the value of notes and the exchange rates between the notes of different banks emerged. This information was published in newspapers and in catalogues called *bank note reporters.*

Most of the time banks maintained convertibility of their notes into gold. But a number of banks tried to develop schemes to minimize the chance that such conversion would be attempted. For example, it is said that some banks located their offices far out in the woods ''where only the wildcats lived,'' yet distributed notes in more populated areas. Such banks were the source of the name for this era in banking history. This kind of expropriation was at its height because the system was essentially one of ''buyer beware.'' The market developed methods for trying to assess the risk of nonconvertibility, but there were no guarantees and the individual was responsible for assessing risk and deciding on the appropriate notes.

During this period there was virtually no national currency as we know it today. Each bank issued its own notes or currency, and the only common denominator was their link to gold. The price of gold was fixed in dollars and, assuming that convertibility was maintained, each dollar note could be converted to a dollar in gold. But individual notes often exchanged at values well below $1. This system of **competing monies** came to an end with the onset of the Civil War and has not existed since.

> The system of **competing monies,** where each bank issued its own notes or currency, existed in the United States until the Civil War.

REFORM: THE NATIONAL BANKING ACT

By 1863 the United States had experienced nearly 30 years of what some people thought was virtual chaos in the banking industry. There was, therefore, considerable sentiment that the system was ripe for reform. Had it not been for the Civil War, this sentiment might not have been sufficient to bring about any significant changes. The government found banking reform to be a convenient way to create a market for the government bonds needed to finance the war. As a result, the **National Banking Act** was first passed in 1863 and amended in the years immediately following.[2]

> **The National Banking Act of 1863** created a national currency and the first federal bank regulatory agency, the comptroller of the currency.

The most important and permanent accomplishment of the National Banking Act was creation of a national currency and the elimination of competing monies. But this was not accomplished by directly distributing a government-produced currency as we have today. Instead, the National Banking Act provided for the

---

[2]See *ibid.* for a perspective on the forces which led to the National Banking Act of 1863.

chartering of national banks, which could issue notes backed by government bonds. These banks were not government banks like the First and Second Banks of the United States, but rather privately owned commercial banks with national rather than state charters. The act as it was amended in 1866 also imposed a 10 percent tax on the notes of state banks, virtually eliminating state bank notes. As a result, the notes of the nationally chartered banks became the national currency. Unlike the notes of state banks issued during the wildcat banking era, national bank notes always traded at par because they were not really backed by the promises of individual issuing banks. Instead, the volume of these notes was directly linked to the bank's holdings of government securities, bearing what was called a *circulation privilege*. Hence the national bank notes were really an indirect form of government-issued money. With this system the government created, at one time, both a ready market for its bonds and a uniform currency.

This method alone was not sufficient for financing the war, so the government also issued a currency of its own, which had no backing of gold. This currency came to be known as *greenbacks*. Greenbacks and national bank notes circulated simultaneously, though not necessarily at the same value. Moreover, banks still generally promised to redeem deposits in gold, but the government did not officially back its own greenback currency with gold. Hence, there was a period during and after the Civil War when the government's promise to settle its claims in gold was abandoned. The resumption of government payments in gold came in 1879. From then until creation of the Federal Reserve in 1913, the system remained largely the same.

In addition to establishing a national currency, the National Banking Act also created the basic banking regulation structure that we have today. First, it required nationally chartered banks to hold reserves behind their deposits in a fixed proportion dependent on the size and location of the bank. This is why it is called a *fractional reserve* banking system. These reserves were maintained in the form of either cash or deposits with other banks. The major difficulty with this system was that these reserves were virtually unavailable when problems of liquidity arose, because there was no provision for adjusting reserve requirements or for extending loans to banks. These reserves were simply not available when they were needed. Large banks often fulfilled the role of a lender for smaller banks, but when liquidity problems spread to the larger banks, the system did not work well.

The National Banking Act also created the office of the Comptroller of the Currency, which still exists today. The comptroller was empowered to maintain minimum capital requirements for national banks and to inspect and restrict their activities and investments. This laid the foundation for the more elaborate regulatory structure we have today.

THE FEDERAL RESERVE SYSTEM

The banking system created by the National Banking Act operated without major changes until the panic of 1907, when the solvency of the financial system came into serious question. This crisis in financial markets led to a major reexamination

The Federal Reserve Act of 1913 created the Board of Governors of the Federal Reserve, the first central bank in the United States.

of the banking system that culminated in the passage of **the Federal Reserve Act of 1913.**

The Federal Reserve System was created out of dissatisfaction with the existing system for ensuring banking system stability. The nineteenth century witnessed a number of banking panics in which people would run on the banks demanding redemption first of their notes in gold, and later, their deposits in either gold or currency. But if the run on virtually any bank is large enough, that bank will be unable to satisfy the demand for conversion, regardless of how sound its loans may be. Even the strongest bank does not hold nearly enough highly liquid assets to satisfy its depositors' demands to convert deposits to currency if enough of them show up at once. Such liquidity problems surfaced every few years throughout the nineteenth century and were particularly severe in 1907. The system created under the National Banking Act was ill-suited to deal with these liquidity problems. Although it led to the end of an era of competing monies, it did almost nothing to assist banks in maintaining their liquidity. The Federal Reserve System was therefore created to fill this void.

The important feature of the Federal Reserve System was its power to control the supply of reserves and therefore the liquidity of commercial banks. As it has developed since 1913, the most important method for exercising this control is through the purchase and sale of United States government securities by the Federal Reserve. But the other method, which was of critical importance at that time, was the ability of the Federal Reserve to extend loans or discounts to member commercial banks. The Federal Reserve had the ability to increase or decrease the liquidity of member commercial banks by extending or contracting its loans to these banks. Banks did not and do not now rely on the Federal Reserve as a major source of funds. Rather, this discounting function of the Federal Reserve provided flexibility in the amount of currency outstanding or in the liquidity of the banking system, as the Federal Reserve was able to act as a **lender of last resort.**

A **lender of last resort** functions as a lender to commercial banks when they experience liquidity problems or runs. The Federal Reserve was designed to serve this role.

From 1913 until 1929 the economy in general and the Federal Reserve in particular were both in their prime. After World War I the economy experienced tremendous growth and prosperity, and the banking system experienced tremendous stability. The Federal Reserve was perceived as a great improvement in bank regulation and there was little sentiment for further change. But in 1929 the stock market crashed, the Great Depression began, and the Federal Reserve's heyday came to an end.

Any reasonable assessment of the Federal Reserve's track record in preserving banking system liquidity during the early years of the Depression must conclude that the system was a dismal failure. Between 1929 and 1933 approximately 9,000 banks failed, roughly half the banks in the United States at the time. This was virtually unprecedented in the history of the country. While there were a number of banking panics throughout the nineteenth century, a general suspension of all banking business for a period as long as a week had never before taken place. Such a banking holiday was declared on March 6, 1933, however, and all banks, including the Federal Reserve System, closed down for a week. In their book Milton Friedman and Anna Schwartz point out the irony of the whole situation:

The central banking system, set up primarily to render impossible the restriction of payments by commercial banks, itself joined the commercial banks in a more widespread, complete, and economically disturbing restriction of payments than had ever been experienced in the history of the country. One can certainly sympathize with (President Herbert) Hoover's comment about that episode: 'I concluded (the Reserve Board) was indeed a weak reed for a nation to lean on in time of trouble.'[3]

It is difficult to provide a concise explanation for the Federal Reserve's failure to maintain the stability of the banking system during this period. The banking system collapse developed in stages between 1930 and 1933. At each stage confidence in the system was further shaken and the crisis became more severe. The initial bank failures were probably due to bad loans as much as anything else. But as the crisis deepened, the demand for conversion of demand deposits into cash intensified at a time when the bond market collapse made the current market value of a large portion of bank assets unusually low. This did not necessarily mean there would be default if those bonds were held to maturity; however, many banks would become insolvent if they had to liquidate those bonds at current low market prices in order to satisfy demands for conversion of demand deposits to currency.

The Federal Reserve could have extended loans on a massive scale to banks facing this difficulty, but it did not. Friedman and Schwartz attribute this failure to a lack of understanding of the situation, and it seems difficult to come to any other conclusion:

> The major reason the System was so belated in showing concern about bank failures and so inactive in responding to them was undoubtedly due to a limited understanding of the connection between bank failures, runs on banks, contraction of deposits, and weakness of the bond markets-connections we have tried to spell out earlier in this chapter. The technical personnel of the New York Bank understood these connections, as undoubtedly many other individuals in the System did also; but most of the governors of the Banks, members of the Board, and other administrative officials of the System did not. They tended to regard bank failures as regrettable consequences of bad management and bad banking practices, or as inevitable reactions to prior speculative excesses, or as a consequence but hardly a cause of the financial and economic collapse in progress.[4]

BANKING LEGISLATION SPAWNED BY THE DEPRESSION

The banking crisis of the early 1930s led to significant reform legislation which altered the nature of the regulation of the depository institutions industry in fundamental ways. The major piece of legislation which was adopted at that time,

---

[3]Excerpts from Milton Friedman and Anna Schwartz, *A Monetary History of the United States 1867–1960,* copyright Princeton University Press, N. J. 1963, pp. 327–28. Reprinted by permission of Princeton University Press.

[4]*Ibid.,* p. 358.

The Banking Act of 1933 reformed the regulation of commercial banking by creating the FDIC.

The Home Owners Loan Act created the FHLBB and the FSLIC, the federal regulator and insurer of savings and loans.

and which has fundamentally altered commercial banking since, is **the Banking Act of 1933.** The most important element of this act was the provision of federal insurance of deposits. Under this law the federal government provided insurance of deposits, originally up to $2,500 and today up to $100,000, for commercial banks that became members of a new agency, the Federal Deposit Insurance Corporation (FDIC). The FDIC became the third federal regulatory agency, in addition to the comptroller of the currency and the Federal Reserve, that dealt with commercial banks. Federally chartered banks were required to join the FDIC, but nearly 97 percent of all (which includes state as well as federal) commercial banks became insured by the FDIC. This percentage has increased to nearly 100 percent in the intervening years.

In addition to the legislation directed toward the commercial banking industry, in 1934 Congress passed the **Home Owners Loan Act,** which established federal home loan banks to regulate and insure savings and loans. While there were many similarities between the regulation of savings and loans and commercial banks, there was a philosophical objective guiding savings and loan regulation with no parallel in commercial bank regulation. Savings and loans were government regulated and protected in order to promote and stimulate housing. Because of this objective, a separate class of depository institutions was created and restricted to serve the home mortgage industry. That purpose has been maintained to this day, though the regulatory system for savings and loans has been altered significantly so that they now have many powers originally reserved for commercial banks. We will focus on the savings and loan and the mortgage finance industry in Chapter 19.

The deposit insurance system created for commercial banks and savings and loans has been tremendously successful. The recurring panics and liquidity crises from the administration of George Washington until the Great Depression have been virtually nonexistent since the provision of deposit insurance. The problem was not resolved by imposing a national currency and creating reserve requirements, nor by giving a central bank authority to expand and contract that currency. But deposit insurance did the job. The impact on the stability of the banking industry is documented in Figure 15–1, which shows the number of bank and savings and loan failures between 1921 and 1985, highlighting the dramatic effect the creation of the FDIC had on bank failures.

In addition to the separation of commercial and investment banking (which was discussed in Chapter 14), at least three other important changes were instituted at this time. The first was the prohibition of interest payments on demand deposits and time deposits above a ceiling set by the Federal Reserve. This prohibition was instituted in order to prevent what many perceived as dangerous competition among banks for depositors' funds. When allowed to compete with interest payments, many believed banks would seek highly risky investments to earn enough return to compensate their depositors. The increased competition was therefore perceived to be the source of excessive risk taking. By restricting payment of interest on deposits, it was believed risk would be reduced.

Second, the government completely phased out national bank notes, which originally came into existence with the National Banking Act of 1863. This was

FIGURE 15–1
Number of bank failures (includes only insured banks after 1935).

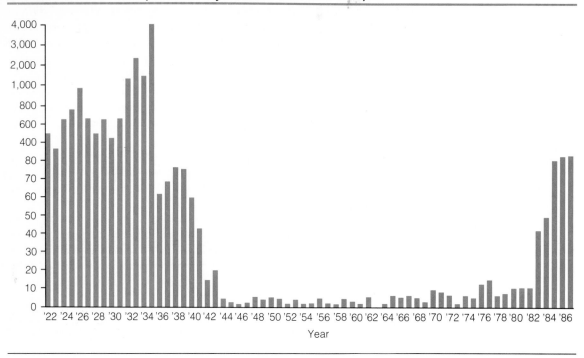

Source: FDIC.

accomplished by retiring the remaining U.S. bonds which, when held by nationally chartered commercial banks, gave them the authority to issue notes. National bank notes had gradually come to be replaced by Federal Reserve notes anyway, which are still used in the United States. With this change the evolution was complete from a currency produced by private institutions, as during the first half of the nineteenth century, to a government monopoly currency.

A final and very important change which took place at that time regarded the role of gold in the banking system. Throughout U.S. history banking system stability hinged on the believability of the promise to redeem notes or deposits in gold. In the nineteenth century banks directly converted notes to gold upon demand. But by the late 1920s the conversion was principally from deposits to currency, and the government stood ready to convert currency to gold, if the demand was made. In 1933 President Franklin Roosevelt essentially nationalized gold by making it illegal, through the power of existing statutes, for private citizens and institutions within the United States to hold gold. All gold was turned over to the U.S. Treasury at the legal price at that time, $20.67 per ounce.

The implications of the nationalization of gold and the enactment of deposit insurance were substantial. The backing behind the bank's deposits became a government promise rather than essentially a promise of the individual bank. Individual banks no longer backed their deposits with gold. Rather, they were compelled to maintain convertibility of their deposits into government-issued currency, which in turn was backed by the good will of the government.[5] But because depositors were insured if private banks reneged on that promise, depositors no longer had an incentive to carefully assess the promises made by individual banks. That responsibility now lay with the government, and in order to fulfill it, a more elaborate system of regulation and control of risk was necessary.

CONTROL OF RISK AND CAPITAL REGULATION

Figure 15–1 indicates that once the deposit insurance system was created in 1933, there was a precipitous decline in the number of bank failures. However, this figure also indicates that since the inception of deposit insurance, the highest failure rates for depository institutions have been in the last few years. The tremendous increase in the number of bank failures, with such cases as Continental Illinois receiving extensive media coverage, has focused considerable popular attention on the stability of commercial banks and savings and loans. The relatively high failure rate for commercial banks in recent years is not a result of some inherent flaw in the deposit insurance system that has finally come to light. It is largely a result of the fundamental market changes for financial services that have forced a major restructuring of the banking and savings and loan industries. This restructuring has already led to some bank and savings and loan failures, and it will undoubtedly lead to still more. However, the restructuring has also pointed to some serious problems in the current regulatory system for depository institutions, particularly pertaining to the deposit insurance system. In the remainder of this chapter we will examine the basic operations of the current regulatory and deposit insurance systems and how they attempt to limit the risk or increase the stability of depository institutions.

REGULATION TO LIMIT RISK

With deposit insurance must come government control of risk. There are essentially three methods of direct regulatory control over risk taking in banks. First, the government directly audits bank loans and investments to be sure they are accurately reported and that they comply with regulations on allowable bank activities. Second, there is direct control over the extent of competition in banking markets. Third, there are restrictions on bank holding companies to limit the lines of business in which they may be engaged.

---

[5]See Benjamin Klein, "The Competitive Supply of Money," *Journal of Money, Credit and Banking,* (November 1974), pp. 423–53, for an analysis of banking regulation in the United States which emphasizes the significance of forced convertibility.

Bank Examination.   The first mechanism for controlling risk includes restrictions on many of the banking activities of banks. Principal among these are the requirements that banks cannot invest in equity securities or directly in real estate. In addition, bank loans to any one customer are constrained so that they cannot exceed 10 percent of the bank's capital. Furthermore, bank investments in bonds are restricted to the higher rating categories. These and other rules are enforced through the process of bank examination by the three federal regulatory agencies.

The division of authority for examination of banks among the three agencies is rather complicated. The comptroller of the currency examines all nationally chartered banks; the Federal Reserve examines all state-chartered banks that are members of the Federal Reserve; and the FDIC examines all banks that are not members of the Federal Reserve System.

In addition, each state has state bank examiners. All of these bank examiners are looking for problems in loans and investments which threaten bank stability and the value of depositors' claims. Such problems may result from fraud or, more frequently, from mismanagement. The FDIC, in cooperation with other two federal regulators, maintains a list of banks it judges may become insolvent. This list of problem banks is used to assess the probability that FDIC insurance will have to be used. The agencies utilize the examination procedure to try to spot difficulties early enough to take corrective action. When examiners discover loans or investments that violate the law or that they consider unsound, they meet with bank management and the board of directors and insist upon changes. The ultimate penalty the regulators wield is to prosecute managers or bank owners for explicit law violations or to take over the bank if they judge that it is becoming insolvent.

Restriction of Competition.   The second mechanism to limit the riskiness of commercial banks has been to limit competition within the banking industry through regulation at both federal and state level. From the time the office of the comptroller was created in 1863 until 1933, it was relatively easy to start a bank. Most state governments were quite willing to grant charters, and the comptroller was equally willing to grant federal charters. As a result, by the late 1920s there were nearly 20,000 banks in the United States. Many of these were small state-chartered banks that had to meet very limited regulatory standards. After the establishment of the FDIC, however, all banks that wanted deposit insurance had to meet its standards. Nearly all banks needed deposit insurance to be perceived as credible and, therefore, to survive. But the FDIC began to demand proof that there was an actual need for the bank's services in order for it to be insured. This concept of need has become the standard criterion for the creation of a new bank today. To show need one must demonstrate that a given market is inadequately served by existing banks and that a new bank will be able to operate profitably.

The simultaneous existence of banks with federal charters and banks with state charters persists to this day and is generally referred to as the **dual banking system.** This system has evolved so that each state has the authority to determine what its banking industry will look like. The system is enhanced by the fact that in 1926 Congress passed the **McFadden Act,** which permits each state to set its

The **dual banking system** refers to the system of joint federal and state regulation of commercial banks.

The **McFadden Act** gave states the right to determine what banks could operate in each state.

own laws on intrastate branch banking and regulate the entry of banks from other states. As a result, each state has a separate banking industry and the rules for creation or expansion vary widely across states. Some states, such as Illinois, have been unit banking states where banks cannot branch statewide. In other states, such as California, statewide branch banking is permitted. Some states, such as Virginia, have only limited branch banking. And some states, such as Arizona, have recently allowed out-of-state banks to enter. For instance, California passed a law in 1986 which will allow banks from other states to enter the California market in 1991.

The traditional laws on branching and the prohibition on banks operating in more than one state are viewed by many as exceptionally archaic restrictions. This view contends that commercial banking is much like a "mom and pop" store and is inefficient as a result. Advocates point to the size distribution of banks and argue that the large number of small banks simply cannot be justified on economic grounds. The majority of banks have less than $25 million in deposits. Only a very small portion of the total number of banks has total deposits of $1 billion. However, most of the total deposits in the country are in the large banks. The top 0.2 percent of the banks hold 37 percent of all the deposits. To most people who have examined this question, it seems that many small banks would not exist were it not for regulatory restrictions, particularly about branching. This view suggests that the branching laws are more a protection of entrenched monopoly position than anything else. But if and when these laws change, there is likely to be a large amount of consolidation in this industry. In fact, as a result of the high rate of banks and savings and loans failures in the 1980s, there has already been substantial relaxation of the regulatory barriers toward consolidation. Those who are worried bring to bear considerable political pressure to preserve the present system. Whether they will be successful in the years ahead remains to be seen.

Bank Holding Company Regulation.   The third mechanism used to control risk is to enforce restrictions on bank holding companies. According to the Bank Holding Company Act of 1956 and its amendments in 1966 and 1970, all bank holding companies are subject to Federal Reserve Board regulation. The Fed restricts the amount of direct control a holding company can exercise on an individual bank, and the law stipulates that bank holding companies can be engaged solely in activities deemed "closely related to banking."

The Federal Reserve Board has been concerned about the diversification of bank holding company activities because it perceives that it may increase the risk to which deposits are exposed. As a result, the Federal Reserve has exercised strict control over the lines of business in which bank holding companies are allowed to enter. These restrictions initially were included in the Bank Holding Company Act of 1956, which gave the Federal Reserve Board the power to approve requests to engage in traditionally nonbanking businesses. But the original law had a number of loopholes, and significant amendments were added in 1970.

Multibank holding companies refer to bank holding companies which own more than one commercial bank.

One loophole was that the law was worded to restrict **multibank holding companies,** leaving holding companies with only one bank unrestricted. This encouraged a large number of banks to form single-bank holding companies so that they could engage in other businesses as they pleased. It also meant that nonbanking firms could seek to acquire banks. This loophole was closed in 1970 when the law was expanded to cover single- as well as multibank holding companies. Today, the Federal Reserve maintains a list of activities permissible for bank holding companies and a list of those specifically forbidden. Many of the permissible activities are in the general financial area, such as mortgage banking, leasing, financial advisory services, credit cards, and data processing services.

The geographic restrictions on banks and the product line restrictions imposed on bank holding companies are facing severe challenges in today's marketplace. Large money-center banks such as Citicorp are seeking to become nationwide providers of consumer financial services, while regional banks are attempting to limit the expansion of their larger competitors. We will look closely at the evolving nature of competition in this market in Part 4.

CAPITAL REGULATION

Minimum capital requirements specify the minimum ratio of equity capital to total assets which must be maintained by commercial banks and savings and loans.

One of the most important mechanisms for limiting the risk to which the guarantor is exposed is the **minimum capital requirement.** Historically, the regulators have not attempted to enforce a standard capital requirement across all U. S. banks. That is, they have not required that all banks must finance, say, 10 percent of the total assets through equity capital. Rather they have tried to see that capital is adequate, given the risk of a bank or a particular class of banks. This resulted in a system where banks governed by different regulators and banks of different size were subject to different capital requirements. However, in June, 1983, the Fed and the office of the Comptroller of the Currency agreed to apply common capital requirements to all commercial banks. The new minimum capital requirement is 6 percent of adjusted total assets. However, the Fed continues to use zones for total capital ratios. The Fed considers banks to be under capitalized if their total capital ratios are less than 6 percent, *marginally capitalized* if total capital ratios lie between 6 and 7 percent, and *adequately capitalized* if total capital ratios exceed 7 percent. The federal bank regulators can also require individual banks to meet higher capital ratios if they are considered to have exceedingly risky loan or investment portfolios. Hence, some discretion is still retained.

Primary capital refers to the ratio of common and preferred stock plus retained earnings to total assets.

Furthermore, the agencies utilize a number of different measures of adequacy of capital. One such measure is the ratio of total capital to total assets of a bank, where total capital includes both the bank's equity value and long-term debt (not deposits). Many people believe that long-term debt should not be counted as capital for regulatory purposes and, hence, measure capital adequacy with the ratio of equity, including common and preferred stock and retained earnings, to total assets. This is referred to as **primary capital.** For the banking industry as a whole, the total capital ratios are significantly above the minimum standards. Data on the capital ratios of commercial banks as of the end of 1984 are shown in Tables 15–1 and 15–2. The average primary as well as total capital ratio (that is, the sum of the individual banks' primary capital ratios divided by the number of banks) for all insured banks in existence at the end of 1984 was 11 percent.

TABLE 15-1
Capital, assets and capital ratios for U.S. commercial banks:
December 31, 1984, report of condition.

	Number of Banks	Capital ($ billions)		Assets ($ billions)	Average Capital Ratios		Aggregate Capital Ratios	
		Primary	Total	Total	Primary	Total	Primary	Total
All U.S. commercial banks	14,404	$174.3	$180.1	$2,443.3	11.0%	11.0%	7.1%	7.4%
By Asset Size:								
Less than $25 million	5,501	8.3	8.4	78.0	14.5	14.5	10.6	10.8
$25 million to $300 million	8,162	49.8	50.5	583.6	8.9	9.0	8.5	8.7
$300 million to $1 billion	466	17.8	18.3	232.2	7.7	7.9	7.7	7.9
$1 billion to $5 billion	209	28.3	29.6	413.4	6.9	7.2	6.8	7.2
Greater than $5 billion	66	70.1	73.3	1,136.0	6.4	6.7	6.2	6.5

TABLE 15-2
Analysis of U.S. commercial banks that do not meet the new capital standards:
December 31, 1984, report of condition.

	Number of Banks Deficient in		Total Number of Deficient Banks	Capital ($ millions)		Assets ($ millions)	Increases in Capital Needed To Achieve New Standards ($ millions)			Decrease in Assets Needed to Achieve New Standards ($ millions)
	Primary Capital	Total Capital		Primary	Total	Total	Minimum Primary Capital	Maximum Secondary Capital	Total	
All banks	242	398	419	$23,767.8	$24,319.8	$430,448.0	$676.1	$1,114.2	$1,790.3	$28,477.5
By asset size:										
Less than $25 million	63	105	108	81.2	83.4	1,671.4	13.8	5.4	19.2	306.0
$25 million to $300 million	141	223	233	946.0	969.7	18,849.1	119.3	63.2	182.5	2,929.7
$300 million to $1 billion	17	34	36	943.1	991.6	18,243.5	93.6	43.8	137.4	2,200.0
$1 billion to $5 billion	16	24	28	2,977.8	3,183.6	57,128.7	264.3	91.6	355.8	5,799.3
Greater than $5 billion	5	12	14	18,819.7	19,061.6	334,555.0	185.2	910.2	1,095.4	17,242.5

Another way to measure the capital adequacy of the banking industry is to divide the total amount of capital of all banks by the total quantity of adjusted total assets of all banks. These measures are shown in the last two columns of Table 15–1. Though there is a noticeable decline from the first measures of aggregate capital ratios, these ratios are still above the 6 percent requirement.

The reason for the differences between these two measures of capital adequacy is apparent from the capital ratios of banks in different size classes. These data indicate that the smaller banks, which are much more numerous, have much higher capital ratios than the larger banks. The banks with assets in excess of $5 billion, which account for 46 percent of total assets, have an aggregate total capital of 6.5 percent.

It is also instructive to examine the condition of the banks that were deficient in capital during 1984. Table 15–2 presents data on the 419 (out of 14,404) banks that were deficient as of December 31, 1984. These banks represented 18 percent of the assets of the entire banking system. This table indicates that the bulk of the assets in deficient banks were accounted for by banks with assets over $5 billion. A bank can attempt to comply with a capital standard either by raising new capital or by decreasing its asset base. Table 15–2 indicates the amount of new capital that would have to be raised or the amount of assets that would have to be eliminated by banks in each size category in order to comply with the 6 percent requirement.

What constitutes an adequate or optimal supply of capital for a bank? This is an exceptionally difficult question. There is not even a clear understanding of what constitutes an optimal capital structure, or mix of debt and equity, for a nonfinancial firm. But for banks, where failure in large numbers imposes a substantial social cost, the problems are even more difficult. In a competitive capital market the market will price all securities to reflect the market's perception of risk and return. As a result, the market extracts a premium from firms that use more risky debt and prices the equity capital of the firm to reflect that risk. But the elements of secrecy surrounding commercial banks, insurance of deposit liabilities, and restrictions and examinations of riskiness make the assessment of such premiums a difficult task for the marketplace. As a result government regulators seek to use capital to provide an additional cushion of protection for depositors against mismanagement, conflicts of interest, and fraud committed by commercial bankers. As such, capital requirements are one more tool used by the regulators to minimize the prospect of major instability in the banking system.

PROBLEMS WITH THE DEPOSIT INSURANCE SYSTEM

Now that we have some understanding of how the current system for controlling risk in depository institutions operates, we can look at the current problems facing the deposit insurance system. The deposit insurance system has faced larger losses in the early 1980s than ever before. Many people believe this system needs extensive reform. Some observers of bank regulation have even labeled the current situation a crisis. We need to understand why deposit insurance is facing such serious problems.

AN ALTERNATIVE BANKRUPTCY SYSTEM

A **bankruptcy or insolvency system** is a legal mechanism for determining when a firm is bankrupt.

One way to view the deposit insurance system is as an alternative **bankruptcy or insolvency system** compared to that available to most U. S. corporations. This system might be better suited to commercial banks than the traditional one. In effect, this bankruptcy system might be more efficient than the alternatives.

Most firms in the United States operate under statutes that allow declarations of bankruptcy if and when a firm runs out of cash. From an economic standpoint, at first glance this appears to be an inappropriate way to define bankruptcy. That is, a firm is bankrupt when the value of its assets falls below the value of its liabilities—when it has negative net worth. However, in general the market does not provide direct estimates of the value of a firm's assets. Instead, it provides estimates of the value of contingent claims on those assets. That is, stock is essentially a call option on the value of the assets of the firm (see Chapter 4). Stock, just like any option, will never have negative value. As long as there is any chance that the firm will survive the bankruptcy process, the stock has positive value. Therefore, it is impractical to attempt to use the economist's conception of when a firm is bankrupt as a practical definition of bankruptcy. The alternative, which has evolved over the years, is for a firm to declare bankruptcy when it is unable to obtain additional credit or cash. In such an instance, the firm cannot find lenders who have sufficient confidence that the value of the firm's assets is in fact in excess of its existing liabilities. When no lenders can be found, then it is bankrupt. Essentially the same system applied to commercial banks prior to the advent of deposit insurance. However, the historical record under that system indicates that depositors tend to lose confidence in a number of institutions at once. This is essentially what happens when there is a run on a group of banks. If a run occurs, a bank can become insolvent even though there may have been no real deterioration in the quality of the bank's assets. In fact, this is Friedman and Schwartz' characterization of what occurred during the Great Depression. Because banks are inherently so vulnerable to this type of instability, the traditional method for determining when a firm is bankrupt is ill-suited to them.

The bankruptcy system operated by the FDIC differs from the traditional bankruptcy system applicable to other firms in a few important respects. First, rather than defining solvency on the basis of liquidity, solvency is determined according to accounting measures of net worth. As long as a bank can maintain its accounting net worth, then it is solvent from a regulatory standpoint. Net worth is accumulated either through retained earnings or through the sale of new stock or certain types of long-term debt in the market. A bank viewed as viable and profitable will generally have little difficulty maintaining regulatory net worth since it has ready access to the market.

There is another interesting and important feature of the bankruptcy system operated by the FDIC and FSLIC. In principle, if the government guarantor could determine precisely when an insured institution reached a level of zero economic net worth, then it could close the institution at precisely that point. Usually, when an institution is closed by the guarantor, it is merged with or sold to another institution. In the savings and loan industry, where there have been a sizable number of failures in recent years (see Chapter 19 for a more detailed discussion of them), the regulators have resorted to a strategy of not selling the failed institution, but arranging for it to be managed by a healthy savings and loan. In either case, if the guarantor could close institutions and recapitalize them at precisely the point when their economic net worth reaches zero, it would not actually incur losses in dealing with failed institutions. The guarantor's only costs would be the administrative costs of running the agency. In this case, the level of premiums charged for deposit insurance would only have to be large enough to cover these administrative costs. A system that worked in this way would be highly efficient and might operate effectively with insurance premiums well below those charged if another type of system were used for banks.

Throughout most of the life of the FDIC and the FSLIC, the actual losses they have incurred have been very low. In effect, they operated a system efficient enough that very low insurance premiums were justified. Table 15–3 shows data on the losses and reserves of the FDIC and the FSLIC from 1934 to 1986. Only in the 1980s did either agency incur significant losses. These data do not necessarily indicate that the deposit insurance system has worked relatively well throughout much of its history. It shows that the banking and savings and loan industries enjoyed an era of tremendous stability from shortly after the creation of these agencies until the early 1980s, when the guarantors began to incur substantial losses. During the long period of stability it appeared that the guarantors needed to charge only a very modest premium for deposit insurance. However, when the health of both the banking and savings and loan industries deteriorated in the 1980s, the prices for deposit insurance appeared to be very low.

PRICING OF DEPOSIT INSURANCE

The basic idea behind deposit insurance is that an agency of the U.S. government assumes the risk-bearing function for individual depositors. Once this function has been transferred to a government agency, that agency must undertake the kinds of activities that a private lender would take to limit its risk exposure. A private debt holder would impose restrictions or covenants on the borrower to limit the borrower's opportunities to impair the interests of the lender. In addition, a private lender would charge a price for a debt that reflected the perceived risk of loss due to insolvency or bankruptcy. An important determinant of the price or interest rate the lender would charge is the amount of capital maintained by the borrower. The more capital the borrower maintained, the smaller the likelihood of insolvency, and therefore, the lower the loan cost would be.

While these basic finance principles guide pricing decisions for most private debt contracts throughout the world, they are not a basis for the operation of the FDIC and the FSLIC. The FDIC and FSLIC do not attempt to assess the risk of

IMPEDIMENTS TO REFORM OF DEPOSIT INSURANCE

Some observers of the deposit insurance system have argued in recent years that it is important, even vital, to modify the system so that deposit insurance prices are related to risk. While proposals have been actively discussed for some time, few actual changes in the system have not moved it in this direction. One reason the current system remains intact is that it is exceptionally difficult to develop a meaningful criterion for precisely distinguishing the riskiness of banks. Recent bank failures have made it clear that bank examiners and regulators are not any more prescient than are bankers about judging good and bad loans. In addition, a number of recent failures have involved fraud. It has proved very difficult to determine fraud until the institution is threatened with insolvency. Furthermore, since many bank assets do not have secondary markets where their value can be readily determined, it is often difficult to determine the value of a bank's assets with any precision. All of these problems make risk assessment a difficult, though not insurmountable, task.

The second reason no changes have been made may be more compelling than the first: a risk-adjusted pricing mechanism would focus public attention on the riskiness of banks. This, in turn, could decrease the stability of the system. The regualtors' purpose is not only to prevent banking defaults as a result of bad loans and mismanagement, but also to avoid banking panics that could precipitate widespread failures. From a historical standpoint, this is the very reason for the existence of regulations.

A third reason the current deposit insurance system has so successfully resisted reform has as much to do with the overall price level for deposit insurance as with the issue of risk adjustment. The basic reason is that deposit insurance is relatively cheap; many insured institutions would find it difficult or impossible to obtain funds in the private marketplace at a cost comparable to the cost of insured deposits. As a result, there is a strong incentive for depository institutions to utilize government-insured debt. Insured debt is attractive because it is, in effect, subsidized. Proposals for reform of the deposit insurance system which would incorporate risk-adjusted pricing also threaten the subsidy's continuation. Therefore, managers and owners of insured depository institutions are not likely to support this type of reform.

The existence of a subsidy within deposit insurance must be placed in context with the costs imposed or benefits conferred by the regulatory system as a whole. For example, reserve requirements (see Chapter 10) impose a cost on depository institutions. The cost arises from the fact that the Federal Reserve pays no interest on the reserves held behind transactions accounts such as demand deposits. This acts like a tax imposed upon the depository institution by the government and raises the cost of accepting deposits or using deposits to fund investments or loans. Other institutions, such as foreign banks, that do not incur this cost have a competitive advantage. Therefore, it is quite possible for a subsidy in one part of the regulatory system to be offset by some cost imposed on insured depository institutions by another part of the regulatory system. Taken as a whole, the costs of the regulatory system will determine whether it is profitable to do business as a regulated and insured commercial bank. At the same time, the costs of funding investments with insured deposits versus other sources of funds will be determined, at least in part, by the costs and benefits implicit in government deposit insurance versus strictly private debt.

insolvency for the institutions they insure and use this assessment to determine the price of deposit insurance. Instead, they set a flat price for deposit insurance for all banks and savings and loans regardless of the riskiness of that institution. The FDIC charges an insurance premium nominally set at one-twelfth of 1 percent of a bank's total domestic deposits. This is the nominal rate because the FDIC allows a credit on this amount so that the effective rate was roughly half of this for a number of years. These premiums build a fund of investments managed by the FDIC that can be drawn upon if a bank fails.

TABLE 15–3
Insured deposits and the Deposit Insurance Fund 1934–1984 (in millions).

Year (December 31)	Deposit Insurance Losses and Expenses	Deposits in Insured Banks[1] Total	Insured	Percentage of Insured Deposits	Deposit Insurance Fund	Ratio of Deposit Insurance Fund to— Total Deposits	Insured Deposits
1985	$6,359.9	$1,974,512	$1,503,393	76.1	$17,956.9	0.91	1.19
1984	1,147.9	1,806,520	1,389,874	76.9	17,161.9	0.95	1.23
1983	834.2	1,690,576	1,268,332	75.0	15,429	0.91	1.22
1982	869.9	1,544,697	1,134,221	73.4	13,770.9	0.89	1.21
1981	720.9	1,409,322	988,898	70.2	12,246.1	0.87	1.24
1980	(34.6)	1,324,463	948,717	71.6	11,019.5	0.83	1.16
1979	(13.1)	1,226,943	808,555	65.9	9,792.7	0.80	1.21
1978	45.6	1,145,835	760,706	66.4	8,796.0	0.77	1.16
1977	24.3	1,050,435	692,533	65.9	7,992.8	0.76	1.15
1976	31.9	941,923	628,263	66.7	7,268.8	0.77	1.16
1975	29.8	875,985	569,101	65.0	6,716.0	0.77	1.18
1974	100.0	833,277	520,309	62.5	6,124.2	0.73	1.18
1973	53.8	766,509	465,600	60.7	5,615.3	0.73	1.21
1972	10.1	697,480	419,756	60.2	5,158.7	0.74	1.23
1971	13.4	610,685	374,568	61.3	4,739.9	0.78	1.27
1970	3.8	545,198	349,581	64.1	4,379.6	0.80	1.25
1969	1.0	495,858	313,085	63.1	4,051.1	0.82	1.29
1968	0.1	491,513	296,701	60.2	3,749.2	0.76	1.26
1967	2.9	448,709	261,149	58.2	3,485.5	0.78	1.33
1966	0.1	401,096	234,150	58.4	3,252.0	0.81	1.39
1965	5.2	377,400	209,690	55.6	3,036.3	0.80	1.45
1964	2.9	348,981	191,787	55.0	2,844.7	0.82	1.48
1963	0.7	313,304[2]	177,381	56.6	2,667.9	0.85	1.50
1962	0.1	297,548[3]	170,210	57.2	2,502.0	0.84	1.47
1961	1.6	281,304	160,309	57.0	2,353.8	0.84	1.47
1960	0.1	260,495	149,684	57.5	2,222.2	0.85	1.48
1959	0.2	247,589	142,131	57.4	2,089.8	0.84	1.47
1958		242,445	137,698	56.8	1,965.4	0.81	1.43
1957	0.1	225,507	127,055	56.3	1,850.5	0.82	1.46
1956	0.3	219,393	121,008	55.2	1,742.1	0.79	1.44
1955	0.3	212,226	116,380	54.8	1,639.6	0.77	1.41
1954	0.1	203,195	110,973	54.6	1,542.7	0.76	1.39
1953	0.1	193,466	105,610	54.6	1,450.7	0.75	1.37
1952	0.8	188,142	101,841	54.1	1,363.5	0.72	1.34
1951		178,540	96,713	54.2	1,282.2	0.72	1.33
1950	1.4	167,818	91,359	54.4	1,243.9	0.74	1.36
1949	0.3	156,786	76,589	48.8	1,203.9	0.77	1.57
1948	0.7	153,454	75,320	49.1	1,065.9	0.69	1.42
1947	0.1	154,096	76,254	49.5	1,006.1	0.65	1.32
1946	0.1	148,458	73,759	49.7	1,058.5	0.71	1.44
1945	0.1	157,174	67,021	42.4	929.2	0.59	1.39
1944	0.1	134,662	56,398	41.9	804.3	0.60	1.43
1943	0.2	111,650	48,440	43.4	703.1	0.63	1.45
1942	0.5	89,869	32,837	36.5	616.9	0.69	1.88
1941	0.6	71,209	28,249	39.7	553.5	0.78	1.96
1940	3.5	65,288	26,638	40.8	496.0	0.76	1.86
1939	7.2	57,485	24,650	42.9	452.7	0.79	1.84
1938	2.5	50,791	23,121	45.5	420.5	0.83	1.82
1937	3.7	48,228	22,557	46.8	383.1	0.79	1.70
1936	2.6	50,281	22,330	44.4	343.4	0.68	1.54
1935	2.8	45,125	20,158	44.7	306.0	0.68	1.52
1934	0.2	40,060	18,075	45.1	291.7	0.73	1.61

[1]Deposits in foreign branches are omitted from totals because they are not insured. Insured deposits are estimated by applying to the deposits in the various types of accounts at the regular Call dates, the percentages insured as determined from the Summary of Deposits survey submitted by insured banks.

[2]December 20, 1963.

[3]December 28, 1962.

The fact that the FDIC and FSLIC charge flat rather than risk-adjusted premiums for deposit insurance has immense implications for how the entire regulatory system for banks and savings and loans must operate. First, the regulators are forced to lean more heavily on direct control of the risk of the loans and investments of depository institutions as a way to limit their risk exposure. Second, there is an incentive for excessive risk taking.

When risk is priced fairly as in most private contracts, it not only provides appropriate compensation to the lender, but it also has an incentive effect for the borrower. The borrower knows that if he undertakes a relatively risky investment, lenders will demand higher compensation for accepting that risk. As a result, the borrower has an incentive to evaluate the risk and return of projects based on their overall payoffs. That is, part of the potential gain for the borrower does not come from a loss that he or she can expect to inflict on the lender. Fair and efficient pricing provides an incentive for lenders not to undertake projects with excessive risk.

However, in a system where the price of debt instruments is not related to the inherent risk, borrowers have a strong incentive to attempt to expropriate lenders. This is one of the types of problems discussed in Chapter 13 which can give rise to regulation. The incentive for borrowers to attempt to expropriate lenders becomes particularly strong when the borrower is highly levered. The reason is very simple. When an investor has a highly levered investment, he is essentially not playing with his own money. If the investment achieves a high payoff, it is to his or her benefit. If the investment turns out to be a disaster and there is a bankruptcy, the investor is protected by limited liability; he or she can only lose the equity that has been invested. As a result, managers and owners of depository institutions who do not have to compensate the FDIC or the FSLIC for the riskiness of the ventures they undertake will have a strong incentive to pursue highly risky investments if the institutions have very little capital. In this case they are not playing with their own money. The guarantor of deposits cannot provide an incentive to avoid highly risky projects by changing the price of deposit insurance as the nature of the bank's investments changes. Therefore, it is compelled to attempt to place direct controls on the riskiness of the institution's investment.

DIVERSIFICATION OF FDIC RISK

One of the fundamental problems facing the deposit insurance agencies is that they are insuring a risk that is not well diversified. Financial institutions tend to experience serious difficulties at the same time. These institutions mirror the financial health of the economy. When significant sectors of the economy are in financial difficulty, the banking industry is threatened with serious losses. When the banking industry as a whole experiences serious losses, the guarantors who insure the debt of these industries are threatened. This risk has a significant systematic element in it. We know that systematic risks are priced in the capital markets on a regular basis. However, if the outcome of a systematic risk is sufficiently bad, the guarantor can become insolvent. Precisely because of this, deposit insurance is provided by a government agency rather than a private firm. No private guarantor could provide a credible complete guarantee for significant systematic risk. Only a government guarantor where the ultimate liability lies with the U. S. Treasury has the ability to provide a credible guarantee.

When the underlying risk accepted by the deposit insurance agencies is not well-diversified, then there can be circumstances when large numbers of institutions have to close simultaneously. Under these conditions a government insurer can have a strong incentive to seek to protect a (finite) insurance fund and fail to close institutions which are determined to have negative net worth. One way to accomplish this is to change the regulatory or accounting definitions for solvency. This is what occurred in the savings and loan industry in the early 1980s. The FHLBB adopted more liberal rules to account for the net worth of savings and loans. As a result, lower levels of capital were required to remain solvent. (See Chapter 19 for a more detailed discussion of the solvency of savings and loans.)

In an economic environment where there are many failing institutions, the regulators presumably take into account the perceived social cost of closing institutions on a large scale. The ability to use discretion about the magnitude of this social cost is a critical element of the federal deposit insurance system. It is apparent that the social cost of a complete failure of the financial system due to widespread withdrawals is intolerably large. However, it is not apparent that the failure of modest or even large numbers of institutions generates a large social cost if those institutions are closed promptly without allowing large negative economic net worth to accumulate. More extensive coverage or more liberal rules for determining closure result in de facto insurance protection for equity owners or for entrenched management. In effect, this means insurance for the existing market and ownership structure of the depository institutions industry. If this view is correct, then the social cost involved in deposit insurance is the cost of avoiding large-scale concentration of firms in the financial services industry.

The way deposit insurers enforce a closure rule in a circumstance where a large number of institutions are experiencing financial difficulty is likely to affect the way those institutions evaluate risk. If managers of institutions perceive that their risk of being closed by the guarantor is minimal as long as they all experience the same risk, then there will be an incentive to collectively take on large risks and underprice those risks. This may partially explain the willingness of many banks to make extensive loans to developing countries with what appear to be relatively low premiums for risk in those loans.

The problems faced by the current system for deposit insurance grow as much out of problems in other aspects of the regulatory system for commercial banks as they do out of deficiencies in deposit insurance per se. The basic problem is that the market for financial services is changing dramatically and is threatening the traditional organization and operation of the banking industry. This change in the financial service marketplace is a central feature of Part 4.

Summary

In this chapter we examined the regulatory system for commercial banks. With the history of banking regulation as background we examined the current regulatory system and discussed some important issues concerning its operation.

The fundamental problem facing depository institutions is the prospect that banking system instability may lead to market failure. This results from the peculiar nature of a deposit as a debt obligation. Like any debt security, the value of the deposit can be influenced by expropriations instigated by the issuer of the claim. The problem with expropriations regarding depository institutions is that it is exceedingly difficult to construct covenants that adequately protect against future increases in the debt issued by the institution. In order to be able to function effectively, a depository institution must have the freedom to increase or decrease deposits as the need arises. This same flexibility makes it impossible to assign collateral to specific deposits.

The first method for dealing with this problem was for banks to back their deposits with gold. Because banks earned their profits from loans, the more gold they held in reserve, the less profitable they could expect to be. During the Civil War this system of strictly private backing for deposits was augmented by the federal government. The Banking Act of 1863 created nationally chartered banks backed by government bonds which were in turn backed by gold. It also created a system of reserves for banks. But banking panics still developed and in 1913 the Federal Reserve System was created. It was given the power to control the supply of reserves in the banking system and, therefore, the liquidity of commercial banks. In spite of the structure created through the Federal Reserve to provide bank liquidity, the largest banking crisis in U.S. history occurred during the 1930s, and the Federal Reserve was unable or unwilling to prevent it.

As a result of the Federal Reserve System's failure to adequately solve the stability problem of deposit intermediaries, the system was fundamentally altered with the Banking Act of 1933. The changes entailed government insurance of the value of bank deposits and government supervision and control of the risk of depository intermediaries. With the institution of deposit insurance, the backing behind bank deposits became a government promise rather than the individual bank's promise. And because depositors were insured if private banks reneged on their own promise, depositors no longer had an incentive to carefully assess how believable the promises were from individual banks. That responsibility now lay with the government. The system of regulating commercial banks was left essentially unchanged until 1980.

On the whole, the system instituted in the 1930s has worked rather well since banking panics have apparently disappeared. However, a number of questions about the operation of this system remain: how should deposit insurance be priced; how extensively should the risk of deposit institutions be regulated; what sorts of barriers to regional and product-line diversification should be allowed; what minimum capital requirements should be required. One of the most important features of the current system of deposit insurance is that both deposit insurance agencies (the FDIC and the FSLIC) do not use risk-adjusted prices for deposit insurance. As a result, deposit insurance prices are not used as an incentive device to encourage managers of insured institutions to avoid excessively risky investments. This has forced regulatory agencies to rely more heavily on direct control of risk through restrictions on allowable activities and on enforcement of capital requirements.

QUESTIONS

1. What does convertibility mean? Explain the nature of the convertibility problem which faced banks throughout most of the nineteenth century.
2. Explain what commercial banking was like during the era of wildcat banking. Why is this period referred to as a time of competing monies?
3. During the wildcat banking era bank notes traded at whatever rate of exchange the market demanded. After the Civil War bank notes of nationally chartered banks traded at par value. Why did this change occur?
4. Contrast the nature of the solution to banking panics contained in the Federal Reserve Act with the nature of the solution which came with the FDIC. How did the FDIC fundamentally change the nature of the financial contract between a bank and its depositors?
5. The banking reform legislation of the early 1930s is sometimes said to have nationalized gold. What does this mean and what is its significance?
6. Deposit insurance and regulatory control of risk are said to go hand in hand. Why is this so?
7. How might the current system for pricing and coverage of deposit insurance be changed? Evaluate the pros and cons.
8. Compare the system for evaluating the solvency or bankruptcy of commercial banks to the system under Chapter 11 of the U. S. bankruptcy statutes which applies to other types of firms. What is the significance of the differences?
9. How does the regulatory system restrict branch banking? How do banks avoid these restrictions? What are the consequences of branching restrictions for the size distribution of commercial banks?
10. What are the current capital requirements for commercial banks? How well do banks actually comply with these requirements?

REFERENCES

Benston, George J. "Economies of Scale in Financial Institutions," *Journal of Money, Credit and Banking,* 4 (May 1972), pp. 312–41.

Black, Fischer, Merton H. Miller, and Richard A. Posner. "An Approach to the Regulation of Bank Holding Companies," *Journal of Business,* 51 (1978), pp. 379–412.

Campbell, Tim S. and David Glenn. "Deposit Insurance in a Deregulated Environment," *Journal of Finance,* 39 (July 1984), pp. 775–84.

Chase, Samuel B., and John J. Mingo. "The Regulation of Bank Holding Companies," *Journal of Finance,* 30 (May 1975), pp. 281–92.

Diamond, Douglas W. and Philip H. Dybvig. "Bank Runs, Deposit Insurance, and Liquidity," *Journal of Political Economy,* 91 (1983).

Friedman, Milton, and Anna Schwartz. *A Monetary History of the United States 1867–1960,* Princeton, N.J.: Princeton University Press, 1963.

Gilbert, R. Alton, Courtenay C. Stone and Michael E. Trebing. "The New Bank Capital Adequacy Standards," *Review,* Federal Reserve Bank of St. Louis (May 1985).

Junker, George R. "A New Supervisory System for Rating Banks," *Quarterly Review,* Federal Reserve Bank of New York, 3 (Summer 1978), pp. 47–51.

Kane, Edward J. *The Gathering Crisis in Federal Deposit Insurance,* Cambridge, Mass.: MIT Press, 1985.

Kareken, John H. "Federal Bank Regulatory Policy: A Description and Some Observations," *Journal of Business,* 19 (January 1986), pp. 3–48.

Kareken, John H., and Neil Wallace. "Deposit Insurance and Bank Regulation: A Partial-Equilibrium Exposition," *Journal of Business,* 51 (1978), pp. 413–38.

Klein, Benjamin. "The Competitive Supply of Money," *Journal of Money, Credit and Banking,* (November 1974), pp. 423–53.

Peltzman, Sam. "Capital Investment in Commercial Banking and Its Relationship to Portfolio Regulation," *Journal of Political Economy,* 78 (1970), pp. 1–26.

Pringle, John. "The Capital Decision in Commercial Banks," *Journal of Finance,* 29 (1974), pp. 779–95.

Santomero, Anthony M., and Ronald D. Watson. "Determining an Optimal Capital Standard for the Banking Industry," *Journal of Finance,* 32 (September 1977), pp. 1267–82.

West, Robert Craig. *Banking Reform and the Federal Reserve 1863–1923,* Ithaca, N.Y.: Cornell University Press, 1974.

16

*I*NNOVATION IN FINANCIAL MARKETS

The process of innovation is especially important in the financial markets of the 1980s. Innovation refers to change—change in financial products, in the institutions that produce or deliver these products, and in the markets where they are traded. Old products and ways of doing business are being discarded and replaced with new and, hopefully, more efficient ones. The 1970s and 1980s have been a time of substantial innovation. We have seen the development of options and financial futures markets, the deregulation of many depository financial institutions, the introduction of a wide variety of new financial instruments and the internationalization of many financial markets. To understand fully how current markets and institutions operate we need to have an understanding of how and why innovation happens.

An important incentive to generate innovations is the profit motive. The innovator generally earns a relatively high return on an innovation. For example, the inventor of the first successful zero-coupon bonds stripped from Treasury bonds reaped benefits in the form of the difference between the price the new securities could command in the market and the cost of acquiring Treasury securities from which the zero-coupon bonds could be created. (We will explain zero-coupon bonds in a few pages.) However, benefits can rapidly diminish after the innovation is introduced into the market. The ability to generate continuing benefits hinges on the innovator's ability to erect barriers to entry in the market for the new product or service. In most financial markets this is very hard to accomplish. In the zero-coupon bond example, it took a very short time for most Wall Street firms to mimic the action of the first issuer of zero-coupon bonds. This meant that the spread or profit margin earned by the innovator was driven down to a more competitive level by the market entry of zero-coupon bonds from other competing investment bankers.

The only continuing source of profit or advantage must lie in the ability to innovate or the ability to spot opportunities for innovation more often than one's competitors. In other words, to benefit from innovation on a consistent basis, you must be a better innovator. This requires a very thorough understanding of the forces which create opportunities and a very sound knowledge of specific markets where innovations may be introduced. It is not obvious that one can have a comparative advantage in innovation. The efficient markets concept would argue that the market for innovation is likely to be competitive like other markets, unless some external force creates barriers to entry.

We begin with a discussion of the process of innovation to find out why it happens or what encourages it. We also want to know how to categorize innovation or how to break it down into its component parts. We will probably learn more from a close look at a few recent examples of innovation than we will from spending too much time on generalities. We will consider securitization of financial products, growth of the NASDAQ market, and development of zero-coupon bonds. ∎

THE PROCESS OF INNOVATION

THE FORCES THAT GENERATE INNOVATION

Innovation is generally a response to a change in some factor in the environment. This is a very broad statement, but it is true for virtually all markets, not just financial ones. The exception to this generalization is the innovation that is simply a new idea. Of the three examples of innovations in this chapter, the closest to this characterization is the zero-coupon bond. The major external factor that affected the viability of zero-coupon bonds was the increased volatility of interest rates in the late 1970s. But to a large degree, zero-coupon bonds represented a clever new idea that simply had not been tried on a large scale before. The idea was tried and it worked.

While the idea that innovation is a response to change in some environmental factor is very general, we can make it more specific by formulating a list of environmental factors. If we look at the major changes in financial markets in the last decade and ones we can foresee in the next decade, they appear to be responses to changes in one or more of these four environmental factors:

1. The level and volatility of inflation and interest rates
2. Technological progress in computers and communications
3. Regulation
4. Tax law.

Probably the largest single cause of innovation in financial markets and institutions in the last decade is increased inflation rates and the resulting increase in the level and volatility of interest rates in the 1970s and early 1980s. Many types of financial products and many financial institutions were designed to be viable only in an environment of relatively low and stable interest rates. But when interest rates increased, many institutions incurred substantial losses. This also caused investors to shift away from products, particularly regulated accounts at commercial banks and savings and loans, that could not effectively compete in the new environment.

In addition, the increased volatility of interest rates in part led to the creation of entire new vehicles for the redistribution of interest rate risk. In particular, financial futures and options became vehicles for transferring risk from one party directly to another, without relying on a bank or other institution to function as an intermediary. In fact, with higher and more volatile interest rates it became less practical for financial intermediaries to bear the risks of fluctuating interest rates to the same extent that they did in the 1950s and 1960s.

At roughly the same time that higher inflation rates were driving up market interest rates, the rate of technological progress in communication and computer technology increased tremendously and significantly affected the cost of providing most financial services. Much of the actual work in financial services involves a matter of recording and communicating transactions. The cost of these services is largely a function of the level of computer and communications technology. With the increasing refinement of the microchip and the computer technology that it made possible, more sophisticated systems for managing financial transactions have become practical. At the same time, improvements in communications systems have reduced the significance of geographic barriers between separate markets both within the United States and across national boundaries.

The changes in the level and volatility of market interest rates and in the technology of financial service delivery were particularly significant because of their impact on the U.S. regulatory system in the 1970s. The regulatory system created in the 1930s determined a set of segmented or specialized financial institutions and markets with geographic and product line barriers. However, by the late 1970s changes in interest rates and technology rendered much of this regulatory system obsolete—or at least raised the cost imposed on society by many

Regulatory arbitrage involves choice of appropriate regulators in order to minimize the cost of regulation.

regulatory restrictions. In practice, opportunities for **regulatory arbitrage** were created. That is, it created opportunities for innovation that avoided costly regulation. Financial institutions adapted to the environment of higher interest rates and new technology by inventing products and services that took advantage of loopholes in the regulations. The process accelerated in the 1980s, not because regulatory avoidance has become fashionable or morally acceptable, but because changes in the environment raised the cost of regulation.

The market response to these changes has caused an additional response from regulatory authorities. Once a loophole is discovered, regulators must decide whether to close it or change the law to allow the new practice. For instance, money market funds originally resulted from two factors: they took advantage of a loophole in regulation, and they were prompted by rates of high inflation and technological progress. Regulators responded to this market innovation by changing bank and savings and loan regulations so that they could compete with money

Regulatory dialectic refers to the process of innovation and regulatory response that results in regulatory reform.

market funds. This process of innovation and regulatory response has been called a **regulatory dialectic** by Ed Kane.[1] Because regulation creates a costly structure, there are incentives to find loopholes in it. When loopholes are discovered, some innovation is introduced, which leads to changes in regulations that generate a renewed search for loopholes.

Another important factor that stimulates innovation is change in tax laws. New tax laws have significant effects on financial products that are successful in the marketplace. For example, Chapter 7 explained that the changes in the tax laws enacted by the Congress in 1986 significantly affect specific financial products. The municipal bond market has been affected by the ceiling placed on the issuance of revenue bonds. This encourages firms to utilize alternatives to revenue bonds for many projects that previously were financed with tax-exempt debt. The tax law also significantly impacts real estate financing by limiting the amount of depreciation and interest expense deductions for real estate investments as well as the amount of write-offs claimed against earned income. These changes significantly affect the ability of real estate syndicators to distribute real estate investments where the principal attraction was tax avoidance. Differences in tax laws from country to country must also be taken into account. In 1982, U.S. tax laws were changed in a way that affected the advantages to corporations of issuing zero-coupon bonds and selling them to U.S. investors. A market for these instruments soon developed in Japan, because the difference between U.S. and Japanese tax laws created an incentive for development of a new zero-coupon bond product.

A TAXONOMY FOR INNOVATION

Product innovation refers to new financial products, such as options, futures and zero-coupon bonds.

Process innovation refers to new types of procedures for managing financial transactions such as point-of-sale terminals, automatic teller machines, and electronic security trading.

Organizational innovations represent new forms of organizations for delivering financial services, such as money market funds.

The innovations in the last decade can be divided into three useful categories: *product, process,* and *organizational innovations.* **Product innovations** refer to new financial products like options, futures, zero-coupon bonds, and Eurobonds. They can be motivated by any of the four environmental factors, although it appears that technological progress is the least likely.

Process innovation, on the other hand, appears to be motivated largely by technological progress. Examples of **process innovation** are credit cards, point-of-sale terminals, electronic funds transfer, automatic teller machines, and electronic security trading. All of these changes in the management of financial transactions have resulted from improved efficiency and reduced cost in computer and communications technology.

Finally, a number of innovations represent organizational changes as much as product or process changes. These types of changes include development of money market funds, municipal bond funds, and financial guarantees. **Organizational innovations** are particularly important as a part of regulatory arbitrage, since a new form of organization can often avoid existing regulatory restrictions.

[1]See Edward Kane, ''Accelerating Inflation, Technological Innovations and the Decreasing Effectiveness of Bank Regulations,'' *Journal of Finance,* 36 (May 1981), pp. 3–32.

A key example is the unitary bank holding company which circumvented the restrictions imposed by Congress on multibank holding companies for a number of years. Another example is the money market fund, which involved a joint venture between a bank and an investment company to avoid restrictions applicable to banks and investment companies as distinct entities.

It is possible to view most organizational innovations as new products as much as organizational changes. For example, financial guarantees are now available on municipal bonds from a number of insurance companies. This type of guarantee has gained more acceptance as municipal bonds have been sold increasingly to individuals rather than institutions. These financial guarantees are a new type of product, but at the same time, they represent a new type of organization participating in the market. The firms that offer these guarantees are subsidiaries of large insurance companies or separate insurance companies specializing in financial guarantees yet obtain financial backing from other, larger firms, including insurance companies and commercial banks. For example, American Municipal Bond Assurance Corporation is partly owned by Citicorp, as well as a number of insurance companies, yet it operates as a separate company providing insurance against default on municipal bonds.

The appropriate form of organization to deliver a specific financial product is determined by the relative costs of using that organizational form versus available alternatives. As any of the environmental factors change, the relative costs of specific types of organizations can be affected. For example, in the last few years a number of Wall Street investment firms have converted from closely held firms or partnerships into publicly held corporations. Some have also been acquired by larger diversified companies. For example, Shearson was acquired by American Express. One important motivation for these changes has been the increased importance of trading operations in the investment banking business. This, in turn, is largely due to the growth of options and futures markets and the introduction of a wide variety of new securities. At the same time, the increased volatility of many asset prices and interest rates has increased the risk of many trading activities. This has resulted in an increased need for capital on the part of the major Wall Street firms which, in turn, has raised the cost of remaining a closely held corporation or partnership. An organization of this type has substantial difficulty raising capital.

Now that we have some understanding of why innovation occurs, we can turn our attention to some examples of innovation.

SECURITIZATION OF FINANCIAL ASSETS

Securitization refers to the transformation of an asset that once had no secondary market into tradeable securities with active secondary markets. Another way to look at it is that securitization is the transformation of an intermediated market into an over-the-counter and ultimately an auction market. A number of assets which were once funded largely through financial intermediaries are now becoming securitized. The market where securitization has gone the farthest is the mortgage market. Chapter 19 is devoted to mortgage finance, so we will not concentrate on the securitization of mortgages here. But auto loans, consumer credit cards, and commercial loans from banks are also becoming securitized. We will discuss these examples as we proceed.

In order to understand how securitization works it is useful to break the process of securitizing a particular asset into its component parts. There are six distinct stages:

1. Originate the asset
2. Service the asset
3. Collect assets and create securities
4. Distribute securities
5. Guarantee the cash flows from those securities
6. Provide liquidity in the secondary market.

Origination of the asset involves the initial creation of the loan or security agreement that requires funding. In the case of a mortgage it involves arranging the loan with the original borrower who is purchasing or refinancing a home. The second stage involves the collection and processing of payments from the borrower. The third stage involves creation of a portfolio of loans out of individual loans. The key to this function is the ability to hedge the risks of the loans against changes in market interest rates until a complete portfolio can be formed and a security can be issued backed by the loans in that portfolio. The fourth stage involves distribution or sale of these securities to investors. The fifth stage entails the splitting off of specific risks and the sale of those risks to specialized investors or guarantors. An insurance company or a bank, for example, may write a guarantee against default on the assets that back the security. This is common practice with mortgage-backed securities. The final stage involves provision of liquidity through maintenance of an active secondary market. This is the dealer's traditional role in a secondary market. That is, the dealer provides liquidity by maintaining a market in the security.

In an intermediated market some of these activities are eliminated, and the remainder are internalized within each institution active in the market. The origination process is not affected significantly by securitization. The debt contract must still be executed regardless. However, in an intermediated market securities are not formed and distributed. Instead, the institution that originates the loan holds that loan in its portfolio. A lender that functions in this way is often referred to as a **portfolio lender.** The third function, that of providing a guarantee, is present in both an intermediated and an over-the-counter market. The distinction regards whether the guarantee is internalized. In an intermediated market, the bank or other type of portfolio lender provides a guarantee to depositors when it issues deposits to fund a loan. For regulated and insured banks and savings and loans there is also a guarantee provided by an agency of the U.S. government (the Federal Deposit Insurance Corporation, for banks, and the Federal Savings and Loan Insurance Corporation, for savings and loans). In a securitized market, the

A **portfolio lender** originates loans and holds them in its loan portfolio.

guarantee may be provided by the same institution that originates the asset or loan, but generally it is not. It may be provided by another firm that also originates its own loans, or it may be provided by a distinct type of institution, generally an insurance company, which is not involved in the origination process. Finally, the last stage in the process, that of providing liquidity, is not a part of an intermediated market. When loans are held in portfolio until maturity (or prepayment), so that a secondary market does not develop, there is no liquidity for the investor and no service to be provided by a dealer.

In an over-the-counter market each of these six distinct functions may be provided by a different type of firm. For example, a commercial bank may originate a loan. The loan may be acquired by another bank and placed in a portfolio. An investment banking firm may create and distribute a security backed by that portfolio of loans. A separate bank or insurance company may provide a guarantee against default on those loans. Finally, a number of investment banking firms, as well as other types of institutions, may operate as dealers in the market for these securitized loans. Moreover, the specific arrangements utilized for any particular type of asset, such as mortgages or commercial loans or even auto loans, vary from case to case. There is no standard or uniform way of structuring securitized financing that applies to all types of assets.

BENEFITS OF SECURITIZATION

Now that we have some understanding of what is involved in securitization, we need to ask what its benefits are. What makes securitization attractive for some types of assets and unattractive for others?

The principal benefit of securitization is a reduction in the cost of operating the market. That is, there can be a gain in efficiency which should result in a lower cost of funds or lower interest rate. To see how securitization can do this, we need to refer to the six components of the securitization process described above. Recall that in an intermediated market each of these stages of the process are either internalized in one institution or they are eliminated. When they are internalized, each institution that operates in the market must be *vertically integrated* to the extent that it provides the entire range of services, from origination through provision of guarantees to depositors. This limits opportunities for specialization that may generate efficiency. Securitization provides an opportunity for and even fosters *specialization,* which can lead to a more cost effective system for funding an asset.

In addition, the regulatory system for commercial banks and savings and loans in the United States has traditionally sheltered these institutions from competition with other types of firms. One way this has been accomplished is by enforcing a separation between banking and commerce and by creating specialized or segmented financial institutions. These institutions are not as diversified as they might be without regulation. In addition, restrictions on geographic expansion have made it possible for many small institutions to survive, where they might not be viable in a less restrictive regulatory environment.

It is important to evaluate the benefits of securitization in light of the impact of current regulatory restrictions on financial intermediaries. Securitization can become attractive simply as a way of avoiding these inefficiencies induced by regulation. Were it not for costly regulation, intermediaries could provide financing at a cost that is competitive with a securitized form of funding. That is, there may be no inherent reason why a securitized market is more cost effective than an intermediated market. Rather, securitization may provide a way to escape or arbitrage the undesirable effects of regulation.

It seems important to single out one of the items on the list of the elements of securitization for special treatment. This is the final item, provision of liquidity. Participants in the market often argue that the main benefit of securitization is that it provides institutions in the market with liquidity. Lenders who previously had no option but to hold assets until they matured can sell them in the market if they need to do so. In addition, institutions can add to their asset portfolio not only by originating new loans, but also by acquiring loans from others. The options to buy and sell assets in the market may be valuable for a number of reasons. For example, an institution may have difficulty attracting deposits to fund existing assets and may therefore need to liquidate assets. It may find new and more attractive investment opportunities that can best be funded by liquidating existing assets. It may change its operating strategy and want to alter the type of assets it holds. It may have more deposit liabilities than it can profitably invest in loans it can orginate on its own. When there is no secondary market for its assets, then none of these options is available.

COSTS OF SECURITIZATION

While securitization has some important benefits, it also has some potential costs. The costs pertain largely to the incentives for monitoring and controlling the risk of default in debt instruments. There are two distinct types of problems that can arise when debt contracts are securitized. These problems are called *adverse selection* and *moral hazard*. We discussed them in Chapter 5, though at that point there was no reference to their importance in securitization. Let's consider adverse selection first.

Adverse selection occurs when the originator of a loan has better knowledge of the quality of loans than investors, and the originator sells only low-quality loans.

Adverse selection is common in many types of insurance arrangements. The problem occurs when one party to a transaction has better information about the nature of its risk than the other party. In the case of securitization, adverse selection can occur when the originator of a loan has better knowledge of the quality of individual loans than investors who might acquire those loans in a secondary market. If the originator has no stake in the outcome of the loans once they are sold in the secondary market, then he or she will have an incentive to keep the loans known to be of relatively low default risk and to sell those known to be of high default risk. If the market as a whole perceives that lenders have an incentive to behave in this way, then they are not likely to acquire loans from these lenders. If no way can be found to limit the originator's incentive to distribute only low quality loans, then the secondary market will fail to function at all.

SECURITIZATION OF AUTO RECEIVABLES

Securitization has progressed the farthest in mortgage markets because the benefits of securitization are very large (including the gains from avoiding costly regulation) while the moral hazard and adverse selection problems with residential mortgages have, thus far, been manageable. In 1986 securitization began to spread to other markets, particularly for auto financing and, to a limited extent, consumer credit card loans. One of the chief reasons auto loans have been securitized is that their costs and benefits are similar to the mortgage industry. This is particularly true with respect to the costs. Like residential mortgages, as long as the auto owner has a significant equity position in the car, there is an incentive to take reasonable care so that the moral hazard problem is not too severe. In addition, it is possible to screen loan applications sufficiently to limit adverse selection problems. On the other hand, the auto finance industry has not been highly regulated like the savings and loan industry, which has been the main source of mortgage credit in the United States. Therefore, there do not appear to be significant gains from avoiding regulation as a result of securitizing auto loans. However, there may be significant benefits derived from the increased liquidity that a securitized auto finance market would generate. The success of securitization of autos will largely depend on how much is gained from liquidity.

As of early 1987, there had been approximately $10 billion of auto-backed securities issued to the public. In addition there was a smaller amount of securities backed by other types of receivables. Table

TABLE 16–1
Asset-Backed Securities.

U.S. Public Issues in 1985				
Date	Issuer	Collateral	Amount (thousands)	Lead Manager
03/07/85	Sperry A	Computer leases	$ 192,455	First Boston
05/15/85	Valley National	Autos	100,499	First Boston
05/15/85	Marine	Autos	60,171	Salomon
08/01/85	Home Federal	Autos	103,205	Salomon
09/12/85	Sperry B	Computer leases	145,805	First Boston
12/12/85	GMAC 1985–A	Autos	524,684	First Boston
12/13/85	Western Financial	Autos	110,000	Drexel
	Total 1985		$1,236,819	

The general nature of the solution to the adverse selection problem is for the loan originator to maintain a stake in their ultimate disposition. A simple way for this to happen is for the originator to offer a guarantee of their credit quality. A less formal way is for originators to develop reputations for not engaging in adverse selection. Reputable originators are perceived to have an incentive to distribute only high-quality loans. Their reputation arises from the fact that if they engage in adverse selection, they may be denied future access to the market.

The moral hazard problem is similar but not identical to the adverse selection problem. **Moral hazard** refers to an originator's incentive to expend effort or resources to reduce the risk of default. This can apply both at the time the loan is

Moral hazard refers to the incentive of an originator to expand effort or resources to reduce the risk of default.

16–1 itemizes most public asset-backed (excluding mortgages) securities issued through the end of 1986. The bulk of them issued thus far have been backed by auto loans originated by General Motors Acceptance Corporation and distributed by First Boston Corporation. There is a significant potential for more issues of the type listed in this table, but it is unclear how this market will develop.

U.S. Public Issues in 1986

Date	Issuer	Collateral	Amount (thousands)	Lead Manager
01/23/86	GMAC	Autos	$ 423,552	First Boston
04/16/86	GMAC	Autos	1,049,490	First Boston
06/18/86	Empire of America	Autos	190,216	First Boston
06/19/86	GMAC	Autos	755,074	First Boston
07/23/86	Chrysler	Autos	250,000	Salomon
07/24/86	NMAC	Light trucks	112,729	First Boston
07/24/86	NMAC	Light trucks	69,701	First Boston
07/24/86	NMAC	Light trucks	5,011	First Boston
08/19/86	GMAC	Autos	354,750	First Boston
08/19/86	GMAC	Autos	725,069	First Boston
10/14/86	ABSC–GMAC*	Autos	2,095,000	First Boston
10/14/86	ABSC–GMAC	Autos	585,000	First Boston
10/14/86	ABSC–GMAC	Autos	1,320,000	First Boston
11/13/86	Western Financial	Autos	191,930	Drexel
11/18/86	Banco Central	Autos	66,614	First Boston
11/18/86	GMAC 1986–F	Autos	326,962	First Boston
12/02/86	ABSC–GMAC	Autos	95,000	First Boston
12/02/86	ABSC–GMAC	Autos	25,050	First Boston
12/02/86	ABSC–GMAC	Autos	60,176	First Boston
12/05/86	Goldome	Computer leases	205,712	First Boston
12/12/86	Bank of America	Autos	514,222	Salomon
12/17/86	GMAC 1986–G	Autos	444,857	First Boston
12/17/86	Sperry C	Computer leases	174,450	First Boston
	Total 1986		$10,040,565	

*Issued by First Boston subsidiary ABSC.

orginated and throughout its duration. In many types of loan agreements, particularly business loans, continual monitoring of the borrower's performance over the life of the loan is as important as good underwriting when the loan is originated. If the originator can sell the loan to another party, then his or her incentive to continue to monitor the loan is eliminated. The apparent way to induce the originator to monitor the loan effectively is to insist that he or she continue to have a significant stake in the loan's outcome. As a result, an originator of loans that require continual monitoring may sell participations in those loans rather than sell the entire loan in a secondary market. The secondary market for corporate or business loans tends to function as a market for participations, for this reason.

Another way to deal with both moral hazard and adverse selection is for a special class of institutions to monitor the originators. There are two types of institutions in U.S. financial markets that serve this purpose. One type is the rating agencies, principally Moody's and Standard and Poor's. The other is private guarantors or insurers of securitized debt. Since these guarantors are legally obligated to pay off if a loan they guarantee defaults, they have a strong incentive to monitor the origination process of lenders whose loans they guarantee so that adverse selection and moral hazard problems are limited. In addition, rating agencies also evaluate the guarantors so there is an additional layer of scrutiny of the credit evaluation process.

In determining whether a market can be successfully securitized, it is necessary to evaluate both the costs and the benefits of securitization. The benefits are essentially gains in efficiency, including benefits provided by liquidity, as well as a possible reduction in the regulation costs. The costs pertain to reduction of the incentives to evaluate and monitor risks properly. In any specific market these costs and benefits may be quite different. Therefore, securitization might be quite successful in one market and might not progress very far in another.

INNOVATIONS IN THE OVER-THE COUNTER MARKET IN EQUITY SECURITIES

THE RISE OF NASDAQ

Over the last decade a number of new types of financial instruments and markets have come into existence. Probably the most conspicuous are new markets for various types of options and futures contracts. However, there has been an interesting and important form of market innovation for one of the oldest and most well-established form of securities traded in the United States, the corporate equity security. The innovation involves a new intensity of competition between rival markets for listing and trading equities. On the one hand there are the established exchanges, principally the New York and American Stock Exchanges (NYSE and AMEX), which are essentially auction markets. These exchanges are facing increasingly stiff competition from the **NASDAQ,** the National Association of Securities Dealers Automatic Quotation System, the over-the-counter market for corporate equities. The NASDAQ was once viewed as a refuge for stocks that could not gain admittance to the major exchanges. Over-the-counter listing was considered something to be outgrown as a company matured. However, in the last few years the NASDAQ has become a highly efficient and potentially viable competitor to the major exchanges. It is both important and interesting to examine the types of innovations introduced in the NASDAQ to improve its efficiency. It is also important to see how the operation of the NASDAQ compares with the operation of the NYSE.

Most trading in corporate equities takes place on one or more of the major stock exchanges in the United States. Of all the exchanges, the greatest publicity

NASDAQ is the National Association of Securities Dealers Automatic Quotation System.

is given to the NYSE because it dwarfs the other exchanges in annual volume of trades executed and value of the securities listed. The second largest is the AMEX, which is not very far behind the NYSE in the total number of securities listed, although the total value of these securities is a fairly small portion of the total value of securities listed on the NYSE. The other regional exchanges are far behind the NYSE both in number of securities and in total value. The same ranking prevails on the volume of trading.

The NYSE is essentially a continuous auction market, but it incorporates a few features of a call-auction and dealers play a significant role. The dealers on the NYSE are referred to as **specialists** because they operate as dealers in particular stocks rather than in all stocks listed on the exchange. The rules of the exchange are designed to limit the specialist's role as a dealer in order to minimize the costs of executing trades on the exchange. Specialists are required to give priority to the execution of orders between public investors rather than trades with themselves. When a specialist receives an order to buy or sell a stock, he or she must first seek to match it with an opposite order from a nonspecialist. The specialist is permitted to execute his or her own order first only if its bid price is higher, or its offering price is lower than the prices of any public order on the exchange. As trading imbalances develop, the dealer is permitted to trade on his or her own account.

There has also long been a market in equities that does not operate through one of the organized stock exchanges. Banks traditionally acted as dealers in these securities (though they no longer do this), and the securities were literally sold over the counter. Hence, this market became known as the "over-the-counter" market. In 1971 the National Association of Securities Dealers, the trade association of securities brokers, implemented an automated quotation system (NASDAQ) for these over-the-counter securities. NASDAQ is a computerized nationwide communications system that provides price quotes for major dealers in over-the-counter securities. As of 1986 the number of securities listed on the NASDAQ system were 4,209 issues, including 2,671 issues on the national market system (explained below) and 1,538 issues not on that system. This is compared to about 2,000 on the NYSE. The NASDAQ system is not identical to the over-the-counter market. Many over-the-counter stocks, usually those infrequently traded, are not listed on NASDAQ, and a few NYSE stocks are listed on NASDAQ. But as a rough approximation, it is useful to think of NASDAQ as the system by which over-the-counter stocks are traded.

Individual dealers in the NASDAQ market hold inventories in the securities listed on NASDAQ and trade as they receive offers to buy or sell. Brokers or others who have access to the NASDAQ system have computer terminals that provide information on prices bid and asked by these dealers. The terminals report the median bid and median asking price of all dealers in the system who trade in a particular stock. In addition, users can obtain the bid and asked price of each dealer in the system. The essential difference between NASDAQ and an exchange like the NYSE is that the NASDAQ system does not carry out or record transactions but merely lists information on dealers' quotations. Exchanges must be

<aside>The **specialist** is the dealer in a particular stock on the New York Stock Exchange.</aside>

completed by telephoning the dealer and carrying out the transaction. This is one important feature distinguishing the over-the-counter from the auction market.

The fundamental difference between the securities listed on the NYSE and the NASDAQ system or other exchanges is in the volume of securities outstanding and the frequency of trades. The NYSE lists only securities that have a large enough volume and are traded frequently enough to warrant the cost of a centralized exchange facility, while the NASDAQ system lists bids on stocks that meet much less stringent requirements. To be listed on the NASDAQ system, securities must have at least two dealers willing to make a market in that security. Listing also involves a fee for the corporation whose stock is listed.

However, NASDAQ has also introduced some marketing innovations that have positioned it to compete more effectively with the NYSE. One of the most important appears to be the adoption of the name **National Market System.** In 1982 the NASDAQ introduced a new level of service for more actively traded securities. This involves a computer system with up-to-the-minute bid and asked prices as well as the latest price at which the stock has traded, the high and low prices for the day, and the current trading volume. For less actively traded stocks, the NASDAQ computer system simply lists the bid and asked prices of individual dealers in each stock and provides a measure of trading volume at the end of each day. Listings for National Market System stocks are printed in the *Wall Street Journal* and other daily papers and do not differ greatly in appearance from NYSE or AMEX listings.

The **National Market System** is the name used by Congress in the 1975 securities reform legislation which directed the SEC to move toward an automated national system for trading securities. It is also used by the NASDAQ market for their market for stocks with high trading volume.

COMPETITION BETWEEN DEALERS ON THE NASDAQ

A critical difference between how the NASDAQ and the NYSE operate is the fact that there is a single dealer in each stock on the NYSE, the specialist, while there may be multiple dealers in a given stock on the NASDAQ. Competition between dealers is permitted on the NASDAQ, while it is limited on the NYSE. In fact, dealer competition is the very essence of the NASDAQ since it represents a computerized communication system among dealers who make a market in various securities. The chief innovation that has made the NASDAQ grow and prosper is the investment in computer technology, which has led to a more efficient system for distributing information about prices offered by competing dealers on stocks in which they make a market.

Some interesting evidence on the pricing of dealer services on the NASDAQ market has been collected since the market began. This market is of particular interest because it allows multiple dealers in each stock, or direct competition among dealers, whereas the NYSE does not. Probably the most comprehensive study of this question was conducted by Hans Stoll, who analyzed the data on the spread in the NASDAQ market and their determinants for a 6-day period in July, 1973. Some background data on the market characteristics for selected dates preceding his sample period are shown in Table 16–2. The table indicates that the middle of 1973 was not a particularly good time for the securities industry. Between April, 1972 and July, 1973, trading volume and average prices fell substantially. In response, percentage spreads between bid and asked prices increased

TABLE 16–2
Background information on the operation of the NASDAQ market on selected dates during 1972 and 1973.

	Date						
	1972				1973		
Variable	4/3	6/27	9/28	12/26	3/27	6/27	7/11
1. NASDAQ composite price index	128	130	129	131	117	100	103
2. NASDAQ share volume for week containing date (millions)	53	38	40	32	33	23	27
3. Median % spread	2.7	2.8	2.9	3.0	3.6	4.2	4.2
Financial stocks	5.1	5.6	6.3	6.7	8.0	10.5	10.5
Industrial stocks							
4. Median $ volume ($100)	101	79	74	80	75	54	101
Financial stocks	75	48	32	39	21	15	22
Industrial stocks							
5. Median price	26	25	26	26	23	19	19.4
Financial stocks	11	10	8.9	8.5	7.3	5.9	5.9
Industrial stocks							
6. Median number of dealers	5	5	5	5	5	5	5
listed	5	5	5	5	4	4	4
Financial stocks							
Industrial stocks							

Note: Median calculated across all non-third-market common stocks.

Source: Hans R. Stoll, "The Pricing of Dealer Services: An Empirical Study of NASDAQ Stocks," *Journal of Finance,* vol. 33 (September 1978), p. 1156.

dramatically, from 5.1 percent to 10.0 percent for the typical industrial stock and from 2.7 percent to 4.2 percent for the typical financial stock. However, the median number of dealers in each stock did not change much at all, remaining four or five throughout the period. This means that the average dealer experienced less trading activity.

During his 6-day sample period, Stoll attempted to explain the variation in observed bid-ask spreads across securities as a function of the following factors: the riskiness of the stock, measured by the variance of its price; the amount of trading based on superior information or the information cost of the dealer, measured by trading volume relative to the number of shares outstanding (on the grounds that this should rise when some people start to trade on special information); the level of order costs; the willingness of dealers to bear risk, measured by a proxy for dealer wealth; and the lack of competition among dealers, measured by the number of dealers in each stock and the concentration of their trading in that stock. As any of these factors increases, so should observed spreads between bid and asked prices.

Using these measures of dealer costs and competition, Stoll was able to account for 80 percent of the variation in observed bid-ask spreads. Futhermore, he showed that each of the factors itemized above has a significant impact on actual spreads in the NASDAQ market. Of particular interest is his conclusion that increased competition does cause a significant decline in the spreads.

To a large degree, NASDAQ's recent growth and success have resulted from the relative efficiency of its computerized system and the competition among dealers. NASDAQ officials are eager to point out that (as of late 1984) 1,800 companies on NASDAQ could qualify for listings on the AMEX and 600 of these could qualify for listings on the NYSE. Each year some companies move from the NASDAQ to the NYSE, but the NASDAQ continues to grow because new companies join the system every year. There have been very few instances of a company defecting from the NYSE to the NASDAQ. However, in order to be listed on the NYSE a company must accept a rule which requires a two-thirds vote of shareholders to delist the stock. Hence, there would appear to be a significant barrier to exit from the NYSE.

It is sometimes argued that the essential difference between NASDAQ and the NYSE is that the NYSE's specialist system limits the liquidity of the market for a particular stock. The reason it may limit liquidity is that the liquidity in each stock is dependent on the actions of a single market maker. If the specialist in a stock runs short of capital, for example, he or she may allow the abrupt price movements which are supposed to be prevented. Another possibility is that when trading volume is heavy the specialist may simply fall behind. These events can lead to halts in trading so that the stock becomes completely illiquid. On the NASDAQ there is virtually never a trading halt to balance orders as occurs on the NYSE.

As time has passed, the differences between the NYSE and the other segments of the secondary market in equities have blurred or diminished. With the advent of NASDAQ the over-the-counter market has become increasingly like the NYSE itself. In addition, the NASDAQ has been an important force compelling the NYSE to change and adopt more efficient procedures. In effect, we are observing competition between the types of markets as trading securities drive each market form toward more efficient methods of operation. Shareholders are likely to benefit from this type of competition.

TIGRS, CATS, AND OTHER ZEROS

Original issue discount bonds are issued with coupon rates which are significantly less than current market interest rates.

Many of the innovations in financial markets represent new types of securities. One of the more interesting such innovations is the **original issue discount bond** (OID), an extreme version of which is the zero-coupon bond. An OID bond is a bond issued with a coupon rate below the going market interest rate for a bond of the same maturity. The zero-coupon bond is the limiting case of an OID, since the coupon rate for such a bond is zero.

Historically, OID and zero-coupon bonds were rather rare financial instruments. Neither the U.S. government nor private corporations issued them. Private corporations did not do so because a corporation financed entirely with zero-coupon debt has no obligation to provide cash flows to bondholders until maturity. Since insolvency is determined by ability to meet cash obligations, an OID bond and particularly a zero-coupon bond provides substantial latitude to corporate borrowers. A corporation financed largely with zero-coupon debt does not have to answer to debtholders for a long time, a situation viewed as very risky for debtholders. However, as interest rates increased to unprecedented levels in the late 1970s and as the volatility of interest rates increased after the change in monetary policy announced by Paul Volcker in October, 1979, both investors and issuers in corporate bonds began to look for new ways to limit interest rate risk. This led to a reevaluation of the attractiveness of OID bonds, especially zero-coupon bonds.

There are two important reasons why OID bonds have become attractive. They provide a way to reduce interest rate risk for investors with specific holding periods, particularly if they are long-term investors. Second, there have been some significant tax advantages to OID bonds. The tax story is an interesting example of how securities evolve in response to the moves and countermoves of investors and tax or regulatory authorities. In this case the tax authorities who have played an important role are both in the United States and Japan. But, before we take up the tax story, consider how OID bonds limit interest rate risk.

INTEREST RATE RISK AND OID BONDS

In order to understand how OID bonds can reduce interest rate risk it is important to see that coupon-paying bonds have two opposing types of risks. First, there is risk surrounding the value of the security if it is sold prior to maturity. If interest rates increase, this is equivalent to a decrease in the value of the coupon-paying bond. Therefore, the holder of the coupon-paying bond is hurt if that bond is sold prior to maturity and prices decline or, equivalently, interest rates increase. At the same time, increasing interest rates have a favorable impact on the income earned on reinvested coupon payments. Higher interest rates mean coupon payments will earn a higher return when they are reinvested. With an OID bond, this reinvestment risk is reduced. In the extreme case of a zero-coupon bond the reinvestment risk is eliminated altogether. For example, if an investor has a specific intended holding period, say 10 years, then she can eliminate both the price risk and the reinvestment risk of the investment by buying a zero-coupon bond with a 10-year maturity. If she buys a coupon-paying bond, even an OID bond, these risks can never be eliminated entirely. We learned in Chapter 9 that an investor can match the duration of a coupon-paying bond with an intended holding period in order to minimize these combined risks. But some risk is still present as long as there are coupon payments.

Table 16–3 illustrates how important the reduction of the coupon interest rate can be when interest rates are high at the time a bond is issued and when there is a risk of a decline in interest rates over the life of the bond. This kind of environment existed in the early 1980s when OID bonds were first offered. Table 16–3 is based on the following assumptions. Suppose a 20-year bond is issued in an environment where market interest rates are 16 percent. Suppose that interest rates

TABLE 16–3
Realized yields to maturity for 20-year bonds with various coupons.

When reinvestment rates drop from 16 percent to 12 percent after ten years

Coupon (in dollars)	Realized Yield to Maturity (in percent)
16	14.248
15	14.254
14	14.261
13	14.270
12	14.279
11	14.290
10	14.303
9	14.319
8	14.338
7	14.362
6	14.392
5	14.435
4	14.493
3	14.581
2	14.728
1	15.029
0	16.000

Source: Andrew Silver "Original Issue Deep Discount Bonds," *Quarterly Review,* Federal Reserve Bank of New York, (Winter 1981–82).

remain at 16 percent for 10 years so that any coupon payments received over the first 10 years of the life of the bond can be reinvested at 16 percent. Then suppose the rate available on reinvested coupon payments declines to 12 percent over the next 10 years of the life of the bond. Table 16–3 shows how the realized or holding period yield on the bond over its 20–year life is affected, depending on the initial level of the coupon rate. The table illustrates that a zero-coupon bond has no change in its holding period yield as a result of the interest rate decline. This results from the fact that the yield is determined solely by the initial bond price and the known maturity value. However, as coupon interest rates increase, the holding period yield falls. If the bond had no discount, that is if the coupon rate were 16 percent, then the holding period yield would be 14.248 percent.

TAX ADVANTAGES OF OID BONDS

When they first began to appear in 1980, OID bonds had some very attractive tax advantages. However, the tax laws pertaining to these bonds have changed since 1980. It is useful to see how the tax laws evolved and how the market both compelled and responded to these changes. First, let's examine the tax advantage to the issuer of an OID bond, according to the tax laws in 1980.

The principal advantage derives from the fact that the IRS allows the issuer to amortize the interest expense over the life of the bond based on a straightline prorating procedure. A straight-line procedure means that the present value of the tax-deductible interest expense will be larger with a discount bond than with a comparable bond without a discount.

In order to see how this works, consider the following example of a two-year $100 conventional bond with a 10 percent coupon paid annually. This will provide the following pretax cash flows to the borrower:

Period	0	1	2
Cash flow	$100	−$10	−$110

The final cash flow is an outflow of $110 since the principal of $100 plus interest of 10 percent must be paid. With this bond the borrower is allowed to deduct $10 in interest expense each period. Now consider raising $100 by issuing a zero-coupon bond. To provide the same 10-percent yield to the investor as the coupon bond above, this bond must repay $121 at the end of the second year. This is because the present value of $121, at 10 percent, is $100. The cash flows for the issuer of the zero-coupon bond are:

Period	0	1	2
Cash flow	$100	0	−$121

However, on this bond the annual amount of interest expense which can be deducted for tax purposes is half of the total interest expense of $21, or $10.50. As a result, the zero-coupon bond generates a tax savings for the issuer.

While the numbers in this example make it appear that this is not much of a tax savings, the actual tax savings available in the early 1980s on bonds with yields in the neighborhood of 16 percent was quite substantial. For example, consider two 20-year bonds both priced to yield 16 percent, but one priced at par or without any discount, and the other with a coupon interest rate of 7 percent. While the bond priced at par sells at $100 (per $100 of face value), the OID bond sells at a value of $46.34. If the issuing corporation is in the 46 percent tax bracket, the after-tax cost of the conventional bond is 8.64 percent (16% × 54%). However, it turns out that the after-tax cost of the discount bond would be 7.95 percent. This is equivalent to the after-tax cost of a conventional bond yielding 14.72 percent before taxes. The issuer in this example could save 128 basis points before taxes by using the OID bond with a 7 percent coupon rate. Table 16–4 illustrates how much savings would be involved for bonds with different maturities and coupon payments issued in a market with yields of 16 and 10 percent. It is apparent from the table that the savings decline with the level of interest rates, and savings are substantially larger if coupon payments are eliminated altogether.

The risk reduction and tax advantages of OID bonds led to a virtual flood of such bonds into the public U.S. bond market beginning in March, 1981, and ending in 1982. The first publicly issued OID bond was issued by Martin Marietta

TABLE 16–4
Comparison of borrowing costs on current coupon bonds and original issue discount bonds.

Bonds issued at various coupons, terms to maturity, and under different market rates of return

Market Rate of Interest (percent)	Coupon Rate (percent)	Term to Maturity (years)	Current Coupon Bond-Equivalent Cost (percent)	Basis Point Saving over Current Coupon Bonds
16	7	20	14.72	128
16	7	30	14.30	170
16	0	20	11.44	456
16	0	30	8.52	748
10	7	20	9.80	20
10	7	30	9.68	31
10	0	20	8.67	133
10	0	30	7.37	263

Source: Andrew Silver "Original Issue Deep Discount Bonds," *Quarterly Review*, Federal Reserve Bank of New York, (Winter 1981–82).

Corporation in March, 1981. Prior to that time all OID bonds were privately issued and generally of low credit quality. After the Martin Marietta issue there were 21 publicly placed high credit quality OID bonds issued by July of 1981, raising a total of $2.0 billion. However, it was not until 1982 that the first corporate zero-coupon bond was issued by PepsiCo for $850 million. The net borrowing cost for this issue was approximately 10 percent, almost four percent or 400 basis points below the prevailing yield at that time on comparable maturity Treasury bonds.

Thus far we have focused on the tax advantage of OID and zero-coupon bonds to the issuers of those bonds under the tax laws applicable in 1981. But the Tax Equity and Fiscal Responsibility Act of 1982 (approved September 3, 1982) changed this situation. It eliminated the tax advantage by eliminating the straight-line prorating of taxes. Issuers of OID bonds would have a tax advantage only if these bonds could be sold to tax-exempt investors. Domestically, the most important tax-exempt investors who had a desire to avoid reinvestment risk were pension funds. However, there was also a significant market for OID bonds in Japan, since Japanese investors had no taxes on capital gains and appreciation of OID bonds was considered at that time a capital gain in Japan. Bonds sold by U.S. issuers outside the U.S. are called **Eurobonds,** even if they are sold in Japan. Therefore, the 1982 tax changes in the U.S. created a market for zero-coupon Eurobonds.

Under Japanese tax law the difference between the sale price and the purchase price of a discounted security is treated entirely as a capital gain as long as the security is sold at least one day prior to maturity. The tax rate on capital gains in

Eurobonds are bonds with dollar-denominated payments issued by U.S. firms and sold outside the United States.

Japan is zero. As a result, a Japanese investor who buys a zero-coupon bond on the date it is issued and sells it one day prior to maturity is able to retain virtually the entire gain on the bond. Since the maximum personal tax rate in Japan on regular income is 75 percent, this represents a considerable advantage. As long as the yields on zero-coupon bonds are not bid up so high by competing issuers that all of this tax advantage accrues to the bond purchasers, it will be advantageous for U.S. firms to sell zero-coupon bonds to Japanese investors. Another important feature of the Japanese tax laws is that Japanese investors are prohibited from purchasing zero-coupon bonds created from U.S. Treasury bonds. This means that corporate bonds face no competition from U.S. Treasury obligations.

THE EMERGENCE OF STRIPPED U.S. TREASURY BONDS

While major U.S. corporations were issuing OID bonds to take advantage of their tax treatment and gain from the risk reduction they provided investors, investment bankers were busy searching for a way to add to the supply of zero-coupon bonds. One possible way was to attempt to transform coupon-paying bonds into zero-coupon bonds. Investment bankers at Merrill Lynch were the first to capitalize on this opportunity. They introduced a new security which they called *TIGRS*. TIGRS were created by acquiring coupon-paying Treasury bonds and **stripping** the coupons. This means that the coupon-paying Treasury bonds were broken into parts; coupon payments or cash flows due on a specific date were combined from a number of distinct Treasury bonds. These cash flows were then used to form a new security with a single cash flow due on the same day as the coupon payment for all of the underlying Treasury bonds. A separate security was created for each of the coupon dates on the underlying Treasury bonds. These new securities were then zero-coupon bonds. They had the added advantage of being free of default risk, since all of the cash flows were obligations of the U.S. Treasury. The issuer of the new securities placed the Treasury bonds in a trust so that investors could be certain that the cash flows would be available as promised.

Stripping refers to the creation of zero-coupon bonds out of the coupon payments from a group of coupon-bearing U.S. Treasury bonds.

This example of financial engineering involves the creation of a new security perceived to be more valuable to the market than the existing securities from which it is created. The new security adds value since it provides real opportunities for risk reduction not previously available. However, the benefits to the innovator of such a product can be short-lived. Once Merrill Lynch created the first stripped zero-coupon bond, it took a very short time for other investment bankers to create their own zero-coupon bonds out of Treasury bonds and market them under their own names. For example, Salomon Brothers introduced their own zero-coupon bonds formed by stripping Treasury bonds and labeled them CATS. As a result, zero-coupon bonds are often generically referred to as **cats.** The profits earned by an originator of zero-coupon bonds depends upon the difference between the selling prices of the zero-coupon bonds created from Treasury bonds and the prices at which those Treasury bonds must be acquired. If real value is added to the market and if there is only one issuer of these zero-coupon bonds, as was the case with Merrill Lynch for a short time, then the issuer reaps the benefit

Cats are the various versions of zero-coupon bonds that Wall Street investment banking firms created by stripping U.S. Treasury bonds.

of the spread between the value of the zero-coupon bonds and the value of the underlying Treasury bonds. However, as new issuers enter the market they will drive down the price of zero-coupon bonds until the benefits accrue to those bond purchasers simply as a result of the competition in the market for creating or issuing zero-coupon instruments.

As you might suspect, this is not the end of the story. Once both zeros were stripped from Treasury bonds and corporate issued zero-coupon Eurobonds, an opportunity developed to attempt to create arbitrage profits as a result of spreads between yields in the U.S. and Eurobond markets. To see how this has been accomplished we will examine a bond issued by Exxon Capital Corporation, a wholly-owned subsidiary of Exxon Corporation.[2] On October 19, 1984, Exxon Capital Corporation issued $1.8 billion principal amount of zero-coupon notes due November 15, 2004, at an annually compounded yield of 11.65 percent. This bond issue yielded net proceeds of $199 million. Exxon Capital then invested the bulk of these proceeds in an issue of stripped or zero-coupon U.S. Treasury bonds that provided exactly the cash needed to pay off the Exxon bond issue on November 15, 2004. During the week before the Exxon bond issue, these stripped Treasury bonds had traded in the over-the-counter market at yields between 11.75 and 11.90 percent. If Exxon had acquired the stripped Treasurys at the yield of 11.75 percent (the higher of the two prices), it would have cost approximately $183 million to acquire $1.8 billion in principal amount of bonds. It would have paid $183 million for title to a certain cash flow which could be used to completely pay off its own bonds issued the following week. This is an arbitrage profit which arises from differences in the yields prevailing in the Eurobond and over-the-counter markets for stripped zero-coupon Treasury bonds within the U.S. As long as there are a number of issuers like Exxon looking for such profits these bonds should be kept to a minimum. The source of the profit is the restriction on Japanese investors by the Japanese government which prevents them from counting gains on zero-coupon bonds created from U.S. Treasury obligations as tax-free gains.

The OID and zero-coupon markets provide an excellent example of the way innovation evolves with interplay between private investors and tax or regulatory authorities. The initial interest in discounted bonds was a result of increases in the level and volatility of interest rates that caused investors with specific holding periods to be willing to pay to avoid the reinvestment risk inherent in coupon bonds. However, tax incentives to issue such bonds also played an important role in the initial growth of the OID market. Moreover, as the U.S. tax laws changed, this created an incentive to shift the distribution to the Eurobond market to arbitrage the differences in the tax laws in different countries. Moreover, the gain

---

[2]For a detailed discussion of this example and the treatment of OID bonds in Japan, see John D. Finnerty, ''Zero Coupon Bond Arbitrage: An Illustration of the Regulatory Dialectic at Work,'' *Financial Management,* (Winter 1985), pp. 13–17.

from supplying viable mechanisms for avoidance of reinvestment risk also prompted private investment bankers to create zero-coupon bonds out of Treasury issues. Unlike the private issues, these could not be marketed to Japan, since Japanese tax laws expressly prohibited treating gains on these instruments as tax-free like the private issues. In 1985 the Japanese government proposed taxing the gains on zero-coupon bonds, though at a lower rate than on regular income. It should be apparent that changes in the tax laws both in the U.S. and abroad can have a significant effect on the nature and extent of innovation in the financial markets.

SUMMARY

In this chapter we examined the process of innovation in financial markets by focusing on the broad environmental factors which can lead to innovation and examining three important examples of recent innovations in financial markets.

There are four important environmental factors which lead to innovation. Often a combination of two or more factors are critical in explaining most innovations. The environmental factors are:

1. The level and volatility of inflation and interest rates
2. Technological progress in computers and communications
3. Regulation
4. Taxation.

Of the four, probably the first one has been the most important factor causing extensive innovation in the last decade. As the level of interest rates increased and as interest rates became increasingly volatile, investors as well as financial intermediaries sought new ways to protect themselves against rate fluctuations. At the same time tremendous technological progress made many of the existing regulatory restrictions on financial institutions and markets obsolete. The combination of these two forces has led to major changes.

The first innovation we considered was securitization of financial assets. Securitization constitutes a transformation of an intermediated market into an over-the-counter and ultimately an auction market. Financial intermediaries which function as portfolio lenders are vertically integrated across the distinct stages of a securitized market. When securitization occurs, each of the specific functions, from origination of the asset to maintenance of liquidity, can be performed by a separate firm.

Securitization is valuable when it can reduce the total cost of operating a market and thereby lower interest rates. This occurs when the specialization generated by securitization creates real gains in efficiency or when the gains from the market liquidity are significant. Securitization can also be valuable when it provides a means of avoiding or arbitraging costly government regulation. Securitization also incorporates some costs. It affects the incentives for those who originate loans to evaluate and monitor credit quality efficiently as well as the incentives for originators to avoid unscrupulous behavior. In markets where these problems are particularly acute, securitization is not likely to be very successful. However, in markets where these problems can be dealt with successfully, securitization can be beneficial.

The second innovation examined was the evolution of the NASDAQ market for corporate equities. Recently, the NASDAQ developed automated systems for displaying information on dealers' bid and asked prices for listed securities which made it a relatively efficient vehicle for executing trades. It also provided competition between dealers in individual securities so that bid and asked prices were influenced by competitive market forces. As the market grew during the early 1980s, it implemented what it has called the National Market System, where securities which meet certain standards for trading volume have up to the minute transaction prices and trading volume available on NASDAQ computer facilities. As a result of the drive for efficiency and the reliance on dealer competition, the NASDAQ is pressing other larger exchanges to modernize trading procedures and limit the opportunities for monopoly returns to specialists on the exchange.

The third example of innovation in this chapter is the market for original issue discount (OID) bonds and especially zero-coupon bonds. The first public offering of highly rated OID bonds occurred in 1980 in response to increased volatility of interest rates. As interest rate risk increased, investors placed a bigger premium on the protection of cash flows from reinvestment risk which is afforded by deep discount bonds. Hence, it became relatively attractive for corporations to issue those bonds. In addition, there was an important tax advantage to corporate issuers that the IRS allowed interest expense to be accrued on a straight-line basis for such issues. However, this advantage was eliminated in the TEFRA tax legislation of 1982. As a result only tax-free investors retained an interest in OID bonds. Of particular importance was the tax treatment of such bonds available to Japanese investors. Japanese tax law stipulated that as long as these bonds were sold at least one day prior to maturity, the gain on the sale qualified as a capital gain. In Japan capital gains are not taxed so this created a tremendous demand by Japanese investors. At the same time corporations were issuing OID bonds, investment banking firms were creating zero-coupon bonds by stripping the coupon payments from coupon-paying Treasury bonds. These new zero-coupon bonds were sold to U.S. investors who had specific intended holding periods and wanted to avoid interest rate risk. Japanese investors were dissuaded from buying these stripped zero-coupon bonds by provisions in the Japanese tax laws which eliminated them from preferential capital gains tax treatment. This meant that there were separate markets for OID bonds in Japan and stripped zero-coupon bonds in the United States. The existence of these two markets created arbitrage opportunities for investors who could issue an OID Eurobond to Japanese investors then acquire stripped Treasury bonds with identical cash flows. The opportunities for profits from such transactions tend to keep yields in the two markets relatively close together. The OID bond example shows how both U.S. and foreign tax laws interact with the effect of changes in desired protection against interest rate risk to influence the evolution of specific financial instruments.

QUESTIONS

1. An important factor which leads to innovation is an increase in the level and volatility of interest rates. Explain the distinction between the impact of a change in the level as opposed to the volatility of interest rates. Give an example of an innovation which results from an increase in the level and another example which results from an increase in the volatility of interest rates. Justify your choice of examples.

2. What does the phrase *regulatory dialectic* mean? Give an example of how the regulatory dialectic is important in innovation.

3. Distinguish between process, product, and organizational innovations. Give an example of at least one innovation which involves all three types of changes.

4. What is a specialist? How do specialists differ from dealers on the NASDAQ? How does this difference affect the operation of the NASDAQ versus the NYSE?

5. What is the National Market System? Why is this name an effective form of strategic innovation for the NASDAQ?

6. Define a trading halt. Why are there trading halts on the NYSE and not on the NASDAQ? What is the significance of trading halts in comparing the relative merits of the two exchanges?

7. What are OID bonds? Why are OID bonds less sensitive to interest rate risk than nondiscount bonds?

8. Explain the tax advantage accruing to issuers of OID bonds if allowed to deduct interest expense on a straight-line basis.

9. Why have OID bonds been sold to Japanese investors since 1982? What important features of the Japanese and U.S. tax codes have determined where these bonds would be sold?

10. Explain the nature of the arbitrage transaction carried out by Exxon utilizing the OID Eurobond market and the U.S. market for stripped Treasury bonds.

11. Describe the six parts of the securitization process. How can there be gains in efficiency via securitization in each of these areas?

12. How are moral hazard and adverse selection relevant to securitization?

13. How does regulation affect the costs and benefits of securitization?

14. Evaluate the costs and benefits of securitization for commercial and industrial loans at commercial banks.

REFERENCES

Finnerty, John D. "Zero Coupon Bond Arbitrage: An Illustration of the Regulatory Dialectic at Work," *Financial Management,* (Winter 1985), pp. 13–17.

Fisher, Lawrence, Ivan E. Brick and Francis K.W. Ng. "Tax Incentives and Financial Innovation: The Case of Zero-Coupon and Other Deep-Discount Corporate Bonds," *The Financial Review,* (November 1983), pp. 292–305.

Johnson, James M. "When Are Zero Coupon Bonds the Better Buy?" *Journal of Portfolio Management,* (Spring 1984), pp. 26–41.

Kane, Edward. "Accelerating Inflation, Technological Innovations and the Decreasing Effectiveness of Bank Regulations," *Journal of Finance,* 36 (May 1981), pp. 3–32.

Louis, Arthur M. "The Stock Market of the Future—Now," *Fortune,* (October 29, 1984), pp. 105–16.

Pyle, David. "Is Deep Discount Debt Financing a Bargain?" *Chase Financial Quarterly,* (Fall 1981), pp. 39–61.

Silver, Andrew. "Original Issue Deep Discount Bonds," *Quarterly Review,* Federal Reserve Bank of New York, (Winter 1981–82), pp. 18–28.

Stoll, Hans R. "The Pricing of Dealer Services: An Emperical Study of NASDAQ Stocks," *Journal of Finance*, 33 (September 1978), p. 1156.

4
PART

CONTEMPORARY FINANCIAL MARKETS AND INSTITUTIONS

Part 4 draws upon the previous chapters in order to analyze the current operation of selected markets and institutions in the United States. The first chapter, Chapter 17, considers how recent deregulation has affected many markets and institutions, particularly commercial banks. Chapter 18 studies the state of the commercial banking industry and how banks compete in the current market environment. Chapter 19 analyzes the mortgage finance market, focusing on the recent development of mortgage-backed securities, the reasons for the securitization of the mortgage market, and its current operations. Chapter 20 describes the current operations of the money market for short-term debt obligations. This chapter surveys the types of money market instruments and describes the growth of money market funds and the swaps market. Finally, Chapter 21 dissects the development of the market for financial futures and exchange-traded options. These markets are among the most important and most interesting financial markets in the world. Chapter 21 explains how these markets developed and how they operate in the mid-1980s. ■

17

REFORM OF THE REGULATORY SYSTEM FOR FINANCIAL INSTITUTIONS

In this chapter we begin our investigation of the actual operation of specific types of financial institutions and markets in the United States. In a sense, all of the material we have covered thus far is really designed to prepare you to understand how specific markets and financial firms operate. Of course, there are so many interesting problems and issues pertaining to individual financial forms or markets that we have to omit more than we can cover. It seems appropriate to start with regulatory reform, or what has been called *deregulation*. In the United States we have a specific set of financial institutions as well as a collection of specific markets that have resulted in large part from regulations imposed by the government. As we learned in Part 3, regulation is one of the principal forces that shapes the organizational structure of financial markets. However, what we did not learn about is the tremendous change currently taking place in the financial regulatory system in the United States. Our purpose is to understand why and how the regulatory system is changing and how this is reshaping financial firms and markets in the United States and around the world.

In Chapters 14 and 15, we learned that new regulations generally are developed in response to crises rather than from rational deliberation on the part of regulators or legislators. The actual process of reform is determined by political power because regulation confers economic advantages and disadvantages. But even with a consensus for change, it is difficult to agree on the appropriate changes.

In the early 1980s there was gradual movement toward complete reform of the system. For awhile it appeared that the changes might be massive, but as the crisis abated, the pressure for immediate reform lessened. As a result, it is difficult to predict how extensive the reform of the next few years may be. What is certain is that we cannot significantly undo what has already been done. To a large degree, the U.S. financial system from the late 1930s until the late 1970s is gone. Some features of the system now being formed are becoming clear. We will also consider why some other changes may be occurring soon and how the changes will affect our current financial system.

In this chapter we will first synthesize the important characteristics of the regulatory system of the 1960s and 1970s, then examine how increased inflation and technological progress impaired the effective operation of that regulatory system. Next we will examine the principal legislative actions taken to reform the regulatory system including the Depository Institutions Deregulation and Monetary Control Act of 1980 and the Garn-St Germain Act of 1982. Finally we will examine three outstanding issues of regulatory reform still being debated: interstate banking, the role of limited service or nonbank banks, and the possible repeal of the Glass-Steagall Act. ■

THE BACKGROUND OF REGULATORY REFORM

Deregulation refers to the change and relaxation of regulations which restrict the activities of U.S. financial institutions.

A good place to start our analysis of regulatory reform is with **deregulation,** the name often given to the changes in regulation proposed or enacted in the last few years. However, the word *deregulation* is quite misleading. It implies that the new set of regulations involves *less* regulation than the old. This is true only in a very limited sense. Some of the changes have eliminated some regulations, such as Regulation Q. Others have increased the powers of some financial institutions, specifically savings and loans. However, as we will discover, a much more appropriate term for describing the effects of most of these changes is **desegmentation**, since much of the reform of the 1980s has tended to reduce or eliminate the distinctions between classes of financial institutions. It is creating a more uniform set of financial institutions that compete in a variety of financial services, rather than a highly segmented set of financial institutions with each one limited in the services it can offer. Some observers have called this the *unisex financial institutions movement*. In order to appreciate why the unisex financial institutions movement has emerged and what it portends for the existing classes of financial firms, we need to summarize the essential features of the regulatory system that existed throughout the 1960s and 1970s, or before the recent reform got underway.

Desegmentation refers to the changes in regulations which reduce the regulatory proscribed distinctions between different types of financial institutions.

BASIC FEATURES OF THE REGULATORY SYSTEM

Since we have already examined the regulatory system for both financial intermediaries and securities markets, we do not need to repeat that discussion here. However, it is extremely important to identify those features of the regulatory system that ultimately became its Achilles heel. Here is a list of five features which made it vulnerable during a period of high inflation and rapid technological progress.

Geographic and product line segmentation of financial services

Competing and overlapping regulatory agencies for distinct types of financial service firms

Creation of a barter system through restriction on competition with interest rates

Selective use of reserve requirements tax and deposit insurance subsidy

Monetary policy directed toward insuring the stability of interest rates.

Segmentation of Services and Overlapping Regulation. A fundamental tenant of regulatory policy toward financial intermediaries has been to restrict competition between institutions. These restrictions have taken two basic forms. First, the McFadden Act of 1926 established the right of each state to regulate the entry of commercial banks domiciled in other states into that state. Given the political power of local banking institutions in each state, this led to a system where, in general, each bank has been allowed to accept deposits in only one state. Furthermore, each state was given the authority to determine its own laws regarding branch banking. As a result, some states, such as Illinois, chose to allow no branch banking at all, while other states, such as California, chose to allow unrestricted branch banking. This system led to geographically segmented institutions and prevented the development of nationwide distribution systems for commercial banking services. While very rigid geographic restrictions were applied to commercial banks and savings and loans, no comparable geographic restrictions were placed on either SEC regulated investment and brokerage firms or on insurance companies.

The system of geographic restrictions was accompanied by a system of product line restrictions which created separate classes of institutions for different financial products or services. We described the distinct types of financial intermediaries which can be found in the U.S. financial system in Chapter 12. Table 17–1 identifies these classes of intermediaries and describes the basic types of assets on the balance sheets of each.

The U.S. financial system is made up of a segmented set of financial institutions, each providing separate financial services, in large part due to government

TABLE 17–1

Principal types of financial institutions in the United States and their major types of assets.

Type of Institutions	Principal Types of Assets
Commercial banks	Commercial, mortgage and consumer loans, Treasury bills, municipal bonds
Savings and loans	Mortgage loans
Credit unions	Consumer loans
Mutual savings banks	Consumer loans, mortgages, corporate bonds
Finance companies	Consumer loans
Investment companies	Corporate equities, bonds and money market instruments
Insurance companies	Corporate bonds and loans, corporate equites, real estate investments

FIGURE 17–1
Structure of the U.S. regulatory system.

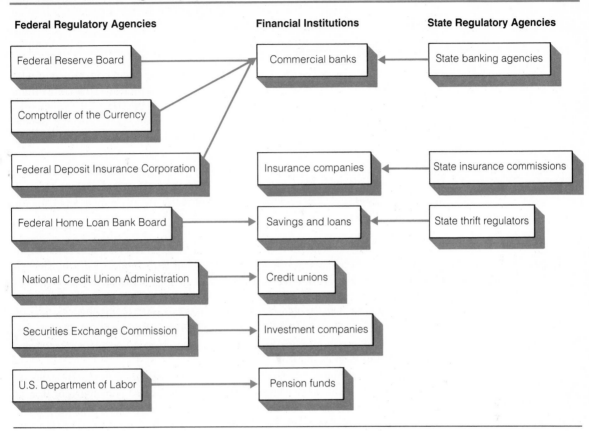

regulation. Moreover, the regulatory system itself is virtually as segmented as the institutions it is intended to regulate. Some types of financial institutions are regulated at both the state and federal level while some, particularly insurance companies, are subject solely to state regulations. Commercial banks have multiple federal regulators, including the Federal Reserve, the Comptroller of the Currency and the FDIC, as well as a state bank regulator in each state. A highly simplified picture of the types of institutions and the regulators they must deal with is presented in Figure 17–1.

The existing regulatory system is almost impossible to explain or justify based on any kind of rational analysis. As we learned in Chapter 15, the current system of bank regulation evolved in response to a sequence of national crises. In each crisis, a new federal regulatory agency was created while the old ones were left intact. By contrast, there is virtually no federal regulation of insurance companies. The only apparent explanation for the differences between the regulation of banks and insurance companies is that a national crisis in the insurance industry has never offered the prospect of widespread bankruptcies threatening the prosperity of the entire country.

There are two alternative views about the virtues of the current overlapping regulatory system for financial institutions. One view is that multiple regulatory agencies for the same institutions, specifically commercial banks, or for competing institutions such as commercial banks and savings and loans, promotes efficient regulation. The basis for this view is that multiple regulators compete with each other and this helps to keep them both honest and efficient. This competition is particularly evident among the various regulatory agencies for commercial banks where there are often differing views about the merits of specific regulations. The alternative view is that multiple regulatory agencies constitute wasteful duplication of effort. In addition, a system of separate regulatory agencies for specific industries creates a greater opportunity for the regulators to become captured by the institutions they are regulating. This accusation has been made with particular strength for the Federal Home Loan Bank Board, which regulates the savings and loan industry.

The Barter System.   The third characteristic of the regulatory system is the barter system created through restrictions on competition with interest rates by depository institutions such as commercial banks and savings and loans. The system of barter common in commercial banking refers to the practice of exchanging services for balances. This system resulted from two factors. The first was the restriction of interest payments on deposit accounts known as **Regulation Q.** The second is the Federal Reserve's policy requiring reserves which do not earn interest and providing services in exchange.

Regulation Q limited the interest rates banks and savings and loans could pay to depositors. This regulation was eliminated in 1982.

Since its inception the Federal Reserve has imposed reserve requirements on commercial banks which are members of the Fed. The exact percentage of reserve requirements can be altered by the Federal Reserve Board. These reserves amount to a tax on the bank because the Federal Reserve pays no interest on the reserves. The banks could invest these funds in Treasury bills or other securities and earn a rate of return, if they were not held in reserve. In exchange for these reserves, the Federal Reserve provided services to commercial banks without charge. These services included check clearing and electronic transfer of funds upon which the federal funds market is based.

A similar type of barter system prevailed in the relationship between banks and savings and loans and their retail customers during the era of Regulation Q. Banks and savings and loans could not compete for deposit balances by offering higher interest rates. As a result, they attempted to attract those deposits by offering services, including convenience, to their customers. For example, there was no direct charge for processing transactions through a checking account. This system was like the one between commercial banks and the Federal Reserve.

Reserve Taxes, Insurance Subsidies, and Monetary Policy.   The next characteristic of the regulatory system is the selective use of the reserve requirements tax and the deposit insurance subsidy. We learned in our discussion of bank regulation in Chapter 15, that the government provides deposit insurance to banks and savings and loans at prices which are not related to the risk taken on by the government. The insurance prices appear to include a significant subsidy relative to the price a bank would have to pay to obtain funds without government insurance. When required reserves do not earn interest, this acts as a tax on institutions which face this requirement. The total cost of regulation for a specific type of financial institution is determined by the aggregate subsidy and tax imposed by various regulations. The important feature of the regulatory system which prevailed in the 1960s and 1970s (and in part still applies today), is that these taxes and subsidies were applied in differing degrees to different classes of institutions. For example, banks of different size had different reserve requirements and banks which were not Federal Reserve members had lower reserve requirements and therefore a lower tax imposed upon them. Savings and loans had no reserve requirements imposed by the Fed and therefore escaped this tax altogether. At the same time, banks and savings and loans (as well as credit unions and mutual savings banks) had access to deposit insurance, but investment companies did not. This created opportunities for **regulatory arbitrage:** institutions had an incentive to change their structure to minimize the total cost of regulation or to shift from one type of regulatory treatment to another as the regulation costs and benefits changed.

Regulatory arbitrage refers to the opportunities for financial institutions to select the most favorable regulators and play one against another.

The final important characteristics of the U.S. regulatory system is a monetary policy directed toward insuring the stability of interest rates. As we learned in Chapters 10 and 11, from the early 1950s through the late 1970s, the Fed conducted monetary policy by attempting to control the federal funds rate. During the first decade or more of this period, this policy appears to have been carried out without any significant concern about the level of monetary aggregates, such as M_1. During the 1970s the Fed expressed concern for both the growth of monetary aggregates and the level of interest rates. However, most observers have concluded that throughout this period the Fed was chiefly concerned with the level of interest rates. This policy had a very important implication for the operation of financial intermediaries such as banks and savings and loans. It meant the Fed was implicitly attempting to guarantee a market environment of stable interest rates. If the Fed could maintain this guarantee, then individual financial institutions could, in turn, offer financial instruments which provided interest rate guarantees to their customers. Principal among these instruments were such things as long-term fixed rate loans. One of the main services which many financial institutions offered their customers was intermediation across time so that the financial institution, rather than that institution's customer, was accepting the risk of fluctuations in market interest rates. This service could be provided with relatively low risk as long as the Fed was able and willing to live up to its implicit commitment to maintain stable interest rates.

WEAKNESSES IN THE REGULATORY SYSTEM

The regulatory system we have been describing was reasonably well suited to an economy where the market for financial services was highly segmented both by geography and by the characteristics of the financial services being provided. It was also well suited to an economy with low rates of inflation and therefore relatively low and stable interest rates. But in the 1970s both of these conditions changed: inflation reached unprecedented levels, and rapid technological progress in both computers and communications transformed a collection of regional markets for financial services into national if not a global market. In order to see how vulnerable the old regulatory system was to these basic changes in the U.S. economy, we need to examine the specific weaknesses in the regulatory system.

The Impact of Inflation.   Probably the most important weakness in the system is that, in a time of high inflation, the Federal Reserve's implicit commitment to provide stable interest rates becomes unworkable. As we learned in Part 2, market interest rates are determined by the real interest rate and by the market's expectation of the future rate of inflation. If the Fed tries to hold down market interest rates in the face of expectations of increasing inflation rates, its efforts would be futile. By concentrating on attempting to maintain low market interest rates, it would lose control of the growth rates of monetary aggregates and thereby exacerbate the inflation problem. The Fed faced precisely this type of situation during the late 1970s. In October, 1979, Chairman Paul Volcker renounced the Fed's long-standing policy of attempting to control market interest rates, in effect, abandoning the Fed's implicit commitment to maintain stable interest rates.

Many financial institutions had based much of their business strategy, either explicitly or implicitly, on the Fed's commitment to maintain stable interest rates. Once this commitment was broken it was no longer feasible for many financial intermediaries to assume significant amounts of interest rate risk. As a result, banking firms moved away from fixed to floating rate loans in both commercial and mortgage lending. Market participants came to rely more heavily on futures and options markets as mechanisms for limiting interest rate risk. In addition, institutions that had not anticipated the changes that inflation would create became unstable and unprofitable.

The difference in performance of Citicorp and Bank of America in the early 1980s illustrates the results of anticipating and failing to anticipate change. Possibly more than any other large financial intermediary, Citicorp anticipated changes in the economic and regulatory environment that occurred in the 1980s. Its chairman during the late 1970s and early 80s, Walter Wriston, is highly regarded for his planning and anticipation of these changes. To a large degree, Citicorp is now highly profitable and growing rapidly because it placed the right bet on how the economic environment would change. In contrast, Bank of America made precisely the opposite bet. Even as inflation accelerated and the Fed backed away from its commitment to stabilize interest rates, Bank of America continued to conduct business in the same ways it always had. It continued to make a large volume of fixed rate mortgage loans and persisted in making business loans at home and abroad as if inflation meant a prolonged era of continued prosperity. Furthermore, once it became apparent that it had made the wrong bet, Bank of America still appeared as if it did not understand the degree to which the market environment had changed. One of those changes resulted from the elimination of Regulation Q. As a result, Bank of America's performance deteriorated in the early 1980s while Citicorp prospered.

The advent of relatively high and volatile interest rates and the elmination of Regulation Q meant depository institutions had to change the way they sought to attract deposit balances. Regulation Q was first scheduled for elimination in 1980 by gradually phasing it out over six years. By 1982 it was apparent that this pace was too slow, and the **Garn-St Germain Act of 1982** eliminated it entirely, leaving banks and savings and loans to compete in new ways. This meant they had to compete with interest rates, where they had been prohibited from doing so before. The methods they had previously used to attract deposits were no longer so valuable. Some of these methods, such as prizes and gifts for new deposits, were easy to abandon, but many institutions had used convenience as their means of competition. And convenience generally meant the development of an expensive branch system for delivering financial services. With the demise of Regulation Q and the change in the nature of the financial services market increasingly toward a national market, the branch systems needed to be overhauled dramatically. In a sense, the barter system, which had been used for so long, was destroyed and a new system with a much larger role for price competition had to replace it.

The barter system between the banks and the Fed also was fundamentally altered at the same time. However, in this case the nature of the change was quite different. Under the barter system the Fed provided services in exchange for reserves that earned no interest. When interest rates were relatively low, as they were by the standards of the late 1960s, these services were not very expensive because the cost of holding reserves was not as large as it became in more recent years, when interest rates rose appreciably. The rise in interest rates made the cost of these services go up, while the benefit the commercial banks derived from these services did not match those increases. Member banks of the Federal Reserve therefore simply chose, in increasing numbers, to withdraw from the Federal Reserve System. They no longer received the services, but they also did not have to hold reserves that earned no interest. The incentive of banks to withdraw from the Federal Reserve system came to be referred to, somewhat euphemistically, as the **membership problem.** The solution to the membership problem adopted by Congress in the Garn-St Germain Act of 1982 was to require all financial intermediaries that offered transactions accounts, including both banks and savings and loans, to be subject to common reserve requirements. These reserves would still not earn interest, however. This was a step toward uniformity in regulation or away from imposing significantly different levels of implicit taxation on different classes of institutions. Nonetheless, the tax itself was not eliminated.

The Impact of Technological Progress.   At the same time that high inflation rates were rendering Regulation Q obsolete, the rapid pace of change in the technology of delivering financial services was also leading to significant changes in the U.S. financial system. The pace of technological progress in communications and computers altered the working definition of what constituted a market for

The **Garn-St Germain Act of 1982** eliminated Regulation Q and gave expanded powers to the savings and loan industry.

The Fed's **membership problem** refers to the incentive of commerical banks to withdraw from the Fed during the period when membership involved higher reserve requirements.

financial services. In the 1950s and even in the 1960s it was reasonable to argue that the market for financial services in one part of the country, say Pittsburgh, was distinct from the market for the same service in another part of the country, say Dallas. There were real obstacles, or at least few economies to be generated, for any firm that attempted to offer banking services in both cities. But as it became possible to computerize an increasingly large portion of bank operations and as the cost of transferring computer information from one part of the country to another declined, the gains in efficiency from geographic expansion of banking firms increased. Furthermore, as the emphasis on both price and quality of service increased with the demise of Regulation Q, the value of brand-name identification and brand loyalty began to become as important in banking as it is in many other lines of business. In the new, post-Regulation Q era, marketing had become an important part of banking, and an important part of marketing was the penetration of new markets with a brand name and a reputation for quality. The geographic segmentation that had been an essential ingredient of the regulatory system was becoming increasingly costly and was a barrier to development of a more efficient financial system.

The same changes in technology and marketing affected the segmentation between product lines enforced by regulation. As we have seen, the U.S. financial system had maintained a separation between broad classes of financial services by erecting barriers prohibiting institutions that specialized in one class from invading the other's turf. Technological progress has blurred the distinctions between the actual processes of producing the services in each of these categories. There appears to be a much more meaningful distinction between financial services marketed to consumers and small businesses and those marketed to corporate customers. Yet within each of these four categories, individual institutions are allowed to operate in both retail and corporate markets.

As the real or economic basis has diminished for segmenting financial services into categories, the pressure from institutions that want to offer all of these services has increased. Sears and Citicorp are prime examples of firms attempting to become nationwide providers of a variety of financial services. These companies, and others who see their interests identified with a movement toward more diversified financial firms, have pressured Congress and the regulatory agencies for changes that break down the barriers between specific financial products. At the same time, many groups of institutions stand to lose from further desegmentation. They are lobbying to maintain features of the old regulatory system that maintain product line segmentation. For example, the insurance industry argues that commercial banks should continue to be prohibited from offering insurance products except for those tied to traditional banking services, such as credit life insurance. The banking industry argues that there is no logical reason to restrict banks from selling and underwriting insurance and that the insurance industry's effort to keep them out is simply an attempt to restrict competition.

By now it should be apparent that the regulatory system put in place in the 1930s is not very well suited to the economic environment that will face the United States in the decades ahead. Some reform of the old system has already taken place, and more will probably be forthcoming.

REFORM OF THE U.S. FINANCIAL SYSTEM IN THE 1980s

The reform of the regulatory system thus far has come in three forms: new laws enacted by the Congress and by state legislatures, changes in regulatory policy by regulators within the scope of existing laws, and reinterpretation of existing laws by the courts. The biggest changes have come in the form of new federal legislation, but that does not mean that the other types of changes have been unimportant. There are two major pieces of federal legislation, one enacted in 1980 and the other in 1982.

The **Depository Institutions Deregulation and Monetary Control Act of 1980** imposed uniform reserve requirements and mandated a gradual elimination of Regulation Q.

THE DEREGULATION LEGISLATION OF 1980 AND 1982

The first important piece of federal reform legislation enacted during the 1980s was the **Depository Institutions Deregulation and Monetary Control Act of 1980.** This legislation, passed by Congress and signed by President Jimmy Carter in March, 1980, involved four principal changes in the regulatory system. These are spelled out in panel A of Table 17–2.

TABLE 17–2
Recent laws affecting depository institutions.

Panel A Principal features of the Depository Institutions Deregulation and Monetary Control Act of 1980.	Panel B Principal Features of the Garn-St Germain Act of 1982.
1. All depository institutions that offer transactions accounts, not simply commercial banks that are members of the Federal Reserve System, must maintain reserves. The law stipulates that banks that were Federal Reserve members in 1980 cannot escape current reserve requirements by withdrawing from the system. It also defines a gradual phasein for reserve requirements on depository institutions that were not previously subject to reserve requirements— that is, they were not member banks in 1980.	1. It mandated that, within 60 days, the regulatory agencies for each distinct type of depository institution authorize those institutions to offer a deposit account fully competitive with accounts available from money market funds.
2. The Federal Reserve must directly price those services provided to commercial banks and make them available to all depository institutions.	2. It eliminated all regulations on interest rates on specific accounts, which permitted savings and loans to pay a higher interest rate than commercial banks, the interest differential.
3. It provided for what amounts to payment of interest on demand deposits by authorizing automatic transfer accounts, NOW accounts, and share drafts. Automatic transfer accounts provide for automatic transfer from savings to checking accounts. NOW accounts are essentially interest-bearing accounts on which checks can be written, as are share drafts at credit unions. It further specified that all of these accounts will be subject to reserve requirements.	3. It gave savings and loans the authority to make commercial loans. They were restricted to make no loan to a single borrower in an amount greater than would be permitted for a national bank with equivalent capital. After January 1, 1984, such loans could comprise as much as 10 percent of an institution's total assets.
4. It required the gradual elimination of interest-rate restriction on deposit accounts over a six-year period.	4. It permitted savings and loans to make consumer loans. These loans could not comprise in excess of 30 percent of the total assets of an institution.
	5. It gave savings and loan holding companies the authority to engage in or acquire insurance underwriting firms. No such authority was granted to bank holding companies.

REGULATORY REFORM ABROAD—THE BIG BANG

Regulatory reform has not been exclusive to the United States. In fact, on October 27, 1987, Britain implemented what has come to be called the *Big Bang*. The Big Bang involves a deregulation of securities trading on the London Stock Exchange which parallels NYSE reform in the early 1970s. Reform of the London Stock Exchange includes elimination of fixed commissions for brokerage services and implementation of a computerized trading system to replace the old trading system on the floor of the exchange. This change represents a major attempt to make the British financial system's stock trading operations competitive with those in the United States and other developed countries. The British were concerned that the London Stock Exchange would disintegrate as a result of a regulatory system that made it uncompetitive with stock trading centers in other parts of the world. If the Big Bang succeeds, it may make London the center of a 24-hour, worldwide market for trading stocks. The change in the rules governing trading on the London Exchange is part of a broader effort to reform and increase the competitiveness of the British financial services industry. Starting in 1983 the British government encouraged mergers among commercial banks, investment banks, and brokers and traders on the London Stock Exchange.

The system that prevailed before the Big Bang protected stockbrokers on the London Exchange with minimum commissions for executing trades. Brokers were prohibited from accumulating inventories of stocks or bonds and trading on their own accounts. In addition, traders on the exchange floor were prohibited from trading with anyone other than the regulated brokers. This system made it difficult for either brokers or traders to develop expertise, build capital, or provide services that investment firms in other countries could provide. The relatively high price of trading stocks on the London Exchange drove trading activities to other countries, even for shares in British companies.

A key part of the current London Stock Exchange is a new computerized stock quotation system. Shortly after this new trading system was introduced in 1987, the vast majority of all trading switched from the floor of the London Stock Exchange to it. Prior to the introduction of this system many trading firms were skeptical about its ultimate success, and they extensively renovated the facilities on the floor of the Exchange. Within only a few months the electronic trading system was so successful that the exchange floor itself became virtually deserted.

The apparent success of the new automated system has not threatened the very existence of the Exchange. Instead, all trades must be reported to the Exchange and cleared through its clearinghouse, and the Exchange has responsibility for enforcing rules against insider trading and other infractions. The most apparent difference is that there simply will not be a need for an exchange floor.

The Deregulation Act of 1980 focused on two basic issues. First it attempted to mandate a gradual deregulation of the liability side of the balance sheets of depository institutions. It indicated that banks and savings and loans should eventually be allowed to compete with interest rates for deposits. Second, it attempted to solve the membership problem of the Federal Reserve by making the reserve requirements tax uniform across all types of institutions that offered transactions accounts. While these changes seemed extraordinarily significant at the time, with hindsight it seems remarkable that they could be viewed as adequate to deal with the problems in the regulatory system. It also seems remarkable, with the benefit of hindsight, to have expected that the market would allow a gradual phase-out of Regulation Q over six years.

In order to understand why the intended six-year phase-out of Regulation Q became impractical, it is only necessary to examine the prime new competitor of

Money market funds are mutual funds which invest in highquality and short maturity securities and offer check writing privileges to their customers.

banks and savings and loans for consumer deposits, the **money market funds.** Money market funds began to grow in the late 1970s as market interest rates increased substantially above the Regulation Q interest rate ceilings on regulated deposit accounts at banks and savings and loans. At the end of 1977 money market funds had total assets of $3.8 billion. However, by the end of 1979, when the 1980 legislation was in preparation, money market fund assets had increased to $43.6 billion. While this increase was sizable, it was still not enough to render a planned gradual elimination of Regulation Q infeasible. However, in the next two years, total money market fund assets increased another four times to a total of $186.8 billion. During this same period interest rates in the United States had reached their historical peak. The combination of unprecedented high interest rates and decreasing market share of consumer savings for traditional depository institutions threatened to create a complete restructuring of the existing financial system. Regulators and Congress were virtually compelled to take some action to speed up the planned phase-out of Regulation Q. They responded with the Garn-St Germain Act of 1982.

The Garn-St Germain Act is a long, detailed piece of legislation with numerous important changes in regulations. Its principal features are summarized in panel B of Table 17–2.

The 1980 and 1982 acts gave banks and savings and loans distinct but roughly similar authority to offer transactions accounts. The 1980 Act (specifically, the Consumer Checking Account Equity Act) enabled **Negotiable Order of Withdrawal (NOW) accounts** which pay interest to be used to effect transfers to third parties. NOW accounts pay interest and may require notice of intention to withdraw; hence, they are different from demand deposits, which pay no interest and are payable upon demand. Section III of the Garn-St Germain Act (known as the Thrift Institution Restructuring Act) allowed savings institutions to accept demand deposits from individuals if used for business purposes and from corporations. However, savings and loans cannot accept individual, nonbusiness demand deposits.

Negotiable Order of Withdrawal (NOW) accounts are similar to demand deposits, but they earn interest and may require notice of an intention to withdraw funds.

INTERSTATE BANKING AND NONBANK BANKS

An important issue not addressed by recent federal legislation is the question of whether interstate banking should be permitted. It now appears that by the early 1990s most restrictions on interstate banking will have been eliminated. But once again, the change is not a result of some rational deliberation about how to improve the regulatory system but instead a response to a crisis. The crisis has two elements to it. The first is that a number of banks and savings and loans have become insolvent or are threatened with insolvency. When a bank gets into trouble, part of the solution is to attract new capital. If interstate banking is prohibited, and a merger or a takeover is required to inject new capital, then the only sources of new capital are banks within the same state. Even in times when other banks are doing well, this kind of merger can decrease competition in a given region. However, when a number of financial institutions in the region are simultaneously experiencing financial difficulties, then it can be very difficult to attract capital within a state. The option of going outside the state to attract capital then becomes attractive.

This option was pursued in the savings and loan industry in 1981 and 1982, when there were widespread failures and few healthy savings and loans that could acquire the failing ones. In these cases the savings and loan regulators were willing to sell failing thrifts to healthy commercial banks or industrial firms, regardless of where they were domiciled. Through this process of auctioning failed institutions Citicorp, for example, was able to acquire savings and loans in California and Florida. This provided the only vehicle available at the time for Citicorp to acquire the rights to deliver financial services to consumers in these states. With the enactment of the Garn-St Germain Act and the enhanced powers for savings and loans it provided, these franchises became nearly as valuable as the right for Citicorp to operate a bank in these states.

The second feature of the crisis, which is hastening the approach of interstate banking, is the fear smaller regional banks and savings and loans have that a few institutions, such as Citicorp, will become national distributors of financial services. Smaller institutions have developed a legitimate concern that they will fall too far behind if Citicorp can be successful in using mechanisms like the acquisition of failing savings and loans to build a national market. At the urging of banks many states have passed laws that have allowed banks within a given region to acquire banks in other cooperating states, yet exclude banks from other states, specifically New York and California. This arrangement has been used extensively in the Southeastern United States to allow state banks to merge into regional banks which may then prepare to be more effective competitors of large institutions such as Citicorp when they do eventually enter that region.

A few states have completely opened their doors to banks from other states. In 1986 Arizona passed a law permitting other banks to enter that state and acquire banks within the state. Banks from other states, particularly California, have been quick to take advantage of the opportunity. In 1986 California passed a law stipulating that banks from other states would be allowed to enter California in 1990. Texas has also welcomed out-of-state banks, but the situation there is rather special. In 1985 and 1986 Texas banks experienced severe losses because of the decline in the energy business. As a result, they were hungry for new capital. Since these problems are reasonably widespread in Texas banks, Texas opted to allow outside banks to enter the state. In December of 1986, New York's Chemical Bank, the seventh largest in the nation, acquired Houston's Texas Commerce Bancshares. During the same week two Dallas banks, Republic Bank and Interfirst, announced they would merge. By the end of 1986, 36 states and the District of Columbia permit out-of-state financial institutions to acquire local banks, though often with some restrictions. In 1982 only four states allowed any such acquisitions.

A **nonbank bank** is a firm that either accepts deposits or makes loans but does not do both.

The interstate banking issue is intimately tied in with the question of how to regulate bank holding companies and even how to define a bank or the **nonbank bank** issue. Existing law regarding bank holding companies restricts these firms to lines of business "closely related to banking." In effect, firms engaged in most lines of commerce cannot be in the banking business or cannot acquire banks. However, no equivalent restrictions apply to unitary savings and loan holding companies, that is, to companies that now only one savings and loan. Any firm, as long as it is approved by the Federal Home Loan Bank Board, can acquire a savings and loan. For example, in 1985 Ford Credit Corporation, a subsidiary of Ford Motor Company, acquired First Nationwide Savings and Loan. Ford did not necessarily acquire a savings and loan because it preferred that to acquiring a bank. It was precluded from acquiring a bank by the current bank holding company laws. There appears to be no logical reason for the distinction in treatment of bank and savings and loan holding companies. Instead, there is a long history of a separation between banking and commerce, while there is no comparable history with savings and loans. As banks attempt to diversify their financial products and expand their geographic areas of operation, the bank holding company laws that restrict their ability to move out of financial services will come under increasing pressure.

A bank holding company is a company which owns one or more banks.

The issue of **bank holding companies** has been complicated by the debate surrounding the appropriate legal definition of a bank. The bank holding company statutes state that, for the purposes of the bank holding company law, a commercial bank engages in two activities: it accepts deposits and makes loans. A bank holding company that would otherwise find it difficult to acquire banks in other states, as well as investment companies that would not be able to acquire a bank at all, could then acquire a bank and curtail its lending. They would then be able to accept deposits and have them insured by the FDIC, but they would not violate the bank holding company statutes since the bank they would operate would be what is called a *nonbank bank*. Alternatively, a bank could acquire a bank in another state solely for the purpose of making loans in that state and not accepting deposits. The office of the comptroller of the currency, which has the authority to grant federal charters for nonbank banks, has chosen to give a liberal interpretation to the statutes. As a result, it has granted charters for limited service banks, which to a certain degree circumvents the bank holding statutes.

In late 1984 a federal court in Florida issued an order barring the comptroller from issuing any more charters for limited service or nonbank banks. In October of 1986, a federal appeals court allowed U.S. Trust Corporation, a bank holding company, to expand its limited service banking activities across state lines by buying a limited service bank in Florida. As a result of that decision, in late 1986 the comptroller filed a motion in federal court in Florida asking that court to vacate its injunction issued in 1984. This issue still has not been settled by the courts.

THE GLASS-STEAGALL ACT

The **Glass-Steagall Act** created a separation between commercial and investment banking.

One of the most important pieces of legislation affecting the current structure of financial institutions in the United States is the **Glass-Steagall Act.** In the 1930s this new law forced banking firms to divest themselves of their securities opera-

THE FED'S VIEW OF REGULATORY REFORM

In 1987 there was a new and relatively unusual contribution to the debate about regulatory system reform for financial institutions. Gerald Corrigan, president of the Federal Reserve Bank of New York, and a long-time associate of then Federal Reserve Board Chairman Paul Volcker, released his own blueprint for regulatory reform. This was unusual in at least two respects. First, the Federal Reserve has generally been opposed to much of the reform movement. Second, neither the Fed as an institution nor its senior officers normally make it a practice to release documents that describe directly how Congress ought to reform regulation. So, on both accounts, the Corrigan report was unique.

The Corrigan report cautioned about two basic risks that may be created by additional deregulation or desegmentation of the financial system. The first risk pertains to the extensive electronic payments system that now handles more than $1 trillion per day in the United States. Corrigan expressed considerable concern about the possibility of a breakdown in this system. He argued that any loosening of regulations or barriers between classes of institutions must not increase the risk of a breakdown in the payments system. Presumably, a breakdown could be triggered by failures of a few key participants in the system, thus necessitating significant intervention by the Fed. However, it is unclear exactly how additional deregulation would affect the prospect that such a situation could develop. This risk seems linked to the solvency of major banking firms already highly regulated by the Fed. It is not easy to see how participation of new entrants into this area or expansion of activities of large commercial banks might materially affect this risk.

Corrigan's other main concern is the threat to the separation of banking and commerce, a critical element in existing laws governing activities of bank holding companies. However, the entry of nonbank firms into consumer or retail banking, principally through their acquisition of savings and loans, has threatened the effectiveness of the bank holding company statutes. Corrigan is concerned that widespread entry of industrial and commercial firms into retail banking would threaten the soundness of the financial system. What is particularly important about Corrigan's position is not simply that regulations must keep some legal separation between banking activities and other activities of firms, but rather that commercial and industrial firms should be effectively prohibited from owning subsidiaries engaged in retail or consumer banking. A more moderate position is to allow commercial and industrial firms to acquire retail banking subsidiaries but with effective separation between the activities of bank and nonbank subsidiaries. Corrigan apparently believes it is impossible to regulate and enforce such separation. Since retail banking firms have access to government deposit insurance, it would be difficult to limit the use of the government's guarantee to strictly banking activities. To make sure that the government's guarantee is not compromised, Corrigan insisted that the legal separation of banking and commerce included in bank holding company statutes be maintained. Since industrial firms can enter the retail banking business through the thrift channel, Corrigan's proposal would require firms such as Ford and Sears to divest themselves of retail financial subsidiaries. Corrigan's views illustrate the lack of agreement and the intense debate that continue about regulatory system reform for financial markets.

---

tions and limit future activities to what is now called commercial, as opposed to investment, banking. The motivations for this separation were principally to prevent conflicts of interest between those who handle depositors' funds and those who underwrite securities as well as to limit the riskiness of the activities of commercial banks.

There is now tremendous pressure building in the U.S. financial system to repeal the Glass-Steagall Act. A consensus seems to be growing that there are now better methods available to limit the kinds of conflict of interest which greatly concerned Congress when Glass-Steagall was passed. Moreover, there is also a consensus emerging that the commercial banking business is changing to such an extent that an inherent part of its business is the underwriting of some types of securities. This change in the banking business is the process of securitization, an issue discussed throughout this book and in the next few chapters. It is probably no longer sufficient for large banks to act simply as portfolio lenders, accepting deposits and using those deposits to fund loans they hold on their books. Many financial markets that have been dominated by financial intermediaries are now being transformed into intermediated markets. This means banks have to act less like portfolio lenders and more like dealers and guarantors of securities. Unfortunately, Glass-Steagall stands directly in their path as they attempt to change.

The statement that there is now a consensus that Glass-Steagall should be repealed may be an overstatement. At the time this is written the Federal Reserve, which regulates bank holding companies, has given only limited support to the repeal of Glass-Steagall. Without the Fed's support, direct repeal of the legislation in Congress may be hard to achieve. However, as we have learned in exploring how other areas of regulation have evolved, sometimes the route to reform of a major form of regulation is circuitous and somewhat surprising. Glass-Steagall appears to be no exception.

Rather than take on all of the restrictions incorporated in Glass-Steagall in a head-on assault, the major money center banks, such as Bankers Trust, Citicorp, Morgan Guaranty, and Chase, have pursued authority to act as dealers only for specific types of securities. They have sought this authority for commercial paper, mortgage-backed and consumer paper-backed securities and municipal revenue bonds. They have always had the authority to operate subsidiaries that act as dealers in U.S. Treasury securities. Therefore, they contend that the movement into trading and underwriting these additional types of issues is a natural extension of their existing authority and their normal lending and investment activities. Commercial paper and mortgage- and consumer paper-backed securities essentially constitute securitized bank loans. Banks have historically been active in these types of loans. Banks have also been active investors in municipal bonds and have underwritten general obligation municipal bonds in the past.

In order to obtain approval for underwriting these securities, a number of bank holding companies that operate in large money center banks have sought approval from the Federal Reserve to establish subsidiaries specifically for such activities. In December, 1986, the Federal Reserve granted authority to Bankers Trust to distribute commercial paper through such a subsidiary. However, the Fed placed restrictions on its activities that stipulated that gross revenue from commercial paper activities cannot exceed five percent of the unit's total gross revenue and that its share of the total dealer-placed commercial paper market cannot exceed five percent.

Also in December, 1986, the New York State Banking Department ruled that state-chartered banks could set up subsidiaries to underwrite corporate and other securities. Since many large money center banks which are owned by holding companies and regulated by the Federal Reserve are state-chartered New York banks, this creates a significant conflict between the state and federal regulatory agencies on this issue. This decision by the New York State Banking Department was made in response to a request from Bankers Trust New York Corp. and J. P. Morgan & Co. for an interpretation of what is known as the *Little Glass-Steagall Act,* a New York state law which is nearly identical to the federal statute of the same name. The state regulatory agency interepreted the law as stipulating that a state-chartered bank can be affiliated with a securities firm as long as underwriting activities that were previously disallowed, such as underwriting muncipal revenue bonds, do not exceed 25 percent of total underwriting activities.

This decision on the part of the New York State Banking Department is yet another example of the way multiple regulatory agencies can be used to move the current regulatory system toward reform. New York banks have had an incentive to pressure the state agency to take a position contrary to the existing position of the Fed. This puts additional pressure on the Fed and Congress to offer a more liberal interpretation of Glass-Steagall. As a result, it appears to increase the probability that the Glass-Steagall Act will be repealed or substantially altered in the next few years.

Summary

This chapter has been concerned with the reform of the regulatory system for financial institutions in the United States, a process that has been referred to as *deregulation. Desegmentation* may be a more appropriate word. Since the Great Depression, when the major pieces of regulation legislation were enacted, the United States has had a set of highly segmented financial firms, both by geography and by product line. Because the barriers that created separate geographic and product markets are now breaking down, the financial institutions of the very near future may be quite different from the ones of the 1960s and 1970s. Two principal changes in the economic environment of the United States have precipitated regulatory system reform: the high rate of inflation and the high interest rates that accompanied it and tremendous technological progress in communications and computers.

Five features of the existing regulatory system made it vulnerable to high inflation and technological progress. The first was the geographic and product line segmentation of financial services. The geographic segmentation has been particularly evident in the commercial banking industry where the McFadden Act (1926) gives each state the right to determine whether banks from another state may enter. Historically most states chose to restrict the entry of other states, and some restricted competition within that state by limiting or prohibiting branch banking. Product line segmentation is also evident where bank holding company laws and the Glass-Steagall Act restrict commercial banks to a specific set of activities and prohibit other firms from owning commercial banks. As the technology for delivering financial services evolved in the last decade, the rationale for maintaining both geographic and product line segmentation of financial services became increasingly tenuous.

The second characteristic of the regulatory system was the competing and overlapping regulatory agencies for specific financial institutions. We learned that this system has both advantages and disadvantages. The duplication involved is costly, and it creates the opportunity for specific regulatory agencies to be captured by the institutions they regulate. An advantage of this system is that competition between the agencies tends to encourage change and reform. Regulated institutions use this structure to try to encourage reform, which we have seen in the recent attempts to reform Glass-Steagall.

The third feature of the regulatory system was the creation of a barter system between depository institutions and those who placed deposits in those institutions as well as between commercial banks and the Federal Reserve. The barter system between banks or savings and loans and depositors was fostered by Regulation Q, which restricted banks and savings and loans from competing for deposits with higher interest rates. These institutions were forced to compete with convenience and other nonprice means to attract customers. At the same time the Fed required banks to hold reserves and yet did not pay interest on those reserves; instead, it offered services to the banks. This worked well as long as the opportunity cost to the banks of holding reserves remained stable, but as interest rates rose with inflation during the 1970s, the opportunity cost of reserves went up accordingly. This meant banks were incurring what amounted to a large tax for being Federal Reserve members.

The fourth feature of the regulatory system was the selective use of this reserve requirement tax and the subsidy implicit in deposit insurance. These two items are important parts of the total cost of regulation imposed on financial firms. If the cost of regulation for one type of firm, say commercial banks who are Federal Reserve members, becomes too high relative to some other type of regulated institution, then the institutions will go to great lengths to change the situation.

The final characteristic of the regulatory system was the implicit commitment made by the Federal Reserve to maintain stable interest rates. For most of the post-World War II era the Fed had conducted monetary policy by attempting to control and stabilize interest rates. As a result, many financial institutions found it profitable to pass on the Fed's implicit commitment to stable interest rates to other participants in financial markets. However, as inflation increased and persisted, the Fed abandoned its long-standing operating procedures of attempting to control interest rates. This made it untenable for financial institutions to continue to offer implicit as well as explicit commitments to the market. As a result, one of the principal services offered by financial institutions was threatened.

A number of major reforms in the regulatory system have been instituted in the last few years. Two pieces of federal reform legislation are the Financial Institutions Deregulation and Monetary Control Act of 1980 and the Garn-St Germain Act of 1982. The earlier piece of legislation mandated that Regulation Q be phased out over six years, that all financial institutions offering transactions accounts would be subject to equivalent reserve requirements, and that the Federal Reserve begin to charge explicit prices for the services it offered to commercial banks.

As it turned out, a planned six-year phase-out of Regulation Q was simply not fast enough, leading Congress to pass the Garn-St Germain Act. This law directed the regulators to implement deposit accounts promptly with terms fully competitive with those offered by money market funds. The law also granted greatly expanded lending and investment powers to savings and loans and unitary savings and loan holding companies.

Three important and still not fully resolved issues of regulatory reform are interstate banking, limited service or nonbank banks, and the Glass-Steagall Act. There has been fairly rapid movement toward interstate banking in 1985 and 1986, as many states have changed laws to allow banks from outside to enter their markets, at least under some conditions. Some states have allowed such entry for reciprocating other states thereby preventing entry of large money center banks, such as Citicorp. The question of whether nonbanking firms and bank holding companies in one state can acquire limited service banks, that is, banks that do not make loans or accept deposits, is currently being considered by the courts. Such acquisitions constitute another move toward desegmentation of financial products and toward interstate banking.

The movement toward repeal of the Glass-Steagall Act is not being pursued head-on by money center banks. Instead, they are attempting to acquire authority to underwrite commercial paper, mortgage-backed and consumer paper-backed securities, and mortgage revenue bonds. With the recent decision by New York state bank regulators to grant such authority to state-chartered banks and with the Fed's decision to grant commercial paper authority to at least some institutions, it appears that Glass-Steagall's repeal is on the way. It now seems the question is how much of and how fast Glass-Steagall will be eliminated.

QUESTIONS

1. How do the two major pieces of federal legislation enacted in 1980 and 1982 differ? In what ways did the 1982 act speed up the provisions of the 1980 act?
2. Why was there a barter system in operation under the regulatory structure for commercial banks which operated during the 1960s and 1970s? What was the Fed's membership problem? How was this problem solved? Discuss the advantages and disadvantages to the solution.
3. What is the difference between deregulation and desegmentation? Why and how has our financial system been segmented?
4. Why and how was our regulatory system for financial institutions vulnerable in a period of high inflation? How did inflation hurt the system?
5. How did the Garn-St Germain Act change the powers of savings and loans versus commercial banks? What is the significance of these changes?

6. How much progress had been made toward interstate banking at the time this book went to press? How much has been made since? Who will be hurt and who will be helped by interstate banking?
7. What is a nonbank bank? Why have these been important as an evolutionary stage to a new form of financial institution?
8. Who would be hurt and who would be helped by repeal of the Glass-Steagall Act?

REFERENCES

Kane, Edward J. "Technological and Regulatory Forces in the Developing Fusion of Financial-Services Competition," *Journal of Finance,* 32 (July 1984), pp. 759–72.

Kareken, John H. "Federal Bank Regulatory Policy: A Description and Some Observations," *Journal of Business,* (1986), pp. 3–48.

Kaufman, George G., Larry R. Mote, and Harvey Rosenblum. "Consequences of Deregulation for Commercial Banking," *Journal of Finance,* 32 (July 1984), pp. 789–802.

Kirkland, Richard I. Jr. "Banks Seek Life Beyond Lending," *Fortune,* (March 3, 1986), pp. 54–7.

Zweig, Phillip L. "New York Rules State-Chartered Banks Can Form Units to Underwrite Securities," *Wall Street Journal,* (December 31, 1986).

18

*T*HE BUSINESS OF BANKING

In this chapter we will focus on the banking business. Our principal objective is to understand how commercial banks compete and attempt to earn a profit in the deregulated or desegmented financial markets now emerging in the United States. During the era when Regulation Q was effective, particularly the late 1970s, the commercial banking business could aptly be described as a spread business. The spread was the difference between the rate of return that could be earned on specific types of loans and the cost of operating the system for generating deposit funds. With the deregulation legislation of the 1980s, the costs of funding loans changed. Eliminating Regulation Q meant banks had to compete directly with competitive rates of return to attract deposit funds. At the same time, technological progress was changing the costs of providing various financial services. If this weren't enough, the relatively high level of interest rates in the 1970s and early 1980s induced many corporate borrowers to assess the cost of borrowing carefully and to look for new avenues to raise funds with minimum cost. Hence, commercial banks have found themselves in an environment where both the demand for their services and the costs of providing them have been changing dramatically.

How will this change affect the banking industry? Some observers predict that within another decade as few as 500 banks will operate in this country, as compared to roughly 14,000 that existed in 1986. Those who espouse this view believe regulation has allowed essentially mom-and-pop banking firms to exist simultaneously with large integrated firms, and few smaller banking firms will survive in the deregulated and competitive market of the future. Some observers also insist that commercial banks will have to become more like investment banks, providing the services of dealers rather than functioning as portfolio lenders. This suggests there are actually two quite distinct banking businesses: one a retail business of providing financial services to consumers and small businesses, the other a wholesale business of providing services to corporate customers and managing investments.

We start this chapter by describing the basic lending activities of commercial banks and what the assets and liabilities of the banking sector looked like in the mid-1980s. We will also examine some of the market characteristics for specific types of bank loans, including loan commitments. Then we will turn our attention to risk management in commercial banks, focusing on how banks manage both credit and funding risks and how the methods for controlling those risks have changed over the years. Finally, in discussing the profitability and valuation of commercial banks or the valuation of bank stocks, we will examine the sources of earnings for banks in the early 1980s and some evidence on how claims on banks are priced in competitive markets. ■

ON- AND OFF-BALANCE-SHEET FINANCING OF COMMERCIAL BANKS

In the traditional view a commercial bank extends loans to consumers and commercial customers and funds them by issuing liabilities largely in the form of deposits. To some extent this is still an accurate characterization of a bank, but it falls far short of telling the whole story. In order to see what modern banks are up to we need to examine the earnings and the asset and liability structure of commercial banks in the 1980s and to look more closely at some of the specific types of loans banks offer. In addition, we need to look off the balance sheet, that is, at the activities of banks that do not show up on their balance sheets, particularly asset sales and commitments.

THE NATURE OF BANK BALANCE SHEETS

The asset side of the balance sheet of commercial banks is composed largely of loans, with approximately one-quarter of the total assets typically invested in marketable securities. Figures 18–1 and 18–2 show the composition of the assets and liabilities of all commercial banks taken together from 1978 to 1986. Panel A of Figure 18–1 shows the total volume of loans and marketable securities. Panel A of Figure 18–2 shows the composition of loans. The figures illustrate that commercial banks extend a wide variety of loans. The largest component of the loan portfolio is commercial or business loans, followed by mortgage loans. **Bank investments** (that is, their holdings of publicly traded securities) are almost exclusively in two types of securities, Treasury bonds and bills and municipal bonds. Banks hold Treasury securities because of their high liquidity. They hold municipal bonds because of their tax advantages. Municipal bonds are free of corporate income taxes, a feature attractive to commercial banks, which, unlike such investors as pension funds, are subject to income taxes. In fact, commercial banks and insurance companies are the largest holders of municipal bonds in the economy,

Bank investments include a bank's holdings of marketable securities, such as Treasury and municipal bonds.

FIGURE 18–1
Principal assets and liabilities of all commercial banks.

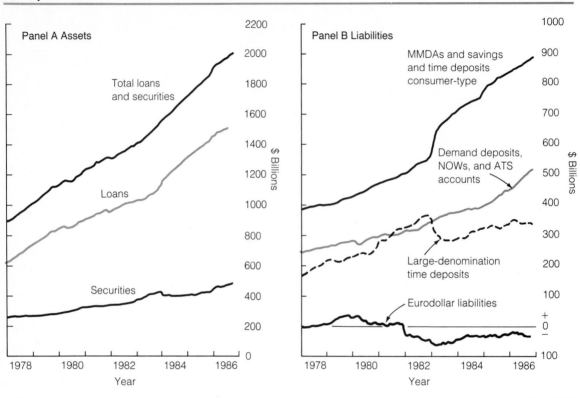

Source: Federal Reserve Chart Book, November, 1986.

though in the last few years holdings of municipal bonds by individual investors and mutual funds have been increasing dramatically. Panel B of Figure 18–2 shows the relative volume of Treasury and municipal investments of commercial banks. It indicates that bank holdings of municipal bonds have been decreasing relative to holdings of Treasury securities, and this reflects decreased reliance on the contribution of after-tax earnings of municipal bonds. In the early 1980s many banks found that they could utilize foreign tax credits and leasing transactions to shelter substantial income from taxation. In addition, some banks had relatively poor earnings in the early 1980s and therefore did not have as much need for tax-exempt income.

On the liability side of the balance sheet, commercial banks derive most of their funds from various types of deposit accounts. The levels of the types of deposit accounts that appear on the books of commercial banks are shown in panel B of Figure 18–1. The largest source of deposits is **money market deposit ac-**

Money market deposit accounts are accounts without interest rate ceilings which were authorized by the Garn-St Germain Act of 1982.

FIGURE 18–2
Principal classes of loans and securities for all commercial banks. Seasonally adjusted, monthly averages.

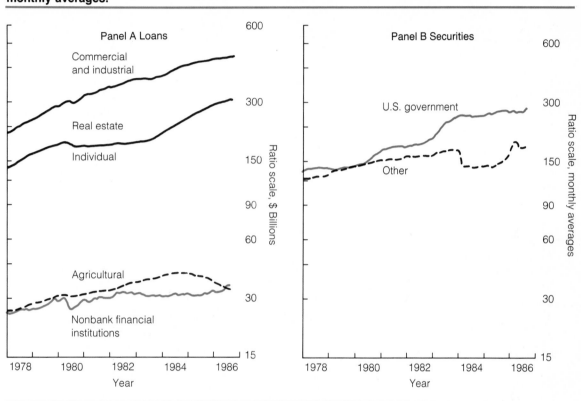

Source: Federal Reserve Chart Book, November, 1986.

NOW and Automatic Transfer Accounts are highly liquid savings accounts earning competitive interest rates.

counts (MMDAs) and savings and time deposits, MMDAs were introduced through the Garn-St Germain Act of 1982. Figure 18–1 shows that this category of deposits increased dramatically in 1983, reflecting the change in regulations. The second largest category of deposits is demand deposits, **negotiated order of withdrawal accounts (NOWs),** and **automatic transfer accounts (ATs).** These are all forms of transaction accounts or accounts with check-writing privileges. The next most important source of deposits is large denomination time deposits or certificates of deposit (CDs). Finally, Eurodollar liabilities represent the smallest fraction of the total. Eurodollar deposits represent overseas liabilities held in foreign branches of U S banks denominated in dollars.

One way to learn more about the bank balance sheet is to examine the terms for commercial and industrial loans. Table 18–1 presents some data on the terms of bank lending of a sort that is collected once every quarter by the Federal Reserve Board. The data here, covering loans made from August 4 to 8, 1986, by

TABLE 18–1
Terms of lending at commercial banks; survey of loans made, August 4–8, 1986[1]. A. Commercial and Industrial Loans[2]

Characteristics	Amount of Loans ($thousands)	Average Size ($thousands)	Weighted-Average Maturity[3] Days	Loan Rate (percent) Weighted-Average Effective[4]	Standard Error[5]	Inter-quartile Range[6]	Loans Made Under Commitment (percent)	Participation Loans (percent)	Most Common Base Pricing Rate[7]
All banks									
1. Overnight[8]	18,440,593	8.119	*	7.07	0.05	6.79–7.18	85.6	2.1	Fed funds
2. One month and under	6,496,558	477	17	7.58	0.13	6.92–7.82	74.0	7.5	Domestic
3. Fixed Rate	5,183,735	763	16	7.35	0.08	6.84–7.52	72.4	8.2	Domestic
4. Floating rate	1,312,824	192	20	8.47	0.18	7.30–9.38	80.5	4.7	Prime
5. Over one month and under a year	9,270,883	99	138	8.61	0.20	7.38–9.42	71.1	6.9	Prime
6. Fixed rate	4,282,589	96	90	8.22	0.35	7.05–9.15	64.9	6.9	Domestic
7. Floating rate	4,988,294	101	179	8.94	0.13	8.24–9.65	76.5	6.9	Prime
8. Demand[9]	5,537,638	156	*	8.65	0.14	7.98–9.38	80.1	7.4	Prime
9. Fixed rate	619,374	226	*	7.62	0.27	7.12–7.76	58.3	10.3	Fed funds
10. Floating rate	4,918,264	150	*	8.78	0.11	8.30–9.38	82.9	7.0	Prime
11. Total short term	**39,745,673**	**273**	**41**	**7.73**	**0.13**	**6.86–8.30**	**79.6**	**4.8**	**Fed funds**
12. Fixed rate (thousands of dollars)	27,611,152	492	18	7.32	0.12	6.83–7.41	79.0	4.2	Fed funds
13. 1–24	320,283	8	112	11.73	0.20	10.38–13.08	19.0	0.0	Prime
14. 25–49	158,047	32	119	10.66	0.24	8.81–12.36	22.9	0.2	Prime
15. 50–99	182,710	67	109	10.43	0.21	9.31–12.28	30.3	0.5	Prime
16. 100–499	433,111	189	80	9.11	0.12	8.25–10.20	44.9	4.3	Prime
17. 500–999	327,159	706	63	9.00	0.32	7.50–11.46	51.0	3.0	Other
18. 1000 and over	26,189,842	8,150	15	7.18	0.06	6.82–7.36	81.3	4.4	Fed funds
19. Floating rate (thousands of dollars)	12,134,521	136	127	8.67	0.11	7.58–9.38	80.9	6.2	Prime
20. 1–24	440,797	9	155	10.07	0.11	9.37–10.49	68.1	1.8	Prime
21. 25–49	458,853	34	153	9.90	0.10	9.18–10.47	65.4	2.1	Prime
22. 50–99	777,538	66	148	9.74	0.10	8.94–10.38	71.5	3.9	Prime
23. 100–499	2,574,700	185	143	9.30	0.06	8.57–9.92	74.9	4.3	Prime
24. 500–999	1,202,075	647	144	9.02	0.07	8.30–9.39	76.6	6.4	Prime
25. 1000 and over	6,680,558	3,935	114	8.07	0.09	7.03–8.84	87.0	7.7	Prime

*Fewer than 10 sample loans.

[1]The survey of terms of bank lending to business collects data on gross loan extensions made during the first full business week in the mid-month of each quarter by a sample of 340 commercial banks of all sizes. A subsample of 250 banks also report loans to farmers. The sample data are blown up to estimate the lending terms at all insured commercial banks during that week. The estimated terms of bank lending are not intended for use in collecting the terms of loans extended over the entire quarter or residing in the portfolios of those banks. Construction and land development loans include both unsecured loans and loans secured by real estate. Thus, some of the construction and land development loans would be reported on the statement of condition as real estate loans and the remainder as business loans. Mortgage loans, purchased loans, foreign loans, and loans of less than $1,000 are excluded from the survey.
As of Dec. 31, 1985, assets of most of the large banks were at least $5.5 billion. For all insured banks total assets averaged $165 million.

[2]Beginning with the August 1986 survey respondent banks provide information on the type of base rate used to price each commercial and industrial loan made during the survey week. This reporting change is reflected in the new column on the most common base pricing rate in table A and footnote 13 from table B.

[3]Average maturities are weighted by loan size and exclude demand loans.

[4]Effective (compounded) annual interest rates are calculated from the stated rate and other terms of the loan and weighted by loan size.

[5]The chances are about two out of three that the average rate shown would differ by less than this amount from the average rate that would be found by a complete survey of lending at all banks.

[6]The interquartile range shows the interest rate range that encompasses the middle 50 percent of the total dollar amount of loans made.

[7]The most common base rate is that rate used to price the largest dollar volume of loans. Base pricing rates include the prime rate (sometimes referred to as a bank's "basic" or "reference" rate); the federal funds rate; domestic money market rates other than the federal funds rate; foreign money market rates; and other base rates not included in the foregoing classifications.

[8]Overnight loans are loans that mature on the following business day.

[9]Demand loans have no stated date of maturity.

Characteristics	Amount of Loans ($thousands)	Average Size ($thousands)	Weighted-Average Maturity[3]	Loan Rate (percent)			Loans Made Under Commitment (percent)	Participation Loans (percent)	Most Common Base Pricing Rate[7]
			Months	Weighted-Average Effective[4]	Standard Error[5]	Inter-quartile Range[6]			
26. Total long term	**$4,635,631**	**203**	**55**	**8.73**	**0.21**	**7.52–9.42**	**77.8**	**10.7**	**Prime**
27. Fixed rate (thousands of dollars)	872,502	85	49	9.03	0.44	6.84–11.02	58.8	2.2	Other
28. 1–99	165,507	18	32	11.84	0.28	11.00–12.68	15.9	0.1	Other
29. 100–499	139,686	196	47	10.72	0.28	9.79–11.63	22.9	1.5	Prime
30. 500–999	44,941	677	42	8.92	0.53	7.50–9.92	57.4	8.5	Prime
31. 1000 and over	522,368	4,919	55	7.69	0.41	6.78–7.97	82.1	2.4	Other
32. Floating rate (thousands of dollars)	3,763,129	300	57	8.66	0.15	7.78–9.38	82.2	12.7	Prime
33. 1–99	215,909	23	47	9.99	0.10	9.11–10.75	46.5	2.3	Prime
34. 100–499	500,447	218	68	9.52	0.19	8.77–9.92	50.9	4.5	Prime
35. 500–999	236,153	659	39	9.05	0.16	8.30–9.92	77.5	11.4	Prime
36. 1000 and over	2,810,620	5,171	57	8.37	0.20	7.39–9.25	90.9	15.1	Prime
Loans made below prime[12]			Days	Effective[4]	Nominal[10]	Prime Rate[11]			
37. Overnight[8]	17,862,669	10,431	*	7.01	6.78	8.00	85.8	2.2	
38. One month and under	5,439,776	2,817	16	7.23	6.99	8.01	75.3	8.2	
39. Over one month and under a year	3,757,206	650	120	7.17	6.95	8.10	80.3	8.1	
40. Demand[9]	1,477,065	1,451	*	7.13	6.91	8.02	80.4	6.8	
41. Total short term	**28,536,716**	**2,733**	**21**	**7.08**	**6.85**	**8.02**	**82.8**	**4.3**	
42. Fixed rate	24,855,428	3,850	14	7.06	6.83	8.01	81.4	4.4	
43. Floating rate	3,681,288	923	85	7.20	6.97	8.08	91.6	3.6	
			Months						
44. Total long term	**1,592,528**	**979**	**62**	**7.33**	**7.12**	**8.25**	**82.8**	**6.9**	
45. Fixed rate	486,433	747	52	7.30	7.11	8.24	79.4	3.1	
46. Floating rate	1,106,095	1,133	67	7.34	7.13	8.26	84.3	8.6	

Source: Federal Reserve Bulletin, February, 1987.

[10]Nominal (not compounded) annual interest rates are calculated from survey data on the stated rate and other terms of the loan and weighted by the loan size.

[11]The prime rate reported by each bank is weighted by the volume of loans extended and then averaged.

[12]The proportion of loans made at rates below prime may vary substantially from the proportion of such loans outstanding in banks' portfolios.

[13]73.4 percent of construction and land development loans were priced relative to the prime rate.

[14]Among banks reporting loans to farmers (Table 5), most "large banks" (survey strata 1 to 3) had over $600 million in total assets, and most "other banks" (survey strata 4 to 6) had total assets below $600 million.

The survey of terms of bank lending to farmers now includes loans secured by farm real estate. In addition, the categories describing the purpose of farm loans have now been expanded to include "purchase or improve farm real estate." In previous surveys, the purpose of such loans was reported as "other".

all commercial banks in the United States, indicate that banks extended about $39.7 billion of short-term loans compared to $4.6 billion of long-term loans. Short-term loans had an average maturity of 44 days, while long-term loans had an average maturity of 55 months. Of the short-term loans $18.4 billion or 46 percent were overnight loans. In addition, 70 percent of the short-term loans were made at fixed interest rates. This means the bank takes on the risk of changing interest rates, at least for loans with maturities longer than one day. Of the long-term loans, 80 percent were made with floating interest rates. The long-term floating rate loans were most commonly based on or tied to the prime interest rate.

The prime interest rate is set by a commercial bank and used as an index in pricing loans with floating interest rates.

The **prime interest rate** was once thought to be the rate charged to a bank's most creditworthy customers. However, it is evident from the table that a sizable portion of the total loan volume is at interest rates below prime. The volume of loans made below prime is particularly large in the short-term loan category—$28.5 billion. Below prime lending has become commonplace in response to increased competition for lending to high-quality borrowers. These borrowers can now issue commercial paper at very tight spreads over the Treasury bill rate. As a result, it has been necessary for banks to reduce the rates they charge to the high-quality segment of the commercial and industrial loan market. Rather than being the rate charged to the highest quality borrower, the prime interest rate is now an index rate used as the base in pricing many floating rate loans. Hence, what matters to a borrower is the spread charged over or under the prime rate and the extent to which a bank's prime rate moves with other market interest rates. Most prime interest rates charged by banks are now closely indexed to market rates, which reflect the cost of specific sources of funds for the bank. However, banks have some incentive to attempt to hold the prime up when market interest rates are falling. If banks' customers can costlessly move from bank to bank in their borrowing, then this incentive is limited. If there are significant costs in such adjustments, then there may tend to be some "stickiness" in the prime, at least on the way down.

Loan commitments are made by commercial banks to lend to a customer according to prearranged terms.

Another interesting feature of bank lending evident in Table 18–1 is the importance of commitments in determining bank lending. In the aggregate, approximately 80 percent of the loans documented in Table 18–1 were made under **loan commitments.** The table also indicates that small loans are much more likely to be made without commitments than larger loans. The distinction between loans of different size is particularly pronounced for short-term loans which are made at fixed rates. In this category, 80 percent of loans over $1 million are made under commitments, while the percentage is much smaller for loans of a lesser dollar magnitude.

Fixed versus floating rate agreements refer to commitments for future loans made at a fixed as opposed to a floating interest rate.

The purpose of the commitment is to provide some insurance to the borrower that funds will be available if and when they are needed. Two major types of commitments may be agreed upon by borrowers and commercial banks. One, referred to as a *line of credit,* is an informal agreement between borrower and lender to provide funds up to a prespecified amount over a prespecified interval. Most lines of credit stipulate that the interest rate will float with the prime rate, and hence they are referred to as *floating rate agreements*. Lines of credit that commit a bank to a specific rate in the future, or fixed rate agreements, are now less common than floating rate agreements. Lines of credit are informal agreements as they are not legally binding upon the bank. Banks scrupulously try to honor most such agreements because their reputation for reliability is at stake, but this type of agreement is not enforceable in court, and banks can legally refuse to honor it. Banks generally require that borrowers with a line of credit maintain balances with the bank as a means of compensating for a line of credit. These balances may be in lieu of or in addition to specific fees paid for the commitment.

The alternative type of commitment is a *revolving credit agreement*. Unlike the line of credit, the revolving credit agreement is a legally binding commitment to provide funds on prespecified terms. As a result, revolving credit agreements often include more detailed specifications for the borrower than a line of credit. In addition, banks generally require that fees be paid to secure a revolving credit agreement.

OFF-BALANCE-SHEET FINANCING

In the mid-1980s a tremendous amount of attention began to be devoted to what is called *off-balance-sheet financing* at commercial banks and other types of financial institutions. Off-balance-sheet financing is sometimes viewed as equivalent to securitization, but this appears to be something of an oversimplification. Four distinct developments fall under the broad heading of off-balance-sheet financing. Only one of these constitutes securitization, as we used the word in Chapter 16. These activites are

1. Loan commitments, such as lines of credit and revolving credit agreements.
2. Investment-related commitments. These are essentially commitments to undertake interest rate or price risks through forward, futures, or options contracts.
3. Guaranties of credit quality through letters of credit.
4. Transformation of nonmarketable assets on the balance sheets of portfolio lenders, such as banks, into marketable securities.

Securitization is the process of transforming assets with no secondary markets into tradeable securities with active secondary markets.

The most dramatic change in the business of financial intermediation now taking place really refers to point 4. This is what we have referred to as *securitization*. **Securitization** entails the transformation of a financial market once dominated by vertically integrated portfolio lenders into an over-the-counter or an auction market. As the market changes there are opportunities for institutions of all types to provide each of the distinct services involved in intermediation: origination of assets, servicing, creation and distribution of securities, guaranteeing the cash flows on those securities, and provision of liquidity in the secondary market. Securitization is valuable because it provides additional liquidity, opportunities for specialization in each of these functions, and, in some markets, a means to avoid costly regulations.

In 1986 securitization of consumer receivables and commercial bank loans began to take place. Securitization has progressed the farthest in the mortgage market (discussed in Chapter 19) where, by the end of 1986, there were in excess of $300 billion of mortgage-backed securities outstanding. With the experience gained in the mortgage market, investment banking firms and portfolio lenders have begun to look for ways to securitize other types of loans, including auto loans, credit card receivables, commercial real estate, and commercial and industrial bank loans. In one form or another, there has long been a secondary market for some of these loans. Banks have long arranged **participations** in their loans with other banks and, more recently, with nonbank firms. For example, Table 18–1 indicates that a little over 10 percent of the long-term loans used for this table involved some kind of participation. However, participation agreements do not constitute marketable securities backed by loans. Participations are not highly standardized instruments and do not afford the liquidity that a relatively large market in asset-backed securities would provide. The value of liquidity gained by securitizing a variety of receivables is one of the principal reasons securitization in this area appears attractive.

A **loan participation** is a sale of part of a loan originated by a commercial bank to another commercial bank or investor.

Another reason derives from the fact that many institutions need to reduce the total volume of assets on their books. For example, in February, 1987, Bank of America made the first public offering of $400 million of securities backed by credit card loans. Bank of America's issue had an expected maturity of approximately two years and was priced at 65 basis points above the Treasury bill rate for the same expected maturity. Prior to this public issue, Banc One of Columbus, Ohio, had made a private offering of credit card receivables. In addition, Republic Bank had made a debt offering of $200 million in 1986 based on credit card loans. But unlike the Bank of America issue, the loans in the Republic issue stayed on Republic's books, and therefore this transaction was not viewed as an actual sale of assets. In the Bank of America case, the credit card receivables were completely removed from the books of Bank of America, and securities owners have no recourse to Bank of America if defaults on the underlying loans exceed the reserves committed by the bank to cover them. However, Standard and Poor's judged that the established reserves were sufficient to cover all but the most extreme possible scenarios for default and awarded the issue an AAA rating.

It is no surprise that Bank of America was the first to make a public offering of this type. It also pioneered the development of mortgage-backed securities issued by a nongovernment-backed entity. In addition, after several years of severe losses it needed to find ways to raise its ratio of capital to assets. Because its stock prices had been driven down as a result of financial difficulties, the option of solving its capital shortage solely by selling new equity was unattractive. As a result, it was looking for ways to get assets off its books. The alternative of stopping making loans was also unattractive since it tends to drive customers to competing banks. The sale of assets provides a relatively attractive alternative, if it can be done on terms that generate a reasonable return to the bank.

A **letter of credit** is an agreement for a commercial bank to make a payment for another party if that party cannot meet its commitment.

Another, very important type of off-balance-sheet item is the letter of credit and standby letter of credit. A **letter of credit** is a commitment issued by a bank to extend credit in some contingency where a borrower cannot meet a financial obligation. The bank issuing the letter of credit is making a commitment to guarantee a lender or investor against the prospect of a borrower's default. There is a legal distinction between a financial guarantee and a letter of credit. Although a bank is legally prohibited from offering an explicit guarantee, it is able to provide what is, for all practical purposes, the same thing through the letter of credit.

Letters of credit are widely utilized in the commercial paper market. In this context they are known as *standby letters of credit*. Letters of credit are issued when an issuer of commercial paper is rated at a relatively low level by rating agencies that evaluate the commercial paper issue. If the issuer purchases a standby letter of credit, then the commercial paper carries the rating of the bank issuing the letter of credit. Hence, letters of credit are essentially providing a rating upgrade to the issuer of the commercial paper, and the standby letter of credit is only as valuable as the rating carried by its issuers. In 1986 Morgan Guaranty was the only commercial bank domiciled in the United States with an AAA rating from Standard and Poor's or Moody's. As a result, Morgan was virtually the only U.S. bank that could provide a standby letter of credit to firms issuing **commercial paper** that would result in the highest rating for that paper. However, there were roughly half a dozen Japanese banks with AAA ratings, and these banks were eager to gain entry into this U.S. market. Therefore, a significant part of the guarantee or letter of credit market in the U.S. was being taken by Japanese banks, and European banks were also important players.

One important issue regarding the use of letters of credit pertains to their treatment by regulatory agencies. Through 1986 regulatory agencies did not impose capital requirements on off-balance-sheet liabilities like letters of credit or loan commitments. Therefore, these were attractive ways to generate income for banks without tying up regulatory capital. However, the regulators have made it clear to the banks that they are highly concerned about the rapid growth of these contingent liabilities. Because they have developed plans for extending capital requirements to these forms of bank liabilities, it is unlikely that this type of business will continue to be attractive.

Commercial paper is a securitized form of short-term borrowing by corporate borrowers.

RISK MANAGEMENT IN COMMERCIAL BANKING

Commercial banks are essentially in the business of managing risks. It is useful to divide the risks faced by a commercial bank into two broad categories, credit risk and funding risk. **Credit risk** refers to the risk of loss due to default or insolvency when a borrower with a loan on the balance sheet defaults or when a loss arises from default by a letter of credit recipient or other contingent liability. **Funding risk** refers to the risk of loss if an asset is funded with a liability that generates a negative spread between the return on the asset and the cost of funding that asset.

Credit risk refers to the risk of default, while **funding risk** pertains to the risk of changes in the cost or availability of bank funds.

MANAGING CREDIT RISK

Losses arising from defaults on loans are among the most serious risks to which commercial banks are exposed. Two basic strategies are used in dealing with credit risk. One strategy attempts to *minimize the losses* generated by defaults.

THE IMPORTANCE OF OFF-BALANCE-SHEET COMMITMENTS

The importance of commitments as a way of doing business in U.S. commercial banks has been increasing in the mid-1980s, particularly for large money center banks. In 1986, the five largest U. S. banks increased off-balance-sheet commitments by 28 percent to approximately $1.2 trillion—more than twice the total assets of $545.5 billion, and more than 40 times the combined equity of these five banks. This magnitude of off-balance-sheet commitments does not simply represent a dramatic increase in assets. In 1985, total off-balance-sheet commitments for the same five banks amounted to $909 billion, or about 174 percent of total assets. It is apparent that, in 1986, commitments grew much more rapidly than did total assets.

Panel A of Table 18–2 shows the total off-balance-sheet commitments in dollars and as a percent of total assets and multiple of shareholders equity for each of these five banks. The table indicates that J.P. Morgan & Co. had the largest total dollar volume of commitments and the highest ratio of commitments to total assets. On the other hand, Bank of America had the lowest ratio of commitments to total assets. This distribution is in part a result of the market's perception of each institution's credit worthiness. J.P. Morgan was the only U. S. bank rated AAA by rating agencies in 1986. On the other hand, Bank of America had the lowest credit rating of any of these five banks. Off-balance-sheet commitments are essentially a business of providing financial guarantees backed by the guarantor's financial resources. To a large extent, a bank's credibility as a guarantor is determined by its credit rating. Therefore, a bank with a high credit rating, as Morgan was in 1986, is in a much better position to compete for commitment business than a bank with a poor credit rating, as Bank of America was in 1986. The relative position of Morgan and Bank of America, shown in Table 18–2,

is in large part determined by their competitive position in the market for commitments.

Panel B of Table 18–2 shows the major categories of commitments for each of the five banks. From this data it is apparent that the largest source of commitments is in foreign exchange. Each of these five banks are major participants in the foreign exchange markets, and they provide services to many customers that involve various types of guarantees and exchange rates. For example, if a bank provides a forward commitment to sell deutsche marks at a specific price in the future, this is an off-balance-sheet commitment. No single category of commitments ranks second in volume for all five banks. Instead, banks have somewhat different profiles of commitments. For example, Citicorp has relatively heavy commitments in futures, options, and money market instruments, as well as in interest rate swaps, while Chase and Bank of America have heavier exposure in loan commitments.

It is not always easy to compile the type of data shown in Table 18–2 because commitments are not reported on the balance sheets of commercial banks. Instead, they are reported in footnotes to the financial statements. There is also no uniform accounting system for commitments across commercial banks. As a result, it is not easy to compare reported numbers of commitments with great accuracy. One reason for the lack of uniformity is that, thus far, there are no capital requirements applicable to off-balance-sheet commitments and therefore only limited reporting is necessary to regulators. However, the amount of off-balance-sheet risk that banks incur is a major factor in the risk-related capital guidelines under consideration by bank regulators in 1987. The Financial Accounting Standards Board is studying a proposal for more complete and uniform disclosure requirements for bank commitments.

Underwriting of a risk refers to the process of evaluating the creditworthiness of a borrower.

This includes screening borrowers in order to determine those who are most likely to default; monitoring the loan agreement over time to maximize the probability the loan will be repaid; and helping the borrower manage financial distress, if it should occur, so that the losses incurred are kept to a minimum. In loans to consumers, the emphasis is on initial screening or **underwriting of the risk** as

TABLE 18–2
Off-balance-sheet financing at commercial banks.

Panel A: Liabilities at five largest banking firms, (year-end 1986, in billions of dollars).

Types of Liability	Citicorp	BofA	Chase	Morgan	Manuf.
Loan commitments	$ 36.8	$ 45.1	$ 26.4	$ 26.1	$ 21.6
Standby letters of credit	22.4	10.5	11.8	7.8	9.2
Others	30.8	2.0	2.5	0.4	1.5
Municipal bond insurance					
Interest rate swaps:					
Notional amount	63.4	11.8	22.0	40.4	37.5
Estimated risk	NA	NA	.455	2.2	0.7
Commitments related to:					
Futures, options, money market instr.	78.9	22.0	6.3	18.0	10.1
Foreign currency sales or purchases	216.3	70.4	104.2	98.0	64.4
Leases	1.4	2.7	1.5	0.8	1.1
Collateral	13.7	5.2		10.5	3.3
Other	3.4			1.0	
Total off-balance-sheet commitments	467.1	169.7	174.7	203.0	148.7
Total assets	196.1	104.2	94.8	76.0	74.4
Total shareholders equity	$ 9.1	$ 4.0	$ 4.3	$ 5.1	$ 3.8

Panel B: Risk at top banks.

	Total ($ Bil.)	% of Total Assets	Multiple Shareholder Equity
Citicorp	$ 467.1	238%	51x
BankAmerica Corp.	169.7	163	42
Chase Manhattan Corp.	174.7	184	41
J. P. Morgan & Co.	203.0	267	40
Manufacturers Hanover Corp.	148.7	200	39
Total for group	$1,163.2	213%	44x

Standby letters of credit do not include letters either secured by marketable securities or which have been participated out to other institutions.

Source: *American Banker,* May 1, 1987.

opposed to continued monitoring, because such loans are generally too expensive to monitor and are generally collateralized by real estate, automobiles, or other consumer durable goods. In loans to businesses, on the other hand, ongoing monitoring and ability to manage a workout situation are very important aspects of effective total risk management.

The second strategy for dealing with credit risk is *effective pricing* of the risk. Banks attempt to assess the riskiness of their customers and then set prices for loans that reflect the risk. High-risk borrowers, whether businesses or individuals, will pay higher interest rates and be subject to restrictions on the amount they can borrow and the uses to which they can put the funds. In loans to businesses, pricing of the loan is dependent upon the nature of covenants and restrictions the loan agreement imposes on the borrower as well as the bank's perception of the underlying risk of default for the borrower's business. In general, the more risky the underlying business of the borrwer, and the higher the leverage of that borrower, the higher the interest rate charged by the bank. However, banks are often reluctant to charge very high interest rates on highly levered loans because high leverage and the high interest rates it would necessitate to provide appropriate compensation to the bank would create an incentive for the borrower to undertake exceedingly risky investments. If the bank perceives this will happen, it will then have to raise interest rates yet farther, creating yet a greater incentive for the borrower to utilize the funds for high-risk investments. This process can easily explode so that beyond some level, it simply does not make sense to make loans to borrowers with high leverage at high interest rates. This process of restricting the amount of leverage and the level of interest rates offered by a bank is referred to as **credit rationing.**

Credit rationing is a restriction of the amount of credit available to a borrower rather than allocation by increasing the loan interest rate as the borrower seeks to borrow more.

When banks price loans they take into account the cost of funding the loan, including the cost of reserve requirements, the expected losses on that class of loans, and the cost of equity capital that must be committed. In order to see how the cost of a loan is analyzed in a typical bank, we will consider a simplified example where a bank is funding a loan to a business borrower with certificates of deposit. Five basic elements of cost are involved in generating and funding that loan. First is the *cost of the funds* utilized in the loan or, in this example, the interest rate on the bank's CDs, say, 7.00 percent. Since CDs must have reserves behind them, the second element of the cost is the *cost of reserve requirements*. Reserve requirements are costly for banks because the Federal Reserve does not pay interest on reserves, thus imposing an opportunity cost equal to the yield that could be earned on reserves. The reserve requirement on CDs is equal to 3 percent. If we assume that the opportunity cost on reserves is equal to 10 percent, then the cost of reserves is 0.10 times 0.03 = 0.3% or 30 basis points. The third element is *operating costs* or overhead necessary to fund the loan. We will assume that this represents 200 basis points. The fourth element is the *level of expected losses* due to default on loans of the risk class of this borrower. We will assume that the bank can expect losses of 50 basis points. The fifth element is the *cost of equity capital*. We will use the capital requirement of 6 percent currently imposed on banks by regulators (see the discussion in Chapter 15), and we will assume that the bank in our example requires a rate of return on equity of 15 percent for the level of risk of the loan being considered. This means that the loan is being funded 94 percent by CDs with a cost of 7.00 percent and 6 percent by equity with a cost of 15 percent. The average cost of the two sources of capital is therefore $0.06 \times 0.15 + 0.94 \times 0.07 = 7.48$ percent, which means that capital

TABLE 18–3
Pricing of a bank loan.

Total Costs of the Bank Loan	
1. Interest expense on CDs	7.00%
2. Reserve requirements	0.30
3. Operating costs	2.00
4. Expected losses on loan	0.50
5. Capital costs	0.48
Interest rate on bank loan	10.28
Spread between loan and CD rate	3.28%

The **all-in interest cost** refers to the total cost of a loan or a credit relationship.

imposes an extra cost of 48 basis points. Table 18–3 summarizes these costs and shows how they are combined to determine the total price of the loan or the **all-in interest cost** of the loan.

Of course, many loans are stated as a markup or spread over a base interest rate. The base interest rate might be the bank's prime interest rate or some other bank's prime rate. It may also be some market interest rate. Many banks use what is called the **LIBOR** (London Interbank Borrowing Rate) for loans, at least for larger corporate customers. This is the rate at which banks around the world lend to each other for very short maturities. If the loan in the example were indexed to the CD rate used in the example, it would be stated as the CD rate plus 328 basis points.

The **LIBOR** refers to the London Interbank Borrowing Rate, a common index used to price loans in international markets.

As we will see when we examine bank profitability, banks have not been very successful during the 1980s in controlling default risk. Bank losses from bad loans have been increasing dramatically, forcing many banks to concentrate particularly hard on developing and maintaining their skills in managing default risk. Since it seems reasonable to expect that the markets for bank services will become even more competitive in the years ahead, these skills will be particularly important.

MANAGING FUNDING RISK

Funding risk arises when the cash flows generated on the asset side of the balance sheet are not perfectly matched with those on the liability side. For example, suppose a bank is funding a commercial and industrial loan that has a maturity of one year with a one year CD. Once the loan is booked and the CD is issued, there is no funding risk. In this example, the cash flows from the loan and the CD are perfectly **term matched.** Suppose, however, that the bank funds the loan with 6-month commercial paper. It then faces the risk that the commercial paper rate may increase and hence its spread on the loan may decline. An increase in a bank's cost of issuing commercial paper might occur because interest rates in general have increased or because the perceived risk of the bank in question has increased. As a third alternative, suppose the bank funds the one-year loan with short-term deposits. The precise volume and cost of available deposits cannot be known in

Term matched refers to matching the maturity of assets and liabilities.

advance. From the bank's vantage point, future deposit volume is determined at least in part by chance. If deposit inflows decline, the bank may have to turn to some alternative source to continue funding the loan, such as an alternative liability like commercial paper, or it could sell some other asset to obtain cash.

Historically, banks had essentially two methods for dealing with a need for additional cash. One method is to liquidate existing assets. With many types of loans, this may be either virtually impossible or exceedingly costly. Some loans simply have no secondary markets, while others have secondary markets, but the loss involved in liquidation may be very large. The cost can be reduced if active secondary markets can be developed, and in some cases this has happened in recent years. But during the 1960s when asset management was widely practiced, few markets had been securitized. As a result, for many years most commercial banks invested in some assets because of their liquidity, principally Treasury securities, because of their active secondary market.

The decision on how extensive the holdings of liquid assets, such as Treasury securities, should be depends upon the costs of holding these securities compared to the alternative means of meeting cash outflows. There are two components to this cost. The first is the *opportunity cost* of revenue lost by not holding more lucrative but less marketable loans or investments. This is really the spread between the rate of return on the liquid asset and the rate of return on the more profitable loan or investment. The second is the *brokerage* or *transaction cost* of selling the liquid asset to satisfy cash outflows. This includes not only the actual cost of selling the asset but the capital losses incurred if the price of the asset has fallen when it is sold. As either of these increases, this alternative will become more expensive.

The maintenance of reserves of liquid assets was once the main tool used by financial intermediaries to deal with funding risk. This method has generally been referred to as **asset management** because the decision is one of how to split assets between the less and more liquid forms. But during the 1970s intermediaries came to rely less intensively on asset management and more on other alternatives. This is reflected in the decline in commercial bank holdings of Treasury securities relative to the less marketable municipal securities during that period, a shift due to development of the money markets and, more recently, the futures markets.

The second method open to banks to deal with a cash shortfall is to acquire new liabilities or what has been called **liability management.** This method became more practical in the late 1960s and 1970s as regulators provided more types of liabilities not subject to interest rate regulations. Hence, over the last three decades banks evolved from relying chiefly upon asset management to relying more heavily on liability management. The option to turn to the money market to satisfy cash outflows is simply the option to borrow short-term funds to satisfy cash drains. During the late 1960s and the 1970s, the money markets developed into efficient sources of very short-term borrowing and lending. Financial intermediaries are able to borrow large amounts of funds with maturities as short as one day through federal funds and repurchase agreements. The risk an intermediary bears in relying on the money market, as opposed to its own holdings of liquid

Asset management refers to the process of managing funding risk by maintaining inventories of highly liquid assets.

Liability management refers to the process of managing funding risk by obtaining funds in the money markets when needed.

assets, is that the cost of obtaining funds in the money market may be high at times when cash flows are least favorable. The advantage of this liability as opposed to asset management is that there is no ongoing opportunity cost of investing in low return assets. The choice between the two alternatives depends upon one's assessment of the relative costs.

In the last decade new ways for banks to manage their funding risk have developed. One method is to *hedge* risks in the financial futures markets; another is to utilize interest rate *swaps*. We have already discussed financial futures in Chapter 9. We will take up swaps in Chapter 20 and futures and options markets again in Chapter 21. But let us briefly review how a hedge can be constructed with Treasury bill futures to deal with funding risk. Suppose a financial intermediary is concerned that there will be a net cash outflow of say $5 million in four weeks. If the manager of the intermediary waits to see whether it develops and finds that it does, he or she will have to borrow the $5 million in the money market and pay the going interest rate four weeks from now, whatever that may be. Also suppose the manager observes that the current interest rate is 9.65 percent and is concerned that this rate will increase. The manager can go to the futures market in Treasury bills and sell a $5 million futures contract to be delivered four weeks later. This means he or she contracts today to deliver a Treasury bill at a prespecified price or yield four weeks later. Now suppose that interest rates do increase above the current 9.65 percent, so that it becomes more expensive to borrow funds when needed. At the same time, this rise in interest rates will mean a fall in the price of Treasury bills. Therefore, when the Treasury bill futures contract matures, it will be possible to buy a Treasury bill and sell it at the contract price for a profit. In a **perfect hedge,** the profit on the Treasury bill futures contract will offset the increase in the cost of borrowing in the money market. If, on the other hand, interest rates go down (and prices of bills go up), there will be a loss on the futures contract, but it will be offset by the reduced cost of borrowing in the money market. In this way, the financial intermediary is able to hedge its risk of future changes in interest rates.

Perfect hedges are hedges where all the risk being hedged can be eliminated.

Even before futures markets developed it was possible to construct such a hedge. The manager in the example could hedge by borrowing (the same as selling short) a 3-month Treasury bill and simultaneously selling it, then after 4 weeks he or she would buy a Treasury bill with the same maturity date. If interest rates corresponding to that maturity rose so that the price of the bills fell, the manager would profit from the transaction and thereby offset the increase in the cost of borrowing. If rates fell, he or she would lose on the short-sale transaction, but the cost of borrowing would fall to offset it. The difficulty with this short-sale procedure for hedging is that it is often more cumbersome and costly than using an organized futures market. Hence the attraction of the futures market is that it makes hedging behavior easier.

Banks have been particularly interested in finding efficient ways to manage funding risk as a result of the increased volatility of interest rates during the late 1970s and early 1980s. This led, in part, to the development of financial futures markets and to the growth of swaps.

PROFITABILITY AND VALUATION OF FINANCIAL INTERMEDIARIES

Now we can turn our attention to an assessment of the performance of commercial banks. First we will examine the recent history of bank profitability. We want to understand how profitable banks have been in the first half of the 1980s and to determine the trends in bank profitability. Then we will consider the problem of valuing commercial banks and, implicitly, other types of financial intermediaries. We will see how some simpler types of financial intermediaries, open- and closed-end funds, are valued, then examine evidence on the forces affecting bank stock prices.

PROFITABILITY OF COMMERCIAL BANKS IN THE 1980s

Table 18–4 presents data that tell an interesting story about the performance of the commercial banking industry in the early 1980s. The first two lines in this table report gross interest income and expense for insured banks. Notice that both

TABLE 18–4
Income and expense as a percent of average net assets for all insured commercial banks, 1981–1985.[1]

Item	1981	1982	1983	1984	1985
Gross interest income	11.93	11.36	9.63	10.23	9.39
Gross interest expense	8.77	8.07	6.38	6.97	6.03
Net interest margin	3.17	3.28	3.25	3.26	3.36
Noninterest income	0.90	0.96	1.03	1.19	1.31
Loss provision	0.26	0.40	0.47	0.57	0.66
Other noninterest expense	2.77	2.93	2.96	3.05	3.17
Securities gains (losses)	0.08	0.06	.00	0.01	0.06
Income before tax	0.96	0.85	0.85	0.83	0.90
Taxes[2]	0.20	0.14	0.18	0.19	0.21
Extraordinary items	0.00	0.00	0.00	0.01	0.01
Net income	0.76	0.71	0.67	0.64	0.70
Cash dividends declared	0.30	0.31	0.33	0.32	0.33
Net retained earnings	0.46	0.40	0.34	0.33	0.37
MEMO: Net interest margin, taxable equivalent[3]	3.53	3.66	3.60	3.73	3.88

[1]Assets are fully consolidated and net of loss reserves. Data are based on averages for call dates in December of the preceding year and in June and December of the current year. In 1984 data are based on averages for call dates at the beginning and end of the year only.

[2]Includes all taxes estimated to be due on income, extraordinary gains, and security gains.

[3]For each bank with profits before tax greater than zero, income from state and local obligations was increased by $[t(1 - t)]$ times the lesser of profits before tax or interest earned on state and local obligations (t is the marginal federal income tax rate). This adjustment approximates the equivalent pretax return on state and local obligations.

Source: Federal Reserve Bulletin, September, 1986.

FIGURE 18–3
Loan loss provisions at commercial banks.

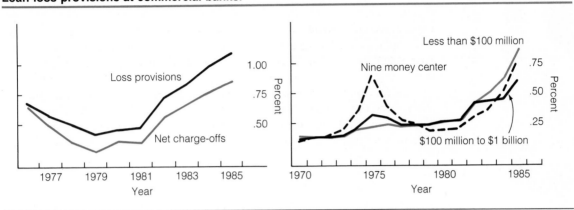

Source: Federal Reserve Bulletin, September, 1986.

were generally declining throughout this period, though there was an increase in 1984, because market interest rates hit their peak in 1981 and declined throughout most of this period. By contrast, net interest margin was increasing during most of this period, though the change was not particularly dramatic. The next two lines in the table document some important changes in the performance of commercial banks. First, noninterest or fee income was increasing. Most commercial banks are placing a significant emphasis on generating a greater portion of total income from fees for services. The data in Table 18–4 show there has actually been an improvement in this area throughout the last five years. However, at the same time, loss provisions from bad loans were increasing. In fact, the increase in loan-loss provisions from 1981 to 1985 is almost identical to the increase in fee income, so that these two items offset each other. In addition, other noninterest or operating expenses have been increasing as banks have modernized their operations to face an increasingly competitive market. The result has been that net income has declined somewhat during this period.

It is particularly interesting to look more closely at loan losses experienced by commercial banks. The loan-loss provisions shown in Table 18–4 represent current revenues commercial banks have diverted from profits to raise or replenish their reserves for loans and lease losses. A closely related balance sheet item, called **loan-loss reserves,** is not shown in Table 18–4. Regulation requires that it be maintained at a level adequate to absorb anticipated losses and not be allowed to drop below zero when bad loans are charged against it. In recent years banks' loan-loss provisions appear to be closely related to their actual charge-offs or actual losses incurred. Both of these items are shown in panel A of Figure 18–3 from 1977 to 1985: both charge-offs and loss provisions began increasing in 1979 and continued to increase throughout this period. Panel B of Figure 18–3 shows the level of loan-loss provisions as a percent of assets for banks in different size

Loan-loss reserves are established to cover losses from future defaults on loans.

classes. The data indicate that banks of all sizes have experienced recent increases in losses. By contrast, loan losses increased principally at money center banks during the recession of 1974–75 but did not spread to smaller banks to a great extent. However, small banks have had the highest losses in the 1980s, largely because they tend to be heavily concentrated in agricultural and, to a lesser extent, energy lending, sectors of the economy that have performed quite poorly in the 1980s.

Return on assets and return on equity for banks in different size classes are shown in Table 18–5. Figure 18–4 shows a longer historical picture of returns on assets for banks in three size classes. The data indicate that banks reached a peak of return on assets in 1979, with performance deteriorating ever since. Of the three size classes, the money center banks have the lowest return on assets while the highest return on assets is generated by banks in the $100 million to $1 billion size range. The large banks other than the money center banks had particularly poor performance in 1983 and 1984. These numbers are strongly influenced by the failure of Continental Illinois in 1983. Continental returned to profitability in 1985, leading to a significant rebound in the return on assets for this entire group of banks. The difference between the return on assets and the return on equity

TABLE 18–5
Profit rates for all insured commercial banks, 1981–1985.

Percent

Type of Return and Size of Bank[1]	1981	1982	1983	1984	1985
Return on assets[2]					
All banks	.76	.71	.67	.64	.70
Less than $100 million	1.14	1.07	.96	.81	.70
$100 million to $1 billion	.91	.84	.84	.88	.84
$1 billion or more					
Money center banks	.53	.53	.54	.52	.45
Others	.66	.60	.54	.53	.77
Return on equity[3]					
All banks	13.09	12.10	11.24	10.60	11.33
Less than $100 million	13.39	12.45	11.12	9.49	8.20
$100 million to $1 billion	12.78	11.74	11.86	12.40	11.71
$1 billion or more					
Money center banks	13.57	13.27	12.57	11.42	9.61
Others	12.80	11.42	10.15	9.66	13.69

[1]Size categories are based on fully consolidated assets at year-end.

[2]Net income as a percent of fully consolidated net assets. Data are based on averages for call dates in December of the preceding year and in June and December of the current year. In 1984 data are based on averages for call dates at the beginning and end of the year only.

[3]Net income as a percent of average equity capital. Data are based on averages for call dates in December of the preceding year and in June and December of the current year. In 1984 data are based on averages for call dates at the beginning and end of the year only.

Source: Federal Reserve Bulletin, September, 1986.

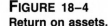

FIGURE 18–4
Return on assets.

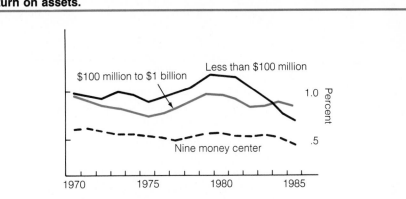

Source: Federal Reserve Bulletin, September 1986.

across size groups shown in Table 18–5 is in part accounted for by the differing degrees of leverage across these groups. Small banks tend to be less levered than large banks. As a result, small banks will have lower return on equity for an equivalent return on assets than larger banks.

Another way to evaluate the performance of commercial banks is to examine their price-earnings ratio, a measure that tells us how much potential for future profitability the market places on commercial banks. That is, a high price-earnings ratio suggests the market has a high degree of confidence that earnings will increase significantly in the future, while a low price-earnings ratio suggests just the opposite. Unfortunately, most commercial banks sell at relatively low price-earnings ratios. According to a recent study of bank profitability by the Federal Reserve Bank of New York, the 17 largest multinational bank holding companies had an average after-tax return on equity of 12.9 percent from 1980 to 1984.[1] This was very close to the 13.1 percent return on equity earned by diversified financial firms, that is, by financial firms other than banks. Yet the bank holding companies had an average price-earnings ratio over the same period of 6.1, while the diversified financial firms had an average multiple of 8.3. One interpretation is simply that the market did not have much confidence in the future of these banks, and another is that the market did not entirely believe that the reported earnings of these banks represented actual earnings. That is, the market may have expected large loan losses down the road. These data on price-earnings ratios suggest that we need to look more closely at how commercial banks are valued in the securities market.

---

[1]See *Recent Trends in Bank Profitability: A Staff Study*, Federal Reserve Bank of New York, (September 1986).

THE CASE OF OPEN- AND CLOSED-END FUNDS

There are a number of special problems encountered in trying to value a financial intermediary such as a commercial bank. An intermediary functions as a portfolio manager and derives revenues from the assets it holds in its portfolio. As a result, the value of the intermediary is dependent upon the value of those assets. As we have seen, these assets often have some special characteristics. By and large, they do not have efficient secondary markets in which they can be easily resold; thus no market sets the value of these outstanding assets. This is true of most loans held by commercial banks and many types of loans held by other institutions. In addition, intermediaries, particularly commmercial banks, might have special information about the assets or loans they hold that the outsider valuing the bank might not have. Most financial intermediaries are also highly regulated, and this has a material impact on the value of the intermediary. Finally, like nonfinancial firms in the economy, most intermediaries have other assets that are a necessary part of the firm's ongoing business. Many of these institutions, particularly commercial banks and savings and loans, have extensive plant and equipment to serve customers. As in valuing any other firm, these assets must be taken into account.

One type of financial intermediary where all of these problems are kept to a minimum is the investment company. These institutions are one of the simplest types of financial intermediaries because the service they provide is essentially one of diversification. Investment companies offer diversified portfolios of securities in which investors can buy shares. These funds are managed by individuals who seek to provide combinations of risk and return attractive to different groups of investors. For example, some funds emphasize more risky securities, while others do not. Some funds are bond funds in that the investments are only in bonds; some are municipal bond funds, which are attractive to high tax bracket investors; and some are money market funds, investing only in money market securities.

Two broad types of investment funds are of particular interest for the purpose of valuing intermediaries: the open-end fund and the closed-end fund. Both types of funds invest in marketable securities. In an open-end fund the fund's owners hold direct claims on the securities managed by the fund. An investor who cashes in his or her share of an **open-end fund** receives a pro rata share of the value of the fund's portfolio at the time of cashing in. In a **closed-end fund** the investor owns a share of the fund as a separate entity, and the fund owns the securities it manages. Closed-end funds therefore have a market value of their own as distinct from the value of the securities they manage. When a person buys into the fund or sells shares in the fund, the shares are exchanged at their market price shares, regardless of the prices of securities owned by the fund. The closed-end fund is similar to most other types of intermediaries in that it owns assets and individuals hold claims on the intermediary rather than directly on the assets. It is different in that the closed-end fund is not subject to the same kind of regulation as depository intermediaries. And the closed-end fund holds assets with active secondary markets, so that unlike other intermediaries, the market value of the assets can be readily determined. The closed-end fund therefore provides an opportunity to ex-

An **open-end fund** is an investment company where the fund owners have a direct claim on the assets in the fund rather than a claim on the legal entity of the fund itself.

A **closed-end fund** is an investment company where the fund owners have a claim on its equity as distinct from the assets owned by the fund.

amine the market's valuation of financial intermediaries, because it is possible to compare the value of the assets held by the closed-end fund directly with the market value of the fund itself.

It is interesting to observe that the value of a closed-end fund is not always the same as the value of the assets owned by that fund. Differences between the market value of the securities owned by the fund and the market value of the fund itself are referred to as **premiums** or **discounts.** The fund is said to be selling at a premium if the fund value exceeds the value of the securities in it. In this case, investors who wish to purchase shares in the fund must pay more than they would pay if they purchased those shares for themselves in the market. The fund is said to be selling at a discount if its value is less than the value of the securities in it. Investors can pay less than the value of the securities owned by the fund if they purchase shares in the fund.

A closed-end fund is selling at a **premium** when the market value of the assets in the fund is more than the value of the fund and at a **discount** when the assets are worth less than the fund.

At first glance one might suspect that, aside from potential difficulties surrounding the accounting procedures in these funds, there ought not be either premiums or discounts. That is, the value of a fund should be the same as the value of the assets it owns. But this is simply not the case. Closed-end funds sell at widely different premiums or discounts, with both substantial variation across funds at one time and in the premium or discount for individual funds at different times. This variability is illustrated in Table 18–6, which shows the discounts (positive sign) and premiums (negative sign) for a sample of funds from 1960 to 1975. The table indicates tremendous variability in the size of the premium or discount.

TABLE 18–6
Year-end discounts* for a sample of large closed-end funds from 1960 to 1975 (%).

ID no.	60	61	62	63	64	65	66	67	68	69	70	71	72	73	74	75
3	14	3	4	9	10	12	6	6	−10	−6	6	15	14	14	25	23
1	30	39	35	34	10	−5	−12	−77	−54	15	−37	−10	6	−26	9	−48
8	12	2	7	8	6	11	19	21	12	14	18	20	17	19	16	22
11	19	10	−1	3	6	7	11	−1	−14	−8	8	12	4	17	13	26
14	−1	−5	−4	−1	6	11	9	−16	−23	−16	−14	8	13	20	22	20
15	2	−23	−28	−13	−3	−2	−18	−19	−32	−51	−16	3	19	34	29	30
18	12	−6	3	6	0	8	12	11	−8	−12	−5	13	7	4	−4	4
16	−2	3	−2	2	10	2	−14	−33	−26	15	12	15	27	39	43	37
19	0	0	5	6	3	−6	0	3	−7	−4	3	14	4	8	10	−2
21	4	5	3	12	21	24	20	19	7	14	15	26	28	23	25	28
22	22	16	19	24	26	33	29	17	7	11	3	7	3	21	26	25
23	23	13	15	21	24	23	25	16	4	2	5	14	19	13	14	22
13†	E	E	34	15	32	27	32	9	−5	−6	−11	−7	8	31	43	16
Average	11	5	7	10	12	11	9	−3	−11	−2	−1	10	13	17	21	16

*Discount = (NAV − MV)/NAV where NAV is the net asset value of the fund, and MV is the market value of the fund's outstanding stock.

†E = fund not traded.

Source: Rex Thompson, "Information Content of Discounts and Premiums on Closed-End Fund Shares," *Journal of Financial Economics,* vol. 6 (1978), p. 158. Reprinted with permission.

THE TAKEOVER MOVEMENT IN CLOSED-END FUNDS

In 1986 closed-end funds began to attract quite a bit of attention from investors. Many of them began to look closely at ways they might generate a profit out of the fact that many closed-end funds were selling at substantial discounts. For example, Table 18–7 presents a listing of closed-end funds and their discounts that appeared in the March 16, 1987, issue of *Business Week.* The problem is it is not an easy task to actually capture the discounts listed in this table. A closed-end fund sells a limited number of shares in the fund and makes no commitment to repurchase them. Therefore, if you buy shares in a closed-end fund, you cannot sell them at the market value of the assets held by the fund unless the fund shares themselves are selling at the same value.

One possible way to capture the value of the discount is to convince the fund management to convert to an open-end fund. However, you cannot necessarily accomplish this simply by buying shares in the fund. However, you can do this if you mount a successful takeover attempt of a closed-end fund, and this is precisely what some investors have attempted. In fact, the *Business Week* article focused on a takeover attempt of the Japan Fund by the son of T. Boone Pickens, the famous corporate raider from Mesa Petroleum. On March 2, 1987, Tom Pickens, announced that he and his partners had acquired a 5.5 percent stake in the Japan Fund. If a raider can successfully take over a fund, he or she could convert it to an open-end fund and then sell interests to the fund for the market value of its assets. For any of the funds listed in Table 18–7 this would represent a sizable profit.

A takeover movement aimed at closed-end funds could potentially drive this form of organization out of existence. In such an action the market is saying it believes the closed-end form is inefficient for managing investors' assets. Whether this type of action can happen depends, in part, on the fund managers' ability to fight takeover attempts and protect their positions. This is an example of the market for corporate control. The managers of closed-end funds exercise some control over those funds, and investors who attempt a takeover are struggling to acquire that control.

The ability to take over banks, which are similar to closed-end funds in some respects, is extensively limited by government regulation. The McFadden Act, the Bank Holding Company statutes, and antitrust laws all combine to make bank takeovers very difficult. In 1986, First Interstate Corporation launched a takeover attempt of Bank America Corporation after Bank of America reported serious losses over several quarters. Under the applicable law, few other firms could have attempted that takeover. The bank holding company laws prohibited any nonfinancial firm from acquiring Bank of America, and California state law prohibited a U. S. bank chartered in another state from doing so. Virtually the only banks that could attempt such an acquisition were California banks and foreign banks, and even these would need the approval of the Board of Governors of the Federal Re-

There are at least four plausible explanations for these premiums and discounts. One possibility: there are sufficient tax considerations that there will be wide and variable differences between the fund value and the value of its assets. This argument relies on the idea that different capital gains occur in different funds because the gains are based on the prices at which the securities were previously acquired. These capital gains will be taxed when the fund shares are sold and the income realized. The magnitude of these unrealized capital gains might account for premiums and discounts. A second possibility is that the difference between the two values is a result of economies in diversifying the fund relative to the cost incurred by individuals. This argues that the value of the shares owned

serve. First Interstate eventually withdrew its offer, claiming that Bank of America's actions had decreased the attractiveness of the acquisition. However, the fact remains that it is very difficult for one bank to challenge a competing bank's management through a takeover. This may be one reason why bank price-earnings ratios are so low.

TABLE 18–7
Closed-end funds that sell at a big discount.

	Fund Assets ($Millions)	Price per Share Mar. 3	Discount from Net Asset Value Percent
Domestic Funds			
Baker Fentress	$397	45¾	18.2%
Gabelli Equity Trust	418	9½	9.1
Gen. Amer. Investors	307	20⅛	10.9
Lehman	859	16⅜	7.8
Liberty All-Star Equity	589	9½	17.7
Zweig	359	9⅝	8.8
Global Funds			
First Australia	$ 59	11⅝	15.4%
France	97	14¼	14.7
Israel Investors	50	25⅜	25.9
Italy	88	12	14.5
Japan	584	17¾	10.5
Mexico	103	4⅞	36.8
Scandinavia	63	9⅜	7.1
Worldwide Value	52	18¼	12.8

Data: Thomas J. Herzfeld Advisors Inc.
Source: *Business Week*, March 16, 1987, p. 113.

by the fund does not include the cost of acquiring them. The third possibility is that the fund value includes the capitalized value of its managers' skills. This will be a positive amount, and thus generate a premium, if the managers are believed to be able to outperform the market. It will be a negative amount, and lead to a discount, if the market believes they will fail to outperform the market, but will generate expenses in so doing. Finally, there is the possibility that the market is simply inefficient in appraising the value of funds and does not act on clear opportunities to trade profitably.

While no one has yet determined exactly what the answer is, some evidence indicates that closed-end funds that sell at discounts tend to generate higher returns than the market average, after adjustment for risk.[2] That is, at least for a time, one could devise simple rules for trading in the market, utilizing funds that sell at discounts and significantly outperform the market as a whole. This is consistent with either the tax argument, the diversification argument, or the inefficiency argument, though it seems unlikely that taxes and diversification can account for it. This conclusion suggests that either some kind of market inefficiency leads to premiums and discounts or that some significant factor determines the prices of risky assets that financial economists have not yet been able to include in their tests. The problem of understanding how intermediaries are valued remains an intriguing and important puzzle.

In the 1980s most closed-end funds have been selling at substantial discounts relative to the value of the assets in the funds. In fact, a number of funds have gone out of existence apparently because persistent discounts made this form of organization unattractive. One possible explanation for the large discounts is that investors perceive the open-end fund is a better form of organization. The deficiency in the closed-end fund is simply that investors cannot control the future actions of the fund managers—that is, there is an agency problem. Specifically, with a closed-end fund investors have given up their most effective tool in disciplining management, their right to take their money out at the market value of the assets in the fund.

VALUING COMMERCIAL BANKS

The case of closed- and open-end funds gives us some insight into how to value more complicated types of financial intermediaries such as commercial banks. A commercial bank is like a closed-end fund. Moreover, commercial banks have had some of the same difficulties as closed-end funds. As we have seen, commercial banks tend to sell at a rather low multiple of their annual earnings or, put another way, their price-earnings ratio tends to be rather low.

One approach to the valuation of commercial banks is to treat the stock in banks just like the stock in any other type of company, at least from a finance point of view (see Chapter 3). That is, we could attempt to explain the rate of return on bank stocks as a function of the return on a diversified portfolio of common stocks plus other factors that might capture systematic risks in the economy. Of particular importance for banks and other portfolio lenders, such as savings and loans, is the level of interest rates. To the extent that commercial banks have balance sheets not perfectly term matched (that is, the maturity of their assets differs from the maturity of their liabilities), they will be exposed to interest rate risk or the risk of unexpected changes in inflation that will alter the economic values of their assets and liabilities.

---

[2]See Rex Thompson, "The Information Content of Discounts and Premiums on Closed-End Fund Shares," *Journal of Financial Economics,* (June 1978), pp. 151–86.

Some interesting empirical analysis of the sensitivity of bank stock returns to the return on a market portfolio and various interest rates has been carried out by Mark Flannery and Christopher James.[3] They collected data on the weekly rates of return on a sample of publicly traded bank stocks from January 1, 1976, until November 1, 1981. The also collected weekly data on three types of interest rates: the return on 8-percent coupon certificates of the Government National Mortgage Association (R_{GNMA}), the return on 7-year Treasury bonds (R_{G7}), and the return on 1-year Treasury bills (R_{TB}). They then filtered the interest rate data so that the interest rate series contained an estimate of only the unexpected changes in interest rates. These unexpected changes in interest rates as well as returns on a market portfolio were used in a time series regression equation designed to explain the return on a portfolio constructed from the bank stocks. Flannery and James estimated the following equation:

$$R_t = \beta_o + \beta_m R_{mt} + \beta_i R_{it} + \epsilon_t ,$$

where

R_t = the holding period return over the period ending at time t,

R_{mt} = the holding period return on an equally weighted portfolio of common stocks over the period ending at time t,

R_{It} = one of the three interest rates defined above

β_m, β_i = the slope coefficients estimated in the regression

β_o = the intercept estimated in the regression

ϵ_t = the error term in the regression.

The results of their empirical analysis are shown in Table 18–8. The first column in the table identifies the interest rate series used in the regression. The second column presents the estimated value of the intercept in the regression and the standard deviation or standard error of that estimated coefficient. The third and fourth columns present the estimated values and standard errors of the coefficients on the market portfolio and the interest rate series. The final two columns are measures of statistical properties of the regression equations. In general we can conclude that when an estimated coefficient is more than twice the size of its standard error, it is reasonable to accept the hypothesis that the true value of the coefficient is different from zero. In this case we can conclude that, since each of the three interest rate coefficients is more than twice its standard error, then bank stocks are influenced by unexpected changes in interest rates, after the effect of the return on the market portfolio on the bank stocks is accounted for.

Flannery and James went on to estimate whether measures of the degree of sensitivity of bank stock returns to interest rates (the β_i's) were dependent upon

[3]See Mark J. Flannery and Christopher M. James, "The Effect of Interest Rate Changes on the Common Stock Returns of Financial Institutions," *Journal of Finance*, 39 (September 1984), pp. 1141–53.

the extent of the maturity mismatch on the books of the individual banks. In this case, rather than estimating a regression using times series of returns for a portfolio of bank stocks, they estimated a regression across the banks using measures of the extent of maturity or term mismatch averaged over time. A measure of the maturity mismatch was constructed by subtracting the dollar value of liabilities subject to repricing within one year from the dollar value of assets subject to repricing within the same period. This was called the *short position*. Then, for each bank in the sample, this measure of the short position was divided by the total market value of equity for that bank, where both were averaged over the entire sample period. Next, the equation described above was estimated for each of the individual banks in the sample so there would be a measure of the interest-rate sensitivity of the bank stock return for each bank, β_i. Then the coefficient estimated in this regression pertaining to the interest rate, β_i, was used as the dependent variable in a regression on the ratio of the short variable to the market value of equity *(MV)*. This procedure determines whether the sensitivity of bank stock prices to interest rates is in turn dependent on the extent of term mismatch for that particular bank. The results from estimating this regression are presented in Table 18–9. Once again, each of the estimated coefficients, for each of the three interest rates, is more than twice its standard error, and each coefficient is negative. This means as the volume of short-term liabilities relative to assets increases, the sensitivity of bank stock returns to unanticipated interest rate changes declines.

The evidence developed by Flannery and James on the factors influencing returns on banks stocks is some of the first empirical work to analyze returns to financial firms with the same empirical tools used in finance to analyze nonfinancial firms. However, we still know very little about how and why bank stocks are valued, and we have no definitive answer to the question of why bank price-earnings ratios are so low. Moreover, there are nearly 14,000 commercial banks

TABLE 18–8
Estimates of interest rate sensitivity for a portfolio of commercial bank stocks[a]. $\tilde{R}_t = \beta_0 + \beta_m \tilde{R}_{mt} + \beta_i \tilde{R}_{it} + \epsilon_t$

Index[b,c]	β_0	β_m	β_i	$\bar{R}^2$	Durbin-Watson Statistic
R_{GNMA}	0.002	0.556	0.133	0.57	1.74
	(0.001)	(0.030)	(0.038)		
R_{G7}	0.002	0.560	0.069	0.56	1.73
	(0.001)	(0.031)	(0.027)		
R_{TB}	0.001	0.555	0.515	0.57	1.73
	(0.001)	(0.031)	(0.160)		

[a]Estimated using weekly data for the period January 1, 1976, to November 1981, $N = 302$.
[b]Interest rate series are the residuals of the AR(3) models.
[c]Standard errors are in parentheses.

TABLE 18–9
Cross-section results.[a,b] $\beta_{ij} = \alpha_0 + \alpha_1 \left(\dfrac{\text{Short}}{MV} \right)_j + \tilde{\omega}_j$

Dependent Variable	α_0	α_1	$\bar{R}^2$	F-statistic
β_{GNMA}	0.143	−0.031	0.30	25.17
	(0.018)	(0.006)		
β_{G7}	0.054	−0.019	0.25	19.10
	(0.013)	(0.004)		
β_{TB}	0.538	−0.124	0.25	19.43
	(0.083)	(0.028)		

[a]Standard errors are in parentheses.
[b]Estimated using cross-sectional data for 67 banks.

in the United States, and only a few of those have publicly traded shares with active trading. Therefore, few banks can be analyzed with the tools empirical of modern finance.

SUMMARY

This chapter focused on three important aspects of the banking business: first, the nature of the basic assets and liabilities of commercial banks as well as their principal off-balance-sheet activities; second, risk management within commercial banks, both credit risk and funding risk; and third, recent trends in the profitability of commercial banks and how banks are valued in the financial markets.

An examination of the balance sheets of commercial banks shows that the largest component of bank loans is business or commercial and industrial loans, followed by mortgage loans. Banks' investments consist largely of holdings of Treasury and municipal debt instruments. Banks invest in Treasuries when they want highly liquid investments and in municipals when they want tax-sheltered income. Banks finance their loans and investments principally with deposit accounts. The most important source of deposits in the 1980s is the money market deposit account and savings and time deposits. Various types of transaction accounts, including demand deposits, are second in importance.

Most commercial and industrial loans are short rather than long term, and most short-term loans are at fixed rates. On the other hand, the vast majority of the longer term loans are made at floating rates tied to the prime interest rate or some market rate. A majority of loans are made under loan commitments of one kind or another, although small loans are less likely to be made under commitments than are large loans.

Off-balance-sheet financing is a term used to refer to a wide variety of bank activities, including loan commitments and securitization of assets on the balance sheets of commercial banks. Securitization has been of interest to commercial banks as a device to improve their ratios of capital to assets. This is particularly true for banks with serious capital deficiencies. In the early 1980s the mortgage market had been extensively securitized. By 1986, securitization was just beginning to develop for many types of consumer receivables, such as auto loans and credit card receivables. Securitization had progressed the farthest with auto loans. If securitization becomes widespread, it could radically change the nature of the banking business.

Risk management in commercial banks can be divided into two broad categories: default risk and funding risk. Banks take essentially two approaches toward default risk. On the one hand, they try to limit the risk of default by screening borrowers and writing and monitoring contracts that minimize the chance of default and the loss if a default occurs. On the other, they try to price default risk efficiently so that they are properly compensated for the risk they take on.

Banks have historically taken essentially two approaches to managing funding risk. The principal method in the 1960s and early 1970s was asset management, which involved the maintenance of a portfolio of highly liquid investments that could be liquidated when necessary in order to satisfy the demand for additional funds. The alternative, liability management, simply entails going to the money markets to obtain new funds as they are needed. The problem banks faced in this area until very recently is that the regulators limited their access to money markets by imposing interest rate and other restrictions on the funds they could raise. Gradually, the regulators have deregulated banks' sources of funds sufficiently to make liability management a viable alternative to asset management. More recently, banks have also turned to the futures markets as a tool for managing funding risk and very recently to the new market for interest rate swaps.

Banks have had difficulties in maintaining profitability during the 1980s. Bank return on assets has suffered from significant increases in loan losses throughout the 1980s, fully offsetting increases in fee income banks have generated during this period. Moreover, banks of all sizes have experienced these difficulties. The large money center banks have the lowest return on assets of all major size classes. Very small banks have also had difficulties due to poor performance of the agricultural sector of the economy. In addition, the relatively poor performance of banks recently does not appear to be taken as an aberration in the securities markets, since bank stocks trade at relatively low price-earnings ratios compared with stocks of other types of firms.

An examination of open- and closed-end mutual funds can aid understanding the valuation of commercial banks and other financial intermediaries. Open- and closed-end funds are really simplified types of financial intermediaries. Closed-end funds often sell at premiums and discounts relative to the value of the assets in those funds, and it is not easy to explain these premiums and discounts. It is difficult to explain premiums and discounts on closed-end funds, where the value of assets is observable. It is even more difficult to value much more complicated intermediaries like commercial banks, where most of the assets owned by commercial banks have no ready market value.

The available empirical evidence on the pricing of bank stocks indicates that rates of return on bank stocks are sensitive to the return on the market as a whole, as well as unanticipated changes in interest rates. Moreover, the evidence indicates that the larger the term or maturity mismatch on the books of a bank, the greater the interest rate sensitivity of that bank's stock. While this may not seem to be very surprising, it has proven to be very difficult to make more definitive statements about the determinants of bank stock returns.

QUESTIONS

1. Describe the patterns in the early 1980s in the composition of bank assets and liabilities. What percentage of bank assets were in loans of various types? How did this percentage change over time? Continue this for other items on bank balance sheets.
2. Of what significance is the prime interest rate in modern pricing of bank loans? How has the use of the prime rate changed over time?
3. What are lines of credit and revolving credit agreements? How important are they in bank lending in the 1980s?
4. Suppose you are given the following information about the costs incurred by a bank: the cost of funds is 6 percent; operating costs are 150 basis points; the cost of equity capital is 18 percent, and the bank is leveraged 95 percent. How would you price a loan to a business borrower where the expected losses for borrowers of this risk class were 75 basis points?
5. Distinguish between asset and liability management. Describe the history of how and why banks have moved from one system to another.
6. Analyze why a bank might prefer interest rate swaps to hedging funding risks in the futures markets.
7. Explain the basic trends in bank profitability in the 1980s. How has the relative importance of interest income versus fee income changed over this period?
8. How have banks of different size performed during the 1980s in both return on assets and return on equity? How can the differences in performance be explained?
9. What are the fundamental difficulties involved in valuing a financial intermediary? What are closed-end funds? Why do they provide an interesting opportunity to explore how financial intermediaries are valued by the market?
10. Explain how intermediaries can use either asset or liability management to handle their liquidity problem.

REFERENCES

Brady, Thomas F. "Changes in Loan Pricing and Business Lending at Commercial Banks," *Federal Reserve Bulletin,* (January 1985), pp. 1–13.

Campbell, Tim S. "A Model of the Market for Lines of Credit," *Journal of Finance,* (March 1978).

Danker, Deborah J. and Mary M. McLaughlin. "Profitability of U.S.-Chartered Insured Commercial Banks in 1985," *Federal Reserve Bulletin,* (October 1986), pp. 618–26.

Flannery, Mark J. and Christopher M. James. "The Effect of Interest Rate Changes on the Common Stock Returns of Financial Institutions," *Journal of Finance,* 39 (September 1984), pp. 1141–53.

Flannery, Mark J. and Christopher M. James. "Market Evidence on the Effective Maturity of Bank Assets and Liabilities," *Journal of Money, Credit and Banking,* (November 1984), pp. 435–45.

Horvitz, Paul M. "Securitization and Bank Capital: An Essay on Two Unrelated Topics," *Journal of Banking and Finance,* (1987).

Thompson, Rex. "The Information Content of Discounts and Premiums on Closed-End Fund Shares," *Journal of Financial Economics,* (June 1978), pp. 151–86.

Recent Trends in Bank Profitability: A Staff Study, Federal Reserve Bank of New York, (September 1986).

19

*M*ORTGAGE FINANCE

Mortgage finance is on the forefront of the revolution occurring in the financial services industry. This revolution is transforming a market once dominated by financial intermediaries, an intermedi- ated market, into what might become an over-the-counter or an auction market. It is the most important example of securitization. You will recall that **securitization** refers to the transformation of assets that once had no secondary market into tradable securities with active secondary markets. Individual mortgages are now combined into portfolios called *pools,* which then market securities. Whereas the individual mortgage is a highly unique asset, mortgage pools are quite homogeneous and subject to the standardization necessary for a secondary market to function.

Securitization represents a radical change in the way the mortgage finance system works. This revolution threatens the viability of many institutions that have been traditional mortgage lenders, specifically savings and loans, historically the mainstay of the mortgage finance business. This specialized class of financial intermediaries was created and protected by federal legislation in order to compel them to function almost exclusively as mortgage lenders. Their traditional method of operation was to fund the acquisition of mortgages by issuing largely short-term deposit liabilities to consumers. With the advent of securitization of mortgages, their way of doing business has been radically altered. Now other, nontraditional mortgage lenders have perceived an opportunity to enter the mortgage finance industry. In this chapter we will examine how this changing mortgage finance system works and the process of securitization in the mortgage finance industry. ■

THE RESIDENTIAL MORTGAGE MARKET IN THE 1970s AND 1980s

In order to understand how the mortgage industry is changing we need to see how the mortgage market has functioned in recent years. The best place to start is with a clear understanding of what mortgages actually finance. It is easy to get the impression that people take out home mortgage loans almost exclusively for the purpose of acquiring homes. This is simply not the case. In fact, it is necessary to look back to the late 1960s to find a time when this was the case. Figure 19–1 shows the volume of increases in mortgage debt on one- to four-family units and new construction of such units from 1948 to 1985. The figure shows quite a striking change. In the early part of the postwar era mortgage debt was consistently less than the volume of new construction. During this period mortgage debt was used to finance the acquisition of new housing. But by the early 1970s the volume of new mortgage financing outstripped the increase in new residential property. Mortgage debt was being used for all sorts of purposes from financing education to funding vacations. It had become a source of consumer financing.

This change did not occur simply because the United States emerged from a time of tremendous unsatisfied demand for housing, as was the case in the early 1950s, but also because of a significant increase in the value of real property, coupled with a decline in the real cost of existing mortgages. In other words, in the 1970s residential property owners found that the market value of their property increased while their mortgage payments remained fixed. The fixed terms of the mortgage at interest rates which proved, with hindsight, to be quite low meant that the real cost of the mortgage was declining. As a result, homeowners chose to borrow against the increased value of their property and use the funds to finance other expenditures. For most individuals in the 1970s, their homes turned out to be the best investment they ever made. Figure 19–1 shows the extent to which they have borrowed against that value.

INTERMEDIARIES IN THE MORTGAGE FINANCE INDUSTRY

What has been good for the borrower has not necessarily been good for either the ultimate supplier of funds or for private institutions that act as intermediaries between borrowers and lenders. With the advent of high inflation rates in the 1970s, to a large degree unanticipated, wealth was transfered from lenders to borrowers. Those who acquired mortgage debt at fixed rates early in the inflationary process benefitted, while those who funded mortgages were hurt. As inflation declined in the early 1980s, financial intermediaries continued to experience financial difficulties resulting from high default rates on mortgages and poor credit quality of many loans. To understand the nature of the difficulties we have to look closely at the industry that funds mortgages in the United States.

The single most important type of institution originating and investing in home mortgages is the savings and loan. In addition, commercial banks, mutual savings banks, insurance companies, mortgage bankers, and a number of govern-

FIGURE 19–1

Residential mortgage debt and construction, annually, 1950–51; seasonally adjusted annual rates, quarterly, 1952.

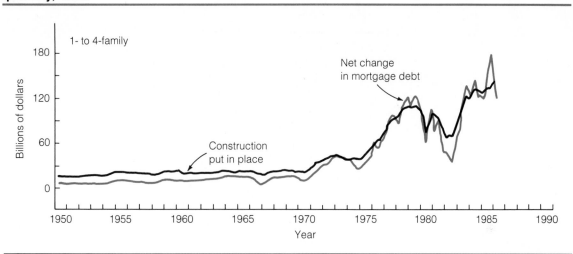

Source: Federal Reserve Chart Book, 1986 annual.

mental and quasi-governmental institutions participate in the market in one capacity or another. Some of these institutions specialize in particular parts of the mortgage market. For example, life insurance companies invest heavily in commercial mortgages but have a relatively small investment in mortgages for single-family residential property. Some other participants, such as mortgage bankers, are not **portfolio lenders**—that is, they do not maintain a portfolio which is invested in mortgages. Instead, mortgage bankers function more as dealers than as financial intermediaries. They acquire mortgages, which are held in inventory until they can be resold in the secondary market. On the other hand, savings and loans have historically served a different role from insurance companies or mortgage bankers. They have acted as portfolio lenders, and most of their funding has gone into single-family dwellings rather than commercial real estate.

> **Portfolio lenders** acquire mortgages and hold them as long-term investments.

The total amount of single family (one- to four-family) home mortgage debt held by each type of institution from 1971 to 1985 is shown in Figure 19–2. The figure shows the largest portion of the total volume of outstanding home mortgages was held by savings and loans, and commercial banks ranked second. But commercial banks have a total portfolio, including nonmortgage loans, that is much more diversified than the portfolio of savings and loans. Savings and loans, on the other hand, have historically been constrained by regulation to invest almost exclusively in residential mortgages. Only since 1982, with the passage of the Garn-St Germain Act, have savings and loans been allowed to diversify to any great extent.

FIGURE 19–2
Residential mortgage debt by type of lender; amount outstanding, end of quarter.

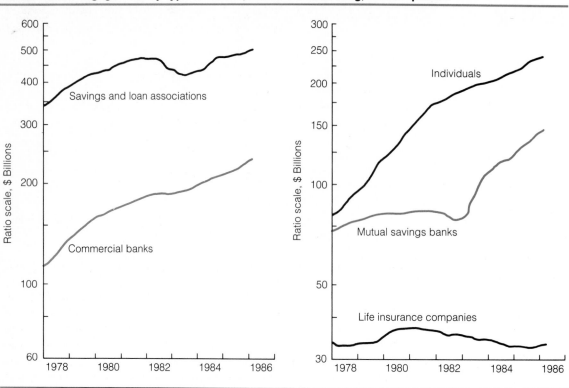

Source: Federal Reserve Chart Book, January 1986.

THE ROLE OF THE REGULATORY SYSTEM FOR SAVINGS AND LOANS

In order to understand how and why the securitization of the residential mortgage industry represents such a dramatic change, it is necessary to know how the regulatory system for savings and loans operated before the Garn-St Germain Act of 1982, which eliminated much of the regulatory structure that had compelled savings and loans to concentrate almost exclusively on residential mortgage lending.

The Federal Home Loan Bank Board (FHLBB) is the federal regulator of the savings and loan industry, while the Federal Savings and Loan Insurance Corporation (FSLIC) is the government insurance corporation for deposits in savings and loans.

The federal regulator of savings and loans is the **Federal Home Loan Bank Board (FHLBB),** and the federal insurer is the **Federal Savings and Loan Insurance Corporation (FSLIC).** Like commercial banks, savings and loans can be chartered and regulated by the state in which they operate, or they can be federally chartered and regulated. Of the roughly 3,200 savings and loans in operation in 1985, slightly less than 44 percent were federally chartered. More than 90 percent were insured by the FSLIC, and these insured institutions account for 98 percent of all deposits.

While many of the regulations imposed upon savings and loans are nearly identical to similar regulations for commercial banks, there are also some very important differences. These differences, motivated by the long-standing intent of the federal government to support housing finance, boil down to the following five points.

1. Savings and loans were required to place all but a small portion of their assets into residential mortgages.
2. Savings and loans were authorized to pay higher interest rates (historically ranging up to one-half of 1 percent) than commercial banks on deposit accounts.
3. The FHLBB has provided a continuing source of funds to savings and loans in the form of advances. A comparable source of funds is not available to commercial banks.
4. The Congress granted special tax treatment to savings and loans.
5. The FHLBB restricted the types of mortgage contracts savings and loans could offer.

The requirement that savings and loans invest only in residential mortgages, aside from some holdings of liquid assets such as Treasury bills, is one of the most direct steps taken by the government to support housing construction. This was accomplished both through direct restrictions on permissible nonmortgage investments and through significant tax advantages to institutions with portfolios concentrated in qualifying mortgage investments. The restrictions limiting investments in nonmortgage assets were relaxed in the Garn-St Germain Act. The tax advantages of a portfolio concentrated in mortgages remain largely intact. These restrictions have meant that roughly 80 percent of all savings and loan assets have been and still are invested in mortgages.

By establishing a lender restricted to investing almost exclusively in mortgages, it was hoped more funds would flow into home mortgages than would otherwise be the case. But the problem with this kind of restriction is that a private institution so constrained is unlikely to be able to compete effectively in the long run with institutions not so restricted. In order to offset this disadvantage, as well as the fact that, unlike commercial banks, saving and loans have historically been unable to offer demand deposits, Congress permitted savings and loans to pay higher interest rates than banks on comparable regulated deposit accounts.

Advances are loans from the Federal Home Loan Bank Board to savings and loans.

The FHLBB has come to assume a supportive role with savings and loans that the bank regulatory agencies do not provide for commercial banks. The FHLBB is a direct supplier of funds to savings and loans through **advances.** These advances have come to represent a sizable portion of the total source of funds for savings and loans. The Federal Reserve provides a service which is similar in some respect through what is called the *discount window*. But loans extended to commercial banks in this way are intended as temporary sources of funds to be used only when a bank has a short-term liquidity problem. Continued reliance on the discount window is a sign of trouble which attracts bank examiners, but this has not been true with use of advances by savings and loans. Advances have been a more permanent source of funds and therefore, in effect, a way of providing federal support for mortgage loans. Total Fed advances were $1.318 billion in December 1985, while total FHLBB advances were $73.888 billion in the same month. As part of the Garn-St Germain Act, savings and loans were given access to loans through the Federal Reserve discount window. However, this is a source of short-term funding in case of liquidity problems only, and it is not comparable to FHLBB advances.

Savings and loans are also regulated through the tax laws. Until the early 1960s savings and loans as well as other thrift institutions, excluding commercial banks, had little need for tax avoidance schemes because other techniques were successful in avoiding almost all taxes. Savings and loans and mutual savings banks were not subject to the federal corporate income tax until 1952. From 1952 until 1962 these institutions were able to avoid almost all federal income taxes through liberal use of bad-debt reserves. **Bad-debt reserves** represent funds set aside to cover possible defauts on loans. Income is tax deductible when it is placed in the bad-debt reserve rather than when a bad debt is actually realized. Therefore, by diverting funds to bad-debt reserves these institutions were able to offset almost all taxable income.

Bad-debt reserves represent funds set aside to cover possible defaults on loans.

Initial revisions in the tax laws pertaining to the deductibility of these expenses were made in 1962, and more extensive revisions were made in the Revenue Act of 1969. The changes incorporated in these acts were significant, leading to a sizable increase in the effective tax rates on savings and loans. The effective tax rate for savings and loans rose from approximately 0.4 percent in 1962 to approximately 24.8 percent in 1974. The 1979 Act provided for a more uniform system of taxation for all financial institutions, particularly with regard to bad-debt reserves. Both the 1962 and 1969 laws defined a number of allowable procedures for computing bad-debt reserves which might be chosen by any financial intermediary and left one additional method open only to savings and loans and mutual savings banks. But the law set requirements for use of this method. Saving and loans must have 82 percent of their assets and mutual savings banks 72 percent in residential mortgages, cash, government securities, and passbook loans. These restrictions were instituted in 1962 and liberalized in the 1969 law so that an institution which had at least 60 percent of its assets in these investments could deduct a smaller percent of its income using the percentage of income method. The income method allows an institution to transfer up to 40 percent of annual income as of 1979 to bad-debt reserves thereby reducing taxable income. This generally allows greater deductions than other methods allowed by the IRS.

The last unique feature of this regulatory system is that the FHLBB restricted the types of mortgages federally chartered savings and loans could offer, and state regulators restricted the allowable contracts for state-chartered savings and loans. It is somewhat difficult to pin down the exact motive for such a restriction. In part it is motivated by a desire to control the risk assumed by insured institutions, and in part it is designed to prevent exploitation of unwary consumers. Specifically, savings and loans were allowed to invest solely in fixed rate mortgages. In 1981, the FHLBB eliminated these restrictions, and since then a number of alternative mortgages have become popular in the marketplace.

PROBLEMS WITH THE SAVINGS AND LOAN REGULATORY SYSTEM

The basic problem historically faced by savings and loans is that they borrowed short and lent long. That is, the average maturity of their loans has been considerably longer than the average maturity of their deposit liabilities. Savings and loans have historically performed the task of intermediating across time. When they extend mortgage loans with maturities of 30 years at a fixed interest rate, they are making a commitment to provide insurance to the borrower against future changes in interest rates. If the lender's liabilities had the same maturity as its mortgage loans, then it would bear no risk in providing that insurance. But when its funds are obtained with an average maturity substantially shorter than the maturity of its loans, it bears the risk that the cost of its funds will increase while the return on its mortgages remains unchanged. In a time when inflation is accelerating, short-term interest rates will tend to increase and the rates of return on existing long-term mortgages will remain unchanged. If this kind of development persists long enough, it can mean disaster for financial intermediaries that invest almost exclusively in fixed interest rate mortgage loans.

It is precisely this problem which afflicted the savings and loan industry in the 1980s. As interest rates rose to unprecedented levels in the early 1980s, savings and loans incurred significant losses resulting from the negative spread between the rate of return on their existing loan portfolios and the cost of funding those new loans in the marketplace. As interest rates declined after 1981 and inflation was reduced significantly, savings and loans began to incur substantial losses due to default on residential mortgages as well as on loans to commercial ventures. It has been estimated that during 1982, when the negative spread between the return on their loan portfolios and the cost of funding those portfolios was at its peak, the accumulated negative net worth of the savings and loan industry rose to between \$100 and \$175 billion.[1] This represents the difference between the value of their assets and the value of outstanding liabilities of these institutions.

Under the current regulatory system, savings and loans can operate with negative real or economic net worth, as measured by the market value of their assets, as long as they maintain positive accounting net worth as measured by the book value of assets. Unlike investment companies regulated by the SEC, savings and loans and commercial banks do not have to record the market value of the assets they manage. A savings and loan will carry its mortgage portfolio on its books at its value when the mortgage loans in the portfolio were originated (less repayments of principal). As a result, there can be a considerable spread between the book value and the market value of the assets for a savings and loan. When interest rates rise, as they did in the late 1970s and early 1980s, the market value of outstanding loans declined significantly below their book value. This means

---

[1]See Edward J. Kane, "A Six-Point Program for Deposit Insurance Reform," *Housing Finance Review*, 2 (July 1983), pp. 269–79.

that savings and loans can have significant negative net worth, measured by the market value of their assets and liabilities, and still have positive net worth measured by book or accounting values. Furthermore, since regulators define the solvency of savings and loans according to their accounting rather than their market net worth, these institutions can continue to operate with negative market net worth unless negative earnings cause their accounting net worth to fall below regulatory limits.

By the middle 1980s a large number of savings and loans had experienced sufficiently severe losses that their accounting net worth had declined below limits considered minimally acceptable by the FHLBB. In fact, the problem had become sufficiently widespread that the FSLIC found it difficult to deal with the situation effectively. The FSLIC had a limited amount of reserves to deal with failed savings and loans. If an institution is closed and sold to another insured savings and loan, the FSLIC is forced to recognize the market value of the losses of the failed institution. It must cover these losses when the institution is sold to another healthy firm. In the mid-1980s the magnitude of these losses substantially exceeded the FSLIC's total reserves. As a result it was forced to allow essentially insolvent institutions to continue to operate, sometimes under management contracts with other healthy institutions, until new resources could be attracted.

The magnitude of the difficulties facing the savings and loan industry are indicated in Table 19–1, which shows the number of institutions, dollar value of their assets, and percent of total assets in various ranges of accounting net worth as measured by generally accepted accounting procedures (GAAP). During most of the period, the FHLBB required savings and loans to have GAAP net worth equal to 3 percent of assets. This is below the 5 percent level required prior to 1981 and less than 6 percent required for commercial banks. A significant portion of the industry did not meet this standard. Moreover, in 1983 and 1984 in excess of two thirds of the industry did not meet a 5-percent net worth standard.

The source of the problem for savings and loans was the government regulation that they invest almost exclusively in long-term fixed rate mortgage loans. Hence, they were precluded from taking the kinds of steps an unrestricted lender might take to reduce exposure to the risk of increasing short-term interest rates. Other institutions, such as most commercial banks, have chosen not to become so heavily committed to mortgages and, thereby, have limited the amount of risk they bear. But to permit savings and loans this option was perceived to be inconsistent with the object of promoting housing construction, an objective that has guided government policy toward savings and loans.

THE ERA OF REGULATION Q

Until the early 1980s regulatory authorities and the Congress attempted to protect savings and loans from increases in the cost of funds by restricting the institutions' competition for consumer deposits with interest rates. Rather than let the cost of

TABLE 19–1
Estimated net worth calculations based on generally accepted accounting principles.*

Year	Number of Institutions NWTL≤0	Assets of Institutions NWTL≤0 ($ thousands)	Percent of Total Assets	Number of Institutions 0<NWTL≤.03	Assets of Institutions 0<NWTL≤.03 ($ thousands)	Percent of Total Assets	Number of Institutions 0<NWTL≤.05	Assets of Institutions 0<NWTL≤.05 ($ thousands)	Percent of Total Assets
1980	17	127,001	0.02	280	35,123,008	5.82	1,357	241,083,868	39.9
1981	65	17,303,469	2.70	653	126,666,356	19.80	1,834	379,804,220	59.4
1982	201	48,716,430	7.10	842	204,252,098	29.77	1,824	504,221,332	73.5
1983	287	78,906,404	9.70	883	242,667,975	29.82	1,770	555,963,440	68.3
1984	434	107,319,626	10.39	856	350,360,796	34.54	1,656	675,539,320	69.1

*Estimated GAAP net worth includes: preferred stock; permanent, reserve, or guaranty stock; paid-in surplus, reserves; undivided profits (retained earnings); net undistributed income; less: deferred net losses (gains) on loans sold;[1] deferred net losses (gains) on other assets sold.[2] The data collected by the Board do not include all data needed to calculate GAAP net worth. As a result, the estimated GAAP net worth may slightly overstate or understate actual GAAP net worth.

[1]For periods prior to 3/84, deferred losses sold is an estimate.

[2]Not collected until 3/84.

Source: John B. Barth, Dan Brumbaugh, Daniel Sauerhaft, and George Wang, "Insolvency and Risk Taking in the Thrift Industry: Implications for the Future," (Paper delivered at the Annual Conference of the Western Economic Association, June 20, 1985), p. 7.

Regulation Q imposed ceilings on the interest rates on deposit accounts at insured depository institutions.

deposits rise with short-term market interest rates, the government placed ceilings on the interest rates savings and loans and commercial banks could pay to depositors. The ceilings were actually intended to protect savings and loans and, to a lesser extent, commercial banks. It was infeasible to attempt simply to protect savings and loans, because commercial banks would then have a sufficient advantage in the consumer deposit market that savings and loans presumably would not be viable institutions. So the government imposed a regulation that specified interest-rate ceilings on both commercial banks and savings and loans. **Regulation Q** is the regulation of the Federal Reserve Board that controlled deposit ceilings at commercial banks. However, a similar regulation coordinated with Regulation Q was imposed by the FHLBB on savings and loans. All of these ceilings have been somewhat loosely referred to as *Regulation Q*.

Disintermediation occurs when depositors withdraw their funds from regulated intermediaries as market interest rates rise above rate ceilings for deposit accounts.

The problem with deposit rate ceilings is that when market interest rates rise above them, as they often did in the 1970s and early 1980s, depositors have a strong incentive to withdraw funds and invest in credit market instruments not subject to similar restrictions. This process is referred to as **disintermediation.** When deposit rate ceilings were first implemented this was only a potential, not an actual, problem. Market interest rates were not particularly volatile then and generally remained at levels that, from the vantage point of the mid-1980s, seem rather low. However, this state of affairs did not last, so the potential problem with deposit ceilings became an all too vivid reality. By the middle 1970s interest rates on short-term U.S. Treasury bills and other short-term marketable instruments rose to unprecedented levels. As a result, there was a tremendous incentive for depositors to withdraw funds from savings and loans or banks and invest in Treasury bills or money market funds.

RECAPITALIZING THE FSLIC

In early 1987 the situation facing the FSLIC took a turn for the worse. The Office of Management and Budget released a report that essentially said the FSLIC was insolvent. This did not surprise anyone who was following the situation. It was similar to the old story that the emperor had no clothes. In 1981 and 1982 when interest rates in the United States were at their peak, savings and loans had a negative net worth of as much as $200 billion based on market value of their assets. However, based on accounting or book values, the situation was not nearly so bleak. The FSLIC had approximately $6 billion in assets to cover potential losses from insolvent savings and loans. If the portfolio of savings and loans had been marked to market or recorded at market value, the FSLIC would have been insolvent long before 1987. But the net worth of savings and loans is measured by regulatory accounting standards rather than market values, and that gave the FSLIC some breathing room.

Unfortunately, the problems in the savings and loan industry were severe enough that the FSLIC could not afford to close all the institutions that needed to be closed, based on regulatory accounting measures of net worth. Instead, from 1982 through 1987, the FSLIC allowed institutions to remain in operation because it did not have sufficient assets to absorb the losses that would be realized if those institutions were closed. In many instances the Federal Home Loan Bank Board replaced the management of these institutions without legally closing them or selling them to other firms. This limited the damage but was not a satisfactory solution to the problem.

To deal with this problem, in 1986 the U.S. Treasury and the Federal Home Loan Bank Board proposed a plan to recapitalize the FSLIC. The plan originally proposed that a new financing corporation be created and capitalized with loans from the Federal Home Loan Banks. This corporation could then borrow funds in the capital markets and pass them on to the FSLIC. The original borrowing power of the corporation was proposed to be between $12 and $15 billion.

This approach was popular apparently because it avoids direct use of Treasury funds to bail out the FSLIC. It also avoids charging higher premiums to solvent institutions to pay for losses incurred by insolvent ones. Managers of strong savings and loans firmly believed they should not be taxed to cover the losses of insolvent institutions.

One problem with this plan was the potential inadequacy of insurance premiums to cover interest expense. In 1985 regular premium income for FSLIC was approximately $700 million while the estimated annual interest cost of the debt service on $12 to $15 billion was $1 billion. A second problem is that the plan does not actually address the underlying difficulties that created the FSLIC's problem. The only way the FSLIC can meet its expenses over time is to reduce its exposure to losses. This requires strong action against poorly managed or highly risky investments by insured institutions. While recapitalization itself may not help provide this more fundamental solution, it may at least remove the obstacle that has made it difficult for the FSLIC to close insolvent institutions.

With the advent of high and volatile inflation and interest rates during the 1970s, the potential problem with deposit rate ceilings became its fatal flaw. The regulators thought something had to be done with disintermediation or housing would suffer such severe problems that the whole purpose for creating and protecting savings and loans would be compromised. The regulators undid the system of deposit ceilings. At first, in 1978, they only partially altered the system by authorizing money market certificates that had interest rates tied to rates on Treasury bills. As a result, when interest rates on Treasury bills rose, depositors who would otherwise have had an incentive to withdraw their funds and place them in Treasury bills no longer had reason to do so. However, a substantial number of deposit accounts were still subject to interest rate ceilings. **The Depository Institutions and Monetary Control Act of 1980** mandated that all Regulation Q ceilings be phased out over a six-year period. However, it soon became apparent that this was not sufficiently rapid to forestall the movement from deposit accounts at banks and savings and loans. Finally, the Garn-St Germain Act of 1982 eliminated deposit ceilings entirely and instructed that regulators authorize banks and savings and loans to offer accounts fully competitive with money market funds. This led to the introduction of new money market accounts at most banks and savings and loans in 1983. Hence, with the passage of the Garn-St Germain Act, both the asset and liability side of the balance sheets of savings and loans had been substantially deregulated.

It is important to understand the basic rationale behind the regulatory system applied to savings and loans that has undergone such significant change in recent years. In effect, the government supported housing through a system where the consumer did not directly bear the inherent risk of the changing costs of funds. But by the early 1980s the market for mortgage finance had undergone such fundamental changes that old modes of operation were no longer viable. New participants had now entered that market, and they operated in different ways.

THE SECONDARY MARKET AGENCIES

Throughout the postwar era the U.S. government has been heavily involved in the mortgage finance industry. You have just seen part of this involvement in the regulatory system for savings and loans, but another form of involvement has become extremely important in recent years. This involvement has taken the form of nurturing the growth of the secondary market for mortgages or, more specifically, **mortgage-backed securities.** The secondary mortgage market has become one of the largest securities markets in the U.S. in recent years, and the government has played a crucial role in fostering this growth. We want to understand how and why this process of securitization is taking place. In order to appreciate this story we need to describe the special role of a number of quasi-governmental agencies as important participants in this market.

A number of quasi-federal agencies are heavily involved in the home mortgage industry. Two of these agencies **the Federal Housing Administration (FHA)** and **the Veterans Administration (VA),** provide loans at attractive interest rates to borrowers and guarantee those loans against default. In addition, three agencies either provide guarantees of credit quality on privately issued securities backed by mortgages or acquire and hold mortgages. These three agencies are the **Federal National Mortgage Association (FNMA or ''Fannie Mae''),** the **Federal Home Loan Mortgage Corporation (FHLMC or ''Freddie Mac''),** and the **Government National Mortgage Association (GNMA or ''Ginnie Mae'').** These three agencies are referred to as quasi-governmental because, to varying degrees,

The Depository Institutions Deregulation and Monetary Control Act of 1980 mandated that Regulation Q ceilings be phased out over a six-year period.

Mortgage-backed securities pay out cash flows generated by a portfolio of mortgages.

The Federal Housing Administration (FHA) and **the Veterans Administration (VA)** are government agencies which provide default guarantees on mortgages.

The Federal National Mortgage Association (FNMA), Federal Home Loan Mortgage Corporation (FHLMC) and **Government National Mortgage Association (GNMA)** are government-sponsored corporations which guarantee and distribute mortgage-backed securities.

they have been transformed into privately owned companies with a government mandate, backing, and control. They each have some form of public supervision and are constrained to pursue public policy objectives. Moreover, they issue or guarantee their own securities, known as *agency securities*. **Agency securities** are issued by agencies of the federal government other than the U.S. Treasury.

The oldest of the three quasi-federal agencies is Fannie Mae. It was originally created in the late 1930s in order to assist the home mortgage industry by purchasing mortgages insured by the Federal Housing Administration. Freddie Mac was established in 1970 in order to fulfill essentially the same purpose but with conventional mortgages, that is, mortgages not backed by FHA. Both of these agencies initially operated by selling agency securities in the market and using the funds to purchase mortgages directly. Fannie Mae has historically operated much like a traditional savings and loan in issuing debt securities with specified maturities, usually shorter than the maturity of the mortgages it was purchasing. Hence, it bought mortgages and funded them with shorter maturity debt and, as a result, accepted substantial interest rate risk. By contrast, Freddie Mac has traditionally issued securities that simply obligated it to pass through the cash flows received from mortgages to the securities' holders. In addition, Freddie Mac guaranteed to pay the promised cash flow if the mortgage was delinquent or in default. Hence, Freddie Mac did not accept the interest rate risk inherent in funding mortgages with short-term liabilities; the only risk it assumed to any large extent was default risk.

Throughout the 1960s and 1970s one of the basic purposes of these quasi-governmental mortgage agencies was to act as a countercyclical source of funds in the mortgage industry. During this period the housing industry tended to experience a pattern of activity determined by fluctuations in market interest rates. When market interest rates rose above the deposit account ceilings enforced by Regulation Q, then savings and loans experienced disintermediation. This limited the availability of funds for mortgage financing, since the housing industry was dependent largely on the savings and loan industry. The secondary mortgage markets emerged during the 1960s and 1970s as the major alternative source of funds for mortgage financing when savings and loans or thrifts became illiquid.

Table 19–2 shows the volume of securities backed by mortgages issued by the three major agencies from 1971 until 1985. GNMA and FHLMC issue virtually all claims as mortgage-backed securities. However, FNMA has a large volume of debt as well as mortgage-backed securities outstanding, so the table understates the total participation of these agencies by the amount of FNMA debt. In December, 1985, FNMA had debt outstanding of $93.9 billion. It is apparent from the table that these agencies represented a very small portion of the total mortgage market in the early 1970s. However, the situation had changed dramatically by the early 1980s. As the secondary mortgage markets grew it became increasingly important to understand the nature of the risks inherent in investing in a mortgage portfolio or a mortgage-backed security.

TABLE 19–2
Outstanding principal balances on mortgage-backed securities ($ billions).

	Issued by		
	GNMA	FHLMC	FNMA
1985	207,198	99,515	54,036
1984	175,589	70,253	35,965
1983	135,801	57,273	25,121
1982	115,831	42,560	14,450
1981	103,007	19,501	717
1980	91,602	13,471	
1979	74,546	12,149	
1978	52,732	9,657	
1977	43,555	5,261	
1976	29,583	2,282	
1975	17,538	1,349	
1974	11,249	608	
1973	7,561	617	

FMMA began to issue mortgage backed-securities in 1981.

RISK MANAGEMENT IN MORTGAGE FINANCE

Prepayment risk is the risk that a mortgage will be prepaid before its maturity, and default risk is the risk that the mortgage borrower will default on the mortgage.

The two important risks involved in holding individual mortgages or mortgage-backed securities are **prepayment risk** and **default risk.** An examination of these two sources of risk will help us see how the market for mortgage-backed securities has developed. The mortgage-backed securities market has been largely concerned with finding ways to manage these two sources of risk effectively.

PREPAYMENT RISK

Prepayment risk arises from the fact that the typical home mortgage borrower has the option to prepay the mortgage when he or she chooses. This is similar to the option to call a bond, which is written into many corporate bonds. Mortgages are prepaid for essentially two reasons. First, if the borrower moves to a new home, the mortgage is usually paid off when the home is sold. Second, if interest rates decline significantly relative to the interest rate on the mortgage, borrowers may prepay simply because they want to reduce their total debt burden. Since prepayment is at the borrower's option, the actual timing of prepayment on any given mortgage is uncertain. Hence, from the vantage point of the investor in either an individual mortgage or a security backed by mortgages, the prepayment option introduces uncertainty into the timing of cash flows from the mortgage. This source of uncertainty is not present in Treasury obligations or even in most corporate obligations. Even if the corporate bond has a call provision, the timing of the exercise of a call on a corporate bond is generally determined by the financial cost of exercising the call option. However, since the prepayment decision on a mortgage is determined by a larger number of factors, more uncertainty surrounds prepayment patterns on mortgages than call provisions on corporate bonds. This uncertainty has historically been a major drawback of residential mortgages as an investment vehicle for institutions other than savings and loans.

What makes prepayment risk such a problem for an investor in mortgages is that prepayments tend to increase when interest rates are declining. As the mortgages in a portfolio prepay, the investor in that portfolio must reinvest those prepayments. If interest rates decline, the rate of return on the reinvested proceeds of the prepayments will decline, hurting the investor. Since prepayments often result when existing mortgages are refinanced to take advantage of decreased interest rates, it can be expected that prepayments will increase as interest rates fall. This is clearly evident in the recent data on prepayment experience. For example, Figure 19–3 shows prepayment rates on mortgage-backed securities issued by

FIGURE 19–3
Prepayment rates and mortgage interest rates (seasoned discount issues[a]. January 79-July 85).

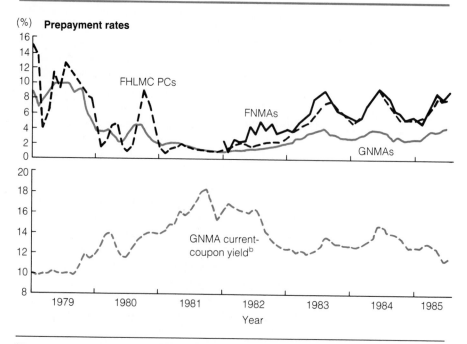

[a]Pools with coupon rates at, or below, the prevailing current coupon, and consisting of loans outstanding for two or more years.
[b]Bond-equivalent yield.

FHLMC, FNMA, and GNMA from 1979 through 1985, during the peak of interest rates in the United States. The upper panel shows prepayment rates for each of these mortgage-backed securities, while the lower panel shows the current GNMA yield. It is apparent from this figure that prepayment rates on all of these instruments were lowest in 1981 and 1982 when interest rates were at their peak and rose significantly as interest rates declined in the last few years of the period.

In order to be able to value a portfolio of mortgages or evaluate a potential mortgage investment, it is exceptionally important to be able to predict prepayment rates. As a result, considerable resources have been expended in recent years both on Wall Street and in academia to attempt to construct statistical models that can explain prepayment patterns. The early studies of prepayments and early pricing systems for mortgages simply assumed that mortgages would prepay according to the historical experience of the Federal Housing Administration (FHA). FHA experience is important since GNMA mortgage pools are largely comprised of FHA guaranteed mortgages. In addition, the largest data base on prepayment experience is for FHA mortgages. Table 19–3 shows the prepayment experience of FHA for mortgages originated from 1957 to 1977 (what are called section 203 30-year home mortgages).

The FHA experience can be used in at least two ways to value a mortgage portfolio. The simpler way is to compute the average life of the mortgages based on FHA experience and then assume that all of them in a specific portfolio will prepay at precisely that point in time. The FHA experience documented in Table 19–3 indicates that the average life of a mortgage is between 14 and 15 years. (Until recently it was common to assume a 12-year life.) We could use the assumption that mortgages will prepay at the end of 15 years to value a specific mortgage portfolio. For example, suppose we had a portfolio of 9 percent mortgages. Also suppose we applied a 14 percent interest rate to the cash flows on those mortgages. The value of this portfolio would be 70.25 per $100 of face value of the mortgages. This is the present value of scheduled interest and principal payments over 15 years and 100 percent prepayment at year 15, all at a discount rate of 14 percent.

A second, and presumably more accurate, method is to assume that the mortgages prepay in a pattern like that defined by FHA experience. This means that FHA prepayment rate in each year would be applied to the total mortgage portfolio so that it would be assumed to prepay gradually. For the same 9 percent mortgage portfolio discussed above, if the 14 percent discount rate is used, it would generate a value of 74.54. This is higher than the value generated using the average life assumption above. The price based on the weighted-average life of a loan will always understate the value of a mortgage portfolio computed by applying the whole schedule of prepayment rates.[2]

---

[2]See Michael Waldman, *The Next Step in Mortgage Security Yields: Applying the Experience of the 1970s,* New York: Salomon Brothers Inc., 1985, for a more detailed treatment of this issue.

TABLE 19-3
1957–1977 FHA experience—survivorship levels for FHA-insured section 203 30-year home mortgages.

Policy Year	Survivors at Beginning of Policy Year	Terminations During Policy Year	Prepayment Rate
1	100,000.0	836.9	0.84%
2	99,163.1	3,100.0	3.13
3	96,063.1	4,170.8	4.34
4	91,892.3	4,603.7	5.01
5	87,288.6	4,908.9	5.62
6	82,379.7	4,955.3	6.02
7	77,424.4	4,668.4	6.03
8	72,756.0	4,398.6	6.05
9	68,357.4	4,093.3	5.99
10	64,264.1	3,783.7	5.89
11	60,480.4	3,595.3	5.94
12	56,885.1	3,399.6	5.98
13	53,485.5	3,240.9	6.06
14	50,244.6	3,126.9	6.22
15	47,117.7	3,055.4	6.48
16	44,062.3	3,028.4	6.87
17	41,033.9	3,036.8	7.40
18	37,997.1	3,057.2	8.05
19	34,939.9	3,073.5	8.80
20	31,866.4	3,105.0	9.74
21	28,761.4	2,953.7	10.27
22	25,807.7	2,793.1	10.82
23	23,014.6	2,624.8	11.40
24	20,389.8	2,450.0	12.02
25	17,939.8	2,270.8	12.66
26	15,669.0	2,089.0	13.33
27	13,580.0	1,906.6	14.04
28	11,673.4	1,725.5	14.78
29	9,947.9	2,181.3	21.93
30	7,766.6	7,766.6	100.0

Source: Actuarial Division, U.S. Department of Housing and Urban Development.

In this example we have computed the value of a mortgage portfolio for a given assumed prepayment pattern and with a given discount rate applied to its cash flows. However, it is important to see that the risk of the prepayment pattern also affects the yield or price of a mortgage portfolio. In this example, we assumed that the relevant discount rate to apply to the assumed cash flow stream from the mortgages was 14 percent. This discount rate should take into account the riskiness of the cash flows or the prepayments. We could also look at it the other way around. That is, the market will set a price for a given mortgage port-folio based in part on the perceived risk of prepayments. Given that price and an assumption about the actual prepayment rate, we can compute a yield for that portfolio. We do this by computing the internal rate of return for the cash flow stream and the current price of the mortgages. If the market demands a premium to bear the risk of future prepayments, this market yield should be above the yield for comparable securities, such as Treasury bonds, that are not subject to prepay-ment risk. We will find that this is the case as we examine yields on mortgage-backed securities in the next section.

An even more sophisticated way to approach the mortgage pricing problem is to take into account the value of the option to prepay the mortgage. One way to view an investment in a mortgage portfolio is as an investment (long position) in an annuity plus a short position in a call option on the annuity. The annuity portion of the investment is equivalent to a sequence of zero-coupon Treasury bonds, one for each scheduled mortgage payment date. The option portion entitles the borrower to retire the annuity, or any portion of it, at anytime. It is a call option (rather than a put) because prepayment is virtually the same as purchasing the annuity for a predetermined exercise price. Unfortunately, valuing the option portion of a mortgage is a highly complex problem. While option pricing models have been applied extensively to other types of security valuation problems, as yet there have been few applications to mortgages.[3] The essence of the difficulty is that mortgage borrowers do not prepay simply to minimize the cost of borrow-ing. That is, they do not prepay in a way that would be suggested by the typical option pricing models (see Chapter 4). Instead, as indicated above, many prepay-ments are due to decisions to move to a new home rather than for refinancing an existing mortgage. Hence, prepayments have proved to be difficult to explain sim-ply using option pricing theory.

DEFAULT RISK

The system that has evolved for dealing with default risk on mortgages and mort-gage-backed securities is unusual compared with the system for handling default risk on most corporate or consumer obligations. A specialized class of institutions, both private and governmental, writes guarantees against default on mortgages. The VA and the FHA provide guarantees on the loans backing GNMA securities and, as noted above, GNMA provides an additional guarantee of timely payment of principal and interest to the securityholder. Private or conventional mortgages may or may not have a guarantee, depending on the extent of leverage of the mortgage. Loans where the borrower has made a down payment of less than 20 percent of the value of the property, or leverage of more than 80 percent, gener-

---

[3]See Kenneth B. Dunn and John J. McConnell, ''Valuation of GNMA Mortgage-Backed Securities,'' *Journal of Finance* 36 (June 1981), pp., 599–616.

ally have guarantees against default provided by a **private mortgage insurance (PMI) company.** Loans leveraged above 80 percent have been viewed as sufficiently risky that government regulators have required independent guarantees be provided for them to savings and loans.

The perception that highly leveraged mortgage loans impose a significant risk on the investors who hold them grew out of the experience of the Great Depression, when default rates on single-family mortgages were as high as 14 percent. During the early 1930s foreclosures were halted by the government when they reached extremely high levels. Moreover, the mortgage insurance industry at that time was wiped out by the high default rates. Mortgage insurance was not used again until the late 1950s, when a new mortgage insurance company called Mortgage Guaranty Insurance Corporation (MGIC) was founded in Milwaukee, Wisconsin. At that time the demand for loans with less than 20 percent down payment had begun to increase. Regulators were persuaded that savings and loans should be allowed to invest in these loans only if they could acquire an independent guarantee against default. MGIC was the first to provide such a guarantee.

During the 1960s and 1970s the mortgage insurance industry proved to be highly profitable because the default rates on mortgages were very low. Table 19–4 shows historical default rates on mortgages guaranteed by MGIC from 1960

TABLE 19–4
Default on insured conventional residential mortgage loans.

Year	Annual Default Incidence as Percent of Total Loans Outstanding in each Year	Total Lifetime Default Incidence as Percent of Loans Originating each Year (as of 1980)
1960	0.012	3.836
1961	0.044	2.734
1962	0.087	2.880
1963	0.234	2.501
1964	0.546	1.923
1965	0.477	1.601
1966	0.430	0.672
1967	0.284	0.481
1968	0.156	0.513
1969	0.101	0.657
1970	0.119	0.871
1971	0.953	0.764
1972	0.113	1.603
1973	0.246	2.006
1974	0.352	2.164
1975	0.394	0.998
1976	0.281	0.648
1977	0.195	0.584
1978	0.142	0.613
1979	0.141	0.743
1980	0.173	0.092

to 1980. Default rates are shown in two ways. The first column shows the annual default rate as a percent of total loans outstanding in each year. The second column shows the lifetime default incidence as a percent of loans originated in any given year. For example, the entry in the second column for 1973, 2.006, indicates the percentage of loans originated in 1973 that had defaulted by 1980. Loans originated in the early 1960s had the highest lifetime default rates. In addition, loans originated in the recession of 1973 and 1974 had relatively high default rates. In other years default rates were much lower.

The relatively low default rates during this period result from the fact that this was an era where most regions in the United States experienced significant appreciation in housing prices. As housing prices increase, borrowers accumulate sufficient equity in their property that they have little incentive to default on their loan. If a borrower should experience difficulties in meeting mortgage payments, there is a strong incentive to sell a house rather than permit foreclosure, as long as there is a significant amount of equity. Hence, high inflation rates lead to low default rates. Low default rates mean relatively high profits for companies that guarantee mortgages against default. However, if the inflation rate declines and the unemployment rate increases, as both did in the early 1980s, then default rates on mortgages will increase and profits for mortgage insurers will decline. Table 19–5 shows aggregate foreclosure rates in the United States from 1965 to 1985 as reported by the Mortgage Bankers Association. This table shows that default rates increased during the early 1980s, compared to the level they achieved in earlier years.

The prospect that high default rates may cause serious problems for some mortgage insurers was highlighted in 1985 when the second largest mortgage insurance company, Ticor Mortgage Insurance, was driven into insolvency. Ticor was exposed to extraordinarily high losses not simply because of the general increase in mortgage default rates experienced throughout the industry, but also because it had provided extensive guarantees on loans originated by a fraudulent institution. The exposure to fraud resulted in such large potential losses that Ticor was forced to withdraw from the mortgage insurance market.

As the mortgage-backed securities market has grown, the role of the mortgage insurer has become increasingly important. For strictly private mortgage-backed securities, that is, securities with no government guarantee, the credit quality of the issue can only be as high as the credit quality of the guarantor who stands behind the pool. Moreover, FHLMC requires private mortgage insurance on all mortgages it buys with leverage over 80 percent. Since it provides a guarantee of its own on the securities it issues, the FHLMC is also keenly interested in the credit quality of the mortgage insurers.

Credit ratings for mortgage-backed securities are an assessment of their guarantors' ability to withstand adverse economic circumstances. Hence, one of the critical factors in the rating process is determining what loss level a guarantor should be able to survive. Standard and Poor's has consistently maintained that an AAA rating should indicate a guarantor can survive a worst case scenario. The Great Depression of the 1930s defines the worst case scenario. Depending upon

TABLE 19–5
Mortgage foreclosures by all lenders†

Year-end	All Mortgage Loans	Conventional Loans	FHA Loans‡	VA Loans
1965	0.40%	0.08%	0.50%	0.40%
1970	0.33	0.08	0.47	0.25
1971	0.46	0.07	0.68	0.30
1972	0.48	0.07	0.75	0.34
1973	n.a.	n.a.	n.a.	n.a.
1974	0.50	0.15	0.57	0.40
1975	0.38	0.16	0.46	0.36
1976	0.40	0.18	0.48	0.41
1977	0.37	0.15	0.46	0.39
1978	0.31	0.13	0.42	0.32
1979	0.29	0.10	0.44	0.38
1980	0.38	0.17	0.53	0.46
1981	0.44	0.24	0.57	0.55
1982	0.67	0.39	0.88	0.76
1983	0.67	0.46	0.84	0.76
1984	0.73	0.47	0.98	0.82
1985	0.81	0.61	1.01	0.88

n.a. = not available.
†Percentage of loans in the foreclosure process.
‡For 1974–1978. FHA loans exclude sections 235 and 237.
Source: Mortgage Bankers Association of America.

the precise time period chosen and the institutions used to measure default incidence, cumulative default incidence during the Depression ranged from 12 to 15 percent. Moreover, it is estimated that the total loss on foreclosed property averaged approximately 40 percent of outstanding loan balances. In order to receive a AAA rating from Standard and Poor's, a mortgage guarantor must demonstrate it could withstand this level of losses. The ability to survive an adverse economic scenario depends both on the initial capitalization of a guarantor and on the income stream assured to that guarantor even in the worst case scenario. Standard and Poor's evaluates both the guarantor's capital and the stability of its future income stream when deciding on a rating.

As the fortunes of the mortgage insurers changed in the early 1980s, they took steps to limit losses from mortgage defaults. One important step was to tighten underwriting standards so that highly risky borrowers and loan terms could be avoided at the outset. Another was to adjust the prices for mortgage insurance to cover the risk involved. The ability of the mortgage insurers to set prices at appropriate levels is constrained by the fact that most market participants want to obtain a sufficient market share that they can obtain perceived scale economies in this business. Hence smaller firms will have an incentive to underprice a given risk in an attempt to gain market share from the largest firms in the market. This type of price competition can make it difficult for the industry to raise prices even if they are below that appropriate for the risk involved. At the same time, these firms are regulated as insurance companies in the individual states in which they operate. Insurance regulations set minimum prices for products in order to limit the ability of insurers to compete. As a result, if prices turn out to be relatively high compared to a fair price for the risk involved, as they appear to have been during the 1970s, it may be difficult for competition to drive them down to a more appropriate level. However, if established prices appear to be too low, as they appear to have been in the early 1980s, the same competitive pressures can make it difficult for prices to rise.

EVOLUTION OF THE SECONDARY MORTGAGE MARKET

In the late 1970s and 1980s the market for mortgage-backed securities grew at a fantastic rate. Figure 19–4, showing the total volume of mortgage-backed securities as a percentage of the total fixed income market including Treasury and corporate bonds, indicates that in just a few years mortgage-backed securities have become a large portion of that market. Moreover, if the total mortgage finance market continues to be securitized, the mortgage portion of the total fixed income market will continue to grow rapidly.

One of the reasons the mortgage-backed securities market has grown so rapidly is the significant innovations in the types of securities offered. Two basic types of securities have been important. The first is the pass-through security. The second and more recent innovation is the collateralized mortgage obligation (CMO).

GROWTH OF THE PASS-THROUGH SECURITY

Pass-through securities pay all the cash flows received on a pool of mortgages, including prepayments, directly to the securityholder.

Beginning in 1970, GNMA began to guarantee the timely payment of principal and interest on securities issued by private mortgage institutions and backed by pools of government-insured or government-guaranteed mortgages. The **pass-through security** is a claim on a share of the income from a specific mortgage pool. The private originators of the individual mortgages generally continue to service the mortgages in the pools, collecting the principal and interest payments and passing them through to the securities holders. A loan originator may also sell the servicing function to another firm. Currently issued GNMA-guaranteed certificates are termed *fully modified*. This means that scheduled payments of principal

FIGURE 19–4
Taxable fixed income securities market (amount outstanding at year end).

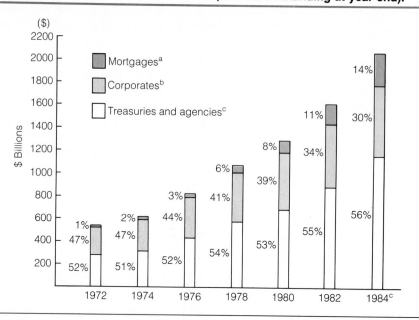

[a]GNMA, FHLMC and FNMA mortgage–backed securities, and publicly sold conventional pass-throughs.
[b]Private placements, convertible bonds, foreign issues sold in the U.S., and straight domestic public issues.
[c]Treasury notes and bonds and nonmortgages agency issues.
[d]As of September 30,1984.
Sources: Board of Governors of the Federal Reserve System; GNMA; FHLMC; FNMA; Lepercq, de Neufize & Co Inc.; M. Waldman and S. Guterman. Mortgage Securities, 1972–1984. Salomon Bros. Inc. Photocopy.

and interest are provided to the security holder, whether or not collected by the mortgage servicer, plus a pro rata share of any prepayments made on the pool of mortgages.

Table 19–3 shows the total volume of pass-through securities guaranteed by GNMA from 1970 until 1985. It is apparent from the data that the volume of GNMA pass-throughs has increased tremendously since being introduced in 1970. During this period, as the volume of pass-throughs increased, the liquidity in the secondary market for these instruments increased as well. The liquidity afforded by a large volume of homogeneous securities outstanding increased the attractiveness of participation in this market for a number of investors.

As the market for GNMA pass-throughs expanded in the early 1970s, FHLMC also introduced its own pass-through, known as a **participation certificate** or **PC.** The outstanding volume of FHLMC mortgage-backed securities that

Participation certifications are pass-through securities issued by FHLMC.

are now principally PCs is shown in the second column of Table 19–3. PCs differ from the pass-throughs guaranteed by GNMA in a number of respects. Probably the most important is that mortgages in the pools backing PCs are conventional mortgages, that is, they do not have guarantees against default risk provided by some U.S. government agency. The second is that FHLMC does not simply provide a guarantee of timely payments on securities issued by private firms, but rather buys mortgages from originators, forms mortgage pools, issues its own securities, and guarantees timely payment of interest. However, unlike GNMA, it does not guarantee timely payment of principal in the event of deliquency or default. As a result, FHLMC is an integrated firm that creates mortgage-backed securities. The extent of vertical integration is limited by the fact that FHLMC does not originate its own mortgages, and it relies on independent dealers to maintain a market in PCs. FNMA now also issues its own pass-through securities, although it was the last of the three agencies to do so. FNMA is funded mostly with short- and medium-term debt rather than through pass-through securities. A number of private institutions have also sold pass-throughs. However, the volume of these security issues is small compared with those of the three quasi-federal agencies.

It is important to see why the pass-through security has become such a popular instrument in the mortgage market. In principle it would be possible to utilize the cash flow pattern commonly found in a bond that has a well-defined maturity and coupon interest payments promised over the life of the bond. However, if mortgage-backed securities were issued in this form, the issuer would accept the risk of mortgage prepayments. With a pass-through security, that risk is transferred to the securityholder. This has worked reasonably well for institutional investors who understand prepayment risk and are willing to accept it. However, many institutions, principally insurance companies and pension funds, have not invested in mortgages to any great extent since the introduction of Regulation Q in the 1960s, and are familiar with the cash flow streams available from corporate and other bonds. Moreover, these investors have not been eager to take on the prepayment risk inherent in the pass-through security. This has created an incentive for institutions who distribute and market mortgage-backed securities to develop new types of mortgage-backed securities that will be attractive to the market portion that has traditionally avoided prepayment risk in pass-through securities. This has led to the creation of a new type of mortgage-backed security, the **collateralized mortgage obligation** or **CMO.**

Collateralized mortgage obligations or **CMOs** are mortgage-backed securities with different priority claims on the cash flows received from a pool of mortgages.

COLLATERALIZED MORTGAGE OBLIGATIONS: A CASE OF INNOVATION

The CMO splits the cash flows generated by a pool of mortgages into separate categories and issues securities with claims to the specialized cash flows generated by an entire pool of mortgages. This kind of innovation is useful if the risk of the entire security can be reduced in the process of dividing it and allocating it to specific securities. Once again, the risk involved is the risk of fluctuations in

REMICS

One of the obstacles that has hindered development of a wider variety of mortgage-backed securities has been the unfavorable tax treatment applied to such securities until the passage of the Tax Reform Act of 1986. For example, before this law was passed, an investment company that invested in mortgages and attempted to manage the mortgage portfolio by changing its composition in any way would be subject to corporate income tax. This is not the case for investment companies managing portfolios of other assets such as corporate bonds. Under this treatment investors in mortgages managed in this way would have double taxation, which was enough to block development of such actively managed mortgage investment vehicles. However, the Tax Reform Act of 1986 authorized development of a new tax entity known as a real estate mortgage investment conduit, or REMIC. REMICS eliminate most of the special provisions in the tax law that inhibited development of efficient and versatile mortgage investment vehicles.

REMICS have important advantages for participants in the mortgage market. REMICS are qualifying mortgage assets for government-regulated thrift institutions. This means investments in REMICS will be treated as qualifying loans for the purpose of computing the addition to reserves for bad debts. This treatment applies to investments in the straight-debt portion of REMICS or in a residual portion of a REMIC like the last tranch of a CMO. .

In the past, interest received by some foreign investors in mortgage pass-through securities was subject to a 30 percent withholding tax. Under the new law, regular interest income in a REMIC is exempt from this withholding requirement, which makes REMICS attractive to foreign investors.

The new REMICS provide greater flexibility regarding the legal form assumed by the issuer of a mortgage-backed security. Under the new law the issuer of a REMIC can take any legal form, including a corporation, a partnership, or a trust. In addition, the securities issued by the REMIC can be of any form including pass-throughs, straight debt, or CMOs. No longer will tax considerations determine the choice of legal form of the issuer.

In the past an issuer of a mortgage-backed security often needed to deposit extra mortgages in the mortgage pool or overcollateralize the issue. This was required for the mortgage-backed security to be considered a debt issue for tax purposes. Without the overcollateralization, the purchaser of the security was judged to be taking a risk like that in an equity security. The new REMICS will automatically be considered debt for tax purposes and the costly overcollateralization requirement will be avoided.

prepayment rates. In a CMO that risk is divided among distinct securityholders who have preferences for cash flows with specific maturities.

Tranches of a CMO refer to the separate classes of securities with different priority claims on the cash flows from the underlying mortgages.

The CMO creates **tranches** or classes of securities. Tranches refer to securities with claims to principal payments generated by the mortgage pool in order of priority. For example, if a CMO has four tranches, the first tranch may have title to all of the principal payments until the securities in that tranch are retired. The second tranch would have a claim on all principal payments generated after the first tranch is retired or paid off. Then the third tranch would have a claim on all of the subsequent cash flows until retired. The fourth tranch would receive the final payments. Throughout the life of the pool all three tranches would accrue interest at the rate specified in the mortgages in the pool. However, as principal payments flow in, they would be allocated to a specific tranch.

Within the CMO structure there is still risk regarding the timing of cash receipt, just as there is in the traditional pass-through security. However, that risk

FIGURE 19–5
The structure of a CMO.

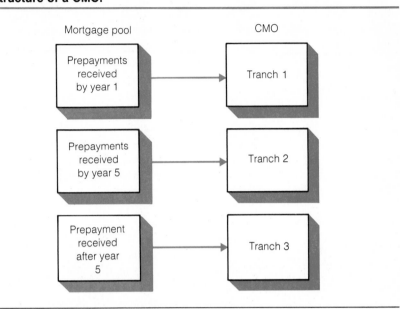

Source: Richard Roll, *Collateralized Mortgage Obligations: Characteristics, History, Analysis,* New York: Goldman Sachs and Company, April, 1986.

has been split up and allocated to specific securities. The CMO reduces the timing uncertainty associated with principal repayments by directing principal to each class of security in order of priority. In addition, the issuer often guarantees a minimum prepayment rate to further reduce the uncertainty of cash flows. Because of the more predictable cash flows, the higher priority CMO securities are like short-term coupon-bearing bonds and the lower priority securities are like intermediate and long-term coupon-bearing bonds. Furthermore, the CMO may make semiannual or quarterly payments rather than monthly payments, as with most pass-through securities. By making CMOs more like coupon-bearing bonds, a broader class of investors has developed a preference for mortgage-backed securities via the CMO.

The difference between the CMO and the standard pass-through is important. With the standard pass-through every securityholder in a given issue receives a prorata share of all cash flows generated by a pool of mortgages. Therefore, every investor has an equivalent share of the total prepayment risk for that pool. However, in a CMO specific tranches bear all of specific parts of the prepayment risk for the entire pool of mortgages, as illustrated in Figure 19–5. This risk partitioning is valuable to the market if there are clienteles who want cash flows with specific maturities that can be matched with a tranch. These investors may be willing to accept some risk that corresponds to a tranch of the CMO. However, they would be willing to accept the entire prepayment risk that is inherent in the traditional pass-through only if they are paid a very high price to do so. Hence, by limiting the magnitude of specific portions of the prepayment risk, the CMO structure can add value to the market.

Table 19–6 shows the total volume of CMOs issued by the end of February, 1986, and indicates what type of institution issued these CMOs. Notice that in 1983 FHLMC was the first to issue CMOs in any volume. Since then a number of other types of institutions have utilized the CMO structure: builders, security dealers such as First Boston or Salomon Brothers, insurance companies, and thrift institutions all now use it. Table 19–7 provides some data on the number of tranches used in the CMOs documented in Table 19–6. Over 80 percent of the CMOs utilize four tranches, and a little over half utilize quarterly cash distributions.

Mean weighted-average life measures the expected maturity of each tranch of a CMO.

Figure 19–6 shows what is called the **mean weighted-average life** of the tranches in the CMOs described in Tables 19–6 and 19–7. The mean weighted-average life measures the expected maturity or life of each tranch of the typical CMO. In order to calculate this number it is necessary to make some assumption about prepayment patterns on the mortgages that provide collateral for the CMO. One possible assumption is that the mortgages will prepay according to the FHA experience described earlier in the chapter. The assumption underlying Figure 19–6 is that mortgages will prepay according to the experience recorded by the Public Securities Association, which differs from the FHA experience. Figure 19–6 shows the mean weighted-average life for CMOs with three, four, and five to ten tranches.

FIGURE 19–6
Mean weighted-average life by number of tranches in CMO.

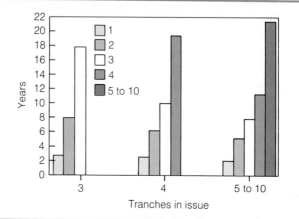

Source: Richard Roll, *Collateralized Mortgage Obligations: Characteristics, History, Analysis,* New York: Goldman Sachs and Company, April, 1986.

TABLE 19–6
CMO issuers and amounts by issuer category and year.

Issuer	1983 Number	1983 Total	1984 Number	1984 Total	1985 Number	1985 Total	First 2 Months 1986 Number	First 2 Months 1986 Total	All Years Number	All Years Total
FHLMC	2	$1,684,675	3	$1,805,025	5	$2,904,760	0	0	10	6,394,460
Builder conduit	1	143,863	8	938,371	25	2,685,355	5	431,730	39	4,200,319
Builder subsidiary	5	884,435	10	1,382,285	14	1,749,203	7	747,021	36	4,772,944
Dealer affiliate	1	500,000	5	1,850,000	1	250,000	3	1,204,100	10	3,804,100
Dealer subsidiary	2	1,000,000	3	1,650,000	10	2,600,000	1	550,000	16	5,800,000
Insurance co. subsidiary	0	0	1	1,250,000	0	0	0	0	1	1,250,000
Mortgage bank subsidiary	1	447,210	5	1,373,520	1	126,700	1	103,516	8	2,050,946
Thrift	0	0	2	765,350	1	100,000	0	0	3	865,350
Thrift conduit	0	0	0	0	7	1,351,075	5	752,325	12	2,103,400
Thrift/originator conduit	0	0	0	0	3	388,641	0	0	3	388,641
Thrift subsidiary	0	0	0	0	18	3,402,741	4	800,100	22	4,203,841
Other*	0	0	0	0	1	200,000	0	0	1	200,000
	12	4,650,183	37	11,025,551	86	15,759,475	26	4,588,792	161	36,034,001

*Indiana Housing Finance Agency.

Source: Richard Roll, *Collateralized Mortgage Obligations: Characteristics, History, Analysis*, New York: Goldman Sachs and Company, April, 1986.

TABLE 19–7
Number of tranches and periodicity of bond payments.

Number of Tranches	Cases	%	Periodicity	Cases	%
3	16	9.9	Monthly	17	10.6
4*	133	82.6	Quarterly	86	53.4
≧5	12	7.5	Semiannual*	58	36.0

*There is one case of two tranches plus serial bonds.

*In one case interest was semiannual and principal was quarterly.

Source: Richard Roll, *Collateralized Mortgage Obligations: Characteristics, History, Analysis*, New York: Goldman Sachs and Company, April, 1986.

FIGURE 19–7
Yield spread versus treasury maturity and frequency of use.

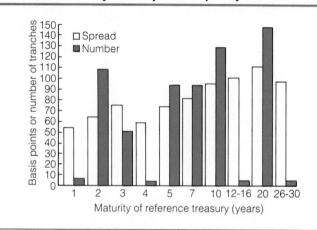

Source: Richard Roll, *Collateralized Mortgage Obligations: Characteristics, History, Analysis,* New York: Goldman Sachs and Company, April, 1986.

Once the mean weighted-average life of a particular tranch of a CMO has been computed, as in Figure 19–6, it is possible to compute the estimated yield on this tranch of the CMO and compare it with the yield on a comparable maturity Treasury instrument. The yield on each tranch of the CMO is calculated as the internal rate of return, given the assumption about prepayments used to calculate the mean weighted-average life and the observed price of that tranch of the CMO. Figure 19–7 compares the yields on specific tranches of CMOs with the corresponding maturity Treasury for all CMOs issued by February, 1986. The figure indicates that the spread between CMO yields and corresponding maturity Treasury bonds increases with maturity. For example, the average spread was 76 basis points when the reference Treasury had three years to maturity, but it increased to 81 basis points for the seven-year maturity, 95 basis points for the ten year and 111 basis points for the twenty year.[4]

The spread between the yield on CMO and corresponding maturity Treasury instruments represents a compensation to the investor for the CMO's prepayment risk. Since the vast majority of CMOs are backed by mortgages guaranteed against default by the government (either GNMA or FHLMC mortgages), the yield spread shown in Figure 19–7 cannot include a significant premium for default risk. The fact that the spread between CMO yields and Treasury yields increase with maturity indicates that the market perceives a higher prepayment risk for longer maturity tranches of the CMO. Since this figure represents a composite of what hap-

---

[4]See Richard Roll, *Collateralized Mortgage Obligations: Characteristics, History, Analysis,* New York: Goldman Sachs & Company, April 1986, for a more detailed treatment of CMOs. Also note that the figures and tables presented here are drawn from Roll.

pened over a three-year period, it obscures the fact that the spreads between yields on each tranch of a CMO and the corresponding maturity Treasury instrument tend to rise and fall with the level of interest rates, a logical consequence of the relationship of prepayment risk to the level of interest rates.

PRIVATIZATION OF SECONDARY MARKET AGENCIES

While it is important to understand the nature of the innovation which the CMO represents, it is also important to note the special role quasi-government agencies have in this market. As we saw in Table 19–6, FHLMC has been one of the major issuers of CMOs, but this fact alone understates the agencies' role. Most CMOs issued by private firms were collateralized with GNMA securities or other government-guaranteed mortgage pools. The reason is simple. These organizations carry agency status and therefore can sell debt at yields that reflect the implicit backing of the U.S. government. This has two important implications. First, it means that the U.S. government is intimately involved in extensive guarantees against default on mortgage debt. This participation goes beyond the direct guarantees issued by FHA and VA to include all conventional loans acquired by FHLMC or FNMA. Second, it means private issuers of mortgage-backed securities face a competitive disadvantage. They must obtain credit ratings from private rating agencies and issue debt priced according to those ratings. In order to obtain a high rating, they must commit capital or hold reserves sufficient to guarantee they can survive a high level of default experience. This requirement is avoided by the quasi-government agencies. Moreover, there is still a positive spread in yields between even AAA-rated private issues and the yields on agency securities. As a result, even if private issuers obtain a AAA rating, they face a cost disadvantage relative to quasi-government agencies.

It is not obvious whether the extensive role played by FHLMC, FNMA, and GNMA in the mortgage markets is harmful or beneficial. Some argue the innovations in this market would not have been feasible without government guarantees. This view asserts that government participation has created a standardized form of security, particularly in the GNMA market, that has permitted a highly liquid market to develop. This view also argues that the credit guarantee provided by the government is essential to a large and thriving mortgage-backed securities market. Moreover, as long as savings and loans have government guarantees on their deposits, withdrawal of the government guarantee on mortgage-backed securities would simply mean that the secondary mortgage market would stagnate, since private guarantees could not compete with government-backed deposits.

An interesting twist of this point of view asserts that the quasi-government agencies represent an efficient subsidy since they avoid the costly and allegedly inefficient private rating process. This argument essentially asserts that the rating agencies represent a bottleneck which has thwarted growth of a large private secondary mortgage market. The basis for this argument is that rating agencies insist private guarantors who want an AAA rating must maintain sufficient capital to withstand a level of losses equal to the Great Depression of the 1930s. Those who believe this is inefficient contend that the government would never allow foreclosure rates to reach this level again. Hence, the capital requirements imposed by rating agencies are onerous. This view suggests government guarantees are efficient since they avoid the level of capital requirements imposed by the private rating agencies. There is considerable support for privatization of the guarantee function now provided by the government from the savings and loan industry. Many managers in this industry view the secondary mortgage market as a source of competition which threatens their institutions, hence, they would like to limit the agencies' growth. It is likely that political battles surrounding the proper role of FLMC, GNMA, and FNMA wil continue.

Summary

This chapter examined the rapidly changing mortgage finance market, beginning with the current state of the traditional supplier of mortgage funds, the savings and loan industry. Regulation put in place in the 1930s has compelled savings and loans to invest almost exclusively in residential mortgages. This regulation consisted of restrictions on types of liabilities offered and the interest rates paid and on types of investments included in the portfolios of savings and loans. The government relied on tax incentives to make mortgage investments attractive to savings and loans, but the result was to expose savings and loans to significant amounts of interest rate risk. When inflation forced interest rates to rise in the late 1970s and early 1980s, they incurred significant losses. Many institutions also experienced serious problems with default in real estate projects they financed. The problems facing the savings and loan industry have been complicated by the fact that the Federal Savings and Loan Insurance Corporation (FSLIC) has had insufficient resources to deal effectively with the large number of insolvent institutions. As a result, a significant number of institutions have operated with little or no capital.

Federal government participation in the mortgage finance industry has not been limited to savings and loans regulation. It has also created and supported a set of specialized mortgage institutions that guarantee mortgages against default and issue mortgage-backed securities. These agencies issue debt obligations with agency status in the debt markets, which means they carry the implicit backing of the U.S. government and therefore have very low premiums for default risk. The three issuers of mortgage-backed securities, GNMA, FHLMC and FNMA, were originally intended to provide a source of mortgage funds when the savings and loan industry experienced disintermediation. However, in the late 1970s, the secondary mortgage market, composed principally of securities issued by these agencies, grew into a major source of mortgage funds.

There are two distinct risks important in mortgage-backed securities: prepayment risk and default risk. Prepayment risk refers to the fact that timing receipt of cash flows on a mortgage is uncertain, since mortgages generally include an option for the borrower to prepay the mortgage. Prepayments occur principally when a home is sold and when interest rates decline so that refinancing is profitable. Since both events are uncertain, the cash flows in a mortgage investment are uncertain. Prepayments tend to increase when interest rates decline, and this is precisely when it is disadvantageous for a lender to reinvest the funds which were invested in a mortgage. Prepayment risk is an important determinant of the yields on mortgage-backed securities.

FHA and VA mortgages have government guarantees against default, the other kind of risk. Conventional mortgages generally have a private default guarantee if leveraged above 80 percent. Companies offering these guarantees are known as mortgage insurance companies.

One of the most important features of the mortgage finance market in recent years is the growth of mortgage-backed securities. The types of securities used in this market are distinct from the types used in either the corporate or the Treasury bond markets. Bonds generally have well-specified cash flows or coupon payments. By contrast, the most popular mortgage-backed security used to date is a pass-through security. The pass-through got its name from the fact that all cash flows from the pool of mortgages backing the security are passed through to securityholders as received so that prepayment risk is borne by the securityholders. The pass-through has been used principally by GNMA and FHLMC for their issues of mortgage-backed securities.

A new type of mortgage-backed security, the CMO, transforms the cash flows from a mortgage pool into a pattern of distributions to securityholders that more closely resembles a corporate or Treasury bond than cash flows from a pass-through security. The CMO splits cash flows generated by a pool of mortgages into separate categories and issues securities with claims on these specialized cash flows on the entire mortgage pool. This adds value to the market since the prepayment risk of each specialized class of claims on the mortgage pool is relatively low. Market participants who prefer cash flows with a specific maturity will be attracted to specific classes of securities in a CMO. Since the uncertainty for each preferred maturity is reduced relative to a pass-through security, the CMO adds value to the overall market.

QUESTIONS

1. Summarize the key regulations imposed on the savings and loan industry which induced them to invest their portfolios largely in residential mortgages.
2. What were the basic features of the Garn-St Germain Act? How has and will this piece of legislation influence the savings and loan industry?
3. What has been the effect of the tax laws on the investment practices of savings and loans?
4. Do savings and loans have to record the market value of their assets on their financial statements? Why or why not? What has been the implication of this practice for determining when a savings and loan is solvent or insolvent?
5. Distinguish between the three mortgage agencies: FHLMC, FNMA and GNMA. How do they differ? How are they similar?
6. What has been the historical pattern of default experienced on conventional mortgages? Who bears the risk of these defaults? Why did the system evolve the way it has?

7. Describe how you would compute the yield on a pass-through security if you knew its price and you assumed that it would prepay according to the pattern in the recent FHA experience? How would this compare to your answer if you assumed all the mortgages in the pool would prepay at year 15?
8. Explain how a CMO works. How can CMOs add value to the market relative to pass-through securities? Who is likely to reap the benefits of the addition of value: the securities brokers, FHLMC or some other market participant?
9. What is the mean weighted-average life of a tranch of a CMO? How would it be computed?
10. If you knew the mean weighted-average life of a tranch of a CMO, how could you compute the yield of that tranch? How would you select the maturity of a Treasury instrument with which to compare it?
11. How do yields on specific tranches of CMOs compare with yields on Treasury instruments? How does the yield spread vary with maturity? Explain the reason for the pattern which you observe.

REFERENCES

Barth, John B., Dan Brumbaugh, Daniel Sauerhaft, and George Wang, "Insolvency and Risk Taking in the Thrift Industry: Implications for the Future," paper delivered at the Conference of the Western Economic Association, June 20, 1985.

Campbell, Tim S. and J. Kimball Dietrich. "The Determinants of Default on Insured Conventional Residential Mortgage Loans," *Journal of Finance,* 38 (December 1983), pp. 1569–82.

Dale-Johnson, David and Terence C. Langetieg. "The Pricing of Collateralized Mortgage Obligations," Working Paper, University of Southern California, 1985.

Dunn, Kenneth B. and John J. McConnell. "A Comparison of Alternative Models for Pricing GNMA Mortgage-Backed Securities," *Journal of Finance,* 36 (May 1981), pp. 471–83.

Dunn, Kenneth B. and John J. McConnell. "Valuation of GNMA Mortgage-Backed Securities," *Journal of Finance* 36 (June 1981), pp. 599–616.

Kane, Edward J. "A Six-Point Program for Deposit Insurance Reform," *Housing Finance Review,* 2 (July 1983), pp. 269–79.

Kane, Edward J. "Change and Progress in Contemporary Mortgage Markets," *Housing Finance Review,* 3 (July 1984), pp. 257–82.

Roll, Richard. *Collateralized Mortgage Obligations: Characteristics, History, Analysis,* New York: Goldman Sachs & Company, April 1986.

Seiders, David F. "The Future of Secondary Mortgage Markets: Economic Forces and Federal Policies," *Housing Finance Review,* 3 (July 1984) pp. 219–348.

Von Furstenberg, George M. "Default Risk on FHA-Insured Home Mortgages as a Function of the Terms of Financing: A Quantitative Analysis," *Journal of Finance,* 24 (June 1969), pp. 459–77.

Waldman, Michael. *Mortgage Securities: 1972–1984 Historical Performance and Implications for Investors,* New York: Salomon Brothers Inc., March 1985.

Waldman, Michael. *The Next Step in Mortgage Security Yields: Applying the Experience of the 1970s,* New York: Salomon Brothers Inc., 1985.

Waldman, Michael, Mark Gordon and Steven Guterman. *The Salomon Brothers Prepayment Model: Impact of the Market Rally on Mortgage Prepayments and Yields,* New York: Salomon Brothers Inc., September 4, 1985.

20

*T*HE MONEY MARKETS

In this chapter and the next one we examine the operation of specific financial markets in the United States. We will focus on two types of markets: (1) the money markets or the markets for short-term liquid debt instruments, and (2) the options and futures markets. Money markets are one of the oldest markets, and they are particularly important for financial institutions, especially commercial banks, since one of their main services is to provide liquidity. Hence, financial institutions' operations are very closely linked with money markets.

We can observe a wide variety of distinct types of financial instruments and forms of market organization in the money markets. Actually, **money markets** consist of a collection of markets where distinct types of short-term financial instruments are traded, such as Treasury bills, commercial paper, and federal funds. Our objective in analyzing these markets, in part, is to develop some institutional knowledge. However, it is also to see some examples of different types of market organization and to observe more examples of innovation in financial markets. Some of the money market instruments exist largely because regulations created them. This is particularly true of the federal funds market which grew out of bank trading in excess reserves. Were it not for reserve requirements, there simply would be no federal funds as we know them. In other cases an over-the-counter market has developed in a particular type of instrument because it was exempted from some kind of regulation. For instance, debt instruments with maturities shorter than 270 days are exempt from SEC registration. Because of this rule, commercial paper has a maturity less than 270 days.

We will examine the operations of the primary and secondary markets for one of the largest volume instruments in the money markets, U.S. Treasury bills, and also examine how dealers in the secondary Treasury securities market operate. Then we will turn our attention to interesting new developments in the money markets, such as growth of money market funds and their effect on the banking system and the development of a market for swaps. ■

OVERVIEW OF MONEY MARKET INSTRUMENTS

Money markets consist of a collection of markets where distinct types of short-term financial instruments are traded.

In one sense the name *money market* is a misnomer because money, per se, is not traded in this market. Money is composed essentially of cash or currency and demand deposits or checking account balances. And these items are not traded in the money market. However, the closest money substitutes that the financial markets have to offer are traded in the money market. As a result, it is useful to think of the money market as determining yields on these close money substitutes and thus indirectly on money itself.

The money market refers to the market for a wide variety of short-term debt instruments, where *short term* generally means securities having maturities of one year or less. Since the instruments in the money market are relatively close substitutes, their yields move quite closely together. Figure 20–1 shows recent yields on some of the most important money market instruments. The money market is a combination of primary and secondary markets. The important feature here is that the asset must be relatively liquid so that it can be turned over quickly at low costs. Also, this normally means it is necessary for the asset to be able to be resold. For assets with very short maturities, however, the resale provision may not be all-important as long as there is little probability of default. As a result, the money market is composed of assets perceived to be liquid, either because they have short maturities with low default risk, or because there is an active secondary market in the asset. To qualify under either of these accounts, an asset must be reasonably homogeneous or standardized and have a sufficient trading volume to make it profitable for dealers to hold it in their inventories. To understand the money market we have to understand the nature of the securities traded in it. Let us now look briefly at some of these securities.

Treasury bills are obligations of the U.S. Treasury which are issued with a maturity of one year or less.

Treasury Bills. The most important type of security in the money market in terms of volume of securities outstanding is **U.S. Treasury bills.** These bills are part of the secondary rather than the primary market in Treasury bills and are available in denominations as low as $10,000, though most Treasury bill trading is in larger denominations. The maturities available range from 30 days to 1 year, and the interest rates in the secondary market are closely related to the rates on new issues of Treasury bills.

Commercial paper is unsecured debt obligations with initial maturities up to 270 days issued by both financial and nonfinancial corporations.

Commercial Paper. This is the name given to the unsecured short-term financial obligations sold to the market by corporations or financial institutions. Trading in commercial paper is principally a primary rather than a secondary market. **Commercial paper** is generally issued with denominations of at least $100,000 and may have a maturity of up to 270 days. Publicly issued securities with longer

FIGURE 20–1

Short-term interest rates: monthly averages, except for discount and prime rates, which are effective dates of change.

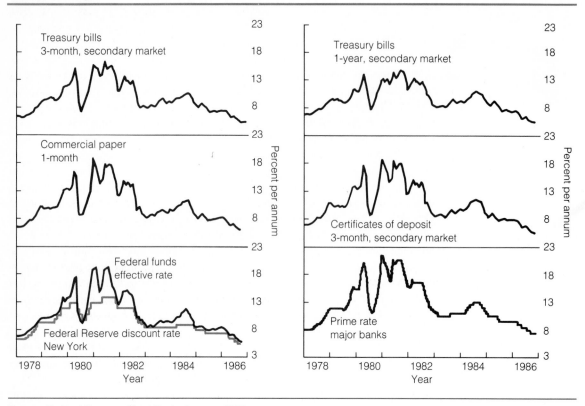

Source: Federal Reserve Chart Book, January 1987.

maturities must be registered with the Securities and Exchange Commission, a costly process that would raise the cost of these short-term debt instruments. The market for commercial paper is generally limited to the more creditworthy corporations and financial institutions. As a result, commercial paper is thought to be a relative low-risk investment.

However, defaults have not been unknown on commercial paper. In 1970 the Penn Central Railroad defaulted on $82 million worth of commercial paper. The market did not suffer any serious long-term difficulties due to this default by a major borrower, though it did encourage lenders to analyze the risks carefully. One mechanism used to limit the amount of risk is for borrowers to have their commercial paper backed by commitments from commercial banks to extend loans, if necessary, at the time the commercial paper matures. Commercial paper backed in this way is called *prime commercial paper*.

Certificates of deposit (CDs) are marketable time deposits at commercial banks.

Certificates of Deposit.   These securities are a marketable type of time deposit originally issued by commercial banks. **Certificates of deposit (CDs)** are issued with a specific maturity and have a minimum denomination of $100,000. The market for CDs began to develop in the early 1960s as a secondary market where existing CDs could be resold. Prior to this time, investors were reluctant to commit large amounts of funds to bank time deposits because of the penalty if funds were withdrawn prior to maturity. With the advent of a secondary market, this problem was essentially eliminated. Still, CDs, like other bank deposits, were subject to restrictions for maximum interest rates (see Chapters 14, 17, and 18). They were, therefore, unattractive in periods when interest rates on other money market securities were above these limits. Between 1970 and 1973, the Federal Reserve phased out the interest rate restrictions paid on deposits over $100,000 or on CDs. With this change, CDs became an important part of the money market both when interest rates were high and low.

Banker's Acceptance.   Historically, bankers' acceptances were one of the first short-term highly marketable assets. They have been used for virtually hundreds of years. A **banker's acceptance** is created to finance goods that have not yet been transported from seller to buyer. The buyer of the goods promises to pay a prespecified amount within a limited period of time, say 90 days. The promise is given credibility if the bank accepts it, because the bank then commits itself to make the payment should the seller default. The banker's acceptance is therefore a commitment from a merchant and from a bank to pay a specified amount at a particular time. This makes these securities of rather low risk. Bankers' acceptances have functioned as a highly liquid short-term asset for many years.

Federal Funds and Repurchase Agreements.   Federal funds and repurchase agreements constitute probably the most liquid and the shortest maturity assets available in the money market. The **federal funds** market started as a market where commercial banks which were members of the Federal Reserve System could borrow and lend excess reserves among one another. Excess reserves are funds which banks hold on deposit with the Federal Reserve to satisfy its reserve requirements. If one bank finds it has an excess in deposits at the Federal Reserve, it can loan these funds to another bank and the exchange is made by the Federal Reserve through its wire transfer service, an electronic mechanism through which funds can be transferred instantly from one bank to another. There is no delay for a check to clear as with other types of transactions. As a result, it became possible to have virtually overnight maturities on federal funds. The market for federal funds has gradually grown to be much broader than merely the borrowing and lending of excess reserves between Federal Reserve System member banks. The federal funds market now involves borrowing and lending between a variety of financial institutions. The fundamental characteristic of the market is that it involves immediately available funds, or funds cleared through the Federal Reserve's wire transfer service.

A closely related market is the market for repurchase agreements (RPs). A **repurchase agreement** involves the sale of a security, usually a Treasury bill, with the simultaneous agreement by the seller to repurchase the security at a prespecified later date. A repurchase agreement is therefore similar to a collateralized

A banker's acceptance is a commitment from a merchant backed up by a commitment from a bank to pay a specific amount of funds at a specific time.

Federal funds constitute short-term borrowing between financial institutions executed through the Federal Reserve's wire transfer service.

A repurchase agreement involves the sale of a security with a simultaneous agreement to repurchase it at a prespecified date.

loan. The seller of the Treasury bill is borrowing funds for a prespecified period. Repurchase agreements are generally of very short maturities, sometimes 1 day, but most often 3 to 14 days. Because of this, they are very similar to federal funds, but RPs involve a larger market. In addition, RPs are used as a substitute for federal funds because of the flexibility of negotiating maturities. Financial and nonfinancial corporations as well as governments borrow and lend through repurchase agreements.

Most of the money market is an over-the-counter market, but the exception is the primary market in Treasury bills. The money market operates over the telephone and most all transactions are carried out by large institutions or corporations so that transactions are relatively large. Because the market's central purpose is to provide highly liquid short-term borrowing and investment opportunities to corporations and financial institutions, it is particularly concerned with executing fast and efficient transactions.

An order is placed in this market through a telephone call to a dealer who quotes a bid or asked price. An order can be placed immediately with a dealer or a customer may shop around for quotations from other dealers. Once an order is placed, the dealer arranges for transfer of title to the securities and an exchange of funds through the customer's bank. Some of the dealers in this market are commercial banks and others are brokerage firms. In either case, they stand ready to quote a price and execute the transaction over the telephone.

In terms of the volume of securities outstanding, the largest component of the money market is made up of Treasury bills. Moreover, because RPs are often collateralized by Treasury bills and federal funds are closely related to Treasury bills, government securities are the dominant portion of the market. Because of the prominence of government securities in the money market, the over-the-counter market in these money market assets is closely tied to the secondary market in government securities, not just the secondary market in Treasury bills.

The money market differs from other markets as it is a conglomeration of markets for distinct securities that have some common characteristics—short maturities, low default risk, and high degree of liquidity. The securities are similar enough that a dealer in one can be a dealer in all of them, yet they are not sufficiently homogeneous to make an auction market an efficient trading method. As a result, they have come to be traded in what operates like a single over-the-counter market.

While the money market operates much like a single over-the-counter market for a variety of different money market instruments, it is still useful to examine the market for Treasury bills in a little more detail.

THE TREASURY BILL MARKET

THE PRIMARY TREASURY BILL MARKET—PURE AUCTION

The primary Treasury bill market is one of the few pure call auction markets for financial assets in operation. Auctions are conducted by the U.S. Treasury at regular weekly intervals. The Treasury decides ahead of time what volume of bills it intends to issue and then auctions them to the highest bidders. At one time the Treasury operated in the reverse manner by setting a price and then seeking buyers, but this was abandoned some years ago in favor of the auction procedure.

Two types of offers to purchase bills are entertained by the Treasury. **Competitive tenders** constitute an offer to buy a specific volume of Treasury bills at a specific price. Buyers who make such offers are generally dealers in the secondary market in government securities or other large institutions that buy in volume and can study the market and forecast the best offer price. If they guess high, they will be assured of securing their bids. If they bid low, then there may be sufficient offers at higher prices to exhaust the Treasury issue. **Noncompetitive tenders** contain no specific offer of a price; instead, they constitute an offer to buy a specific volume of securities at the average price prevailing in that auction, whatever it might be. The Treasury places maximum limits on the size of noncompetitive tenders for bills. This stood at $500,000 in the mid-1980s. By comparison, the average size of competitive tenders often exceeds $20 million.

In the Treasury bill auction, the procedure used to determine what orders will be accepted is as follows: the Treasury accepts all noncompetitive tenders first then turns to the competitive tenders. It proceeds through the competitive tenders from highest to lowest bid until all available bills have been sold or the issue is fully subscribed. It then computes the average price of all competitive tenders and applies that price to the noncompetitive tenders.

While neither the Treasury nor the Federal Reserve has collected historical data on the composition of noncompetitive tenders, the Federal Reserve Bank of New York did conduct a special study of those making noncompetitive tenders in the New York Federal Reserve district for the auction on July 20, 1978. In this 1978 auction more than 85 percent of the total number of noncompetitive tenders came from individuals rather than financial institutions or corporations; this represented 70 percent of the total dollar volume of such tenders. Of these tenders from individuals, more than 40 percent of the volume came in amounts greater than $100,000, though many of these large offers came from estates or trust accounts managed by commercial banks.[1]

The purity of the primary auction market for Treasury bills leaves no room for dealers, although dealers are certainly one of the more important customers in this primary market. They purchase new Treasury bills to support their inventories for resale in the secondary market, which is an over-the-counter rather than an auction market. Unlike the secondary market in equities, the trading process is not continuous, so no imbalances develop between buyers and sellers that can be resolved by dealers. In the primary Treasury bill market imbalances are resolved by the low bidders going without. They can then wait for the next primary auction, or they can turn to a dealer in the secondary Treasury bill market.

Competitive tenders refer to bids to buy Treasury bills in the Treasury's weekly auction at a price offered by the bidder; **noncompetitive tenders** refer to bids to buy Treasury bills at the average price prevailing in that auction.

---

[1]See Charles M. Sivesind, "Noncompetitive Tenders in Treasury Auctions: How Much Do They Affect Savings Flows?" *Quarterly Review,* Federal Reserve Bank of New York, vol. 3 (Autumn 1978), pp. 34–8.

THE SECONDARY MARKET IN TREASURY BILLS

The secondary market in Treasury securities is referred to as an over-the-counter market because there is no centralized exchange facility. But this market underwent tremendous changes in the 1970s, and it is now closer to an auction market than it once was. Trading in the market is generally broken down into the interdealer market and the customer market. The **customer market** includes trading with all other nondealer participants. The **interdealer market** includes trades directly between dealers and trades between dealers arranged through a broker. Brokers are used in the interdealer market in order to maintain confidentiality or anonymity about the other trading party's identity. Direct dealer trades declined in significance through the 1970s, but trading with brokers increased. The sum of the two represented a little more than 50 percent of all trades in the mid-1980s.

In the early 1960s and 1970s the market operated over the telephone. The traders working for each dealer firm would quote prices and make exchanges with other dealers, with brokers or with other types of customers. Customers would have to search for the best price to buy or sell by calling separate firms and asking for quotes. There was no centralized facility for exchange or for displaying quotations of bid or ask prices. Beginning in the mid-1970s this system began to change. At that time dealer firms began to implement automated quotation systems as a result of private entrepreneurial activity. The automated quotation system involved two separate systems, one used in the interdealer market and one available to dealers and nondealer customers of brokers. The system, used exclusively in the interdealer market, facilitates automated quotation of bid and ask prices as well as automated execution of trades. It eliminates the need for dealers to search for the best prices among themselves. Like the similar system envisioned for the NYSE, it provides automatic exchanges at the best available prices. With the use of this facility the interdealer market has become essentially an auction market.

The billboard system used outside the interdealer market provides only display of bid and ask prices. There is no ability to actually conduct an exchange through the system. A dealer displays his or her price on the quotation system, and a customer interested in an exchange at that price must call the dealer to conduct the exchange. These billboard systems can be rented by anyone interested in the market. A billboard system like this is essentially an advertising device; it reduces the cost of searching for alternative prices which is borne by the customers in an over-the-counter market. This billboard system is most economical for securities that are very actively traded.

DEALERS IN THE TREASURY SECURITY MARKET

The official dealers in Treasury securities are those firms which the Federal Reserve Bank of New York (FRBNY) classifies as dealers. The FRBNY has a central position in this market because it conducts all trades in Treasury securities for the Federal Reserve System. And the principal mechanism through which the Fed-

The **customer market** for Treasury bills is the market where purchasers are not dealers in Treasury bills. The **interdealer market** is the market among dealers.

eral Reserve conducts monetary policy is by the purchase and sale of Treasury securities. Most dealers in the Treasury bill market also act as dealers in at least a selection of other instruments, as we will see in examining data on dealer transactions and dealer inventories.

As a result of its special position vis-a-vis dealers, the FRBNY has, in effect, become the regulator of the dealers in this market. In 1985 a U.S. government securities dealer known as E.S.M Government Securities Inc. of Fort Lauderdale, Florida, went into bankruptcy. E.S.M was not one of the official dealers monitored by the FRBNY. However, a number of other financial institutions took sizable losses as a result of the E.S.M. collapse, causing considerable attention to be focused on the operations of Treasury dealers and their regulation. It also caused market participants to take new precautions to limit their loss exposure with individual dealers.

The FRBNY receives daily statistical reports from all dealers it recognizes and trades with. In addition, it maintains daily phone contact with these dealers and visits the firms periodically. There are generally about 35 dealers reporting to the FRBNY, many of which are generally commercial banks. Unlike other areas of securities trading, the Glass-Steagall Act did not exclude commercial banks from operating as U.S. Treasury securities dealers. A firm is invited to join the official list when the FRBNY concludes that it has sufficient business volume across the maturity spectrum of available securities and it is adequately capitalized and managed.

Dealers in this market chiefly earn their profits off the spread between bid and asked prices on the securities they trade and from the gains or losses in particular securities. In addition, dealers attempt to earn a higher interest rate on their securities inventory than they must pay for funds to support that inventory. When this yield spread is favorable to the dealer, it is referred to as **positive carry.** Their ability to generate a positive carry hinges on the shape of the yield curve because their investments tend to be spread across the maturity spectrum, while their funding is obtained with a very short maturity. The profit earned from trading depends upon the magnitude of the market spread and how successfully dealers have managed their positions. As the volatility of Treasury yields increased in the late 1970s and early 1980s, dealers became particularly interested in using Treasury bill futures and other futures and options to hedge the risks of their positions. Such hedging activities are now an integral part of the dealer's risk management.

Dealers in Treasury securities generally also act as dealers in other types of money market instruments, such as bankers' acceptances and certificates of deposit. Table 20–1 presents data on transactions and positions of inventory for dealers who reported to the Federal Reserve Bank of New York during 1985. The table shows the average daily trading volume and average daily positions in a variety of money market and related instruments during 1985 for FRBNY authorized dealers. The table also shows the same data for futures and forward positions. It indicates that the largest volume of transactions during 1985 were in Treasury bills and that trading volume declines as the maturity of the Treasury

Positive carry refers to a positive spread between the yield on a dealer's inventory of securities and the cost of funding that inventory.

TABLE 20–1
Transactions and positions of U.S. government securities dealers, averages of daily figures for 1985 ($millions).

Type of Instrument	Transactions	Positions
Cash Market:		
Treasury bills	32,900	10,075
Other less than 1 Year	1,811	1,050
Treasury 1–5 years	18,361	5,154
Treasury 5–10 years	12,703	−6,202
Treasury over 10 years	9,556	−2,686
Total Treasury	$75,331	
Transactions with dealers	3,336	
Transactions with brokers	36,222	
Transactions with others	35,773	
Federal agency securities	11,640	22,860
Certificates of deposit	4,016	9,192
Bankers acceptances	3,242	4,586
Commercial paper	10,018	5,570
Futures Market:		
Treasury bills	5,561	−7,322
Treasury notes, bonds	6,069	4,465
Federal agencies	240	−722
Forward Market:		
Treasuries	1,283	−911
Federal agencies	3,857	−9,420

obligation lengthens. The next largest volume of trading was in commercial paper and agency securities. *Agency securities* are debt instruments issued by U.S. government agencies. Most of these agencies are involved in mortgage financing which was discussed in some detail in Chapter 19. The data in Table 20–1 reveal that FRBNY-authorized dealers had the largest inventory position in Treasury bills. This makes sense since they had the largest trading volume in this security as well. But they also had a correspondingly large short position in Treasury bill futures, which means they were hedging a significant portion of their Treasury bill inventory. By contrast, dealers had a short cash position in Treasury coupon-bearing debt (debt with a maturity longer than one year), while they had offsetting long positions in futures contracts in Treasury coupon debt. This demonstrates the importance of hedging operations to the dealer function.

The Treasury market is actually only one of the broader money markets. We could spend a lot of time on each of these markets. However, there are a number of excellent treatments of the details of each of the instruments in the money markets. (For example, see Marcia Stigum, *The Money Market.*) Therefore, it is probably more useful to examine some innovations that have developed in the money markets in the last few years.

MONEY MARKET MUTUAL FUNDS

Money markets in the United States are a collection of constantly changing markets for distinct securities. The process of change or innovation in these markets was particularly rapid in the late 1970s and 1980s. One of the more interesting new developments in the money markets is the growth of money market funds. Some observers of financial markets have called the money market fund the most important development in retail banking, or in delivery of financial services to consumers, in this century. One reason this innovation is important is because it has been so successful, at least as measured by the magnitude of funds money market funds have attracted in such a short time. From a base of less than $4 billion in 1975, money market fund assets grew to roughly $220 billion by the end of 1981. But these new institutions are also important for another reason as well—they have posed an extremely serious threat to traditional depository institutions, such as savings and loans and commercial banks. Let's try to understand the nature of this threat as well as how depository institutions and regulators have responded to the growth of money market funds.

SOME BASIC FACTS

Money market mutual funds are open-end investment companies which invest only in short-term money market instruments. An **open-end investment company** invests in other securities and sells direct claims on the securities portfolio maintained by the fund to the public. By contrast, a closed-end fund sells shares in the distinct legal entity that constitutes the fund. We examined how closed-end funds are valued in Chapter 18. There are many types of mutual funds, both open- and closed-end. The unique feature of money market funds is that they invest in high quality short-term credit obligations so that the assets in their portfolios have relatively little default or interest rate risk. This makes them attractive to both institutional and individual investors who want an investment that offers little risk of price fluctuations and has low default risk.

Most money market funds operate in a relatively standard manner, though there are some differences across funds. Investors generally are allowed to purchase and redeem shares without paying a sales charge. The expenses incurred by the fund are deducted daily from the fund's gross income. Most funds have a minimum initial investment ranging from $500 to $20,000. The yield on the fund depends on the yield earned on the securities in the fund. The portfolio of the money market fund is **marked-to-market** each day; this means that the portfolio is valued each day based on the values of the individual assets in it. Most money market funds have check writing privileges which allow fund investors to write checks (with a $500 minimum) against their holdings in the fund. The check writing process is generally arranged through a joint venture of the investment company offering the fund and a commercial bank.

Table 20–2 provides some basic information on a selection of money market funds available in 1985. This is excerpted from a larger table published regularly

Money market mutual funds are open-end investment companies which invest only in short-term money market instruments.

An **open-end investment company** holds a portfolio of securities and sells direct claims on it to the public.

Marking a portfolio to market means recording the market value of a securities portfolio on the books of the firm that owns them.

TABLE 20–2
Money market funds as of September, 1985.

Portfolio Average Maturity (days)	Fund/Distributor	Date Started	Investment Results		Total Assets		Minimum Initial Investment	Annual Expenses per $100
			Latest 12 Months					
			Total Return	Return from Income Dividends	6/30/85 ($ millions)	% Change '85 vs. '84		
	FORBES government money fund companies			8.6%				
	FORBES tax-free money fund composite			5.3%				
	FORBES general money fund composite			8.9%				
General money market funds								
49	Prudential-Bache Money-Mart Assets52/Pru-Bache	6/76	—	9.3%	$3,324	13%	$1,000	$0.52‡
57	Putnam Daily Dividend Trust/Putnam	9/76	—	9.1	270	-2	1,000	0.85
29	Renaissance Assets Trust-MM/First of Mich	7/82	—	9.1	136	147	1,000	0.63‡
1	Reserve CPA-Primary/Reserve Partner	9/83	—	8.7	10	0	1,000	1.00‡
48	Reserve Fund-Primary/Reserve Partner	11/71	—	8.9	1,560	-8	1,000	0.91‡
42	LF Rothschild Earnings & Liquidity/Rothschild	4/82	—	8.9	336	7	2,500	0.73
25	RPF of America-MM Fund/Venture	9/76	—	8.1	13	49	1,000	1.23‡
25	Safeco Money Market Mutual Fund/Safeco	4/82	—	9.2	36	6	1,000	0.93
40	Scudder Cash Investment Trust/Scudder	7/76	—	8.9	1,027	4	1,000	0.66
15	Security Cash Fund/Security	10/80	—	8.1	47	-34	1,000	1.00
35	Selected Money Market-General/Prescott, Ball	10/77	—	8.5	22	-18	1,000	1.27
28	Seligman Cash Magement-Prime/Seligman	1/77	—	8.8	342	-21	1,000	0.94
37	Sentinel Cash Management Fund/Equity Services	10/81	—	8.9	39	10	1,000	0.75
25	Sentry Cash Management Fund/Sentry	6/81	—	8.8	27	-9	1,000	0.94
44	Shearson Daily Dividend/Shearson	6/79	—	9.0	3,507	-2	2,500	0.70
46	Shearson FMA Cash Fund/Shearson	2/82	—	9.0	1,123	71	15,000	0.70
21	Short Term Assets Reserve/Moseley	12/84	—	—*	74	—	1,000	0.61‡
50	Short Term Income Fund-MM/Reich & Tang	1/80	—	8.9	353	39	5,000	0.86‡
23	Short-Term Yield Secs/AIM Distributor	5/78	—	8.4	14	-20	1,250	1.00
14	Sigma Money Market Fund/Delfi Capital	9/80	—	8.6	7	-54	500	1.00‡
39	Standby Reserve Fund/Cowen	11/81	—	9.2	273	24	2,000	0.76
15	State Bond Cash Management Fund/State Bond	2/82	—	8.3	4	-3	1,000	1.00‡
34	SteinRoe Cash Reserves/Stein Roe	10/76	—	9.0	759	-19	2,500	0.72
60	Summit Cash Reserves Fund/ML Funds	12/82	—	9.0	495	19	5,000	0.78‡
12	Sutro MM Fund/Sutro	2/82	—	8.6	110	20	2,000	1.20
36	Transamerica Cash Reserve/Transamerica	8/80	—	9.3	239	-36	500	0.50
16	Trinity Liquid Assets Trust/Russell	1/83	—	9.1	275	0	1,000	0.60‡
44	Trust for Cash Reserves/Milwaukee Co	2/80	—	8.7	150	3	1,000	1.05
45	Tucker Anthony Cash Mgmt Fund/Tucker Anthony	4/81	—	8.9	470	41	2,500	0.64
15	20th Century Cash Reserve/20th Century	3/85	—	—*	12	—	none†	1.01
33	UMB Money Market-Prime/Jones & Babson	11/82	—	9.1	80	65	1,000	0.53
45	United Cash Management/Waddell & Reed	8/79	—	8.9	323	-7	1,000	1.06‡
35	USAA Mutual-MM Fund/USAA	2/81	—	9.1	259	14	1,000	0.73
48	Value Line Cash Fund/Value Line	4/79	—	9.1	454	-16	1,000	0.82
27	Vanguard MM Trust-Insured/Vanguard	2/83	—	8.6	54	75	1,000	0.90
41	Vanguard MM Trust-Prime/Vanguard	6/75	—	9.4	166	-87	1,000	0.48
42	Vantage Money Market-Cash/Smith Barney	10/82	—	9.1	290	77	none†	0.66
37	Webster Cash Reserve/Kidder	8/79	—	9.1	1,371	21	1,500	0.67
44	Working Assets Money Fund/Working Assets	8/83	—	8.3	63	200	1,000	1.10‡

Funds are added to this guide when they exceed $5 million in net assets and deleted when they drop below $2 million. *Fund not in operation for full period. †Most funds are no load. Some funds are offered as part of an integrated financial service account which has a minimum initial investment. ‡Fund has 12b-1 plan pending or in force. 52Formely MoneyMart Assets.

Source: Forbes, September 16, 1985, p. 149.

by *Forbes* on all money market funds available to the public. The table indicates when the fund was started, its total assets, annual expenses, average maturity, and rate of return earned in the last 12 months. This table illustrates that the average maturity of assets in the funds is relatively short; no fund on this page has a maturity longer than 60 days. Moreover, the table illustrates that the funds earned very similar rates of return during this period. Since the assets in these funds are of relatively low risk, there is less lattitude for the kinds of differences in performance across funds which might be found in mutual funds that invest in corporate equities.

DEVELOPMENT OF MONEY MARKET FUNDS

The first money market fund offered shares to the public in 1972. In 1974, there was a significant increase in interest rates on short-term money market securities such as Treasury bills, commercial paper, and certificates of deposit. Those relatively high interest rates encouraged investors to look for new ways to invest funds in safe and liquid but high-yielding investments. Money market funds emerged to satisfy that demand. By the end of 1975, there were 35 funds offering shares to the public with total assets of slightly under $4 billion. Money market funds experienced no additional growth until interest rates began to increase again. From 1977 until 1982 money market funds experienced tremendous growth as interest rates accelerated to record high levels. The growth in money market fund assets is documented in Table 20–3, which shows the level of assets each year from 1977 until 1986.

The reason money market funds were able to grow as interest rates increased on money market securities is that commercial banks and savings and loans were constrained by Regulation Q. *Regulation Q* was maintained by the Federal Reserve Board to limit interest rates that commercial banks could pay on most time and savings accounts. Regulations similar to those enforced by the Federal Reserve were applied to savings and loans by the Federal Home Loan Bank Board. (See Chapter 19 for a more detailed discussion of Regulation Q and the savings

TABLE 20–3
Money market fund assets ($ billions).

Date	Total Outstanding Assets
1985	241.1
1984	230.4
1983	181.4
1982	233.6
1981	186.8
1980	75.8
1979	43.6
1978	10.3
1977	3.8

and loan industry.) The intent of Regulation Q was to protect depository institutions from the potentially adverse consequences of competing for savings deposits by raising interest rates. In large part, the concern about such competition arose from the fact that savings and loans were constrained by regulation to invest in long-term fixed rate mortgages funded with largely short-term deposits. If these institutions were compelled to pay relatively high rates on savings deposits to attract funds, their profitability and ultimately their solvency could be threatened. In the early 1980s, this is precisely what happened to savings and loans. But, in the mid-1970s, the policy of the bank and savings and loan regulators was to protect these institutions by enforcing Regulation Q.

The inherent flaw in Regulation Q was that if market interest rates rose substantially above the interest rate ceilings on deposit accounts the depositors would withdraw their funds from these regulated institutions. In the 1960s and early 1970s when this process of disintermediation occurred, depositors with modest amounts of funds had relatively few alternatives. Depositors with more than $100,000 could choose certificates of deposit that were free of Regulation Q ceilings. The interest rate ceilings on these types of deposits were eliminated by the Federal Reserve in 1963. In 1974, when interest rates rose above Regulation Q ceilings, depositors with less than $100,000 who wanted high return risk-free investments were largely constrained to invest in Treasury bills. These had a minimum denomination of $10,000 and were the most readily understandable and accessible investments open to individuals used to placing funds in banks and savings and loans.

Traditional banks and savings and loan customers were being driven out of these depository institutions to invest in Treasury obligations because of high market interest rates and regulatory ceilings on deposit accounts. This fact created a market opportunity for firms that were not subject to Regulation Q, the investment companies and brokerage firms regulated by the SEC. Those firms did not face the same constraints that banks and savings and loans did, however, the retail customer base of most brokerage firms was, and still is, quite different from that of most banks and savings and loans. Most depositors who wanted to avoid Regulation Q ceilings wanted the safety and convenience they were used to with depository institutions, and they also wanted the liquidity provided by being able to transfer funds into accounts where they could write checks.

The brokerage firms responded to this market situation by offering money market funds that provided most of the advantages of deposit accounts at commercial banks and savings and loans, without some of the inconveniences—particularly Regulation Q. Money market funds effectively satisfied consumer demand by providing safety almost as high as that available with government insurance of deposits at commercial banks and savings and loans. Since money market fund portfolios are highly diversified, of very short maturity, and are invested largely in high-quality paper, they involve very little risk. Moreover, since money market funds do not promise a specific yield, they are not subject to runs in the same sense as commercial banks. There is never any point to pulling out funds from a money market fund to get the promised return before other investors do the same and drive the fund into insolvency. This is not feasible with a money market fund since there is no promised rate; investors simply receive pro rata shares of the total earnings of the fund. Furthermore, all money market funds are regulated by the SEC and subject to their supervision so that fraud is limited.

Money market funds also provided the liquidity and convenience that investors demanded by effectively using new technology for delivery of financial services and by exploiting loopholes in regulations regarding bank and investment company activities. Rather than attempting to compete with banks and savings and loans by building a physical distribution system, such as a branch network, most firms which offered money market funds dealt with customers principally through the mails and over the telephone. Once their customers became familiar with this method of doing business, they found it more efficient than dealing with a local bank or savings and loan office. Moreover, this distribution system proved to be substantially less expensive than maintaining a branch system.

The check writing privilege is an important part of why they were such successful innovations. However, the investment company which offers the fund does not directly provide the transactions services involved in check writing privileges. It is generally offered through a joint venture with a commercial bank. The first such joint venture was arranged by Merrill Lynch with BancOne Corporation of Columbus, Ohio. BancOne is one of the more successful small banks in the United States, having concentrated on research and development in data processing and consumer services. It pioneered the development of automated processing of checks and VISA debit cards for Merrill Lynch's tremendously successful money fund, the Cash Management Account (CMA). By 1985, 160 banks and other financial institutions used its processing for credit card and money market fund transactions. Without the regulatory arbitrage of combining the transactions services of a commercial bank and the investment management of a money fund in a joint venture, it is unlikely that money market funds would have been nearly as successful as they are today.

The rapid growth of money market funds posed a serious threat to the banking and savings and loan industries; they represented a major invasion of the turf of the depository institutions by the brokerage industry. Money funds were attracting traditional customers away from banks and savings and loans with both effective new financial instruments and a low-cost delivery system. Many retail bankers feared they might lose customers permanently. The success of money market funds constituted a major victory for the securities industry in the continuing war regarding how and to what extent investment and commercial banking should be separated. The bank and savings and loan lobbies had no effective alternative in this case but to pressure the Congress and regulators to eliminate Regulation Q.

In 1982 the Congress passed the Garn-St Germain Act that directed bank and savings and loan regulators to implement a new account fully competitive with money market funds as quickly as possible. The new accounts authorized by Garn-St Germain are called **money market deposit accounts** (MMDAs). There is no interest ceiling on these accounts, though there are restrictions on the number of automatic or telephone transfers. In the first six weeks after these accounts were

Money market deposit accounts are commercial bank accounts authorized by the Garn-St Germain Act to compete with money market funds.

offered in December 1982, they generated flows into commercial banks that averaged $35 billion per week. Part of the MMDAs represented a recapturing of the market share of the consumer investment business back from the money market funds. But the bulk of the increase in MMDAs appears to have come from other deposit accounts at depository institutions. In fact, an inspection of Table 20–3 indicates that the total decline from 1982 to 1983 in money market fund assets was only $52 billion, less than the first two weeks of increase in MMDAs in 1983.

Money market funds have been a successful innovation for a number of reasons. The case of the money funds illustrates how competitive firms respond to market opportunities and how these actions, in turn, compel the regulators to reform the regulatory system.

THE NEW MARKET FOR SWAPS

A new market has developed in the 1980s, the market for swaps. It is debatable whether to include this in this chapter on the money market. Some might argue that swaps should be placed in a different category than the money market. However, swaps are one of the more interesting new financial products in the last few years and an example of the innovation we discussed in Chapter 16.

THE NATURE OF SWAPS

An **interest rate swap** involves an exchange of obligations to make interest payments on debt obligations between two borrowers.

A *swap* involves a trade of financial obligations between two parties. The most common types of swaps currently utilized in financial markets are interest rate swaps. In an **interest rate swap** parties trade obligations to make payments to lenders or bondholders. One party in the swap may have an obligation to make interest payments which are tied to a short-term interest rate, while the other party may have been committed to interest payments based on a long-term interest rate, such as the 20-year Treasury bond rate. If the first party would prefer a long-term obligation and the second party would prefer a short-term obligation, then it makes sense for them to swap interest payments.

A **currency swap** involves an exchange of fixed amounts denominated in different currencies.

The **counterparties** are the parties which agree to an exchange of financial obligations.

Swaps began to be commonly used in the the early 1980s. One of the first types of swaps was the **currency swap**, involving the exchange of cash flows between two parties to the swap, or **counterparties** as they are called when they are denominated in different currencies. Suppose, for example, that two companies each had fixed interest rate obligations on outstanding debt, but company A had debt denominated in dollars while company B had debt denominated in deutsche marks. The two companies could swap their obligations so that company A had a deutsche mark-denominated interest rate obligation while company B had a dollar-denominated obligation. Actually, a more common variety of currency swap might well include some change in the nature of the interest obligation. That is, company A might have a floating rate dollar-denominated obligation, and company B might have a fixed rate deutsche mark-denominated obligation. Then a

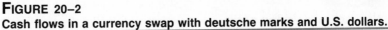

FIGURE 20–2
Cash flows in a currency swap with deutsche marks and U.S. dollars.

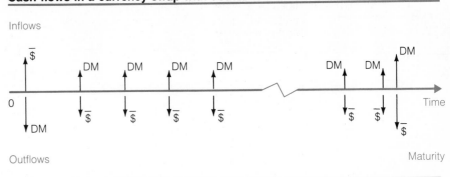

swap would entail both a change in the currency and in the interest rate maturity used to determine the obligation. The cash flows involved in this kind of currency swap are illustrated in Figure 20–2, which shows the cash flows to a company receiving deutsche marks and paying dollars in a fixed currency swap. Notice that the company receives an inflow of dollars and must pay out the equivalent value in deutsche marks at the time the swap is arranged. There is an exchange of dollars for deutsche marks throughout the life of the swap, and at the end, the principal is exchanged once again. It is not necessary that the principal values be exchanged at the beginning and the end, however, the net change in the relative value of the currencies must be exchanged.

Interest rate swaps were developed after currency swaps, but by 1987, the interest rate swap market had grown much larger than the currency swap market. Though no statistics report the total volume of various types of swaps, it is generally perceived that the interest rate swap market had grown to more than $200 billion by 1986. The interest rate swap market has grown within the United States and between firms in the United States and other parts of the world, also called the *Euromarket*.

There appear to be four basic reasons for the growth of the interest rate swap market:

1. Interest rate swaps have been a convenient and flexible way for institutions to restructure balance sheets to reduce the mismatch between the maturities of assets and liabilities.
2. Interest rate swaps have become a device to create a link between distinct markets or firms with differential access to fund sources.
3. Interest rate swaps provide a way to reduce the total funding cost for a company due to differences in spreads between ratings for short- and long-term debt.
4. Interest rate swaps can minimize the costs of regulation and tax laws.

FIGURE 20–3
Interest rate swap between two banks

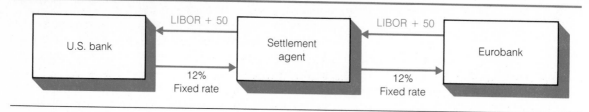

USING SWAPS FOR BALANCE SHEET RESTRUCTURING

Our discussion of how interest rate swaps work and how they are used will focus on these four points and some examples that illustrate them. To illustrate the first two points, consider the situation facing a typical U.S. bank or savings and loan that generates significant funds from short-term deposits such as money market certificates that are repriced every six months. The U.S. bank has a portfolio mismatch problem because its customers prefer to borrow for long maturities. It needs to find a way to minimize the risk inherent in the mismatch of maturities. One way is to offer variable rate loans, but the demand for these loans is considerably less than the demand for long-term fixed rate loans. A second alternative is to utilize the futures markets to hedge risk, but the futures markets entail at least some basis risk, therefore the bank is interested in evaluating other alternatives.

At the same time the U.S. bank has more short-term liabilities than assets, a bank in Europe has exactly the opposite problem. It has access to a large volume of long-term fixed rate funds through the Eurobond market. It has a sizable demand for loans with variable rates matched to LIBOR (London Interbank Offered Rate). Both banks can meet their objectives by using an interest rate swap. To illustrate, suppose the U.S. and Eurobank agree to a $10 million interest rate swap. Also suppose that the U.S. bank agrees to pay a fixed interest rate of 12 percent every 6 months for 5 years on the $10 million, called the *notional* amount. At the same time, the Eurobank agrees to pay the U.S. bank LIBOR plus 50 basis points on the same notional amount over the same period. The two banks will not actually exchange cash equal to the total amount of the promised interest payments; instead, they will exchange the net difference between these obligations. Therefore, if Libor is 10.5 percent during one 6-month period, then the U.S. bank would pay the Eurobank $50,000 (1% × $10 million per year or ½% × $10 million for six months). This transaction is illustrated in Figure 20–3.

There is generally a third party in an interest rate swap besides the two firms swapping interest payments. The third party acts as a settlement agent, collecting and paying obligated cash flows when they are due. This third party is usually also a bank. It has no obligation to pay the cash flows due unless it also acts as a guarantor in the swap. The bank which arranges the transaction and acts as a settlement agent will collect a service fee that is generally collected up front and is related to both the size and difficulty of the transaction. In addition, if the bank provides a guarantee against default, it will also collect a fee.

The interest rate swap in this example is an attractive alternative for two reasons. First, it is a relatively flexible way to alter the nature of the maturity mismatch on the books of both banks. It might be possible to accomplish the same thing with interest rate futures. However, the swap transaction can be tailored to meet the specific needs of individual parties to the transaction, an advantage if the participants are unconcerned with liquidity. That is, unlike a future, there is no secondary market for a swap. The **standardization** of the futures contract has made it possible to create highly liquid instruments with active secondary markets. However, this standardization means that the futures contract cannot be highly flexible. This creates the opportunity for the swap transaction. Secondly, the swap is valuable because it creates a link between the European market or bank and the U.S. bank. In effect, the swap links institutions operating in different markets or with different access to funds, creating the internationalization or globalization of financial markets.

Standardization refers to common terms in contracts such as futures contracts which allow the development of liquidity.

USING SWAPS TO REDUCE THE COST OF DEBT

An often cited advantage of interest rate swaps is the potential for reducing the total financing cost for the two counterparties. The opportunity for cost reduction arises from differences in risk premiums between high- and low-quality borrowers using short versus long maturity debt. In both the short-term or floating rate market and the long-term bond market, borrowers with higher perceived probability of default have to pay higher premiums to borrow. However, evidence indicates that the premiums are substantially higher for the same quality borrower in the long-term market than in the short-term market. Table 20–4 presents the actual spreads between Baa and Aaa rated 20-year fixed rate corporate bonds from 1982 to 1985. During the same time, the average spreads for comparable quality issues in the short-term floating rate market were in the neighborhood of 50 basis points. Some observers argued that the interest rate swap market was created largely as a device to take advantage of or arbitrage this spread.

To see how a swap can be used in this way, let's consider an example of a Baa rated firm which can borrow in the short-term market at a rate equal to the Treasury bill rate plus 50 basis points and an Aaa rated borrower that can borrow at Treasury plus 25 basis points.[2] This example is illustrated in Figure 20–4. We will also assume that in the long-term bond market the spread between the rates charged, or the quality spread, is 150 basis points for a 5-year bond. If the high-quality firm had to pay 11.5 percent for a new 5-year bond issue, then the lower-quality firm would have to pay 13 percent. The idea behind the swap in this

---

[2]This example and the related discussion draws heavily on James L. Bicksler and Andrew H. Chen, "An Economic Analysis of Interest Rate Swaps," *Journal of Finance* (July 1986), pp. 645–55.

TABLE 20–4
Quality spread (Baa—Aaa).

Date	1982	1983	1984	1985
Jan	1.92	2.15	1.45	1.18
Feb	1.91	1.94	1.51	1.10
Mar	2.24	1.88	1.42	1.13
Apr	2.32	1.78	1.50	1.28
May	2.38	1.63	1.46	1.43
Jun	2.11	1.63	1.50	1.46
Jul	2.19	1.24	1.71	1.46
Aug	2.61	1.13	1.76	1.45
Sep	2.69	1.18	1.69	—
Oct	2.61	1.21	1.31	—
Nov	2.62	1.20	1.19	—
Dec	2.31	1.18	1.27	—
Avg	2.33	1.51	1.48	1.31
Min	1.91	1.13	1.19	1.10
Max	2.69	2.15	1.76	1.46

Source: James L. Bickslen and Andrew H. Chen, "An Economic Analysis of Interest Rate Swaps," *Journal of Finance* (July 1986).

situation is for the high-quality borrower to issue a 5-year bond, although it would prefer a shorter maturity issue, then swap the cash flows with the lower-quality firm that issues a short maturity obligation. The cost savings for the lower quality firm is then shared between the two firms, and both come out with a lower cost of funds than they otherwise would. To complete the example, suppose the Aaa firm issues a bond of $100 million at 11.5 percent then swaps with the Baa firm issuing short-maturity debt. The Baa firm agrees to pay the Aaa firm 12 percent and receives the 6-month Treasury bill rate in exchange. The Aaa firm incurs a net cost of the Treasury rate less 50 basis points. Had it simply gone directly to the short-term market, it would have paid the Treasury bill rate plus 25 basis points. Therefore, it saved 75 basis points in total financing cost.

The Baa firm reduced its cost of borrowing through the swap: it will receive the Treasury bill rate from the Aaa firm, and it will pay out 12 percent. Since it borrowed in the short-term market at the Treasury bill rate plus 50 basis points, its net cost will be 12.5 percent for a 5-year fixed rate loan. Had it gone directly to the long-term market, it would have paid 13 percent. As a result, it reduced its cost of funds by 50 basis points. The combined savings of 125 basis points was split between the Aaa firm and the Baa firm 75–50, respectively.

The example illustrates one of the most common advantages behind interest rate swaps—a reduction in the total cost of borrowing. However, the example makes clear that the cost savings is generated because of differences in pricing default risk in short-term and long-term markets for debt. Does this discrepancy represent some kind of mispricing or inefficiency in the market? One possibility

FIGURE **20–4**
**Fixed/floating rate swap. The Baa corporation raises funds in a floating rate
market and promises to pay the Aaa corporation a fixed rate interest, while
the Aaa corporation raises funds in a fixed rate market and promises to pay
the Baa corporation a floating rate interest.**

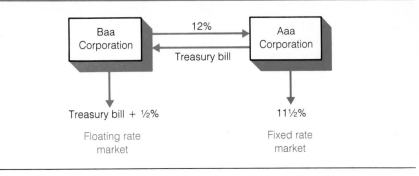

is that there is some kind of segmentation between short-term and long-term markets, much as in the segmentation theory of the term structure of interest rates
(see Chapter 8). According to this view, the interest rate swap is a device for
arbitraging away that mispricing by bridging the gap between the two markets.
Another possibility is that some of the Baa firm's default risk has been shifted
from the financial markets to the Aaa firm in the transaction. However, the Aaa
firm is never obligated to pay off the principal of the loan incurred by the Baa
firm. Instead, the maximum exposure of either firm is to the interest payment due
from the other firm the next period. If the Baa firm defaults on its obligation to
pay 12 percent to the Aaa firm, the swap is terminated and the Aaa firm is left
with long-term debt rather than the short-term obligation created through the
swap. Hence, each counterparty faces the potential risk that a default on the agreement will force it to accept the interest rate obligations to which it is committed
in public markets. The perception of the nature and extent of this risk may affect
the initial swap terms or pricing.

SWAPS AS DEVICES FOR AVOIDING REGULATION COSTS

A final motivation for swaps is avoiding costs of regulation and tax laws. In some
circumstances swaps are desirable because simpler vehicles that accomplish the
same thing are restricted by regulation or have undesirable tax consequences. One
often-cited example pertains to the Japanese government's restrictions on the ability of Japanese pension and investment funds to diversify internationally. In order
to avoid such restrictions, a class of instruments known as dual currency yen/
dollar issues have been introduced where borrowing and interest payments are in
yen but the principal repayment is in dollars. This type of bond has been exempt
from Japanese government restrictions. However, the issuer might not want ex-

SWAPS COME IN MORE FLAVORS THAN JUST PLAIN VANILLA

The swaps we have discussed so far are essentially swaps of fixed or floating rate debt or swaps of one currency for another. These are referred to as *plain vanilla swaps.* As you might imagine, the market has come up with a variety of different types of swaps. There are essentially three ways to make a swap more exotic. One is to change the nature of the instruments used to define the swap. A second is to add options onto it. A third is to combine swaps into packages or portfolios of swaps.

One type is a *basis swap,* where two counterparties swap floating rate obligations tied to two different interest rates. A common example is to swap a floating rate obligation tied to the 6-month LIBOR rate with a floating rate obligation tied to the 30-day prime commercial paper rate. The pricing would depend on the market's estimate of the likely spread between the 6-month LIBOR and the 30-day commercial paper rate. For example, the market might set a price so that the counterparty paying commercial paper would pay the 30-day commercial paper rate plus 30 basis points. The other counterparty would then pay the 6-month LIBOR. The two counterparties would just break even if the 6-month LIBOR turned out to be 30 basis points above the commercial paper rate over the life of the swap.

Another variety of swap is extendable and putable swaps. Suppose counterparty A is swapping floating rate debt to counterparty B for 5-year fixed rate debt. The swap agreement might be written for a 3-year maturity but include an option for counterparty A to extend the swap another two years. This option to extend the swap is valuable. As a result, the interest rate that counterparty A will pay to counterparty B will be reduced by an amount that represents the value of the option to extend. With a putable swap, counterparty A may choose to execute a swap for five years but keep the option to terminate it after three years. Once again, the option is valuable so the interest rate counterparty A will pay will be reduced.

A final example of an exotic swap involves a notional amount that does not remain constant over the life of the swap. For example, suppose a borrower has a fixed rate amortizing loan initially set at $100 million but declines by $25 million per year over four years. If this borrower wants to swap the fixed rate obligation for a floating rate obligation, it would not be appropriate to enter into a 4-year swap for $100 million. Instead, it would be best to have the notional amount of the swap decline each year by $25 million. This actually is a package of four separate swaps, each having a notional amount of $25 million but the maturities begin at one year and stretch to four years. Each separate swap is matched with one annual obligation on the amortizing loan.

posure to the risk of changes in the yen/dollar exchange rate. In order to protect its position, the issuer could also issue a yen-denominated zero-coupon bond with the same maturity date as the principal in the dual currency bond. Now the issuer can offset its obligations to make payments in yen, which consist of both principal and interest, by swapping those into a dollar obligation. It is left with a fixed-rate debt obligation solely in dollars. However, it has benefited from a relatively attractive cost to the dual currency bond which arises because of Japanese government regulations on diversification. These dual currency bonds generally have lower yields because they are one of the few avenues open to Japanese investors for international diversification. The issuer of the dual currency bond is generally the beneficiary of this lower yield.

SUMMARY

Money markets include markets for a wide variety of short-term debt instruments having a maturity of one year or less. Some of the most important money market instruments include Treasury bills, commercial paper, certificates of deposit, federal funds and repurchase agreements, and bankers' acceptances. In the beginning of the chapter we described some of the principal instruments in the money market, but it omitted a lot of institutional detail. There are excellent sources available which provide extensive descriptive information on money markets and the securities traded in them.

We examined the operation of the primary and secondary market for Treasury bills. The primary Treasury bill market is a call auction market where the U.S. Treasury sells bills once a week. The price of bills is determined by competitive bids submitted to the Treasury. In addition, the Treasury accepts noncompetitive tenders at the average price of bills in the weekly auction.

The secondary market for Treasury securities is an over-the-counter market where dealers sell bills to investors. The Federal Reserve Bank of New York maintains a list of authorized Treasury dealers who do business with the Fed. They must report their activity and inventory to the Fed daily. We examined the inventory and trading activity of official dealers in order to get a picture of the amount of trading, the size of their positions, and the extent of hedging in each major type of security in which they make market.

Money market funds emerged as a way for investors who had previously placed funds in commercial banks and savings and loans to avoid the regulations restricting the interest rates those institutions could pay. As inflation rates drove interest rates in the 1970s above the ceilings imposed by Regulation Q, depositors sought alternative ways to invest funds. One of the few relatively low risk and highly liquid investments available was Treasury bills. Brokerage firms found they could create mutual funds which invested in high-quality and short maturity debt obligations and thereby offer the public a high-return and low-risk alternative investment. In order to compete effectively with depository institutions, these funds had to provide the liquidity normally generated by check writing privileges and the close proximity of a local office of the depository institution. Brokerage firms were able to provide this level of liquidity by arranging joint ventures with commercial banks that combined check writing privileges with money funds. In addition, most funds made effective use of telephone and mail services to substitute for costly branch systems. As a result, the money market funds accumulated in excess of $200 billion in assets in less than 5 years. This unprecedented growth forced Congress to eliminate Regulation Q in order to preserve the viability of the commercial banking and savings and loan industries. Therefore, as a part of the Garn-St Germain Act of 1982, the Congress instructed regulators to allow commercial banks and savings and loans to offer a deposit account fully competitive with money market funds. The new money market deposit accounts attracted substantial new deposits, but the market position of the money market funds was too well established to be threatened by them. This example demonstrates how financial institutions find comparative advantages through differences in regulatory treatment and how regulations evolve in response to innovations by regulated institutions.

In the early 1980s a very large market for interest rate swaps developed. We learned what interest rates swaps are, the basic mechanics of how they work, and four basic reasons why swaps are utilized. These reasons are (1) Interest rate swaps are a convenient and flexible way for institutions to restructure balance sheets to reduce the mismatch between maturities of assets and liabilities; (2) Swaps have created a link between distinct markets or between firms with differential access to sources of funds; (3) Swaps reduce the total funding cost for a company due to the differences in spreads between ratings for short- and long-term debt; and (4) Swaps minimize the costs of regulation and tax laws.

QUESTIONS

1. Explain the differences between Treasury bills, bankers' acceptances, commercial paper, and federal funds.
2. Explain how the primary market for Treasury bills operates. What makes this market so pure?
3. How do dealers in the secondary market for Treasury bills earn a profit? What is positive carry and how important is it?
4. Explain how money market funds took advantage of a loophole in regulations for banks and investment companies. Why did money market funds grow so rapidly?
5. Why did commercial banks and savings and loans fear money market funds? How did regulations on banks and savings and loans change to deal with the emergence of money market funds?
6. What is the difference between an interest rate swap and a currency swap? Why were interest rate swaps so popular during the early 1980s?
7. Suppose a borrower has swapped a long-term debt obligation for a short-term debt obligation with another firm and the other firm defaults. What is the nature of the risk exposure of each firm in this transaction?
8. Why might a bank prefer to use a swap to reduce its term mismatch as opposed to using futures markets? Are there any advantages in swaps not present in futures markets?
9. Do you think the market is mispricing risk when it charges larger risk premiums in the long-term corporate bond market than in the short-term market? Swaps are used to lower the total premium paid for risk by the high-quality firm borrowing long and swapping with a low-quality firm that borrows short. Does this mean the swap counterparties are mispricing risk? Why or why not?

REFERENCES

Bicksler, James and Andrew H. Chen. "An Economic Analysis of Interest Rate Swaps," *Journal of Finance* (July 1986), pp. 645–55.

Garbade, Kenneth D. "Electronic Quotation Systems and the Market for Government Securities," *Quarterly Review,* Federal Reserve Bank of New York, 3 (Summer 1978), pp. 13–20.

————, and William L. Silber. "Price Dispersion in the Government Securities Market," *Journal of Political Economy,* 84 (1976), pp. 721–40.

————, and ————. "Structural Organization of Secondary Markets: Clearing Frequency, Dealer Activity and Liquidity Risk," *Journal of Finance,* 34 (June 1979), pp. 577–94.

Hervey, Jack L. "Bankers' Acceptances," *Business Conditions,* Federal Reserve Bank of Chicago (May 1976), pp. 3–11.

Lucas, Charles, Marcos T. Jones, and Thom B. Thurston. "Federal Funds and Repurchase Agreements," *Quarterly Review,* Federal Reserve Bank of New York (Summer 1977), pp. 33–48.

Merton, William C. "The Market for Large Negotiable CDs," *Quarterly Review,* Federal Reserve Bank of New York, (Winter 1977–1978), pp. 22–34.

Sivesind, Charles M. "Noncompetitive Tenders in Treasury Auctions: How Much Do They Affect Savings Flows?" *Quarterly Review,* Federal Reserve Bank of New York, 3 (Autumn 1978), pp. 34–8.

Smith, Clifford, and Lee Wakeman. "The Evolving Market for Swaps," *Midland Corporate Finance Journal,* (Winter 1986), pp. 20–32.

Stigum, Marcia, *The Money Market,* Homewood, Ill.: Dow Jones-Irwin, 1983.

21

OPTIONS AND FUTURES MARKETS

The markets for options and futures contracts are particularly interesting for a number of reasons, but especially because much innovation occurred in the 1970s and 1980s. Innovation came in the form of new products, including options and futures contracts on different types of financial instruments from Treasury bills to currencies to stock indexes. Second, many competing exchanges trade options and futures contracts, and these markets compete with each other to attract trading activity. As a result, we can see competition both between various types of financial instruments as well as between types of markets. Third, options and futures markets present an interesting case study in the effects of government regulation. A separate regulatory agency, the Commodity Futures Trading Corporation, has jurisdiction over futures markets. The policies of this and other agencies have a significant impact on how futures and options markets operate.

Options and futures markets draw on almost every topic in this book. They provide an excellent example of how market organization changes over time as well as a case study in innovation in both products and market form. This chapter studies how markets for options and futures work and how they are organized. There are a number of excellent references that present mechanics of the trading processes and details of various types of contracts used in these markets for those who want more information.[1]

The chapter traces the evolution of futures and options markets and discusses why these markets have developed so rapidly in the last few years. It describes the various exchanges on which financial futures are traded and the open-outcry trading process of these exchanges. We will

---

[1]For an excellent reference on futures see Robert W. Kolb, *Understanding Futures Markets,* Glenview, Ill.: Scott, Foresman and Company, 1985. For an excellent reference on options, although written at a much higher level than the book by Kolb on futures, see John Cox, and Mark Rubinstein, *Options Markets,* Englewood Cliffs, N.J.: Prentice-Hall, Inc, 1985.

also document the growth of various types of futures contracts in financial instruments and compare their operation with futures contracts in commodities.

As in the futures markets, there are a number of distinct exchanges on which options contracts are traded. We will describe the basic features of these exchanges and trading practices on the major exchanges, particularly the Chicago Board Options Exchange, plus discuss the topics of programmed trading and the triple witching hour. ■

THE GROWTH OF MARKETS FOR FUTURES AND OPTIONS

Before examining the operations of the U.S. futures and options markets, we want to understand what services futures and options markets provide to the investor that cannot easily be duplicated elsewhere. We will then analyze how both types of markets operate and compete.

THE VALUE OF FUTURES AND OPTIONS EXCHANGES

The markets for futures and options contracts have been one of the high-growth businesses of the 1970s and 1980s largely because they provided new avenues for investors to hedge risks and make specific types of investments which were either costly or not available without these markets. In many cases it is possible to structure what amounts to the same financial transaction without trading one of the futures or options contracts on the organized exchanges. The point is that the options and futures contracts existing on the exchanges are not necessarily the only way to hedge risks or construct specific types of investments, but the exchanges offer some very important advantages. The most important are liquidity and minimal credit risk.

Liquidity refers to the fact that there is an active secondary market in the specific contracts offered on organized futures and options exchanges. In fact, one of the reasons the exchange exists is to provide a secondary market so that investors will have liquidity. However, liquidity has its cost. In order to generate it, a contract must be standardized so there cannot be tremendous flexibility in the terms of contracts on the exchanges. The greater the flexibility, the less standardization and, therefore, the less liquidity. Since liquidity is one of the basic reasons for having exchanges where futures contracts can be traded, liquidity inherently means a lack of flexibility.

The second advantage of exchange-traded options and futures contracts is they reduce the credit risk facing the contract parties. Every futures or options contract is actually a contract with the exchange or with a **clearinghouse** rather than a contract between the two parties who are short and long the future or the buyer and the writer of an option. The clearinghouse bears the credit risk of all the

A **clearinghouse** is the entity with which individual futures and options contracts are made for exchange-traded contracts.

parties to contracts on that exchange. Therefore, the exchange and the clearing-house have an incentive to devise rules and procedures to limit their risk exposure. Many of the rules pertaining to options and futures trading are actually mechanisms designed to limit credit risk. If each party to a futures or options contract were exposed to the risk of default by the other party of the contract, this could significantly impair how willing many potential investors would be to engage in options and futures transactions. For example, if the purchaser of a put option on an individual stock were dependent solely on the put writer's promise to pay off if the put were exercised at a gain, the purchaser would be very concerned about the writer's ability to meet its obligations and the enforceability of the options contract. However, with exchange traded options, the purchaser of the put actually has a contract with the clearinghouse or the exchange where the option is traded. Therefore, the purchaser need only worry about the credit quality of the exchange, which is not nearly as significant an issue. In effect, by centralizing and properly controlling credit risk, the clearinghouse acts as an insurance agency for participants in the options and futures markets.

THE EVOLUTION OF MARKETS FOR FINANCIAL FUTURES

An important theme in the latter half of this book is competition between types of markets or organizational forms for markets, such as the NASDAQ and the NYSE competing for trading equities and commercial banks and investment banks competing to provide financial services to corporations and consumers. Competition between types of markets is particularly evident in the futures and options markets. A number of different exchanges compete for trading volume in a wide variety of different types of futures and options contracts. Hence, in this market not only does competition and innovation pertain to specific types of financial instruments, but it is also between the exchanges which trade those instruments.

Trading in futures contracts on organized exchanges is a relatively recent innovation. Beginning in October, 1975, the Chicago Board of Trade introduced a futures contract in GNMA mortgage-backed securities. Within a few months new futures contracts on both Treasury securities and commercial paper had also been introduced. There is now active trading in futures contracts on the following five types of debt instruments:

1. U.S. Treasury bills
2. U.S. Treasury notes and bonds
3. GNMA mortgage pass-through securities
4. Prime quality commercial paper
5. Bank certificates of deposit (CDs)

In addition, there is now active trading in futures contracts on indexes such as the Standard and Poor (S&P) 500 Index, the NYSE Index, and an index of municipal bond returns. Moreover, financial futures contracts are traded on the following exchanges:

1. Chicago Board of Trade
2. International Monetary Market of the Chicago Mercantile Exchange (IMM)
3. Amex Commodities Exchange (ACE)
4. Commodity Exchange (COMEX)
5. New York Futures Exchange

While trading in futures contracts on financial instruments is a relatively recent phenomenon, trading in futures contracts on commodities has been going on for many years. In fact, the first four of the five exchanges listed began as exchanges for commodity futures. Only the New York Futures Exchange, which is a part of the New York Stock Exchange, has grown sepecifically to handle financial futures. However, financial futures, including futures on indexes, now generally account for more than 50 percent of aggregate trading volume on these exchanges.

Futures contracts on commodities evolved principally to protect farmers from the risk of price fluctuations in the commodities they produced. To see how futures provide farmers with insurance, consider the example of a midwestern corn farmer. The farmer faces a long sequence of risks surrounding farm productivity. It might not rain. The crop might suffer from some disease. The cost of harvesting equipment might rise, the cost of farm labor might go up, and taxes might increase. Most of these risks are difficult for the farmer to insure against or redistribute throughout the economy. However, a farmer also faces the risk of changes in the aggregate price of corn, and he or she can insure against this risk by selling corn futures short. Then, if the price of corn increases, he or she loses money on the futures contract but makes up the loss through increased profit on the crop. If the price of corn falls, he or she makes money on the futures contract, which covers the decline in value of the crop. Farmers generally find such hedging to be valuable because they are better able to handle the risks they cannot insure if they can hedge the risks of their product price. Precisely because farmers value this type of insurance, commodities futures exchanges, generally located in Chicago, have emerged to provide efficient vehicles for this kind of hedging. Once these futures markets were in place, it was a natural extension of their traditional function to innovate in developing financial futures contracts.

The **Commodity Futures Trading commission (CFTC)** is the federal regulatory agency responsible for regulation of futures trading.

The futures exchanges are regulated by the **Commodity Futures Trading Commission (CFTC),** which has many of the same oversight responsibilities for futures markets that the SEC does for the securities markets. However, the CFTC also has responsibility for approving the introduction of new futures contracts. For a futures contract to be approved, it must be demonstrated that it will serve some useful economic purpose, such as making hedging of some risk possible. This requirement is apparently motivated by a concern that the futures markets not become simply a vehicle for speculation. The CFTC also has responsibility for regulating procedures on the trading floor and for settling limits on allowable daily price fluctuations.

The CFTC has long been a controversial agency and was involved in a long dispute with the SEC over jurisdiction of option trading. In addition, the CFTC has generally had very meager funds allocated to carry out its responsibilities so that it has relied on self-regulation to a much greater extent than has the SEC. In recent years it has not been particularly concerned with insider trading. Moreover, the futures exchanges utilize procedures which do not currently include automated records of actual transactions. As a result, it is difficult to conduct the kinds of trade investigations that have led to identification and prosecution of insider trading by the SEC.

THE EVOLUTION OF THE OPTIONS MARKETS

The history of the market for options is rather different from that for futures contracts. No auction market for options on stocks existed until April 26, 1973, when the Chicago Board Options Exchange (CBOE) was created. Prior to that time options on exchange-traded stocks were traded over the counter, to the extent that they existed at all. There are now five exchanges where options contracts are traded: the CBOE, the American Stock Exchange (AMEX), the Philadelphia Stock Exchange (PHLX), the Pacific Stock Exchange (PSE), and the New York Stock Exchange (NYSE).

The over-the-counter market in options was generally viewed as a failure. Its lack of success is generally attributed to the high costs of trading and the lack of liquidity it provided. The costs of carrying out the trade were as much as 25 percent of the option cost. Roughly half of this fee was in the form of a dealer bid-ask spread to cover costs incurred by the dealer. The other half was for insurance or a performance bond to insure against the prospect that the option writer would be able to pay off the option if exercised. Since, under this system, exercise of an option generally required liquidation of the underlying security and reinvestment of the funds, additional commissions were incurred by the option purchaser. These costs were sufficiently high to prevent much active writing of options contracts.[2]

When the CBOE was created in 1973, a total of 48 options was traded in 16 underlying securities at three different maturities. Average daily contract trading volume during May of 1983 was 1,584. By March, 1974, monthly contract volume on the CBOE was greater than the entire 1973 volume of the previous over-the-counter market. By the end of 1986 average daily contract volume on the CBOE was 712,877. Clearly, the CBOE has become a sucessful innovation.

The innovation of **exchange-traded options** was such an apparent success so quickly that other exchanges including the American Stock Exchange, Philadelphia Stock Exchange, and the Pacific Stock Exchange also introduced trading in options. These exchanges, plus the CBOE, offered options contracts solely in individual equity securities until 1982 when new options contracts were introduced on other types of instruments. In principle, an option or a futures contract can be traded on anything that is measurable. For example, we could have an option

Exchange-traded options are traded on an organized exchange rather than over the counter.

---

[2]See John C. Cox, and Mark Rubinstein, *ibid.*

contract on the U.S. unemployment rate or annual snowfall in Snowbird, Utah. It is easy to imagine that there would be more interest in trading some types of options contracts than others. Interest generally arises when the underlying security is a risk which someone wants to hedge, as in the case of farmers hedging the price of agricultural commodities. In the U.S. in 1987 there were exchange-traded options on agricultural commodities, metals, financial instruments, and foreign currencies, and on indexes such as the S&P 500.

Another type of innovation that has grown with development of new types of exchange-traded options is the *option on the future*. In order to understand it we have to consider the four possible types of contracts for any underlying security. Let's consider Treasury bonds as an example. We have a cash market in Treasury bonds. We also have a futures market in Treasury bonds and an options market in Treasury bonds. But we also have an options market in the futures contracts in Treasury bonds. In fact, if you examine the daily *Wall Street Journal* quotations, you will find three categories of futures and options price quotes: futures prices, futures options, and listed options quotations including foreign currency and index options.

There is no particular mystery behind the idea of an option on a future. As discussed, an option can be on anything that is measurable. There can be good reasons in some markets to use futures rather than the cash item as the underlying security, particularly in commodities since there may be more liquidity all year round in a given futures contract than in the cash market. In addition, if the underlying security were delivered, it would be preferable to take delivery of the future rather than the actural commodity. These reasons suggest that, for commodities at least, it may be preferable to have an option on the futures contract rather than an option on the commoditity. And this is the way the markets actually work. There are exchange-traded options on agricultural commodity futures and on metal futures, but no options on the actual commodities. In the case of indexes there is little basis for preferring the index over the future on the index if the future were always highly liquid. In 1987 options on indexes were more common than options on index futures; however, both types existed for the NYSE and S&P 500 indexes. Both can survive as long as there is sufficient liquidity in each type of option. The trading volume in these instruments appears to be large enough for both to exist; the same is true of Treasury notes and bonds and some foreign currencies.

It may seem like the marketplace simply did not discover the possibility of developing options and futures contracts on such a wide variety of underlying assets until 1982. Acutally, this is not the case at all. To introduce a new class of options contracts, regulatory approval is necessary, and prior to 1982, it was not clear what regulatory agency had authority to grant such approval and supervise trading in the new contracts. The two agencies involved were the SEC and the Commodities Futures Trading Commission (CFTC). For a number of years there was an ongoing dispute between these agencies over regulatory authority. As a result, proposals for new options contracts submitted to regulators as early as 1980 waited for approval until 1982 giving competing exchanges an opportunity to develop essentially similar products. This difficulty was resolved in October, 1982, when President Ronald Reagan signed a law which gave the SEC jurisdiction over options contracts on securities traded on organized exchanges and on options on foreign currency. The CFTC was given jurisdiction over options on financial futures.

The delay in regulatory approval had important implications for the viability of the competing exchanges' entry into the new business of trading options on instruments other than individual stocks. A critical element in the success of a new financial asset is the development of liquidity. Generally, the first entrant in a new financial market has a significant advantage since it can develop liquidity surrounding its product. Once liquidity develops in a particular instrument, it is difficult for a new entrant to enter the market successfully. The relative value of the old and new instruments will depend on the ability to resell the instruments quickly and with little cost. In effect, liquidity becomes a barrier to entry in the business of trading financial instruments.

*F*UTURES MARKETS

Since the first financial futures were introduced by the Chicago Board of Trade in 1975 the trading volume in financial futures has grown dramatically. In order to understand how the futures markets operate we need to examine the terms of some of the most important types of financial futures. We will focus on Treasury bills and bonds, but these are only a few of the financial instruments that have active futures trading.

THE NATURE OF FUTURES CONTRACTS

Chapter 4 presented a sample of futures prices from the *Wall Street Journal* in Table 4–1. Similar quotes solely for Treasury bills, notes, and bonds are shown in Figure 21–1. The prices are from the March 27, 1987, issue of the *Wall Street Journal* and pertain to the preceding trading day, March 26, 1987. Each contract has a description printed in bold-face type which identifies the contract being traded, the exchange on which it is traded (in parentheses), the dollar amount of a contract, and the units in which the price is stated. For example, the Treasury bill contracts are traded on the International Monetary Market (IMM) in $1 million units. The Treasury bill on which the futures contract is written is a 90-day bill. This means the seller of a (short) futures contract is obligated to deliver a 90-day bill when the futures contract matures. The opening price for a June future is stated as 94.44 percent. This is an index used by the IMM that is not comparable to the actual cash price of a Treasury bill. The quotations are reported for futures contracts that mature in June, September, and December of 1987 and March, June, and September of 1988. For each contract the opening price is shown first, followed by the high and low prices reached during trading. The **settlement price**

The **settlement price**, the closing price for a trading day, is used to determine the change in value of futures contracts from one day to the next.

FIGURE 21–1
Futures market quotes.

TREASURY BONDS (CBT) – $100,000; pts. 32nds of 100%							
June	100-13	100-25	100-13	100-23	+ 14	7.928 – .044	192,839
Sept	99-13	99-26	99-13	99-24	+ 15	8.025 – .048	13,051
Dec	98-16	98-26	98-15	98-24	+ 13	8.128 – .041	3,779
Mr88	97-25	97-28	97-23	97-27	+ 13	8.221 – .043	3,680
June	96-26	97-00	96-22	97-00	+ 14	8.310 – .047	3,293
Sept	95-29	96-05	95-29	96-04	+ 13	8.403 – .044	1,744
Dec				95-11	+ 14	8.488 – .047	527

Est vol 135,000; vol Wed 125,793; open int 233,373, +1,972.

TREASURY NOTES (CBT) – $100,000; pts. 32nds of 100%							
June	103-24	103-30	103-24	103-29	+ 6	7.439 – .027	44,841
Sept	103-02	103-07	103-02	103-06	+ 6	7.540 – .027	5,092
Dec				102-18	+ 7	7.629 – .031	260

Est vol 11,000; vol Wed 7,239; open int 54,213, +976.

TREASURY BILLS (IMM) – $1 mil.; pts. of 100%							
						Discount	Open
	Open	High	Low	Settle	Chg	Settle Chg	Interest
June	94.44	94.45	94.39	94.43	+ .02	5.57 – .02	29,938
Sept	94.49	94.50	94.47	94.49	+ .02	5.51 – .02	5,757
Dec	94.53	94.53	94.46	94.49	+ .01	5.51 – .01	1,698
Mr88	94.46	94.46	94.40	94.45	+ .01	5.55 – .01	739
June	94.34	94.37	94.30	94.35	....	5.65	293
Sept	9	....	....	94.19	– .02	5.81 + .02	130

Est vol 5,745; vol Wed 5,814; open int 38,574, +91.

S&P 500 INDEX (CME) 500 times index							
June	305.50	305.70	302.65	303.40	– .20	305.70 228.90	95,994
Sept	307.20	307.50	304.70	305.35	– .10	307.50 229.90	1,532
Dec	308.00	309.20	306.80	307.30	– .05	309.20 243.20	922

Est vol 70,300; vol Wed 69,149; open int 98,453, +1,129.
Index (prelim.) High 302.72; Low 300.38; Close 300.93 +.55

NYSE COMPOSITE INDEX (NYFE) 500 times index							
June	173.15	173.35	171.85	172.15	– .10	173.35 131.05	9,661
Sept	174.30	174.50	173.15	173.25	– .05	174.50 133.55	1,059
Dec	175.25	175.25	174.25	174.30	+ .05	175.25 140.30	391

Est vol 11,721; vol Wed 9,368; open int 11,123, +410.
The index: High 171.63; Low 170.49; Close 170.77 +.27

KC VALUE LINE INDEX (KC) 500 times index							
June	273.90	274.20	271.60	272.50	– .15	274.20 219.50	7,083
Sept	272.50	273.10	271.00	271.20	– .45	273.10 221.70	328

Est vol 2,000; vol Wed 1,894; open int 7,475, +595.
The index: High 274.22; Low 273.32; Close 273.64 +.31

MAJOR MKT INDEX (CBT) $250 times index							
Apr	467.00	471.70	466.50	468.40	+ 2.00	471.70 397.90	5,457
June	468.40	473.60	468.40	470.10	+ 1.95	473.60 381.00	766

Est vol 15,000; vol Wed 11,181; open int 6,297, +80.
The index: High 469.85; Low 464.05; Close 466.51 +2.36

Source: *Wall Street Journal*, March 27, 1987, p. 36.

is the closing price of that day's trading, and the change (chg) represents the change from the previous day's settlement price. In the Treasury bill futures section of the table, the settlement price is also expressed in terms of a discount interest rate as used in the cash market for Treasury bills. (Discount rates, Treasury bill prices, and market yields were discussed in Chapter 6, so you might want to reread it.) The final column shows open interest, the total number of contracts for this maturity which are outstanding. Note that the futures contract on the IMM is for Treasury bills with 90 days to maturity. Bills with other maturities are available in the cash market, but they are not used as the underlying security in futures contracts traded on organized exchanges.

Open interest is the total number of contracts outstanding for a given future.

It is interesting to examine the pattern of **open interest** shown for Treasury bills, notes, and bonds in the Figure 21–1. For each type of future the largest amount of open interst is in the nearest contract, and it falls off continuously as we move to contracts with maturity dates farther out in time. The pattern we observe indicates that most traders are interested in hedging or speculating for relatively near-term changes in interest rates. Market participants probably feel less comfortable with predictions of changes in interest rates for longer maturities and therefore have less desire to take positions for longer maturities. In addition, they always have the option to hedge at a later time with a shorter maturity contract. It also appears there are more contracts for notes and bonds outstanding than for bills. However, the bill contracts are in $1 million units, while the note and bond contracts are in $100,000 units. Therefore, there is not such a large discrepancy in the dollar volume of contracts outstanding.

The IMM index price for Treasury bills shown in the *Wall Street Journal* is computed as follows:

$$\text{IMM index} = 100\% - \text{Discount rate}.$$

For example, the settlement index price for the June Treasury bill futures contract is

$$94.43\% = 100\% - 5.57\%.$$

This is not the price of a Treasury bill. The difference is accounted for by the fact that the discount rate only applies to 90 days. To determine the price for 90-day Treasury bills at maturity which is implied by the discount rate of 5.57 percent, we have to solve for the price of the bill just as we did in Chapter 6. The price of the bill is determined as:

$$\begin{array}{c}\text{Price} \\ \text{of} \\ \text{bill}\end{array} = \$1,000,000 - \frac{0.0557 \times \$1,000,000 \times 90}{360} = \$986,075.$$

For every change in the discount rate, or equivalently in the IMM index, of 1 basis point, the price of the Treasury bill futures contract changes by $25. This means it is fairly simple to inspect the change in daily settlement prices as quoted by the *Wall Street Journal* to see what happened to the actual price in the futures contract. For example, Figure 21–1 shows the settlement index on the June bill future increased by 2 basis points from March 25 to March 26 so the price of the bills in the futures contract increased by $50.

Similar information is presented for Treasury notes and Treasury bonds; however, there are a few differences. First, the prices are stated in thirty seconds of 100 percent rather than simply in percent. For example, the June Treasury bond future had a settlement price of 100 and 23/32. Futures prices are quoted this way because the cash prices in Treasury notes and bonds are stated in this manner. Second, instead of reporting a discount yield, as with Treasury bills, the yield to maturity corresponding to the settlement price is presented.

With Treasury bond futures the futures contract is not written on a bond with a specific maturity in mind. The maturity of the underlying bond depends upon the exchange rules specifying what can be delievered to close out a futures contract. Rules of the Board of Trade stipulate that delivery can be any bonds with $100,000 in face value that have at least 15 years remaining until maturity or until the first possible date they may be called. The $100,000 is face value, not market value. The fact that the rules are stated in face value means there will generally be quite a few bonds that can be used to close out a futures contract at maturity. This insures the market liquidity. It creates some interesting problems, however, since bonds with the same maturity and face value may have quite different market values if they have different coupon rates. As a result, futures traders are keenly interested in picking the least expensive Treasury bond to deliver when a futures contract matures, and the strategy involved has become an important aspect of trading.

MARGIN AND RESETTLEMENT

A number of important features of the operations of futures markets contribute to their efficiency. One of these is the enforcement of *margin requirements*. Actually, there are two types of margin requirements, the *initial margin* and the *maintenance margin*. In order to understand how these margin requirements work, we also need to understand the process of daily resettlement used on the futures exchanges.

The **initial margin** refers to the amount which must be deposited with the broker when the futures contract is initially acquired. The margin amount may be in the form of cash, Treasury bills, or a bank letter of credit. The amount of the initial margin requirement varies from contract to contract. For most agricultural commodities the amount is generally 5 percent of the face value of the contract. However, for Treasury bills the amount is generally $2,000 for a $1 million contract. It may seem like this is very little protection against the prospect of a default on a sizable obligation. However, the initial margin actually only covers the loss exposure for the first day the contract is outstanding, because the futures exchanges require daily resettlement.

Daily resettlement means futures traders must realize any gain or loss on the value of their futures contract each day. To see how this works, suppose you had taken short positions in 10 June Treasury bill futures contracts on March 25, 1987. Given an initial margin of $2,000 per contract, you would have to deposit $20,000 on March 25. We know from Figure 21–1 and our discussion above that the settlement price increased from March 25 to March 26 by 2 basis points. This was a loss of $50 per contract for anyone with a short position in the June future. Since you have a short position in 10 contracts, this means that you would lose $500. Therefore, your actual margin on deposit on March 26 would now be $19,500.

Since the market operates with daily resettlement, your broker will determine whether you have sufficient margin to face the events of the next day. This means he or she will now have to determine your maintenance margin. The **maintenace margin** is generally 75 percent of the initial margin. Therefore, the maintenance margin would be $15,000, and you clearly would have enough to satisfy this new requirement. However, if you had a two basis point loss each day, you would need to deposit additional margin after only ten trading days. Since your maintenance margin is less than your initial margin, you might want to reduce your actual margin. If you keep only the required margin each day, then you will have to make new deposits any day you experience a loss. To ease the logistics of this process, brokers generally require that you maintain another account so they can transfer funds from it to your margin account.

The imposition of margin requirements is one of the major devices utilized by the futures exchanges to control the credit risk inherent in futures trading. In addition, the use of a central clearinghouse for all trades on an exchange is also an essential feature of the futures markets. Individual futures contracts are agreements between the trader, the broker, and the clearinghouse. They are not con-

---

The **initial margin** refers to the amount of funds that must be deposited with a broker when a futures contract is purchased.

Daily resettlment means futures traders must realize any gain or loss on the value of their futures contract each day.

The **maintenance margin** refers to the amount of funds that must be maintained on account with a broker when holding a futures contract.

TRIPLE WITCHING AND PROGRAM TRADING

One of the features of new types of options and futures contracts that has attracted public attention is program trading. Linked with this is the *triple witching hour,* the times when stock index futures are deliverable *and* options on stock indexes mature. When these two events occur simultaneously, some interesting things happen in the cash market for stocks in the index in question.

Program trading is an efficient way to take advantage of one of the basic equilibrium relationships governing futures markets. We discussed futures pricing in Chapters 4 and 9, though we never applied it to a future on a stock index. Suppose you are deciding how much of a cash position to take in stocks that make up the index, and you are also holding a futures contract on the index. Actually, you don't need to buy all the stocks in the index. It is quite sufficient to buy a much smaller portfolio, called a basket, that imitates the behavior of the entire index. If you take equivalent positions in both the basket and the futures contract, then you will have locked in a certain return. Since this return is risk free, you have an opportunity for arbitrage profit if the return you can get is anything other than the prevailing risk-free rate. The futures price must differ from the current spot price for the underlying assets only by the risk-free rate, net of any dividends that you know will be paid to stocks in the basket. Any deviation from this relationship creates an arbitrage opportunity. Program trading involves development of computer programs that constantly monitor prices of futures on stock indexes and the basket which mimics behavior of the index itself. Whenever computer programs operated by Wall Street firms spot a discrepancy between the price of the index future and the price of the basket, they initiate a trade to take advantage of the mispricing. Large institutions specialize in this because they have instantaneous access to the necessary data and they can execute large-scale trades to cover the cost of developing the price of the monitor systems.

A very important aspect of this trading makes these arbitrage actions risk free. At the time the futures contract expires, the current price of the future must equal the current price of the basket in the cash market because at maturity the futures contract is a commitment to buy or sell at a specific price. There would be a sure loss or gain if that price were anything other than the prevailing cash price. Hence, any program trading can lock in a sure profit if the relationship does not hold and if the arbitrageurs wait until maturity of the futes contract to close it out. Most arbitrageurs hold contracts until the last moment to close them out. Since these positions are closed out in the last few minutes of trading on the maturity date of the futures contract, program traders will also be very active in the cash market for the basket of stocks at the same time. Once they close out their futures position, they must also close out their cash position to eliminate exposure to risk of changes in the price of the basket. Hence, there is also very active trading in the stock market for the stocks in the basket when the futures are closed. As long as the program traders have offsetting positions in both the index future and the basket, they have no risk.

Since program traders must unwind both the cash position in the basket and their futures position at the same time, large price swings on the stock exchanges usually occur when index futures mature. Triple witching occurs when options on indexes mature at the same time as the futures and investors in options and futures attempt to close out their positions simultaneously. Price swings that result from program trading have caused substantial concern about the operation of financial markets. The volatility created by program trading strikes some observers as being dangerous to the entire market. It will be interesting to see whether the market is capable of remedying this perceived problem before trading restrictions occur in either futures or options on indexes.

tracts between the two parties who are short and long the future. Each of the futures exchanges has a clearinghouse, and brokers on the exchange must be members of the clearinghouse to place orders on the exchange. In addition, the exchanges also enforce other rules designed to limit the risk exposure of market participants and to standardize the contracts. One such rule is a limit on price movements during any trading day. The exchanges enforce such rules allegedly to prevent large price swings that could wipe out margins, and change these price limits as they choose.

THE OPEN OUTCRY AUCTION PROCESS

The **open outcry auction** is the process of trading futures where bids to buy or sell must be transmitted to anyone on the floor of the exchange participating in trading a particular contract.

The futures exchanges utilize a trading process called an **open outcry auction.** To see how the open outcry process works, let's return to the example of Treasury bills available on March 26, 1987. Suppose you knew that you were going to borrow money in June and were concerned that interest rates might increase between late March and June. Therefore, to hedge your risk you take a short position in Treasury bill futures. Recall that you make money on a short position in Treasury bill futures when the price falls, which is equivalent to an increase in the yield on Treasury bills. Therefore, the short position hedges your risk of an increase in interest rates. Suppose the company you work for will need to borrow $10 million. Therefore, you decide to hedge the entire risk and buy 10 futures contracts. Once you have made your decision to hedge, you call your broker and place an order. The broker then contacts the firm's agent, known as a **pit broker,** on the floor of the IMM where the June Treasury bill futures are traded and executes your order. The trading pit works by pit brokers verbally arranging a trade, hence the name *open outcry*. (Actually, due to the noise from a large number of pit brokers simultaneously screaming orders at each other, a system of hand signals has evolved for order communication.) The other party to the trade could be a hedger like you—concerned about interest rates falling, who therefore wants a long position in Treasury bill futures. It could be a speculator who does not have any inherent risk exposure to interest rates but is betting on the future change in rates. Either of them would be represented by another pit broker. Alternatively, your pit broker might trade with an exchange member who is trading for his or her own account and does not represent any other investor.

Pit brokers are the agents on the exchange floor who trade futures contracts.

The distinguishing feature of the open outcry auction is that any offer to buy or sell a futures contract must be made to all of the traders in the pit where that contract is traded. This is very different from the system of specialists that prevails on the New York Stock Exchange. There, all trading in a particular security takes place through a specialist in that stock. The specialist holds an inventory in order to be able to buy and sell with anyone, but sellers and buyers can only execute trades through that specialist. On the futures exchanges anyone in the pit can bid on any contract. Once a verbal agreement has been made between two individuals in the pit, they report the trade to the clearinghouse. The transaction is then between the clearinghouse and the purchaser of the futures contract.

As trading in financial futures has increased, considerable pressure has developed to change the open outcry system of trading. One complaint is simply that the existing system of verbal agreements and hand signals followed by written records of orders is too slow and inefficient. As a result, the Chicago Board of Trade and the Chicago Mercantile Exchange are considering installing electronic order routing and execution systems. Another difficulty with the existing system is that pit brokers are allowed to trade simultaneously for their own and customers' accounts. Critics contend that this creates an inherent conflict of interest.

In the current system it is difficult if not impossible to spot many potential types of abuse since the exchanges have no electronic record of transactions. It is difficult to determine to what extent the open outcry process actually requires pit brokers to offer trades to all those in the pit. It is alleged that pit brokers often arrange trades with just a few others in the pit without seeking widespread bidding on the transaction.

Another problem is that futures exchanges do not currently allow block trading of futures contracts. Block trading involves trades of large numbers or blocks of contracts. The desire for it is directly related to the growth of trading in stock index futures. With the growth in trading, there is increased participation in the futures market by Wall Street firms who are used to trading other types of securities, particularly equities, where block trading is now common practice. To understand why this issue has developed, it is interesting to take a closer look at stock index futures.

STOCK INDEX FUTURES

Stock index futures are futures contracts on a stock index, such as the S&P 500.

One of the more important futures contracts introduced in the last few years is the **stock index future.** This is a futures contract written on an index of returns on portfolios of stocks. Four stock index futures are actively traded. Quotes on the prices of these futures contracts for March 26, 1987, are taken from the *Wall Street Journal* shown in Figure 21–1. The four indexes are the *Standard & Poor's 500,* the NYSE, the Value Line Index, and the Major Market Index, which is designed to closely approximate the Dow Jones Index. To define the actual value of the contract, the index used in the contract must be multiplied by some dollar amount. For example, the S&P 500 future is defined as the value of the index times $500. The NYSE and the Value Line futures also use $500, while $100 is used for the Major Market Index. A special characteristic of stock index futures is that the underlying asset is never delivered to close out the future. Since the index itself is not an asset, delivery could only be arranged with the portfolio of assets used to construct the index. Actual delivery of this portfolio would be difficult and would therefore reduce the liquidity of the futures contract. Instead of delivery at maturity, the maturity date involves simply another day of resettlement where margins are eliminated and all gains and losses are paid off. To see how different these contracts actually are, it is necessary to examine the degree to which the indexes are correlated. Table 21–1 shows correlation coefficients computed among the various indexes. While some of these indexes are very closely related, there is still a considerable discrepancy between them.

Stock index futures have been particularly useful as devices to hedge risk in individual stock positions or portfolios of stocks.[3] Their popularity is documented

---

[3]See Robert W. Kolb, *op. cit.,* for an excellent discussion of the appropriate approach to this problem.

TABLE 21-1
Correlations among the indexes. Based on data from the period February 1, 1971–March 31, 1982.

	S and P 500	Value Line	NYSE	Dow-Jones
S and P 500	1.000			
Value Line	0.882	1.000		
NYSE	0.989	0.928	1.000	
Dow-Jones	0.729	0.507	0.644	1.000

Source: Chicago Mercantile Exchange, "Inside S and P Stock Index Futures," p. 6.

by the tremendous growth in trading volume in these futures contracts, as shown in Figure 21–2. Stock index futures are useful because they provide a very efficient vehicle for trading systematic risk. Recall from Chapter 3 that the risk of any individual asset or portfolio of assets can be decomposed into two components, systematic and unsystematic risks. The measure of the systematic risk of an asset is the asset's beta. The beta measures the sensitivity of the return on an individual asset to the return on some diversified portfolio.

To see how stock index futures might be used, suppose you had a relatively large portfolio to manage. (You might hope it is for yourself, but more likely imagine you are employed as a portfolio manager.) Also suppose you became rather pessimistic about the future course of the market and you wanted to limit your exposure to market declines. One way to do this is simply to sell part of your portfolio, but this is a rather unattractive alternative if for no other reason

FIGURE 21-2
Volume of stock index futures. Daily dollar volume of trading in the Standard & Poor's 500 stock index futures contract[1].

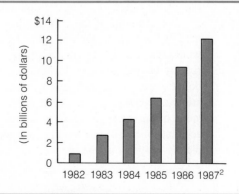

[1]Based on year-end contract price multiplied by average daily trading volume for the year
[2]Year to date
Source: *Chicago Mercantile Exchange*

WALL STREET TAKES A BATH ON OVER-THE-COUNTER OPTIONS

You may recall from Chapter 9 that in April, 1987, Merrill Lynch & Co. reported a $275 million loss as a result of an unhedged position in mortgage-backed securities. The loss occurred because of a large unanticipated increase in interest rates during April, 1987. When we first discussed this, we did not specify the securities that proved to be so troublesome for Merrill Lynch. Apparently Merrill Lynch had accumulated a large position in mortgage-backed securities known as IOPOs. These securities have interest payments stripped from the principal payments in the underlying mortgages. Then separate securities with claims only on the principal and only on the interest are sold to investors. Merrill Lynch had retained a large position in the principal portion of these instruments. Mortgage-backed securities are subject to prepayment risk, which is concentrated in the principal-only portion of IOPOs. As a result, these securities are highly sensitive to interest rate changes. The prepayment provision is a type of option where the gain from exercising the option is a function of the level of interest rates. However, there is no exchange where options that are identical to the option implicit in the principal portion of a mortgage are traded. As a result, it is difficult to hedge the prepayment risk in the principal portion of IOPOs directly. Thus Merrill Lynch was exposed to significant interest rate risk that it could not effectively lay off in other markets.

Other Wall Street firms also suffered large losses as a result of the dramatic interest rate changes during that month. Though the exposure of other firms was different from that of Merrill Lynch, the basic reason for the loss was the same—a major change in value of the underlying security in an over-the-counter option written by the investment banking firm. First Boston was among the firms who experienced this type of loss. As of June, 1987, First Boston's trading losses during April and May totaled between $80 and $100 million. The difficulties First Boston encountered were because of an unusually large and rapid drop in the value of long-term Treasury bonds. The price of 30-year Treasury bonds fell eight points in the two-week period ending April 23, 1987, creating a particularly difficult problem for First Boston as it was writing over-the-counter options on 30-year Treasury bonds. These options were tailored to individual customer preferences and therefore could not be hedged easily in the market for exchange-traded options. When the price of Treasury bonds fell in April, First Boston's customers chose to exercise them.

than the transactions costs involved. A much simpler alternative is to hedge the risk of the effect of changes in the market as a whole on your portfolio.

For example, if the beta of your portfolio were 1.3 with respect to the Standard & Poor's 500, then you could expect that any one-dollar change in the index would result in a $1.3 change in the value of your portfolio. You could hedge this risk by buying stock index futures. Notice that you would not want to buy one dollar worth of the S&P index future for every dollar of portfolio you held. There are two reasons for this. First, the value of the futures contract is 500 times the value of the index. Second, you need to account for the beta of your portfolio. To account for these, you should compute the number of contracts necessary to completely hedge your risk as:

$$\text{Number of contracts} = \frac{\text{Value of portfolio}}{\text{Value of contract}} \times \text{Portfolio beta}.$$

Again, notice that the value of the futures contract is the value of the index times 500. Therefore, if the value of the index is, say, 120 and if you have a portfolio worth $10,000,000 to hedge, then you can compute the number of contracts necessary to hedge your risk as:

$$217 = \frac{\$10,000,000}{120 \times 500} \times 1.3.$$

You can also use stock index futures to eliminate the systematic component of an investment in a particular stock. For example, suppose you have some information (not inside information) which makes you believe some event will positively affect the future returns of a particular company. You want to invest to get the benefit of that information. But you want to protect yourself against the prospect that the market as a whole might change and affect the price of the stock in which you are interested. You can accomplish this by buying the stock and selling the stock index future short. Again, to determine the number of contracts you want, you need to take account of how the value of the index is defined and the beta of your stock with respect to that index.

These examples should make it clear that stock index futures have a lot of practical value, and because of that practical value, they have become so popular. One interesting aspect of the growth of these indexes is that they have forged a link between the stock markets and the futures markets. The people who use the stock index futures are trading and managing portfolios of stocks. Hence, the participants in the equity markets are now interested in influencing the operations of the futures exchanges and in developing competing markets.

THE MARKET FOR EXCHANGE-TRADED OPTIONS

Like futures contracts, options are traded on a number of U.S. exchanges. We learned early in this chapter that options are traded on the CBOE, the AMEX, and PHLX, the PSE, and the NYSE. Now we want to explore how these options markets operate and compete for business.

THE STRUCTURE OF OPTIONS CONTRACTS

In specifying an option contract a number of terms must be clearly defined including the identity of the underlying security, the maturity date, and the strike or exercise price. In the U.S., options contracts are called American options. This means the option may be exercised any time prior to maturity. The alternative is a European option, which can be exercised only at maturity. Options are available in the U.S. on a variety of different types of instruments, but this discussion will focus principally on options on individual stocks.

Options on a given underlying stock can have a variety of maturity dates. There are three expiration cycles or schedules of maturity dates used on exchanges that trade options. They are a January/April/July/October, February/May/August/November, and March/June/September/December. On any given date, options are available with the three expiration dates of the cycle nearest to that date. The longest maturity an exchange-traded option can have is nine months. Option contracts always expire on the Saturday immediately following the third Friday of their expiration month.

Each of the exchanges chooses the strike prices for which it will offer options for a particular underlying security. Their freedom is restricted by rules established by the SEC. Allowable strike prices are in integers divisible by 5, plus or minus 2.5 points for securities where the underlying price is less than $100 and 5 points if the price is over $100. The exchange may use larger intervals if it chooses. The total number of options available for a particular security are essentially determined by the market demand to acquire and trade those options. For securities with a large outstanding volume and active trading and where there is a perception that the price variance of the underlying security is large, there may be more options listed than for smaller stocks. For example, on March 27, 1987, there were options contracts available on the CBOE at eleven strike prices for IBM while there were only three for Payless.

Options contracts are generally for round lots of 100 shares of the underlying security. This means the option contract represents a right to buy or sell 100 shares of the underlying security. The underlying securities must meet a number of requirements: they must be traded on a national exchange and meet minimum standards for number of shares outstanding and volume of trading, and they must have a minimum stock price of $10 and a record of not defaulting on debt obligations.

Figure 21–3 presents a listing of options quotations for IBM on the CBOE taken from the *Wall Street Journal* of March 27, 1987. The quotations are in a matrix form where rows correspond to different strike prices and columns to different maturity dates for calls and puts. Underneath the IBM name the number 154 is repeated for each row of the listed options, because it is the closing price on the NYSE for the previous day. The next column defines the various strike prices where options quotes are presented. The next six columns show the prices

FIGURE 21–3
Puts and calls on IBM.

CHICAGO BOARD

Option & Strike NY Close Price		Calls–Last			Puts–Last		
		Apr	May	Jul	Apr	May	Jul
I B M	110	r	s	4/-3/4	r	s	1/16
154	115	41 3/8	s	r	r	s	3/16
154	120	35 1/2	s	37 1/2	1/16	s	1/4
154	125	29 1/4	s	32	1/16	s	3/8
154	130	25	s	26 1/2	1/16	s	11/16
154	135	19 1/4	s	22 1/2	1/8	s	1 1/8
154	140	14 3/4	16 1/8	18 1/4	1/4	7/8	2
154	145	10 1/4	11 1/2	14 1/4	3/4	2	3 1/4
154	150	6 1/2	8	10 3/4	2	3 3/4	5
154	155	3 5/8	5 5/8	8 1/4	4 3/8	5 5/8	7 1/2
154	160	1 15/16	3 1/2	6 1/2	6 7/8	8 1/2	10 1/2

Source: *Wall Street Journal,* March 27, 1987. p. 40.

of calls and puts trading on the CBOE at each strike price and maturity date. The price is quoted on a per share basis so that to determine the price of an options contract for 100 shares, the listed price must be multiplied by 100. The options prices shown represent the last trade of the day. If the letter *r* is shown, as it is for the IBM call at $110 maturing in April, the option is available for trading but did not trade that day. The letter *s* means no option with that particular combination of strike price and maturity date is available on the exchange. Notice that there are no May calls for IBM with strike prices below $140.

OPTION TRADING

The procedures for trading options used on the various exchanges differ to some degree so we will concentrate on procedures used on the CBOE. To see how the trading process works, suppose you want to purchase a call on IBM. (Remember a call is an option to buy a stock at a prespecified price, while a put is an option to sell a stock at a prespecified price.) Suppose you do not have a position in the underlying security. Then you are called **naked** in the option. If, for example, you owned the stock and bought a put on it, you would have what is called a **covered position** in the put. If the price of the underlying security falls below the exercise price, the potential gains from the put will be offset by the loss in value in the stock itself. (You might want to review the diagrams on payoffs on puts and calls in Chapter 4 if you don't follow this.) If you also have no short positions or have not already written a call option in the same security, then your purchase of the call is an opening purchase transaction, which means you are buying a call that you have not already written.

A **covered position** is a position in an option as well as in the underlying security. A **naked position** involves an option with no simultaneous position in the underlying security.

In order to purchase the call, you will need to go to a broker. The broker who takes your order will transmit your order to a floor broker. The **floor broker,** who is a member of the CBOE, goes to the place on the exchange floor, or the post, where IBM call options are traded and acts as your representative in attempting to obtain the best price for your purchase of the IBM call. The floor broker may trade with an order book official, a market maker, or another floor broker. An order book official is an exchange official who trades only for public customers—that is, he or she does not maintain an inventory in his or her own name or trade on a personal account. A **market maker** is an exchange member who trades only for his or her own account and does not trade for public customers. The floor broker and the other party with whom he or she trades on the exchange floor execute a verbal agreement and record the transaction with the exchange at the end of the day.

A **floor broker** is a broker permitted to execute orders on the floor of the CBOE.

A **market maker** is a CBOE member who trades only for his or her own account and does not trade for public customers.

A **market order** must be filled at the best price as soon as possible, while a **limit order** requires the broker to execute the order only if he or she can do so at or better than a prespecified price.

Orders can take either of two forms: a market order or a limit order. When a floor broker receives a **market order,** he or she is instructed to fill the order at the best price as soon as possible. When a floor broker receives a **limit order,** he or she is instructed to fill the order only if it is possible to do so at or better than a prespecified price. In addition, both types of orders can have a variety of different contingencies attached. For example, either type of order may be made contingent on the price level of the underlying security. In addition, orders for spe-

PROGRAM TRADING AND PORTFOLIO HEDGING AFTER THE CRASH OF 1987

In the aftermath of the October, 1987, stock market crash, attention was focused on the link between stock markets and futures and options markets. Many observers argued that the decline was so steep and the market so volatile partly because of program trading and portfolio insurance. Program trading is the system set up by market participants to automatically take advantage of any discrepancies between prices of stocks in the cash markets on the NYSE and the value of a futures contract on an index of the same stocks, such as the Standard and Poor's 500. When the futures contract on the S&P 500 and the value of the stocks in the index diverge, there is an opportunity for a risk-free arbitrage. A computerized system automatically executes trades in the futures and stocks via computer links between the exchange and a firm that holds a seat on the exchange. As much as 30 percent of daily stock trading volume in recent years is done by program trading.

Prior to Monday, October 19, program trading had generally kept the spread between index futures and the underlying stocks quite narrow. However, during the week of the crash this relationship fell apart because program trading was stopped by regulators and exchange officials. After a 23 percent decline in the DJIA on Monday, the NYSE restricted use of its electronic routing system for transferring orders to buy and sell securities from member firms. Index futures contracts then began to move around wildly.

Figure 21–4 shows the behavior of the S&P 500 futures contract and the value of the underlying securities. It also indicates the extent to which the futures contract is above or below the value of the stock market, measured in percent. The figure illustrates wide disparities between stock and futures markets throughout the week of October 19.

Stock futures arbitrage is particularly important for portfolio insurance. Portfolio insurance is a strategy for protecting a stock portfolio against declines in the market. One way to acquire such protection is to buy a put contract on the S&P 500 or other index. However, portfolio insurance uses a procedure of dynamic hedging to mimic the payoffs from purchasing such an option. The dynamic hedging strategy is similar to the idea Black and Scholes originally used to explain the price of an option as a leveraged position in the underlying asset. Portfolio insurers sell insurance based on such dynamic hedging partly because the fund manager does not pay an insurance fee as would occur if an exchange-traded put were bought on an index. Portfolio insurers have utilized hedges in index futures markets rather than the stock market largely because the transactions costs are lower.

On Tuesday, October 20, portfolio insurers' hedging strategies required that they sell significant quantities of index futures as a result of the decline in stock prices on Monday. However, because pro-

---

A **straddle** is a simultaneous position in a put and a call in the same underlying security.

cific calls and puts may be linked together. For example, an order may be placed for a **straddle,** a simultaneous purchase of a put and a call on the same underlying security at the same strike price. A straddle may be attractive to an investor who believes a significant change in the price of the underlying security will occur but does not know which direction that change is likely to be.

When an option is purchased, the investor must put up the entire purchase price of the option. At first glance, this seems like a heavy restriction on the amount of margin involved in the purchase. With regular stock purchases current regulations require at least 50 percent of the purchase price be paid with cash, or a 50 percent margin requirement. However, by purchasing a call option on a stock you are indirectly acquiring the stock itself. In effect, you have equal claim on all increases in the price of that stock above the exercise price, just as if you owned

FIGURE 21–4
Futures to Cash Spread in S&P 500.

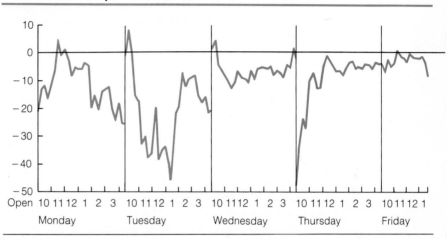

Source: *Wall Street Journal*, Oct. 26, 1987, p. 18.

gram traders' activities were restricted, the large sales of futures contracts precipitated a significant decline in the futures to cash spread (Figure 21–4). As a result, portfolio insurance strategies were not as effective in protecting against adverse market moves as many users thought they would be.

A significant part of the problem pertains to the differences in practices and origins of the stock market as opposed to the futures and options markets—a focus of this chapter. Much of the drama during the week of October 19 resulted from the perception that the NYSE might close and, in fact, trading was closed in a number of securities that make up the indexes on which futures contracts are based. Much reform after the market crash should be directed at integration of the markets for assets and contingent claims on those assets.

it. In addition, the value of the option is generally far less than the value of the stock itself. For example, consider the call options on IBM in Figure 21–3. The April call on IBM at a strike price of $155 sells for $3 5/8, while the price of the underlying stock is $154. Hence, you can acquire access to nearly all the increases in the future price of the stock through April for a very small fraction of its purchase price. When writing an option it is necessary to make a deposit against the prospect that a loss will be incurred. However, the price paid by the option purchaser can be used as part of this deposit, and Treasury bills can be deposited as well. Therefore, the deposit is an interest-bearing asset for the option writer.

When a transaction in options is executed by the floor broker, the transaction is then cleared at the end of the day through the Options Clearing Corporation (OCC). The OCC handles all options trades on the CBOE, AMEX, PHLX, and

PSE. In order for an exchange member to clear trades, he or she also must become a member of the OCC, which imposes a minimum capital requirement and payment of fees. Members must put up margin to the OCC for options where it represents the writer. In addition, deposits must be made with the OCC at least equal to the amount of the purchase price of every option purchased on the exchange until that transaction is cleared by the exchange. These two requirements of margin and deposits protect the OCC against defaults on transactions both at the time of purchase and when the option writer has to pay the purchaser if the option is exercised. Recall that the introduction of a centralized clearinghouse was an important innovation of exchange-traded options that reduced the cost of trading options relative to the over-the-counter market.

The procedure for executing trades on the CBOE and on the PSE, involving market makers and order book officials, resembles the open outcry auction process on the commodity exchanges. The CBOE pioneered development of exchange-traded options and followed the lead of the commodity exchanges in a number of respects. By contrast, the AMEX and PHLX utilize a system closer to the specialist system used on the New York Stock Exchange. Here we see once again, as in the competition between NASDAQ and the NYSE and between the various commodities exchanges, that the various options exchanges compete both with product development and the nature of the exchange process. The CBOE was the pioneer in developing exchange-traded options, and it remains the principal exchange, accounting for more than half of all options trading. The tremendous growth of exchange-traded options in general has provided an environment where a number of exchanges can successfully participate in this market. It is not at all clear how many separate exchanges will continue to operate if and when the growth of options trading materially slows down.

To summarize the principal features of exchange-traded options that have made options markets such successful innovations, we can identify at least four major advantages of exchange-traded options relative to the over-the-counter form of trading. They are:

1. Liquidity provided by highly standardized options contracts
2. Increased efficiency in managing credit risk resulting from introduction of the Options Clearing Corporation
3. Improved disclosure and surveillance of trading activities by centralized auction markets
4. Reduced transactions costs from the efficient trading process on the options exchanges

SUMMARY

The markets for futures and options contracts illustrate almost every principle dealt with throughout this book. They are excellent examples of innovation, they show how regulatory decisions can influence the evolution of market forms, and they show how a market can change from the over-the-counter form of organization to the auction form. They are also one of the most complicated types of markets in the current world financial system.

Both futures and options have been traded on over-the-counter markets, but in the last decade highly active auction markets have developed to increase liquidity and reduce credit risk generated by arranging contracts through a centralized clearinghouse. The standardization that accompanies the auction market makes the high degree of liquidity possible, but it also reduces flexibility, which is present in an over-the-counter market. The clearinghouse can reduce the cost of trading in the market since it introduces efficient systems for minimizing the risk of default on individual futures and options contracts.

Futures on financial instruments were first introduced in 1975, and they are currently traded on five exchanges. By contrast, the first organized options exchange, the CBOE, started trading options on specific stocks in April, 1973. The volume of options contracts on the CBOE increased rapidly from the outset. The CBOE first introduced options contracts on underlying assets other than individual stocks in 1982. Regulatory agencies delayed granting approval to new options contracts until a jurisdictional dispute about regulatory authority of the CFTC and the SEC was settled. The delay allowed time for other exchanges to prepare competing options contracts, and as a result, options contracts on a variety of instruments are traded on several different exchanges.

Initial margin requirements can be relatively modest for futures contracts because of the process of daily resettlement, where futures traders must realize gains and losses on the contracts daily. As a result, they must comply with a maintenance margin imposed each day. The actual trading process on the futures exchanges is called open outcry: when brokers come to the pit, they call out the order to buy or sell a contract. They must trade with anyone else in the pit who wishes to trade with them. There is considerable debate about the efficiency and potential for abuse in the process, and futures exchanges are considering a number of changes to automate trading and limit opportunities for abuse.

The final portion of the chapter analyzed how options contracts are specified and how to read the options quotes in the *Wall Street Journal*. An example of IBM options prices from the *Wall Street Journal* showed how pricing differs from that of futures contracts. In the trading process for contracts on the major options exchanges, particularly the CBOE, there are initial margin requirements but no daily resettlement. A central clearinghouse is used by four of the five major options exchanges. The trading process on the CBOE and PSE is similar to the open outcry process on the futures exchanges. However, other options exchanges utilize a system much like the specialist system on the NYSE. Since the CBOE pioneered options trading and has the largest portion of the total market, most trading in options and futures is through the open outcry system. Recently, program trading and triple witching have developed. Program trading is a highly organized and automated effort to trade on any perceived mispricing in the futures and options markets. However, it can create tremendous need to trade underlying stocks when index futures and options mature. Because the traders have perfectly hedged positions, they are unconcerned about the impact of their trading activity on the actual level of stock prices. A large amount of program trading can lead to large volume and large price swings in the equity markets when stock index futures and options contracts mature at the same time. The high trading volume and price volatility have attracted considerable public attention.

QUESTIONS

1. What is a clearinghouse? Why is it an important part of exchanges for trading options or futures?
2. What are the costs and benefits of standardization? How did standardization reduce the costs of options trading as the market was transformed from an over the counter to an auction market?
3. What regulatory agencies have jurisdiction over options and futures exchanges? How did the current allocation of responsibility evolve?
4. Compare the open outcry system with the specialist system. Where are these two systems used in the futures and options markets?
5. Is it possible to have an option on a future? When would it be preferable to have an option on the cash asset rather than on the future?
6. Suppose the settlement discount rates on two different days for a Treasury bill future are 6.26 percent and 6.36 percent. What are the corresponding actual prices on the futures contracts on these days? How much did the futures prices change from one day to the next?
7. Describe the initial and maintenance margin. How do they work? Why do the futures markets use daily resettlement? Is the same process used on the options markets? Why?
8. Explain why stock index futures are valuable tools for portfolio managers.
9. Compare margin requirements on the CBOE, the CBT, and the NYSE. Can you explain how and why they differ?
10. What is triple witching? Do you think triple witching represents a problem which requires more extensive regulation? What do you think is the solution to this problem?

REFERENCES

Cox, John C. and Mark Rubinstein, *Options Markets,* Englewood Cliffs, N.J.: Prentice-Hall, Inc., 1985.

Kane, Edward J. "Market Incompleteness and Divergence between Forward and Futures Interest Rates," *Journal of Finance,* (May 1980), pp. 221–34.

Kolb, Robert W. *Understanding Futures Markets,* Glenview, Ill.: Scott, Foresman and Company, 1985.

McMurray, Scott, "Merc's Trading Crush in Its Financial Futures Raises Call for Reforms," *Wall Street Journal,* (March 13, 1987), p. 1.

Phillips, Susan M. "Regulation of Futures Markets," in *Market Making and the Changing Structure of the Securities Industry,* edited by Amihud, Ho, and Schwartz, Lexington, Mass.: Lexington Books, 1985.

Scarf, Douglas. "The Securities and Commodities Markets: A Case Study in Product Convergence and Regulatory Disparity," in *Market Making and the Changing Structure of the Securities Industry,* edited by Amihud, Ho, and Schwartz, Lexington, Mass.: Lexington Books, 1985.

22

CONCLUSION

The last 21 chapters have covered a lot of territory. As you have gone through these chapters it may have been easier to grasp the details about how financial markets work than to identify and place the important issues in perspective. There are two important questions to answer regarding all of this material. They are: What are the most important things we have learned? What are the most important things we do not yet understand? The answers are very subjective, and the answers in this chapter are my answers to these questions. Now that you have almost finished this book, you should be in a position to provide some answers of your own. After all, 21 chapters have clearly indicated that there are few aspects of financial markets on which all observers agree.

In order to keep the topical structure of this book in perspective, in this last chapter we will proceed through each of the five parts of the book. For each part we will examine two important things we have learned and two important unanswered questions. ∎

WHAT WE LEARNED ABOUT THE VALUE OF ASSETS

How Time and Uncertainty Affect the Value of Distinct Types of Assets.
Chapter 2 explained that an asset is essentially a claim on a future stream of income. The basic ingredient in determining the value of assets is the real interest rate, and two forces influence this rate. The first is the set of real investment opportunities open to market participants. Real investments involve the production of some real capital goods that can be used to produce goods or services in the future. The second involves the attitudes of individuals in the economy toward present as opposed to future consumption. These two forces determine an equilibrium interest rate that represents the rate of return on real investment, the rate at which individuals prefer to trade current for future consumption, and the interest rate on financial contracts.

Markets can take the uncertainty about future income streams into account in pricing assets. The uncertainty that surrounds future income can be measured specifically. We also found that we can represent the way individual make investment decisions as a trade-off between the expected return of an asset and its risk. The risk borne by any individual depends upon the portfolio of assets which that individual holds because diversification reduces the risk of a portfolio of assets. As a result, the market value of any asset is based on its contribution to the portfolio risk of those individuals who hold it. Some types of assets have payoffs contingent on the values of some other underlying assets, such as options and futures. We learned how to evaluate the payoffs on options and futures and how these securities are priced in competitive markets.

How Markets Utilize Information. The second important feature of financial markets emphasized in Part 1 was the way markets produce and aggregate information. In order for the value of any asset to be determined in a market, the market participant must have some information about the income stream which may accrue to that asset. This information is produced and distributed to the market in a variety of ways—for instance, direct distribution to the market or provided with other valuable services, as in the case of financial intermediaries. All market participants form judgments of future returns based on the available information, and the market aggregates this information so that prices represent aggregates of individual judgments. Because there is competition for information to estimate future returns on assets, there is pressure for information to be produced and distributed efficiently. Efficient markets have a competitive return on producing and distributing information.

IMPORTANT UNANSWERED QUESTIONS

Are We Missing Something in Our Theory of How Risky Assets Are Priced? Part 1 analyzed the risk and expected return of an asset and how to combine assets into portfolios. With this it explained the theory—known as the capital asset pricing model—of how the marketplace actually values risky securities. The theory is built upon some rather elaborate and even distasteful assumptions, and the predictions it generates do not conform well with the observable world. The question is, what is missing from this theory? Is an important piece of the real world left out of it? Is the theory really fundamentally untestable and, hence, not really a theory at all, as some have charged? Is there a more practical or a better theory? We simply do not yet know.

How Does the Market for Information Function? We know that financial markets aggregate available information into asset prices, but we know very little about how this is done, probably because we know very little about the market for information itself. Information is produced and distributed in a number of ways, ranging from direct sale, as in the *Wall Street Journal,* to more complicated mechanisms, as with financial intermediaries. But we do not know why each form of information is made and what the return on it may be. These are very important issues because financial markets bring information together to determine prices. We know much more about the assets themselves and the markets in which they are traded than we do about the information that determines their prices.

WHAT WE LEARNED ABOUT THE DETERMINANTS OF MARKET INTEREST RATES

Why Nominal Rates Differ from the Real Interest Rate. Part 2 identified the most important factors that account for the level of observed nominal interest rates. All nominal rates can be thought of as the real rate plus premiums for special factors that distinguish the security in question. The important factors that determine these premiums are: (1) the expected rate of inflation, (2) the risk of the security, (3) the security's tax treatment, (4) relative security supplies, and (5) the security's maturity. Part 2 explained each of these factors and how they affect the yield on securities. We also surveyed empirical evidence on the relative importance of these factors in determining various nominal rates. In recent years the most obvious factor causing changes in nominal rates has been the expected rate of inflation. As actual and expected inflation rates have fluctuated, nominal interest rates have adjusted accordingly.

Similarly, it is relatively simple to see how differential tax treatment affected securities by examining the differences in yields on comparable municipal and corporate bonds. Municipal bonds have consistently lower yields because they are free from federal income taxes. In the case of differences in maturity, or the term structure of interest rates, differences in nominal yields are evident from inspections of yield curves at different points, but specific reasons for these differences are not so evident. While we can identify alternative explanations of the term structure, it is not as easy to establish which is correct. The Federal Reserve influences interest rates by implementing monetary policy for the nation's economy. We examined the mechanics of its operations as well as the competing interpretations of how monetary policy influences interest rates. Monetary policy can influence the real interest rate, at least temporarily, and it can influence the market's expectations of inflation, which in turn influences nominal rates.

How to Hedge Financial Risks Using Futures and Options Markets.   It is not enough to understand the market forces that determine market interest rates since most participants are concerned about how they can manage the risk of changes in future interest rates. Futures and options markets are used to hedge these types of risks. Hedging creates an investment with payoffs that offset an investor's risk exposure. In principle, a given risk exposure can be totally offset with a perfect hedge; however, in practice most hedges involve some kind of basis risk, either from a mismatch in the maturity of a hedge and the futures or options contract used, or because the asset being hedged and the instrument used to hedge are different. In either case, hedging strategy involves creation of a hedge which effectively manages the basis risk.

IMPORTANT UNANSWERED QUESTIONS

Do Changes in Inflation Expectations or the Real Rate Explain Short-term Changes in Observed Nominal Rates?   While we have a fairly clear understanding of what factors determine nominal interest rates, we do not understand the relative importance of each factor in explaining specific changes in nominal rates as well—particularly in explaining changes in short-term rates, such as Treasury bill rates. For example, a reduction in Treasury bill rates, such as between March and June, 1980, when 90-day bill rates fell from 14 to 7 percent, might be attributed to a reduction in the expected rate of inflation, but it also might be a change in the real interest rate. In all likelihood both the real rate of interest and the expected rate of inflation are changing simultaneously. And as they do, the nominal rate of interest changes accordingly. However, because we do not actually observe the *ex ante* real interest rate demanded by the market, it is exceedingly difficult to determine the actual cause of any particular change in nominal interest rates. In long-run equilibrium, the real interest rate demanded on financial transactions must be the same as the real rate of return on the economy's capital stock, but this does not mean that the two real rates do not diverge. During such periods the *ex ante* real rate demanded on financial contracts may fluctuate considerably and thereby cause changes in nominal rates. But we do not know how large changes in the real rate may be relative to changes in the expected rate of inflation.

How Significant are Liquidity Premiums in the Term Structure?   A similar question pertains to the relationship between short- and long-term interest rates. Long-term interest rates are determined in part by the market's expectation of future short-term rates, but if market participants are risk-averse, then they will demand a premium to bear the risk of changes in future short-term rates—a liquidity premium. How important are these liquidity premiums in determining observed long-term rates? What is the relative importance of changes in the real rate and changes in inflation expectations in determining changes in short-term nominal rates? The underlying difficulty is that we do not directly observe liqudity premiums in the market, just as we do not directly observe the *ex ante* real interest rate. The challenge is to devise some way to measure liquidity premiums to see whether supply-and-demand pressures at each maturity have a significant impact on the term structure. In addition, it would be desirable to be able to measure and even predict this impact on a regular basis. As yet we can do this only very imperfectly.

WHAT WE LEARNED ABOUT FORCES SHAPING THE STRUCTURE OF FINANCIAL MARKETS

A Taxonomy of Markets. Part 3 organized the maze of U.S. financial markets into a coherent classification system or taxonomy. Markets were divided into three basic types according to the way the exchange of assets actually takes place, as auction, over-the-counter, and intermediated markets. We explored the features of each type of market, the reasons why each market is used, and examples of each type of market. The value of this kind of taxonomy is that, first, it allows us to make sense out of the complex financial world and, second, it shows how a particular market is supposed to work, so that we can evaluate the efficiency of markets and understand how markets evolve from one form into another. This process of change is particularly important as the pace of innovation has increased in the 1980s and undoubtedly will continue.

The Rationale for Regulation of Financial Markets. Part 3 explored the principal features of the regulatory system for financial markets. But it also attempted to explain why it came into existence and to identify problems that can arise in an unregulated market that can interfere with its operation or cause it to fail altogether. There are two basic sources of the problems which can provide a logical or economic justification for regulation. The first pertains to development of monopoly power and the second pertains to the function of financial markets as information collectors and distributors. Much of our regulatory system is designed to limit monopolistic practices, particularly that part which applies to auction and over-the-counter markets. But an important additional purpose is to regulate information distribution and the individuals and institutions which possess special information. This understanding of the economic rationale for regulation is exceptionally important to make sense out of the maze of regulations that currently exist and to evaluate the merits of each component of that regulatory system. Regulation is costly and can be used to protect as well as eliminate vested interests. In addition, regulation is one of the most important forces shaping the structure of our financial markets and institutions.

IMPORTANT UNANSWERED QUESTIONS

How Thoroughly Will Technological Changes Alter the Operation of Financial Markets in the Years Ahead?   Technological change has been so rapid during the twentieth century that new industries have been created and old ones become obsolete almost before many participants realized what was happening. It has also been a crucial determinant of the types of U.S. financial markets which have prospered.

For much of the nineteenth century commercial banks were virtually the only significant type of financial market. Not until the corporate form of organization began to prosper did auction markets like the New York Stock Exchange emerge to trade corporate securities. As communication systems improved, over-the-counter markets grew to be strong competitors of the auction market. As the economy expanded after the Great Depression of the 1930s, the problems of assessing the expected returns and risk for a wide variety of different securities became more complicated. A set of financial intermediaries began to specialize in these activities, and their growth was further augmented by a system of insurance and government control that shifted risk from the marketplace to the government.

Two important changes in the 1970s and 1980s have caused financial markets to adapt again. The first major technological process is the system of communicating and processing information. Progress ranges from the evolution of low-cost minicomputers to the advent of telecommunications technology, which permits swift, low-cost transfer of information electronically. These changes altered the need for regional financial markets and institutions and blurred the distinction between auction and over-the-counter markets. The second major element of technological change is the advent of high inflation rates, a change that certainly cannot be viewed as progress. It fundamentally changed the nature of the risks that each security holder and institution bears in every financial transaction. During the 1990s the institutions and markets must adapt to these changes. How extensive this adaptation will be and who will gain and lose from it remains an unsolved but fascinating question.

How Much Responsibility for Regulating the Flow of Information Should Be Granted to the Government?   Financial markets can suffer from serious problems if information is not widely distributed throughout the market or if those entrusted with special information misuse it. The trend has been toward increased regulation of information distribution and of financial institutions that make decisions for those who may be less well-informed. Yet many argue that the distribution and use of information is now overregulated. Much of the criticism has been directed at disclosure laws, but it also applies to regulation of investment companies and financial intermediaries. Defenders of current regulation are inclined to view the period before the 1930s as an unnecessarily unstable period. That instability is attributed in part to imperfect information distribution and to fear of market failure resulting from perceived conflicts of interest. The important question is whether it would be possible to deregulate the distribution and use of information substantially without creating real or perceived conflicts of interest.

WHAT WE LEARNED ABOUT CONTEMPORARY FINANCIAL MARKETS AND INSTITUTIONS

The Importance of Deregulation in Reshaping U.S. Financial Institutions.   Part IV focused on the operation of specific financial institutions and markets and examined the deregulation or reform of the regulatory system for financial institutions and markets. We are moving away from a system based on product line and geographic segmentation of financial services toward a nationwide and even global market for financial services with fewer restrictions on the activities of firms participating in this market. We identified the principal reform legislation in the U.S., the Depository Institutions Deregulation Act of 1980 and the Garn-St Germain Act of 1982 and traced the progress made within courts and regulatory agencies on such important issues as interstate banking and repeal of the Glass-Steagall Act. The changes that have already taken place constitute a major restructuring of the U.S. financial system that will force all institutions to be more competitive.

The Nature of Competition in Specific Financial Markets.   A major task in Part 4 has been to examine the contemporary operation of specific types of financial markets, including commercial banking, mortgage finance, money markets, and futures and options markets. Our focus has been on understanding how these markets operate and how competitors in these markets conduct their business. Commercial banks must increasingly compete on the basis of efficiency in managing funding and default risks. Mortgage finance markets are evolving from a highly regulated market of portfolio lenders, chiefly savings and loans, into an over-the-counter market for mortgage-backed securities. Participants in this market can specialize in any of the steps in the securitization process, from origination to servicing to maintenance of a secondary market in mortgage-backed securities. Here, the crucial areas of risk management are prepayment risk and default risk. Innovation is important in the money market where money market funds have emerged as major participants in the management of portfolios. New products, such as interest rate swaps, are creating new opportunities for innovative financing and risk management. Finally, we examined how the options and futures markets operate and their trading procedures. Once again, the pace of innovation has been rapid in these markets.

IMPORTANT UNANSWERED QUESTIONS

Should We Stop Protecting Special Financial Institutions?   The regulatory system that emerged in the 1930s led to a set of instituions that serve specialized purposes and clienteles. The important feature is that they did not emerge and prosper in a competitive market environment, but instead were protected by the government through the regulatory system. The prospect of deregulation poses the important question, should these institutions continue to be protected or should more competition be allowed? If competition is encouraged through such devices as the elimination of restrictions on interstate commercial bank branching and effective repeal of the Glass-Steagall Act, then a vastly different intermediation industry might well result. The extent that this change should be encouraged and allowed and how different institutions should be regulated and insured is likely to be extremely important during the 1990s.

How Far Will Securitization Progress?   One of the most important practical problems facing financial markets is how securitzation will affect the U.S. financial system. Securitization has become widespread in the mortgage markets and is spreading to other types of financial instruments. Securitization is beneficial if it can provide increased liquidity and if there are gains from specialization that cannot be achieved in a market dominated by portfolio lenders. However, we do not know how extensive the gains from securitization may be in particular markets. We also do not know how severely securitization will threaten the viability of existing financial institutions, particularly commercial banks. Since commercial banks are protected by a government insurance corporation and since commercial banks have traditionally been an important part of our financial system, securitization is especially important.

A APPENDIX

*T*IME AND THE VALUE OF ASSETS

This appendix examines the importance of the time distribution of future income for the value of assets. The basic strategy is to devise a procedure for converting the stream of income which will accrue to an asset in the future into a single value of that asset today. We refer to this as capitalizing the income stream of the asset, and the value of the asset is the capitalized value.

The problem of uncertainty aside, it would be a trivial task to capitalize the income stream of an asset if market participants were unconcerned about the differences between equal amounts of income paid at different points in time, or if market participants consider a dollar paid one year from now to be worth the same today as a dollar paid two years from now (adjusted for inflation). The asset value would simply be defined as the sum of the income flows that accrue in each future period. This can be expressed algebraically as (assuming no change in the price level)

$$\text{Value} = \sum_{t=1}^{N} I_t, \qquad \text{A–1})$$

where I is the income that accrues in period t and $\sum_{t=1}^{N}$ means to add up all the values of I_t, allowing t to assume the values 1 through N. For example if $N = 3$ and $I_1 = 15$, $I_2 = 12$ and $I_3 = 7$, then the value equals 34. But the process of capitalizing income streams is not as simple as Equation (A–1) suggests. The reason is that there is a positive interest rate in the world, which means the market as a whole is concerned with differences between equivalent amounts of money received in distinct time periods.

*I*NTRODUCTION TO PRESENT VALUE

This section analyzes the concept of present value, while the next section extends these ideas and introduces the internal rate of return.

FOUR PRESENT VALUE PROBLEMS

We will examine four types of problems dealing with present and future value and use them to consider the concept of internal rate of return. We will consider the simpler form first then consider the complications after we have dealt with the basic structure of the four problems.

Problem 1. Suppose we place $1 in the bank at an interest rate of i for N years. What will the value of that dollar be at the end of the N years? First of all we will consider the very simple case where N is equal to one. In this instance, the value of the dollar at the end of the year, which we will refer to as the future value (FV), is

$$FV = 1(1 + i). \qquad (A-2)$$

This is simply the expression for simple interest defined in Chapter 2. If the dollar is left on deposit for more than one period earning the interest rate of i per period, then we must simply compound the interest to arrive at the future value. At the end of N years the future value is

$$FV = 1(1 + i)(1 + i) \ldots (1 + i). \qquad (A-3)$$

This can be rewritten as

$$FV = 1(1 + i).^N \qquad (A-4)$$

For example, if the interest rate is 10 percent and N is equal to 10 years, then $FV = \$1.00(1.10)^{10} = \$2.59$.

Problem 2. Suppose we place $1 in the bank every year for N years. What will be the value of that stream of deposits at the end of the N years? This problem can be viewed as the sum of a sequence of problems identical to problem 1. At the end of N years the value of the first dollar deposited is $1(1 + i)^N$; the value of the second dollar deposited is $1(1 + i)^{N-1}$, and so forth. The future value of the stream of dollars can therefore be expressed as:

$$FV = 1(1 + i) + 1(1 + i)^2 + 1(1 + i)^3 + \ldots + 1(1 + i),^N \qquad (A-5)$$

which can be simplified to read:

$$FV = \sum_{t=1}^{N} 1(1 + i).^t \qquad (A-6)$$

For example, if $N = 5$ and $i = 5$ percent, then

$$
\begin{aligned}
FV &= \$1.05 + (1.05)^2 + (\$1.05)^3 + (\$1.05)^4 + (\$1.05)^5 \\
&= \$1.05 + \$1.103 + \$1.158 + \$1.216 + \$1.276 \\
&= \$5.80.
\end{aligned}
$$

Problem 3. Problems 3 and 4 are concerned with the present value (*PV*) rather than the future value. If we reverse question 1, we ask the following: What is the value today of $1 received *N* periods from now? To answer we merely reverse the answer to question 1. The present value of the dollar is equal to the discounted value of the dollar:

$$PV = \frac{1}{(1 + i)^N}.$$
(A–7)

This is another way of saying that there is an amount, *PV*, which if invested for *N* years at *i* percent, will have a value of $1 at the end of *N* years. For example, if *N* is equal to 10 and *i* is equal to 5 percent, then the present value of the dollar is $1/(1.05)^{10} = 0.61$.

Problem 4. The reverse to question 2 is the following: what is the value today of a stream of income of $1 received at the end of each period for *N* periods? It is important to note whether the dollar is received at the beginning or the end of the period. In problem 2 we implicitly assumed the deposit was made at the beginning of the period. In this problem, we assumed the deposit was made at the beginning of the period and the dollar is received at the end of each period, just as was assumed in problem 3. This distinction may seem a little awkward at first, but it is standard practice in present value calculations. This problem is merely a sequence of problems like problem 3. The value of the first dollar received is $1/(1 + i)$; the value of a second dollar received is $1/(1 + i)^2$; and so on until the value of the last dollar received is $1/(1 + i)^N$. The present value of the stream of income can therefore be expressed as :

$$PV = \sum_{t=1}^{N} \frac{1}{(1 + i)^t}.$$
(A–8)

For example, if *i* is equal to 5 percent and *N* is equal to 5, then

$$PV = \frac{1}{(\$1.05)} + \frac{1}{(\$1.05)^2} + \frac{1}{(\$1.05)^3} + \frac{1}{(\$1.05)^4} + \frac{1}{(\$1.05)^5}$$
$$= \$.952 + \$.907 + \$.864 + \$.823 + \$.783$$
$$= \$4.33.$$

These four questions and the formulas which accompany them are summarized in Table A–1.

GENERALIZING THE FOUR PROBLEMS AND THE CONCEPT OF ANNUITY

The computational burden involved in computing either the present value or the future value of a stream of income is apparent from the example in problem 4 above. If *N* is relatively large, then the computations involved are burdensome.

TABLE A–1
Summary of the four basic questions of present and future value.

Question	Formula for the Answer
Future Value Questions	
1. What is the future value of $1 invested for N years at i %?	$FV = 1(1 + i)^N$
2. What is the future value of $1 invested every year for N years?	$FV = \sum_{t=1}^{N} 1(1 + i)^t$
Present Value Questions	
3. What is the present value of $1 received N years from now?	$PV = \dfrac{1}{(1 + i)^N}$
4. What is the present value of $1 received every year for N years?	$PV = \sum_{t=1}^{N} \dfrac{1}{(1 + i)^t}$

Fortunately, there is a relatively simple procedure that can be used to avoid these difficulties when the problem has the simplifying feature of problems 2 and 4, that the amount received each period is the same. In these problems the amount received each period was $1, but it could be any amount. As long as the amount each period is the same, the stream of income is referred to as an annuity. In this instance the computational burden can be reduced substantially. To see how this reduction can be accomplished we will first generalize the solutions for the four problems and then explain the procedure for dealing with annuities.

A limiting feature of these four problems as described is the amount of income in each period is restricted to $1. This simplifies the initial statement in the present equations, but the actual income per period can be any amount. Therefore we can generalize each of the solutions to the four problems for an arbitrary amount of income. In problems 1 and 3, where there is only one payment, we can symbolize the payment with A. In problems 2 and 4, where there are N payments, each of which might be different, each will be represented by A_t in time period t. Each of the solutions may not be rewritten for this more general income stream by substituting A at A_t in the earlier equations.

Problem 1:

$$FV = A(1 + i).^N \tag{A–9}$$

Problem 2:

$$FV = \sum_{t=1}^{N} A_t(1 + i).^t \tag{Ȧ–10}$$

Problem 3:

$$PV = \frac{A}{(1 + i)^{N.}} \tag{A–11}$$

Problem 4:

$$PV = \sum_{t=1}^{N} \frac{A_t}{(1 + i)^t.} \tag{A–12}$$

Equations (A–10) and (A–12) will be referred to as the future and present value equations. They indicate the basic procedure for valuing an income stream when problems involving uncertainty about the income stream are ignored. Notice that Equations (A–9) and (A–11) are simply a special case of Equations (A–10) and (A–12) where $A_t = 0$ for all values of t except $t = N$. In these special cases the subscript can be dropped altogether.

In order to use Equations (A–10) and (A–12) for the future and present value of an income stream, it is important to be familiar with some of the available procedures that greatly simplify computing these values. Most of these computations are easily performed on electronic calculators, but they may also be obtained from tables of simple present values and annuities. An annuity table is presented in Table A–2.

Equations (A–10) and (A–12) describe annuities if one simplifying restriction holds: the income stream is a constant so that the subscript of t on A may be dropped. The restriction can be written algebraically as $A_j = A_k$, for all values of j and k from 1 to N. For example, a constant income stream would be \$1,000 per year for 10 years, while a nonconstant stream would be \$1,000; \$2,000; \$2,500; \$212. When the income stream is constant, it is referred to as an *annuity*. In this case, it is possible to use an annuity procedure on a calculator or an annuity table to determine either the present or future value of the annuity. The simplicity in computation gained with an annuity can be seen from Equation (A–12) as follows. Where A_t is constant for all t, and the subscript is omitted, then the equation can be written as:

$$PV = \sum_{t=1}^{N} \frac{A}{(1 + i)^t}. \qquad (A–13)$$

But this can be simplified by extracting A from the summation:

$$PV = A \sum_{t=1}^{N} \frac{1}{(1 + i)^t}. \qquad (A–14)$$

It is now possible to compute the value of the second part of the right-hand term

$$\sum_{t=1}^{N} [1/(1 + i)^t],$$

for any value of i and N.

These terms can be computed ahead of time and are then available to be used with any value of A. This is why an annuity table or a calculator is useful. Tables contain the values of

$$\sum_{t=1}^{N} [1/(1 + i)^t],$$

for a selection of i and N. One can therefore simply look up the relevant entry in the table and multiply it by the value of the periodic payment A. The annuity table in Table A–2 contains these terms indexed by i and N. For example, an annuity of $1,000 per year for 10 years at 10 percent has a present value of $6,145, where the annuity factor is 6.145.

ADDITIONAL FEATURES OF PRESENT VALUE

NET PRESENT VALUE

The concept of present value is used in setting almost all prices in financial markets. In fact, the prices of financial assets are the discounted values of expected future earnings adjusted for risk. In addition, the present value procedure is the principal technique that can be used to evaluate an investment. However, when used in this context, we need to amend the procedure slightly by distinguishing between the total or gross present value of an asset and the net present value of an asset. What we have discussed so far is actually the gross present value. To see the distinction let's consider an example.

Suppose we are considering whether to undertake an investment that promises to pay $10,000 per year each year for 10 years. Also suppose that the interest rate that represents our opportunity cost is 12 percent. Finally, suppose that the asset that yields this future stream of income can be purchased for $50,000. The question we have to ask ourselves is, what is the asset worth to us? We can determine this by computing the gross present value (GPV). The value is determined as indicated in equation (A–12):

$$GPV = \sum_{t=1}^{10} \frac{10,000}{(1.12)^t}$$
$$= \$56,502.$$

We cannot tell from the gross present value alone whether we should purchase this asset. We must compare the gross present value with the purchase price or the cost of the asset. We will label this cost C. Now we can define the difference between these two as the net present value (NPV).

$$NPV = GPV - C. \qquad (A–15)$$

In the example, the NPV is

$$NPV = \$56,502 - \$50,000 = \$6,502.$$

The net present value measures the difference between the present value of the future revenues and the cost of the investment. It is therefore a measure of economic value.

Net present value can be used to define a simple rule for evaluating investments. An investment is worthwhile if it has positive economic value or a positive net present value when evaluated at an appropriate discount rate. If the discount

TABLE A-2
Annuity tables.

Panel A: Discount factors: Present value of $1 to be received after t years $= 1/(1 + r)^t$.

Number of Years							Interest Rate per Year								
	1%	2%	3%	4%	5%	6%	7%	8%	9%	10%	11%	12%	13%	14%	15%
1	.990	.980	.971	.962	.952	.943	.935	.926	.917	.909	.901	.893	.885	.877	.870
2	.980	.961	.943	.925	.907	.890	.873	.857	.842	.826	.812	.797	.783	.769	.756
3	.971	.942	.915	.889	.864	.840	.816	.794	.772	.751	.731	.712	.693	.675	.658
4	.961	.924	.888	.855	.823	.792	.763	.735	.708	.683	.659	.636	.613	.592	.572
5	.951	.906	.863	.822	.784	.747	.713	.681	.650	.621	.593	.567	.543	.519	.497
6	.942	.888	.837	.790	.746	.705	.666	.630	.596	.564	.535	.507	.480	.456	.432
7	.933	.871	.813	.760	.711	.665	.623	.583	.547	.513	.482	.452	.425	.400	.376
8	.923	.853	.789	.731	.677	.627	.582	.540	.502	.467	.434	.404	.376	.351	.327
9	.914	.837	.766	.703	.645	.592	.544	.500	.460	.424	.391	.361	.333	.308	.284
10	.905	.820	.744	.676	.614	.558	.508	.463	.422	.386	.352	.322	.295	.270	.247
11	.896	.804	.722	.650	.585	.527	.475	.429	.388	.350	.317	.287	.261	.237	.215
12	.887	.788	.701	.625	.557	.497	.444	.397	.356	.319	.286	.257	.231	.208	.187
13	.879	.773	.681	.601	.530	.469	.415	.368	.326	.290	.258	.229	.204	.182	.163
14	.870	.758	.661	.577	.505	.442	.388	.340	.299	.263	.232	.205	.181	.160	.141
15	.861	.743	.642	.555	.481	.417	.362	.315	.275	.239	.209	.183	.160	.140	.123
16	.853	.728	.623	.534	.458	.394	.339	.292	.252	.218	.188	.163	.141	.123	.107
17	.844	.714	.605	.513	.436	.371	.317	.270	.231	.198	.170	.146	.125	.108	.093
18	.836	.700	.587	.494	.416	.350	.296	.250	.212	.180	.153	.130	.111	.095	.081
19	.828	.686	.570	.475	.396	.331	.277	.232	.194	.164	.138	.116	.098	.083	.070
20	.820	.673	.554	.456	.377	.312	.258	.215	.178	.149	.124	.104	.087	.073	.061
25	.780	.610	.478	.375	.295	.233	.184	.146	.116	.092	.074	.059	.047	.038	.030
30	.742	.552	.412	.308	.231	.174	.131	.099	.075	.057	.044	.033	.026	.020	.015

Number of Years							Interest Rate per Year								
	16%	17%	18%	19%	20%	21%	22%	23%	24%	25%	26%	27%	28%	29%	30%
1	.862	.855	.847	.840	.833	.826	.820	.813	.806	.800	.794	.787	.781	.775	.769
2	.743	.731	.718	.706	.694	.683	.672	.661	.650	.640	.630	.620	.610	.601	.592
3	.641	.624	.609	.593	.579	.564	.551	.537	.524	.512	.500	.488	.477	.466	.455
4	.552	.534	.516	.499	.482	.467	.451	.437	.423	.410	.397	.384	.373	.361	.350
5	.476	.456	.437	.419	.402	.386	.370	.355	.341	.328	.315	.303	.291	.280	.269
6	.410	.390	.370	.352	.335	.319	.303	.289	.275	.262	.250	.238	.227	.217	.207
7	.354	.333	.314	.296	.279	.263	.249	.235	.222	.210	.198	.188	.178	.168	.159
8	.305	.285	.266	.249	.233	.218	.204	.191	.179	.168	.157	.148	.139	.130	.123
9	.263	.243	.225	.209	.194	.180	.167	.155	.144	.134	.125	.116	.108	.101	.094
10	.227	.208	.191	.176	.162	.149	.137	.126	.116	.107	.099	.092	.085	.078	.073
11	.195	.178	.162	.148	.135	.123	.112	.103	.094	.086	.079	.072	.066	.061	.056
12	.168	.152	.137	.124	.112	.102	.092	.083	.076	.069	.062	.057	.052	.047	.043
13	.145	.130	.116	.104	.093	.084	.075	.068	.061	.055	.050	.045	.040	.037	.033
14	.125	.111	.099	.088	.078	.069	.062	.055	.049	.044	.039	.035	.032	.028	.025
15	.108	.095	.084	.074	.065	.057	.051	.045	.040	.035	.031	.028	.025	.022	.020
16	.093	.081	.071	.062	.054	.047	.042	.036	.032	.028	.025	.022	.019	.017	.015
17	.080	.069	.060	.052	.045	.039	.034	.030	.026	.023	.020	.017	.015	.013	.012
18	.069	.059	.051	.044	.038	.032	.028	.024	.021	.018	.016	.014	.012	.010	.009
19	.060	.051	.043	.037	.031	.027	.023	.020	.017	.014	.012	.011	.009	.008	.007
20	.051	.043	.037	.031	.026	.022	.019	.016	.014	.012	.010	.008	.007	.006	.005
25	.024	.020	.016	.013	.010	.009	.007	.006	.005	.004	.003	.003	.002	.002	.001
30	.012	.009	.007	.005	.004	.003	.003	.002	.002	.001	.001	.001	.001	.000	.000

E.g.: If the interest rate is 10 percent per year, the present value of $1 received at the end of year 5 is $0.621.

TABLE A–2 (continued)

Panel B: Future value of $1 by the end of t years $= (1 + r)^t$.

Number of Years	Interest Rate per Year														
	1%	2%	3%	4%	5%	6%	7%	8%	9%	10%	11%	12%	13%	14%	15%
1	1.010	1.020	1.030	1.040	1.050	1.060	1.070	1.080	1.090	1.100	1.110	1.120	1.130	1.140	1.150
2	1.020	1.040	1.061	1.082	1.102	1.124	1.145	1.166	1.188	1.210	1.232	1.254	1.277	1.300	1.323
3	1.030	1.061	1.093	1.125	1.158	1.191	1.225	1.260	1.295	1.331	1.368	1.405	1.443	1.482	1.521
4	1.041	1.082	1.126	1.170	1.216	1.262	1.311	1.360	1.412	1.464	1.518	1.574	1.630	1.689	1.749
5	1.051	1.104	1.159	1.217	1.276	1.338	1.403	1.469	1.539	1.611	1.685	1.762	1.842	1.925	2.011
6	1.062	1.126	1.194	1.265	1.340	1.419	1.501	1.587	1.677	1.772	1.870	1.974	2.082	2.195	2.313
7	1.072	1.149	1.230	1.316	1.407	1.504	1.606	1.714	1.828	1.949	2.076	2.211	2.353	2.502	2.660
8	1.083	1.172	1.267	1.369	1.477	1.594	1.718	1.851	1.993	2.144	2.305	2.476	2.658	2.853	3.059
9	1.094	1.195	1.305	1.423	1.551	1.689	1.838	1.999	2.172	2.358	2.558	2.773	3.004	3.252	3.518
10	1.105	1.219	1.344	1.480	1.629	1.791	1.967	2.159	2.367	2.594	2.839	3.106	3.395	3.707	4.046
11	1.116	1.243	1.384	1.539	1.710	1.898	2.105	2.332	2.580	2.853	3.152	3.479	3.836	4.226	4.652
12	1.127	1.268	1.426	1.601	1.796	2.012	2.252	2.518	2.813	3.138	3.498	3.896	4.335	4.818	5.350
13	1.138	1.294	1.469	1.665	1.886	2.133	2.410	2.720	3.066	3.452	3.883	4.363	4.898	5.492	6.153
14	1.149	1.319	1.513	1.732	1.980	2.261	2.579	2.937	3.342	3.797	4.310	4.887	5.535	6.261	7.076
15	1.161	1.346	1.558	1.801	2.079	2.397	2.759	3.172	3.642	4.177	4.785	5.474	6.254	7.138	8.137
16	1.173	1.373	1.605	1.873	2.183	2.540	2.952	3.426	3.970	4.595	5.311	6.130	7.067	8.137	9.358
17	1.184	1.400	1.653	1.948	2.292	2.693	3.159	3.700	4.328	5.054	5.895	6.866	7.986	9.276	10.76
18	1.196	1.428	1.702	2.026	2.407	2.854	3.380	3.996	4.717	5.560	6.544	7.690	9.024	10.58	12.38
19	1.208	1.457	1.754	2.107	2.527	3.026	3.617	4.316	5.142	6.116	7.263	8.613	10.20	12.06	14.23
20	1.220	1.486	1.806	2.191	2.653	3.207	3.870	4.661	5.604	6.727	8.062	9.646	11.52	13.74	16.37
25	1.282	1.641	2.094	2.666	3.386	4.292	5.427	6.848	8.623	10.83	13.59	17.00	21.23	26.46	32.92
30	1.348	1.811	2.427	3.243	4.322	5.743	7.612	10.06	13.27	17.45	22.89	29.96	39.12	50.95	66.21

Number of Years	Interest Rate per Year														
	16%	17%	18%	19%	20%	21%	22%	23%	24%	25%	26%	27%	28%	29%	30%
1	1.160	1.170	1.180	1.190	1.200	1.210	1.220	1.230	1.240	1.250	1.260	1.270	1.280	1.290	1.300
2	1.346	1.369	1.392	1.416	1.440	1.464	1.488	1.513	1.538	1.563	1.588	1.613	1.638	1.664	1.690
3	1.561	1.602	1.643	1.685	1.728	1.772	1.816	1.861	1.907	1.953	2.000	2.048	2.097	2.147	2.197
4	1.811	1.874	1.939	2.005	2.074	2.144	2.215	2.289	2.364	2.441	2.520	2.601	2.684	2.769	2.856
5	2.100	2.192	2.288	2.386	2.488	2.594	2.703	2.815	2.932	3.052	3.176	3.304	3.436	3.572	3.713
6	2.436	2.565	2.700	2.840	2.986	3.138	3.297	3.463	3.635	3.815	4.002	4.196	4.398	4.608	4.827
7	2.826	3.001	3.185	3.379	3.583	3.797	4.023	4.259	4.508	4.768	5.042	5.329	5.629	5.945	6.275
8	3.278	3.511	3.759	4.021	4.300	4.595	4.908	5.239	5.590	5.960	6.353	6.768	7.206	7.669	8.157
9	3.803	4.108	4.435	4.785	5.160	5.560	5.987	6.444	6.931	7.451	8.005	8.595	9.223	9.893	10.60
10	4.411	4.807	5.234	5.695	6.192	6.728	7.305	7.926	8.594	9.313	10.09	10.92	11.81	12.76	13.79
11	5.117	5.624	6.176	6.777	7.430	8.140	8.912	9.749	10.66	11.64	12.71	13.86	15.11	16.46	17.92
12	5.936	6.580	7.288	8.064	8.916	9.850	10.87	11.99	13.21	14.55	16.01	17.61	19.34	21.24	23.30
13	6.886	7.699	8.599	9.596	10.70	11.92	13.26	14.75	16.39	18.19	20.18	22.36	24.76	27.39	30.29
14	7.988	9.007	10.15	11.42	12.84	14.42	16.18	18.14	20.32	22.74	25.42	28.40	31.69	35.34	39.37
15	9.266	10.54	11.97	13.59	15.41	17.45	19.74	22.31	25.20	28.42	32.03	36.06	40.56	45.59	51.19
16	10.75	12.33	14.13	16.17	18.49	21.11	24.09	27.45	31.24	35.53	40.36	45.80	51.92	58.81	66.54
17	12.47	14.43	16.67	19.24	22.19	25.55	29.38	33.76	38.74	44.41	50.85	58.17	66.46	75.86	86.50
18	14.46	16.88	19.67	22.90	26.62	30.91	35.85	41.52	48.04	55.51	64.07	73.87	85.07	97.86	112.5
19	16.78	19.75	23.21	27.25	31.95	37.40	43.74	51.07	59.57	69.39	80.73	93.81	108.9	126.2	146.2
20	19.46	23.11	27.39	32.43	38.34	45.26	53.36	62.82	73.86	86.74	101.7	119.1	139.4	162.9	190.0
25	40.87	50.66	62.67	77.39	95.40	117.4	144.2	176.9	216.5	264.7	323.0	393.6	478.9	581.8	705.6
30	85.85	111.1	143.4	184.7	237.4	304.5	389.8	497.9	634.8	807.8	1026	1301	1646	2078	2620

E.g.: If the interest rate is 10 percent per year, the investment of $1 today will be worth $1.611 at the end of year 5.

TABLE A–2 (continued)

Panel C: Present value of $1 *per year* for each of *t* years = $1/r - 1/[r(1 + r)^t]$.

Number of Years	Interest Rate per Year														
	1%	2%	3%	4%	5%	6%	7%	8%	9%	10%	11%	12%	13%	14%	15%
1	.990	.980	.971	.962	.952	.943	.935	.926	.917	.909	.901	.893	.885	.877	.870
2	1.970	1.942	1.913	1.886	1.859	1.833	1.808	1.783	1.759	1.736	1.713	1.690	1.668	1.647	1.626
3	2.941	2.884	2.829	2.775	2.723	2.673	2.624	2.577	2.531	2.487	2.444	2.402	2.361	2.322	2.283
4	3.902	3.808	3.717	3.630	3.546	3.465	3.387	3.312	3.240	3.170	3.102	3.037	2.974	2.914	2.855
5	4.853	4.713	4.580	4.452	4.329	4.212	4.100	3.993	3.890	3.791	3.696	3.605	3.517	3.433	3.352
6	5.795	5.601	5.417	5.242	5.076	4.917	4.767	4.623	4.486	4.355	4.231	4.111	3.998	3.889	3.784
7	6.728	6.472	6.230	6.002	5.786	5.582	5.389	5.206	5.033	4.868	4.712	4.564	4.423	4.288	4.160
8	7.652	7.325	7.020	6.733	6.463	6.210	5.971	5.747	5.535	5.335	5.146	4.968	4.799	4.639	4.487
9	8.566	8.162	7.786	7.435	7.108	6.802	6.515	6.247	5.995	5.759	5.537	5.328	5.132	4.946	4.772
10	9.471	8.983	8.530	8.111	7.722	7.360	7.024	6.710	6.418	6.145	5.889	5.650	5.426	5.216	5.019
11	10.37	9.787	9.253	8.760	8.306	7.887	7.499	7.139	6.805	6.495	6.207	5.938	5.687	5.453	5.234
12	11.26	10.58	9.954	9.385	8.863	8.384	7.943	7.536	7.161	6.814	6.492	6.194	5.918	5.660	5.421
13	12.13	11.35	10.63	9.986	9.394	8.853	8.358	7.904	7.487	7.103	6.750	6.424	6.122	5.842	5.583
14	13.00	12.11	11.30	10.56	9.899	9.295	8.745	8.244	7.786	7.367	6.982	6.628	6.302	6.002	5.724
15	13.87	12.85	11.94	11.12	10.38	9.712	9.108	8.559	8.061	7.606	7.191	6.811	6.462	6.142	5.847
16	14.72	13.58	12.56	11.65	10.84	10.11	9.447	8.851	8.313	7.824	7.379	6.974	6.604	6.265	5.954
17	15.56	14.29	13.17	12.17	11.27	10.48	9.763	9.122	8.544	8.022	7.549	7.120	6.729	6.373	6.047
18	16.40	14.99	13.75	12.66	11.69	10.83	10.06	9.372	8.756	8.201	7.702	7.250	6.840	6.467	6.128
19	17.23	15.68	14.32	13.13	12.09	11.16	10.34	9.604	8.950	8.365	7.839	7.366	6.938	6.550	6.198
20	18.05	16.35	14.88	13.59	12.46	11.47	10.59	9.818	9.129	8.514	7.963	7.469	7.025	6.623	6.259
25	22.02	19.52	17.41	15.62	14.09	12.78	11.65	10.67	9.823	9.077	8.422	7.843	7.330	6.873	6.464
30	25.81	22.40	19.60	17.29	15.37	13.76	12.41	11.26	10.27	9.427	8.694	8.055	7.496	7.003	6.566

Number of Years	Interest Rate per Year														
	16%	17%	18%	19%	20%	21%	22%	23%	24%	25%	26%	27%	28%	29%	30%
1	.862	.855	.847	.840	.833	.826	.820	.813	.806	.800	.794	.787	.781	.775	.769
2	1.605	1.585	1.566	1.547	1.528	1.509	1.492	1.474	1.457	1.440	1.424	1.407	1.392	1.376	1.361
3	2.246	2.210	2.174	2.140	2.106	2.074	2.042	2.011	1.981	1.952	1.923	1.896	1.868	1.842	1.816
4	2.798	2.743	2.690	2.639	2.589	2.540	2.494	2.448	2.404	2.362	2.320	2.280	2.241	2.203	2.166
5	3.274	3.199	3.127	3.058	2.991	2.926	2.864	2.803	2.745	2.689	2.635	2.583	2.532	2.483	2.436
6	3.685	3.589	3.498	3.410	3.326	3.245	3.167	3.092	3.020	2.951	2.885	2.821	2.759	2.700	2.643
7	4.039	3.922	3.812	3.706	3.605	3.508	3.416	3.327	3.242	3.161	3.083	3.009	2.937	2.868	2.802
8	4.344	4.207	4.078	3.954	3.837	3.726	3.619	3.518	3.421	3.329	3.241	3.156	3.076	2.999	2.925
9	4.607	4.451	4.303	4.163	4.031	3.905	3.786	3.673	3.566	3.463	3.366	3.273	3.184	3.100	3.019
10	4.833	4.659	4.494	4.339	4.192	4.054	3.923	3.799	3.682	3.571	3.465	3.364	3.269	3.178	3.092
11	5.029	4.836	4.656	4.486	4.327	4.177	4.035	3.902	3.776	3.656	3.543	3.437	3.335	3.239	3.147
12	5.197	4.988	4.793	4.611	4.439	4.278	4.127	3.985	3.851	3.725	3.606	3.493	3.387	3.286	3.190
13	5.342	5.118	4.910	4.715	4.533	4.362	4.203	4.053	3.912	3.780	3.656	3.538	3.427	3.322	3.223
14	5.468	5.229	5.008	4.802	4.611	4.432	4.265	4.108	3.962	3.824	3.695	3.573	3.459	3.351	3.249
15	5.575	5.324	5.092	4.876	4.675	4.489	4.315	4.153	4.001	3.859	3.726	3.601	3.483	3.373	3.268
16	5.668	5.405	5.162	4.938	4.730	4.536	4.357	4.189	4.033	3.887	3.751	3.623	3.503	3.390	3.283
17	5.749	5.475	5.222	4.990	4.775	4.576	4.391	4.219	4.059	3.910	3.771	3.640	3.518	3.403	3.295
18	5.818	5.534	5.273	5.033	4.812	4.608	4.419	4.243	4.080	3.928	3.786	3.654	3.529	3.413	3.304
19	5.877	5.584	5.316	5.070	4.843	4.635	4.442	4.263	4.097	3.942	3.799	3.664	3.539	3.421	3.311
20	5.929	5.628	5.353	5.101	4.870	4.657	4.460	4.279	4.110	3.954	3.808	3.673	3.546	3.427	3.316
25	6.097	5.766	5.467	5.195	4.948	4.721	4.514	4.323	4.147	3.985	3.834	3.694	3.564	3.442	3.329
30	6.177	5.829	5.517	5.235	4.979	4.746	4.534	4.339	4.160	3.995	3.842	3.701	3.569	3.447	3.332

E.g.: If the interest rate is 10 percent per year, the present value of $1 received at the end of each of the next 5 years is $3.791.

rate reflects the opportunity cost to the investor, then all investments with positive net present value will make a positive contribution to that investor's total worth.

THE INTERNAL RATE OF RETURN

There is another way to view the relationship between the income stream an asset generates and its present value. Instead of taking an interest rate as given and using it to discount the future income to arrive at present value, we can use the value of an asset and its future income stream to derive its rate of return. We can define the interest rate as the internal rate of return when we take the present and future values as given and solve for the interest rate that satisfies the present value equation. In the case of the present value equation for a single payment, Equation (A–11), if we are given the payment to be received N periods hence, A, and the value of the payment today, PV, then we can solve for i^*, the interest rate earned on this asset and defined as the internal rate of return. By solving for i^* in Equation (A–11), we conclude that:

$$i^* = N\sqrt{\frac{A}{PV}} - 1. \qquad\qquad (A\text{--}16)$$

We can also use net present value to provide an equivalent definition of the internal rate of return. The interest rate that yields a zero net present value for an investment is the internal rate of return. This is the same as saying that it is the interest rate that yields a present value of future income equal to the cost of an asset.

To understand this definition of the internal rate of return, return to the example about net present value in the preceding section that involved an investment with a stream of $10,000 per year for 10 years and a cost of $50,000. The net present value of this investment when discounted at 12 percent was $6,502. We could also compute the net present value for this investment at a selection of alternative discount rates. If we did so, these combinations of net present value and discount rate could be plotted in a diagram such as Figure A–1. The vertical axis measures net present value in dollars and the horizontal axis measures the discount rate. The downward-sloping line illustrates that the net present value declines as the discount rate increases. The internal rate of return is the discount rate which yields a net present value of zero. In this example, the internal rate of return is approximately 15 percent; this is the point where the downward-sloping line crosses the vertical axis. This is the same thing as saying that the internal rate of return is the discount rate that yields a present value of zero for the future income on the $50,000 investment.

The only substantive difference between the concepts of present value and internal rate of return is the choice about what is a given and what must be derived. When we solve for the present value, the interest rate is taken as given. This interest rate is often called a discount rate, but it is not referred to as an internal rate of return. Conversely, when the present value is taken as given, we

FIGURE A–1
Present value of an investment which pays $10,000 per year for 10 years and costs $50,000. The figure shows that the internal rate of return is approximately 15 percent.

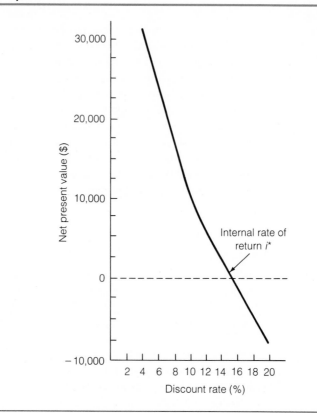

can solve for the implied interest rate according to Equation (A–16), and we label this the internal rate of return. The present value and the internal rate of return may therefore be thought of as the flip side of the same coin. If we know the interest rate or yield that the market demands, then we can determine an asset's value in dollars. Conversely, if we know the value placed on an asset by the market, we can determine the yield the market is demanding. We cannot determine one without the other.

The internal rate of return is relatively easy to define analytically and compute when there is a single future payment involved, as in Equation (A–16). It is not nearly as straightforward when there is a stream of future income, as is the case for the present value equation, Equation (A–12). We must resort to more complicated procedures to derive the value of the internal rate of return. To determine the internal rate of return in this instance we merely state that if we know the current value of the asset, *PV*, and we know the cash flow stream, A_t, then an interest rate, i^*, will exist that satisfies Equation (A–12):

$$PV = \sum_{t=1}^{N} \frac{A_t}{(1 + i^*)^t}.$$

(A–17)

But to say that such an interest rate exists is not to show how to determine what its value is. Analytically, that is a rather complicated task. There is a relatively simple procedure for estimating the internal rate of return that is essentially a method of hunt and peck. Basically the procedure is as follows. Choose an interest rate arbitrarily and determine the present value of the income stream A_t based on that interest rate. If the present value computed is higher than the actual value of the asset, then increase the interest rate and repeat the calculations. Generally, this converges on the accurate internal rate of return. One way to accomplish this is by using the present value tables, or, if the cash flow stream is an annuity, most financial calculators will compute it automatically. For example, if the present value of an asset is $10,000 and the income stream is $1,200 per year for 10 years, then the internal rate of return is 3.5 percent.

For assets with income in more than one future period, the internal rate of return is not always well defined. There might be more than one internal rate of return or no internal rate of return. For example, suppose you are considering an investment project with the following cash flow: year 1, − $40,000; year 2, + $25,000; and year 3, − $25,000. This project has two internal rates of return, 25 percent and 400 percent. The problem is that Equation (A–17) is a polynomial of order *N*. The task of solving for i^* requires identification of the roots of the polynomial.[1] If there are multiple roots of the polynomial, then, in effect, there are multiple internal rates of return. In these cases the multiple roots obscure the meaning of the results, but, fortunately, it is easy to tell by inspecting the income stream when multiple roots are a possibility. They might occur only when there is negative income in some future periods. If all future values of A_t are positive, then there will be a single internal rate of return. The implication is that it is best to avoid the internal rate of return altogether if future income in some period is negative.

Finally, it is important to reemphasize that present value and internal rate of return are merely reverse sides of the same coin. The concept that lies behind them is that each asset has a value that can be expressed directly in dollars if we know the yield demanded by the market. Conversely, it can be expressed in the form of an interest rate if we know the dollar value placed on it. There simply cannot be one without the other.

---

[1]See Eugene F. Fama and Merton H. Miller, *The Theory of Finance*, New York: Holt, Rinehart and Winston, 1972, pp. 137–43, for a more detailed discussion of difficulties surrounding the internal rate of return.

TAKING ACCOUNT OF THE FREQUENCY OF COMPOUNDING

One final complication can be introduced into the procedure for determining present and future values: interest may be compounded more than once per period. The real complication here is that we have a common unit for comparison. But the compounding may be more frequent than annually, and when it is, we do not generally change the interest rate to express it on a quarterly, monthly, or daily basis. Changes in the frequency of compounding alter the present and future values and the effective annual interest rate earned.

To see what happens as the frequency of compounding is increased, we will modify the present and future value equations for the case of a single payment to accommodate an arbitrary frequency. But the same modifications apply to the more general cases of multiple payments as described in Equations (A–10) and (A–12). Suppose that compounding takes place m times per year at an annual interest rate of i, or an interest rate of i/m per compounding. The present value of A dollars received N periods from now would be

$$PV = \frac{A}{(1 + i/m)^{mN}} \qquad \text{(A–18)}$$

For example, if the annual interest rate is 12 percent and compounding is done once per quarter, then the present value of \$1,000 received one year hence is $PV = \$1,000/(\$1.03)^4 = \$888.49$.

It is quite possible to imagine compounding so frequently that it virtually becomes continuous or that the frequency of compounding approaches infinity. In this case, it is necessary to examine what happens as m approaches infinity in Equation (A–18). While we will eschew dealing with all the mathematics involved in evaluating this equation as m approaches infinity, we can neatly summarize the form of the equation which results.[2] The present value of A dollars received in N years when compounding is continuous at an annual interest rate of i can be expressed:

$$PV = \frac{\$1,000}{e^{iN}} = \$1,000(e^{-iN}), \qquad \text{(A–19)}$$

where e is called the natural logarithm and has the value 2.718. Similarly, the future value of \$1,000 invested today on the same terms would be

$$FV = \$1,000(e^{iN}). \qquad \text{(A–20)}$$

If, for example, i is 10 percent, N is 2 years, and A is \$1,000, then the present value is $[\$1,000/(2,718.2)] = \$818.74$. Had the compounding been annual, the

---

[2]For a more complete treatment of the case of continuous compounding, see J. Hirshleifer, *Investment, Interest, and Capital*, Englewood Cliffs, N.J.: Prentice-Hall, 1970.

present value would be $826.44. Therefore, increasing the frequency of compounding from annual to continuous decreased the present value by $7.70.

PERPETUITIES

The purpose of capitalizing an income stream into a present value is applicable to virtually all assets in the market. For example, the present value equation provides the basic framework for valuing equity securities. But particularly in the case of equities, and with some other assets as well, the time horizon for the income stream is not precisely defined. That is, many assets do not have a specific maturity that defines the point that the income stream terminates. Instead, the asset generates income for an indefinite future. One way to deal with assets that have no specific termination point is to assume that they will go on forever. Such assets are usually referred to as *perpetuities*. While few if any things actually go on forever, the assumption is not really that troublesome because in any present value equation with a positive interest rate, events—that is, inflow of dollars—become increasingly less significant today, the farther in the future they take place. The fact that dollars received in the future are discounted by one plus the interest rate raised to the power of the time interval involved, means that the significance, today, of future income will decline rapidly as the time interval increases. Only if the income stream itself is growing can this perpetuity assumption lead to real difficulties.

In order to examine how the value of assets is determined when those assets are assumed to go on forever, we will ignore the prospect of growth in the income stream accruing to an asset and examine the present value of a perpetual but constant income stream. That is, we will examine an annuity with an infinite maturity. There is at least one real world example of such an annuity. For many years the British Treasury has sold bonds called consols, which are promises to pay a constant stream of income forever. The prices and yields of these securities are determined using the basic present value equation, but now the maturity, N, equals infinity. The price of the consol is therefore defined as:

$$PV = \sum_{t=1}^{N} \frac{A}{(1 + i)^t},\tag{A-21}$$

where i is the market yield on a consol and A is received at the end of each period. To simplify this equation we can multiply both sides by $(1 + i)$, which yields:

$$PV(1 + i) = A + \frac{A}{(1 + i)} + \frac{A}{(1 + i)^2} + \ldots + \frac{A}{(1 + i)^{N-1}}.\tag{A-22}$$

Subtracting Equation (A-21) from Equation (A-22), we obtain

$$PV(1 + i) - PV = A - \frac{A}{(1 + i)^N}.$$

As N approaches infinity, as in the case of the perpetuity, $A/(1 + i)^N$ approaches zero. As a result PV can be simplified to:

$$PV = \frac{A}{i},\qquad\qquad\text{(A–23)}$$

or the yield can be expressed as:

$$i = \frac{A}{PV}.\qquad\qquad\text{(A–24)}$$

This simply says that the yield on a perpetuity is equal to the ratio of the periodic payment to the asset's current value. If, for example, A = \$600 and PV = \$12,000, then i = 5 percent.

PRESENT VALUE OF BONDS AND STOCKS

There are a wide variety of different types of debt instruments traded in financial markets. Each such debt instrument has a price and a market interest rate, or yield. The price is the present value of the future income stream accruing to the bond if held to maturity and discounted at the market yield for that bond. Similarly, the market yield is simply the internal rate of return for the same income stream, given the market price of the bond. These prices and yields are quoted regularly in the financial press, and it is important to see more precisely how they are computed.

One quite common type of debt instrument is the *coupon bond*. We discussed the distinction between a coupon and market interest rate earlier. Coupon interest is the promised interest payment paid periodically on a bond. It is generally stated as some percentage of the face or maturity value of the bond. For example, a 5 percent coupon bond with a face value of \$10,000 would pay \$500 every year to the bond owner until the bond matured. At maturity the bondholder would receive the face value of \$10,000.

To see how the market prices a coupon bond, we will consider an example with the following characteristics. The bond has a maturity value of \$100,000 with a 5 percent coupon interest rate paid semiannually. The bond was originally issued with a maturity of 20 years; there are now exactly 10 years remaining to maturity, and the current date is January 1, 1987. We want to ask two questions about this bond. First, we want to know what the market price of this bond would be given the yield on 10-year bonds. Then we want to know what the yield would be if we know the bond price. The market computes the value of a bond both in terms of a dollar price and market yield. Given one, we can determine the other, and we want to see how this is done in our example.

The first thing we need to do in order to determine the price or the yield for the bond is carefully define the income stream that will accrue to it. With a 5 percent coupon rate, the bondholder will receive \$5,000 per year in interest. But because this bond stipulates semiannual payments, $2,500 will be received every 6 months. In addition, at the end of 10 years, or on January 1, 1997, the bond-holder will receive the $100,000 maturity value. The cash flows received on each future date are shown in the table below:

	July	Jan.	July	Jan.	. . .	July	Jan.
Date	87	88	88	89		96	97
Cash flow	$2,500	$2,500	$2,500	$2,500		$2,500	$102,500

In order to determine either the market price or yield we need to set up the present value equation for this bond. From the time path of future payments to the bond-holder we know that there are 19 periods, each 6 months long, when the bond-holder will receive $2,500 per period. In the twentieth period the bondholder will receive $102,500. The present value equation therefore can be written as:

$$PV = \sum_{t=1}^{19} \frac{\$2,500}{(1+i/2)^t} + \frac{\$102,000}{(1+i/2)^{20}}.$$

We have to discount the annual interest rate by half because we are compounding every six months rather than annually, due to the fact that coupon payments are made every six months.

We can use this equation to solve for either the market price of the bond or the yield, given the other value. If the market yield on this bond is 7 percent, then the price of the bond is determined as follows:

$$PV = \frac{\$2,500}{1.035} + \frac{\$2,500}{(1.035)^2} + \frac{\$2,500}{(1.035)^3} + \ldots + \frac{\$2,500}{(1.035)^{19}} \frac{\$2,500}{(1.035)^{20}}$$
$$= \$85,787.$$

On the other hand, if the bond price is $95,000, then the market yield must be determined through the hunt-and-peck procedure described above. It turns out to be approximately 5.7 percent. There is no shortcut except to use trial and error, unless you have a calculator which will do it for you.

VALUING EQUITY SECURITIES

The value of a perpetuity provides the basis for valuing any income stream that is presumed to last forever but not expected to be constant. The equity security is an example of this situation. The stream of income that accrues to an equity security is composed of the dividend payment and the capital gain or loss on the stock price. As a result, the current price is the capitalized value of future dividends and capital gains and losses. But the price at any point in the future is, in turn, dependent on dividends or capital gains on losses even further in the future. The implication is that the current price is really the capitalized value of future dividends as long as the firm continues to exist, plus the value of the firm at termination if it should be sold. If we assume that the firm goes on forever, then the current value is virtually the capitalized value of future dividends. The general present value equation for the equity value of the firm, ignoring uncertainty and the magnitude of future dividends, can then be written as:

$$PV = \sum_{t=1}^{N}\frac{D_t}{(1+i)^t},$$ (A–25)

where D_t is the dividend payment anticipated in time period t. The only distinction between this case and the perpetuity considered earlier is that the dividend payments are subscripted for time, indicating that they will be distinct values each period.

If we can say nothing more about the way future dividends will evolve over time, then Equation (A–25) is essentially the end of the story about time and the value of assets. But if we can postulate a regular pattern about the evolution of dividends, we can simplify the equation considerably. One way is to assume that dividends grow at some constant rate, say, g. Then if dividends are initially at a level of D_0, the dividend payment in any future period t can be written:

$$D_t = D_0(1+g)^t$$ (A–26)

Substituting this into Equation (A–25) yields

$$PV = \sum_{t=1}^{N}\frac{D_0(1+g)^t}{(1+i)^t}.$$ (A–27)

This equation for the value of an equity security can now be simplified, just as Equation (A–21) could for the value of a British consol, if i is greater than g. That is, we can simplify the equation if the discount rate is greater than the rate of growth of dividends. If this were not the case, then the value of the asset would be infinite, because the numerator grows at a faster rate than the denominator. But if i exceeds g, then the denominators in Equation (A–27) will increase faster than the numerators, and PV will have a finite value.

To see this, consider an example where dividends are growing at 10 percent from an initial amount of $10 and i is only 5 percent. We only need to write out a few terms of Equation (A–27) to see the effect:

$$PV = \frac{10(1.1)}{1.05} + \frac{10(1.1)^2}{(1.05)^2} + \frac{10(1.1)^3}{(1.05)^3} + \cdots$$
$$= \frac{11}{1.05} + \frac{12.00}{1.1025} + \frac{13.31}{1.1576} + \cdots$$
$$= 10.48 + 10.98 + 11.50 + \cdots.$$

As we add more terms, they keep getting larger, which means there will be no finite for *PV* if the firm goes on forever.

When *i* is greater than *g* the following result for the value of the asset as *N* approaches infinity:[3]

$$PV = \frac{D_1}{(i - g)},$$ (A–28)

or for its rate of return:

$$i = \frac{D_1}{PV} + g.$$ (A–29)

These are directly analogous to Equations (A–23) and (A–24). For example, the equity price is equal to the dividends in the next period, discounted as if they would be perpetual, at a rate equal to the discount rate net of the rate of growth in dividends. This approach to valuation, known as the Gordon growth model, is one of the principal tools used for valuing equity securities in the market.

To illustrate the use of Equation (A–28) for the value of equity securities, let's suppose we are examining a company with a fairly long history of dividend payments. From this history we can formulate an estimate of the future growth rate in dividends. There are a number of ways we might do this, but probably the simplest is to compute the growth rate in each past year then utilize the average of those past growth rates. This assumes that the future will be like the past, which it might not be. If we have good evidence about how the future will differ, then use it. But without such evidence, the average probability represents a reasonable estimate of the future. Suppose that these computations show the average growth rate for dividends has been 6 percent. Next suppose that the discount rate which represents opportunity cost is 10 percent. Finally, suppose that the company we are examining has announced that dividends will be $2.50 per share next year. We can use these numbers to compute the value of the company's equity shares as follows:

---

[3]Multiply both sides of Equation (A–27) by $(1 + i)/(1 + g)$ and subtract Equation (A–27) from the result. This yields:

$$\frac{PV(1 + i)}{(1 + g)} - PV = D_0 - \frac{D_0(1 + g)^N}{(1 + i)^N}.$$

As long as *i* exceeds g, then as *N* approaches infinity, $D_0(1 + g)^N / (1 + i)^N$ approaches zero. As a result, we can write:

$$PV \frac{1 + i}{1 + g} - 1 = D_0$$

$$PV \frac{(1 + i) - (1 + g)}{1 + g} = D_0$$

$$PV \frac{(i - g)}{(1 + g)} = D_0$$

$$PV = \frac{D_1}{1 - g}.$$

$$PV = \frac{\$2.50}{0.10 - 0.06} = \$62.50 \text{ per share.}$$

Few companies actually have constant growth rates for dividends. Most companies might have high growth in dividends for a while, but it proves hard to sustain this, and the growth rate generally falls. Therefore, the assumption of a constant growth rate employed in the Gordon growth model is quite unrealistic. In fact, we are generally quite uncertain about what the future growth rate will be for most companies, and this element of uncertainty is as important as the element of time in determining value.

SUMMARY

In this appendix we examined the connections between time and value. The central question is, how do we translate the stream of income which accrues to an asset into a value of that asset at a point in time, either today or some time in the future?

All problems involving present and future value can be divided into four basic types of problems. Real world problems may be a simple example of one of these types or a combination of them. The solution to each problem can be stated in a relatively simple equation.

Of course, these four problems are simplifications of the types of problems in the real world. Therefore we examined some ways that basic present and future value problems can become more complicated. First of all future income might not be constant. If it is constant, then it is relatively simple to compute present or future value. But if not constant, while the computations can still be made, they are more cumbersome. We learned that interest can be compounded as frequently as we choose, and we learned how to alter formulas to take this into account. We also learned how to distinguish between net present value and gross present value. Net present value provides a simple rule of thumb for determining whether an investment is worth undertaking. Finally, we found that the internal rate of return was the interest rate which results in a net present value of zero for a particular investment. Net present value and internal rate of return are simply alternative ways of thinking about the same problem—they are flip sides of the same coin. However, the internal rate of return has the potential to be quite misleading. Whenever possible, it is best to stick with net present value.

We applied what we learned about present value and interest rates to a few examples of financial assets in the marketplace. We used present value to compute the yield or price of a bond and, in the process, learned what the yield and price meant. We also applied these concepts to the determination of the price of a share of stock. Unlike most bonds, a share of stock has no well-defined maturity date. Therefore, we employed the idea of a perpetual income stream to determine the value of the stock.

A good understanding of the subject of present value is critical for understanding financial markets. Almost every decision made and every aspect of the market hinges on present value. Moreover, the tools used to analyze present value are relatively concrete and easy to master. Therefore, it is worth getting a firm foundation in this subject matter before we move on to the more difficult topics of uncertainty and value.

QUESTIONS

1. What would be the price of an 8 percent coupon Treasury bond with semiannual coupon payments that had 14 years to maturity and a face value of $1,000 if the market interest rate is 12 percent?

2. Suppose you are considering whether to invest in some income (rental) property. You plan to hold the property for 5 years and sell it for $140,000. You also expect to collect $5,000 in rent every 6 months of that 5-year period. The first payment will be received in 6 months. The current asking price is $100,000. Suppose your alternative use of funds is to invest in Treasury bonds which yield 12 percent for a 5-year maturity. Which investment would you choose?

3. Reconsider question 2. Suppose you were in the 30 percent tax bracket and you could depreciate the property for tax purposes. Suppose you could deduct 10 percent of the purchase price from your taxes every year you owned the property. Now which alternative would you choose?

4. You expect to retire in 20 years. At the time you retire you want enough money invested to pay you $40,000 per year for 15 years. You do not expect to live more than 15 years past retirement, so you are not worried about funds after that point. Over the next 20 years you can invest funds each year at a 12 percent return. If you are going to invest a constant amount each year, how much would that be?

5. Explain the differences between simple and compound interest and between simple interest and interest on a discount basis.

6. Suppose you bought a Treasury bond with 5 years to maturity, a coupon rate of 8 percent, and a face value of $100,000. When you bought it, market interest rates were at 10 percent, and they have now fallen to 6 percent. What happened to the price of your bond?

7. Suppose you were going to buy a home worth $100,000, and you intended to finance it with an $80,000 mortgage. The mortgage has a maturity of 30 years and an interest rate of 12 percent. What would your monthly payments be? Suppose you were in the 40 percent tax bracket and could deduct interest expense. What would be the after-tax cost of your mortgage? How much would you be able to deduct during the first year of the mortgage?

8. Suppose you used a credit card. There is a flat charge of $30 per year regardless of how much the card is used and a percentage charge of 1.5 percent per month on the balance outstanding. You had exactly $1,000 outstanding on this card for an entire year. What would be the actual annual interest rate on the $1,000?

B APPENDIX

UNCERTAINTY AND VALUE

Appendix B functions as a supplement to Chapter 3 on the pricing of risky assets and develops some of the more technical issues on this topic. We will begin with a discussion of how to measure the expected return and standard deviation of returns for a risky asset when it can be combined into a portfolio. Then we will examine how to measure the beta of an asset. Finally, we will discuss the formal assumptions that support the capital asset pricing model.

MEASURING RISK AND RETURN

In order to understand how to value risky assets and choose among them, it is necessary to have some methodology for measuring the risk and expected return of those assets. We will focus on the example of three assets, labeled A, B and C, introduced in Chapter 3 and examine the probability distributions on returns for each of these projects. Then we will evaluate how to measure expected return and develop a measurement for the risk of these assets.

THE PROBABILITY DISTRIBUTION ON RETURNS

Risk and expected return are based on the probability distributions that determine the future return on each asset. We will define probability distributions for each of our three hypothetical investments that constitute our available choices. These probability distributions show five possible returns for each asset and the probability that each of these returns will occur. To explain the probability distribution we will confine our attention, momentarily, to only one of the assets, asset A. The five possible returns for it are shown in column Asset A of Table B–1. The highest return is $8,500 and the lowest is $5,500. The probability that each outcome will occur is shown in the third column, labeled probability of occurrence of each state. In this example, the probability of both the highest and lowest return is 10 percent. The five possible returns for asset A depend on states of the world that correspond to possible future courses of the economy, from deep recession to major boom. Actually, the possible returns could have been represented more simply if only three states were considered: recession, normal, and boom. Or, the possible returns could have been represented in more detail by considering many more states. You can use as many states of the world as you think are appropriate to best represent the problem under consideration.

Table B–1 also shows probability distributions for the other two assets available in our example. The alternative returns in each state of the world for assets B and C are listed in the last two columns of the table. The convenience of using states of the world should now be apparent. By stating the probability of each state of the world and the outcome for each asset in each state, only one column of probabilities is necessary.

The probability distributions on returns for each asset are only estimated probabilities. Each investor must formulate his or her own estimates of these probabilities. There is generally substantial information available for formulating these estimates. But you cannot go to *The Wall Street Journal* and look up the probability distribution for future returns on IBM, although you can acquire information about IBM from it and utilize it to formulate a probability distribution like those in Table B–1. But that probability distribution is still your estimate.

It will make our future work much simpler if we can develop a notation to refer to a particular asset, state of the world, probability of occurrence, and future return. Therefore, we will number the states of the world 1 through 5, beginning with deep recession and ending with major boom, as shown in Table B–1. We have already identified the assets with the letters A, B, and C. We will refer to the return on asset A in the first state of the world as $_1R_A$. In the example, $_1R_A = \$5,500$. We can use this notation to refer to the return on any asset in any state of the world, such as asset B in normal time, $_3R_B = \$7,000$. Finally, we need a notation for the probabilities of each of the five states of the world. We will use the symbol $P_3 = 0.4$. All the other states of the world may be referred to by adjusting the subscript; for example, $P_1 = 0.1$. Now that we have a system of notation we can utilize the probability distributions shown in Table B–1 to measure the expected return on each investment.

MEASURING EXPECTED RETURN

The expected return is supposed to represent our best estimate of what the future actual return will be. Another way to look at it is if we had to pick a single number which would be our forecast of the future return, this would be it. A

TABLE B–1
Uncertain returns on three investments.

State of the World Description	Number	Probability of Occurrence of Each State	Returns (in $) on Each Asset in Each State of the World		
			Asset A	Asset B	Asset C
Deep recession	1	0.1	5,500	3,000	13,000
Mild recession	2	0.2	6,000	5,000	11,000
Normal	3	0.4	7,000	7,000	9,000
Minor boom	4	0.2	8,000	9,000	7,000
Major boom	5	0.1	8,500	11,000	5,000

procedure that accounts for the entire probability distribution is to define the expected return as the weighted average of all possible returns in the probability distribution, where the weights are the probabilities that each return will occur. Before we can define the expected return with algebra, we need some notation to represent expected return. The symbol $E(R_A)$ will represent the expected return on asset A. We can define $E(R_A)$ as follows:

$$E(R_A) = \sum_{i=1}^{N} P_i(_iR_A) \tag{B–1}$$

Equation (B–1) says that the expected return is equal to the sum of the products of the individual probabilities and returns for each state of the world. We can illustrate how this formula is used with the probability distribution for investment A in Table B–1. The formula says that the subscript i should assume the numbers of the alternative states of the world, 1 through 5. Then the probability of each state occurring is multiplied by the return in that state. These five products are added together as follows:

Illustration of Equation (B–1)

$P_1 \times {}_1R_A = 0.1 \times 5,500$

$P_2 \times {}_2R_A = 0.2 \times 6,000$

$P_3 \times {}_3R_A = 0.3 \times 7,000$

$P_4 \times {}_4R_A = 0.2 \times 8,000$

$\underline{P_5 \times {}_5R_A = 0.1 \times 8,500}$

$\sum_{i=1,}^{N} P_i(_iR_A) = 7,000$

$E(R_A) = 7,000.$

We can compute the expected return for each of the other projects in a similar manner. All the expected returns are presented in Table B–2, which shows investments A and B both have the the same expected return of $7,000. But investment C has an expected return of $9,000. If expected return were the only criterion for choosing or valuing investments, then investment C is the best one. In addition, we could conclude that its value should be $9,000, for this is what it is expected to pay.

TABLE B–2
Expected return, variance and standard deviation for three investments.

Investment	Expected Return	Variance	Standard Deviation
A	$7,000	850,000	922
B	7,000	4,800,000	2,191
C	9,000	4,800,000	2,191

MEASURING RISK

The basic idea behind measuring risk is to express quantitatively how much the actual return can vary. We have defined a best guess of the future return, but this best guess tells us nothing about the variability of returns or how spread out the possible returns are around the expected value. You can easily see what variability means by examining a graphical representation of probability distributions. Before we examine plots of the distributions in Table B–1, let's examine some extreme cases of probability distributions with different amounts of variability. An example of such extremes is presented in Figure B–1, which illustrates three different probability distributions. The probability of each outcome is shown on the vertical axis, and the corresponding outcome is shown on the horizontal axis for each of the three distributions. All of the distributions have the same expected value but vastly different amounts of variability. Distribution 1 has the least variability because it is the most concentrated around the expected value. In distribution 1 the probability is small that returns very far away from the expected value will actually occur. Distribution 2 has more variability, so it is less peaked or concentrated around its expected value. Finally, distribution 3 has the most variability, as it is the flattest of the distributions.

Now that we have an intuitive idea of what variability means, we can develop a way to measure it. The accepted measure of the variation of a probability distribution is known as the *variance*. First, we will examine a formal algebraic definition of the variance and then examine how it is computed and interpreted by applying it to the three sample investments in Table B–1. The standard notation for the variance is the Greek letter sigma raised to the second power, σ^2. We need to add a subscript to indicate which probability distribution we are referring to, so we will use σ_A^2 to refer to the variance of the future returns to investment A. The variance is defined as follows:

FIGURE B–1
Three probability distributions with the same expected value but different amounts of variability.

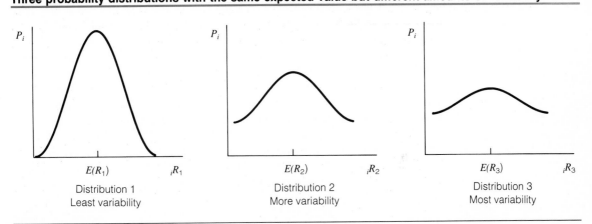

$E(R_1)$ $_iR_1$	$E(R_2)$ $_iR_2$	$E(R_3)$ $_iR_3$
Distribution 1	Distribution 2	Distribution 3
Least variability	More variability	Most variability

$$\sigma_A^2 = \sum_{i=1}^{N} P_i[(R_A - E(R_A)].^2 \tag{B-2}$$

Another similar measure that is used almost interchangeably with the variance is standard deviation. This is simply the square root of the variance and is symbolized as σ_A.

We can utilize the probability distribution for returns on investment A to see how to compute the variance. For each of the possible returns, we subtract the expected return on the investment from that return and square the difference. Then we multiply that squared difference by the probability of that outcome. Finally, we add up all of these terms. The standard deviation is then computed by taking the square root of the variance. These computations are illustrated below for asset A, and the variances and standard deviations of all three investments are shown in Table B-2.

Illustration of Equation (B-2)

$$P_1 \times {}_1R_A - E(R_A)^2 = 0.1 \times (5,500 - 7,000)^2$$
$$P_2 \times {}_2R_A - E(R_A)^2 = 0.2 \times (6,000 - 7,000)^2$$
$$P_3 \times {}_3R_A - E(R_A)^2 = 0.4 \times (7,000 - 7,000)^2$$
$$P_4 \times {}_4R_A - E(R_A)^2 = 0.2 \times (8,000 - 7,000)^2$$
$$P_5 \times {}_5R_A - E(R_A)^2 = 0.1 \times (8,500 - 7,000)^2$$

$$\sigma_A^2 = \sum_{i=1}^{N} P_i[R_A - E(R_A)]^2 = 850,000$$
$$\sigma_A = \sqrt{850,000} = 922.$$

To see how the variance and standard deviation actually measure the variation of a probability distribution, it is useful to compare the variances and standard deviations of the three projects in our example with the visual impression of their variation shown in Figure B-2. This figure shows the same type of graphical representation of probability distributions presented in Figure B-1. We know from Table B-2 that B and C have the same variance and standard deviation and that investment A has a smaller variance. B and C have the same amount of risk, and they both have more risk than investment A. Figure B-2 indicates that investments B and C have the same amount of variation or dispersion. That is, they are spread out to the same extent, though they have different expected returns. Judging by the standard deviations, B and C are a little more than twice as risky as investment A. This is also consistent with the figure in that the probability distributions for B and C appear to be about twice as spread out as the distribution for A. It is misleading to judge the relative amount of risk directly from the variance, because, as we can tell from Equation (B-2), the variance includes the square of every deviation of each possible occurrence about the expected value. As a result the variance will tend to exaggerate relative riskiness. If B has twice as much risk as A according to the standard deviation, it will have four times as much according to the variance.

FIGURE B–2
Probability distributions for the three investments in Table B–1.

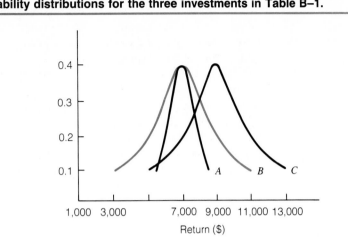

RISK AND RETURN IN PORTFOLIOS OF ASSETS

As we learned in Chapter 3, when assets can be combined into portfolios, investors can take advantage of the benefits of diversification to reduce the total risk to which they are exposed. Chapter 3 stated the equation for the variance of a portfolio of two assets, but it did not provide much motivation for this equation. Here we will provide some background for this and focus on the appropriate measure of risk of individual assets when held in a portfolio, the beta of the asset.

To deal with portfolios of assets, we need to make one important change in the example in this discussion: we need to deal with rates of return rather than total returns measured in dollars. When a portfolio of assets is made for an investor, that investor may purchase only a small portion of each asset or some share of each asset. Therefore we need to be able to work with the return per share or per dollar invested in the asset, so we must introduce the price paid for each asset. Therefore we will assume that each of the three assets initially presented in Table B–1 can be purchased for $50,000. We can then compute the rate of return for each asset in each state of the world by dividing each payoff in Table B–1 by $50,000. Table B–2 contains the payoff for each asset in each state of the world in a percentage of rate of return form. To accommodate rates of return, we must introduce a little more notation. The symbol $_1r_A$ will represent the rate of return on asset A in state of the world 1. Now we can simply replace the dollar return with the rate of return in all of our computations. Note that the expected rate of return for each asset is given in panel B of Table B–2, as are the variances and standard deviations. Also note that we use the symbols σ^2_{rA} and σ_{rA} for the variance and standard deviation of the rates of return.

MEASURING THE RELATIONSHIP BETWEEN ASSETS

We will work with two measures of the relationship between the rates of return on assets called the covariance and the correlation coefficient. Actually what we want to use is the correlation coefficient, but to understand the correlation coefficient, we must first develop the covariance.

The covariance is very similar to the variance. The variance of an asset is computed by subtracting the expected value from each of the possible outcomes for a particular probability distribution and then squaring that difference. The covariance between two assets is computed similarly, except the deviations of the possible outcomes from their expected values for two different outcomes are multiplied together. The symbol for the covariance between the rates of return on two assets, A and B, is written $\sigma^2 r_{A \cdot B}$. The formula for this covariance is the following:

$$\sigma^2{}_{rA \cdot B} = \sum_{i=1}^{N} P_i[{}_i r_A - E(r_A)][{}_i r_B - E(r_B)]. \tag{B-3}$$

The computations involved in the covariance are illustrated below.

Illustration of Equation (B–3)

$$P_1[{}_1 r_A - E(r_A)][{}_1 r_B - E(r_B)] = 0.1 \times (0.11 - 0.14)(0.06 - 0.14)$$
$$P_2[{}_2 r_A - E(r_A)][{}_2 r_B - E(r_B)] = 0.2 \times (0.12 - 0.14)(0.10 - 0.14)$$
$$P_3[{}_3 r_A - E(r_A)][{}_3 r_B - E(r_B)] = 0.4 \times (0.14 - 0.14)(0.14 - 0.14)$$
$$P_4[{}_4 r_A - E(r_A)][{}_4 r_B - E(r_B)] = 0.2 \times (0.16 - 0.14)(0.18 - 0.14)$$
$$P_5[{}_5 r_A - E(r_A)][{}_5 r_B - E(r_B)] = 0.1 \times (0.17 - 0.14)(0.22 - 0.14)$$

$$\sigma^2{}_{rA.B} = \sum_{i=1}^{N} P_i[{}_i r_A - E(r_A)][{}_i r_B - E(r_B)] = .0008.$$

The covariances for the alternative combinations of investment A, B, and C are shown in Table B–3 which is the same as Table 3–2. We are now working with rates of return rather than dollar returns, thus the numbers involved will be smaller. Suppose we try to interpret these numbers. The covariance between A and B is positive while the other two are negative. This tells us that the return on B tends to be high when the return on C is low, and the return on B is high when the return on A is high. But we would also like to be able to infer something about the strength of the relationship between the probability distributions from these numbers. That is, we would like to know whether A and B have a very close relationship so that as A goes up B goes up by a similar amount. Unfortunately, we cannot judge this from the covariance since the size of the number in the covariance is not meaningful.

To remedy this problem it is possible to use the correlation coefficient. The difference between these two measures of the relationship between probability distributions is that the correlation coefficient is computed by dividing the covariance by the product of the standard deviation of the two distributions in question.

TABLE B-3
Returns on three investments.

Panel A: Uncertain Rates of Return on Three Investments

State of the World Description	Number	Probability of Occurence	Rate of Return on Assets in Each State of the World		
			Asset A	Asset B	Asset C
Deep recession	1	0.1	0.11	0.06	0.26*
Mild recession	2	0.2	0.12	0.10	0.22
Normal	3	0.4	0.14	0.14	0.18
Minor boom	4	0.2	0.16	0.18	0.14
Major boom	5	0.1	0.17	0.22	0.10

Panel B: Expected Rate of Return, Variance, and Standard Deviation for Three Investments

	Asset A	Asset B	Asset C
$E(r)$	0.14	0.14	0.18
σ^2_r	0.00034	0.00192	0.00192
σ_r	0.01844	0.04382	0.04382

*Rate of return on asset C calculated as follows: 13,000/50,000 = 0.26.

We will symbolize the correlation coefficient with $\mathcal{P}_{A.B}$. The formula for the correlation coefficient is

$$\mathcal{P}_{A.B} = \frac{\sigma^2_{rA.B}}{\sigma_{rA}\,\sigma_{rB}}. \tag{B-4}$$

For example, the correlation coefficient between A and B can be computed as:

$$\mathcal{P}_{A.B} = \frac{0.0008}{0.01844 \times 0.04382} = 0.99.$$

The correlation coefficient is a standardized unit of measurement, which the covariance is not, so the correlation coefficient is always a percentage. It never exceeds +1 or is less than −1. A large positive fraction indicates a strong positive relationship between the two probability distributions, while a small fraction, either positive or negative, indicates a weak relationship. Finally, a large, in absolute value, negative fraction indicates a strong negative relationship. The correlation coefficients for each of the investment combinations are shown along with the covariance in Table B-3. We can tell from these correlation coefficients that all three assets have strong relationships between them. Between B and C the relationship is a perfect negative one; every movement away from the expected value of B is perfectly matched by the movement in the opposite direction of C. The other relationships are not quite as close but are still very strong.

MEASURING PORTFOLIO RISK AND RETURN

Now we can turn our attention to the portfolio of an investor. In order to keep the example as simple as possible we will limit ourselves to portfolios which contain only two assets. Everything we do with two assets we can do with three or more, but the algebra becomes more cumbersome as more assets are added to the port-folio.

For a portfolio with two assets, say A and B, we will assume that the investor commits x percent of his or her wealth to asset A and y or $(1 - x)$ percent of wealth to asset B. Then the rate of return actually received on the portfolio will be

$$r_p = xr_A + yr_B, \qquad \text{(B--5)}$$

where r_A is the actual rate of return earned by asset A and r_B is the actual rate of return earned by asset B. The rate of return on the portfolio is the weighted av-erage of the rates of return on asset A and B, where the weights are the proportion of the investor's wealth invested in these two assets.

There are two properties of expectations of the return that make it possible to determine the equation for the expected return of the portfolio. The first property is that the expectation of a sum of two random variables is equal to the sum of the expectations of those variables. A random variable is one determined by a probability distribution; r_A is a random variable and x is not. Therefore, the ex-pected rate of return on the portfolio, which is defined as

$$E(r_p) = E[xr_A + yr_B], \qquad \text{(B--6)}$$

can be written, using this rule, as

$$E(r_p) = E(xr_A) + E(yr_B). \qquad \text{(B--7)}$$

The second property is that the expectation of the product of a constant and a random variable is equal to the product of the constant and the expected value of the random variable, or

$$E(xr_A) = xE(r_A). \qquad \text{(B--8)}$$

The expected rate of return on the portfolio can be expressed as the weighted sum of the expected rate of return on the two assets that comprise the portfolio, where the weights are the portion of wealth committed to each asset:

$$E(r_p) = xE(r_A) + yE(r_B). \qquad \text{(B--9)}$$

For example, this implies that a portfolio made up of 50 percent shares in asset A and 50 percent in asset C would have an expected rate of return of 16 percent: $E(r_p) = 0.5 \times 0.14 + 0.5 \times 0.18$.

Next we need to define the risk of the investor's portfolio just as the variance of the returns of any single asset is defined. It is written as follows:

$$\sigma^2 r_p = \sum_{i=1}^{N} P_i [r_p - E(r_p)].^2 \qquad (B–10)$$

Next, to get to the form of variance that captures the effect of diversification, we have to go through considerable algebraic manipulation. These manipulations are not essential to understand the ultimate result, so they are relegated to a footnote.[2] The expression that results from these manipulations is

$$\sigma^2_{r_p} = x^2\, \sigma^2_{rA} + y^2\, \sigma^2_{rB} + 2xy\, \mathcal{P}_{A.B} \sigma_{rA} \sigma_{rB}. \qquad (B–11)$$

This is the same equation presented in Chapter 3 as Equation (3–1) to interpret how diversification reduces risk.

COMPUTING THE BETA OF A SECURITY

Next, it is important to see how to compute beta for a given security using the procedure for computing the estimate of a coefficient in a linear regression model. The pricing equation shown as Equation (3–2) in Chapter 3 is an example of a linear regression where r_A is regressed on r_M. The formula for the computation of β_A is much easier to state than it is to derive. It is

$$\beta_A = \frac{\sigma^2_{rA.M}}{\sigma^2_{rM}}, \qquad (B–12)$$

where $\sigma^2_{rA.M}$ represents the covariance between the rates of return on asset A and the market portfolio.

As an initial illustration of the procedure for computing beta, we can turn to the example used above. We must have data or observations on r_A and r_M to compute an estimate of beta. Table B–2 presents some hypothetical data on the rates of return on three assets corresponding to five alternative states of the world. If we also had corresponding rates of return for the market portfolio in each state of the world, then we could use Equation (B–12) to compute the beta for any of the three assets in Table B–2. Table B–4 presents data on the rate of return on the market portfolio in each of the five states of the world. It also repeats the probability of each state of the world and the rate of return on asset A.

Using the information in Table B–4 and recalling the definition of the covariance from Equation (B–3), we can compute the value of β_A as follows:

$$\frac{\sum_{i=1}^{5} P_i[_ir_A - E(r_A)][_ir_M - E(r_M)]}{\sum_{i=1}^{5} P_i[_ir_M - E(r_M)]^2}.$$

The numerator is equal to

$(0.1 \times 0.03 \times 0.03)$ $+ (0.2 \times 0.02 \times 0.01) + 0 + (0.2 \times 0.02 \times 0.01)$
$+ (0.1 \times 0.03 \times 0.03)$
$= 0.00026.$

The denominator is equal to 0.00022.
This implies

$$\beta_A = \frac{0.00026}{0.00022} = 1.18.$$

This example links the concept of systematic risk to our discussion of investment decisions and the value of risky assets in Chapter 3. The example shows how to quantify the risk of each of the assets available when they are held as one of the assets in a large portfolio. It is important, however, to see how the concept of beta can be used to quantify the risk of an asset traded in organized markets. Table B–5 shows the annual rate of return on IBM stock from 1969 to 1978. We can use these data to compute the beta for IBM. Table B–5 also shows the rate of return for the Standard & Poor's Composite Index, which we will use as a proxy for the market portfolio.

The only difference between this computation and the one performed for asset A is that past performance must be substituted for estimates of outcomes in alternative states of the world. Implicit in this substitution is the idea that past performance is an appropriate basis for estimating the future performance of an asset. If the systematic risk has changed, then this is not a useful procedure. In effect, we

TABLE B–4
Uncertain rates of return on investment A and the market portfolio.

Description of State of the World	Probability of Occurrence	Rates of Return in Each State of the World	
		Asset A	Market Portfolio
Deep recession	0.1	0.11	0.03
Mild recession	0.2	0.12	0.05
Normal	0.4	0.14	0.06
Minor boom	0.2	0.16	0.07
Major boom	0.1	0.17	0.09
$E(r_A) = 0.14$			
$E(r_M) = 0.06$			

TABLE B–5
Rates of return on IBM and on the Standard & Poor's Composite Index.

	Rate of Return on IBM		Rate of Return on Common Stocks*
	Percent Return		Percent Return
1969	1.9		−8.5
1970	−6.8		4.0
1971	8.9		14.3
1972	18.5		19.0
1973	0.4		−14.7
1974	−30.8		−26.5
1975	−1.7		37.2
1976	37.2		23.8
1977	8.7		−7.2
1978	7.2		6.6
Average over the period	4.35	Average over the Period	4.8

*Source: Roger Ibbotson, and Rex A. Singuefield, *Stocks, Bonds, Bills and Inflation: Historical Return (1926–1978),* Financial Analysts Research Foundation, 1979.

are treating the past returns as sample values from the same probability distribution that will determine future returns. If this assumption is reasonable, then we can derive a measure of beta that is a valid measure of the future risk of the security.

One procedural change results from the fact that we have no estimates of individual probabilities as we did for the states of the world in Appendix A's example. Therefore, when we compute the covariance of the rate of return on IBM and the rate of return on the market, as well as the variance of the market, we weight the past events equally rather than attempt to assign specific probabilities. For instance, we compute the variance of the rate of return on the market according to the following equation:

$$\sigma^2_{rM} = \sum_{t=1}^{N} [t_{rM_t} - E(_{r_M})]^2/N.$$

The subscript t refers to the past annual observations on the rate of return, rather than the alternative states of the world, and N refers to the number of past observations (10 in this case), rather than the number of states of the world. Because all past observations are weighted equally, the sum of the squared deviations around the expected rate of return is divided by N. This is equivalent to multiplying each individual deviation by $1/N$.

The computations for determining the variance of the rate of return on IBM and the covariance between the two are not shown, though the procedure is identical. Note that the expected rate of return on IBM is 4.35 percent. Then σ^2_{rM} is computed as follows:

$$\sigma^2_{rM} = [1969_{rM} - E_{(rM)}]^2 \text{ or } (-8.5 - 4.8)^2$$
$$[1970_{rM} - E_{(rM)}]^2 \text{ or } (4.0 - 4.8)^2$$
$$[1971_{rM} - E_{(rM)}]^2 \text{ or } (14.3 - 4.8)^2$$
$$[1972_{rM} - E_{(rM)}]^2 \text{ or } (19.0 - 4.8)^2$$
$$[1973_{rM} - E_{(rM)}]^2 \text{ or } (14.7 - 4.8)^2$$
$$[1974_{rM} - E_{(rM)}]^2 \text{ or } (-26.5 - 4.8)^2$$
$$[1975_{rM} - E_{(rM)}]^2 \text{ or } (37.2 - 4.8)^2$$
$$[1976_{rM} - E_{(rM)}]^2 \text{ or } (23.8 - 4.8)^2$$
$$[1977_{rM} - E_{(rM)}]^2 \text{ or } (-7.2 - 4.8)^2$$
$$[1978_{rM} - E_{(rM)}]^2 \text{ or } (6.6 - 4.8)^2$$
$$\sigma^2_{rM} = 3.39\%.$$
$$\sigma_{rM} = 18.4\%.$$

Similar computations will disclose that the value of the covariance between the two rates of return, $\sigma^2 r_{IBM} \cdot r_M$ is 2.29 percent. If we substitute these into the equation for the value of beta we find that beta is equal to

$$\text{IBM} = \frac{2.29}{3.39} = 0.68.$$

THE CAPITAL ASSET PRICING MODEL (CAPM)

As we learned in Chapter 3, the capital asset pricing model (CAPM) leads to a specific equation that explains how the market prices individual securities. In order to understand what the CAPM has to say and how we can use it, let's carefully examine the key assumptions which go into the theory.

ASSUMPTIONS OF THE CAPM

Four fundamental assumptions form the basis of the CAPM. Once you read them, you will see they are clearly unrealistic, for any theory incorporates simplifications of reality which make it unrealistic. The relevant test of the theory is whether we acquire an improved understanding of how the market operates by making these admittedly unrealistic assumptions. You will have to judge that when we finish. The assumptions are:

1. All investors are averse to risk and choose portfolios that give the optimal combinations of expected return and risk, as measured by standard deviation.
2. Investors agree about the probability distributions of returns on assets.
3. One asset exists that is free of risk with a rate of return, r_F. All investors may borrow or lend unlimited amounts at this risk-free rate.
4. Assets offer a return on a single period only.

The first assumption says that people choose portfolios of assets the way we described them in Appendix A. If they are risk-averse, then each individual's attitude toward risk, or trade-off between risk and return, can be represented with indifference curves in a diagram showing expected return and standard deviation of alternative portfolios of assets. These indifference curves were illustrated in Chapter 3.

We can go further in describing the set of possible investments from which investors can choose. In Figure 3–7 we examined the alternative portfolios that could be constructed from the three assets in the example. If two assets had a correlation coefficient of -1, then the set of possible portfolios looked like a V on its side with the bottom of the V lying on the horizontal axis. If the assets were not perfectly correlated, then the set of portfolios looked like a curve that did not reach the horizontal axis. In the real world of possible portfolios few assets have correlation coefficients of -1. As a result, the possible portfolios that individuals can construct from all the assets available in the market have combinations of expected return and standard deviation represented by a curve as shown in Figure B–3. Actually curve *GH* only shows the best combinations of expected return and standard deviation. There are an infinite number of possible portfolios, such as the one represented by point *L,* that are inside line *GH*. These portfolios are always inferior to some portfolio on the line because the one on the line will have both less risk and more expected return. The line therefore represents the *efficient frontier,* which includes all portfolios that are not clearly inferior to some other possible portfolio.

FIGURE B–3

Efficient frontier of a portfolio. The curve *GH* illustrates the efficient frontier of a set of available portfolios. Portfolios to the right of the line, such as *L,* are available, but they are inferior to those on the frontier.

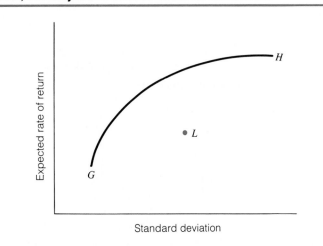

FIGURE B–4
Optimal portfolio on the efficient frontier. *P** illustrates the optimal portfolio for an individual with the indifference curves shown. The optimal portfolio is the point of tangency between the efficient frontier and an indifference curve.

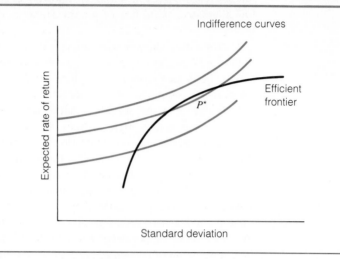

Assumption 1 simply says people choose their portfolios from this efficient set and their trade-off between risk and return can be represented with indifference curves. We can illustrate the choice of a hypothetical individual from the efficient set with Figure B–4. This figure shows a sample of indifference curves and the efficient set drawn in Figure B–3. The optimal portfolio for this hypothetical individual is the one labeled *P**. This point is the point of tangency between line *GH* and an indifference curve of the individual. It is optimal because it cannot reach a higher indifference curve.

The second assumption says all market participants agree about the estimates of future return and standard deviation for all assets in the market. All individuals see the same efficient set of possible portfolios. As a result, the only thing that separates individuals is their attitudes toward risk. In terms of Figure B–4, the only thing that separates individuals is that they have different indifference curves.

The third assumption introduces an asset free of risk. In addition, it stipulates that individuals can borrow and lend at the risk-free interest rate on that asset. The real world counterpart of the risk-free asset is a Treasury bill, which is thought to be free of default risk. The prices of Treasury bills can increase or decrease over time, but this sort of risk of price changes is not really a part of this analysis, because assumption 4 rules out multiple future periods. The existence of a risk-free asset alters the set of portfolios from which individuals can choose. Figure B–5 shows how the set of possible portfolios is altered. The key to this change is that the risk-free asset plots on the vertical axis with return at r_F because it has no risk. In addition it can be combined with any portfolio of risky assets in any proportion. The most efficient combinations are ones that involve portfolio M and the risk-free asset. These portfolios fall on the line that intersects r_F and is tangent to the set of risky portfolios at point M. Any portfolio on this line will be superior to any portfolio beneath the line, for the same reason portfolios on the efficient frontier are superior to those inside it. An investor can move from point M in either direction by borrowing or lending at the risk-free rate r_F. Borrowing means a movement up the line away from r_F, and lending or investing in the risk-free asset involves a movement down the line toward point r_F.

Now we can represent the choice of any individual for this modified set of possible portfolios, just as we did in Figure B–4 where there was no risk-free asset. The optimal portfolio for the individual with the indifference curves shown in Figure B–5 is the one at point N, for at this point this individual has reached the highest indifference curve possible. This portfolio represents a combination of the risk-free assets at point M. The implication is that when investors agree on the probability distributions on assets in the market, and when there is a risk-free asset that can be borrowed or lent, then no investor will ever choose a portfolio of risky assets other than the one at point M. This is the market portfolio. However, different investors will combine that portfolio in different proportions with the risk-free asset, depending upon their attitudes toward risk. It is their risk-return preference, represented by the shape of their indifference curves, which will determine how much of the market portfolio of risky assets and how much of the risk-free assets will be purchased.

FIGURE B–5

Portfolio choice with a risk-free asset. This figure shows how the available combinations of risk and expected return are altered when a risk-free asset is available. Everyone will now choose an optimal portfolio along the line from r_F to I. The individual in this example chooses portfolio N.

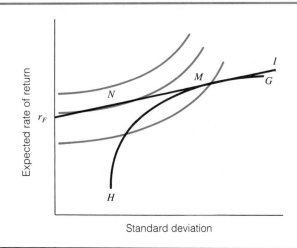

RISK PREMIUMS IN THE MARKET FOR EQUITY SECURITIES

As explained in Chapter 3, the capital asset pricing model (CAPM), is the preeminent theory of the determinants of risk premiums on equity securities. The basic question at issue is whether the CAPM provides an adequate explanation of the differences in observed premiums. That is, can the risk premiums on equity securities observed in the market be adequately explained as a function solely of the systematic risk of the securities? If so, then it is possible to accept the CAPM as a reasonably good description of reality. If they cannot, then some additional factors other than systematic risk must be included in the analysis.

To be specific about what we mean by the risk premium on equity securities and by the systematic risk, we return to the CAPM. It asserts that all assets will be priced so that their expected return is equal to the risk-free interest rate plus the product of the beta of the security and the excess of the rate of return on the market portfolio over the risk-free interest rate. This means asset A is priced according to:

$$E(r_A) = r_F + [E(r_M) - r_F] \beta_A.$$

This can be transformed into an equation for testing the determinants of risk premiums simply by moving the risk-free rate to the left-hand side of the equation, and by introducing an additional intercept term (α):

$$E(r_A) - r_F = \alpha + [E(r_M) - r_F] \beta_A. \tag{B–13}$$

The CAPM asserts that the risk premium of a particular security is equal to the market price of risk $[E(r_M) - r_F]$ times the measure of the security's risk (β_A). But Equation (B–13) incorporates an additional term, α. The α acts as a proxy for other factors that might be important for risk premiums but are excluded from the CAPM and cannot be specifically measured by other available data. The object of the test is to determine whether α is equal to zero. If tests indicate that it is equal to zero, then these factors are considered insignificant. The security's variance can also be used to measure the security's unsystematic risk.

There is one other serious problem that must be dealt with before such tests can be performed. The problem is that Equation (B–13) includes the expected rate of return on security A and $E(r_M)$, and these are never observed in the market. The actual ex post return is observed each period, but the ex ante expected return is not. Those who have conducted statistical tests of the CAPM have dealt with this by assuming that, over the long run, all assets constitute a fair game. In a fair game the expected rate of return is equal to the average actual return over the long run. In any single period, the actual return may be above or below the expected return. But over time, in a fair game, high returns will balance low returns and, on average, the asset will actually return its expected value. The idea of a fair game is essentially the idea of an efficient market, as discussed in Chapter 5. If the market were not a fair game, then you could expect to earn excess returns and the market would not be efficient. Therefore, tests of the determinants of risk premiums based on the CAPM also implicitly assume that markets are efficient. As a result, it is possible to rewrite the empirically useful form of Equation (B–13) without the expectation for the return on asset A, as long as this holds only for average returns over long periods:

$$r_A - r_F = \alpha + (r_M - r_F)\,\beta_A, \qquad (B–14)$$

where r_A and r_M are the actual ex post rates of return on assets A and M.

Tests of this type of equation for observed risk premiums on equities have been conducted by many researchers. Their results have led to a general consensus on at least two basic conclusions. First, measures of unsystematic risk do not significantly contribute to the explanation of observed risk premiums. By and large, whenever the variance of the security's return is added to Equation (B–14), it does not add significantly to the statistical explanation of the risk premium. On the other hand, these tests uniformly conclude that α is not equal to zero.

An example of this kind of empirical test is presented in Figure B–6. This figure shows the average monthly return on 10 portfolios of securities (vertical axis) graphed against the systematic risk of the portfolios (horizontal axis) for the period 1931 to 1965. The slope of the line in the figure is an estimate of the market price of risk $(r_M - r_F)$, just as $(r_M - r_F)$ measures the slope in Equation

FIGURE B–6

Average monthly returns versus systematic risk for the 35-year period 1931–1965 for ten portfolios and the market portfolio.

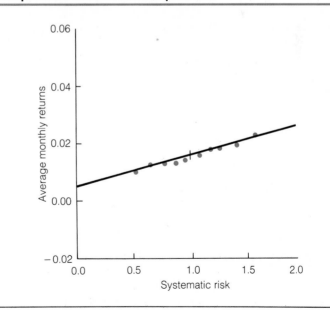

(B–14). The intercept term in the figure is an estimate of α and is greater than zero.

These kinds of results compel us to reject the capital asset pricing model as a completely satisfactory description of the way equity securities are priced. Evidently something has been left out. While there is considerable conjecture about what the missing factor or factors might be, at this time there is little consensus or reliable evidence.

Acknowledgments

Figure 4–2, pp. 80–81: from "Financial" and "Chicago Board." Reprinted by permission of *The Wall Street Journal,* June 3, 1986. Copyright © Dow Jones & Company, Inc., 1986. All Rights Reserved. **Table 5–1,** p. 111: From "The Behavior of Stock-Market Prices" by E. F. Fama, *The Journal of Business,* Vol. 38, January 1965, p. 72. Reprinted by permission of The University of Chicago Press. **Figure 5–3,** p. 117: "The Market's Tumultuous Week." Reprinted by permission of *The Wall Street Journal,* October 26, 1987. Copyright © Dow Jones & Company, Inc. 1987. All Rights Reserved. **Table 6–3,** p. 144: "Asset Returns and Inflation," by E. F. Fama and William G. Schwert, *Journal of Financial Business,* 1977, p. 123. **Figure 6–2,** p. 148: "Foreign Exchange." Reprinted by permission of *The Wall Street Journal,* March 7, 1987. Copyright © Dow Jones & Company, Inc., 1987. All Rights Reserved. **Figure 6–4,** pp. 154–55: "Perspective on the Dollar." Reprinted by permission of *The Wall Street Journal,* April 15, 1987. Copyright © Dow Jones & Company, Inc., 1986. All Rights Reserved. **Table 7–4A,** p. 171: "BankAmerica." Reprinted by permission of *The Wall Street Journal,* June 9, 1987. Copyright © Dow Jones & Company, Inc., 1987. All Rights Reserved. **Table 7–4B,** p. 171: "Foreign Debt Problem." Reprinted by permission of *The Wall Street Journal,* June 16, 1987. Copyright © Dow Jones & Company, Inc., 1987. All Rights Reserved. **Figure 8–3,** p. 197: "Treasury Bill Yields." Reprinted by permission of *The Wall Street Journal,* June 26, 1987. Copyright © Dow Jones & Company, Inc., 1987. All Rights Reserved. **Figure 9–4,** p. 232: "Mortgage Rate Crosscurrents." Reprinted by permission of *The Wall Street Journal,* April 30, 1987. Copyright © Dow Jones & Company, Inc., 1987. All Rights Reserved. **Figure 11–4,** p. 283: "Money Growth vs. the Fed's Targets." Reprinted by permission of *The Wall Street Journal,* July 11, 1986. Copyright © Dow Jones & Company, Inc., 1986. All Rights Reserved. **Figure 11–6,** p. 295: "The Falling Dollar." Reprinted by permission of *The Wall Street Journal,* November 10, 1987. Copyright © Dow, Jones & Company, Inc., 1987. All Rights Reserved. **Table 16–2,** p. 409: From "The Pricing of Dealer Services: An Empirical Study of NASDAQ Stocks" by Hans. R. Stoll, *The Journal of Finance,* Vol. 33, September 1978, p. 1156. Copyright © 1978 by The American Finance Association. Reprinted by permission. **Table 18–2,** p. 453: "Off-Balance-Sheet Liabilities at Five Largest Banking Firms" and "Off-Balance-Sheet Risk at Top Banks," from *American Banker,* May 1, 1987. Copyright © 1987 by American Banker Inc. All rights reserved. **Table 18–6,** p. 463: From "Information Content of Discounts and Premiums on Closed-End Fund Shares," *Journal of Financial Economics* by Rex Thompson, 1978, p. 158. Copyright © 1978 Elsevier Science Publishers B. V. (North Holland) Reprinted by permission. **Table 18–7,** p. 465: "Closed-End Funds That Sell At A Big Discount." Reprinted from March 16, 1987 issue of *Business Week* by special permission, copyright © 1987 by McGraw-Hill, Inc. **Figure 19–5,** p. 497: From *Collateralized Mortgage Obligations: Characteristics, History, Analysis,* by Richard Roll. Reprinted by permission of Goldman, Sachs and Richard Roll. **Figure 19–6,** p. 499: From *Collateralized Mortgage Obligations: Characteristics, History, Analysis,* by Richard Roll. Reprinted by permission of Goldman, Sachs and Richard Roll. **Tables 19–6 and 19–7,** p. 499: From *Collateralized Mortgage Obligations: Characteristics, History, Analysis,* by Richard Roll. Reprinted by permission of Goldman, Sachs and Richard Roll. **Figure 19–7,** p. 500: From *Collateralized Mortgage Obligations: Characteristics, History, Analysis,* by Richard Roll. Reprinted by permission of Goldman, Sachs and Richard Roll. **Table 20–2,** p. 516: From "The Mutual Fund Survey of 1985," *Forbes,* September 16, 1985. Excerpted by permission of Forbes Magazine. Copyright © Forbes, Inc., 1985. **Table 20–4,** p. 523: From "An Economic Analysis of Interest Rate Swaps" by James Bicksler and Andrew H. Chen, *Journal of Finance,* July 1986, Vol. XLI, No. 3, p. 649. Copyright © 1986 The American Finance Association. Reprinted by permission. **Figure 21–1,** p. 537: "Futures Prices." Reprinted by permission of *The Wall Street Journal,* March 27, 1987. Copyright © Dow Jones & Company, Inc., 1987. All Rights Reserved. **Figure 21–3,** p. 546: "Listed Option Quotes from the Chicago Board of Exchange," Reprinted by permission of *The Wall Street Journal,* Inc., 1987. All Rights Reserved. **Figure 21–4,** p. 549: "After a Wild Start, the Futures Market Calmed Down," Reprinted by permission of *The Wall Street Journal,* October 26, 1987. Copyright © Dow Jones & Company, Inc., 1987. All Rights Reserved.

INDEX